Wine Lover's Companion

By
Ron Herbst
and
Sharon Tyler Herbst

D1025706

BARRON'S

Special thanks to Ron Herbst for his help in creating the maps.

All inquiries should be addressed to:
Barron's Educational Series, Inc.
250 Wireless Boulevard
Hauppauge, New York 11788

International Standard Book No. 0-8120-1479-0

Library of Congress Catalog Card No. 94-40845

Library of Congress Cataloging-in-Publication Data

Herbst, Ron.
    Wine lover's companion/by Ron Herbst and Sharon Tyler
Herbst.
        p. cm.
    Includes bibliographical references.
    ISBN 0-8120-1479-0
    1. Wine and wine making—Dictionaries. I. Herbst, Sharon Tyler.
II. Title.
TP546.H47   1995
641.2'2'03—dc20   94-40845
                                                        CIP

PRINTED IN THE UNITED STATES OF AMERICA

5678   9770   987654321

CONTENTS

ACKNOWLEDGMENTS

Our heartfelt thanks to:

The world's talented, hardworking winemakers who, thankfully, share their exquisite labors of love. Particular affection goes to the countless neighboring California vintners with whom we've enjoyed both hospitality and wine.

Michael Boyd, for the wine knowledge he so generously shares, and for his wonderful shop, Michael's Wine Cellar, in Corte Madera, California.

Phil Hicks, for his thoughtful contribution toward the phonetics in this book.

Oscar Anderson and Holly Hartley, for their years of excellent, professional biweekly winetastings, which always expand our knowledge.

Liza Burby, our editor and guiding light at Barron's, for her expertise and wisdom every step of the way and, just as important, for her warmth, good humor, and understanding.

Sara Black (hardworking copyeditor), Donna Jones (incredibly eagle-eyed proofreader), Gina Crawford (talented production manager), and all the behind-the-scenes people at Barron's who were involved in the artwork, layout, printing, editing, and everything else it took to bring this book together.

And, for sharing the passion—Gale Bach, Kathy Benson, Walt and Carol Boice, Mary Lynn Boyd, Marilee Brand, Jerry Bucher, Ted Campagna, Ron Cutler, Louie DeMattei, Lotta Ekman, Lisa and Lou Ekus, Dave and Peg Flanders, Rick Fox, Bill Hassenzahl, Barry Herbst, Ruth Hicks, Max Hinchman, Lee and Susan Janvrin, Marvin Lamb, Judy Lockwood, Judy MacGregor, Larry Michalak, Bob Nichol, Kent Rosenbloom, Kevin Roberts, Emma Swain, Dennis Swanson, Joel Teller, Alan Tobey, Bob Tripp, Mark van Norman, Stuart and Kirsten Williams, and Dan and Kimberley Young.

INTRODUCTION

"One not only drinks wine, one smells it, observes it, tastes it, sips it and one talks about it."
—*King Edward VII*

It's clear from this quote that Great Britain's popular King Edward VII, a well-known *bon vivant,* was a true enophile. The fact that he so obviously loved wine gives us a feeling of kinship, for so do we. The love affair we've long had with wine has developed over the years into a deep and lasting involvement. Of course, our passion certainly is fueled by living just 45 minutes away from where most of America's fine wine originates—California's Napa and Sonoma Valleys.

Our easy access to the wonders of much of California's wine-growing country (the North Coast and Central Coast) is a constant joy. Who can blame us for so loving these viticultural edens, with their glorious seasonal changes. One of our favorite times of year is early spring, when dazzling yellow wild mustard separates the rows of dormant, naked brown vines. In the summertime the vines are lush with verdant leaves and the tiny bud clusters begin their transformation into plump, succulent grapes all but bursting with juice. The harvest begins in late summer to early fall and the crush permeates the air with the perfume of grapes and yeast, a fragrance so heady it's intoxicating. The heart of autumn brings a veritable artist's palate, rich with hues of copper, russet, crimson, and gold. Finally comes winter, when the hardworking vines can at last relax and take a well-deserved rest.

The magic of these viticultural seasons is mirrored around the world in areas such as Bordeaux and Burgundy in France, Tuscany in Italy, Rioja in Spain, and the Hunter Valley in Australia. But our love of wine and the areas that produce it weren't the genesis for writing *Wine Lover's Companion.* The idea actually came to us one day after a couple of closely related events. The first occurred when a friend was recounting a conversation he had overheard at his gym. "Mine," one man apparently said, "was young, vigorous, supple, and full-bodied, with a great nose and terrific legs." To which the second man replied, "Yeah, well, just my luck that the one I brought was in a dumb stage." Our friend chauvinistically told us that he assumed the men were discussing women. "You can imagine my surprise," he said, "when I discovered the subject was wine!" We laughed, recounting some of the colorful terms we hear at our biweekly winetastings. Not long afterward, another friend was angrily recounting how a "rude" coworker had corrected her pronunciation of the wine, Pouilly-Fuissé. Still piqued, she said, "I wish there were a wine book with phonetic pronunciations like there are in Sharon's *Food Lover's Companion*." We looked at each other. M-m-m-m-m . . . what a great idea!

And so we began to think about just what such a book should include. From the start we knew we wanted *Wine Lover's Companion* to be eminently user-friendly—an approachable guide to the wonderful world of wine, which is every bit as intriguing and changeable as the culinary universe. We wanted it to be filled to the brim with a rich, complex blend of vineal facts and detail so the wine world would be less enigmatic and much more enjoyable. We also wanted *Wine Lover's Companion* to be thorough and accurate, with the information presented in the same concise, nonesoteric style as that of *Food Lover's Companion*. And, of course, our book had to be a wine lover's "companion"—as much fun to browse through as it was easy to use. Whew! *Big order,* we thought. And then we got to work.

Two years later we presented our editor with this A-to-Z wine-reference book, packed full of over 3,500 terms that detail wine facts, tips, historical lore, and phonetic pronunciations, all wrapped up in a small, tidy package. We took great pains *not* to editorialize (though we were often tempted), but to simply present the facts in a clear, educational fashion. It's our hope that this book will equip wine enthusiasts with the facts needed to transform them from inexperienced to informed and supply accomplished enophiles with new insights and quick reminders. With *Wine Lover's Companion* as a guide, anyone can learn to speak the language of wine with ease. Whether ordering it in a restaurant, buying it at a wine shop, or enjoying it at a friend's house, dealing with wine will no longer be intimidating.

Wine Lover's Companion offers myriad facts and details such as: grape varieties used for making wines; wine-growing regions around the world; explanations of wine label terms; historical wine lore; wine-making techniques; winetasting terms for a wine's appearance, flavor, and bouquet; etymological origins; foreign wine terms; bottle sizes; how to store wine; what comprises a winetasting; sizes and styles of glasses; and much, much more. With *Wine Lover's Companion* you can quickly reference listings like **Caymus Vineyards**—a California winery famous for Cabernet Sauvignon wines—or **Piedmont**—a winemaking region in northern Italy—or **flinty**—a sensory term used to describe a characteristic found in some extremely dry white wines. Or you can look up winemaking terms like **Brix, dosage,** and **must,** or flip to another page to see if **Ruby Cabernet** is the same grape variety as **Cabernet Sauvignon**.

And *Wine Lover's Companion* just might save you embarrassment by telling you how to pronounce correctly some of those often formidable wine terms. We think the phonetic pronunciations will be one of the most frequently used parts of this book and have used the "sounding-out" method to make them even easier (*see* Pronunciation Guide, page xiii). Hopefully, you'll never again be frustrated when trying to figure out how to pronounce a wine word. For instance, this book tells you that the way to say **Montrachet** is "maw*n*-rah-SHAY," that **Graves** is "GRAHV," and that **kir** is pronounced "KEER."

Don't forget to check the back of *Wine Lover's Companion* for an assortment of charts, tables, and glossaries on a variety of subjects including winetasting terms, grape varieties, wine aromas, styles and sizes of wineglasses and bottles, optimum wine-serving temperatures, official wine classifications, wine styles, and maps of the world's major wine regions.

Writing *Wine Lover's Companion* has been a great gift to both of us. In the end, however, what we found most difficult about writing this book was . . . well, to stop writing. Although we would have loved to include every single one of the world's wineries, vineyards, châteaus, etc., we simply could not (our heartfelt apologies to those we had to leave out). Doing so would have created a book so huge and unwieldy that you couldn't easily carry it to the wine store or read it in bed or take it to a winetasting—and one of our primary parameters for this book was that it be companionable.

In closing, we pass on *Wine Lover's Companion* to you, the reader, with the hope that it will increase your wine knowledge and awareness and, most of all, deliver a great deal of pleasure in the reading. Our parting wish is that all your wines be as wonderful as the one about which Irish satirist Jonathan Swift exclaimed, "This wine should be eaten; it is too good to be drunk."

Ron Herbst
Sharon Tyler Herbst
Greenbrae, Calif.
1995

HOW TO USE THIS BOOK

ENTRIES ARE ARRANGED alphabetically and are cross-referenced. Alphabetization is by letter, rather than by word, so that multiple-word entries are treated as single words. For instance, the listing **closed** is positioned between **Clos du Val** and **Clos Fourtet**. Common-usage acronyms and abbreviations appear in their natural alphabetical order. For example, **A.P.Nr.** follows **apéritif** and precedes **appellation**.

Entries are in lowercase, unless capitals are required for the proper form of the word (German nouns are always capitalized). All but the most basic words have pronunciations (*see* Pronunciation Guide, page xiii). A term with several meanings will list all its definitions in numerical order within the main listing.

Words such as *en, i, il, la,* and *les* are handled as the word *the*. For instance, the listing for **La Mission-Haut-Brion** is in the *M* section, following the entry for **Mission**. Likewise, the listing for **Mis au Domaine** comes before that of **Mis en Bouteille**. French châteaus can be found throughout this book under their individual names; for example, **Château Margaux** is listed under **Margaux, Château**. The exception is when the word *château* is an essential part of the name, as in **Château-Chalon**, or when it's an American winery, such as **Chateau St. Jean** (note that American wineries do not use the ^ diacritical mark in "chateau").

CROSS-REFERENCES are indicated by SMALL CAPITALS and may appear in the body of a definition, at the end of a definition, or in lieu of a definition.

Cross-references are used within the body of a definition when the term may not be familiar to the reader or to point out that there is additional information relevant to a term. For instance, the listing for **late harvest** states: ". . . Such grapes have a higher sugar content (a minimum of 24° BRIX), particularly if they've been infected with BOTRYTIS CINEREA. . . ." Common entries such as **California, temperature,** or **wine** are not characterized with SMALL CAPITALS as cross-references. A cross-referenced word will be capitalized only once in each listing. Cross-references at the end of a definition refer to entries related to the word being defined.

When a word is fully defined elsewhere, a cross-reference rather than a definition is listed. For example, the listing for **magnum** will say *see*

WINE BOTTLES. In the world of wine, many terms have more than one name, often depending on the region in which they're used. Cross-referencing is particularly extensive in *Wine Lover's Companion* because of the myriad synonyms for many terms (like grape varieties), as well as confusing, multifarious designations, such as those for German wine labels. For example, the terms **Blauburgunder**, **Pinot Nero**, and **Spätburgunder** are all cross-referenced to **Pinot Noir**, the more commonly known name of this grape. Different spellings of a term are also cross-referenced. **Silvaner**, for instance, refers the reader to the more common spelling of **Sylvaner**.

ITALICS are used in this book for several reasons. One is to point out that the term being defined also goes by another name. The Hungarian wine **Tokay**, for example, is also labeled as *Tokaji* or *Tokaji Aszu*. Additionally, italics are used to indicate foreign words and publication titles and to highlight cross-references at the end of a listing (the end of the entry for **maceration** states "*See also* CUVAISON; CARBONIC MACERATION").

BOLDFACE PRINT is used not only for main-entry headings but for subentries within a definition as well. For example, the definition for **Muscat** uses boldface to highlight the headings of the various types of this grape (such as **Muscat Blanc à Petits Grains** and **Muscat of Alexandria**), which are defined within the body of that entry. Boldface print is also used to highlight words like names of special brands or second labels.

BRACKETS surround an entry's pronunciation, which immediately follows the listing and precedes the definition. (*See* the Pronunciation Guide on the next page for complete information.)

PRONUNCIATION GUIDE

All but the most basic words are accompanied by pronunciations, which are enclosed in brackets [—]. We've always thought that the standard phonetic alphabet and diacritical marks such as a tilde (~), diaeresis (¨), breve (˘) and circumflex (^) slow readers down because they must often look up the symbol in a chart at the front of a book to see how it affects a word's pronunciation. As advocates of the most direct route, we use the "sounding-out" phonetic method, with the accented syllable indicated by capital letters. On a word like **Auslese**, for example, the common dictionary-style phonetic is *ous' lā zə,* which would force most readers to look up the sounds represented by the diacritics. In this book, however, the word is simply sounded out as *OWS-lay-zuh.*

A list of the basic sounds employed in this book's pronunciations follows:

a as in **can** or **add**
ah as in **father** or **balm**
ay as in **date** or **face**
ch as in **church** or **beach**
ee as in **steam** or **beer**
eh as in **set** or **check**
g as in **game** or **green**
i as in **ice** or **pie**
ih as in **if** or **strip**
j as in **gin** or **juicy**
k as in **cool** or **crisp**
o as in **odd** or **bottle**
oh as in **open** or **boat**
oo as in **food** or **boo**
ow as in **cow** or **flour**
uh as in **love** or **cup**
y as in **yellow** or **yes**
zh as in **beige** or **vision**

Note: A single *i* is used for the long i sound, as in *pie.* The exception to the single i rule is when an *i* is followed by a consonant, in which case, an *e* is appended. For example, both *i*'s are long in the word **weinkellerei**, which is phoneticized *vine-KEHL-ler-ri.*

Foreign Sounds

eu A sound made with the lips rounded as if to say *oo* (as in *food*) while trying to say *a* (as in *able*).

n, m An italicized *n* or *m* is used to indicate that the *n* or *m* is not pronounced and that the preceding vowel has a nasal sound.

r An italicized *r* indicates that the *r* sound should be diminished, with a sound more like *w*.

rr The appearance of *rr* indicates the sound of a rolling *r*.

bboccato [ah-boh-KAH-toh] Italian for "lightly sweet," indicating that a wine contains a small amount of RESIDUAL SUGAR. This word is used to describe a wide range of wines from semisweet to medium-DRY.

L'Abeille de Fieuzal *see* DE FIEUZAL, CHÂTEAU

Abfüller; Abfüllung [AB-few-ler; AB-few-lung] German words for "bottler" and "bottling." For example, *erseugerabfüllung* on a wine label means "bottled by the proprietor," which is equivalent to ESTATE BOTTLED in the United States.

Ablan *see* PALOMINO

abocado [ah-boh-KAH-doh] The Spanish word for "semisweet," indicating that the wine contains some RESIDUAL SUGAR.

Abruzzi; Abruzzo [ah-BROOD-dzee] Abruzzi (*Abruzzo* in Italian) is a very mountainous region located east of Rome on the Adriatic Sea about midway down the coastline. The main grape variety used for white wines is TREBBIANO, but there are a multitude of other white grapes allowed including BOMBINO BIANCO, MALVASIA, and Pinot Grigio (PINOT GRIS). MONTEPULCIANO is the main grape for ROSSO and ROSATO, followed by SANGIOVESE. There are two DOCs in this area, TREBBIANO D'ABRUZZO and MONTEPULCIANO D'ABRUZZO.

Abtsberg *see* MAXIMIN GRÜNHÄUS

AC Abbreviation for APPELLATION D'ORIGINE CONTRÔLÉE.

Acacia Winery [uh-KAY-shuh] California winery established in 1979 that is situated on the NAPA VALLEY side of the CARNEROS AVA and produces about 50,000 cases of wine a year—primarily CHARDONNAY. It has its own 50-acre Marina Vineyard planted in Chardonnay and purchases Chardonnay and PINOT NOIR grapes from other growers. In addition to Carneros AVA-designated Chardonnay and Pinot Noir wines, Acacia Winery offers several different VINEYARD-DESIGNATED bottlings, including Chardonnay from its own Marina Vineyard and Pinot Noir from Madonna and St. Clair vineyards. Wines from Iund, Lee, and Winery Lake vineyards are no longer offered. In 1986 Acacia became part of Chalone, Inc., which also owns CARMENET VINEYARD and CHALONE VINEYARDS and is involved in a joint venture with Paragon Vineyards in EDNA VALLEY VINEYARDS.

acescence; acescent [uh-SEHS-uhns; uh-SEHS-uhnt] A wine with *acescence* has a sharp, sweet-and-sour tang, sometimes accompanied by a vinegary smell. *Acescent* characteristics are indicative of the presence of ACETIC ACID and ETHYL ACETATE.

acetaldehyde [as-ih-TAL-duh-hide] Colorless, volatile, and water-soluble, acetaldehyde is a natural element found in grapes and wine. It has a pungent fruitlike odor and is present in small amounts in good TABLE WINE and in high amounts in OXIDIZED wines. Oxidation is a detriment in a normal table wine but intentional in wines like SHERRY or MADEIRA. Most acetaldehyde eventually converts to ETHANOL, the ALCOHOL found in wine. If oxygen is introduced too fast or in excessive amounts, the production of acetaldehyde can temporarily cause a reaction like BOTTLE SICKNESS or, worse, give wine a permanent sherrylike trait.

acetic [uh-SEE-tihk] A sensory term used to describe wines that have an excess of acetic acid (*see* ACIDS), which contributes a sweet, slightly vinegary odor and a sharp, tart flavor. Such wines are said to have ACESCENCE.

acetic acid [uh-SEE-tihk] *see* ACIDS

acetification [uh-SEE-tuh-fih-KAY-shuhn] The process of wine turning into vinegar. This most often occurs because of spoilage, when acetic bacteria convert ALCOHOL to acetic acid (*see* ACIDS) and ETHYL ACETATE.

acetobacter [uh-SEE-tuh-bak-tuhr] A microorganism that, when wines are exposed to oxygen, creates acetic acid (*see* ACIDS).

acetone [AS-ih-tohn] A word sometimes used as an adjective to describe a wine that has a sharp but slightly sweet and fruity smell. This is generally caused by ESTERS, most commonly ETHYL ACETATE.

acidic [uh-SIHD-ihk] A term used to describe a wine's tart, slightly acerbic taste and a harsh feeling in the mouth. This undesirable characteristic is caused by excess ACID in the wine.

acidity *see* ACIDS

acids Acids occur naturally during the growing of grapes and as part of the FERMENTATION process. Wines show lower levels of acid when there are hot growing seasons or when the grapes come from hotter VITICULTURAL regions. Conversely, cooler regions or cooler growing seasons produce wines with higher acid levels. In the proper proportion, acids are a desirable trait and give the wine CHARACTER, much as a dash of vinegar or lemon juice heightens the flavor of many foods. Too much acid leaves a sharp, tart taste in the mouth, while too little makes wine seem flat and lifeless. The three predominant acids in wine are **tartaric**, **malic**, and **citric**, all of which are intrinsic to the grape. Tartaric acid is the principal acid in grapes and is a component that promotes a crisp flavor and graceful AGING in wine. A moderate amount of a wine's acid comes from malic acid, which contributes fruitiness, and a small amount comes from citric acid. Wine also contains minute to trace amounts of other acids, which are produced during fermentation, including: **acetic**, **butyric**, **capric**, **caproic**, **caprylic**, **carbonic** (in SPARKLING WINES), **formic**, **lactic**, **lauric**, **propionic**, and **succinic**. The least desirable acid in wine is **acetic acid**, which, when present in more than a nominal amount, gives wine a sour or vinegary aspect (*see* ACETIC; VOLATILE ACIDITY). **Volatile acids** (such as acetic and butyric) are those that can be altered—for instance, they can evaporate. **Fixed acids** are fruit acids (such as malic and tartaric) that are organic to the grape. **Total acidity**, also called *titratable acidity,* is the sum of the fixed and volatile acids, which is determined by a chemical process called **titration**. In the United States the total acidity is usually expressed in terms of tartaric acid, even though the other acids are measured. Total acidity is expressed either as a percentage or as grams per liter. The proper acid level of a wine varies, with sweeter wines generally requiring somewhat higher levels to retain the proper BALANCE. Some labels make note of a wine's acidity. For dry TABLE WINE the acceptable range is usually 0.6 to 0.75 percent; for sweet wine it's 0.7 to 0.85 percent. In some areas (usually warm growing regions where acidity is lower) like California, natural grape acids can legally be added to wine to increase the acidity. This acid adjustment process is called **acidulation**. In a well-made wine, acidity will not be noticeable. *See also* PH; MALOLACTIC FERMENTATION; TARTRATES.

acidulation *see* ACIDS

adamado [a-duh-MAH-doh] The Portuguese word for "sweet."

adega [ah-DAY-gah] Portuguese term referring to a winery, cellar, or warehouse where wine is made, BLENDED, or AGED.

adulterated wine Wine that has been modified with an inordinate amount of allowable ingredients or with unapproved substances.

aeration [ay-RAY-shun] The process in which air is deliberately introduced to wine, as in DECANTING, or in swirling the wine in a glass.

aestivalis *see* VITIS AESTIVALIS

Affentaler [AH-fen-tah-ler] The shortened name of *Affentaler Spätburgunder Rotwein,* a German red wine made from Spätburgunder

A

(PINOT NOIR) grapes in the BADEN region. The wine, which ranges from DRY to sweet, can be of QbA or QmP quality. Affentaler is produced in the area south of Baden-Baden around the villages of Bühl and Eisental. The word *Affental* translates to "monkey valley," which is why the Affentaler wine bottles bear an embossed image of a monkey.

Africa For the most part, Africa's excessive climate isn't very hospitable for wine grapes. They generally are grown only at the northern and southern ends of the continent, the farthest points from the Equator. *See also* ALGERIA; MOROCCO; TUNISIA; SOUTH AFRICA.

aftertaste Usually the hallmark of a COMPLEX wine, the aftertaste is the flavor that lingers in the back of the throat or nasal passages after a wine is swallowed. *See also* FINISH; LENGTH.

aggressive A tasting term used to describe a wine that's slightly harsh on the palate, usually due to high TANNINS or ACID.

aging; age The process of maturing wines so that they can improve. Those wines that benefit from aging become less harsh, less TANNIC, SMOOTHER, and more COMPLEX. Once wines complete FERMENTATION, they begin to change, mainly as a result of air contact but also because the natural components of the new wine begin interacting with one another. All ROSÉ wines and most white and LIGHT red wines should be bottled soon after fermentation and drunk while still young. But aging is necessary for some wines to reach their full potential. These include most fine red wines (such as those from France's BORDEAUX and RHÔNE regions, California's better CABERNET SAUVIGNONS and ZINFANDELS, and Italy's BAROLOS and BRUNELLO DI MONTALCINOS) and many white wines (SAUTERNES, BURGUNDIES, and some California CHARDONNAYS). Wines begin the aging process in the tanks or vats where they go through fermentation. After that, most high-quality wines receive some sort of wood aging and then bottle aging. **Wood aging** is a process of maturing wine in barrels or casks prior to bottling. This process allows young wines to SOFTEN and absorb some of the wood's flavors and TANNINS; the wine's flavors become concentrated because of slight evaporation. In modern winemaking, wood aging has become very complex, with considerations like size of container, origin and type of wood, and barrel-making techniques. Although the best sources for barrel oak are still being debated (*see* OAK), the small oak barrel has evolved as today's container of choice. **Bottle aging** further develops the nuances of wine. After a wine is bottled, the first few weeks of aging allow it to recover from BOTTLE SICKNESS. The length of further aging depends upon the type of wine. Many, including rosé, light white, and light red wines, are at their best soon after bottling and don't require further aging. White wines like California Chardonnay do well with a minimum of 6 to 12 months aging, whereas French white Burgundy and Sauternes develop better with extended bottle aging. Long-lived red wine—such as California Cabernet Sauvignon and Zinfandel, French Bordeaux, Italian Barolo, and vintage PORT—improve for many years, sometimes decades. Such wines evolve beautifully in the bottle as their tannins soften and the flavor and BOUQUET become more intriguing and complex. At some point, however, the wine hits its peak and begins declining in quality, making bottle aging no longer beneficial.

Aglianico [ah-LYAH-nee-koh] One of the higher-quality red wine grapes found in southern Italy, mainly in CAMPANIA and BASILICATA. Aglianico is thought to have been planted in this region as early as the seventh century B.C. The best 100 percent Aglianico wines come from TAURASI, followed by those from AGLIANICO DEL VULTURE; both have DOC status. The wines from these two DOCs are noted for their ROUGHNESS when young due to high TANNINS, noticeable ACIDITY, and a dense concentration of flavors; they're definitely built for AGING. As these wines mature, they can exhibit great BALANCE, with subtle fruit flavors and EARTHY, TARRY, and CHOCOLATY characteristics. FALERNO DEL MASSICO also produces excellent wines that use a high proportion of Aglianico in their blend. Unfortunately, much of the wine produced from Aglianico grapes is unexciting and of lesser quality.

Aglianico del Vulture DOC [ah-LYAH-nee-koh del VOOL-too-reh] The only DOC zone in Italy's BASILICATA region. Although this DOC covers AMABILE and SPUMANTE versions, it's the STILL, DRY wines that are most highly regarded. These red wines are made from the AGLIAN-ICO grape that's grown here and in the neighboring region of CAMPANIA (*see* TAURASI DOC). The better vineyards are on the east slope of Monte Vulture, an extinct volcano in the northern part of Basilicata. When young, the Aglianico del Vulture wines are noted for their ROUGHNESS, which is due to high TANNINS, noticeable ACIDITY, and a dense concentration of flavors. As they mature, these wines can show great BALANCE, with subtle fruit flavors and EARTHY, TARRY, and CHOCOLATY characteristics. They can AGE for 7 to 10 years or longer.

Agliano *see* ALEATICO

agrafe; agraffe [uh-GRAF] A metal clasp used to hold the temporary cork in place during BOTTLE FERMENTATION when making SPARKLING WINE via the METHODE CHAMPENOISE. The agrafe has, in most instances, been replaced by the CROWN CAP.

Ahr [AHR] With only slightly over 1,000 acres planted, Ahr is the fourth smallest of the thirteen German ANBAUGEBIETE (quality-wine regions). It's located on the river Ahr, a tributary of the Rhine, just south of the city of Bonn in western Germany. Winemaking in the Ahr region goes back to Roman times, and the region claims Germany's first cooperative cellar, which local growers established in 1868. Even though it is located the farthest north of all the Anbaugebiete, over 70 percent of its vineyards are planted with red varieties, which is unusual because of the cooler climate. The main varieties here are Spätburgunder (PINOT NOIR) and PORTUGIESER, and the red wines are usually pale and lightly flavored. The main white varieties are RIESLING and MÜLLER-THURGAU. Even though Ahr's white wines are usually better than the reds, they're not as good as those made from the same varieties in some of the southern regions. Most of the wines are consumed locally and few are exported. Ahr has one BEREICH, **Walporzheim/Ahrtal**; one GROSSLAGE, **Klosterberg**; and forty-three EINZELLAGEN. The principal wine-producing towns are Ahrweiler and Bad Neuenahr (the region's capital).

aigre [AYGR] French for "sour" or "vinegary." In wine parlance, *aigre* refers to an ACETIC trait.

aimable [ay-MAHBL] A French term used in winetasting to describe a pleasant, well-BALANCED wine.

Airén [i-REHN] A white grape that is Spain's and the world's most widely planted grape variety. Airén blankets central Spain's hot, arid regions of LA MANCHA and VALDEPEÑAS and is used for both red and white wines. The Airén grape's reputation for creating dull white wines is still widely dependable but—thanks to modern equipment and new winemaking techniques—these wines have recently gained a better image. There are now white Airén wines being produced that are light, crisp, fruity, and slightly aromatic. Spain's Valdepeñas region, which has a good reputation for red wines, actually grows much more Airén than it does the local red-grape favorite Cencibel (TEMPRANILLO). In fact, often a small amount of Airén is blended with the Cencibel to create the region's popular red wine. Much of the blander white wine made from Airén is processed further to create BRANDY. Airén is also known as *Lairén, Manchega,* and *Valdepeñera Blanca.*

Aix *see* COTEAUX D' AIX-EN-PROVENCE

Ajaccio AC [ah-YAHT-choh] An APPELLATION that encompasses the wines made in the hills around the city of Ajaccio on the west coast of the French island of CORSICA. The appellation designation covers red

A

and ROSÉ wines made primarily from the local Sciacarello grape and white wines made primarily from VERMENTINO and Ugni Blanc (TREBBIANO).

Alba [AHL-bah] An important wine town of about 30,000 people situated in the wine-producing area south of Turin in Italy's PIEDMONT region. There are several Italian DOCs that use Alba in their name—BARBERA D'ALBA, DOLCETTO D'ALBA, NEBBIOLO D'ALBA, and Dolcetto di Diano d'Alba. The well-known DOCGs of BAROLO and BARBARESCO are also near Alba. In addition to red wines, the area around Alba is also known for its white truffles.

Albana [ahl-BAH-nah] Grown principally in northern Italy's EMILIA-ROMAGNA region and environs, this white wine grape has been cultivated in this area since the thirteenth century. The wines it produces are of extremely variable quality and rarely considered great. ALBANA DI ROMAGNA wines are designated DOCG (Italy's highest official classification); however, many experts question this high ranking. At their best, Albana wines are SMOOTH yet CRISP, with hints of nuttiness. The Albana grape is processed into many styles of wine including AMABILE, DRY, PASSITO, SPARKLING, and sweet. Albana is also known as *Biancame, Greco di Ancona,* and *Greco* (although it's totally unrelated to the true GRECO variety used in GRECO DI TUFO).

Albana di Romagna DOCG [ahl-BAH-nah dee roh-MAH-nyah] When the wines from this area were upgraded from DOC to DOCG status in 1987, the event sparked lots of controversy. Many wine reviewers had hoped the DOCG designation would be reserved for outstanding high-quality wines, and the Albana di Romagna wines weren't viewed as such. At their best, these wines, which are made from the ALBANA grape, are SMOOTH yet CRISP, with hints of nuttiness. Their quality, however, is quite variable, and the wines are generally not considered world class. The area for producing these wines is extremely large and is located in the EMILIA-ROMAGNA region in northern Italy. Albana di Romagna covers the vineyards surrounding over twenty villages between Bologna and Rimini. The DOCG designation allows many styles of wine including AMABILE, SECCO, PASSITO, and DOLCE. The SPUMANTE wines may still only be classified as DOC.

Albany *see* LOWER GREAT SOUTHERN REGION

Albariño *see* ALVARINHO

albariza *see* JEREZ-XÉRÈX-SHERRY Y MANZANILLA DE SANLÚCAR DE BARRAMEDA DO

Alcamo DOC [AHL-cah-moh] A DOC that is located in the western part of SICILY and includes the vineyards surrounding the village of Alcamo and eleven other small villages. The wines, also called *Bianco Alcamo* or *Bianco d'Alcamo*, are made mainly from Catarratto grapes but use small amounts of others like Damaschino, Grecanico, and TREBBIANO. Many are of mediocre quality, but several producers make CRISP, LIVELY wines with class and CHARACTER.

Alcanol *see* MACABEO

Alcayata *see* MONASTRELL

alcohol [AL-kuh-hawl] Alcohol is the intoxicating element produced by the yeast FERMENTATION of certain carbohydrates—the sugar in fruit, in the instance of wine. If a wine is fully fermented, from 40 to 45 percent of the grapes' sugar content is converted into carbon dioxide and from 55 to 60 percent is converted into **ethyl alcohol** (the only alcohol suitable for drinking). Therefore, a wine whose grapes were picked at 23° BRIX will end up with 12.6 to 13.8 percent alcohol if VINIFIED completely DRY. Ethyl alcohol, also known as *ethanol,* lends little if any flavor to wine but must be present in the right proportion to give wine a desirable BALANCE. Wine with a low alcohol level might be too sweet because not enough of the grape's sugar was converted. This results in RESIDUAL SUGAR, an undesirable trait in some wines. Wines with excessive alcohol are characterized by a burning sensation in the mouth and are, in fact, referred to as HOT. Wines with full, concentrated fruit flavors can withstand higher alcohol levels without becoming hot; more delicate wines don't fare as well. The United States requires that **alcohol by volume** information be included on wine labels. For TABLE WINE, the United States requires a minimum alcohol level of 7 percent and a maximum of 14 percent. The label variance can be up to 1.5 percent. For example, a wine stating "Alcohol 12.5% By Volume" can legally range anywhere from 11 to 14 percent. However, wines cannot exceed the upper or lower limit. The alcohol-by-volume range for SHERRIES is 17 to 20 percent; for PORTS it's 18 to 20 percent. The label variance for both of these FORTIFIED wines is 1 percent.

alcohol by volume *see* ALCOHOL

alcoholic A term used to describe a wine's hot, burning taste accompanied by a sharp, biting sensation in the mouth. This undesirable trait is caused when an elevated ALCOHOL level is not balanced by other wine components. *See also* HOT.

alcool [al-KOOL] The Italian and French word for "alcohol."

Alderbrook Vineyards Winery that consists of about 55 acres (actually owned by partner Mark Rafanelli of the winemaking family) located in the southern end of the DRY CREEK VALLEY AVA. Founded in 1982, the 30,000-case winery makes wine from its own CHARDONNAY, SAUVIGNON BLANC, SEMILLON, and MUSCAT grapes. It also purchases grapes to produce GEWÜRZTRAMINER, PETITE SIRAH, and ZINFANDEL wines. Alderbrook has a reputation for good-quality wines at reasonable prices.

Aleatico [ah-leh-AH-tee-koh] An Italian red grape that some theorize is a variation of the MUSCAT family because of its flowery Muscat characteristics. Its noncharacteristic deep color, however, seems to discount this theory. The wines created from this grape are RICH, sweet, ALCOHOLIC, and well-ROUNDED. There are two DOCs focused on this variety—Aleatico di Puglia in southern Italy and Aleatico di Gradoli in LAZIO, northwest of Rome. Aleatico wines that are FORTIFIED as LIQUOROSOS can serve as less expensive PORT substitutes. This grape is also called *Agliano, Allianico, Moscatello,* and *Muscateller.*

Alejandro Fernandez *see* RIBERA DEL DUERO DO

Alella DO [ah-LEH-lyah] A small DO zone located on the outskirts of Barcelona in the CATALONIA region in northeast Spain. As the urban sprawl of Barcelona grows toward the small village of Alella, the vineyards around it are disappearing and being replaced with houses. In 1989 this designated area, which has been shrinking since the 1970s, added the vineyards of four other towns to increase its size. This move has been criticized because the added vineyards aren't as good those in the original zone. Alella primarily produces semisweet and DRY white wines. The main white grapes used in them are Pansa Blanca (XAREL-LO) and Garnacha Blanca (GRENACHE). A small amount of red and ROSÉ wines are produced from Ulle de Llebre (TEMPRANILLO) and Garnacha Tinta (GRENACHE), along with some Pansa Rosado. The area's white wines, which should be drunk young, are considered its best.

Alexander Valley AVA A VITICULTURAL AREA just north of San Francisco in northern Sonoma County. It borders the Russian River from just south of Healdsburg, north to the Sonoma-Mendocino County line. Alexander Valley temperatures are somewhat on the warm side because fog's not as prevalent as in other growing areas. It generally falls into the Region III category (*see* CLIMATE REGIONS OF CALIFORNIA). The region, however, is versatile enough to do well with a wide variety of grapes including CABERNET SAUVIGNON, CHARDONNAY, GEWÜRZTRAMINER, MERLOT, RIESLING, SAUVIGNON BLANC, and ZINFANDEL. Among the notable wineries in this area are ALEXANDER VALLEY VINEYARDS, CLOS DU BOIS, GEYSER

PEAK, Gauer Estate, JORDAN, MURPHY-GOODE, SIMI, and CHATEAU SOUVERAIN. Producers such as SILVER OAK CELLARS, which is based in the Napa Valley, make Cabernet Sauvignon with an "Alexander Valley" designation, meaning the grapes came from this growing region.

Alexander Valley Vineyards Winery owned by the Wetzel family and consisting of about 130 acres in the middle of the ALEXANDER VALLEY AVA. The vineyard is planted mainly with CABERNET SAUVIGNON, CHARDONNAY, and MERLOT, although it also has small amounts of CHENIN BLANC, GEWÜRZTRAMINER, PINOT NOIR, RIESLING, and ZINFANDEL. The winery was built in 1975 (the vineyards were already in place) and now produces about 50,000 cases annually. The Cabernet Sauvignon wines (usually with a small amount of Merlot blended in) are generally the most consistent and highly regarded.

Algeria [al-JEER-ee-uh] Algeria, along with its neighbors TUNISIA and MOROCCO, was once a significant wine producer. During the time it was a colony of France, Algeria produced good-quality wines. Because Algeria's Muslim-dominated population drank little alcohol, most of its wine was exported to France, either in bottles or in bulk to be blended with French wine. Since Algeria's independence in 1962, when most of the French left, wine quality has dropped, exports have dwindled, and production has diminished. The 900,000 acres of vineyard land has been reduced to less than 40,000, and wine production has been reduced to less than 1 percent of the pre-1962 levels. The French established a VDQS system with twelve regions, which have since dropped to seven (now called quality zones). They are Aïn Bessem-Bouria, Coteaux du Zaccar, Medea, Monts du Tessalah, Coteaux de Tlemcen, Coteaux du Mascara, and an area around the villages of Aïn Merane, Mazouna, and Tanghrite. These last three areas generally produce the best wines. The grape varieties grown in Algeria include ALICANTE BOUSCHET, CARIGNAN, CINSAUT, CLAIRETTE, GRENACHE, MOURVEDRE, SYRAH, Ugni Blanc (TREBBIANO), and, occasionally, CABERNET SAUVIGNON.

Alianca *See* CAVES ALIANCA

Alicante *See* ALICANTE BOUSCHET; ALMANSA DO; GRENACHE

Alicante Bouschet [al-eh-KAN-tay (Fr. ah-lee-KAHNT) boo-SHAY] Frenchman Louis Bouschet de Bernard and his son Henri created this prolific HYBRID vine that produces intensely colored, red-fleshed grapes. They developed Alicante Bouschet in 1866 by crossing GRENACHE and Petit Bouschet (the latter variety a cross of Teinturier du Cher and ARAMON). By itself, the Alicante Bouschet grape produces wines that are decidedly unexciting. It's cultivated mainly to add color to wines made from less vivid varieties. This grape is widely planted in the MIDI region of southern France and in North Africa. It was quite popular in California during PROHIBITION (for use by home winemakers), where there are still a number of acres planted, mainly in the CENTRAL VALLEY. This grape is sometimes simply called *Alicante*, but shouldn't be confused with the ALICANTE DO wines of southeastern Spain. Nor should it be confused with the wine called *Bouchet*, which is the name used for CABERNET FRANC in BORDEAUX'S SAINT-ÉMILION.

Alicante DO [al-eh-KAN-tay (Fr. ah-lee-KAHNT)] DO located in the Alicante province in the Levante region of southeastern Spain, south of the VALENCIA DO. Alicante consists of two areas, a large one spreading out to the west of the city of Alicante and a smaller one, referred to as La Marina, northeast of the city. The larger area produces mostly BIG, full-bodied (*see* BODY) red wines, as well as some ROSÉS from MONASTRELL and Garnacha Tinta (GRENACHE). The DRY, white wines, made from Verdil and Merseguera grapes, aren't particularly well regarded. The smaller zone, La Marina, produces good sweet, white wines made from Moscatel (MUSCAT). A unique wine called **Fondillon** is also produced in the Alicante area. It's a RANCIO-style wine made from the Monastrell grape and AGED for 6 to 10 years in barrels. The ALCOHOL content is a potent 16 to 18 percent.

Alicante Ganzin *see* RUBIRED

Aligoté [ah-lee-gaw-TAY] White wine grape that is widely cultivated in and around BURGUNDY. It's considered less important and distinguished than the CHARDONNAY grape, and, in most cases, wines developed from the Aligoté are not as rich or long-lived as those from Chardonnay. Older Aligoté vines have been known to produce some very nice wines, which often exhibit citrusy and, occasionally, nutty characteristics. Burgundian wines made from this grape are labeled BOURGOGNE ALIGOTÉ AC or, when they come from the village of Bourzeron in the COTE CHALONNAISE, BOURGOGNE ALIGOTÉ DE BOURZERON AC. The Aligoté grape is losing out to Chardonnay, and vineyard plantings have been reduced in the last 15 years. However, it remains popular in some eastern European countries including Bulgaria and Rumania. The Aligoté grape is also called *Blanc de Troyes, Chaudenet Gris,* and *Plant Gris*.

Allianico *see* ALEATICO

Almansa DO [ahl-MAHN-suh] The Almansa DO is situated in Spain's CASTILLA-LA MANCHA region east of the LA MANCHA DO and next to the Levante. Although there's a small amount of white wine made from Merseguera grapes, about 75 percent of the wine produced is red, made with MONASTRELL, Cencibel (TEMPRANILLO), and Garnacha Tintorera. This last variety, which is also called Alicante here, has red flesh and imparts lots of color, flavor, and TANNINS to the blends. It appears to be unrelated to the Garnacha Tinta (GRENACHE). Although the Garnacha Tintorera grape gives these Almansa wines a special character, the better red wines use only a small amount of it.

Aloxe-Corton [ah-loss kor-TAWN] An important wine-producing village at the northern end of the CÔTE DE BEAUNE district in France's BURGUNDY region. The most celebrated wines come from the vineyards on Montagne de Corton, a vast hill rising above the village. This area's red wines are made from PINOT NOIR grapes, the whites from CHARDONNAY. Within Aloxe-Corton (and extending into the villages of LADOIX-SERRIGNY and PERNAND-VERGELESSES) are the two GRANDS CRUS of CORTON (red wines) and CORTON-CHARLEMAGNE (white wines). The wines from these grand crus are ranked among the world's finest, with the reds from Corton considered some of the best and longest aging in Burgundy, and the white wines from Corton-Charlemagne compared favorably to other top white wines from the region. Within the grand cru of Corton, there are twenty-seven other individual grand cru vineyards in addition to le Corton vineyard. These vineyards may simply use Corton on the label or add their name to Corton, as in Corton Bressandes or Corton Clos du Roi. Nine of these same vineyards are also permitted to produce grand cru white wines under the Corton-Charlemagne AC. Aloxe-Corton also has a number of fine PREMIER CRU vineyards. The wines produced under the general village appellation of Aloxe-Corton AC are also generally of good quality.

Alsace [al-SASS; (Fr. Al-ZASS)] Located on the German border in northeast France, east of CHAMPAGNE and north of BURGUNDY, Alsace is one of France's most beautiful wine regions. Its vineyards extend along the foothills of the Vosges Mountains, and numerous picturesque villages like Eguisheim, Kayserberg, and Riquewihr dot the landscape. Alsace, which consists of the modern French DÉPARTEMENTS of Haut-Rhin and Bas-Rhin, is not your usual French winemaking region because of the extensive use of VARIETAL WINE labeling on bottles. The Alsace APPELLATION was the first in France to implement varietal labeling, which is a system similar to that in the United States and therefore easier for Americans to understand. Alsace also differs from other French winemaking regions because of its widespread German influence. Germany ruled this region from 1870 until 1919, and its influence persists not only in the Germanic names, but also in the tall, slender, green MOSELlike bottles and in the bias of the approved grape varieties—GEWÜRZTRAMINER, RIESLING, SYLVANER, PINOT GRIS, PINOT BLANC, PINOT NOIR, and MUSCAT. Unlike the Germans, however, Alsace VINTNERS make DRY wines with higher ALCOHOL content and usually with riper, more scented fruit. Almost all Alsatian wines are varietal wines and must be 100 percent of the chosen grape variety. The exception is **Edelzwicker**, which means "noble wine," and consists of a blend of the approved white Alsace grape varieties. Pinot Noir is the only approved grape for red wine. Because this grape variety has difficulty in fully ripening in this climate (except during warmer years), Pinot Noir often appears as a ROSÉ wine. Since the 1985 VINTAGE, the very best Alsatian vineyards have been designated Alsace GRAND CRU, a distinct appellation for which 51 vineyards have qualified so far. These vineyards are allowed to put "Grand Cru" on their labels. SPARKLING WINES have their own appellation—CRÉMANT D'ALSACE AC. LATE HARVEST wines, made from late-picked grapes with higher sugar levels and more pronounced flavors, are bottled under the appellation **Alsace Vendange Tardive**. A specialty of the Alsace region, the rich, extremely flavorful VENDANGE TARDIVE wines are usually vinified totally dry. **Sélection de Grains Nobles** are wines made with late harvest grapes that are affected by BOTRYTIS CINEREA, which results in very sweet and concentrated wines. Alsace Grand Cru, Vendange Tardive, and Sélection de Grains Nobles appellation wines can be made only from Gewürztraminer, Riesling, Pinot Gris, and Muscat.

Altenberg *see* KANZEM

Altesse [ahl-TESS]
Good-quality white wine grape cultivated mainly in and around France's SAVOIE region, where it's also called *Roussette*. Vines from this variety are thought to have been brought to the Savoie from CYPRUS in the Middle Ages. Altesse wines are described as full-bodied (*see* BODY) and AROMATIC with SPICY, PEPPERY characteristics. This grape is often blended with other varieties to produce desirable white wines. A substantial portion of the Altesse crop finds its way into SPARKLING WINES. The Savoie village of Seyssel is well known for its SEYSSEL MOUSSEUX sparkling wines, which are described as CREAMY, with a sharp peppery bite. Altesse is sometimes referred to as *Maconnais* or *Altesse Vert*.

Alto Adige DOC [AHL-toh AH-dee-zhay]
DOC zone that covers most of the northern portion of Italy's TRENTINO-ALTO ADIGE region, Alto Adige. It's located in northeastern Italy, bordered by LOMBARDY on the west, VENETO on the east, and Austria on the north. Many of the vineyards are planted on steep hillsides as the Alps drop down toward the

Adige River and its tributary, the Isarco. Alto Adige, which is also known as **South Tyrol** or **Südtirol**, is officially bilingual, with a German-speaking majority that still has strong ties to Austria (which ceded this area to Italy in 1918). The Alto Adige wines reflect this bilingual approach in their labels—a wine made from the PINOT BLANC grape might be referred to as both Weissburgunder and Pinot Bianco (both of which mean Pinot Blanc). There are seventeen VARIETAL WINES—Cabernet (from CABERNET SAUVIGNON and CABERNET FRANC), CHARDONNAY, LANGREIN (labeled as *Lagrein Rosato* or *Lagrein Kretzer* for ROSÉ wines and *Lagrein Scuro* or *Lagren Dunkel* for red wines), MALVASIA (also labeled *Malvaier*), MERLOT, MUSCAT (labeled *Moscato Giallo* or *Goldenmuskateller* for white wines and *Moscato Rosa* or *Rosenmuskateller* for rosé wines), MÜLLER THURGAU (also labeled *Riesling-Sylvaner*), Pinot Blanc (labeled *Pinot Bianco* or *Weissburgunder*), PINOT GRIS (labeled *Pinot Grigio* or *Rulander*), PINOT NOIR (labeled *Pinot Nero* or *Blauburgunder*), WELSCHRIESLING (also labeled *Riesling Italico*), RIESLING (labeled *Riesling Renano* or *Rheinriesling*), SAUVIGNON BLANC, SCHIAVA (also labeled *Vernatsch*), SYLVANER, and GEWÜRZTRAMINER (also labeled *Traminer Aromatico*). SPUMANTE is also made from some of these approved grapes.

Alvarinho [ahl-vah-REE-nyoh] Low-yielding, high-quality white wine grape grown in Portugal's VINHO VERDE, as well as in Spain's Galicia region, where it's called *Albariño*. Although reasonably productive, these grapes are so thick skinned that only a small amount of juice can be extracted from them. Alvarinho grapes can produce CREAMY, rich wines with complex flavors of apricots, peaches, and citrus. Although Alvariho wines are some of the most expensive and highly prized white wines in both Portugal and Spain, this variety is rarely cultivated elsewhere.

amabile [ah-MAH-bee-lay] An Italian word describing wines that are medium-sweet. Amabile wines are usually less sweet than those labeled DOLCE but sweeter than ABBOCCATO.

Amador County [AM-uh-dor] Important California wine-producing area located in the Sierra Foothills, north of Calaveras County and west and slightly south of Sacramento. There are two smaller VITICULTURAL AREAS in the county, FIDDLETOWN and SHENANDOAH VALLEY, and the large SIERRA FOOTHILLS AVA, which also includes parts of several other counties. Amador County is very warm in most parts, generally rating a Region III classification and sometimes a Region IV (*see* CLIMATE REGIONS OF CALIFORNIA). By a very considerable margin, ZINFANDEL is the most widely planted grape variety here. The second most popular

A

grape is SAUVIGNON BLANC. Tiny amounts of CABERNET SAUVIGNON, CHARDONNAY, and a variety of other grapes are also grown. Some of the better-known wineries include Amador Foothill, Montevina, Santino, and Shenandoah.

amaro [ah-MAH-roh] An Italian word used to describe wines that are bitter or very DRY. The words *amarognolo* or *ammandorlato,* which denote a bitter, toasted-almond flavor, are considered more flattering.

amarognolo *see* AMARO

amarone *see* RECIOTO

Amboise [ahm-BWAHZ] A quaint little town in France's TOURAINE AC that produces higher-quality wine and is allowed to append its name to the label—Touraine-Amboise. The white wines are made from CHENIN BLANC and resemble those from VOUVRAY. The red and ROSÉ wines are made from CABERNET FRANC, GAMAY, and MALBEC. The Touraine province is known as the "château country," and Amboise has a well-known château that's quite popular.

Ambonnay [ahm-baw-NAY] An important wine-producing village located in the Montagne de Reims area of France's CHAMPAGNE region. Ambonnay, whose vineyards are planted with PINOT NOIR, is one of only seventeen villages to have obtained a GRAND CRU rating of 100 percent (*see* CHAMPAGNE for explanation of percent system).

ambra *see* MARSALA DOC

amelioration [uh-MEEL-yuh-RAY-shuhn] A catchall term for various methods of improving a wine, some of which are illegal in commercial winemaking. These methods include adding sugar, water, and/or acid to the grape juice or wine to correct deficiencies. Most countries have regulations pertaining to these practices with regard to commercial winemaking.

American Viticultural Area (AVA) A system implemented in 1983 designed to identify U.S. wines in a fashion similar to the French APPELLATION D'ORIGINE CONTRÔLÉE (AOC or AC) system. Unlike the French regulations, however, the rules governing American VITICULTURAL AREAS (under the jurisdiction of BATF—Bureau of Alcohol, Tobacco, and Firearms) are extremely lax. An AVA is defined strictly by a geographic area, whereas in France the parameters are much more precise. A French AOC identifies the grape varieties that may be grown in a geographic area, the maximum production per acre, the minimum level of alcohol required for wines produced in the area, and so forth. The only requirement for wines utilizing an AVA on the label is that 85 percent of the grapes must be grown in that viticultural area. Growers must petition the BATF to designate an area as an AVA. The Bureau's decision is based on such characteristics as an area's topography, soil type, microclimate, elevation and, to some extent, historical precedent. AVAs range in size from several hundred acres to several million; some reside within other larger AVAs. For example, California's NAPA VALLEY is an AVA that encompasses other AVA's including HOWELL MOUNTAIN, STAGS LEAP DISTRICT, and RUTHERFORD BENCH. It also includes part of the CARNEROS AVA, whose area spills over into SONOMA COUNTY.

Americano *see* ISABELLA; TICINO

Amézola de la Mora [ah-meh-ZOH-lah deh lah MOR-uh] Located in Spain's RIOJA DO, this BODEGA was founded in 1986 and is one of the new breed of producers to spring up in this area. It produces only red wines from TEMPRANILLO, Mazuelo (CARIGNAN), and Viura (MACABEO). The highly regarded wines are AGED for at least 4 years (some longer), and some French oak barrels are used in the aging process. The proprietary brand names used for these wines are Viña Amézola and Señorío Amézola.

Amiral de Beychevelle *see* BEYCHEVELLE, CHÂTEAU

ammandorlato *see* AMARO

amontillado *see* SHERRY

amoroso *see* SHERRY

Les Amoureuses *see* CHAMBOLLE-MUSIGNY

ampelography [am-peh-LAW-gra-fee] The study and classification of grape varieties.

amphora [AM-fuhr-uh] An ancient earthenware vessel used by the Greeks and Romans to store wine. It usually had two handles and an oval body and was tapered to a point at the base. In order for it to stand upright, the amphora was seated on a round foot or base.

Ampurdán-Costa Brava DO [ahm-poor-DAHN KOH-stah BRAH-vah] A small DO located at the very northeastern tip of Spain in the CATALONIA region. Its northern border is France, the Mediterranean is east of it. The region consists of many small landowners, and most of the wines are made by thirteen large cooperatives. Cavas del Ampurdán is a BODEGA that AGES and bottles much of this wine for the cooperatives. Ampurdán-Costa Brava DO produces mostly ROSÉ but also red and white wines. The red wines are made using Garnacha Tinta (GRENACHE) and Cariñena (CARIGNAN); rosé wines use those grapes plus the two white VARIETIES, MACEBEO and XAREL-LO. White wines are made from these last two grapes. There are a variety of styles including FORTIFIED WINES and RANCIOS. There are also CAVA DO wines produced under the Castillo de Perelada label.

Amtliche Prüfungsnummer [AM-tlish-eh PROOF-unz-snoo-mer] A German phrase meaning "official test number," usually abbreviated on a wine label as A.P.Nr. The Amtliche Prüfungsnummer indicates that the wine has met the minimum standards required by the law. It's granted by an official testing control center where the wine is tasted and the results of a chemical analysis (performed by an officially recognized laboratory) reviewed. The number, which must appear on the label, identifies the control center that tested the wine, bottling location, bottler's registration number, bottler's application number (indicating the wine lot), and year the wine was tested (not the VINTAGE year).

Anbaugebiet; pl. Anbaugebiete [AHN-bow-geh-beet] A German term referring to a growing region for quality wine, either QbA (QUALITÄTSWEIN BESTIMMTER ANBAUGEBIET) or QmP (QUALITÄTSWEIN MIT PRÄDIKAT). There are now thirteen of these regions, and their regional name is required on labels of quality wines. Eleven were initially established in 1971 by German law in an effort to meet European Common Market rules. They are AHR, BADEN, FRANKEN, HESSISCHE BERGSTRSSE, MITTELRHEIN, MOSEL-SAAR-RUWER, NAHE, RHEINGAU, RHEINHESSEN, RHEINPFALZ, and WÜRTTEMBERG. Two more Anbaugebiete were recently added from the former East Germany—SAALE-UNSTRUT and SACHSEN. Each Anbaugebiet may be further divided into BEREICHE (districts), GROSSLAGEN (general sites), and EINZELLAGEN (individual sites or vineyards).

Andalusia; Sp. Andalucía [an'dl-OO-zhuh] A well-known region covering the southernmost part of Spain. Andalusia encompasses eight provinces and spans from the Atlantic Ocean to the Mediterranean. There are four DO areas—MONTILLA-MORILES, MÁLAGA, CONDADO DE HUELVA, and JEREZ-XÉRÈX-SHERRY Y MANZANILLA DE SANLÚCAR DE BARRAMEDA. The best-known potables from the region are FORTIFIED WINES, the most famous of which is SHERRY.

Anderson Valley AVA An AVA located in California's Mendocino County, north of Sonoma County and San Francisco. The area starts just south of Booneville and extends northwest for about 25 miles ending close to the Pacific Ocean at its northwest tip. Most of the Anderson Valley Viticultural Area is a cool growing area—a Region I to Region II rating (*see* CLIMATE REGIONS OF CALIFORNIA). It does well with PINOT NOIR, CHARDONNAY, GEWURTRAMINER, and RIESLING; CABERNET SAUVIGNON, MERLOT, and ZINFANDEL are also grown. In addition to STILL WINES, the region has shown that it can grow the style of grape required for good SPARKLING WINES as demonstrated by those from Scharfenberger Cellars and ROEDERER ESTATE. Other well-known wineries include HANDLEY CELLARS, HUSCH VINEYARDS, and Navarro Vineyards.

S. Anderson Vineyards Winery that was founded in 1979 by the late Dr. Stanley Anderson and his wife Carol. It consists of 32 acres located at the northern end of the STAGS LEAP DISTRICT AVA, with another 70 acres in the CARNEROS AVA. The winery produces highly regarded SPARKLING WINE in BRUT, BLANC DE NOIRS, and ROSÉ styles. The sparkling wines and a CHARDONNAY are produced from grapes grown in Anderson's own vineyards. A limited amount of excellent CABERNET SAUVIGNON is made from grapes purchased from neighboring Stags Leap vineyards.

Andre Sparkling Wine *see* E & J GALLO WINERY

anejo; anejado por [ah-NYAY-yoh; ah-nyay-YAH-doh por] Spanish terms for "old" or "aged," and for "aged by."

angelica wine [an-JEHL-ih-kuh] An inexpensive FORTIFIED wine, typically made from MISSION or MUSCAT grapes and enhanced with BRANDY. Angelica wine usually contains 10 to 15 percent RESIDUAL SUGAR. It's associated with California, its name being a reference to the city of Los Angeles.

L'Angélus, Château [sha-TOH lahn-zhay-LEUS] With approximately 65 acres, this BORDEAUX chateau is one of the largest in SAINT-ÉMILION. It has a GRAND CRU CLASSÉ ranking and has produced such excellent wines in recent years that some feel L'Angélus should be upgraded to a PREMIER GRAND CRU CLASSÉ. The approximate blend for its red wines is 50 percent CABERNET FRANC, 45 percent MERLOT, and 5 percent CABERNET SAUVIGNON. Château L'Angélus produces about 7,000 to 13,000 cases of red wine per year and has a SECOND LABEL **Carillon de L'Angélus**. Wines from better VINTAGES can AGE for up to 10 to 12 years.

Anghelu Ruju [AHN-jeh-loo ROO-yoo] Italian term that means "red angel." Anghelu Ruju is a delicious PASSITO wine produced by Sella

& Mosca, a large wine estate on the island of SARDINIA. It's made from Connonau grapes that have been dried on mats for 2½ to 3 weeks to concentrate their sugars and flavors. The result is a sweet, high-ALCO-HOL (about 18 percent) wine that has some resemblance to PORT.

d'Angludet, Château [sha-TOH dah*n*-gloo-DAY] Château located in the MARGAUX AC that is one of BORDEAUX's very good CRUS BOUR-GEOIS EXCEPTIONNELS. It has approximately 75 acres, which are planted with about 60 percent CABERNET SAUVIGNON, 30 percent MERLOT, and small amounts of both CABERNET FRANC and PETIT VERDOT. British-born Peter A. Sichel, who purchased the property in 1961, has made dramatic improvements in the quality of the wine. Many feel Château d'Angludet deserves to be moved up to CRU CLASSÉ status. Wines from the better VINTAGES can AGE for 15 to 20 years. The CHÂTEAU produces about 12,000 to 13,000 cases of red wine each year and has a SECOND LABEL, **Domaine Baury**.

angular Winetasting term that describes wines that generally leave a tart flavor impression on the palate. Such wines, which are usually young and DRY, lack the SOFT, SUPPLE qualities of their counterparts.

Anjou [ah*n*-ZHOO] Area that is located in the central LOIRE near the city of Angers and is part of a larger growing region known as Anjou-Saumur. Anjou is best known for its rosés—ROSÉ D' ANJOU AC (a sweetish, pale pink wine produced from Cot (MALBEC), GAMAY, GROSLOT, and Pineau d'Aunis grapes) and CABERNET D'ANJOU AC (generally regarded as a higher-quality rosé made from CABERNET FRANC and CABERNET SAUVI-GNON). White wines from Anjou have traditionally been on the sweet side, made mostly from CHENIN BLANC (locally called *Pineau d'Anjou* or *Pineau de la Loire*). Recently, drier styles made with up to the legal maximum of 20 percent CHARDONNAY and/or SAUVIGNON BLANC have produced attractive, fruity wines. Beside the basic Anjou APPELLATION, white wines are produced in a number of smaller appellations in the area including BONNEZEAUX AC, COTEAUX DE L'AUBANCE AC, COTEAUX DU LAYON, QUARTS DE CHAUME, and SAVENNIÈRES AC. Red wines are made from Cabernet Franc, Cabernet Sauvignon, and Gamay, and those from the basic Anjou appellation are gaining in reputation. The **Anjou-Villages AC** is made up of forty-six villages scattered throughout Anjou that produce higher-quality red wines made from Cabernet Franc and Cabernet Sauvignon. There are also a number of white and rose SPARKLING WINES made by the MÉTHODE CHAMPENOISE and produced under the **Anjou Mousseux AC** and the higher-quality CRÉMANT DE LOIRE AC.

Annaberg *see* KALLSTADT

annata [an-NAH-tah] Italian term for "year of the vintage."

año [AHN-yoh] Spanish term for "year."

anthocyanins The pigments that contribute the red colors in wine and grapes.

antioxidant [AN-tee-AHK-sih-dehnt] In winemaking, reference to additives such as ascorbic acid and sulfur dioxide. When added in the right quantities, these substances limit the effect of oxygen contact with wine during various winemaking processes such as RACKING, FILTERING, and bottling.

Antonio Barbadillo   *see* BARBADILLO, ANTONIO

AOC Abbreviation for APPELLATION D'ORIGINE CÔNTROLÉE.

apéritif [ah-pehr-uh-TEEF; ay-pehr-ee-TEEF] A French term referring to a light alcoholic drink taken before a meal to stimulate the appetite. Popular apéritifs include CHAMPAGNE, VERMOUTH, SHERRY, and FORTIFIED and flavored wines such as Lillet and Dubonnet.

A.P.Nr. Abbreviation for AMTLICHE PRUFÜNGSNUMMER.

appellation [ap-puh-LAY-shuhn; Fr. ah-pel-lah-SYAW*N*] In the wine world, a designated growing area governed by the rules and regulations established by its federal government and local governing body. Such rules vary from country to country but are somewhat similar in their attempt to stimulate the production of quality wines. These regulations are established by the APPELLATION D'ORIGINE CÔNTROLÉE (AOC) in France, the DENOMINAZIONE DI ORIGINE CONTROLLATA (DOC) in Italy, the DENOMINAÇÀO DE ORIGEM CONTROLADA (DOC) in Portugal, the DENOMINACIÓN DE ORIGEN (DO) in Spain, and the AMERICAN VITICULTURAL AREA (AVA) in the United States.

Appellation Côntrolée   *see* APPELLATION D'ORIGINE CÔNTROLÉE

Appellation d'Origine Contrôlée (AOC or AC) [ah-pehl-lah-SYAW*N* daw-ree-JEEN kaw*n*-traw-LAY] The top category in the French system for ensuring quality wines. Appellation d'Origine Contrôlée, which means "Appellation of Controlled Origin," is sometimes shortened to Appellation Contrôlée and abbreviated as either AOC or AC. The French initiated the Appellation d'Origine Contrôlée system in 1935 as a means of safeguarding the more quality-conscious winemakers, vineyards, and areas from unethical producers who were taking advantage of the better-known names. Although the French AC system can't guarantee the quality of a producer's wine, it can control most of the elements that go into making it. This is accomplished by the demanding criteria necessary for qualifying as an AC. These criteria fall into the following seven categories: 1. the land—acceptable vineyard acreage is precisely defined based on centuries of recorded usage and issues such as the land's soil, configuration, and altitude; 2. the grape varieties—defined for each geographic area and based on historical data, clarifying which varieties perform well in particular soils and climates; 3. Vitacultural practices—this category considers such things as the number of vines per HECTARE, pruning techniques, and fertilization methods; 4. permissible YIELD—because large yields decrease the grapes' quality, and one way to improve caliber is to restrict the crop, maximum yields are established for each AC; 5. alcohol content—all ACs must guarantee a minimum alcohol level, which means that the grapes must reach a certain ripeness (sugar content), which in turn ensures flavor, although in some areas it's legal to add sugar (CHAPTALIZE) to reach the required alcohol level; 6. winemaking practices—each AC has regulations regarding winemaking procedures, usually based on historical practices that produced favorable results; 7. official tasting—since 1979 tasting panels sample all wines that apply for AC status. Wines that meet all seven of these criteria are entitled to use the phrase Appellation Contrôlée on their labels; not following these regulations disqualifies a wine from AC status. Multiple ACs can exist within the geographic area of a larger AC. Such is the case with the PAUILLAC AC, which is within the HAUT-MÉDOC AC, which is within the BORDEAUX AC. Generally, the smaller ACs produce the highest-quality wines. The categories below Appellation d'Origine Contrôlée are, from top to bottom: VIN DÉLIMITÉ DE QUALITÉ SUPÉRIEURE, VIN DE PAYS, and VIN DE TABLE. Although the French system is being paralleled by other countries, so far none seem to be as successful. These include the AMERICAN VITICULTURAL AREA (AVA) in the United States, the DENOMINAZIONE DI ORIGINE CONTROLLATA (DOC) in Italy, the DENOMINAÇÃO DE ORIGEM CONTROLADA (DOC) in Portugal, and the DENOMINACIÓN DE ORIGEN (DO) in Spain.

appley; apples Sensory term that describes a wine's smell in several ways. A **green apple** scent, for example, signals that immature grapes went into the wine, while the smell of **ripe apples** is indicative of some CHARDONNAYS, and an **old apple** fragrance is often found in sweet Tokay wines.

A.P.Nr. *see* AMTLICHE PRÜFUNGSNUMMER

Aprilia DOC [ah-PREE-lyah] DOC zone that is south and slightly east of Rome in the CASTELLI ROMANI district of Italy's LATIUM region. Three wines are made here: A DRY red from MERLOT; a dry ROSATO from

SANGIOVESE; and a dry white from TREBBIANO. The named grape must make up at least 95 percent of the grapes used.

Apulia [ah-POOL-yuh] Located in Italy's southeast section, Apulia (*Puglia* in Italian) is the wine region lying in the "heel" of Italy's boot-shaped land mass. There are numerous grape varieties grown in the Apulia region. The primary red grapes are Negroamaro, Primitivo (*see* ZINFANDEL), MALVASIA Nera, and UVA DI TROIA. The white grape varieties, led by Verdeca, include Bianco d'Alessano, BOMBINO BIANCO, Malvasia Bianca, and TREBBIANO. The wine output from this area is tremendous and usually competes with SICILY for the largest production of Italy's twenty wine regions. The quality of the wines, however, is generally not very high. This is somewhat evidenced by the tiny amount of DOC-quality wine produced (less than 2 percent of the region's total production), although many of the region's good wines are not qualified to be DOCs. Apulia's twenty-four DOCs include CASTEL DEL MONTE, **Locorotondo**, **Martina Franca**, **Salice Salentino**, and **San Severo**. Much of this region's wine production is further processed into VERMOUTH or other APÉRITIF-type wine.

Aquileia DOC [ah-kwee-LAY-ah] A DOC area located in the southern part of the FRIULI-VENEZIA GIULIA region in northeastern Italy. The DOC covers a ROSATO plus thirteen different VARIETAL WINES, which must contain at least 90 percent of the main grape variety. The varietal wines are Cabernet (from Cabernet Sauvignon and Cabernet Franc), CABERNET SAUVIGNON, CABERNET FRANC, CHARDONNAY, MERLOT, Pinot Bianco (PINOT BLANC), Pinot Grigio (PINOT GRIS), Refosco dal Peduncolo Rosso (MONDEUSE), Riesling Renano (RIESLING), Sauvignon (SAUVIGNON BLANC), TOCAI FRIULANO, Traminer Aromatico (GEWÜRZTRAMINER), and VERDUZZO FRIULANO. The Rosato is mainly Merlot but can include up to 30 percent of some of the other approved red grapes. Most Aquileia wines have a light to medium BODY and should be drunk fairly young.

Aramon [ah-rah-MAWN] This high-yielding, red wine grape is extensively planted in France's LANGUEDOC-ROUSSILLON region. It's responsible for immense amounts of inferior wine, most of which has low alcohol and little flavor—France's contribution to the notorious European WINE LAKE. Because Aramon produces such pale red wine, a more darkly colored variety such as ALICANTE BOUSCHET is usually added for color. France is encouraging the replanting of many areas like the Languedoc-Roussillon with more respectable varieties. As a result, Aramon acreage has been decreasing over the last 25 years. Aramon is also known as *Pisse-vin, Plante Riche,* and *Ugni Noir.*

Arbois [ahr-BWAH] A large APPELLATION located in the Jura region of eastern France surrounding the town of Arbois. White wines are made from SAVAGNIN and CHARDONNAY. Light red and ROSÉ wines are made from Trousseau, PINOT NOIR, and Poulsard grapes. A good SPARKLING WINE, **Arbois MOUSSEUX**, is made by MÉTHODE CHAMPENOISE from Chardonnay grapes.

d'Arche, Château [sha-TOH DAHRSH] A DEUXIÈME CRU (second growth) CHÂTEAU located in the COMMUNE of Sauternes in France's BORDEAUX region. It has 70 acres planted with approximately 90 percent SÉMILLON and 10 percent SAUVIGNON BLANC. When environmental conditions permit BOTRYTIS CINEREA to attack the grapes, sweet DESSERT WINES are produced under the SAUTERNES AC. The wines from Château d'Arche have improved significantly since 1981, when new ownership took over. These wines can AGE for up to 15 years. About 4,000 cases are produced each year, and the château has a SECOND LABEL, **d'Arche-Lafaurie**.

Aretini *see* CHIANTI DOCG

Argentina Even though Argentina is the world's fifth largest wine-producing country, a great majority of the wine is inexpensive and ordinary. Most of Argentina's wine is consumed within the country, which also happens to have one of the higher per capita consumption rates. The largest growing region is in the Mendoza province, which produces 70 percent of Argentina's wine and 85 percent of its quality wine. Rio Negro, San Juan, and Salta are some of the other growing regions. Most of the growing areas are not far from the Andes Mountains where they have access to water for irrigation from the melting snows. Red wines account for a majority of Argentina's wines. Criolla (MISSION) is the most widely planted red grape variety, followed by MALBEC. There are a variety of other red grapes planted in Argentina—BARBERA, BONARDA, CABERNET SAUVIGNON, MERLOT, NEBBIOLO, PINOT NOIR, SANGIOVESE, SYRAH, and TEMPRANILLO. Widely grown white varieties, which are used mostly for FORTIFIED WINES, are PALOMINO, Torrontes, and PEDRO XIMÉNEZ. There is also acreage planted with CHARDONNAY, CHENIN BLANC, SÉMILLON, and SAUVIGNON BLANC, most of which go into higher-quality white wines, particularly from the Rio Negro area.

argol [AHR-guhl] A natural tartar produced during FERMENTATION that appears as little crystals in wine vats and sometimes in bottles. Argols can sometimes be found clinging to a cork when it's extracted.

Arinto [ah-RIHN-toh] Cultivated in Portugal, this good-quality white wine grape is known for its high ACIDITY, even when grown in the hottest areas. A well-made Arinto wine can be very aromatic with a fresh citrus feature. Arinto is a recommended variety throughout much of Portugal. Many growers, however, prefer to plant higher-yielding but lower-quality varieties. Arinto is also known as *Pedernão*.

Arkansas In the early 1900s, Arkansas enjoyed abundant vineyards, mostly of CONCORD grapes, a native American variety of the VITIS LABRUSCA species. Unfortunately, wines from these grapes don't have the popular appeal of VITIS VINIFERA species (the basic European varieties like CABERNET SAUVIGNON and CHARDONNAY). Today, Arkansas winemaking is mostly from HYBRIDS and vitis vinifera grapes. The state has about 5,000 acres of vineyards producing a variety of STILL WINES (including Cabernet Sauvignon and Chardonnay) as well as SPARKLING WINES. The Wiederkehr Winery, which was started in the late 1800s, is in operation today by the founder's descendants. It has shifted from American varieties and hybrids to grapes like Cabernet Sauvignon, RIESLING, and MUSCAT. Post Winery and Mount Bethel are other wineries in the state.

Armagnac [ahr-muhn-YAK] A fine French BRANDY from the Armagnac region, which is situated southeast of BORDEAUX. The region consists of three subregions—Bas-Armagnac, Tenareze, and Haut-Armagnac. Although almost as highly regarded as COGNAC, Armagnac is of a different style. It's distilled only once and therefore has a lower alcoholic strength (generally about 53 percent alcohol) than Cognac (about 70 percent), which undergoes a double distillation process. This single distillation also leaves more flavoring elements in the distilled spirit. Armagnac employs the local black oak for AGING instead of the Limousin oak used for Cognac. Black oak imparts more flavor to the Armagnac and allows for faster aging. The result is that Armagnac is silky smooth but fuller-flavored than Cognac, although it generally doesn't have the finesse of the finest Cognacs.

Arneis [ahr-NAYZ] White wine grape that originated (and is still primarily grown) in the Roero hills of Italy's southern PIEDMONT, just north of ALBA. Once nearly extinct, Arneis has made a comeback in recent years. It can produce very good wines with PERFUMY characteristics of apples, pears, and a hint of licorice. The wines, usually sold as ROERO ARNEIS DOC, are in limited supply.

aroma In the wine world, the traditional definition of aroma is the simple, fruity smell of the grape variety. Today's broader definition combines a wine's varietal fragrance plus any changes that develop during FERMENTATION and AGING. The traditional difference is that a young wine will show its varietal aroma in a more pronounced way. However, in a mature wine—where some of the grape's intrinsic fragrance has been replaced by other characteristics—the smell transmutes into a BOUQUET. *See also* NOSE.

aromatic Winetasting term that describes a wine with a rich, spicy, or herbaceous aroma and flavor, generally derived from certain grape varieties such as SAUVIGNON BLANC and MUSCAT.

arresting fermentation A technique of preserving RESIDUAL SUGAR in wines by stopping FERMENTATION. There are several methods to arrest fermentation including chilling the wine to the point where YEASTS become inactive and using a CENTRIFUGE to remove the yeast cells prior to completing fermentation.

arroba [ah-ROH-bah] A Spanish measure used for grapes and the resulting wines. It's equivalent to just over 25 pounds of grapes (about one basketful), which yields about 4¼ gallons.

arrope *see* MALAGA DO

L'Arrosée, Château [sha-TOH lah-roh-SAY] A GRAND CRU CLASSÉ château located in the SAINT-ÉMILION AC in France's BORDEAUX region. It has nearly 40 acres planted with about 50 percent MERLOT, 35 percent CABERNET SAUVIGNON, and the rest CABERNET FRANC. The wines were relatively unknown until recently, but good performance in the 1980s has resulted in an increased following. L'Arrosee produces about 4,000 to 5,000 cases of red wine annually and has a SECOND LABEL, **Les Coteaux du Château L'Arrosée.**

Arrowood Vineyards & Winery A winery founded by Dick Arrowood, the longtime (1974 to 1990) winemaker at CHATEAU ST. JEAN. He was still at Chateau St. Jean when he started building his own winery in the SONOMA VALLEY near the town of Glen Ellen in 1986. He has now shifted his attention to his own winemaking activities, producing mostly CABERNET SAUVIGNON and CHARDONNAY, both of which are highly regarded. The winery has only 4 acres of its own, planted in CABERNET FRANC, MERLOT, MALBEC, and PETIT VERDOT. It buys grapes from a multitude of vineyards—Chardonnay from six different vineyards in various areas like the ALEXANDER VALLEY, RUSSIAN RIVER VALLEY, and Sonoma Valley and Cabernet Sauvignon from at least twelve different vineyard locations. The Arrowood MERLOT, first released in 1988, received critical acclaim for its initial releases. Arrowood is now making small amounts of VIOGNIER, as well as RIESLING in a LATE HARVEST style. **Domaine du Grand Archer** is Arrowood's SECOND LABEL.

Arroyo Grande AVA [uh-ROY-oh GRAN-day] AVA located in central California about halfway between San Francisco and Los

Angeles. It's southwest of San Luis Obispo, encompasses the town of Arroyo Grande, and extends to the northeast. The western part of the area has a long cool growing season, a Region I rating (*see* CLIMATE RE-GIONS OF CALIFORNIA), but the eastern part of the area is warmer and falls into Region III. CHARDONNAY is the most popular variety by a considerable amount, followed by PINOT NOIR and other grapes like CABER-NET SAUVIGNON, SAUVIGNON BLANC, SÉMILLON, and ZINFANDEL. One of the area's wineries is Maison Deutz, a joint venture between the French Champange company Deutz, and Wine World, Inc. (who also own BERINGER VINEYARDS in the NAPA VALLEY). Other highly regarded wineries include Saucelito Canyon Vineyard and Talley Vineyards.

Arroyo Seco AVA [uh-ROY-oh SEH-koh] Small VITICULTURAL AREA located in Monterey County, California, southeast of Monterey. Arroyo Seco, which is a subzone in the larger MONTEREY AVA, begins just south of Soledad and extends to south of Greenfield. The major grapes grown here are CHARDONNAY and RIESLING. Jekel Vineyard and Ventana Vineyards are two of the best-known wineries in this area.

Artigues-Arnaud *see* GRAND-PUY-DUCASSE, CHÂTEAU

asciutto [ah-SHOO-toh] An Italian word that, when used to describe STILL WINES, means "very dry."

Asprino [ah-SPREE-noh] A DRY, LIGHT, lower-ALCOHOL wine produced in the BASILICATA and CAMPANIA regions of Italy. This VINO DA TAVOLA (table wine) is made from the Asprinio grape.

assemblage [ah-sahm-BLAHJ] The French term for "assembling," referring to art of BLENDING. In BORDEAUX assemblage describes the activity of judging the wines made from different lots (which can come from different varieties, the same variety from different parts of the vineyard, or grapes picked at different times and therefore showing different levels of sugar) and determining which lots are suitable for a CHÂTEAU'S final wines. In some cases, the wine will go into the premium brand; in other cases, it'll go into a SECOND LABEL or even be sold off in BULK. In a poor year, a château may decide not to produce any of its premium brand wines at all. In CHAMPAGNE, a similar process is employed (particularly with NON-VINTAGE champagnes) in order to achieve a "house style" that's consistent from year to year. This requires reviewing batches of wines from different vineyards, grapes, and years to blend the appropriate CUVÉE.

Assmannshausen [AHS-mahns-how-zuhn] A German village located in the RHEINGAU region, north of RÜDESHEIM, where the Rhine shifts north toward the town of Koblenz. Assmannshausen produces a famous and expensive red wine made from Spätburgunder (PINOT NOIR). Internationally, these wines are not as well received as they are in Germany because they're generally lighter and can be sweet.

Asti [AH-stee] Name of an important wine-producing town and province situated south of Turin in Italy's PIEDMONT region. In addition to the ASTI SPUMANTE DOCG (which produces the area's famous SPARKLING WINE of the same name), several other DOCs and DOCGs use Asti in their names—BARBERA D'ASTI, Dolcetto d'Asti, Freisa d'Asti, Grignolino d'Asti, and MOSCATO D'ASTI.

Asti Spumante DOCG; Asti [AH-stee spoo-MAHN-teh] Located in the southeastern portion of the PIEDMONT region near the town of Asti, this DOCG area produces Italy's most famous SPARKLING WINE. Asti Spumante shares this DOCG with a related wine, **Moscato d'Asti**, which is made similarly, but in a FRIZZANTE (instead of fully sparkling) style. In 1994, when Asti Spumante was upgraded to DOCG status, its name was simplified to *Asti*. These wines, which are generally semisweet to sweet, are so popular that the amount produced by this DOCG is now second only to the CHINATI DOCG. The wines are made in a modified version of the CHARMAT or *autoclave* process. In this process the grape MUST is filtered and then stored in tanks at near freezing temperatures so that FERMENTATION can't begin. The producers make batches according to demand so that the resulting wines can be as fresh as possible. To produce the wine, the must is allowed to warm and then is innoculated with yeast so that fermentation can begin. This process all occurs inside large sealed tanks so that the carbon dioxide produced during fermentation isn't lost. Once the desired ALCOHOL and RESIDUAL SUGAR levels are reached, the wine is rapidly chilled to stop fermentation. The wine is then filtered, bottled, and corked—ready for shipment. The main difference between the Asti Spumante DOCG wines and the Moscato d'Asti DOCG wines is that fermentation of Moscato d'Asti wines is stopped sooner so that the residual sugar content is higher, the alcohol level is lower, and the wine is less effervescent because less carbon dioxide is produced. Additionally, Asti Spumante is normally packaged like CHAMPAGNE with a wired-down cork, and Moscato d'Asti generally has the standard cork used by most STILL WINES. The wines are made from the MUSCAT grape (called *Moscato Bianco* or *Moscato di Canelli* in this region), and the resulting wine has a fresh grapey taste. Asti Spumante and Moscato d'Asti wines should be drunk young and fresh. Other DOC wines made in the region near the town of Asti include BARBERA D'ASTI and Dolcetto d'Asti.

astringent; astringency A wine that has a harsh, dry, mouth-puckering effect created by excess TANNINS. High ACIDITY can produce a similar reaction. Wines with astringency may SOFTEN as they mature.

asztalibor; asztali bor [AHS-tah-lih-bahr] The Hungarian term for "common TABLE WINE" (*bor* means wine).

Aszú [ah-SOO] The Hungarian term for grapes infected with BOTRY-TIS CINEREA and therefore shriveled and full of concentrated flavors and sugar. TOKAY ASZÚ (or *Tokaji Azsú*), the famous DESSERT WINE, is made from botrytis-infected FURMINT grapes.

atmosphere; atm Atm is the abbreviation for *atmosphere,* which in the wine world is the measurement for pressure used to produce SPARKLING WINES. Technically, it's the normal air pressure at sea level, approximately 14.7 pounds per square inch. In the production of a standard sparkling wine such as CHAMPAGNE or SPUMANTE, the pressure should be 6 atms. A CRÉMANT-style sparkling wine has about half that pressure, and some FRIZZANTE-style Italian wines may have only 2 atms of pressure.

attack Winetasting parlance for the first impression of a wine on the palate.

attenuated [uh-TEN-yoo-ay-td] A wine that's heading over the hill, demonstrated by a loss of FRUIT and BODY, can be referred to as attenuated.

Attica An important wine-producing region situated near Athens in southeastern Greece. The grapes used are the local varieties—Savatiano, Mandilaria, and Rhoditis. Most of the production is made into RETSINA.

Au Bon Climat [oh bohn klee-MAHT] A 10,000-case winery that specializes in CHARDONNAY and PINOT NOIR wines. Au Bon Climat is situated just inside SAN LUIS OBISPO COUNTY where it dips down into the adjacent SANTA BARBARA COUNTY, west of Santa Maria in central California. The winemaking facility is located on the Bien Nacido Vineyard, which supplies Au Bon Climat with Chardonnay and Pinot Noir grapes. This winery generally receives praise for its Chardonnays—the standard bottlings, the Talley Reserve and Bien Nacido Reserve, as well as its Talley Reserve and Benedict Reserve Pinot Noirs.

Les Arvelets *see* FIXIN

Aubance *see* COTEAUX DE L'AUBANCE AC

Aube *see* CHAMPAGNE

Aude [OHD] A large DÉPARTEMENT in France's LANGUEDOC-ROUSSILLON, or *Midi,* as it's sometimes called. Aude, located in southern France along the Mediterranean not too far from the Spanish border, produces millions of bottles of very ordinary wine, most of it red wine made from CARIGNAN, CINSAUT, and GRENACHE. Along with départements of HÉRAULT and GARD, Aude contributes to what is called the European WINE LAKE—huge amounts of nondescript wine. There are signs that the quality is improving, in part due to increased planting of popular varieties like CABERNET SAUVIGNON, CHARDONNAY, and SAUVIGNON BLANC. Under existing APPELLATION rules, these varieties cannot qualify for higher classification so the wines made from them must be sold as VIN DE PAYS. The best-known appellations in Aude are BLANQUETTE DE LIMOUX (which produces decent SPARKLING WINE via MÉTHODE CHAMPENOISE), CORBIÈRES, MINERVOIS, and FITOU.

Auflange *see* NIERSTEIN

Aurora; Aurore [aw-ROAR-ah; aw-ROAR] White wine grape that is one of the most widely planted varieties in the northeastern United States, where the cool climate suits its early ripening properties. Aurora is a French-American HYBRID, officially known as **Seibel Hybrid 5279**. It's used to make SPARKLING WINES, as well as OFF-DRY, STILL WINES.

Ausbruch A quality category for Austrian wines. Wines allowed into this category are made from grapes that have been infected with BOTRYTIS CINEREA and then dried naturally. The botrytis and drying shrivels the grapes, thereby concentrating the sugar. The superior wine made from these grapes is very sweet but has enough ACID for proper BALANCE. The required sugar levels place Ausbruch wines between BEERENAUSLESE and the highest-quality level, TROCKENBEERENAUSLESE.

Auslese [OWS-lay-zuh] The German word for "selection," used in the wine trade to describe specially selected, perfectly ripened bunches of grapes that are hand-picked and then pressed separately from other grapes. Auslese is one of the six subcategories of QmP (QUALITÄTSWEIN MIT PRÄDIKAT) and ranks above KABINETT and SPÄTLESE but below BEERENAUSLESE, EISWEIN, and TROCKENBEERENAUSLESE. To attain the Auslese category, the natural sugar content of the grapes must reach a certain minimum (83 to 105° OECHSLE, approximately 20 to 25 percent sugar by weight), depending on the region and the variety. The grapes are often subject to BOTRYTIS CINEREA (called *Edelfäule* in

German), which can give them that extra push toward the high sugar levels. The superior wine made from these grapes is sweet and expensive and is generally categorized as a DESSERT WINE.

Ausone, Château [sha-TOH oh-ZON] A famous CHÂTEAU of the SAINT-ÉMILION AC in France's BORDEAUX region. Château Ausone is a PREMIER GRAND CRU CLASSÉ and ranks with Château CHEVAL BLANC as one of the two top châteaus of Saint-Émilion. They're both compared with the FIRST GROWTHS of the MÉDOC—Châteaus LAFITE-ROTHSCHILD, LATOUR, and MOUTON-ROTHSCHILD. Château Ausone is named after the Roman poet Ausonius who lived in the Bordeaux area during the fourth century (but most likely not on this site). Its vineyard consists of about 17 acres planted almost evenly with CABERNET FRANC and MERLOT. Château Ausone produces only around 2,300 cases of red wine per year. Better VINTAGES of this hard-to-find wine can age for 35 to 50 years.

austere; austerity A tasting term used to describe wine that's somewhat HARD and lacking in FRUIT and richness. Such austerity is usually due to excess TANNINS, sometimes ACID. It's most often found in young, immature wines and will sometimes SOFTEN during AGING.

Australia Although Australia has had vineyards since the late 1700s, it wasn't until the late 1950s that Australian winemakers really started to focus on TABLE WINES. By the 1980s Australian wines finally began to get the attention of the rest of the world. As in California, the European (particularly French) grape varieties are the most popular. Shiraz (SYRAH) is the most widely planted red grape, followed by CABERNET SAUVIGNON, GRENACHE, and PINOT NOIR. MUSCAT is the leading white variety, followed closely by CHARDONNAY and RIESLING along with SÉMILLON, TREBBIANO, SAUVIGNON BLANC, and COLOMBARD. A fair amount of PALOMINO and PEDRO XIMÉNEZ is still grown for the production of Australian SHERRY. SULTANA is also widely grown, and although most of the production is used for table grapes or raisins, some finds its way into BULK WINES. Australia is quite large—the subcontinent is about four-fifths the size of the United States. However, the vineyard land, like the population, is clustered mainly in the southeast and the southwest. The vast quantity of wine comes from areas collectively known as the Riverlands, which are located along the Murry and Murrumbidgee Rivers in the states of New South Wales, South Australia, and Victoria. These areas are Riverina and Murrumbidgee Irrigation Area (MIA) in New South Wales, Riverland in South Australia, and Sunraysia in Victoria. The better-quality wines come from a variety of distinct areas: HUNTER VALLEY and MUDGEE in New South Wales; Geelong, Goulburn Valley, Great Western, Milawa, Rutherglen, and YARRA VALLEY in Victoria; Adelaide,

BAROSSA VALLEY, Clare Valley, COONAWARRA, Padthaway, and SOUTHERN VALES in Southern Australia; and the LOWER GREAT SOUTHERN REGION, MARGARET RIVER, and Swan Valley areas of Western Australia. In Queensland the only area of note is the Granite Belt. On the Australian island of Tasmania, with its somewhat cooler climate, there are high viticultural hopes for areas like Pipes River and Tamar Valley in the north and Coal River, Derwent Valley, Huon Valley, and the East Coast on the south portion. If an Australian wine label indicates a single grape variety, the wine must be made of at least 80 percent of that grape. If the label indicates multiple varieties—such as Cabernet-Shiraz, Shiraz-Cabernet or Semillon-Chardonnay—the varieties must be listed in descending order of quantity. If the label indicates that the wine is from a particular region, 80 percent of it must be from that region. A wine blended from wines of different regions (which many Australian winemakers prefer) must label the regions in descending order of volume. VINTAGE Australian wine must be at least 95 percent from that vintage.

Austria The world of wine in Austria is similiar to that of Germany in many ways, but it's also quite different. Austria is generally warmer than Germany, and therefore the grapes ripen more fully, which produces stronger wines. Austrians also generally like their wines drier (*see* DRY). Since the wine scandal of 1985, where traces of poisonous diethylene glycol were found in wines that were supposed to contain only natural sugars, tougher laws (very similiar to those in Germany) were enacted. The Austrian quality categories are similiar to Germany's—Qualitätswein (*see* QUALITÄTSWEIN BESTIMMTER ANBAUGEBIET), Prädikatswein (*see* QUALITÄTSWEIN MIT PRÄDIKAT), KABINETT, SPÄTLESE, AUSLESE, EISWEIN, BEERENAUSLESE, AUSBRUCH (not found in Germany), and TROCKENBEERENAUSLESE. In most cases, the Austrian requirements are somewhat stricter—for example, higher required sugar levels. If the name of a RIED ("vineyard") is used on the label, 100 percent of the wine used must be from that vineyard location. This is also true for any local or regional name. If a variety or vintage appears on the label, 85 percent of the wine must come from the named grape or vintage. Per capita, Austrians consume over three times the wine of the United States. In fact, they consume more than they produce so wines must be imported to fill the gap. More than 80 percent of the Austrian wine produced is white. The most popular white grape is GRÜNER VELTLINER, which produces pale, CRISP, light- to medium-bodied (*see* BODY), slightly SPICY wines of good quality. Other popular white varieties are GEWÜRZTRAMINER, Muscat-Ottonel (MUSCAT), Rhine Riesling (RIESLING), MÜLLER-THURGAU, Weissburgunder (PINOT BLANC), WELSCHRIESLING, Rotgipfler, Zierflander, and Neuburger (a cross of Pinot Blanc and SYLVANER). The red wines, which are usually very light, are made from Blauburgunder (PINOT NOIR), PORTUGIESER, Blaufränkisch, and Zweigelt. Austria produces most of its wines in the eastern part of the country. Over half is produced in the region of Niederösterreich (or Lower Austria), followed by Burgenland and then Steiermark (or Styria) and Vienna. Most of the wines produced from the various regions are dry. The exceptions are the sweet, BOTRYTISED wines from Burgenland, which are sometimes compared to those from SAUTERNES.

autoclave [AW-tuh-klayv] Italian name for the sealed tanks used in the CHARMAT PROCESS (bulk process) of producing SPARKLING WINES. Occasionally the process itself is referred to as autoclave. ASTI SPUMANTE sparkling wines rely heavily on the use of the autoclave.

autolysis [aw-TAHL-uh-sihss] A decomposition of dead yeast cells that occurs in wines that are aged SUR LIE ("on the LEES"). Winemakers believe that certain wines—like those made with CHARDONNAY or SAUVIGNON BLANC grapes—benefit from autolysis because they gain complexity during the process. Autolysis affects SPARKLING WINES made via MÉTHODE CHAMPENOISE because yeast cells and a mixture of sugar and wine (DOSAGE) are added to create a second fermentation in the bottle. The sparkling wine is then aged with the yeast cells in the bottle (sometimes for up to 10 years), which adds complexity to both BOUQUET and flavor.

autovinification [AW-toh-vihn-ih-fih-KAY-shun] The use of large, pressure-locked stainless steel or concrete tanks (called autovinificators) during the FERMENTATION of PORT. The naturally produced gases create enough pressure to force open the locks, pumping the juice up and over the CAP (seed, skins, stems, etc.) and thereby extracting TANNINS, color, and full fruit flavors. This technique replaces the traditional method of using long poles to push the cap down into the juice.

Auxerrois *see* MALBEC

Auxerrois Blanc [awk-sehr-WAH (oh-zher-WAH) BLAHN (BLAHNGK)] A white wine grape grown primarily in France's ALSACE region. The good-yielding Auxerrois Blanc produces a rather bland, high ACID, and high-ALCOHOL wine, which is most often used as a blend for EDELSWICKERS. There's some confusion about its name because, in various locales, MALBEC is called *Auxerrois,* CHARDONNAY is called *Auxerrois Blanc,* and PINOT GRIS is called *Auxerrois Gris.*

Auxerrois Gris *see* PINOT GRIS

Auxey-Duresses AC [awk-SAY dew-RESS] A minor wine-producing APPELLATION centered around the village of Auxey-Duresses in the CÔTE DE BEAUNE area of France's BURGUNDY region. This area produces good wines—reds from PINOT NOIR and white wines from CHARDONNAY—but they're overshadowed by the superb wines of neighboring MEURSALT. Auxey-Duresses contains several PREMIER CRU vineyards, but much of the wine produced in this appellation is sold under the name Côte de Beaune-Villages AC.

AVA *see* AMERICAN VITICULTURAL AREA

Avellino *see* FIANO DI AVELLINO DOC

Ayala *see* CHAMPAGNE

abcock Vineyards A 50-acre California winery in SANTA YNEZ VALLEY, not far from Lompoc. The vineyards are planted with CHARDONNAY, GEWÜRZTRAMINER, PINOT NOIR, RIESLING, and SAUVIGNON BLANC. Babcock Vineyards is also developing parcels with the Italian varieties of SANGIOVESE, VIOGNIER, and VERNACCIA. In addition, Babcock buys grapes from other growers in the Santa Barbara area. This winery receives high praise for its Babcock Vineyards-labeled Gewürztraminer, Grand Cuvee Chardonnay, and Sauvignon Blanc, as well as the **11 OAKS RANCH**-labeled Sauvignon Blanc. Babcock Vineyards' SECOND LABEL for lesser wines is **RIVER BREAK**.

Bacchus [BAK-uhs] 1. A white wine grape that is a very successful cross of MÜLLER-THURGAU and a SYLVANER-RIESLING HYBRID. Bacchus generally produces wines with good BODY, CHARACTER, and AROMA but low ACIDITY. The best ones show MUSCATlike attributes. Most Bacchus wines are blended with Müller-Thurgau and go into lower-quality LIEBFRAU-MILCH. 2. The god of wine in classical mythology; also called DIONYSUS.

Bacharach, Bereich *see* MITTELRHEIN

back blending The New Zealand term for adding SÜSSRESERVE (sweet unfermented grape juice) to sweeten a wine.

backward A term used to describe wine that's not as developed as expected for its age and style.

Baco, Maurice [BAH-koh] A late eighteenth-century French hybridist who developed a number of HYBRIDS that are still in use today including BACO BLANC and BACO NOIR.

Baco Blanc [BAH-koh BLAHN (BLAHNGK)] White French-American HYBRID that is grown mainly in France's ARMAGNAC district, where it replaced FOLLE BLANCHE, which had GRAFTING and BLACK ROT problems. Baco Blanc was developed by French hybridizer Maurice Baco who CROSSED the American hybrid Noah with Folle Blanche. Baco Blanc is very prolific and produces the highly ACIDIC, low-alcohol wines much sought after by the BRANDY makers of Armagnac. It's also known as *Baco 22A* and *Piqupoul de Pays*.

Baco Noir [BAH-koh NWAHR] A French-American HYBRID developed by French hybridizer Maurice Baco by crossing FOLLE BLANCHE with a native American vine. Baco Noir is grown in the eastern United States, primarily in New York State. It produces red wines that range from light, fruity styles that are reminiscent of BEAUJOLAIS' GAMAY to slightly heavier versions that are more suggestive of light BORDEAUX-style wines. Much of the modest Baco Noir acreage finds its way into BLENDS.

Badacsonyi [BAH-dah-CHAW-nyih] Hungary adds an *i* to the end of the names of its high-quality wine-producing regions, thereby identifying the wine's source. Badacsonyi refers to wines coming from the Mount Badacsony area in western Hungary on Lake Balaton's north shore. The best known of these wines is Badacsonyi Kéknyelü, made from the KÉKNYELÜ grape. Others are Badacsonyi Szürkebarát (PINOT GRIS) and Badacsonyi FURMINT.

Bad Dürkheim [baht DUHRK-hime] An important German wine center as well as a spa town. The name *bad* translates to "bath" or "spa" and usually indicates an area with mineral springs. Bad Dürkheim is located west of the city of Mannheim in the RHEINPFALZ region. The vineyards around Bad Dürkheim, which is also famous for its annual Sausage Fair, are known for producing excellent RIESLING wines. There are three GROSSLAGEN—Feuerberg, Hochmess, and Schenkenböhl. The EINZELLAGE Spielberg is one of the best sites.

Baden [BAHD-uhn] A large German ANBAUGEBIET (quality-wine region) that is the southernmost of the thirteen Anbaugebiete, with its southern edge touching up against the Swiss border. The major portion of Baden starts along the river Main, just north of Heidelberg, and extends south about 300 kilometers (180 miles) to the city of Basel. Most of the vineyards are situated in the southern portion, from the spa-resort town of Baden-Baden to Basel. One small part of Baden sits next to the FRANKEN Anbaugebiete, which is farther north, and another section is around Bodensee (also called Lake Constance). Baden's climate is the warmest of the thirteen Anbaugebiete and, as a result, over 70 percent of Germany's Spätburgunder (PINOT NOIR) vines are planted here. MÜLLER-THURGAU is the most widely planted variety, with Rülander (PINOT GRIS) quite popular as well. The area's warm climate contributes to wines that are generally more ALCOHOLIC and less ACIDIC than those from other parts of Germany. The unusual ROSÉ wine, BADISH ROTGOLD, which is a local specialty, is made from a combination of Spätburgunder and Rülander grapes. The pale pink WEISSHERBST wines, generally made from Spätburgunder, are also a local favorite. Baden contains 7 BEREICHE (including KAISERSTUHL-TUNIBERG and MARKGRÄFLERLAND), 16 GROSSLAGEN, and over 300 EINZELLAGEN. Production in Baden is carried out primarily by cooperative cellars including the huge **Badischer Winzerkeller**, Europe's largest wine-producing cellar.

B

Badischer Winzerkeller, Bereich   *see* BADEN

Bad Kreuznach [baht KROYTS-nahkh] The center of Germany's NAHE wine region, Bad Kreuznach is also a spa-resort town (*bad* translates to "bath" or "spa"). In addition, it gives its name to the BEREICH **Kreuznach**, which covers the southern portion of the Nahe ANBAUGE-BIETE. **Kronenberg** is the well-known GROSSLAGE, whose vineyards surround Bad Kreuznach. Some of the best EINZELLAGEN include **Brückes**, **Kahlenberg**, **Krötenpfuhl**, and **Steinweg**.

Badisch Rotgold [BAHD-ish ROHT-golt] A quality ROSÉ wine that used to be quite popular in Germany's BADEN region. It's made by combining Rülander (PINOT GRIS) and Spätburgunder (PINOT NOIR) grapes and then PRESSING and FERMENTING them together.

Badstube, Grosslage Bernkasteler   *see* BERNKASTEL

Baga [BAH-guh] Portugal's most widely cultivated red wine grape variety. It's particularly heavily planted in BAIRRADA, where it accounts for 80 to 90 percent of the region's red wine production. Baga is also widely grown in the regions of DÃO, DOURO (where its known as *Tinta Bairrada*), and Minho. Although extremely productive, Baga generally produces only medium-quality wines. These deeply colored wines are very TANNIC and ASTRINGENT, especially when VINIFIED in the traditional way by leaving the skins *and* stalks in the fermenting juice for a week or longer. Newer processing methods, which use only the skins (and for shorter periods) during fermentation, produce rich, colorful wines that are fragrant and fruity and certainly not as ROUGH.

Baiken   *see* RAUENTHAL

Bairrada DOC [bi-RAH-dah] A DENOMINAÇÃO DE ORIGEM CONTRO-LADA (DOC) area located in northern Portugal near the Atlantic coast, west of the DAO DOC and south of Oporto. The region is known for its TANNIC, high-ACID red wines made primarily from the BAGA grape along with PERIQUITA, Bastardo and Tinta Pinheira. The best of these wines will, with AGING, become SOFTER and richer. Newer techniques have been introduced to remove grape stalks prior to FERMENTATION and to shorten the period that the skins are in contact. This method produces rich, colorful wines that are fragrant and fruity and much less tannic. About 90 percent of the wines produced are red. Small amounts of SPARKLING WINE and white STILL WINE are also produced. Grapes used for the white wines are mainly local varieties and include Bical, Maria Gomes, and Rabo de Ovelha.

baked A winetasting term describing an aromatic characteristic exemplified by a warm-earth smell. It's sometimes found in VINTAGES produced during a hot growing season when extreme sun exposure can cause moisture-deprived grapes to dehydrate. In MADEIRA (*see listing*) wines, a process called *estufagem* "bakes" the wines, which produces their characteristic tangy, burnt-caramel flavor.

baking A term that relates to MADEIRA wine production. Baking refers to a process called *estufagem*. During this procedure, the wines are placed in hot rooms or heated tanks (*estufas*) where they're allowed to bake slowly for a minimum of 90 days. The finer Madeiras are stored in wooden casks and left in attics or other extremely warm areas for years to slowly develop the tangy, burnt-caramel, slightly bitter flavor that's unique to this wine.

balance; balanced Balance in wine is created when all the components—ACID, ALCOHOL, FRUIT, TANNINS etc.—are in perfect harmony. In a well-balanced wine, none of these elements overpowers another. The perfect balance in a particular wine depends on its origin and style.

Balaton [bah-lah-TAWN] Term that refers to Europe's largest lake, Lake Balaton, located in western Hungary. It also refers to the general wine-producing region surrounding the lake. Specific growing districts around Lake Balaton include Badacsony (BADACSONYI) and Balatonfüred-Csopak.

Balbi *see* PROSECCO

Balestard-la-Tonnelle, Château [sha-TOH bah-les-STAR lah toh-NELL] CHÂTEAU that is ranked as a GRAND CRU CLASSÉ and is located east of the town of SAINT-ÉMILION in France's BORDEAUX region. It produces about 5,000 cases of red wine a year from its 26 acres, which are planted with about 65 percent MERLOT, 20 percent CABERNET FRANC, and the rest CABERNET SAUVIGNON and MALBEC. Wine from better VINTAGES can AGE for about 15 years. The SECOND LABEL is **Les Tourelles de Balestard**.

balling scale *see* BRIX

Balthazar *see* WINE BOTTLES

Balzac *see* MOURVÈDRE

Bandol AC [bahn-DAWL] An APPELLATION for red, white, and ROSÉ wines that covers the area around the resort town of Bandol, located between Marseille and Toulon on the Mediterranean coast in France's Provence region. The MOURVÈDRE variety is the principal component (comprising at least 50 percent) in the BANDOL red and rosé wines, with GRENACHE, CINSAUT, and SYRAH generally used in the blend. The red wines, which are considered some of the best in Provence, must be AGED in wood for a least 18 months and can handle extensive BOTTLE AGING (10 years or so). The white wines, made from CLAIRETTE, UGNI BLANC, BOURBOULENC, and SAUVIGNON BLANC are rather neutral in character and account for only about 5 percent of the total wine production.

Banyuls AC [bah-NYUHLS] An APPELLATION in the LANGUEDOC-ROUS-SILLON in southern France known for its rather unusual fortified wines, which are classified as VIN DOUX NATUREL. Many of the vineyards are located in the sheer rocky terraces of the Pyrenees as they sweep down into the ocean close to the Spanish border. Even though Banyul wines are sometimes vinified moderately DRY, they're best when sweet. They must contain at least 15 percent alcohol and be made from a minimum of 50 percent GRENACHE grapes. Banyuls GRAND CRU must be made from a minimum of 75 percent GRENACHE and aged in wood for 30 months. RANCIO is a variation that's purposefully OXIDIZED by placing small barrels of wine in the sun during summertime. This procedure gives the wine a tawny color and a rich but unique flavor. Banyuls wines are consumed as both APÉRITIFS and DESSERT WINES.

Barbacarlo [bahr-bah-KAHR-loh] The name of a wine made by the Italian wine estate **Lino Maga**, which originally produced Barbacarlo and later claimed (and won) the exclusive rights to the name. Lino Maga is located in the OLTREPÒ PAVESE DOC, which is in the southwest corner of LOMBARDY, south of Pavia. Barbacarlo is made from a blend of BARBERA, CROATINA, Uva Rara, and Ughetta. At one time, Barbacarlo was included in the approved list of Oltrepò Pavese DOC wines, but now only Lino Maga can use it.

Barbadillo, Antonio [bahr-bah-DEE-lyoh] Based in the town of Sanlúcar de Barrameda, Spain, Antonio Barbadillo is the oldest and largest of the SHERRY firms. Although privately owned, an 11 percent share is held by HARVEYS. Antonio Barbadillo makes a broad range of sherries, the best of which are the *manzanilla*-style wines. The firm is now producing a DRY, white table wine called Castillo de San Diego, which isn't particularly well regarded.

Barbaresco DOCG [bar-bah-RESS-koh] One of the small number of DOCG areas in Italy, Barbaresco shares this status in northwestern Italy's PIEDMONT region with BAROLO, ASTI SPUMANTE, and GATTINARA. The DOCG zone encompasses the villages of Barbaresco, Tresio, and Neive, just east of Alba. The wines, which are made from the NEBBIOLO grape, must be AGED for 2 years, one of which is in wooden barrels. A RISERVA must be aged for 3 years, one of those in wood. Considered some of Italy's best, these wines have rich, spicy flavors, and, although DRY, they have a perfumed sweetness. Barbaresco wines are often compared to Barolo wines because they're both made from Nebbiolo grapes. In the comparison, Barbaresco wines are usually regarded as more elegant and refined; the Barolos are thought to be more robust and longer-lived.

Barbera [bar-BEH-rah] Italian red wine grape that can produce marvelous wines but that has become so plentiful in some of the hotter growing regions around the world that its image is beginning to tarnish. Barbera wines from these hotter areas—such as southern Italy and California's SAN JOAQUIN VALLEY—are high in ALCOHOL and ACID. They have little flavor and are used mainly as BLENDING WINES. Superior Barbera wines can exhibit a ripe currant flavor with a nuance of SMOKINESS. Five DOCs in Italy's PIEDMONT region produce the most noteworthy Barbera wines. Two of them—BARBERA D'ALBA and BARBERA D'ASTI—make wines that are 100 percent Barbera, while Barbera del Monferrato, Colli Toronesi, and Rubino di Cantavenna may produce blended wines. Good Barbera wines are also made by the DOC's of OLTREPÒ PAVESE in Lombardy and COLLI BOLOGNESI and COLLI PIACENTINI in Emilia (look for GUTTURNIO). The PIEDMONT region uses Barbera grapes to produce **Verbesco,** a light, DRY, slightly effervescent (FRIZZANTE) white wine made as a BLANC DE NOIR.

Barbera d'Alba DOC [bar-BEH-rah DAHL-bah] DOC located in the PIEDMONT region in northwestern Italy near the town of Alba. The wines from this area are regarded as some of the best made from the BARBERA grape. Although they're some of the more robust of the Barberas, they should be drunk within 3 to 4 years of the VINTAGE date.

Barbera d'Asti DOC [bar-BEH-rah DAH-steel] Wines produced in Italy's PIEDMONT from the vineyards around the towns of Asti, Alexandria, and Casale Monferrato. These wines are generally regarded as slightly less full-bodied (*see* BODY) than those from BARBERA D'ALBA, even though both are made from the BARBERA grape. They should be drunk young.

Barca Velha *see* FERREIRA

Barco Reale *see* CARMIGNANO DOCG

Bardolino DOC [bar-doh-LEE-noh] DOC area that lies in the western part of the VENETO region in northeast Italy. It encompasses vineyards on the southeastern shore of Lake Garda, in and around the town of Bardolino. The grapes used for these ROSSO and ROSATO wines are mainly CORVINA, Rondinella, Molinara, and Negrara. Although the blend of grapes used is similar to that for the better-known VALPOLICELLA DOC wines, Bardolino wines are usually not as full-bodied (*see* BODY). Wines labeled **Bardolino Classico** are made with grapes from a smaller site (the original Bardolino area) that's thought to have better vineyard land. **Bardolino Chiaretto** is the name for the ROSÉ wine, which is made in both DRY and SPUMANTE (sparkling) versions. **Bardolino Novello** is a young, fresh wine that must be bottled prior to the end of the VINTAGE year (like a French BEAUJOLIAS NOUVEAU).

barnyard A smell in wine that's analogous to a barnyard or farmyard. This characteristic can be caused by less-than-sanitary barrels or winemaking procedures or by a spoilage yeast called BRETTANOMYCES.

Barolo DOCG [bah-ROH-loh] Many view the red wines from Barolo as Italy's best—so much so that they're sometimes called the "King" of Italian wines. The Barolo DOCG area lies just southwest of Alba and includes the vineyards on the steep hills around the towns of Barolo, Castiglione Falletto, Serralunga d'Alba, Monforte d'Alba, and La Morra. It's one of the small number of DOCG areas in Italy, sharing this status in northwestern Italy's PIEDMONT region with BARBARESCO, ASTI SPUMANTE, and GATTINARA. Like the Barbaresco DOCG, the grape used here is the NEBBIOLO. DOCG rules require Barolo wines to AGE for a minimum of 3 years, two of which must be in wooden barrels. RISERVA wines require 4 years; Riserva Speciale wines must have 5 years. Young Barolos, which are tough, TANNIC, and need 5-plus years to SOFTEN, are somewhat of an acquired taste. Once they SOFTEN and open up, however, they're RICH, full-bodied (*see* BODY) and COMPLEX and can have earthy, truffly, and CHOCOLATY characteristics with an aroma reminiscent of violets.

Barossa Valley [bah-ROH-suh] One of the most important wine-producing regions in Australia. It's located in the state of Southern Australia, about 35 miles northeast of the city of Adelaide. The climate is generally warm and dry, but the eastern hills offer a cool growing area. The most popular grape grown for white TABLE WINES is RIESLING, followed by SÉMILLON and CHARDONNAY. PALOMINO and PEDRO XIMÉNEX are still grown for use in FORTIFIED wines, which have historically been a part of this area's winemaking tradition. The most popular red grape here is Shiraz (SYRAH), along with GRENACHE, CABERNET SAUVIGNON, Mataro (MOUVÈDRE), and others. Well-known wineries include Basedows, Kaiser Stuhl, Krondorf, Peter Lehmann, Orlando,

Saltram, Seppelt & Sons, Tollana, Wolf Blass, Yalumba, and, of course, Penfolds—maker of one of Australia's most famous wines, GRANGE HERMITAGE.

barrel A wooden container of varying size used to AGE, store, and sometimes FERMENT and ship wine. OAK is the wood of choice, although redwood and chestnut are sometimes used. BARRIQUES, BUTTS, FEUILLETES, HOGSHEADS, PIÈCES, and PUNCHEONS are some of the names for different barrels used in the wine-producing process. *See also* COOPERAGE.

barrel aging *see* AGING

barrel fermentation; barrel-fermented The process of fermenting wines in small barrels instead of large vats or stainless steel tanks. The barrels are usually made of **oak** and are about 60 gallons in size, although larger ones are used occasionally. Even though barrel fermentation is more expensive and less controllable than fermentation in larger tanks, it's thought to imbue wine with rich creamy flavors, delicate oak characteristics, and better aging capabilities. On the downside, this technique contributes to some loss of fruit flavor. Barrel fermentation is usually associated with white wine grapes like CHARDONNAY and SAUVIGNON BLANC, although occasionally CHENIN BLANC and SÉMILLION are processed this way. *See also* FERMENTATION.

barrica [bahr-REE-kah] The Spanish name for the wooden barrels similar to the French BARRIQUES.

barrique [ba-REEK] The term used in BORDEAUX to specify the 225-liter (almost 60-gallon) oak barrels that are used for storing and aging wine. It's similar in size to the PIÈCE used in BURGUNDY.

barro [BAH-roh] *see* JEREZ-XÉRÈX-SHERRY Y MANZANILLA DE SANLÚCAR DE BARRAMEDA DO

Barsac AC [BAHR-sak; ba*r*-SAK] The largest of the five townships within the SAUTERNES district, Barsac is the most recognizable APPELLATION after Sauternes itself. It's part of France's BORDEAUX region and is located approximately 25 miles from the city of Bordeaux. Because Barsac is part of the Sauternes appellation, producers may also use "Sauternes" on their label, although most top producers simply use "Barsac." Like their Sauternes neighbors, Barsac wines are sweet and luscious, although generally lighter and more refined. The best producer is Château CLIMENS followed by Châteaus COUTET and DOISY-VÉDRINES and then by Châteaus BROUSTET, DOISY-DAËNE, and NAIRAC. The very rare Cuvée Madame from Château Coutet is specially produced in exceptional years and thought by some to be second only to the renowned Château D'YQUEM.

Bartles & Jaymes *see* E & J GALLO WINERY

Basilicata [bah-see-lee-KAH-tah] An obscure region located in southern Italy next to APULIA, CALABRIA, and CAMPANIA. Of Italy's twenty regions, Basilicata is the third smallest wine producer and has only one DOC, ALIANICO DEL VULTURE, which produces a well-regarded red wine from the AGLIANICO grape. This region's principal grapes for red and ROSÉ wines are Aglianico, Aglianicone, and MALVASIA Nera; for white wines they're Asprinio and Malvasia Bianca.

basket *see* DECANTING

Bas-Médoc *see* MÉDOC

Bassermann-Jordan, Weingut Dr. von [VINE-goot] A well-known German wine estate located near Deidesheim in Germany's RHEINPFALZ region. The estate consists of nearly 100 acres spread out over several different vineyards in the BEREICH Mittelhaardt/Deutsche, all planted with RIESLING. The site has been important since 1250, but it didn't come into the Jordan family until 1816 when Andreas Jordan acquired it. His granddaughter's husband, Dr. Fredrich von Bassermann-Jordan, made the wine estate famous with his meticulous care in winemaking. Weingut Dr. von Basserman-Jordan's wines are highly regarded on an international level by Riesling connoisseurs.

Basses Mourottes *see* CORTON; CORTON-CHARLEMAGNE

bastard A sweet wine of uncertain origin that was popular in England during the sixteenth century. It's thought to have come from either Spain, Portugal, or the Portuguese island of MADEIRA. The wine is said to have been made from the Bastardo grape (hence the name), which is still grown in parts of Portugal.

Batailley, Château [sha-TOH bah-TIE-yay] A CINQUIÈME CRU (fifth growth) located in the PAUILLAC AC in France's BORDEAUX region. Château HAUT-BATAILLEY and Château Batailley were part of the same property until 1942, when it was split. The château produces good red wines from its 128 acres, and, because it's not well known, they're thought to be a relatively good value. The vineyards are planted with about 70 percent CABERNET SAUVIGNON, 20 percent MERLOT, and the rest CABERNET FRANC and PETIT VERDOT. Between 22,000 and 25,000 cases of red wine are produced annually. The best Château Batailley wines can AGE for up to 25 years.

Bâtard-Montrachet AC [bah-TAHR mohn-rah-SHAY] A 29-acre GRAND CRU vineyard located in the CÔTE DE BEAUNE just east of the famous LE MONTRACHET vineyard in France's BURGUNDY region. Although mostly associated with the village of PULIGNY-MONTRACHET, part of the vineyards are in the village of CHASSAGNE-MONTRACHET as well. These wines, made from CHARDONNAY grapes, are among the world's best and most expensive white wines. The best examples have honeyed aromas, rich and concentrated flavors with lots of fruit, and deserve 8 to 10 year of AGING.

Baumé [boh-MAY] A system used by the French and other Europeans to measure SPECIFIC GRAVITY, which indicates the sugar content of unfermented grape juice. One degree Baumé is equivalent to 1.8° BRIX (the measurement system used in the United States). The Baumé measurement system helps winemakers forecast the finished wine's potential alcohol content, with 1° degree roughly equal to 1 percent alcohol when the wine is fully fermented. Germany has a similar system measured on the OECHSLE scale.

Bearn AC [bay-ARN] This APPELLATION, which lies in Basque country in the Pyrenees in southwest France, covers red, white, and ROSÉ wines. Red and rosé wines are made from various grapes including CABERNET SAUVIGNON, CABERNET FRANC, Tannat, and Manseng Noir. White wines are produced from Gros Manseng, Petit Manseng, and Courbu. Within the Bearn area are the appellations of IROULEGUY, JURANÇON, and MADIRAN. Generally these are pretty basic wines; the best are the rosés and the sweet white wines from Jurançon.

Beaujolais [boh-zhuh-LAY] The Beaujolais area, located in the southern part of France's BURGUNDY region, starts just north of Lyons and extends for about 35 miles north to the city of Mâcon. Beaujolais is different from most of Burgundy because of its focus on the GAMAY grape for its red wines, instead of PINOT NOIR. As with many of the France's regions, years of experience have proven which grape is best for an area, and for the granite-laden hills of Beaujolais it's Gamay. To date, no other location in the world has been able to produce Gamay-based wines as well as Beaujolais. Most of the wines from Beaujolais are red, with tiny amounts of ROSÉ and white. Beaujolais winemakers employ a different red winemaking process called *macération carbonique* (*see* CARBONIC MACERATION), a technique used during primary FERMENTATION to make light red wines with intense color, a fresh fruity flavor, and low TANNINS—in short, a wine that can be drunk early. Most wines for the basic APPELLATION **Beaujolais AC** are produced in the southern part of the region. These wines must contain minimum alcohol levels of 9 percent for red and rosé wines and 9½ percent for white. **Beaujolais Supérieur AC** wines, which are produced in the same areas as the Beaujolais AC, must have lower yields per acre (usually an indicator of higher-quality wines) and minimum alcohol levels that are 1 percent higher. The next highest-quality appellation is **Beaujolais-Villages AC**, a collection of thirty-nine villages with superior vineyard sites in the northern part of Beaujolais. The highest-quality level is comprised of ten individual, CRU-status villages, each with its own individual appellation. They are BROUILLY, CHÉNAS, CHIROUBLES, CÔTE DE BROUILLY, FLEURIE, JULIÉNAS, MORGON, MOULIN-À-VENT, RÉGNIÉ, and SAINT-AMOUR. These villages produce the best and most expensive wines, with Moulin-a Vent, Morgon, and Chenas considered the most full-bodied (*see* BODY) and longest AGING. **Beaujolais Nouveau** is a special category of 7- to 9-week-old wine that's released annually on the third Thursday of November. This "new" wine, sometimes called **Beaujolais Primeur**, is meant to be drunk very young. It's made from the better grapes of the basic Beaujolais appellation and is usually quite good.

Beaulieu Vineyards (BV) [BOOL-yuh] Also known simply

as *BV,* Beaulieu Vineyards is one of NAPA VALLEY'S most famous wineries. It was established in 1900 by Georges de Latour, who was one of the early innovators with French grape varieties, especially CABERNET SAUVIGNON. Beaulieu Vineyards survived the United States PROHIBITION act by selling sacramental wines to the Catholic church. Staying in business this way meant that when Prohibition was lifted in 1934, Beaulieu was in a good position to restart its normal wine business. In 1938 André Tchelistcheff, a Russian-born French-trained ENOLOGIST who became the "Dean" of Napa Valley winemakers, joined Beaulieu as its winemaker. He continued in this position for 35 years. In 1941 barrels of the Georges de Latour-made 1936 VINTAGE Cabernet Sauvignon were released. This was a year after the great man had died, and the Private Reserve wine was named after him. For several decades the George de Latour Private Reserve Cabernet Sauvignons were some of the most esteemed wines produced in this country—they did much to establish the Napa Valley's reputation. In 1969 de Latour's heirs sold Beaulieu Vineyards to Heublein, which subsequently increased the winery's production to about 450,000 cases annually. In addition to the Private Reserve Cabernet Sauvignon, Beaulieu Vineyards produces Rutherford and Beau Tour bottlings of this same variety. All are AGED in American oak. It also produces a Reserve PINOT NOIR and a CHARDONNAY from the winery's CARNEROS vineyards.

Beaulieu-sur-Layon *see* COTEAUX DU LAYON

Beau-Mayne *see* COUVENT-DES-JACOBINS, CHÂTEAU

Beaumes-de-Venise [bohm duh vuh-NEEZ] A small attractive village in the southern RHÔNE best known for its sweet MUSCAT DE BEAUMES-DE-VENISE, a VIN DOUX NATUREL style of white wine. The red wines, made from CINSAUT, GRENACHE, SYRAH, and MOURVÈDRE, and bottled as CÔTES DU RHÔNE-VILLAGES AC wines, are generally good and hearty.

Beaune [BOHN] An important French town that many consider the wine capital of the CÔTE D'OR, if not of all BURGUNDY. It's not only in an area of important vineyards but also houses many influential wine merchants. Beaune gives its name to the southern portion of the Côte d'Or, CÔTE DE BEAUNE. The **Beaune AC** itself produces mainly red wines from the PINOT NOIR grape. Most of these wines, although they'll AGE 5 to 10 years, are made in a SOFTER, low-TANNIN style that allows them to be appreciated young. Even though there are no GRAND CRU vineyards in the Beaune AC, there are number of PREMIER CRU vineyards—many of them excellent. Usually included in the top tier are **Les Boucherottes**, **Les Bressandes**, **Les Cents Vignes**, **Clos du Roi**, **Le Clos des Mouches**, **Les Fèves**, **Les Grèves**, **Les Marconnets**, and **Les Teurons**.

Beaunois *see* CHARDONNAY

Beauregard, Château [sha-TOH boh-ruh-GAHR] This property, which actually has a beautiful seventeenth century château, is located in the POMEROL AC in France's BORDEAUX region. It's not classified because the Pomerol châteaus have never been classified, like those of the MÉDOC, for example. It produces about 5,000 cases of red wine each year from its 32 acres. The vineyard is almost evenly divided between MERLOT and CABERNET FRANC, although there are small amounts of CABERNET SAUVIGNON and MALBEC. Wines from the best years can AGE for 10 to 12 years. The SECOND LABEL is **Domaine des Douves**.

Beauroy *see* CHABLIS

Beauséjour, Château [sha-TOH boh-say-ZHOOR] Château Beauséjour is also referred to as Château Beauséjour-Duffau-Lagarrosse to eliminate confusing it with the neighboring Château BEAU-SÉJOUR-BÉCOT. Both were formerly part of a larger SAINT-ÉMILION parcel simply called Beauséjour. Owned by the Duffau-Lagarrosse family, Château Beauséjour is considered the better of the two and has PREMIER GRAND CRU CLASSÉ ranking. The CHÂTEAU consists of 17 acres

B

planted with MERLOT (55 percent), CABERNET FRANC (25 percent) and CABERNET SAUVIGNON (20 percent). It produces about 3,000 cases of red wine each year, the best of which can AGE for about 15 years. The SECOND LABEL of Château Beauséjour is called **La Croix de Mazerat**.

Beau-Séjour-Bécot, Château [sha-TOH boh-say-ZHOO*R*-bay-koh] Part of a larger property that was split up in 1869—the other portion being the Château BEAUSÉJOUR (Duffau-Lagarrosse). This CHÂTEAU was demoted from the status of PREMIER GRAND CRU CLASSÉ to GRAND CRU CLASSÉ in the 1985 reclassification of SAINT-ÉMILION châteaus. Although some critics think that prior to 1985 the quality of the wines weren't high enough to warrant a premier grand cru classé ranking, the real reason for the downgrade seems to relate to the addition of two adjacent châteaus, La Carte and Des Trois Moulins, to Château Beau-Séjour-Becot's acreage. Both were ranked only as grand cru classé châteaus, and it appears that the authorities didn't want the automatic upgrading of these new vineyards to take place. The château now consists of about 40 acres planted with approximately 70 percent MERLOT, 24 percent CABERNET FRANC, and 6 percent CABERNET SAUVIGNON. It produces about 6,500 to 7,000 cases of red wine annually. The AGING capability of the better wines is about 10 to 12 years. The SECOND LABEL is **Tournelle des Moines**.

Beerenauslese [BAY-*r*uhn-OWS-lay-zuh; BEH-*r*uhn-OWS-lay-zuh] The German term for "selected berries," used in the wine trade to describe specially selected, overripe grapes that are hand-picked and then pressed separately from other grapes. Beerenauslese is one of the six subcategories of QmP (QUALITÄTSWEIN MIT PRÄDIKAT) and ranks above KABINETT, SPÄTLESE, and AUSLESE but below TROCKENBEERENAUSLESE. To attain the Beerenauslese category, the natural sugar content of the grapes must reach a certain minimum (110° to 128° OECHSLE, approximately 26 to 30 percent sugar by weight), depending on the region and the variety. The grapes are usually infected with BOTRYTIS CINEREA (called *Edelfäule* in German), which shrivels them, thereby concentrating the sugar. The superior wine made from these grapes is very sweet but has enough ACID for proper BALANCE. Beerenauslese wines are quite rare, extremely expensive, and considered one of the world's top DESSERT WINES. These wines will AGE for many years, during which they develop even more complexity.

beeswing [BEEZ-wing] Named for its translucent appearance, beeswing is a flaky deposit sometimes found in older, BOTTLE-AGED wines, particularly PORT. Such wines are usually DECANTED, thereby eliminating the residue.

Belair, Château [sha-TOH bel-EHR] A PREMIER GRAND CRU CLASSÉ château located in the SAINT-ÉMILION AC in France's BORDEAUX region. It's owned by the same owners of its famous neighbor, Château AUSONE. After a long period of very average wines, the quality of Château Belair wines seems to have improved during the 1980s. The 32 acres are planted with about 60 percent MERLOT and 40 percent CABERNET FRANC. This CHÂTEAU produces about 4,500 to 5,000 cases of red wine each year. Better wines from this château can AGE for 12 to 15 years. The non-VINTAGE **Roc-Blanquant** is the château's SECOND LABEL.

Bel Arbors *see* FETZER VINEYARDS

Belgrave, Château [sha-TOH bel-GRAHV] CHÂTEAU located in the COMMUNE of Saint-Laurent-et-Benon, part of the HAUT-MÉDOC AC in France's BORDEAUX region. Although Château Belgrave is a CINQUIÈME CRU (fifth growth), some critics have felt for years that it should be downgraded. Since 1980 new owners have been modernizing the estate and improving the wines. Each year, Château Belgrave produces about 20,000 to 25,000 cases of red wine from it 136-acre parcel. CABERNET SAUVIGNON makes up about 60 percent of the vineyard, followed by MERLOT with 35 percent and PETIT VERDOT with 5 percent. The better wines can AGE in the range of 10 to 12 years.

Beli Pinot *see* PINOT BLANC

Bell Cayon *see* BURGESS CELLARS

Belle Epoque *see* CHAMPAGNE

Bellet AC [behl-LAY] A tiny APPELLATION in France's PROVENCE region, located in the hills behind Nice near the French Riviera. It produces red, white, and ROSÉ wines from the 100-plus acres that qualify for AC status. Red grapes are CINSAUT, GRENACHE, and the local varieties Braquet and Folle (or Fuelle) Noire. White grapes are the local Rolle and small amounts of CHARDONNAY.

Bellina *see* ISABELLA

bench grafting *see* GRAFTING

Benmore Valley AVA *see* LAKE COUNTY

bentonite [BEN-tn-ite] A powdery clay found in Wyoming, South Dakota, and Germany that is used as a FINING agent to clarify wines (especially white). When added to wine, bentonite settles to the bottom carrying with it any suspended particles.

B

Benziger of Glen Ellen A 150,000-case winery located near the town of Glen Ellen in California's SONOMA VALLEY. The Benziger family is focusing on its Benziger and Imagery lines after selling its Glen Ellen line (approximately 3.5 million cases) to Heublein in 1993. The Benzingers kept the winery and about 85 acres of vineyard, which is planted with CABERNET SAUVIGNON, CHARDONNAY, MERLOT, and SAUVIGNON BLANC, all of which go into their Sonoma Valley bottlings. Purchased grapes are used for a SONOMA COUNTY group of wines, which include the previously mentioned varieties plus PINOT BLANC. Their **Imagery** series includes wines made from some unusual grape varieties such as ALEATICO and Trousseau (TROUSSEAU GRIS). It also has a PORT wine made from ZINFANDEL.

Bereich [beh-RIKH] The German word for "region." Under the German wine laws established in 1971, a Bereich is a district or sub-region within an ANBAUGEBIET (quality-wine growing region). There are forty-three Bereiche throughout the thirteen Anbaugebiete. Within a Bereich there are GROSSLAGEN (general sites) and EINZELLAGEN (individual sites or vineyards). If a wine label carries a Bereich name (instead of a Grosslage or Einzellage), it's considered to be of satisfactory quality (much like a French regional wine from ANJOU, BORDEAUX, BURGUNDY or CÔTES-DU-RHÔNE). However, the higher-quality wines will generally carry the name of an individual vineyard (Einzellage) from one of the better Bereiche.

Berg *see* ERSHERNDORF; RÜDESHEIM

Bergerac [behr-jeh-RAK] The town that gives its name to the surrounding region and sits on the Dordogne River just over 60 miles from the city of Bordeaux. The Bergerac APPELLATIONS abut the BORDEAUX region and use many of the same grapes. **Bergerac AC** produces red wines that are made from CABERNET SAUVIGNON, CABERNET FRANC, and MERLOT and that are similiar to lighter Bordeaux reds. MUSCADELLE, SAUVIGNON BLANC, and SÉMILLON are the main white varieties and are used in the basic **Bergerac Sec AC** wines. **Côtes de Bergerac AC** wines are required to have a higher minimum alcohol content and are generally of better quality. The **Côtes de Bergerac Moelleux AC** is for sweet wines produced in the Bergerac area. Other appellations in the Bergerac area include MONBAZILLAC, MONTRAVEL, PÉCHARMANT, ROSETTE, and Saussiggion.

Beringer Vineyards Located in St. Helena, California, this historic NAPA VALLEY winery was started in the 1876 by Jacob and Frederick Beringer. Today the Rhine House and the old stone winery that they built have been refurbished by Wine World Inc., a division of Nestlé, the Swiss-based giant. Wine World, which took over in 1971, has poured millions of dollars into Beringer, refurbishing old facilities, building new ones, and buying vineyard land in Napa Valley and KNIGHTS VALLEY. Today, Beringer produces over 1.3 million cases of wine a year, much of it under the **Napa Ridge** and **Los Hermanos** brands. Beringer's highly regarded premium wines are led by a trio of CABERNET SAUVIGNONS (Private Reserve, Chabot Vineyard, and Knights Valley), a MERLOT from HOWELL MOUNTAIN, and two CHARDONNAYS (Private Reserve and Proprietor Grown). Beringer makes a wide assortment of other wines including a GEWÜRZTRAMINER, a ZINFANDEL, a FUMÉ BLANC, a SAUVIGNON BLANC-SÉMILLON blend, and a LATE HARVEST wine made from Sauvignon Blanc and Sémillon called **Nightingale** (named after former head winemaker, Myron Nightingale). Large volumes of WHITE ZINFANDEL and CHENIN BLANC are also made. Beringer puchases grapes to meet its needs in addition to using the grapes from its own 3,100 acres. Nestle's Wine World subsidiary also owns Château Souverain, Meridian, and part of Maison Deutz.

Berliquet, Château [sha-TOH behr-lee-KAY] CHÂTEAU located very near the village of SAINT-ÉMILION in France's BORDEAUX region. It was the only one to be upgraded to GRAND CRU CLASSÉ status in the 1985 reclassification. It has about 21 acres planted with about 75 percent MERLOT, 15 percent CABERNET FRANC, and 10 percent CABERNET SAUVIGNON. About 3,200 to 4,000 cases of red wine are produced each year, and the AGING potential for the better VINTAGES is 10 to 12 years.

Bernkastel [BEHRN-kah-stl] The name Bernkastel applies to a town, a BEREICH, and as part of two GROSSLAGEN. The town is situated on the Mosel River in Germany's MOSEL-SAAR-RUWER region and is noted for its narrow, picturesque streets. The town, which is also known as Bernkastel-Kues (Kues is the larger town across the river), is located near many important vineyard sites, including the world-famous DOCTOR vineyard. **Bereich Bernkastel** is one of the five Bereiche in the Mosel-Saar-Ruwer region and covers the vineyards around the middle portion of the Mosel River area, what's often referred to as the Mittelmosel. The Bereich begins northeast of Trier and encompasses the area to the northeast, including Bernkastel-Kues, and ends just short of ZELL. Ten Grosslagen are included in the Bereich, including two that encompass vineyards around the town of Bernkastel. These two, which are entitled to add Bernkasteler in front of their name, are Bernkasteler **Badstube** and Bernkasteler **Kürfustlay**.

berrylike An intense, ripe, sweet-fruit characteristic found in some young wines such as those made from ZINFANDEL, CABERNET SAUVIGNON, and MERLOT. Such a trait most often suggests blackberries, black cherries, mulberries, raspberries, or strawberries.

Beychevelle, Château [sha-TOH beh-shuh-VEHL] A well-known CHÂTEAU located in the SAINT-JULIEN AC in France's BORDEAUX region. It's said that the château's name comes from the French expression, *baissez les voiles,* which means "strike sail." This name refers to the one-time owner of the property, the Duke of Epernon, Grand Admiral of France, and his requirement that passing ships strike their sails in respect. In the CLASSIFICATION OF 1855, Château Beychevelle was given a QUATRIÈME CRU (fourth growth) rating, but many wine lovers feel that the ranking would be higher if done today (prices also reflect this theory). The 175 acres are planted with approximately 60 percent CABERNET SAUVIGNON, 28 percent MERLOT, and the rest CABERNET FRANC and PETIT VERDOT. This château produces approximately 25,000 to 30,000 cases of red wine each year, and wines from the best VINTAGES can AGE for 20 to 25 years. Château Beychevelle uses two SECOND LABELS, **Amiral de Beychevelle** and **RESERVE DE L'AMIRAL.**

Biancame *see* ALBANA

bianco; Bianco [BYAHN-koh] 1. The Italian word for "white," *vino bianco* meaning "white wine." 2. In Italy, the term *Bianco* (with a capital *B*) is also used to indicate a white wine that's made from specific, approved grape varieties, which can differ depending on the DOC and region.

Bianco Alcamo; Bianco d'Alcamo *see* ALCAMO DOC

Bianco di Custoza DOC [be-YAHN-koh dee koos-TOH-tzah] DOC that makes a DRY white wine from a blend of TREBBIANO, GARGANEGA, TOCAI, CORTESE, MALVASIA, and Riesling Italico (WELSCHRIESLING). These wines, once thought to be a cheaper, lesser-quality alternative to those from the SOAVE DOC, have established themselves as high-quality contenders (except against the better Soave Classico wines). Bianco di Custoza is located on the southeastern shore of Lake Garda in the eastern portion of Italy's VENETO region (in the same area as the BARDOLINO DOC).

Bienvenues-Bâtard-Montrachet AC [byan-veh-NOO bah-TAHR mohn-rah-SHAY] A 9-acre GRAND CRU that is located in France's BURGUNDY region and situated in the village of PULIGNY-MONTRACHET in the CÔTE DE BEAUNE. The vineyard is bordered on two sides by the larger and better-known BÂTARD-MONTRACHET vineyard. The wines from these two vineyards are often compared, although the Bâtard-Montrachet is usually considered superior. Still, the rich, flavorful Bienvenues-Bâtard-Montrachet wines, made from CHARDONNAY grapes, are among the world's best white wines and are priced accordingly.

big A winetasting term for a RICH, full-bodied (*see* BODY) wine that's concentrated, intensely flavored, and assertive. Big wines are usually high in ALCOHOL but have good BALANCE. *Massive* is a term used for exceptionally big (and magnificent) wines.

Bigney *see* MERLOT

Bikaver *see* EGRI BIKAVÉR

Bildstock *see* NIERSTEIN

Billecart-Salmon *see* CHAMPAGNE

Bingen [BING-uhn] An important wine town directly across from RÜDESHEIM, where the Nahe River joins the Rhine River. Its name is also used for the BEREICH that covers this area. Both are part of the RHEIN-HESSEN region, with **Bereich Bingen** covering the northwestern portion of the Rheinhessen. The Bereich contains six GROSSLAGEN, including Grosslage Sankt Rochuskapelle, of which the vineyards around the town of Bingen are a part. The town's best-known vineyard is the 87-acre **Scharlachberg** (which means "scarlet hill," referring to its red soil). RIESLING grapes produce the area's top wines, which can be among the best from the Rheinhessen region.

Bischöflichen Weingüter [BIHSH-uhf-lihkh-uhn VINE-goot-uhr] This 260-acre German wine estate was established in 1966 by combining the estates of three independent charitable organizations—Bischöfliches Priesterseminar, Bischöfliches Konvikt, and the Hohe Domkirche. Since that time, the management group has leased four other church-related estates. The vineyards of the Bischöflichen Weingüter, which is based in Trier in the MOSEL-SAAR-RUWER regions, are scattered around various locations in the region. The grapes are PRESSED in several locations; the juice is then brought to Trier for FERMENTATION and AGING. RIESLING covers 97 percent of the vineyards, along with a small amount of Spätburgunder (PINOT NOIR). These internationally known wines are of very high quality.

Bischofsberg *see* RÜDESHEIM

bishop A type of MULLED WINE, usually made with PORT, sugar, oranges and cloves, which are combined and heated.

bitter; bitterness Bitterness in wine can be due to TANNINS, chemical salts, oxidized polyphenols, bacteria, and even some grapes, such as GEWÜRZTRAMINER, which have a bitter note in their flavor. Even though a slight bitterness can contribute BALANCE to a sweet wine, an overtly bitter characteristic is considered a fault if it dominates a wine's flavor or AFTERTASTE.

black currant *see* CASSIS

Black Muscat *see* MUSCAT

black rot Any of a variety of fungal diseases that attack both grapes and vines. Usually brought on by hot, extremely humid weather, black rot discolors leaves and stems and causes the grapes to shrivel and turn brownish-black. Copper sulfate is the common treatment.

Blagny [blah-NYEE] A tiny village that straddles the borderline of the MEURSAULT and PULIGNY-MONTRACHET appellations in the CÔTE DE BEAUNE district of France's BURGUNDY region. Both areas have PREMIER CRU vineyards for white wines, which are made from CHARDONNAY and labeled either Puligny-Montrachet, Meursault, or Meursault-Blagny. The Blagny APPELLATION is only for red wines made from PINOT NOIR grapes.

blanc [BLAH*N* (BLAH*N*GK)] French for "white."

Blanca-Roja *see* MALVASIA

blanc de blanc [BLAH*N* duh BLAH*N*; BLAH*N*GK duh BLAH-*N*GK] French phrase meaning "white wine from white grapes." The term originated in France's CHAMPAGNE region (where most champagnes are made from a combination of the white CHARDONNAY grape and the red PINOT NOIR grape) to describe champagne made entirely from Chardonnay. Blanc de blancs are usually light and delicate. The term also refers to STILL WINES. *See also* BLANC DE NOIR.

Blanc de Cabernet Sauvignon *See* CABERNET BLANC

blanc de noir(s) [blah*n* (blah*n*gk) duh NWAHR] The French term meaning "white wine from red grapes." In particular, the phrase *blanc de noir* is used with those CHAMPAGNES (and other SPARKLING WINES) that are made entirely from the PINOT NOIR grape. Occasionally this phrase refers to STILL WINES made from CABERNET SAUVIGNON, Pinot Noir, or ZINFANDEL. In the United States, however, these BLUSH WINES usually go by other names such as BLANC DE PINOT NOIR, CABERNET BLANC, or WHITE ZINFANDEL. Blanc de noirs are produced by quickly removing the skins from the juice after the grapes have been pressed. This technique prevents the pigment in the grape's dark skin from transferring too much color to the wine. These wines may vary in hue from pale pink to apricot to salmon; seldom are they clear or "white." *See also* BLANC DE BLANC.

Blanc de Pinot Noir [blahn (blahngk) duh PEE-noh NWAHR] One of the names used for BLUSH WINE, describing that made from PINOT NOIR grapes.

Blanc de Troyes *see* ALIGOTÉ

Blanc Fumé [blahn (blahngk) foo-MAY] Around the village of Pouilly-sur-Loire, in the central part of France's LOIRE region, Blanc Fumé is the name used for the SAUVIGNON BLANC grape. Wine from this grape is usually labeled POUILLY-FUMÉ AC, and occasionally, **Blanc Fumé de Pouilly AC**. *Blanc* is French for "white," *fumée* means "smoke," and it's said the name comes from the SMOKY (also known as FLINTY) quality of these wines.

Blanchots [blahn-SHOH] One of the seven GRAND CRU vineyards in CHABLIS. Blanchots consists of just over 30 acres and sits southeast of the other six grand cru vineyards.

blanco [BLAHNG-koh] Spanish for "white."

Blanquette *see* CLAIRETTE

Blanquette de Limoux AC [blahn-KEHT duh lee-MOO] APPELLATION for sparkling wines made in the hills surrounding the town of Limoux in Southern France's LANGUEDOC-ROUSSILLON region. Mauzac, also called Blanquette, is the main grape, of which the wines must contain at least 80 percent. CLAIRETTE, CHENIN BLANC, and CHARDONNAY make up the balance. The wines, sometimes referred to as *vins mousseux*, are primarily made by MÉTHODE CHAMPENOISE although the *méthode rurale* (RURAL METHOD) is still occasionally used. Blanquette de Limoux wines, which are generally quite good, are described as having a "green apple" or "cidery" flavor.

blau [BLOUW] German for "blue." The word *blau* is often used in wine-producing circles to refer to grapes used to produce red wines, such as Blauer Portugieser (PORTUGIESER) or Blauer Spätburgunder (PINOT NOIR).

Blauburgunder *see* PINOT NOIR

Blauer Klevner *see* PINOT NOIR

Blauer Limberger *see* BLAUFRANKISCH

Blauer Portugieser *see* PORTUGIESER

Blauer Spätburgunder *see* PINOT NOIR

Blaufränkisch [blouw-FRAHN-keesh] A red-wine grape widely planted in Austria and in smaller amounts in Germany's WÜRTTEMBERG region, where its called *Blauer Limberger,* and in Hungary, where it's known as *Kékfrankos.* It's not, as sometimes thought, the same variety as GAMAY. Blaufränkisch, which buds early and ripens late, doesn't do well in the colder climates. The wines it produces are lighter-styled reds, usually with plenty of ACIDITY. Blaufränkisch is also known as *Limberger* and *Lemberger.*

Blaye [BLA-yuh] A historic town on the Gironde estuary across from the HAUT-MÉDOC in France's BORDEAUX region. It's the center of a large wine-growing region of the same name that has three appellations. **Blaye AC** (or *Blayais*) and **Côtes de Blaye AC** produce white wines using SÉMILLON, SAUVIGNON BLANC, and COLOMBARD as the main grape varieties. For the most part, these wines are fairly undistinguished. **Premières Côtes de Blaye AC** produces mostly red wines from MERLOT, CABERNET SAUVIGNON, CABERNET FRANC, and MALBEC and a small amount of white wine. Although this is the inferred superior appellation for this region, many of the better white wines use only the Côtes de Blaye designation. The quality of the red wines is increasing but, except in isolated cases, they still have a reputation of being below-average wines.

blending The process of combining different wines with the goal of creating a composite that's better than any of the wines separately. The wines used for blending might be from different varieties (for instance, CABERNET SAUVIGNON, MERLOT, and CABERNET FRANC), different regions (such as NAPA VALLEY and PASO ROBLES), varying types of COOPERAGE (some new barrels, some older barrels, barrels from different forests or coopers, etc.), and even different VINTAGES (as in non-vintage CHAMPAGNE created by combining wines from different years).

blending wine Also called a cutting wine, a blending wine is added, in small quantities, to other wines to enhance them or to correct deficiencies in them. For example, wines with high alcoholic content are often added to wines with low alcoholic content and wines with dark color to those lacking color. In France a blending wine is called a *coupage.*

blind tasting *see* WINETASTING

blush wine Called BLANC DE NOIR or ROSÉ in France, "blush wine" is an American generic name given to wines that vary in color from pale pink to apricot to salmon. Such wines are generally produced from red grapes by quickly removing the skins from the juice after the grapes are pressed. This technique stops the transfer of color from the dark pigments in the grape's skin, and the wine continues its processing as for white wine. Introduced in the United States in the late 1970s, blush wines found popularity in the early 1980s as the white-wine boom took off and producers searched for a channel for the red-grape surplus. Today, some producers create blush wine by mixing red and white wines. Blush wines usually go by other names, such as BLANC DE PINOT NOIR, CABERNET BLANC, WHITE ZINFANDEL, or PINOT VIN GRIS. Most of these wines are slightly sweet, although some are quite DRY with just a whisper of RESIDUAL SUGAR. Wines labeled VIN GRIS are usually fairly dry and often have some wood aging.

Boal; Bual [boo-AHL; boh-AHL] 1. A white wine grape historically associated with the island of MADEIRA. Boal is now found there only in limited quantities. After PHYLLOXERA attacked the Madeira vineyards in the 1870s, and the vineyards were eventually replanted, the classic Madeira varieties like Boal were replaced with the hardier TINTA NEGRA MOLE. However, because of Common Market labeling regulations (see below), Boal is expected to make a comeback. 2. After MALMSEY, Boal is the darkest and and richest of the Madeira wine styles. Originally made primarily with the Boal grape, this style of Madeira has recently utilized more Tinta Negra Mole, especially in the cheaper versions. However, in 1986, Portugal entered the Common Market, whose regulations required that by 1993 any Madeira wine naming a variety on its label would have to contain at least 85 percent of that grape. This labeling requirement has caused an upsurge in replanting of the classic vines such as Boal. Wines labeled "Boal-style" can contain less than the required 85 percent and most likely contain more Tinta Negra Mole.

Boca DOC [BOH-kah] A DOC in the Novara hills near the village of Boca, just north of GATTINARA in Italy's PIEDMONT region. It makes DRY red wines from NEBBIOLO, Vespolina, and BONARDA grapes. These wines must have 3 years of AGING, two of which must be in wooden barrels.

bocksbeutel [BAWKS-boy-tuhl] A squat, flagon-shaped green or amber bottle used for quality wine (QbA or QmP) from Germany's FRANKEN region. Badisches Frankenland, a wine produced in the northern part of German's BADEN region, also uses a bocksbeutel. *Bock* is the German word for "goat," and it's said that the bottle is patterned after the scrotum of that animal. Others feel that the name is taken from a bag used to carry religious books called a **Bockesbeutel** in Low German.

Bockstein *see* OCKFEN

bodega [boh-DAY-gah] A versatile Spanish term used for "wine cellar," as well as "winery," "wine storage area," and "wine-producing firm."

boden [BOH-duhn] A German word meaning "soil" or "ground." Like the French GOÛT DE TERROIR, *bodengeschmack,* which means "taste of the soil," refers to wines with an earthy flavor that reflects the soil in which the grapes were grown. RIESLING grapes grown in slate-based terrain, such as that found in the MOSEL-SAAR-RUWER region, are said to absorb a slate flavor and transmit it to the wines.

body; bodied The perception of TEXTURE or WEIGHT of a wine in the mouth, which is a combination of elements including ALCOHOL, EXTRACT, GLYCEROL, and ACID. A wine with a RICH, COMPLEX, well-ROUNDED, LINGERING flavor is considered **full-bodied**; one that's watery or lacking in body is called **light-bodied** or thin; a **medium-bodied** wine ranks in between. Not all wines strive for a full-bodied characteristic, namely those whose hallmark may be FINESSE, such as CHAMPAGNE. Dessert wines, like rich SAUTERNES, are considered full-bodied partly because the RESIDUAL SUGAR adds weight and texture.

Böhlig *see* WACHENHEIM

Bolgheri DOC [bohl-GEH-ree] Located southeast of Livorno in Italy's TUSCANY region, this DOC includes the sloping coastal vineyards south of the village of Bogheri. The DRY rosé (ROSATO) wines produced here are highly regarded. They're made primarily from SANGIOVESE, blended with some CANAIOLO and other red grapes. The dry white wines (BIANCO) are made chiefly from TREBBIANO, blended with VERMENTINO and other white grapes. This is the region that produces the super-Tuscan (*see* TUSCANY) wines—SASSICAIA and Ornellaia.

Bollinger [BAWL-in-jer; BOHL-in-jer] Based in Ay, France, Bollinger is one of the great CHAMPAGNE houses. It produces about 1.5 million bottles per year and is known for high-quality wines. Even Bollinger's lower-end non-vintage Spécial Cuvée Brut consistently receives high ratings. Bollinger's top wine is the vintage **R.D.** (*recemment degorge,* "recently disgorged"), which spends up to 10 years aging in the bottle with its yeast cells (SUR LIE) a process that develops the complex, TOASTY quality sought by many champagne enthusiasts.

Bollinger also makes **Vieilles Vignes Françaises,** a very rare VINTAGE wine produced from a small plot of ungrafted, pre-PHYLLOXERA PINOT NOIR vines in Ay. Other vintage Bollinger sparkling wines include Année Rare, Brut, Grand Année, and Grand Année Rosé.

Bombino Bianco [bom-BEE-noh BYAHN-koh] White wine grape that is grown in southeast Italy, primarily in APULIA and ABRUZZI but also in MARCHE and LATIUM. Bombino Bianco generally produces bland, low-ALCOHOL wines used primarily with other grape varieties for BLENDS, and sometimes for VERMOUTH. In Abruzzi, a DOC called TREBBIANO D'ABRUZZO uses this grape, which is also called *Trebbiano d'Abruzzo* (although it's unrelated to TREBBIANO). Some producers in this DOC carefully prune the Bombino Bianco vines, thereby reducing the YIELD and generating more flavorful grapes, which result in wines that can be quite good. The better examples exhibit CREAMY and CITRUSY characteristics. Bombino Bianco is also known as *Zapponara Bianca.*

Bonarda [baw-NAHRR-dah] 1. The shortened name given to *Bonarda Piemontese,* a red wine grape grown in Italy's PIEDMONT region. Though once widely planted in Piedmont, this grape fell out of favor over the years. Only recently has it been making a slight comeback. Bonarda Piemontese wines are generally LIGHT, FRUITY, and immediately drinkable. This variety is also known as *Bonarda di Chieri* and *Bonarda di Gattinara.* 2. A synonym for a grape variety officially known as CROATINA.

Bonarda dell'Oltrepo Pavese *see* CROATINA

Bonarda di Chieri *see* BONARDA

Bonarda di Gattinara *see* BONARDA

Bonarda Piemontese *see* BONARDA

bond; bonded A *bond* is a federal permit to commercially produce and store wine. A *bonded winery* is an enterprise that produces and stores wine under a bond that guarantees payment of the federal excise tax.

Bon Marché *see* BUEHLER VINEYARDS

Bonnes Mares AC [bawn MAHR] A famous GRAND CRU vineyard located in the CÔTE DE NUITS area of France's BURGUNDY region. Of its 37 acres of PINOT NOIR grapes, 33.5 acres are in the village of CHAMBOLLE-MUSIGNY, and 3.7 acres are in MOREY-SAINT-DENIS. Bonnes Mares AC red wines are full-bodied (*see* BODY) TANNIC and can AGE for 10 to 20 years.

They're quite different from the wines from the village's other grand cru vineyard, MUSIGNY, which are lighter, more elegant and earlier maturing. Most critics agree that Bonnes Mares AC red wines can be some of the best in the world.

Bonnezeaux AC [bawn-ZOH] Small APPELLATION that nestles in the ANJOU region of France's LOIRE Valley. Located within the larger CÔTEAUX DU LAYON appellation, Bonnezeaux is one of the two premier DESSERT WINES from the Loire—QUARTS DE CHAUME is the other. Both have GRAND CRU status. The grapes used are CHENIN BLANC which, in better years, are attacked by BOTRYTIS CINEREA (noble rot). This mold produces shriveled, raisiny, intensely sweet grapes that in turn create rich, luscious wines. The naturally high acidity of the Chenin Blanc grape helps these wines AGE—some for 20 years or more—and they're best with some BOTTLE AGING.

Bonny Doon Vineyard Randall Graham bought his vineyard land in the SANTA CRUZ MOUNTAIN area in 1981 and started one of the more unique wineries in California. Bonny Doon produces an assortment of wines that are markedly different from those produced by most wineries. Bonny Doon's singular reputation was established with the release of its **Le Cigare Volant**, a red CHÂTEAUNEUF-DU-PAPE-style wine. The wine's name, which refers to a flying saucer, makes fun of an official French proclamation in the 1950s that outlawed UFOs from landing in the vineyards of the Châteauneuf-du-Pape area. Le Cigare Volant, which is made from GRENACHE, MOUVÈDRE, and SYRAH, was followed by a number of unique wines including: **Clos de Gilroy**, a Grenache wine made from grapes grown around the town of Gilroy; **Old Telegram**, a Mouvèdre wine name after France's famous Le Vieux Telegraph; **Le Sophiste**, a white wine made from MARSANNE and ROUSSANNE grapes; and **Vin Gris de Cigare**, a OEIL DE PERDRIX-style wine. Bonny Doon is also branching out with its **Ca' Del Solo** label, which is focued on Italian-type wines. There's also a line of EAUX DE VIE in various fruit flavors.

Boone's Farm *see* E & J GALLO WINERY

bor [bahr] Hungarian for "wine."

Bordeaux [bohr-DOH] An area in southwest France considered by most wine enthusiasts as the world's greatest wine-producing region because of the large quantity (ranging from 500 to 750 million bottles annually) and the high quality of the wines. This large region essentially covers the same territory as the DÉPARTEMENT of GIRONDE. At its center lies the seaport city of Bordeaux, which sits on the Garonne

River upstream from the Gironde estuary, which empties into the Atlantic Ocean. The Bordeaux region's fame dates back some 2,000 years when Romans first sang the praises of its wines. The wide popularity of Bordeaux wines in the United Kingdom (where they're called CLARETS) can be traced back to the period from 1152 to 1453, when the English owned this region, which was acquired through a royal marriage and then lost in the 100 Years' War. Bordeaux gains most of its fame from its red wines, which generally make up over 75 percent of the production. Nevertheless, the region's rich, sweet white wines from SAUTERNES are world renowned, and its DRY white wines from GRAVES have a serious following. Bordeaux's primary APPELLATIONS (*see also* APPELLATION D'ORIGINE CONTRÔLÉE), which cover the entire region, are **Bordeaux AC**—for red, white, and ROSÉ wines—and **Bordeaux Supérieur AC**—a designation for red and rosé wines that requires lower grape yields and slightly higher alcohol levels than basic Bordeaux. However, Bordeaux is broken up into many districts and contains numerous individual appellations. The five main districts that have individual appellations are POMEROL, SAINT-ÉMILION, Graves, Sauternes, and, most important of them all, MÉDOC. Within Médoc there are many individual COMMUNES with specific appellations as well. Some of them, like MARGAUX, PAUILLAC, SAINT-ESTÈPHE, and SAINT-JULIEN, are quite well known. Minor Bordeaux districts with appellations include BLAYE, BOURG, ENTRE-DEUX-MERS, and PREMIÈRES CÔTES DE BORDEAUX. There are over fifty individual appellations in Bordeaux, and, generally, the smallest ACs produce the highest-quality wines. There are also thousands of individual CHÂTEAUS—some are quite impressive, while others are simply tiny farmhouses. This number has resulted in attempts at classifying the better châteaus in addition to using appellations as a quality guide. At the top of the list sit the CRU CLASSÉ (classed growths) whose classifications are, for the most part, quite old and frequently raise questions regarding the accuracy of the rankings in today's environment. For example, the CLASSIFICATION OF 1855 divided the crus classés for the Médoc red wines into five subcategories—PREMIER CRU (FIRST GROWTH) through CINQUIÈME CRU (fifth growth)—and the white wines of Sauternes into two subcategories—*premier cru* (first growth) and DEUXIÈMES CRU (second growth). The quality of the wines from châteaus ranked in the second through fifth growths has changed over the years, but there hasn't been any official classification change. However, the first growth châteaus—HAUT-BRION, LAFITE-ROTHSCHILD, LATOUR, MARGAUX, and MOUTON-ROTHSCHILD (added in 1973)—have continued to maintain their standards for high quality (and high prices). Over the years, additional cru classé classifications were declared for other areas like Graves and Saint-Émilion. Today there are less than 200 châteaus classified as crus classés and the Pomerol district châteaus have never been classified. This has not deterred wine lovers from seeking out the higher-quality wines— Pomerol's Château PÉTRUS is consistently one of the most desired and expensive of all Bordeaux wines. Below the cru classé ranking is another grouping of classifications called CRU BOURGEOIS, which ranks several hundred better Bordeaux châteaus not included in the cru classé. Below this are thousands of châteaus of lesser stature grouped together as PETITS CHÂTEAU (the categories of CRU ARTISAN and CRU PAYSAN are no longer commonly used). The primary red grape varieties used in Bordeaux are CABERNET SAUVIGNON, CABERNET FRANC, MERLOT, and occasionally MALBEC and PETIT VERDOT. In fact, it may surprise many American ENOPHILES to learn that Merlot has almost twice as much acreage as Cabernet Sauvignon. SAUVIGNON BLANC, SÉMILLON, and MUSCADELLE are the primary white grapes. Bordeaux winemakers tend to blend grape varieties when making their wines, as opposed to the most common practice in the United States of making VARIETAL WINES. It should be noted that winemakers in the United States have recently started to make more blended wines and have coined the term MERITAGE for those that use the approved Bordeaux grape varieties. In general, the vineyards of Saint-Émilion and Pomerol are planted more heavily in Merlot and thus produce SOFTER, more SUPPLE wines, whereas the vineyards of Médoc and Graves favor the Cabernet varieties and produce more intense, TANNIC, and long-lived wines.

Bordeaux Blend [bohr-DOH] A term used for blended wines made with two or more of the traditional BORDEAUX grape varieties. The Bordeaux red grapes are CABERNET FRANC, CABERNET SAUVIGNON, Carmenere, Gros Verdot, MALBEC, MERLOT, PETITE VERDOT, and St. Macaire; white grapes are SAUVIGNON BLANC (Sauvignon Musque), MUSCADELLE (Sauvignon Vert), and SÉMILLON. In the United States, such blends are referred to as MERITAGE wines, providing they meet certain requirements.

Bordeaux mixture [bohr-DOH] Known as *bouillie bordelaise* in France, a Bordeaux mixture is a compound of copper sulfate, slaked lime, salt, and water. It's used throughout Europe and other parts of the world as a spray to combat MILDEW, especially powdery mildew.

Bordo *see* CABERNET FRANC

bota [BOH-tah] 1. A Spanish term referring to a goatskin bag that holds about a liter of wine. The bota has a nozzle on one end—when the bag is squeezed, the wine is forced out and into one's mouth. 2. A Spanish wine barrel equivalent to a sherry BUTT, holding about 132 U.S. gallons.

botrytis cinerea [boh-TRI-tihs sihn-EHR-ee-uh] Also called *noble rot,* this beneficial mold develops on grapes under certain environmental conditions. However, under the wrong circumstances (such as unripe grapes), **gray rot** develops and spoils the grapes. When carefully cultivated, botrytis causes the grape to shrivel, concentrating and intensifying both sugar and flavor. In addition, the acid levels remain high, which prevents the resulting wines from being cloyingly sweet. Most winemakers are exhilarated when noble rot descends on their grapes because it gives them fruit from which to make very elegant, intensely flavored DESSERT WINES. In California, botrytised wines are usually referred to as LATE HARVEST or SELECT LATE HARVEST. In France, where noble rot is called *pourriture noble,* the best-known beneficiaries are the famous wines of SAUTERNES. Noble rot is called *Edelfäule* in Germany, where winemakers are experts at producing a large variety of elegant wines such as TROCKENBEERENAUSLESE and BEERENAUSLESE. The renowned Hungarian TOKAY Aszú is also a popular botrytis-infected wine. In Italy, botrytis cinerea is called *muffa nobile.* A wide range of grape varieties are subject to the positive effects of noble rot. These include CHENIN BLANC, FURMINT, GEWÜRZTRAMINER, HÁRSLEVELÜ, OPTIMA, ORTEGA, RIESLING, SAUVIGNON BLANC, SCHEUREBE, and SÉMILLON.

botrytised [boh-TRY-tihsd] Description of wines that have a sweet, uniquely aromatic, honeyed characteristic in both flavor and fragrance. This trait is caused by grapes that have been infected with a mold known as BOTRYTIS CINEREA.

bottle *see* WINE BOTTLES

bottle aging *see* AGING

bottled by By itself, the phrase *bottled by* indicates that the winery played a very small part in the wine's production. The most likely role was simply to purchase and bottle wine made somewhere else. *See also* ESTATE BOTTLED; GROWN, PRODUCED AND BOTTLED BY; MADE AND BOTTLED BY; PRODUCED AND BOTTLED BY.

bottle fermentation; bottle-fermented Reference to the second fermentation that occurs in the bottle during the production of SPARKLING WINE via MÉTHODE CHAMPENOISE. *See also* FERMENTATION.

bottle shock *see* BOTTLE SICKNESS

bottle sickness A reaction that occurs in wine immediately after corking, resulting from the large amount of oxygen it absorbed during bottling. Bottle sickness can also be caused if sulfur dioxide was added during the bottling process. The effect on the wine is a flat flavor and aroma, sometimes accompanied by an off-putting odor. Bottle sickness, sometimes referred to as *bottle shock,* dissipates within a few weeks. *See also* ACETALDEHYDE.

bottle stink A stale, somewhat stinky odor that sometimes exists when a cork is first withdrawn from the bottle. Bottle stink usually dissipates fairly quickly.

bottling dosage *see* DOSAGE

Bouchaine; Bouchaine Vineyards; Chateau Bouchaine [boo-SHAYN] Located in the CARNEROS REGION of NAPA VALLEY, this winery has gone through several name changes—Chateau Bouchaine, Bouchaine Vineyards and, finally, simply Bouchaine. This winery primarily produces PINOT NOIR and CHARDONNAY made from grapes from its 31-acre Carneros vineyard. It also purchases grapes from other growers in Carneros and the NAPA VALLEY. Bouchaine's Chardonnays are currently their most highly regarded wines. They also makes a tiny amount of GEWÜRZTRAMINER from grapes purchased from the RUSSIAN RIVER area. Partners in this venture are publisher Austin Kiplinger and DuPont heir Gerret Copeland. Bouchaine's SECOND LABEL is **Q. C. FLY**.

Bouche *see* CABERNET FRANC; CABERNET SAUVIGNON

Les Boucherottes *see* BEAUNE

Bouchet *see* CABERNET FRANC; CABERNET SAUVIGNON

Aux Boudots *see* NUITS-SAINT-GEORGES

La Boudriotte *see* CHASSAGNE-MONTRACHET AC

Bougros [boo-GROH] One of the seven GRAND CRU vineyards in CHABLIS. Bougros consists of just over 35 acres and is adjacent to and northwest of LES PREUSES.

bouquet Today's classic usage for the term bouquet is the complex fragrance that develops in a wine through fermentation and aging, specifically bottle aging. *See also* AROMA; NOSE.

Bourg [BOOR] A small town in France's BORDEAUX region located north of the city of Bordeaux and across the Gironde River from MARGAUX. It's in the BLAYE region but has its own appellation, **Côtes de**

Bourg AC, whose wines have a better reputation than the rest of Blaye. Red wines, which represent the largest percentage of production, are made from MERLOT, CABERNET FRANC, CABERNET SAUVIGNON, and MALBEC grape varieties. Although these wines don't have the reputation of those produced across the river in MÉDOC, they're full-flavored, pleasant, and moderately priced.

Bourgeois *see* CRU BOURGEOIS

Bourgogne AC [boor-GON-yuh] A general regional APPELLATION for red, ROSÉ, and white wines. It covers all the wines produced in France's BURGUNDY region that, although they don't qualify for a higher-rated appellation, meet the qualifications of this basic appellation. Red Burgundy (*Bourgogne Rouge*) must be made from PINOT NOIR, although the GAMAY grape variety is allowed in BEAUJOLAIS; in the Yonne DÉPARTEMENT, the local varieties Tressot or Cesar are also approved. CHARDONNAY is the main variety used for white Burgundy (*Bourgogne Blanc*), although PINOT BLANC and PINOT GRIS are also approved varieties. Bourgogne AC wines are usually not as interesting as those with village or vineyard appellations, but they're generally good and moderately priced. The best are usually from single growers who couldn't put their wine into premium labels because it didn't quite meet specifications. *See also* BOURGOGNE ALIGOTÉ AC; BOURGOGNE GRAND ORDINAIRE AC; BOURGOGNE PASSE-TOUT-GRAIN AC; BURGUNDY.

Bourgogne Aligoté AC; Bourgogne Aligoté de Bouzeron AC [boor-GON-yuh ah-lee-goh-TAY] These APPELLATIONS are specifically for the ALIGOTÉ variety, a white-wine grape cultivated in some parts of BURGUNDY. Compared to CHARDONNAY, Aligoté is not as important or distinguished, and, in most cases, the wines it produces aren't as rich or long-lived. Some Aligoté wines can be sharp and sour, but older Aligoté vines have been known to produce some very pleasant wines that exhibit citrusy and, occasionally, nutty characteristics. Burgundian wines made from this grape are labeled **Bourgogne Aligoté AC** or, when they come from the village of Bourzeron in the northern CÔTE CHALONNAISE, **Bourgogne Aligoté de Bourzeron AC**.

Bourgogne Grand Ordinaire AC [boor-GON-yuh grah*n* ohr-dee-NEHR] The general regional APPELLATION, known as BGO, that is rarely used today. Its requirements are even lower than those for the BOURGOGNE AC, so most winemakers opt for the latter. The grape varieties are the same as allowed for Bourgogne AC wines, with the addition of MELON DE BOURGOGNE for white wines. In the

Yonne DÉPARTEMENT, the local Sacy grape variety is also allowed in white wines. As the name implies, the wines are fairly ordinary.

Bourgogne-Hautes Côtes de Beaune *see* HAUTES-CÔTES DE BEAUNE

Bourgogne-Hautes Côtes de Nuits *see* HAUTES-CÔTES DE NUITS

Bourgogne Mousseux AC *see* CRÉMANT DE BOURGOGNE

Bourgogne Passe-Tout-Grain AC [boor-GON-yuh pahss too GRA*N*] An APPELLATION that covers the entire BURGUNDY region for wines that are comprised of at least one-third PINOT NOIR and up to two-thirds GAMAY grapes and that are fermented together. This is primarily a red wine AC, although a small amount of ROSÉ is also produced. The wine from this AC is fairly basic and ordinary; however, ongoing vineyard replanting is gradually increasing the available Pinot Noir grapes, which in turn is improving wine quality. Most of Bourgogne Passe-Tout-Grain AC wines come from the CÔTE CHALONNAISE, with small amounts from CÔTE D'OR.

Bourgueil AC [boor-GEUH-yuh] One of the few APPELLATIONS in the LOIRE Valley focused on red wines. Located in the TOURAINE region, the area around the village of Bourgueil—like that of its neighbors CHINON and SAINT-NICOLAS-DE-BOURGUEIL—is dry enough to grow CABERNET FRANC and limited quantities of CABERNET SAUVIGNON. The wines from this AC are normally light and fruity. They're certainly no match for better BORDEAUX reds, but hot years can produce good, full-bodied (*see* BODY) wines with AGING capabilities of 10 to 15 years.

Bourguignon Noir *see* GAMAY

Bouscaut, Château [sha-TOH boo-SKOH] A large CRU CLASSÉ located in the PESSAC-LÉOGNAN AC in the GRAVES district of BORDEAUX. It consists of 111 acres and annually produces about 15,000 cases of red wine and about 7,000 cases of white. Both red and white wines are viewed as good but not inspiring. The red grapes used are about 50 percent MERLOT, 35 percent CABERNET SAUVIGNON, and 15 percent CABERNET FRANC. The white wines are made from around 60 percent SÉMILLON and 40 percent SAUVIGNON BLANC. The AGING capability for the red wines is about 10 to 12 years and for the whites about 5 to 6 years. This CHÂTEAU uses the SECOND LABEL, **Valoux**, for lower-quality batches of wine.

Bousse d'Or *see* VOLNAY

Bouzy [boo-ZEE] An outstanding wine-producing village on the Montagne de Reims in France's CHAMPAGNE region. Its vineyards have GRAND CRU status with a top rating of 100 percent under the region's percentage system (*see* CHAMPAGNE for more infomation). The grapes are PINOT NOIR, most of which are used to produce SPARKLING WINE, although a small amount of still red wine is bottled under the CÔTEAUX CHAMPENOIS AC.

Boyd-Cantenac, Château [sha-TOH boyd kah*n*-tuh-NACK] This 44-acre TROISIÈME CRU (third-growth) CHÂTEAU is located in the COMMUNE of Cantenac in the MARGAUX AC in France's BORDEAUX region. Until 1960 it was part of a larger single property (which included Château CANTENAC-BROWN) known as Château Boyd. Some feel that Château Boyd-Cantenac's inconsistent red-wine results in recent years haven't been up to third-growth quality. This château produces 7,000 to 8,000 cases each year from vineyards that are planted with about 67 percent CABERNET SAUVIGNON, 20 percent MERLOT, 7 percent CABERNET FRANC, and 6 percent PETIT VERDOT. Production of these wines is actually performed at Château POUGET, which is also owned by Boyd-Cantenac's proprietor, Pierre Guillemet. Wines from better VINTAGES can AGE for up 18 to 20 years. This château should not be confused with Château BRANE-CANTENAC.

Bramaterra DOC [brah-mah-TEHR-uh] DOC located in Italy's PIEDMONT region just to the west of GATTINARA near the villages of Roasio and Villadel Bosco. The DRY, red wines—made from NEBBIOLO, CROATINA, BONARDA, and Vespolina—are much lighter and more elegant than those from BAROLO or GATTINARA. They require 2 years AGING, with 18 months in wood barrels. A RISERVA requires 3 years, with 2 years in wood barrels.

brambly; bramble *see* BRIARY

Branaire-Ducru, Château [sha-TOH brah-NEHR doo-KROO] A QUATRIÈME CRU (fourth growth) CHÂTEAU located in SAINT-JULIEN. It's right next to Château BEYCHEVELLE in the MÉDOC district of France's BORDEAUX region. The château's 118 acres are planted with about 60 percent CABERNET SAUVIGNON, 25 percent MERLOT, 10 percent CABERNET FRANC, and 5 percent PETIT VERDOT. Each year this estate produces about 19,000 to 20,000 cases of red wine, which, although actually labeled *Château Branaire* (Duluc-Ducru), is commonly refered to as Château Branaire-Ducru. The better VINTAGES can age for about 15 years. The SECOND LABEL is **Château Duluc.**

branco [BRAHN-koh] Portuguese for "white."

brandy A liquor distilled from wine and aged in wood, which contributes flavor and color. The finest of all brandies is COGNAC, closely followed by ARMAGNAC. The name *brandy* comes from the Dutch *brandewijin,* meaning "burned (distilled) wine." Brandy can also be made from fermented fruits other than grapes (such as the apple-based Calvados), but they are generally qualified by adding the name of the fruit, as in apple brandy. The term brandy by itself generally refers to those made from grapes.

Brane-Cantenac, Château [sha-TOH brahn kah*n*-teh-NAHK] This is a DEUXIÈME CRU (second-growth) CHÂTEAU located west of Cantenac in France's BORDEAUX region's MARGAUX AC. Brane-Cantenac's reputation has been tarnished by a series of mediocre wines in the past, but it began to rebound slightly in the 1980s. The estate consists of about 210 acres planted with approximately 70 percent CABERNET SAUVIGNON, 15 percent MERLOT, 13 percent CABERNET FRANC, and 2 percent PETIT VERDOT. The château produces some 30,000 to 35,000 cases of red wine annually, some of which is bottled under one of the two SECOND LABELS of **Château Notton** or **Château de Fontarney**.

Brauneberg [BROUW-nuh-beh*r*k] A well-known village located just southwest of its more famous neighbor, BERNKASTEL, on the Mosel River in Germany's MOSEL-SAAR-RUWER region. Vineyards belonging to the village are in BEREICH Bernkastel and GROSSLAGE Kurfürstlay. **Juffer** is the most famous EINZELLAGE, and the wines from this vineyard are very expensive. Wines from this village have had an esteemed reputation for centuries.

Braune Kupp *see* WILTINGEN

Braunfels *see* WILTINGEN

brawny A sensory term often applied to MUSCULAR, young red wines that are full-bodied (*see* BODY) and high in TANNINS and ALCOHOL. AGING such wines usually helps SOFTEN their rough edges, thereby producing some degree of finesse.

Brazil Brazil is a huge country but, relatively speaking, it doesn't make much wine. What it does make is fairly ordinary, and most of it is consumed locally. A majority of the wines are made from native American grapes, HYBRIDS, or CROSSES. Some of the more popular are CONCORD, ISABELLA, NIAGARA, and SEYVAL BLANC. Recently, VITIS VINIFERA vines such as BARBERA, CABERNET SAUVIGNON, CABERNET FRANC, CHARDONNAY, MERLOT, MUSCAT, NEBBIOLO, PINOT BLANC, RIESLING, SÉMILLON and TREBBIANO have been planted. They do best in areas far from the Equator, where the climate is cooler. Brazil's biggest growing region is in Rio Grande do Sul, Brazil's southernmost state.

breathe; breathing When the cork is removed from the bottle and the wine is exposed to outside air, the wine begins to "breathe," or aerate. The aeration process is accelerated when the wine is DE-CANTED into another vessel (a DECANTER) or poured into a wineglass, allowing even more air access to the wine. There is some debate about the benefits of letting wine breathe. Advocates believe that the practice allows wines to SOFTEN (especially younger red wines with high TANNINS) and the BOUQUET to evolve and develop COMPLEXITY. Detractors say breathing dulls the wine's flavor and diminishes its liveliness. There's no argument that many wines simply don't benefit from breathing—generally most white and ROSÉ wines, as well as many lower-quality reds. Wines that do benefit are usually higher-quality VINTAGE red wines and some superior whites from BURGUNDY. Care should be taken with very old wines in that too much aeration may cause them to lose some of their fragile bouquet and flavor.

breed A term used by ENOPHILES to describe the best and most refined wines, prized for their CHARACTER, COMPLEXITY, and high quality. A wine of breed will have a superior heritage and be made from the best varieties. The French term for breed is *race.*

Breganze DOC [breh-GAHN-zeh] Located in the VENETO region in northeast Italy, this DOC zone is north of Vicenza and encompasses the vineyards around the village of Breganze. This DOC produces five VARIETAL WINES—Cabernet (made with CABERNET FRANC and CABERNET SAUVIGNON), Pinot Bianco (PINOT BLANC), Pinot Grigio (PINOT GRIS), Pinot Nero (PINOT NOIR) and Vespaiolo. Breganze DOC also produces blended red and white wines. The BIANCO combines Pinot Bianco, Pinot Grigio, Riesling Italico (WELSCHRIESLING), Sauvignon (SAUVIGNON BLANC), TOCAI, and Vespaiolo. The ROSSO is made with Cabernet Franc, Cabernet Sauvignon, Gropello, MERLOT, Marzemino, and Pinot Nero.

Brenton *see* CABERNET FRANC

Les Bressandes *see* BEAUNE; CORTON

brett *see* BRETTANOMYCES

brettanomyces; brett [breht-tan-uh-MI-sees; BREHT] A spoilage yeast that grows on grapes and in wineries. Because brettanomyces (*brett,* for short) is almost impossible to eradicate, most winemakers take great pains to avoid it. If it does happen in wine, vintners generally use special filters to reduce the prospect of continued growth in the bottle. Low levels of this pesky yeast can add complexity to a wine's aroma, while overt amounts can ruin it. Brett gives wine a horsey, BARNYARD aroma that some people love, others detest, and many don't even detect. A wine greatly degraded by brettanomyces can take on unpleasant odors that are variously described as resembling mouse droppings, a sweaty saddle, or burnt beans. A wine overly imbued with brett tends to get worse as it AGES. An organism called *dekkera* is virtually identical to brettanomyces and produces the same odoriferous results.

briary [BRI-uh-ree] An adjective used to describe wines—usually those with high TANNINS and ALCOHOL—that give an impression on the palate of being PRICKLY and AGGRESSIVE with a spiciness akin to black pepper. The term *brambly* or *bramble* is sometimes used synonomously.

Bricco Manzoni [BREE-koh man-ZOH-nee] A highly regarded VINO DA TAVOLA from the PIEDMONT region in northwestern Italy. It's produced by the wine estate of Podere Rocche dei Manzoni in the BAROLO DOC area of Monforte d'Alba from about 80 percent NEBBIOLO and 20 percent BARBERA.

brick red A descriptor for the color of some red wines that signals maturity. The brick-red hue is detectable most obviously at the MENISCUS, or rim of the wine in a glass.

Bridgehampton Winery A winery located on the South Fork of Long Island in New York State. It does best with CHARDONNAY and LATE HARVEST RIESLING but also produces CABERNET SAUVIGNON, MERLOT, and SAUVIGNON BLANC wines.

bright; brightness A descriptive term used for wines (generally young ones) with a fresh, fruity character.

brilliant An adjective used to describe a wine of superior clarity, which is usually accomplished through intense filtering.

British Sherry *see* BRITISH WINE

British Wine The term *British Wine* (or *British Sherry*) indicates that imported MUST or grape concentrate was used to make the wines, as opposed to ENGLISH WINE, which uses grapes grown in England.

Brix [BRIHKS] Named for A. F. W. Brix, a nineteenth-century German inventor, the Brix scale is a system used in the United States to measure the sugar content of grapes and wine. The Brix (sugar content) is determined by a HYDROMETER, which indicates a liquid's SPECIFIC

GRAVITY (the density of a liquid in relation to that of pure water). Each degree Brix is equivalent to 1 gram of sugar per 100 grams of grape juice. The grapes for most TABLE WINES have a Brix reading of between 20° to 25° at harvest. About 55 to 60 percent of the sugar is converted into ALCOHOL. The estimated alcohol that a wine will produce (called **potential alcohol**) is estimated by multiplying the Brix reading by 0.55. Therefore, a 20° Brix will make a wine with about 11 percent alcohol. The **Balling** scale was a comparable measurement procedure that has since been replaced by the Brix system.

Brochon *see* CÔTE DE NUITS

Brouilly AC [broo-YEE] This is the largest and southernmost of the ten CRUS in France's BEAUJOLAIS region. It includes five villages surrounding Mont de Brouilly and has almost 3,000 acres of vineyards. Made from GAMAY grapes, these wines are delicate and fruity with nuances of strawberries, bananas, and peaches. Though perhaps lighter than some of the other crus, they're still considered to be fairly typical of Beaujolais wines. CÔTE DE BROUILLY is a different cru located next to Brouilly.

Broustet, Château [sha-TOH broo-STEH] This is a DEUXIÈME CRU (second growth) CHÂTEAU located in the SAUTERNES AC in France's BORDEAUX region. It consists of almost 40 acres planted with 63 percent SÉMILLON, 25 percent SAUVIGNON BLANC, and 12 percent MUSCADELLE. When the environment permits BOTRYTIS CINEREA to infect the grapes, Château Broustet produces sweet DESSERT WINES under the SAUTERNES AC. If the conditions aren't suitable for sweet wines, it produces a DRY white wine, **Vin Sec de Château Broustet**, which has the GRAVES or Graves Supérieures APPELLATION. This château produces 2,000 to 3,000 cases of white wine per year. Its top-caliber wines will age for up to 20 years. Château Broustet has the SECOND LABEL of **Château de Ségur**.

browning An older red wine will be a deep ruby color with a tinge of brown on the edges. Although it may be quite enjoyable, a wine that shows browning will usually not improve with additional AGING.

Brown Muscat *see* MUSCAT

brown sherry *see* SHERRY

David Bruce Winery This California winery, which is located in the SANTA CRUZ MOUNTAINS, was started in the early 1960s by David Bruce, a San Jose dermatologist. After apprenticing with pioneering winemaker MARTIN RAY, Bruce planted 25 acres of his own vineyards in the hills above Los Gatos. He's experimented with a number of grapes, but today the winery focuses primarily on ESTATE-BOTTLED CHARDONNAY and PINOT NOIR. It also makes a CABERNET SAUVIGNON and a Chardonnay with a California APPELLATION. David Bruce's wines have been controversial over the years, but wines from recent vintages have generally been praised, particularly the estate-bottled Pinot Noir.

Brückes *see* BAD KREUZNACH

Bruderberg *see* MAXIMIN GRÜNHÄUS

Brunello *see* SANGIOVESE

Brunello di Montalcino DOCG [broo-NELL-oh dee mawn-tahl-CHEE-noh] The wines from Brunello di Montalcino are regarded as some of Italy's best. They're made totally from a SANGIOVESE clone, a strain of Sangiovese Grosso called *Brunello* ("little dark one"), so named for the brown hue of its skin. The wines are BIG, deep-colored, and powerful, with enough TANNINS and STRUCTURE to be quite LONG-LIVED. Brunello di Montalcino wines have one of the longest AGING requirements in Italy—4 years, 3½ of which must be in wooden barrels. The RISERVA must age for 5 years. Brunello di Montalcino is one of the small number of DOCG areas in Italy and one of the five (along with CHIANTI, CARMIGNANO, VERNACCIA DI SAN GIMIGNANO and VINO NOBILE DI MONTEPULCIANO) located in the TUSCANY region. This DOCG zone encompasses the vineyards around the hillside town of Montalcino, which is south and slightly east of Siena in the southern portion of Tuscany. The wine owes its beginning to Ferruccio Biondi-Santi who, in the 1860s, planted Brunello on the hills with the belief that he could produce great wines. His family continues the tradition today under the Biondi-Santi label. *See also* ROSSO DI MONTALCINO DOC.

brut [BROOT] A term applied to the driest (*see* DRY) CHAMPAGNE and other SPARKLING WINES. Brut wines are drier (contain less RESIDUAL SUGAR) than those labeled "extra dry." **Extra Brut** denotes a wine that's extremely dry, sometimes totally dry. Totally dry sparkling wines (those that aren't sweetened with a little DOSAGE) are also sometimes called *Brut Nature* or *Brut Integral*.

Brut de Lafaurie *see* LAFAURIE-PEYRAGUEY, CHÂTEAU

Bual *see* BOAL

budwood A shoot or stem of a plant bearing buds suitable for bud grafting.

Buehler Vineyards [BYOO-ler] This 61-acre winery, situated in the east mountains of California's NAPA VALLEY near Lake Hennessey, was founded in 1978 by John Buehler, Sr., a retired engineer. The vineyard was planted mainly with ZINFANDEL and CABERNET SAUVIGNON plus a tiny bit of PINOT BLANC, although Buehler has recently given up their Pinot Blanc effort. With the advent of a WHITE ZINFANDEL and Buehler's SECOND LABEL **Bon Marché**, the winery's production is now at about 30,000 cases per year. John Buehler, Jr., now administers the operation of Buehler Vineyards.

Buena Vista Winery [BWAY-nuh VIHS-tah] Old, historic California winery established in 1857 by AGOSTON HARASZTHY. The winery was dormant during PROHIBITION and up until about 1943. The original facility, now serving as a visitor's center, is located east of the town of Sonoma in the SONOMA VALLEY AVA. A modern production facility is located in the SONOMA COUNTY portion of the CARNEROS region and consists of 1,700 acres, of which almost 1,000 are planted with vines. Germany's A. Racke Co. is the current owner, with Marcus and Anne Moller-Racke managing the operation. Buena Vista produces a broad range of regular and Private Reserve bottlings, which are based primarily on CABERNET SAUVIGNON, CHARDONNAY, MERLOT, and PINOT NOIR varieties. The winery purchases grapes from other areas to produce other VARIETAL WINES. Buena Vista's production is nearing the 250,000-case level. **Domaine Buena Vista** is this winery's SECOND LABEL. In 1991 the Rackes acquired the **Haywood Winery**, and moved wine production to the Buena Vista Winery. RAVENSWOOD took over the winery facility formerly used by Haywood Winery.

Bugey VDQS [boo-JAY] This small area (625 acres) with VDQS status is located in the DEPARTEMENT of Ain next to SAVOIE in eastern France. It produces red and ROSÉ wines, mainly from GAMAY, PINOT NOIR, MONDEUSE, and Poulsard. The main grape varieties for white wines are JACQUÈRE, CHARDONNAY, and ALTESSE. Generally, the wines from the Bugey area are light but good, and the white wines in particular are improving as Chardonnay begins to play a more important role. Most wines are labeled **Vin du Bugey VDQS**, although wine made from Chardonnay and Altesse, called *Roussette* locally, can be labeled **Roussette de Bugey VDQS**. The word *cru* can be added to the label of wines from specified villages where the established vineyard YIELDS are lower and the minimum ALCOHOL level is higher. Sparkling (MOUSSEUX) and semi-sparkling (PÉTILLANT) wines are labeled Vin du Bugey Mousseux or Vin du Bugey Pétillant.

Buisserate *see* JACQUÈRE

Bulgaria [buhl-GEHR-ee-uh] This is an important wine-producing country in eastern Europe. Of the eastern European countries, Bulgaria has done the best job of getting wines into the markets of western Europe and the United States. This success is related to establishing approved growing regions (similiar to APPELLATIONS) and modernizing the wine-producing industry. But it is primarily due to Bulgaria's quicker adaptation to popular western grapes like CABERNET SAUVIGNON and MERLOT (which are now the top two red varieties here), along with ALIGOTÉ, CHARDONNAY, GEWÜRZTRAMINER, PINOT GRIS, RIESLING, and WELSCHRIESLING. Wines are also still made from eastern European varieties like the white Dimiat, Mistket, and Rkatzitelli and the red Gamza, Mavrud, Melnik, Pamid, and Tamianka. Bulgarian wines of a **Declared Geographical Origin** (DGO) must be labeled with one of twenty-six specifically approved wine-producing district designations. Of these DGOs, the best areas for white wines are Khan Krum, Novi Pazar, Preslav, Shumen, Targovishte, and Varna. The best DGOs for red wines include Assenovgrad, Lorzitza, Oriachovitza, Pavlikeni, Pleven, Plovdiv, Sakar Mountain, Stambolova, Suhindol, and Svischtov. **Controliaran** wines, the highest-quality level, must be from an approved vineyard site in one of the twenty-six DGOs and be from a specified grape variety. Currently there are twenty-one approved Controliran wines—Assenovgrad Mavrud, Harsovo Melnik, Kahn Krum Traminer, Liaskovetz Aligote, Lozitza Cabernet, Novi Pazar Chardonnay, Novo Selo Gamza, Oriachovitza Cabernet-Merlot, Pavlikeni Gamza, Preslav Chardonnay, Rozovata Dolina Misket, Russe Riverside White, Sakar Merlot, South Coast Rosé, Stambolovo Merlot, Suhindol Gamza, Sungulare Misket, Svischtov Cabernet Sauvignon, Treasure of Kralevo, Varna Chardonnay, and Yantra Valley Cabernet Sauvignon. Use of the word *Reserve* on the label requires 2 to 3 years of AGING for white varieties and 3 to 4 years for red varieties.

bulk; bulk wine Although sometimes erroneously used to describe wine sold in jugs or boxes, the term *bulk wine* actually refers to wine that's not yet packaged for retail sale.

bulk process *See* CHARMAT PROCESS

bung A plug that's used for sealing a wine barrel. It's inserted into the **bung hole,** through which wine can be added or withdrawn.

Burger *see* ELBLING

Burgess Cellars [BER-jihss] California winery located on Howell Mountain (although its elevation is too low to be part of the HOWELL MOUNTAIN AVA) on the east side of the NAPA VALLEY. In the early

1970s, Tom Burgess purchased this 20-acre property, which was the original Souverain Winery made famous by Lee Stewart. An additional 50-acre vineyard (Triere Vineyard) was acquired in 1979. Today the winery focuses on three VARIETAL WINES—CABERNET SAUVIGNON, CHARDONNAY and ZINFANDEL—all of which are highly regarded. The Cabernet Sauvignon, called Vintage Selection, usually has MERLOT and CABERNET FRANC blended with it. **Bell Canyon** is the SECOND LABEL for Burgess.

Burgundac Crni *see* PINOT NOIR

Burgunder *see* SPÄTBURGUNDER

Burgundy [BER-gun-dee] 1. Burgundy, one of the world's most famous wine-growing areas, is located in eastern France, southeast of Paris. *Bourgogne,* as it's called in France, consists of five basic regions—CHABLIS in the north, the CÔTE D'OR, the CÔTE CHALONNAISE, the MACÔNNAIS, and BEAUJOLAIS, which is farthest south. The Côte d'Or is futher divided into two well-known sections—CÔTE DE BEAUNE in the south and CÔTE DE NUITS in the north. Burgundy and its wines have a long history going back at least to the time when the Romans ruled this region. In the fourteenth and fifteenth centuries the Grand Duchy of Burgundy flourished, controlling an area that included what are now parts of Belgium, the Netherlands, Luxembourg, and a large portion of northern France. It was a rich and powerful empire, and the great Dukes of Burgundy savored the region's marvelous wines as part of their opulent lifestyle. The Burgundy region has established a reputation over centuries not only for its fine wines but also its marvelous food. The wines vary considerably from region to region throughout Burgundy, but the focus is on three grape varieties—PINOT NOIR and GAMAY for red wines and CHARDONNAY for whites. Though others varieties are grown—such as the white ALIGOTÉ, PINOT BLANC, SAUVIGNON BLANC, and Sacy and the red Cesar—they're being replaced in many areas by the three most prominent grapes. Gamay is the dominant red grape in Beaujolais, while Pinot Noir prevails in the other regions. The very best red wines come from the GRANDS CRUS in the Côte d'Or. Chardonnay is grown throughout the region and reaches its zenith in the Côte de Beaune. Although the wines made of Pinot Noir and Chardonnay get most of the attention, there are more wines produced in Beaujolais (where they make Gamay-based wines) than in all of the remaining Burgundy region. In some ways, the Burgundian system for identifying quality wines is much more straightforward than that of BORDEAUX. In addition to the APPELLATION D'ORIGINE CONTRÔLÉE (AC), Bordeaux uses a complex and inconsistent château classification system. Burgundy uses only the AC system to classify regions, villages, and individual vineyards into appellations, the theory being that the smaller and more precise the appellation, the higher the general quality of the wine. At the lowest quality level (usually), the AC system starts with general regional appellations that cover all of Burgundy, such as BOURGOGNE AC, BOURGOGNE ALIGOTÉ AC, BOURGOGNE GRAND ORDINAIRE AC, and BOURGOGNE PASSE-TOUT-GRAIN AC. Less general are the specific regional appellations like Chablis AC, Beaujolais AC, HAUTE-CÔTES DE BEAUNE AC, and HAUTE-CÔTES DE NUITS AC. Next up on the quality scale are the village appellations, which allow single villages to use their name on the label (for example, GEVREY-CHAMBERTIN, GIVRY, MEURSAULT, POMMARD, and VOLNAY). In the Beaujolais region there are ten villages (called CRUS) with the right to specific village appellations: BROUILLY, FLEURIE, MORGON, and MOULIN-À-VENT, to name a few. Some vineyards are now adding the vineyard name after the village name to further differentiate themselves. Ranking next to the top of this appellation progression are the PREMIER CRU (first growth) vineyards, which are individual vineyard sites that have historically produced superior wine. (Note that premier cru is the very top rating for châteaus in Bordeaux.) Burgundy premier cru wines use the village name, the vineyard name, and the term *Premier Cru* on the label. The only exception is when the wine is a blend of several premier cru vineyards, in which case the village name and the term *Premier Cru* appear. At the very top of the quality hierarchy are the GRANDS CRUS (great growths), which are the few very select sites that traditionally produce exceptional wines. Grand cru wines need only the vineyard name and the term *Grand Cru* on the label. Burgundy's seemingly straightforward ranking of appellations deteriorates, however, because the ownership structure in Burgundy, triggered by events that began with the French Revolution in the late eighteenth century, results in myriad small owners. The oft-used example is Clos de Vougeot, a 125-acre grand cru vineyard that now has around eighty different owners, each with a small parcel. The quality of wines made from this vineyard by the multitude of producers varies widely, yet all have the right to call their wine Clos de Vougeot, Grand Cru. It's thought that many of the best producers do a better job with their premier cru vineyards than some of the poorer producers with their grand cru vineyards. The same holds true with the best producers and their village-appellation vineyards versus the lesser producers with premier cru vineyards. So, although the appellation system is fairly straightforward, the true Burgundy lover studies the individual producers to determine which wines they like best. 2. Burgundy is also a generic name used for ordinary, inexpensive red wine made outside of France in countries like Australia, South Africa, and United States. Although many of the bulk producers in these countries are starting to call these wines Red Table Wine, the word *Burgundy* still appears on a number of wine bottle labels.

Burgundy basket *see* DECANTING

Burgweg *see* NAHE

Bürklin-Wolf, Weingut, Dr. Located in Germany's RHEINPFALZ region, this acclaimed wine estate is based in WACHENHEIM and owns over 270 acres scattered throughout some of the best vineyards in the region. The estate produces wines ranging in style from TROCKEN and HALBTROCKEN to magnificient BEERNAUSLESEN, EISWEIN, and very rare TROCKENBEERENAUSLESEN. The vineyards are planted with MÜLLER-THURGAU, EHRENFELSER, Weissburgunder (PINOT BLANC), GEWÜRZTRAMINER, SCHEUREBE, Spätburgunder (PINOT NOIR), and RIESLING, which produces the superior wines. The estate has been in the same family for over 400 years.

burning *see* HOT

burnt matches *see* SULFUR

La Bussiere *see* MOREY-SAINT-DENIS

butt A very large CASK used for wine or other SPIRITS. A butt normally holds 132 gallons and is commonly used to ship SHERRY.

Buttafuoco *see* OLTREPÒ PAVESE DOC

buttery A descriptor used to describe the smell and, sometimes, flavor of melted butter in a wine, most often CHARDONNAY. The term *buttery* is also used to describe the golden color of some wines.

butyric [byoo-TIHR-ihk] Derived from butyric acid (*see* ACIDS) and found in some spoiled wines, a butyric characteristic is evidenced by the odor of rancid butter.

Buzet AC [boo-ZAY] APPELLATION in southwest France that is right next to ARMAGNAC, not far from BORDEAUX. Formerly called **Côtes de Buzet**, it achieved AC status in 1973. Its main grapes are those of Bordeaux—CABERNET SAUVIGNON, CABERNET FRANC, MERLOT, and MALBEC for red and ROSÉ wines; SÉMILLON, SAUVIGNON BLANC, and MUSCADELLE for whites. The red wines, which dominate the area's production, are similiar to good Bordeaux wines but are but moderately priced. The series of good vintages in the 1980s have helped this little-known appellation gain attention. Most of the wines come from a large cooperative, **Caves Réunis des Côtes de Buzet**, at Buzet-sur-Baise. It produces good wines under the Cuvee Napeoleon label.

BV *see* BEAULIEU VINEYARDS

Byron Vineyard & Winery Located in the SANTA MARIA VALLEY AVA in central California, this winery was started in 1984 by Byron Kenneth Brown, who up until then had been the winemaker at Zaca Mesa Winery. After growing to between 15,000 and 20,000 cases of wine per year, Byron Vineyard & Winery was sold to ROBERT MONDAVI WINERY in 1990. Ken Brown is still managing the operation, which now annually produces about 30,000 cases of wine. Byron Vineyard & Winery has about 120 acres planted with CABERNET SAUVIGNON, CHARDONNAY, PINOT NOIR, SAUVIGNON BLANC, and tiny plots of MARSANNE and VIOGNIER. The Reserve Chardonnay is very highly regarded.

abernet Blanc [KA-behr-nay BLAH*N* (BLAH*N*GK)] One of the names used for a BLUSH WINE (white wine made from red grapes) produced from CABERNET SAUVIGNON grapes. Such wines are also known as *Blanc de Cabernet Sauvignon* and *Cabernet Blush*.

Cabernet Blush *see* CABERNET BLANC

Cabernet d'Anjou AC [KA-behr-nay dah*n*-ZHOO] An APPELLATION for ROSÉ wine located in the ANJOU region in the central part of France's LOIRE Valley. These almost DRY, raspberry-flavored wines are based on CABERNET FRANC grapes (with some CABERNET SAUVIGNON) and regarded with more respect than the sweet ROSÉ D'ANJOU AC wines that are also produced in this region.

Cabernet di Pramaggiore *see* LISON-PRAMAGGIORE

Cabernet Franc [KA-behr-nay FRAH*N* (FRAH*N*GK)] Although similar in structure and flavor to CABERNET SAUVIGNON, this red wine grape is not quite as full-bodied (*see* BODY), and has fewer TANNINS and less ACID. It is, however, more AROMATIC and HERBACEOUS. Unlike Cabernet Sauvignon, Cabernet Franc grows in cooler climates and ripens early. Therefore, it can be particularly important if weather conditions create a less-than-perfect Cabernet Sauvignon crop. Under such circumstances, the French have found that the addition of Cabernet Franc might salvage the VINTAGE. In BORDEAUX, Cabernet Franc is most often blended with MERLOT and Cabernet Sauvignon; it's usually not the dominant grape in these blends. The most noteworthy examples of French wines made primarily from Cabernet Franc grapes are those from Château CHEVAL BLANC, whose vineyards are planted with about 66 percent Cabernet Franc and 33 percent Merlot. In the United States, Cabernet Franc has not been widely planted, mainly because the weather in California yields consistently higher-quality Cabernet Sauvignon grapes than in France. Only recently has its popularity grown as a flavor enhancer for wines based on Cabernet Sauvignon. Cabernet Franc is also called *Bordo, Bouchet, Brenton, Carmenet,* and *Trouchet Noir.*

Cabernet Sauvignon [ka-behr-NAY soh-vihn-YOHN (soh-vee-NYAW*N*)] If not the king, as many argue, Cabernet Sauvignon is certainly the most successful and popular of the top-quality red wine grapes. It is the primary grape of most of the top vineyards in BORDEAUX'S MÉDOC and GRAVES districts. It's also the basis for most of California's superb red wines. This reputation for excellence has launched a Cabernet Sauvignon popularity boom around the world.

There's been heavy planting (which continues) in Chile, Australia, and eastern Europe, especially Bulgaria. In addition, Cabernet Sauvignon has begun making inroads into areas of Spain and Italy where local grapes have dominated for centuries. The flavor, STRUCTURE, COMPLEXITY, and longevity of wines made from the Cabernet Sauvignon grape are what makes it so popular. Its fruity flavors have been described as cherry, black cherry, black currant (cassis), and raspberry. In addition, other flavor descriptors include MINTY, CEDAR, and bell pepper; the word TOBACCO is often used to describe older vintages. The ACIDS and TANNINS found in a Cabernet Sauvignon wine help form the basis for its structure and longevity. In Bordeaux, Cabernet Sauvignon is most often blended with one or more of the following: MERLOT, CABERNET FRANC, PETIT VERDOT, or MALBEC. In California, wines are more often made with 100 percent Cabernet Sauvignon grapes, although the trend recently has been toward some blending, as in Bordeaux. In Australia, there is a predilection to blend Cabernet Sauvignon with SHIRAZ, which is widely grown there. Although the Cabernet Sauvignon grape has been grown in Italy for over 150 years, it has only recently become more popular. Italian winemakers are now blending small amounts of Cabernet Sauvignon with the local top red wine grape, SANGIOVESE. They also make a few top-quality wines with a majority of Cabernet Sauvignon. In Spain, there are blends of the local favorite, TEMPRANILLO, and Cabernet Sauvignon. There are a multitude of well-made Cabernet Sauvignon-based wines made throughout the world. Among the most notable wines are those from France's CHÂTEAU LAFITE-ROTHSCHILD, CHÂTEAU LATOUR, CHÂTEAU MOUTON-ROTHSCHILD, and CHÂTEAU MARGAUX and California's BEAULIEU VINEYARDS, CAYMUS VINEYARDS, HEITZ WINE CELLARS, and ROBERT MONDAVI WINERY. Although known as Cabernet Sauvignon throughout most of the world, in parts of France this grape is also called *Bouche, Bouchet, Petit-Cabernet, Sauvignon Rouge,* and *Vidure. See also* RUBY CABERNET.

Cabinet *see* KABINETT

Cabrières *see* COTEAUX DU LANGUEDOC

Caccione Nero *see* CANAIOLO

Cadarca *see* KADARKA

Ca' Del Solo *see* BONNY DOON VINEYARD

Cadet-Piola, Château [sha-TOH kah-DAY PYOH-luh] A relatively unknown GRAND CRU CLASSÉ château located in the SAINT-ÉMILION AC in France's BORDEAUX region. It's small (17 acres) and produces only about 3,000 cases of red wine each year. These wines aren't quite as SOFT as most Saint-Émilion wines, probably because the blend is slightly lower in MERLOT and slightly higher in CABERNET SAUVIGNON. The blend is approximately 51 percent Merlot, 28 percent Cabernet Sauvignon, 18 percent CABERNET FRANC, and 3 percent PETIT VERDOT. Those familiar with these wines think highly of them, particularly the VINTAGES since the 1980s. **Château Chevaliers de Malta** is the SECOND LABEL.

Cadillac AC [kah-dee-YAHK] A small APPELLATION located in the area around the picturesque little town of Cadillac in the southern end of the PREMIERES CÔTES DE BORDEAUX in France's BORDEAUX region. It sits on the Garronne River across from CÉRONS and BARSAC. The appellation is only for white wines made from SÉMILLON, SAUVIGNON BLANC, and MUS-CADELLE, which must be semisweet or sweet (minimum of 1.8 percent RESIDUAL SUGAR). Although some of the grapes in the Cadillac AC are infected by BOTRYTIS CINEREA, the resulting wines aren't generally as intense or luscious (nor are the prices as high) as those from SAUTERNES, which is just across the river.

Cahors AC [kah-OR] Located in southwest France, this APPELLATION produces red wines, mainly from MALBEC (locally called Auxerrois) BLENDED with small amounts of MERLOT and Tannat. Cahors has a reputation for its "black wines," which are made with grapes from hillside vineyards and are so named because they're very dark, TANNIC, and LONG-LIVED. Newer vineyards on the valley floor produce much lighter-style red wines.

Le Caillou, Château [sha-TOH kah-YOO] A DEUXIÈME CRU (second growth) CHÂTEAU located in the SAUTERNES AC in France's BORDEAUX region. The French word *caillou* means "pebble," and the vineyard soil in this area is full of them. The château has about 37 acres planted with about 90 percent SEMILLON and 10 percent SAUVIGNON BLANC. BOTRYTIS CINEREA will attack the grapes with the right climatic conditions, allowing the production of sweet DESSERT WINES under the Sauternes AC. If this is not possible, then DRY white wine under the label **Vin Sec de Château Caillou** is produced. The dry wines must use the the GRAVES or Graves Supérieures appellation on the label. The sweet wines are generally a lighter, more elegant style and will AGE for up to about 10 years. Château Le Caillou occasionally uses a SECOND LABEL **Château Petit-Mayne**.

Les Caillerets *see* CHASSAGNE-MONTRACHET AC; VOLNAY

Les Cailles *see* NUITS-SAINT-GEORGES

Caillou Blanc du Château Talbot *see* TALBOT, CHÂTEAU

Cain Cellars [KAY*N*] California winery located high up on the mountain in the SPRING MOUNTAIN AVA, west of the town of St. Helena in the NAPA VALLEY. Started by Jerry Cain in 1983, the winery is now owned by Jim Meadlock. The focus of Cain Cellars is on the following four wines: CHARDONNAY, made with grapes puchased from CARNEROS; a SAUVIGNON BLANC wine called **Musque**; **Cain Five**, a red wine made from the five BORDEAUX grape varieties—CABERNET SAUVIGNON, CABERNET FRANC, MERLOT, MALBEC, and PETIT VERDOT; and Cain Cuvée, a lighter style red made from the same five grapes. Cain Cellars has about 120 acres planted with the five red varieties and produces about 15,000 cases annually of primarily red wines.

Cain Five *see* CAIN CELLARS

Cairanne [keh-RAH*N*] A small village in the southern portion of France's RHÔNE region. It's entitled to use the CÔTES DU RHÔNE-VILLAGES AC, and wine labels usually also include the village name. These wines generally exhibit dark color, spicy fruit, and enough TANNINS to age well. The main grapes used are GRENACHE, SYRAH, CINSAUT, and MOUR-VÈDRE.

Cakebread Cellars California winery in the heart of the NAPA VALLEY just northwest of the town of Oakville. Founded by Jack Cakebread in 1973, the winery now has about 75 acres planted with CABERNET SAUVIGNON and SAUVIGNON BLANC. PHYLLOXERA infestation has forced the replanting of this vineyard, and more Sauvignon Blanc vines have been added so that the winery can increase production of its highly regarded Sauvignon Blanc wines. CHARDONNAY and ZINFANDEL wines are made from purchased grapes. Production is between 45,000 and 55,000 cases a year.

Calabrese *see* SANGIOVESE

Calabria [kah-LAH-bree-uh] The wine region lying in the "toe" of Italy's boot-shaped land mass. This beautiful, mountainous region is still quite antiquated in terms of winemaking technology and gener-ally produces mediocre wine. There are eight DOCs in the Calabria re-gion, the best known being CIRÒ, Greco di Bianco, and Melissa. The primary grapes are Gaglioppo and Marsigliana for red and rosé wines, and GRECO for white wines.

calcium alginate beads *see* RIDDLING

Caldaro *see* LAGO DI CALDARO

Calera Wine Company [ka-LEHR-uh] After working in France's BURGUNDY and RHÔNE regions, Josh Jensen set out to find a California vineyard site with a limestone subsoil like those in Burgundy so that he could focus on PINOT NOIR wines. He settled on a site south of Hollister and inland from Monterey Bay in the Gavilan Mountains. This winery's vineyard is the only one in the Mount Harlan AVA. Calera Wine Company now produces several Pinot Noirs including the Central Coast (from Santa Barbara area grapes) and four that are VINEYARD-DESIGNATED (from various vineyard microclimates) as Jensen, Reed, Selleck, and Mills. There's also an estate-bottled CHARDONNAY called Mount Harlan Vineyard, as well as a Central Coast Chardonnay. Calera planted VIOGNIER vines in 1983, the first wines of which were the 1987 VINTAGE. All Calera Wine Company wines—Chardonnay, Pinot Noir, and Viognier—from their own vineyards are very highly regarded. They're also in limited production and therefore difficult to find. The winery has just under 50 acres planted with these three varieties and produces just under 20,000 cases of wine a year.

California The California wine industry is said to have started during the period from 1769 to 1823 when the Franciscan monks began planting vineyards as they worked their way from southern to northern California establishing their missions. Unfortunately, the grape they planted was the MISSION, which produces wines of poor to medium quality. It wasn't until about 1830 that Jean-Louis Vignes began to import higher-quality VITIS VINIFERA grapevines. In the 1850s and 1860s, AGOSTON HARASZTHY expanded the effort by trying to determine which grape varieties would work best in various locations in the state. To this end, he imported thousands of cuttings of about 300 different grape varieties. In addition to planting these vines in SONOMA COUNTY, he sold cuttings in various parts of the state, primarily in the San Francisco Bay and Los Angeles areas. The California wine-producing industry went through numerous ups and downs over the next 80 years, but the PHYLLOXERA infestation in the 1890s and PROHIBITION from 1920 to 1933 severely curtailed wine business growth. The industry continued to grow sporadically from 1933 on, but most of the production was fairly ordinary wine from the giant CENTRAL VALLEY. At the time, most wines were made from grapes like THOMPSON SEEDLESS, Emperor, and Flame Tokay, which could also be used for table grapes or raisins. This trend began to change in the 1960s when Joe Heitz started HEITZ WINE CELLARS in 1964, Dick Graf established CHALONE VINEYARD in 1965, and ROBERT MONDAVI left the family (CHARLES KRUG) winery and established his own in 1966. At that time, the boom for quality wine took off, with dramatic increases in acreage allotted to grapes like CABERNET SAUVIGNON and CHARDONNAY. Today Chardonnay is the most widely planted wine grape, with over 56,000 acres, followed closely by French COLOMBARD, with just slightly less. (This compares with a 1959 total of about 80,000 acres for all of California's wine grapes.) After Chardonnay and French Colombard, the white grapes in order of total acreage are CHENIN BLANC, SAUVIGNON BLANC, RIESLING, GEWÜRZTRAMINER, PINOT BLANC, and MUSCAT. The most widely planted red grape (with about 35,000 acres) is ZINFANDEL, which barely edges out Cabernet Sauvignon. These two are followed in order of total acreage by GRENACHE, BARBERA, CARIGNANE, PINOT NOIR, MERLOT, RUBY CABERNET, PETITE SIRAH, GAMAY, GAMAY BEAJOLAIS, and SYRAH. Today, California produces about 95 percent of the wine made in the United States. Although it now competes favorably in producing some of the world's finest wines, it also still produces plenty of ordinary wine. Over 75 percent of California wine production comes from the hot Central Valley. Much of this wine is still undistinguished, although the quality is higher than in the past because of modernized equipment and better crop selection. For fine California wines, the climate of the cooler growing areas along the coast are best. Because of this, the NAPA VALLEY has become one of the premier wine-producing areas in the world. But it is not alone in the production of fine wine, as evidenced by other areas of the NORTH COAST in the counties of LAKE, SONOMA, MENDOCINO, SOLANO, and SONOMA. As the California wine industry continues to grow, other quality VITICULTURAL AREAS are being discovered, including numerous locations in the CENTRAL COAST region and selected areas in the SIERRA FOOTHILLS. California has many AMERICAN VITICULTURAL AREAS (AVA), however, this system is still in its infancy, and there are myriad confusing issues to be resolved. In an effort to define growing areas around the state, California uses a system known variously as degree days, heat summation method, Winkler Scale and Regions I–V (*see* CLIMATE REGIONS OF CALIFORNIA).

Calistoga Vineyards *see* CUVAISON WINERY

Calon-Ségur, Château [sha-TOH   kah-law*n*-say-GYOO*R*] TROISIÈME CRU (third growth) CHÂTEAU located on the northern side of SAINT-ESTÈPHE in the MÉDOC district of France's BORDEAUX region. It's the northernmost CLASSED GROWTH in Bordeaux. Legend has it that in the eighteenth century, the Marquis de Ségur (who owned Calon-Ségur, Château LATOUR, and Château Lafite, which is now Château LAFITE-ROTHSCHILD) said, "I make my wine at Lafite and Latour but my heart is in Calon." The Château Calon-Ségur labels are imprinted with a red heart, apparently to immortalize this thought. This large estate has about 124 acres planted with about 65 percent CABERNET SAUVIGNON, 25 percent MERLOT, and 10 percent CABERNET FRANC. The château produces about 18,000 to 22,000 cases of red wine each year. The SECOND LABEL is **Marquis de Ségur**.

Caluso Passito DOC [kah-LOO-soh pah-SEE-toh] DOC area located in the northern part of Italy's PIEDMONT region north of Turin. The vineyards are located in 35 different villages in and around the town of Caluso. The rich, sweet DESSERT WINES are made from the ERBALUCE grape by the PASSITO process—grapes are dried on mats so that their sugars and flavors are concentrated before they're made into wine. The wines are then AGED for a minimum of 5 years (different VINTAGES may be combined). This area also produces **Caluso Passito Liquoroso**, a wine FORTIFIED with grape ALCOHOL to a minimum alcohol level of 17.5 percent. *See also* ERBULANCE DI CALUSO DOC.

Caluso Spumante *see* ERBALUCE DI CALUSO DOC

Cambria Winery *see* KENDALL-JACKSON VINEYARDS

De Camensac, Château [sha-TOH kah-mahn-SAHK] Although this CHÂTEAU is ranked as a CINQUIÈME CRU (fifth growth), it's relatively unknown. Some suggest that, until recently, the château has been making lackluster wines, which may account for its obscurity. It's located in the COMMUNE of Saint-Laurent, which is part of the HAUT-MÉDOC AC in France's BORDEAUX region. Château de Camensac (sometimes referred to simply as Château Camensac) consists of approximately 155 acres of vineyard planted with about 60 percent CABERNET SAUVIGNON, 20 percent MERLOT, and 20 percent CABERNET FRANC. The château produces about 20,000 to 26,000 cases of red wine, and the best VINTAGES can AGE for 12 to 15 years.

Camobraque *see* FOLLE BLANCHE

Campania [kahm-PAH-nyah] A wine-producing region that runs along the eastern coast of southern Italy and encompasses Naples and the surrounding area. Naples is the major city of Campania, Italy's second most populous region. Most Campania wines are mediocre at best, as somewhat evidenced by the less than 1 percent of the total wine production that qualifies for DOC status. There are ten DOCs in the area including CAPRI, FALERNO DEL MASSICO, FIANO DI AVELLINO, GRECO DI TUFO, ISCHIA, LACRYMA CHRISTI DEL VESUVIO, Solopaca and TAURASI. The standout among premium wine producers in this region is the family-run firm of Mastroberardino, which produces over half the DOC wine. The primary varieties here are AGLIANICO and Piedirosso for red and

ROSÉ wines, and Asprinio, Fiano, GRECO, and Falanghina for white wines.

Campden tablets *see* POTASSIUM METABISULFITE

Campo de Borja DO [KAHM-poh day BOR-hah] A small DO located in the Aragón region in northern Spain, west of the city of Zaragoza in the Ebro Valley. Like much of this region, Campo de Borja is known for its heavy, high-ALCOHOL (from 13 to 18 percent) red wine, much of which is sold off in bulk as a BLENDING WINE. In addition to the large volumes of red wine, about 20 percent of the production is ROSÉ; there's also a small amount of white wine. The main grape for red wine is Garnacha (GRENACHE). The white wines are made from MACABEO (which is also used in small amounts in the red wines) and Moscatel (MUSCAT). Producers in Campo de Borja are experimenting with different grapes, lower-alcohol wines, and shorter AGING periods in attempt to produce the lighter, fruiter wines that are more popular today.

El Campo de Tarragona *see* TARRAGONA DO

Campo Fiorin [KAHM-poh FYOH-rihn] This is a VINO DA TAVOLA wine made by Masi, a wine estate located in Italy's VENETO area and a well-known VALPOLICELLA producer. Campo Fiorin could qualify as a Valpolicella DOC wine, but Masi prefers it to be highlighted as a special RIPASSO PROCESS wine—information that isn't allowed on a Valpolicella DOC wine label. The Ripasso process adds COMPLEXITY, color, and TANNINS, which results in a much richer, weightier (*see* WEIGHTY) wine than a traditional Valpolicella.

Campo Viejo [KAHM-poh VYAY-hoh] One of the largest BODEGAS of the RIOJA DO in northern Spain. It's owned by Bodegas y Bebidas (previously known as *Savin*), the largest wine company in Spain. Campo Viejo produces nearly 2 million cases of wine each year. The basic red wines are good, the RESERVA and GRAN RESERVA are very good, and the *Marqués de Villamagne Gran Reservas* are the best. TEMPRANILLO is the primary red variety, but Garnacha Tinta (GRENACHE), Mazuelo (CARIGNAN), and GRACIANO are also used. Small amounts of white wines are made from Viura (MACABEO). This bodega is also experimenting with wines made from CABERNET SAUVIGNON, PINOT NOIR, and CHARDONNAY. Most wines are aged in American oak.

Canada Canada is not a very large wine producer and, in fact, consumes about five times what it produces. The severe climate is very limiting in areas where grapes can be successfully grown. However, a couple of regions are starting to emerge as quality-wine producers—

southern Ontario and the Okanagan Valley in British Columbia. The climate of both these areas is tempered by the surrounding lakes. Southern Ontario produces about 85 percent of Canada's wines and has three quality growing areas—Pelee Island, Lake Erie North Shore, and the Niagara Peninsula (this last area produces over 75 percent of all Canadian wines). Most grapes are HYBRIDS like DE CHAUNAC, MARECHAL FOCH, SEYVAL BLANC, and VIDAL BLANC or American varieties like CATAWBA, CONCORD, Elvira, or NIAGARA. Canada grows limited amounts of VITIS VINIFERA grapes including CHARDONNAY, GAMAY, GEWÜRZTRAMINER, PINOT NOIR, and RIESLING. Canadian wineries are allowed to add grapes from other countries to their wine production.

Canaiolo [kah-nah-YAW-loh; kah-nay-YOH-loh] A red wine grape grown in Italy's TUSCANY, UMBRIA, LATIUM, MARCHE, and EMILIA-ROMAGNA regions. *Canaiolo Nero*, as it's officially known, produces slightly bitter, rather bland wine that becomes part of the traditional BLEND for CHIANTI wine. Chianti's DOCG rules for allowable grapes were changed in 1984, and Canaiolo's role was reduced from the 10–30 percent range to less than 10 percent. Naturally, this stimulated an acreage reduction in some areas. This variety, sometimes called *Cagnina*, is occasionally made into a red DESSERT WINE by that same name. Canaiolo has many synonyms including *Caccione Nero, Tindilloro, Uva Canina*, and *Uva Merla*.

Canard-Duchêne *see* CHAMPAGNE

Candel *see* D'ISSAN, CHÂTEAU

Canon, Château [sha-TOH kah-NAW*M* PREMIER GRAND CRU CLASSÉ château that is considered by many to be one of the best in the SAINT-ÉMILION AC. It produces only about 6,500 to 8,000 cases of red wine from its 44 acres. The blend for these wines is approximately 55 percent MERLOT and 45 percent CABERNET FRANC. In the best VINTAGES, these wines, which are described as RICH, full-bodied (*see* BODY), and TANNIC, can AGE for up to 25 years. The SECOND LABEL from this château is **Clos J. Kanon**. This Château Canon should not be confused with other Château Canons located in the CANON-FRONSAC AC in the BORDEAUX region.

Canon-Fronsac AC [kah-NAW*N* fwaw*n*-SAK] Small APPELLATION for red wines that is found at the southern end of the FRONSAC district in France's BORDEAUX region, not far from SAINT-ÉMILION. In the eighteenth and nineteenth centuries, the wines from this area were better known than the now-more-famous POMEROL. MERLOT is the dominant grape, followed by CABERNET FRANC, CABERNET SAUVIGNON, and small amounts of

C

MALBEC. The Canon-Fronsac hillside vineyards generally produce better wines than the neighboring Fronsac appellation, as indicated by the required ½ percent higher minimum ALCOHOL content. Wines from both appellations are reputed to be BIG and full-flavored, though somewhat HARD and TANNIC; they requiring extensive AGING. A new SOFTER style and the improved quality of recent vintages have created renewed interest in this area.

Canon-la-Gaffelière, Château [sha-TOH kah-NAW*N* lah gahf-LYEH*R*] CHÂTEAU located in the SAINT-ÉMILION AC in France's BORDEAUX region. It was awarded GRAND CRU CLASSÉ status in the 1955 Saint Émilion Official Classification but produced rather mediocre wines until changes began in 1984. The château consists of approximately 48 acres and produces 8,000 to 10,000 cases of red wine. The wines are made up of about 55 percent MERLOT, 40 percent CABERNET FRANC, and 5 percent CABERNET SAUVIGNON. A SECOND LABEL **Côte Mignon-La-Gaffèliere** is used for LIGHTER wines. Wines from recent VINTAGES are capable of aging from 12 to 14 years.

canopy The "curtain" of leaves and shoots formed by a grapevine.

Cantelaude *see* GISCOURS, CHÂTEAU

Cantemerle, Château [sha-TOH kahn-teh-MEH*RL*] CHÂTEAU that is classified as a CINQUIÈME CRU (fifth growth). Many wine lovers would agree that it should be upgraded to a DEUXIÈME CRU (second growth) or TROISIÈME CRU (third growth). Château Cantemerle, which is surrounded by a beautiful wooded park, is the second major château just north of the city of Bordeaux, heading into the MÉDOC. The quality of the château's wines has always been very good, but it took a dip in the 1970s prior to the Cordier firm beginning its supervision in 1980. Recent vintages have been quite good. The estate's 131 acres produce about 20,000 to 25,000 cases of red wine annually. The varieties used are generally 45 percent CABERNET SAUVIGNON, 40 percent MERLOT, 10 percent CABERNET FRANC, and 5 percent PETIT VERDOT. Better wines from this château can AGE for 16 to 18 years. The château uses a SECOND LABEL, **Villeneuve de Cantemerle**, for its lesser wines.

Cantenac *see* MARGAUX AC

Cantenac-Brown, Château [sha-TOH kahn-teh-NAK BROWN] Château Cantenac-Brown and Château BOYD-CANTENAC were originally part of a larger single property known as Château Boyd, which was split in 1860. This TROISIÈME CRU (third growth) CHÂTEAU is located in the COMMUNE of Cantenac and is part of the MARGAUX AC in France's BOR-

DEAUX region. Some feel the red wines from this château have been inconsistent and not up to third-growth quality. Château Cantenac-Brown produces 12,000 to 16,000 cases each year from its 100 acres. The vineyards are planted with about 67 percent CABERNET SAUVIGNON, 25 percent MERLOT, and 8 percent CABERNET FRANC. Wines from best VINTAGES can AGE for up 18 to 20 years. The château uses two SECOND LABELS, **Château Canuet** and **Château Lamartine**. This château should not be confused with Château BRANE-CANTENAC.

cantina [kan-TEE-nuh] Italian for "cellar" or "winery."

cantina sociale [kan-TEE-nuh soh-CHAH-lay] Italian for a "cooperative cellar" or "cooperative winery." Sometimes abbreviated as CS, cantina sociale is also called *cantina cooperativa*.

Canuet *see* CANTENAC-BROWN, CHÂTEAU

cap In winemaking, the mass of grape solids (skins, stems, seeds, pulp, etc.) that floats on the surface of the juice during the FERMENTATION of red wine. The cap needs to be broken up and pushed down into the wine frequently to help extract color, flavor, and TANNINS, as well as to ensure that the cap doesn't dry out and develop unwanted bacteria. In some wineries, workers employ the old method of using a long paddle to punch down the cap into the wine several times a day during active fermentation. Newer techniques include pumping the juice over the cap, thereby breaking it up and forcing it down into the juice. There are also specially designed tanks with screens fixed part way up in the tank. These screens stop the cap from rising to the top, thereby keeping it suspended in the juice. Other specially designed tanks rotate periodically, blending the cap and juice together.

Cap de Haut *see* MAUCAILLOU, CHÂTEAU

Cape Riesling *see* CROUCHEN

Capri DOC [KAH-pree] DOC situated on the island of Capri south of Naples in the Gulf of Naples. It produces red wines mainly from Piedirosso grapes and white wines from Falanghina, GRECO, and Biancolella; these wines are considered fairly ordinary.

capsule [KAP-suhl; KAP-sool] The wrapping that covers the cork and neck of a wine bottle. Historically, the favored material for capsules has been lead, but concerns over lead's safety are causing its gradual replacement. Other alternatives are plastic, tin, aluminum, and laminates. Recent innovations by ROBERT MONDAVI WINERY may lead to elimination of the tradional capsule. The winery's newest bottle features a natural-paper and beeswax cap that's attached directly to the cork.

En Caradeux see PERNAND-VERGELESSES

carafe [kuh-RAF] A simple clear glass (occasionally metal) container with a wide mouth used for serving wine or other beverages. Restaurants often use carafes to serve inexpensive wines. Carafes can also be used to decant older wines that have thrown SEDIMENT; however, finer wines are customarily transferred to a more elaborate container, such as a DECANTER.

carafe wine [kuh-RAF] Another name for HOUSE WINE. Generally a young, inexpensive wine served in restaurants, usually in a CARAFE. In France this is referred to as a *vin de carafe*.

Caramany *see* CÔTES DU ROUSSILLON

caramel An adjective used to describe wines, such as MADEIRA, that have a rich, burnt-sugar aroma and flavor.

Caramino [kah-rah-MEE-noh] The proprietary name of a wine made by Luigi Dessilani & Figli from 30 to 50 percent NEBIOLO, 10 to 30 percent Vespolina, and up to 40 percent Bonarda (CROATINA). Caramino is regarded as one of the best wines from the Fara DOC, which is southeast of the GATTINARA DOCG in the Norvara hills in northwest part of Italy's PIEDMONT region.

carbonation [kar-buh-NAY-shuhn] A method of making SPARKLING WINE (and other beverages) by injecting it with carbon dioxide. This technique is the least effective way to create effervescence and is used only for inexpensive wines. Such wines must be labeled "carbonated" in the United States, *gazéifie* in France. They're characterized by large, crude bubbles that quickly lose their effervescence, whereas MÉTHODE CHAMPENOISE sparklers have smaller, more refined and longer-lived bubbles.

carbon dioxide A colorless, odorless, incombustible gas, carbon dioxide (CO_2) is one of the two byproducts of FERMENTATION, the other being ALCOHOL. Yeast acts on the natural grape sugar and converts 40 to 45 percent of it to carbon dioxide, which in most cases escapes into the air. In the production of SPARKLING WINES, however, carbon dioxide is purposely trapped in the wine to create effervescence.

carbonic maceration [kar-BAHN-ihk mas-uh-RAY-shuhn] Also called *macération carbonique*, this technique is used during primary FERMENTATION to produce light red wines with low tannins, intense color, and fresh, fruity flavors and aromas. Such wines—like French BEAUJOLAIS—should be consumed early. The carbonic maceration process begins by dumping whole bunches of freshly picked, uncrushed grapes into large vats filled with carbon dioxide and, if native yeasts are undesirable, a good wine yeast. In this process, the bottom grapes are crushed by the weight of the grapes above them, and fermentation begins with the exuded juice. This beginning fermentation develops more carbon dioxide gas, which envelops the upper layers of uncrushed grapes and blocks air exposure that normally would occur. Soon, fermentation begins within the whole grapes, and they begin to ooze more juice. Finally, the whole batch is pressed, and fermentation is finished in a standard way.

Carbonnieux, Château [sha-TOH kar-baw-NYEUH] CRU CLASSÉ château located in the PESSAC-LÉOGNAN AC in the GRAVES area of BORDEAUX. With about 175 acres, it's one of the larger properties in Graves. This CHÂTEAU produces about 18,000 to 25,000 cases of red wine and 15,000 to 20,000 cases of white wine. The red wine is BLENDED with about 55 percent CABERNET SAUVIGNON, 30 percent MERLOT, 10 percent CABERNET FRANC, and 5 percent MALBEC; the white wine is blended with about 65 percent SAUVIGNON BLANC, 30 percent SÉMILLON, and 5 percent MUSCADELLE. This château is better known for the quality of its white wines than for its reds, although the latter has improved significantly during the last 4 to 5 years. White wines from the better VINTAGES will AGE for 10 to 12 years; red wines for age 8 to 10 years. Château Carbonnieux uses the SECOND LABEL **Château La Tour-Léognan**.

carboy [KAHR-boy] A large narrow-necked bottle of glass, plastic, or earthenware often used with a FERMENTATION LOCK as a SECONDARY FERMENTATION vessel.

Carcavelos DOC [kar-kuh-VEH-lyoosh] A small Portuguese DENOMINAÇÀO DE ORIGEM CONTROLADA (DOC) located just west of Lisbon near the seaside resort of Estoril. Carcavelos is known for its sweet, white FORTIFIED WINES made from local grape varieties of Boais, Cerceal do Douro, Galego Dourado, and Rabo de Ovelha. They also make an almost-DRY style that's more appropriate as an APÉRITIF.

de Cardaillan *see* DE MALL, CHÂTEAU

Cardinale *see* KENDALL-JACKSON VINEYARDS

Carignan; Carignane [kah-ree-NYAH*N*] Although this red grape originated in northern SPAIN'S CARIÑENA district, it's become the most widely grown red grape in FRANCE, especially throughout the LANGUEDOC-ROUSSILLON region. It's also extensively grown in other countries ringing the Mediterranean including Italy, Spain, Algeria, and Israel. It was also once the most widely planted red grape in California (where it's spelled *Carignane*), mostly in the San Joaquin Valley. With its high yields, Carignan produces more red wine than any other grape variety—most of it very ordinary. This grape is noted for its deep purple color, high TANNINS, and high ALCOHOL. At its best, it produces wines that are FRUITY and SPICY. Carignan is most often blended with wines from softer grapes, primarily GRENACHE and CINSAUT. In France most of these wines end up as VIN DE TABLE or VIN ORDINAIRE—"ordinary TABLE WINES." Carignan is also called *Carignano, Cariñena, Mazuelo, Monestel,* and *Roussillonen.*

Carignan Rosos *see* GRENACHE

Carillon de L'Angelus *see* L'ANGELUS, CHÂTEAU

Carinena *see* CARIGNAN

Cariñena DO [kah-ree-NYEH-nah] A DO encompassing the town of Cariñena in northern Spain's Aragón region. It produces large quantities of red and ROSÉ wine made primarily from Garnacha Tinta (GRENACHE), TEMPRANILLO, and Cariñena (CARIGNAN). The Cariñena grape, which is also called *Mazuelo,* is thought to have originated in this region, but is now more widely planted in France. White wines are made from Viura (MACABEO), Garnacha Blanc (GRENACHE), and Moscatel Romano (MUSCAT). Because of this region's dry, hot weather, the grapes ripen quickly, which results in high-ALCOHOL wines. Although the minimum alcohol content for this DO was lowered from 14 to 12 percent, the maximum is still 18 percent.

Carmelin *see* PETIT VERDOT

Carmel Valley AVA VITICULTURAL AREA located in Monterey County, California. It's southeast of the city of Monterey and the resort town of Carmel and west of the Salinas Valley. Though Carmel Valley is a large area, it has only a few wineries including Durney Vineyard and Château Julien. Carmel Valley generally falls into a Region I classification (*see* CLIMATE REGIONS OF CALIFORNIA), although it's a bit warmer (and does better with red wines) than the north end of Salinas Valley.

Carmenet *see* CABERNET FRANC

Carmenet Vineyard [kar-meh-NAY] California winery that is part of Chalone, Inc., which also owns CHALONE VINEYARD, and ACACIA

WINERY and is involved in a joint venture (with Paragon Vineyards) in EDNA VALLEY VINEYARDS. Carmenet has around 55 acres of vineyard situated on a beautiful site high in the mountains just north of the town of Sonoma in SONOMA VALLEY. It produces BORDEAUX-style wines, and its red wines, predominately CABERNET SAUVIGNON blended with MERLOT and CABERNET FRANC, are generally quite highly regarded. The SAUVIGNON BLANC wines (blended with some SÉMILLON) have not, however, been as consistent. Carmenet has switched to its Edna Valley Vineyards affiliate as its primary source for its white grapes, so the quality of these wines may become more uniform. Current annual production is around 30,000 cases.

Les Carmes Haut-Brion, Château [sha-TOH lay KAHRM oh-bree-OHN] Very small 9-acre property located in the PESSAC-LÉOGNAN AC in GRAVES near the famous chateaus HAUT-BRION and LA MISSION HAUT-BRION. It produces only about 1,500 cases of high-quality red wine. The blend of grapes is approximately 60 percent MERLOT, 20 percent CABERNET SAUVIGNON, and 20 percent CABERNET FRANC. These wines can AGE for up to about 20 years.

Carmignano DOCG [kahr-mee-NYAH-noh] Small area that was just recently upgraded to DOCG status. It's one of only a small number of DOCG areas in Italy and one of five (along with CHIANTI, BRUNELLO DI MONTALCINO, VERNACCIA DI SAN GIMIGNANO, and VINO NOBILE DI MONTEPULCIANO) located in the TUSCANY region. It's located just west of Florence inside the northeast section of the CHIANTI Montalbano subzone. These red wines, which are similiar to those from Chianti, use a variety of grapes—SANGIOVESE being predominate. Carmignano wines differ from Chiantis in that they must include between 6 and 10 percent CABERNET SAUVIGNON grapes, which have been justified for DOCG qualification because they've been grown here since the 1700s. ROSATO and VIN SANTO wines from Carmignano have DOC status. **Barco Reale**, a lighter version of the Carmignano DOCG red wines, is expected to soon receive DOC status since Carmignano red wines have been upgraded to DOCG status.

Carnelian [kahr-NEEL-yuhn] A red wine grape that is the result of a CROSS of GRENACHE with an earlier hybrid of CABERNET SAUVIGNON and CARIGNAN. This variety was developed in California during the early 1970s in an attempt to produce a grape that would do well in hot climates and still have Cabernet Sauvignon characteristics. The result was not widely successful, and there are only modest plantings of this grape. To the disappointment of all, the generally LIGHT, rather bland Carnelian wines did not acquire the desired Cabernet Sauvignon traits.

Carneros AVA; Los Carneros AVA [kahr-NEH-rohs] Also known as *Los Carneros,* this AVA lies at the northern end of San Pablo Bay (the northern section of San Francisco Bay) and includes vineyards in both SONOMA and NAPA COUNTIES. Because of the Bay's cooling effects, and the fog that the hotter inland areas draw over the land, Carneros has become an increasingly popular growing area. Its climate is ranked a Region I (*see* CLIMATE REGIONS OF CALIFORNIA), although some areas protected from the cooling breezes can be warmer. The dominant grapes in Carneros are PINOT NOIR and CHARDONNAY, and about one-third of these find there way into SPARKLING WINE. Small amounts of CABERNET SAUVIGNON and MERLOT are grown here as well. Carneros has attracted foreign investment in the form of three sparkling wine facilities: Codorníu Napa from the Spanish giant CODORNÍU; DOMAIN CARNEROS from the French CHAMPAGNE house TAITTINGER; and Gloria Ferrer from another Spanish firm FREIXENET. Other well-known Carneros wineries include ACACIA, BOUCHAINE, BUENAS VISTA, CARNEROS CREEK, Macrostie, Kent Rasmussen, Roche, SAINTSBURY, Schug, Sonoma Creek, and Truchard Vineyards. The Carneros area supplies many wineries not located in the AVA itself. Carneros is Spanish for "sheep."

Carneros Creek Winery [kahr-NEH-rohs] CARNEROS AVA winery founded in 1972 by Francis Mahoney and Balfour Gibson. It produces highly regarded PINOT NOIR wines in three price ranges: **Signature Reserve** is the most expensive, followed respectively by the **Los Carneros** and **Fleur de Carneros**. Usually, the Los Carneros CHARDONNAY is also quite well received. This winery also makes CABERNET SAUVIGNON from purchased grapes, currently from the Truchard Vineyards in the CARENEROS area. Carneros Creek Winery has about 21 acres of its own and produces between 20,000 and 25,000 cases of wine a year.

Les Carriéres *see* CORTON

Les Carruades de Lafite *see* LAFITE-ROTHSCHILD, CHÂTEAU

casa vinicola [KAH-suh vee-nee-KOH-luh] The Italian term for a wine house or a firm that makes wine primarily from purchased grapes.

cascina [kah-SHEE-nuh] The northern Italian term for a farm or estate that makes wine.

casein [KAY-seen; KAY-see-ihn] A form of milk protein used for FINING wines. Casein is often obtained in the form of powdered skim milk.

cask [KASK] 1. A large, strong, barrel-shaped, leak-proof container generally used for storing wines and other SPIRITS. Most wine casks are made of oak. 2. This term is also used to describe the quantity such a container holds.

cask number; cask # A cask number is often used to denote a very special wine, such as STAG'S LEAP WINE CELLARS "Cask 23," which is a RESERVE-style CABERNET SAUVIGNON. In the true sense, a cask number is supposed to indicate that a wine spent its entire aging period in one cask and that the wine was produced in limited quantities. However, there's no legal requirement as to how this term is used, and it's too often employed simply as a marketing ploy.

cassis [ka-SEES] A sensory term used to describe the rich, black currant flavor and aroma found in some wines, such as those made from CABERNET SAUVIGNON grapes.

Cassis AC [kah-SEES] APPELLATION that surrounds the resort town of Cassis located on the Mediterranean just southeast of Marseille in France's PROVENCE region. Although this appellation also covers red and ROSÉ wines made from GRENACHE, CINSAUT and MOURVÈDRE, white wines are predominate and make up a majority of the production. The best examples of these white wines, which are made from Ugni Blanc (TREBBIANO), CLAIRETTE, MARSANNE, and a small amount of SAUVIGNON BLANC, are FRESH, LIGHT, DRY, and FRAGRANT. Wines from the Cassis AC should not be confused with crème de cassis liqueur, which is made from a European black currant called *cassis*.

Castelhão Frances *see* PERIQUITA

Castel del Monte DOC [kas-TEHL del MON-tay] A well-known DOC located in Italy's APULIA region. It's located in the hilly region west of Bari not far from the Adriatic. It covers ROSSO, BIANCO, and ROSATO wines; the reds and rosés are highly regarded. UVA DI TROIA is the main grape for the red wines, which also include AGLIANICO, MONTEPULCIANO, Pinot Nero (PINOT NOIR), and SANGIOVESE. Bombino Nero is the dominate grape for the rosé wine, which can also include most of the aforementioned red grapes. The white wine, which is made from mainly from Pampanuto, is considered rather bland.

Casteller DOC [kass-TEH-ler] DOC located in the Trentino province, which is part of the TRENTINO-ALTO ADIGE region in northeastern Italy. It covers a wide area and includes vineyards around twenty-seven different villages in the province. The rather ordinary, DRY, light red wine produced here is made from SCHIAVA, LAMBRUSCO, and MERLOT. It should be drunk young.

Castelli di Jesi *see* VERDICCHIO DEI CASTELLIDI DI JESI DOC

Castelli Romani [kah-STEHL-ee roh-MAH-nee] A group of hills southeast of Rome in the LATIUM region, just north of the COLLI ALBANI DOC. The Castelli Romani hills contain a number of DOCs—including FRASCATI, MARINO, MONTECOMPATRI-COLONNA, and Zagarolo—which help supply wine to the populace of Rome.

castello [kahs-TEHL-loh] Italian for "castle." The word *castello* can be used only on labels of DOC/DOCG wines.

Castilla-La Mancha [kahs-TEE-yuh lah MAHN-chuh] A huge wine-growing region in the center of Spain. It includes the provinces of Albacete, Cuenca, Ciudad Real, Guadalajara, and Toledo plus the cities of Madrid and Toledo. The summer climate is so hot and forbidding that the YIELD is very low. Yet there are so many acres of vineyard planted that this region generates almost half of all the wine produced in Spain—most of it white. The main white grape is the AIRÉN, and this vast region helps Airén claim the title of the world's most widely planted grape variety. Cencibel (TEMPRANILLO) is the region's most widely planted red variety. Much of the wine produced is sold in bulk as a BLENDING WINE to other Spanish regions and even other European countries. Large quantities find their way to distilleries for further processing into ALCOHOL. Castilla-La Mancha contains five DO areas—ALMANSA, LA MANCHA (Europe's largest designated quality-wine-producing area), MÉNTRIDA, VALDEPEÑAS, and VINOS DE MADRID.

Castillon *see* CÔTES DE CASTILLON AC

Catalonia; Sp. Cataluña [katl-OH-nee-uh; katl-OHN-yuh (Sp. kah-tah-LOO-nyuh)] An extensive and well-known region in the northeastern part of Spain. Its northern border is adjacent to France, and the Mediterranean is to the east. Catalonia is an autonomous bilingual region whose people speak both Spanish and the local Catalan. The region covers four provinces—Barcelona, Gerona, Lérida, and Tarragona—and it's capital is the city of Barcelona. Catalonia has eight DO areas making STILL WINE—ALELLA, AMPURDÁN-COSTA BRAVA, CONCA DE BARBERÀ, COSTERS DEL SERGRE, PENEDÈS, PRIORATO, TARRAGONA, and TERRA ALTA. The CAVA DO, which has multiple locations spread throughout northern Spain producing SPARKLING WINE via MÉTHODE CHAMPENOISE, is centered in Catalonia.

Catawba [kuh-TAW-bah] This light red grape is native to North America and thought to be a natural HYBRID of other indigenous varieties. It's believed to have first been found along North Carolina's Catawba River, hence its name. It's popular on the East Coast of the United States, particularly in the FINGER LAKES region of New York State.

Catawba grapes produce light-colored juice in various shades of pink, with flavor characteristics of the native VITIS LABRUSCA. They're used in ROSÉ and white STILL WINES, as well as in inexpensive SPARKLING WINES.

Cava DO; cava [KAH-vah] Cava is the official name for SPARKLING WINE produced in designated areas in various parts of northern Spain. The use of the word *cava* came about as a result of legal conflicts with France over the use of the word *champan*, Spain's translation of the French *champagne*. The word *cava* (which is Catalan for "cellar") was chosen to identify sparkling wines because almost all such wines in Spain are made in the Catalan region. Unlike other Spanish DOS, the Cava DO, which was established in 1986, has multiple geographic areas. In fact, 159 villages spread over eight provinces have been authorized for cava production. These areas are in northern Spain, mostly in the PENEDÈS portion of the CATALONIA region around Barcelona (where 90 percent of the cavas are made). Wines must also be made by the MÉTHODE CHAMPENOISE in order to qualify for Cava DO status. Méthode champenoise sparkling wines that aren't geographically qualified for Cava DO status are called *vino espumoso natural método tradicional.* Most Cava DO wines use MACABEO, PARELLADA, and XAREL-LO grapes; however, the best wines use large amounts of CHARDONNAY and/or PINOT NOIR in the CUVÉE. CODORNÍU, RAIMAT (owned by Codorníu) and Segura Viudas (owned by FREIXENET) are some of the wine companies producing cava with Chardonnay as a major component. Unfortunately, the three most commonly used grapes don't AGE well, yet Cava DO rules require a minimum aging of 9 months. This means that many of these wines are dull and bland with an earthy character—they should be drunk as young as possible while there's still some fruit flavor.

Cavas del Ampurdán *see* AMPURDÁN-COSTA BRAVA DO

cave [CAHV] The French term meaning "cellar." Although often referring to an underground storage place, the word *cave* is also used to identify a collection of wines wherever they are stored.

cave cooperative *see* COOPERATIVE

Caves Aliança [KAH-vehr ehr-LYERN-ser] One of the largest wine companies in Portugal. It is based in northern Portugal's BAIRRADA region and produces red, ROSÉ, and white STILL WINES, SPARKLING WINES make up a large percentage of the production.

Caves Réunis des Côtes de Buzet *see* BUZET

Caymus Vineyards [KAY-muhss] Established by Charles Wagner in 1972, this NAPA VALLEY winery is renowned for the intensity of its rich, lush CABERNETS. It also produces highly regarded PINOT NOIR, SAUVIGNON BLANC, ZINFANDEL, and **Conundrum**, a proprietary white wine that's a blend of MUSCAT, CHARDONNAY, SÉMILLON, and Sauvignon Blanc. The wines currently sold under Caymus' good-value SECOND LABEL **Liberty School** are a CHARDONNAY and Cabernet as well as the **Three Valley Select**—a blend of Chardonnay, Sauvignon Blanc, and Muscat. Caymus has 65 acres of its own planted mainly with Cabernet Sauvignon but buys grapes from other growers for some of its wines. Caymus Vineyards' production is about 50,000 cases per year, plus an additional 75,000 to 80,000 for the Liberty School label.

Cayuga White [kay-YOO-guh; ki-YOO-guh] A white wine HYBRID created by the New York State Agricultural Office at its Geneva experimental station by crossing SEYVAL BLANC (a European hybrid) with a native American vine. It's grown mostly in New York's FINGER LAKES region and is named after that region's Cayuga Lake.

cedar A characteristic of some wines reminiscent of cedarwood, most often found in the BOUQUET of fine red wines, such as those from BORDEAUX and some California CABERNET SAUVIGNONS. A cedarlike quality can also be detected in some OAK-aged white wines. The term *cigar box* is synonymous for cedar.

cellar *see* WINE CELLAR

cellared by An imprecise term that appears on some wine labels, usually meaning that the winery purchased the wine from somewhere else and then bottled and AGED it prior to release. Since there's no requirement for the length of aging, this term it doesn't necessarily mean the wine received special attention. *See also* BOTTLED BY; ESTATE BOTTLED; GROWN, PRODUCED AND BOTTLED BY; MADE AND BOTTLED BY; PRODUCED AND BOTTLED BY.

Cellukork *see* CORKS

Cencibel *see* TEMPRANILLO

centiliter *see* METRIC

Central Coast AVA A huge VITICULTURAL AREA covering vineyards from Los Angeles to San Francisco. The counties it covers are Alameda, Monterey, San Benito, San Luis Obispo, Santa Barbara, Santa Clara, and Santa Cruz. There are numerous smaller AVAS within the large Central Coast area. Some winemakers use the smaller AVA names on their labels, although those who use grapes from more than one of the smaller AVAs must use the Central Coast AVA.

Central Valley Huge California growing area that runs inland from north of Chico (which is north of Sacramento) to south of Bakersfield. The Central Valley can actually be broken into two parts—the **Sacramento Valley** at the north and the **San Joaquin Valley** at the south. The area is so large (it encompasses 55 percent of California's vineyard acreage) and the yields are so bountiful that over 75 percent of California's total wine production comes out of this region. There are three VITICULTURAL AREAS in the valley—MADERA, MERRITT ISLAND, and CLARKSBURG. Most of the wine from the Central Valley is pretty ordinary, but implementation of modern winery facilities has gradually improved the quality. Because of the Central Valley's high temperatures and short growing season, ACID in the grapes isn't fully developed, which is why high-acid grapes like BARBERA, CHENIN BLANC, and French Colombard (COLOMBARD) have been planted in increasing numbers. The leading red varieties are ZINFANDEL and GRENACHE, followed by Barbera, CARIGNANE, RUBIRED, RUBY CABERNET, CABERNET SAUVIGNON and MERLOT. Other white varieties include CHARDONNAY, SAUVIGNON BLANC, and MALVASIA.

centrifuge; centrifuging [SIHN-truh-fyooj] A high-speed, rotating apparatus that separates substances of varying densities through centrifugal force. **Centrifuging** is used in winemaking to remove yeast cells from a wine before it completes the FERMENTATION process. It's also used instead of other processes (such as FILTERING) to remove particles from wine.

Les Cents Vignes *see* BEAUNE

Centurion [sihn-TOOR-ee-uhn; sihn-TYOOR-ee-uhn] This red wine grape is a cross (similar to CARNELIAN) of CARIGNAN, CABERNET SAUVIGNON, and GRENACHE. It was developed in California for hotter growing areas and has been planted on a limited basis in California's CENTRAL VALLEY. Like Carnelian, Centurion didn't acquire enough Cabernet traits to make it valued, and it's received only limited acceptance.

cepa [THEH-pah] A Spanish term literally meaning "vine" or "root"; also often used to mean "grape variety."

cepage [say-PAHZH] French for "grape variety."

cerasuolo [cheh-rah-SWAW-loh] Italian for "cherry red" or "cherry-colored." Cerasuolo is used to describe some darker ROSÉ wines.

Cérons AC [say-RAWN] Small APPELLATION located southeast of the city of Bordeaux along the Garonne River that abuts BARSAC and is surrounded by the much larger appellation GRAVES. Cérons AC produces only sweet white wines, similiar to those from SAUTERNES though not as intense, sweet, or expensive. The grapes used are SÉMILLON, SAUVIGNON BLANC, and MUSCADELLE. Decreasing interest in sweet wines has led many producers in this area to shift to DRY white wines, which must be labeled with the Graves appellation.

Certan-de-May, Château [sha-TOH seh*r*-tah*N* duh MEH] Small unclassified CHÂTEAU located in the POMEROL AC in BORDEAUX next to famous neighbors like Château PÉTRUS and VIEUX-CHÂTEAU-CERTAN. It shares the same soil and climate as its celebrated neighbors and, since 1974, has produced such excellent wines that it's considered one of Pomerol's top châteaus. Unfortunately, only about 2,000 cases of these RICH, CONCENTRATED wines are produced from this 12-acre estate. The grape blend used is approximately 65 percent MERLOT, 25 percent CABERNET FRANC, and 10 percent CABERNET SAUVIGNON. The best VINTAGES can AGE for 20 years or more.

Certan-Giraud, Château [sha-TOH seh*r*-TAH*N* zhee-*R*OH] Small unclassified CHÂTEAU located in the POMEROL AC in BORDEAUX. It has famous neighbors including Châteaus CERTAN-DE-MAY and PÉTRUS and VIEUX-CHÂTEAU-CERTAIN. Château Certan-Giraud shares the same soil and climate as that of its illustrious neighbors, and, although inconsistent, it frequently produces excellent wines. The château consists of 17 acres planted with about 65 percent MERLOT and 35 percent CABERNET FRANC. It produces between 3,500 and 4,000 cases of red wine each year. The best VINTAGES can AGE for about 10 years. Some wine is produced under a SECOND LABEL **Clos du Roy**.

Cerveteri DOC [chayr-veh-TEH-ree] Located northwest of Rome in Italy's LATIUM region, this DOC zone produces both ROSSO and BIANCO wines. The reds are made from SANGIOVESE, MONTEPULCIANO, Cesanese, Carignano (CARIGNAN), CANAIOLO Nero, and BARBERA. The white wines are a blend of numerous white varieties but predominately TREBBIANO and MALVASIA.

Chablais [shah-BLAY] One of the three main growing areas in the Swiss canton of VAUD. Chablais is located just north of the canton of VALAIS and just south of Lake Geneva in the valley of the Rhône. It's a white wine area where the dominant grape is CHASSELAS (locally known as *Dorin*). This area's best wines come from the villages of Aigle and Yvorne.

Chablis [sha-BLEE; shah-BLEE] 1. Small growing district located 110 miles southeast of Paris that encircles the town of Chablis in France's BURGUNDY region and produces some of the world's best known white wines. Chablis' vineyards, which are fairly far north, are closer to the CHAMPAGNE region than they are to most of the rest of Burgundy. There are between 6,000 and 7,000 acres with AC status. This acreage has increased in recent years because of improved methods of protecting the vineyards when the temperature drops below freezing, which isn't uncommon in this northerly region. CHARDONNAY is the approved grape for Chablis' appellations, which are, in increasing order of quality, **Petit Chablis AC**, **Chablis AC**, **Chablis Premier Cru AC**, and **Chablis Grand Cru AC**. The majority of the production comes from the Chablis AC vineyards followed by those of the Chablis Premier Cru AC vineyards. There are forty vineyards with PREMIER CRU status, but some smaller premier cru vineyards have the right to use the names of certain larger, better-known premier cru vineyards so that the practical number of names in use is around twenty. The best known of these are **Beauroy**, **Fourchaume**, **Les Fourneaux**, **Côte de Léchet**, **Mont de Milieu**, **Montée de Tonnerre**, **Montmains**, **Mélinots**, **Vaillons**, **Vaucoupin**, **Vau de Vey**, and **Vosgros**. The best wines come from the seven grand cru vineyards—BLANCHOTS, BOUGROS, LES CLOS, GRENOUILLES, LES PREUSES, VALMUR, and VAUDÉSIR, which cover a total of about 250 acres. The term *grand cru* appears on the labels of these special wines, followed by the name of the originating vineyard. They can rank among the best white wines in Burgundy, and therefore in the world, but Chablis wines are at the mercy of the weather more than any place else in Burgundy. Cool growing seasons inhibit the Chardonnay grapes from fully ripening, whereas warm seasons can produce luscious ripe grapes that produce magnificent wines. Chablis wines are somewhat different from other Burgundy white wines in that they're generally known for being drier (*see* DRY) and slightly more AUSTERE and for having a FLINTY or mineral quality. Oak-barrel AGING lends added complexity and a hint of vanilla. However, most producers in Chablis VINIFY only in stainless steel tanks, thereby achieving their desired goal of wines that are CRISP and more precise. As with other parts of Burgundy, wine quality varies even from the same PREMIER CRU or GRAND CRU vineyard so it's best to get to know the various producers. 2. Chablis is also a generic name used for ordinary inexpensive white (sometimes pink) wine made outside of France in countries like the Australia, South Africa, and the United States. Unlike the French originals, these generic wines are made from various grape varieties and sometimes even include red grapes. They're usually medium sweet to sweet.

chai [SHEH; SHAY] A French term usually referring to an above-ground building for storing wine. Although CAVE and chai are often used interchangeably, cave more typically denotes underground cellars.

Chalk Hill AVA APPELLATION that is just east of the town of Windsor in SONOMA COUNTY, California, and is a subzone of and encompasses the northeast corner of the larger RUSSIAN RIVER AVA. Chalk Hill differs from the rest of the Russian River area in that it's warmer (the hills block the cooling ocean breezes) and the soil is white, derived from volcanic ash. While most of the Russian River area is rated as a Region I growing area, Chalk Hill is considered a Region II (*see* CLIMATE REGIONS OF CALIFORNIA). The more widely planted varieties are the white grapes, CHARDONNAY and SAUVIGNON BLANC. Balvarine Vineyards and Chalk Hill Winery are this area's best-known wineries. Rodney Strong Vineyards also has land in this area and produces a Chalk Hill designated Chardonnay.

Chalone AVA [shuh-LOHN] AVA located in Monterey County, California. It is home to only one winery—CHALONE VINEYARD, which is in the hills southeast of Salinas and northeast of Soledad. Because the area sits above the Salinas Valley fog, it has higher temperatures than the valley floor. The Chalone VITICULTURAL AREA falls into the Region II or Region III category (*see* CLIMATE REGIONS OF CALIFORNIA), depending on a particular year's weather. CHARDONNAY and PINOT NOIR are the area's major grapes, followed by CHENIN BLANC and PINOT BLANC.

Chalone Inc. *see* CHALONE VINEYARD

Chalone Vineyard [shah-LOHN] The only winery in the CHALONE AVA, Chalone Vineyard is situated high in the rugged Gavilan Mountains east of Salinas, California. It's part of **Chalone, Inc.**, which also owns CARMENET VINEYARD and ACACIA WINERY and is involved in a joint venture (with Paragon Vineyards) in EDNA VALLEY VINEYARDS. The stock of Chalone, Inc. is traded publicly, and the company exchanged shares with Domaines Baron de Rothschild, owners of Lafite-Rothschild. Founded in 1965 by Richard Graff, Chalone Vineyard has developed a reputation for consistently high-quality wines. Much of their character comes from substantial limestone deposits in the soil and an arid climate. Chalone Vineyard has nearly 200 acres of vineyards planted mainly with CHARDONNAY, but also PINOT NOIR, PINOT BLANC, CHENIN BLANC, and CABERNET SAUVIGNON. Reserve wines produced from older Pinot Noir and Chardonnay vines are generally sold entirely to stockholders and are usually difficult to find otherwise. The winery annually produces between 25,000 and 30,000 cases of wine, predominately Chardonnay. Chalone's SECOND LABEL is **Gavilan**, a name that's also been used in the past by Carmenet Vineyard.

Chambertin [shah*m*-behr-TA*N*] A world-famous, GRAND CRU vineyard located in the village of GEVREY-CHAMBERTIN in the CÔTE DE NUITS district of France's BURGUNDY region. This 32-acre PINOT NOIR vineyard adjoins a 38-acre parcel called **Clos de Bèze**, which is also a GRAND CRU vineyard and whose wine may use **Chambertin AC** or **Chambertin-Clos de Bèze AC** on their labels. Chambertin may not be called Chambertin-Clos de Bèze, however. The Clos de Bèze vineyard was initially cleared and planted back in the seventh century by monks from the Abbey of Bèze, which owned the land. Legend has it that it wasn't until the twelfth century that Chambertin was planted by a Monsieur Bertin, who felt that he could also make good wines if he grew the same grape varieties as his famous next door neighbor. His vineyard was called Champ de Bertin ("Bertin's field") and later shortened to Chambertin. The Chambertin wines were one of Napoleon's favorites and it's said that he insisted that they be available to him even during his various military campaigns. As with most of Burgundy's vineyards, both Chambertin and Clos de Bèze have had numerous owners, twenty-three and eighteen respectively. Unfortunately, quality varies from producer to producer and, although Chambertin has been called "King of Wines," less accomplished vintners don't make wines that live up to that reputation. The quality of wines from Clos de Bèze is considered higher and more consistent than those from Chambertin. The best wines from these two vineyards are quite powerful. They have CONCENTRATED fruit flavors, intense, rich, perfumed aromas, and long AGING capabilities. There are seven other GRANDS CRUS that may use Chambertin on their labels followed by their vineyard name. They are CHAPPELLE-CHAMBERTIN, CHARMES-CHAMBERTIN, GRIOTTE-CHAMBERTIN, LATRICIÈRES-CHAMBERTIN, MAZIS-CHAMBERTIN, MAZOYÈRES-CHAMBERTIN, and RUCHOTTES-CHAMBERTIN.

Chambertin-Clos de Bèze AC *see* CHAMBERTIN

Chambolle-Musigny [shah*m*-BAWL mew-see-NYEE] Well-known village located in the the CÔTE DE NUITS district of France's BURGUNDY region. It's one of the smaller villages in this famous area and contains approximately 550 vineyard acres, all planted in PINOT NOIR except for a ¾-acre plot that grows CHARDONNAY. The highest-quality wines are from two well-known GRAND CRUS—BONNES MARES AC and MUSIGNY AC—and they produce wines of quite different styles. The Musigny wines are flavorful but better known for their elegance and finesse; they can be drunk relatively young. Wines from Bonnes Mares, however, are full-bodied (*see* BODY), TANNIC, and require AGING a number of years before they mature. The small plot of Chardonnay is planted in Musigny. It produces very good wines, but they're limited, very expensive, and generally not the quality of other top GRAND CRU white wines. Chambolle-Musigny also has twenty-four PREMIER CRU vineyards with **Les Amoureuses** and **Les Charmes** generally regarded as the two finest. Chambolle-Musigny AC wines, though generally light and elegant, normally have good STRUCTURE.

Chambourcin [shahm-boor-SAN] Red wine HYBRID that was introduced in 1963 by Joannes Seyve and that has gained favorable acceptance, particularly in France's LOIRE region. Chambourcin produces good-quality, ruby-colored wines that have a reasonably full, slightly herbaceous flavor and aroma. This grape is VINIFIED both as a ROSÉ and a red wine. Chambourcin is also known as *Joannes Seyve 26205.*

chambrer [shahn-BRAY] A derivative of the French word *chambre* ("room"), the term *chambrer* means "bring to room temperature." It's associated with the older traditional environment where cellars were very cool (55°F or less) and dining rooms were frequently about 60°F. Bringing to room temperature meant simply taking the bottle of wine out of the wine cellar several hours before serving so that it could warm to this room temperature. Today, dining rooms are usually much warmer and most wines are better when served at 65°F or less, so bringing them to room temperature could make them too warm. *See also* TEMPERATURE.

Champagne; champagne [sham-PAYN (Fr. shahm-PAH-nyuh)] 1. Even though effervescent wines abound throughout the world, *true* champagne comes only from France's northernmost wine-growing area, the Champagne region, just 90 miles northeast of Paris. This renowned region consists of four main growing areas—**Montagne de Reims, Côtes des Blancs, Vallée de la Marne**, and the **Aube**—and a fifth area that's evolving, **Côte de Sézanne**. Because it's so far north, Champagne's cool weather creates a difficult growing environment for grapes. The main grape varieties—red PINOT NOIR and MEUNIER (Pinot Meunier) and white CHARDONNAY—all require warmer weather for optimum development. Grapes that don't fully ripen tend to have high acidity and less-developed flavors, which just happens to be the perfect formula for SPARKLING WINES. The chalky soil in this region further contributes its magic to create just the right flavor composition in these grape varieties. In the Champagne region, the villages and their associated vineyards are classified (from 80 to 100 percent) according to the quality of the grapes produced. Of the approximately 270 villages, only 17 have obtained GRAND CRU ratings of 100 percent. The next level, called PREMIER CRU, consists of villages with ratings from 90 to 99 percent. The remaining villages have ratings of between 80 to 89 percent. Most of the better-known champagne houses buy grapes to supplement their own vineyards, and this precentage rating system helps set the prices growers receive. Although **Dom Pérignon**, the seventeenth-century cellarmaster of the Abbey of Hautvillers, didn't invent sparkling wines, he is acknowledged for greatly improving the process. He's credited for his work in preventing champagne bottles and corks from exploding by using thicker bottles and tying the corks down with string. Even then, it's said that the venerable monk lost half his champagne through bursting bottles. Dom Perignon is also celebrated for developing the art of blending wines to create champagnes with superior flavor. Today, some champagne makers mix as many as thirty to forty or more different base wines to create the blend, or CUVÉE. Most major champagne houses strive for a cuvée that's consistent from year to year. Good champagne is expensive not only because it's made with premium grapes, but also because it's made by the MÉTHODE CHAMPENOISE. This traditional technique requires a second fermentation in the bottle, as well as some 100 hand operations (some of which are mechanized today). **Vintage champagnes** are made from the best grapes of the harvest in years when the *chef de cave* of an individual champagne house feels the grapes are better than average. Wines from the declared year must comprise at least 80 percent of the cuvée for vintage champagnes, with the balance coming from reserve wines from prior years. Vintage champagnes must be aged for 3 years prior to their release. **Non-vintage champagnes**, which make up 75 to 80 percent of those produced, are blends of 2 or more years. They're usually made in a definitive house style, which is maintained by meticulous cuvée blending. ROSÉ champagnes are generally made by adding a small amount of red still wine to the cuvée, although some producers extract color by MACERATING the juice with red grape skins. These sparkling wines are usually full-flavored and full-bodied (*see* BODY) and have an intriguing salmon-pink color. The pale pink, full-flavored **BLANC DE NOIRS champagnes** are made entirely from the red Pinot Noir and/or Meunier grapes. **BLANC DE BLANCS champanges**, which are usually more delicate and the lightest in color, are made entirely from Chardonnay grapes. **CRÉMANT champagnes**, which are made with only slightly more than half the pressure of standard sparkling wines, have a creamier mouth-feel. Champagne can be LIGHT and FRESH,

TOASTY to YEASTY, and DRY to sweet. A champagne's BOUQUET and flavor gain complexity through a process called AUTOLYSIS, whereby the wine ages with the yeast cells in the bottle (sometimes for up to 10 years) before being DISGORGED. A sugar-wine mixture, called a DOSAGE, added just before final corking, determines how sweet a champagne will be. The label indicates the level of sweetness: BRUT (bone dry to almost dry—less than 1.5 percent sugar); EXTRA SEC or EXTRA DRY (slightly sweeter—1.2 to 2 percent sugar); sec (medium sweet—1.7 to 3.5 percent sugar); DEMI-SEC (sweet—3.3 to 5 percent sugar); and DOUX (very sweet—over 5 percent sugar). The last two are considered DESSERT WINES. **Grande Marque** is a French term for "great brand" and is used unofficially to refer to the best champagne houses. An organization called the *Syndicat des Grandes Marques* has twenty-four members and most of the better-known firms belong, including: **Ayala, Billecart-Salmon, J. BOLLINGER, Canard-Duchêne, Deutz, Charles Heidsieck, Heidsieck Monopole, Henriot, KRUG, Lanson, LAURENT PERRIER, Mercier, MOËT & CHANDON, MUMM, PERRIER-JOUËT, JOSEPH PERRIER, PIPER HEIDSIECK, POL ROGER, Pommery and Greno, LOUIS ROEDERER, RUINART, Salon, TAITTINGER,** and **VEUVE CLICQUOT-PONSARDIN.** Some of these Grandes Marques produce a premium brand—an expensive, high-end sparkling wine—variously known as **cuvée de prestige** or **cuvée spéciale**. Moet & Chandon was the first to produce such a wine with their **Dom Perignon** bottling. Today there are numerous offerings including **Diamant Bleu** from Heidsieck & Co., **Comtes de Champagne** from Taittinger, **Grand Siècle** from Laurent-Perrier, **Cristal** from Louis Roederer, **Grand Cuvée** from Krug, and **Belle Epoque** from Perrier-Jouët. STILL WINES are also made in the Champagne region. The **Coteaux Champenois AC** covers red, white, and rosé still wines made from the three primary champagne grapes—Pinot Noir, Meunier, and Chardonnay. These wines don't have a great reputation primarily because the grapes used aren't generally fully ripe. The **Rosé des Riceys AC** covers Pinot Noir-based rosé still wines made around Les Riceys in the Aube. Though hard to find and relatively expensive, these wines are more full-flavored because the Aube, which is warmer than other parts of the Champagne region, produces riper grapes. 2. Champagne is also used as generic name for sparkling wines made in some areas outside of France. Most countries bow to French tradition by not using the word *champagne* on their labels. Their sparkling wines are called by other names such as SPUMANTE in Italy, SEKT in Germany, and *vin mousseux* (*see* MOUSSEUX) in other regions of France or by simply using the term *sparkling wine*. In the United States and some South American countries, it's legal to use the term *cham-*

pagne for sparkling wine. However, most top-quality, U.S. sparkling-wine producers don't use the term but rather indicate that the wines were made by the French *méthode champenoise. See also* Opening and Serving Champagne and Sparkling Wines, page 591.

champana *see* CAVA

Les Champans *see* VOLNAY

champenois *see* METHODE CHAMPENOIS

Les Champs Fulliot *see* MONTHÉLIE

Chancellor [CHAN-suh-luhr; CHAN-sluhr] Red-wine grape that is a French-American hybrid widely grown in the eastern United States. Chancellor, also known as Seibel 7053, produces fruity but somewhat bland red wines.

Chandon *see* DOMAINE CHANDON

chapeau [sha-POH] French term for "CAP," referring in the wine world to the mass of grape solids that floats on the juice's surface during the FERMENTATION process.

Chapelle-Chambertin AC [shah-PEHL shah*m*-behr-TA*N*] A small GRAND CRU vineyard located in the village of GEVRY-CHAMBERTIN in the CÔTE DE NUITS district of France's BURGUNDY region. It takes its name from a chapel built by the monks from the Abbey of Bèze. Its 13.6 acres of PINOT NOIR grapes generally produce the lightest red wines of this village's grands crus. *See also* CHAMBERTIN.

Chappellet Vineyard [shap-pehl-LAY] California mountain winery in the NAPA VALLEY just east of Lake Hennessey. It was founded in 1969 by Donn and Molly Chappellet. There are 110 acres of terraced vineyards, and the winery produces between 25,000 and 30,000 cases of wine a year. Chappellet's standard offerings are CABERNET SAUVIGNON, CHARDONNAY and CHENIN BLANC. RIESLING, which was previously offered, has been dropped, while MERLOT is occasionally made. Eight acres of recently planted SANGIOVESE grapes should start producing wines fairly soon.

chaptalization [shap-tuh-luh-ZAY-shuhn] The procedure of adding sugar to grape juice or MUST prior to or during FERMENTATION; also called *sugaring.* When natural grape sugars aren't high enough to produce reasonable ALCOHOL levels (sugar is converted to alcohol during fermentation), chaptalization is used to attain the necessary sugar levels. Chaptalization is usually practiced when grapes don't fully ripen, which can happen in cool weather regions or poor growing seasons. When used properly, chaptalization allows the production of full, rich wines with sufficient alcohol levels to give them BALANCE. This procedure is legal (with certain restrictions) in France and Germany, but illegal in California and Italy, although addition of GRAPE CONCENTRATE is allowed. Chaptalization is legal in other parts of the United States such as Oregon and New York.

character A term applied to a wine with distinctive, obvious features, either pertaining to its style or its variety. Although character has nothing to do with a wine's quality, one without it is considered dull. *See also* VARIETAL CHARACTER.

Charbono [shar-BOH-noh] An uncommon red-wine grape grown in California's NAPA VALLEY and MENDOCINO COUNTY. Charbono wines are very dark in color, lackluster in flavor, and tend to be both TANNIC and ACIDIC. Charbono is thought to have links to *Corbeau* (or *Charbonneau*), a rare French variety.

Chardonnay [shar-dn-AY; shar-doh-NAY] Just as CABERNET SAUVIGNON has become the most popular high-quality red-wine grape, Chardonnay has taken the lead for first-class white-wine grapes—and with even greater ardor. Although some argue that the RIESLING grape produces the finest white wines, it's Chardonnay that is being extensively planted throughout the world. In addition to being highly prized, Chardonnay is easy to grow and quite versatile. It's high in EXTRACT and, unless picked late, has good ACID levels. The wide range of growing soils, as well as the winemaker's influence, produces a diverse spectrum of Chardonnay wines with varying characteristics. Their flavors can be described as BUTTERY, CREAMY, NUTTY, SMOKY, and STEELY; popular fruit descriptors include APPLEY, lemon, melon, and pineapple. Chardonnay's origins are difficult to determine but—as with many popular wines—its reputation was established in France, particularly in the BURGUNDY region. The highly prized Chardonnay wines from CHABLIS, CORTON CHARLEMAGNE, MÂCON, MEURSAULT, MONTRACHET, and POUILLY-FUSSÉ are imitated by winemakers around the world. Chardonnay is also an important grape in the CHAMPAGNE district where it's picked before fully ripe while it still has high ACID and understated fruit flavors—the perfect combination for champagne. California has adopted this grape with a fervor and has come into prominence with its delightful Chardonnay wines from wineries such as ACACIA, CHALONE, KISTLER, ROBERT MONDAVI, MOUNT EDEN, and STONY HILL. In addition to the hundreds of wineries in California, there are some 200 wineries producing Chardonnay wines in other parts of the United States. Chardonnay has also seen a tremendous planting surge in Australia, with excellent wines from several wineries including Petaluma and Leeuwin. As this grape's popularity grows, new vineyards of Chardonnay are being planted throughout the world in Italy, Lebanon, New Zealand, Spain, South Africa, and other parts of France. Chardonnay is also called *Beaunois, Gamay Blanc, Melon d'Arbois, and Pinot Chardonnay*. It's sometimes mistakenly referred to as PINOT BLANC, which is a different variety.

En Charlemagne; Le Charlemagne *see* CORTON; CORTON-CHARLEMAGNE

Charmat; Charmat process [shar-MAH; shar-MAHT] A bulk method for making SPARKLING WINES developed around 1910 by Frenchman Eugène Charmat. The Charmat process involves faster and less expensive production techniques using large pressurized tanks throughout production. These interconnecting tanks retain the pressure (created by the production of CARBON DIOXIDE during FERMENTATION) throughout the entire process. For many winemakers, the Charmat process replaces the expensive MÉTHODE CHAMPENOISE technique of secondary fermentation in bottles, thereby enabling them to produce inexpensive sparkling wines. Charmat wines can be good (although, once poured, they often lose their bubbles quickly) but are usually not as esteemed as méthode champenoise sparkling wines. The Charmat process is superior, however, to the technique used by some producers of simply pumping carbon dioxide gas into STILL WINE (like carbonated soft drinks are made). The Charmat process is also called *bulk process* and in the United States, wines may be labeled "Bulk Process" or "Charmat Process" (the latter being preferred). In France this process is also called *cuve close*; in Italy it's known as *metodo charmat* or sometimes *autoclave* (the Italian name for the sealed tanks). In Spain it's called *granvas,* and in Portugal, *método continuo.*

Les Charmes *see* CHAMBOLLE-MUSIGNY; MEURSAULT

Charmes-Chambertin AC [SHARM shahm-behr-TA*(N)*] A well-known GRAND CRU vineyard located in the village of GEVRY-CHAMBERTIN in the CÔTE DE NUITS district of France's BURGUNDY region. The grand cru adjoining it, **Mazoyères-Chambertin,** may legally use the name Charmes-Chambertin on its wine labels and most producers do. Few producers actually use Mazoyères-Chambertin AC on their labels so it isn't well known, and the two parcels are often viewed as one large (76-acre) vineyard (referred to as Charmes-Chambertin). Because of the size of the production from the two parcels, Charmes-

Chambertin is one of the better known of grands crus of Gevery-Chambertin. These wines are highly prized, ranking only slightly behind those of the neighboring grands crus of CHAMBERTIN and CHAMBERTIN-CLOS DE BÈZE.

Chassagne-Montrachet   AC [shah-SAHN-yuh mohn-rah-SHAY] A significant village in the southern part of the CÔTE DE BEUNE in France's BURGUNDY region. Although best known for its CHARDONNAY-based white wines, the 1,100-plus acres in Chassagne-Montrachet actually produce more red wines, which are made from PINOT NOIR. Chassagne-Montrachet has one GRAND CRU vineyard (CRIOTS-BÂTARD-MONTRACHET) and nearly half of each of two others (LE MONTRACHET and BÂTARD-MONTRACHET). Many consider Le Montrachet's top white wines the best in the world, and those from the other two grand cru aren't far behind. Wines from the Chassagne-Montrachet AC and the village's thirteen PREMIER CRU vineyards are of generally high quality and, because the Chassagne-Montrachet doesn't have the notoriety of the neighboring village of PULIGNY-MONTRACHET, prices are somewhat less. The best premier cru vineyards for white wines include **Les Caillerets**, **Les Embrazées**, **Morgeot**, **Les Grandes Ruchottes**, and **Les Vergers**. Because of the attention focused on the white wines, the red wines are sometimes overlooked. There are no grand cru red wines, but the red wines from the Chassagne-Montrachet AC and the premier cru vineyards can be quite good and reasonably priced relative to other red Burgundies. The best premier cru vineyards for red wines include **Clos Saint-Jean**, **La Boudriotte**, **La Maltroie**, and **Morgeot**.

Chasselas [shas-suh-LAH] A very ancient white wine grape that is grown in Switzerland and in small sections of France, Germany, Italy, and New Zealand. Chasselas—one of the oldest cultivated varieties—is thought to have originated in the Middle East. Even though this grape's still one of Switzerland's leading varieties, Chasselas' acreage in general has dwindled over the years. Chasselas wines are low in ACID and ALCOHOL and generally lacking in CHARACTER. There are numerous subvarieties of this grape, one being the *Chasselas Dore*, which is cultivated on a very limited basis in California. As with many older grape varieties, Chasselas is known by a variety of names including *Dorin, Fendant, Gutedel, Marzemina Bianca, Perlan,* and *Weisser Gutedel*.

Chasse-Spleen, Château [sha-TOH shahs SPLEEN] An outstanding CRU BOURGEOIS EXCEPTIONNEL château located in the MOULIS AC in the MEDOC district of BORDEAUX. According to legend, the CHÂTEAU'S

name came from Lord Byron's assertion that its wine cured his spleen attacks. The 173-acre estate produces about 17,000 cases of Château Chasse-Spleen red wine each year, which is said to be comparable to the wines of many of the CRU CLASSÉ châteaus. These wines are a blend of approximately 60 percent CABERNET SAUVIGNON, 35 percent MERLOT, 3 percent PETIT VERDOT, and 2 percent CABERNET FRANC. Wines from the best VINTAGES can AGE for 15 to 18 years. Another 16,000 to 17,000 cases of wine is produced under the château's SECOND LABEL, **L'Ermitage de Chasse-Spleen**.

château [sha-TOH] Although this is the French word for "castle," in wine parlance château refers to "wine estate" or "vineyard." The name is most often used in France's BORDEAUX region. The buildings occupying the wine estate or vineyard range from simple farmhouses to true castlelike structures. The French only allow the word château to appear on a label name when an authentic vineyard with the traditional use of the name has produced the wine. Châteaus can be found throughout this book under their individual names, for example: Château Margaux is listed under MARGAUX, CHÂTEAU. The exception is when the word château is an essential part of the name, as in CHÂTEAU-CHALON, or when it's an American winery, such as CHATEAU ST. JEAN. Note: American chateaus do not generally use the diacritical mark ^ above the first a.

château bottled *see* ESTATE BOTTLED

Château-Chalon AC [sha-TOH shah-LAWN] Vineyard located in the Jura region in eastern France. This tiny APPELLATION specializes in VIN JAUNE (yellow wine), which is made from a rather rare, high-quality white grape called SAVAGNIN. AGED for 6 years, vin jaune undergoes a process simliar to SHERRY, whereby a film of YEAST covers the wine's surface, which prevents OXIDATION but allows evaporation and the subsequent concentration of the wine. The result is a sherrylike wine with a delicate, nutty richness that can age for decades. Unlike sherry, Château-Chalone wines are not FORTIFIED. Most wine critics feel that they're not as quite good as the better Spanish sherries.

Château-Grillet AC [sha-TOH gree-YEH] A celebrated vineyard located in France's northern RHÔNE region. The 6½-acre plot, which has its own APPELLATION, is planted entirely with VIOGNIER grapes. The MICROCLIMATE appears to be just right for this variety because some of the best Viognier wines are produced here. These DRY white wines have a floral BOUQUET, a hint of apricot in the flavor, and a spicy FINISH. Only a small amount is produced so these wines are generally expensive.

Chateau La Grande Roche *see* FORMAN VINEYARD

Châteaumeillant VDQS [shat-toh-may-AHN] An area with
VDQS status for making red and ROSÉ wines made from GAMAY. It's located around the village of Châteaumeillant, south of the city of Bourges in central France's Cher DÉPARTEMENT. The wines, which are a lighter style, are seldom seen outside of the local area.

Chateau Montelena [sha-TOH mawn-teh-LEE-nuh] California
winery located at the far north end of the NAPA VALLEY (north of Calistoga). It seems to do equally well with both CHARDONNAY and CABERNET SAUVIGNON wines. Chateau Montelena, which was originally built in 1882, was revitalized starting in 1969 by Jim Barret and his partners. The winery received international recognition in 1976, when its 1973 Chardonnay won first place in a much-publicized winetasting in Paris that included renowned white wines from France's BURGUNDY region. Chateau Montelena's winemaker at the time was Mike Grgich, who's now a partner in his own winery, GRGICH HILLS. The winery produces three highly regarded wines—two Chardonnays (one from the Napa Valley and the other from ALEXANDER VALLEY) and an estate-grown Cabernet Sauvignon. A small amount of ZINFANDEL wine is also made, and a new Cabernet, Calistoga Cuvee, was recently introduced. Chateau Montelena has about 100 acres of vineyard planted primarily with Cabernet Sauvignon vines. Their annual production is about 30,000 cases of wine.

Châteauneuf-du-Pape AC [shah-toh-nuhf-doo-PAHP] Impor-
tant APPELLATION that surrounds the village of Châteaneuf-du-Pape, which is located in between Orange and Avignon in the southern portion of France's RHÔNE region. Its name means "new castle of the pope," referring to the summer palace built in the area during the 1300s and used by the popes from Avignon. In 1923 Châteauneuf-du-Pape was the first area to adopt strict rules for grape growing and winemaking. These rules were the basis for France's national system, APPELLATION D'ORIGINE CONTRÔLÉE, which was implemented in 1936. Châteauneuf-du-Pape AC permits thirteen red and white grapes; it's quite unusual for a French AC to have so many varieties. GRENACHE, the dominant variety in the area, exists in both a red (Grenache Noir) and white (Grenache Blanc) form. Other red varieties include CINSAULT, Counoise, MOURVÈDRE, Muscardine, SYRAH, Terret Noir, and Vaccarèse. Permitted white varieties are Bourboulenc, CLAIRETTE, Picardan, ROUSSANNE, and Piquepoul (or Picpoule)—this last variety had a red version but it's not widely grown. Red wines make up approximately 97 percent of this appellation's production; however, the white varieties may

be used in red wines, mainly to SOFTEN some of the bigger, bolder wines. The minimum ALCOHOL level of 12½ percent is the highest minimum of any AC. Generally, it's not difficult to reach this alcohol level because of the warm climate. The area's stony soil retains the day's heat into the evening hours, which allows the grapes to ripen to their fullest. Fully ripened grapes have a high sugar content that can convert into higher alcohol levels. Châteauneuf-du-Pape's red wines are traditionally BIG, RICH, and full-bodied (*see* BODY) with SPICY, raspberry flavors. They're capable of AGING for 5 to 20 years. A lighter BEAUJOLAIS-style red, made with CARBONIC MACERATION, is also produced. The white wines are usually CRISP with flavors that hint of peaches, pears, melons, and, sometimes, licorice. Wines with the papal coat of arms embossed on the bottle above the label indicate that they are ESTATE BOTTLED.

Chateau Ste. Michelle [sha-TOH saynt mih-SHELL] The biggest winery in the state of WASHINGTON, Chateau Ste. Michelle produces between 700,000 and 800,000 cases of wine per year. It's also part of Stimson Lane, a subsidiary of UST Inc. (owners of U.S. Tobacco), which also owns Washington's Columbia Crest winery and California's CONN CREEK and VILLA MT. EDEN, both located in the NAPA VALLEY. Chateau Ste. Michelle, which was founded in 1934, made fruit and berry wines but not much grape wine until it was puchased by U.S. Tobacco in 1974. It now owns 3,000 acres of vineyard land and three separate winemaking facilities. The winery offers a broad spectrum of wines including CABERNET SAUVIGNON, CHARDONNAY, CHENIN BLANC, GEWÜRZTRAMINER, MERLOT, RIESLING, SAUVIGNON BLANC, SÉMILLON, and SPARKLING WINE under the **Domaine Ste. Michelle** label. Chateau Ste. Michelle, which has a great reputation for good-quality wines at good prices, is moving into the high-quality, higher-priced arena with its RESERVE and VINEYARD-DESIGNATED wines.

Chateau St. Jean [sha-TOH saynt JEEN] Established in 1973, Chateau St. Jean was one of the first in SONOMA COUNTY to build a modern winery (complete with stainless steel tanks) and to produce VINEYARD-DESIGNATED wines. Dick Arrowood, now owner of his own winery, ARROWOOD VINEYARDS AND WINERY, was the winemaker at Chateau St. Jean for 16 years. This winery gained its reputation with CHARDONNAY wines from vineyards like Belle Terre and Robert Young. With the recent VINTAGES of CABERNET SAUVIGNON, however, it's now showing that it can make red wines as well. In addition to the numerous vineyard-designated Chardonnay wines, Château St. Jean also makes other white wines including SAUVIGNON BLANC, RIESLING, and LATE HARVEST versions of GEWÜRZTRAMINER and Riesling. SPARKLING WINE is produced from a different facility located near Graton, California, which is west of Santa Rosa. The main winery, which is just north of Kenwood in the Sonoma Valley, produces between 175,000 and 200,000 cases of wine (mostly white) per year. Château St. Jean was puchased in 1984 by the Japanese company, Suntory International.

Chateau Woltner [sha-TOH WALT-ner] After laying idle for almost 60 years, this California winery was revitalized by a French couple, Francis and Françoise DeWavrin-Woltner, following the sale of their Château LA MISSION-HAUT-BRION in France's BORDEAUX region. (Oddly enough, the original winery and estate was built in the 1880s by two Frenchmen, Messieurs Brun and Chaix.) Once the DeWavrin-Woltners puchased this property in 1980, they began to transform it into a CHARDONNAY-only estate. Today, Chateau Woltner produces five different Chardonnay wines—Estate Reserve, St. Thomas Vineyard, Titus Vineyard, Frederique Vineyard, and Howell Mountain. The 181-acre estate, which is located on HOWELL MOUNTAIN in the NAPA VALLEY, has about 55 acres currently planted. Production is between 10,000 and 12,000 cases per year. The VINEYARD-DESIGNATED wines are some of California's most expensive Chardonnays.

Chatillon-en-Diois AC [shah-tee-YAWN ahn dee-WAH] An obscure APPELLATION located near the village of Die on the eastern (middle) edge of France's RHÔNE region. Red and ROSÉ wines are produced from GAMAY, PINOT NOIR and SYRAH; white wines are made from ALIGOTÉ and CHARDONNAY.

Chauche Gris *see* TROUSSEAU GRIS

Chaudenet Gris *see* ALIGOTÉ

Chaume *see* COTEAUX DU LAYON

Les Chaumes *see* CORTON

Les Chaumes de la Voirosse *see* CORTON

De Chaunac [duh SHAW-nak] A red HYBRID grape that is widely grown in the eastern United States and further north in Canada's Ontario province. De Chaunac, also known as *Seibel 9549*, is the most extensively planted variety in New York's FINGER LAKES region. This grape produces fairly fruity wines of ordinary quality; much of it is futher processed into SHERRY.

Chautauqua *see* NEW YORK STATE

Cheilly-les-Maranges *see* CÔTE DE BEAUNE

Chelois [shehl-WAH] A French-American HYBRID also known as *Seibel 10878*. Chelois is popular in the mid-western and eastern United States, particularly in the FINGER LAKES region of New York. It's made into LIGHT red or ROSÉ wines.

Chénas AC [shay-NAH] The smallest of the ten CRUS in France's BEAUJOLAIS region. These GAMAY-based wines are full-bodied (*see* BODY) and concentrated, with more intense color but less fruitiness than some of the lighter-style wines from other Beaujolais crus. They usually benefit from 2 years or more of AGING and peak at about 5 years. Wines from Chénas are very similiar in style to those from its larger and better-known neighbor to the south, MOULIN-À-VENT. Because portions of Chénas are in Moulin-à-Vent, growers can sell their wines under either label. It's even been suggested that Chénas be absorbed by Moulin-à-Vent. Because many producers opt for Moulin-à-Vent on the label, wines labeled Chénas aren't well known and are difficult to find.

Chenin Blanc [SHEN-ihn BLAH*N* (BLAH*N*GK)] French white-wine grape that is the basis for many superior wines coming out of France's LOIRE region. These include lively, DRY wines from SAVENNIÈRES; medium-sweet wines from VOUVRAY; rich, LATE HARVEST wines from COTEAUX DU LAYON; and fragrant SPARKLING WINES from SAUMUR. French Chenin Blanc has an intense, fascinating aroma; its high ACID enables some of these wines to balance the sweetness and age for years. Two notable areas from the Coteaux du Layon are QUARTS DE CHAUME and BONNEZEAUS, where BOTRYTISED grapes produce intensely sweet, rich, flavorful wines. Although sometimes called *Pineau de la Loire* or *Pineau d'Anjou*, Chenin Blanc is not related to PINOT NOIR. Chenin Blanc is widely grown outside of France in South Africa and California and is planted to a lesser extent in Chile, Australia, and New Zealand. In the mid-1960s, it was discovered that South Africa had been growing this grape for years but referred to it as *Steen* or *Stein*. Unfortunately, most of the Chenin Blancs produced around the world don't compare to the quality of the top French efforts—particularly those from hotter growing areas, which produce grapes that are much more neutral and much less exciting. Wines from cooler regions can be well balanced with delicate, FLORAL characteristics and hints of melon. Because of the grape's high acid content, Chenin Blanc wines outside of France are often combined with other wines in order to cut Chenin Blanc's sharpness and enliven the final blend. Chenin Blanc is also called *Gros Pineau de Vouvray* and *Pineau de Savennières*.

cherry An aroma and flavor characteristic reminiscent of fresh cherries that is often found in ZINFANDELS and PINOT NOIRS.

Cheval Blanc, Château [sha-TOH shuh-vahl BLAN] A famous BORDEAUX château located in the SAINT-ÉMILION AC. It's usually compared with the FIRST GROWTHS of the MÉDOC—Châteaus LAFITE-ROTHSCHILD, LATOUR and MOUTON-ROTHSCHILD. Château Cheval-Blanc is a PREMIER GRAND CRU CLASSÉ and ranks with Château AUSONE as one of Saint-Emilion's top two châteaus. *Cheval blanc* means "white horse," which apparently refers to the fact that, prior to the 1830 split of the larger property, this was the stable area of Château FIGEAC. Cheval Blanc has 89 acres, which makes it one of the larger Saint-Émilion estates. It produces 12,000 to 14,000 cases of red wine each year. The dominance of CABERNET FRANC (about 66 percent) in these wines is unusual for a major CHÂTEAU. The rest of the blend is approximately 33 percent MERLOT and 1 percent MALBEC. Because of this blend, Château Cheval Blanc wines are usually RICH, fruity, and full-bodied (*see* BODY), with very distinctive, fragrant BOUQUETS. Better VINTAGES of these wines will AGE 20 to 30 years; a great vintage will age for 40 years or more. The château uses a SECOND LABEL **Le Petit Cheval** for its lighter wines.

Chevalier de Lascombes *see* LASCOMBES, CHÂTEAU

Chevalier de Malle *see* DE MALLE, CHÂTEAU

Chevalier de Malta *see* CADET-PIOLA, CHÂTEAU

Chevalier de Védrines *see* DOISY-VÉDRINES, CHÂTEAU

Chevalier-Montrachet AC [shuh-vahl-YAY mohn-rah-SHAY] Esteemed 18-acre GRAND CRU vineyard that is located in France's BURGUNDY region and sits just above the famous LE MONTRACHET grand cru vineyard in the village of PULIGNY-MONTRACHET in the CÔTE DE BEAUNE. This sloping vineyard with its stony, chalky soil produces some of the best white wines in the world from the CHARDONNAY grapes. The wines are intense and SPICY with a unique GOÛT DE TERROIR (earthy flavor). Many wine lovers not only believe that the best white wines from Chevalier-Montrachet rank second only to the best from Le Montrachet but that the former also produces more top-quality wines. Although quite expensive, Chevalier-Montrachet wines aren't nearly as costly as those from Le Montrachet.

Cheverny VDQS [sheh-vehr-NEE] Cheverny is a VDQS area located in France's LOIRE Valley southwest of the village of Blois. It produces red and ROSÉ wines from GAMAY, CABERNET FRANC and CABERNET SAUVIGNON, and white wines from CHARDONNAY, CHENIN BLANC, SAUVIGNON BLANC, and Romorantin.

Chevrier *see* SÉMILLON

chewy Descriptor for wines that are RICH, DENSE, INTENSE, and full-bodied (*see* BODY). Such wines (which are generally red) give a mouth-filling impression that make them seem almost thick enough to chew; they are also sometimes referred to as FLESHY or MEATY.

Chianti DOCG [kee-AHN-tee; KYAHN-tee] 1. Large well-known wine-producing area located in TUSCANY in central Italy. Chianti is one of only a small number of DOCG areas in Italy and one of five (along with CARAMIGNANO, BRUNELLO DI MONTALCINO, VERNACCIA DI SAN GIMIGNANO and VINO NOBILE DI MONTEPULCIANO) located in the Tuscany region. The Chianti DOCG is a single APPELLATION but is divided into seven subzones, the most famous being **Chianti Classico**, which runs from the Florence area south to the Siena region. The remaining six subzones are: **Chianti Aretini**, **Chianti Colli Fiorentini**, **Chianti Colli Senesi**, **Chianti Colline Pisane**, **Chianti Montalbano**, and **Chianti Rufina**. The wines from Chianti Classico, which are usually identifiable by a black rooster (*gallo nero*) on the label, are generally more well known and of better quality than those from the other six areas. A wine made in one of the subzones may be labeled either with the name of the subzone or simply with that of Chianti. If a wine is produced outside one of the seven subzones, but within the Chianti area, it may only be labeled "Chianti." A federation called **Chianti Putto** is made up of growers located in the subzones outside Chianti Classico—their labels often sport a pink cherub called a *putto*. Chianti's STURDY, DRY red wines were once instantly recognizable by their squat, straw-covered bottles called FIASCHI. However, Chianti wines—particularly those from better producers—are now more often found in the traditional Bordeaux-type bottle. Only a few VINTNERS use the straw-based bottle, which today usually designates a cheaper, and often inferior, product. Chianti wines are made from four grape varieties—SANGIOVESE, CANAIOLO, TREBBIANO, and MALVASIA. Today, however, CABERNET SAUVIGNON is being added to some Chianti blends. The word RISERVA on the label indicates that the wine is of superior quality and has been aged for at least 3 years before being released. 2. Chianti is also a generic name used for ordinary, inexpensive red wine made outside of Italy in countries like the Argentina and the United States.

chiaretto [kyah-REH-toh] 1. The Italian term for "light red." 2. The name for the lively but delicate ROSÉ wines made from GROPPELLO in the DOC of Riviera del Garda Bresciano (LOMBARDY region).

Chiavennasca *see* NEBBIOLO

Chile [CHIHL-ee; CHEE-leh] Chilean vineyards were first established in the mid-sixteenth century by Spanish missionaries. These viticultural pioneers planted the grape known as *Pais*, which is similiar to the MISSION grape widely grown in California and the Criolla variety grown in Argentina. For the next 300 years the Pais was Chile's primary grape and still comprises about half the total vineyard land. In 1851 a Spaniard, Silvestre Ochagavía, brought in French wine experts, followed by cuttings of CABERNET FRANC, CABERNET SAUVIGNON, MALBEC, MERLOT, PINOT NOIR, SAUVIGNON BLANC, and SÉMILLON. Other varieties were subsequently planted, including CHARDONNAY, GEWÜRZTRAMINER and RIESLING. The next four decades saw the establishment of numerous wineries that are still prominent estates today including: Cousiño Macul (1861), San Pedro (1865), Errazuriz (1870), Santa Rita (1880), Concha y Toro (1883), and Viña Undurrage (1885). These six wine estates plus those of Caliterra, Los Vascos, Santa Carolina, Saint Morillon, and Walnut Crest account for almost 90 percent of the Chilean wines exported to the United States. Chile seems to have an ideal environment for growing grapes. The vineyards have never been infected with PHYLLOXERA and seem to be permantly protected by the Andes Mountains, the oceans, and the desserts. To the envy of viticulturists in other areas like France and California, this means that Chilean vineyards can be planted with original rootstock, rather than having to be grafted onto those that are phylloxera-resistant. Most of the vineyards are in the central section of the country from about 50 miles north of the city of Santiago to about 150 miles south. From north to south these growing areas are: the Aconcagua Valley; the famous Maipo Valley, which has vineyards within sight of downtown Santiago; Casablanca, near the coastal city of Valparaiso; Rancagua District; Colchagua District; Curicó District; and the Maule Valley. Most of the areas are dry and aren't beleaguered by rains spoiling the harvest. But they do have plenty of water from the melting snows of the Andes. The tremendous potential of the Chilean wine industry is attracting the investments of several foreign wine-producing companies including Spain's Miguel TORRES, France's LAFITE-ROTHSCHILD, and California's FRANCISCAN VINEYARDS.

Chiles Valley A small California growing area that's considered a subzone of the NAPA VALLEY AVA. It's located east of the towns of St. Helena and Calistoga and southeast of the HOWELL MOUNTAIN AVA. The surrounding hills block the fog that the Napa Valley receives, which means Chiles Valley is hotter and has a shorter growing season. ZINFANDEL is the grape that grows best in this area.

chilling wine *see* TEMPERATURE

Chinon AC [shee-NOH*N*] Located in the TOURAINE area, Chinon is one of the few villages in the LOIRE valley focused on red wines, which some wine lovers feel are the Loire's best. Like its neighbors BOURGUEIL and SAINT-NICOLAS-DE-BOURGUEIL, this picturesque village with its medieval hilltop fortress grows CABERNET FRANC (known locally as Brenton) and minor amounts of CABERNET SAUVIGNON. Although normally LIGHT and fruity with a heady raspberry aroma, these red wines have enough BODY to age a few years. Hot years can produce good, full-bodied wines with AGING capabilities of 10 to 15 years. The Chinon APPELLATIONS also makes ROSÉ wines and white wines made from CHENIN BLANC grapes. Chinon is known as the birthplace of François Rabelais, sixteenth century satirist and humorist, who was an ardent admirer of Chinon wines and coined the phrase "taffeta wines," meaning that they are soft and smooth.

Chiroubles AC [she-ROO-bl] Of the ten CRUS in France's BEAUJOLAIS region, Chiroubles produces the softest and lightest wines. Located between the crus of MORGON and FLEURIE, Chiroubles is one of the smallest crus at less than 700 acres. The best Chiroubles wines, which are meant to be drunk very young, are highly sought after; they can be fairly expensive for Beaujolais wine.

chocolaty; chocolate A rich chocolate aroma and flavor sometimes found in CABERNET SAUVIGNONS, ZINFANDELS, and other red wines.

Chorey-lès-Beaune AC [shaw-REH lay BOHN] appellation located in France's BURGUNDY region in the CÔTE DE BEAUNE district just north of the city of Beaune. Although the village of Chorey-les-Beaune has no GRAND CRU or PREMIER CRU vineyards, area producers make highly rated red wines from the principal variety PINOT NOIR.

Christian Brothers Winery, The Formerly a major winery in the NAPA VALLEY, Christian Brothers Winery is now the label for a line of inexpensive wines produced from their facility in the town of Madera just northwest of Fresno in the SAN JOAQUIN VALLEY. The original Christian Brothers Winery was established in 1882 in Martinez, California, by the teaching order, Brothers of Christian Schools. In the 1920s it moved to the Napa Valley. At one point it was producing about 1 million cases each of wine and BRANDY annually. It had three wine-producing facilities in the Napa Valley, plus one in the CENTRAL VALLEY for making both wine and brandy. In 1989 Christian Brothers Winery was sold to Heublein, a subsidiary of the British giant, Grand Metropolitan. Heublein has since divested itself of some of its

Christian Brothers' Napa Valley holdings including the Mont La Salle facility, which it sold to the HESS COLLECTION, and the historic Greystone Cellars, which is now the home of the new west coast branch of the Culinary Institute of America. Heublein also owns INGLENOOK and BEAULIEU VINEYARDS.

Chusclan *see* CÔTES DU RHÔNE

cigar box *see* CEDAR

Cinqueterre DOC [CHEENG-kweh-TEH*R-r*uh] Italian word that means "five lands" and refers to the five fishing villages that dot the coast of the LIGURIA region in northwest Italy. This DOC area includes the steeply terraced vineyards around the town of La Spezia and the five villages of Monterosso, Vernazza, Corniglia, Manarolo, and Riomaggiore. The rather mediocre, DRY white wine made here is at least 60 percent Bosco and up to 40 percent of Arbarola and VERMENTINO. Producers also make limited amounts of the highly regarded **Sciacchetrà** wine, a PASSITO version made from the same grapes. Sciacchetrà can range from AMABILE (medium-sweet) to DOLCE (sweet) and also comes in a LIQUOROSO version.

cinquième cru [sa*n*-kyem KROO] French phrase that means "fifth growth," signifying the lowest category of the MÉDOC area's CRUS CLASSÉS (classed growths), which were established in the CLASSIFICATION OF 1855. At that time, eighteen châteaus were given the *cinquième cru* classification, and that number remains unchanged today.

Cinsaut; Cinsault [SAN-soh] Red-wine grape that is the fourth most widely planted in France. It's extensively grown throughout LANGUEDOC-ROUSSILLON, with particular emphasis in AUDE, HÉRAULT, and GARD. Because Cinsaut can withstand very hot weather and is highly productive, it contributes greatly to the huge volumes of wine from this area. Cinsaut grapes create wines that are light in BODY and neutral in flavor. Because of their high ACIDITY and low TANNINS, Cinsaut wines are usually BALANCED with a blend of GRENACHE and/or CARIGNIN (in Languedoc-Roussillon and surrounding areas). In the southern RHÔNE where its YIELD is strictly controlled (a limited volume per acre), Cinsaut produces wines that are more deeply colored, concentrated, and flavorful. Here, Cinsaut is blended with a variety of other grape varieties including CLAIRETTE, Grenache, MOURVÈDRE, MUSCADINE, and SYRAH. This grape was once heavily grown in North Africa (particularly Algeria) and is still widely cultivated in South Africa. The South Africans also crossed Cinsaut with PINOT NOIR to create PINOTAGE.

Cinsaut is also called *Espagne, Hermitage, Malaga, Ottavianello, Oeillade, Picardan Noir,* and *Prunella.*

Cirò DOC [CHEER-oh] The best-known DOC in southern Italy's CALABRIA region. It's said that the ancient Greeks served these wines (then called *Cremissa*) to Olympic winners. Many consider the past reputation to be better than the current one. The Cirò DOC produces ROSSO, BIANCO, and ROSATO wines. The main varieties used for the red and rosé wines are the red Gaglioppo and the white TREBBIANO and GRECO grapes. The white wines are made from Greco and Trebbiano. Cirò DOC red RISERVA wines have been AGED for 3 years.

Citran, Château [sha-TOH see-TRAHN] A large CRU BOURGEOIS EXCEPTIONNEL located in the HAUT-MÉDOC AC in France's BORDEAUX region. This 210-acre estate produces from 35,000 to 42,000 cases of high-quality red wine. The grape variety mix is approximately 58 percent CABERNET SAUVIGNON and 42 percent MERLOT. The wines from better VINTAGES can AGE for 10 to 12 years. **Villeranque** is the SECOND LABEL for Château Citran.

citric acid *see* ACIDS

citrusy; citrus A winetasting term describing wines with a citrusy (generally grapefruit, lemon, or lime) smell and flavor characteristics. Such wines aren't necessarily high in ACID.

de Clairefont *see* PRIEURÉ-LICHINE, CHÂTEAU

Clairette [kleh-RHEHT] White wine grape that is widely cultivated in southern France. It is also known by its full name *Clairette Blanc.* Clairette is one of the white grape varieties allowed by the French government for use in the red CHÂTEAUNEUF-DU-PAPE and the white CÔTES-DU-RHÔNE wines. Its name is tied to the AOCs of Clairette du Languedoc and Clairette de Bellegarde in the Languedoc-Roussillon region and to the CLAIRETTE DE DIE in the central RHÔNE. By themselves, Clairette wines are generally high in ALCOHOL, low in ACID, and rather bland. The Clairette de Die SPARKLING WINES have a good reputation, but that's primarily because the BLEND includes Muscat Blanc à Petits Grains (MUSCAT), which provides the distinctive aroma and flavor. Clairette is also grown in Australia, where it's known as *Blanquette,* as well as in South Africa, where it's known as *Clairette Blanche.*

Clairette de Die AC; Clairette de Die Tradition AC

[kleh-RHEHT duh DEE] APPELLATIONS, centered around the village of Die on the eastern edge of France's RHÔNE region that produce SPARKLING WINES. **Clairette de Die AC** wines are made from the CLAIRETTE grape using the MÉTHODE CHAMPENOISE; **Clairette de Die Tradition AC** wines are made with at least 50 percent MUSCAT grapes and the rest Clairette via the **méthode dioise** (also called **méthode tradition**). Méthode dioise is a variation of the RURAL METHOD and unique to this appellation. To create effervescence using this method, the MUST is chilled (which slows FERMENTATION) before the wine is bottled. Once the chilled, bottled wine begins to warm, the fermentation process is renewed. As with *méthode champenoise*, the by-product of this fermentation is carbon dioxide, which creates bubbles in the bottled wine. The *méthode dioise* technique for removing sediment is to decant and FILTER the wines under pressure, which eliminates the sediment while retaining as much effervescence as possible. The wines are then rebottled. The Muscat-based wines usually receive higher praise than the Clairette-based ones.

Clairette Ronde *see* TREBBIANO

Clairette Rosé *see* TREBBIANO

La Clape [lah KLAHP] The vineyards surrounding this village are part of the COTEAUX DU LANGUEDOC AC but have CRU status, which indicates that the wines are of better quality and allows the name "La Clape" to be added to the label. This area is located along France's Mediterranean coast near Narbonne. The white wines, made from Bourboulenc, CLAIRETTE, GRENACHE Blanc, and Terret Noir, are considered quite good because of the chalky soil, which contributes a unique flavor composition. The soil, which is unique for this area, is a result of the unusual mountain that rises up dramatically in this fairly flat region. The red and ROSÉ wines, which are made from CARIGNAN, CINSAULT, and GRENACHE, are LIGHT and should be drunk young.

Clare Riesling *see* CROUCHEN

claret [KLAR-eht] 1. A term used by the English when referring to the red wines from BORDEAUX. 2. Elsewhere, the word *claret* is sometimes used as a general reference to light red wines. Even though "claret" sometimes appears on labels, it has no legal definition.

clarete [klah-REH-teh] A Spanish term for light red wines. Clarete has no official definition or application.

clarity Descriptor for a wine that is brilliant, without any cloudiness or haziness—factors that generally signal a flaw in the wine. A clear wine will occasionally have some sediment in the shoulder or the bottom of the bottle, which is acceptable, especially in older wines.

Clarksburg AVA California AVA that is southwest of the city of Sacramento, stretching southward for about 16 miles and includes the MERRIT ISLAND AVA subregion. Although it's part of the generally hot CENTRAL VALLEY, Clarksburg's climate is moderated by the Sacramento River delta and breezes from San Francisco Bay. It's generally considered a Region II growing area (*see* CLIMATE REGIONS OF CALIFORNIA). The variety that does best in this area is CHENIN BLANC.

classed growth; classified growth The English translation of the French "CRU CLASSÉ," signifying a top-ranked vineyard in the Bordeaux CLASSIFICATION OF 1855. This famous classification system ranked the red wines of the MÉDOC and the white wines of SAUTERNES.

classic A broad wine term used to suggest that a wine is consistent with the established characteristics of that particular wine's type and style. Even though the term is sometimes used on wine labels (for example, "Classic Cabernet"), it has no official definition.

classico [KLA-sih-koh; KLAH-see-koh] 1. The Italian term for "classic." 2. An area within a larger geographic region defined by the Italian classification system (DOC); also the wines from that area. Such a terrritory is usually the oldest in terms of grape cultivation and wine production and often has the best wines within the larger region. The famous CHIANTI CLASSICO DOCG, located within the larger CHIANTI DOCG, is such an area.

Classification of 1855 The famous Classification of 1855 was completed as part of the Paris Exhibition that same year. It was intended as a temporary means to determine which BORDEAUX wines would be exhibited. Although unofficial rankings had long been in practice, for some reason the Classification of 1855 took hold and is still in use today. To arrive at the rankings, a group of brokers used a system based on the price each wine traditionally brought in the market. Only the red wines of the MÉDOC and white wines of SAUTERNES were rated. The wines from other Bordeaux growing areas—like GRAVES, POMEROL, and SAINT-ÉMILION—were not deemed prestigious enough for consideration (the only exception being CHÂTEAU HAUT-BRION from Graves). Among the thousands of châteaus in Bordeaux, only sixty from the Médoc and one from Graves were ranked as CRUS CLASSÉS (classed growths) for their red wines. This red-wine category was further divided into five subcategories: four châteaus were classified as PREMIERS CRUS (first growths); fifteen as DEUXIÈMES CRUS (second growths); fourteen as TROISIÈMES CRUS (third growths); ten as QUARTIÈMES CRUS (fourth growths); and eighteen as CINQUIÈMES CRUS (fifth growths).

These rankings have held firm except for the upgrade in 1973 of CHÂTEAU MOUTON-ROTHSCHILD from a second to a first growth. For the Sauternes-area white wines, there are only two cru classé subcategories—first growth and second growth. Of the twenty-four classified châteaus, eleven were designated as first growth and twelve as second growth. Château D'YQUEM was elevated to a class all by itself—known variously as *Premier Grand Cru, Grand Premier Cru,* and *Premier Cru Supérieur*—and is allowed to put "Premier Grand Cru Classé" on its label, although it doesn't. The first-growth châteaus may also put "Premier Grand Cru Classe" on their labels; those with second-through fifth-growth classification may only label their wines "GRAND CRU CLASSÉ." Pricing was the initial criteria for ranking and, for the most part, that still holds true. However, today it's not uncommon to find many fourth and fifth growths that sell for more than second and third growths; first growths command an even proportionately higher premium than in the 1850s. Since cru classé rankings are tied to a château and not to a specific vineyard, wine from a particular site can actually change classifications if the vineyard should change hands from one château to another. Therefore, wines from a vineyard that was previously classified as fifth-growth can rise to first-growth status if a first-growth château purchases the land from which the wine is made. Classifications for Saint-Émilion and Graves were not made until the twentieth century (*see both listings for details of these classifications*); the Pomerol area has never been classified. *See also* CRU ARTISAN; CRU BOURGEOIS; CRU CLASSÉ; CRU PAYSAN; PREMIER GRAND CRU CLASSÉ.

clavelin [klav-LA*N*] A short fat bottle traditionally used in France's Jura region for VIN JAUNE from the CHÂTEAU-CHALON AC and in some of the region's other ACs. The clavelin holds 62 centiliters (equivalent of about 21 ounces) and is also used for more robust potables like EAU DE VIE.

clean A clean wine is one without faults, either in smell or flavor.

Clear Lake AVA Located north of SONOMA and NAPA COUNTIES and east of MENDOCINO COUNTY, this extremely large AVA area encompasses the territory around California's largest lake, Clear Lake. This viticultural area's climate, which consists of hot days and cold nights, categorizes it as a Region II or Region III (*see* CLIMATE REGIONS OF CALIFORNIA), depending on the area location. SAUVIGNON BLANC grapes seem to do best, although CABERNET SAUVIGNON, CHARDONNAY, and ZINFANDEL are also planted. KENDALL-JACKSON VINEYARDS started out here and still has about 80 acres of vineyard land. Despite the large size of the Clear Lake AVA there are only a few wineries here.

Le Clémentin du Pape-Clément *see* PAPE-CLÉMENT, CHÂTEAU

Clerc-Milon-Rothschild, Château [sha-TOH klehr mee-LAW*N* rawt-SHEELD (rawth-CHILD)] A CINQUIÈME CRU (fifth growth) CHÂTEAU in the PAUILLAC AC of BORDEAUX. There's no château building, just a vineyard situated between Châteaus MOUTON-ROTHSCHILD and LAFITE-ROTHSCHILD. In 1970 this château was purchased by Baron Philippe de Rothschild, owner of Château Mouton-Rothschild. Improvements to the property have obviously paid off, as some of the VINTAGES from the 1980s have been highly rated. The vineyard consists of approximately 70 acres planted with about 70 percent CABERNET SAUVIGNON, 20 percent MERLOT, and 10 percent CABERNET FRANC. From 10,000 to 15,000 cases of high-quality red wine are produced each year. Recent vintages, which have produced more full-bodied (*see* BODY) wines, are capable of AGING for 15 to 20 years.

Clevner *see* PINOT BLANC

climat [klee-MAH] 1. French for "climate." 2. A Burgundian term referring to a specifically defined vineyard area, usually an individual field. Such a vineyard area is distinguished by various factors including soil, drainage, angle of the slope, bearing of the sun, and altitude. *See also* TERROIR.

Climate Regions of California A method for classifying wine climate regions that was developed in the 1930s at the University of California at DAVIS by Professors A. J. Winkler and Maynard Amerine. This system is referred to variously as *degree days, heat summation method, Winkler Scale,* and *Regions I–V.* The method is based on the theory that no vine shoot growth occurs below 50°F and that each degree a day averages above 50°F is considered a *degree day.* For example, if during a 24-hour period the temperature ranges from 57° to 81°F, the average is 69°F, which is equivalent to 19 degree days (69 minus 50). The *heat summation* (sum of all the degree days between April 1 and October 31) of a growing region determines its classification, which is described in total degree days. There are five climate region classifications, which suggests that California has growing environments that are comparable to the various traditional winemaking regions throughout the world. **Climate Region I** (up to 2,500 degree days) is the coolest and is similiar to regions like CHAMPAGNE and CÔTE D'OR in France and the RHINE in Germany. It includes portions of the following areas: ANDERSON VALLEY, CARNEROS, EDNA VALLEY, Marin, MENDOCINO, MONTEREY, NAPA, RUSSIAN RIVER VALLEY, SANTA CLARA, SANTA CRUZ MOUNTAINS, and SONOMA. Suggested varieties for Region I include CABER-

NET SAUVIGNON, CHARDONNAY, PINOT NOIR, RIESLING, and SAUVIGNON BLANC. **Climate Region II** (from 2,500 to 3,000 degree days) is similiar to France's BORDEAUX region and includes portions of the following areas: ALEXANDER VALLEY, Anderson Valley, CHALK HILL, Edna Valley, Mendocino, Monterey, Napa, POTTER VALLEY, Russian River Valley, Santa Clara, and Sonoma. Suggested varieties include those for Region I plus MERLOT. **Climate Region III** (from 3,000 to 3,500 degree days) is equivalent to France's RHÔNE region and includes portions of the following areas: ALAMEDA, Alexander Valley, CONTRA COSTA, EL DORADO, KNIGHT'S VALLEY, LAKE, MCDOWELL VALLEY, Mendocino, Monterey, Napa, PASO ROBLES, PLACER, REDWOOD VALLEY, RIVERSIDE, SAN BENITO, Santa Clara, and Sonoma. Suggested varieties include CARIGNAN, RUBY CABERNET, Sauvignon Blanc, SÉMILLON, and ZINFANDEL. **Climate Region IV** (3,500 to 4,000 degree days) is similar to southern Spain and includes portions of the following areas: AMADOR, CALVERAS, El Dorado, Fresno, MERCED, Riverside, SACRAMENTO, San Diego, SAN JOAQUIN, and YOLO. Suggested varieties include BARBERA, EMERALD RIESLING, Ruby Cabernet, and those used for PORT-style wines. **Climate Region V** (more than 4,000 degree days) is the hottest region and is similar to North Africa. It includes portions of the following areas: Amador, Calveras, Fresno, Kern, MADERA, Merced, Sacramento, San Bernardino, San Diego, San Joaquin, Stanislaus, and Tulare. Suggested varieties include SOUZÀO, TINTA MADERA, and VERDELHO. The authors of this approach have acknowledged that within these broader regions there are MICROCLIMATES capable of growing other varieties. Other states, such as OREGON and WASHINGTON, also use this method to classify their regions.

Climens, Château [sha-TOH klee-MAHS] An outstanding PRE-MIER CRU (first growth) CHÂTEAU located in the BARSAC AC, which is part of the SAUTERNES AC in France's BORDEAUX region. Some feel that Château Climens is second only to Château D'YQUEM in the Sauternes area. The 62-acre vineyard is planted with 98 percent SÉMILLON and 2 percent SAUVIGNON BLANC. When the right climatic conditions exist, BOTRYTIS CINEREA attacks the grapes. This allows the production of DESSERT WINES, which are considered some of the most elegant and well balanced in the entire region. Better VINTAGES will AGE for up to 20 years or more. Château Climens, which produces about 5,000 to 6,500 cases of white wine each year, uses a SECOND LABEL of **Les Cyprès de Climens**.

Cline Cellars Although now located in the SONOMA COUNTY portion of the CARNEROS region, Cline Cellars originated east of San Francisco in Contra Costa County near Oakley. Fred Cline was actually a grower before he started making wines. One of the varieties he grew was MOURVÈDRE, which was originally called *Mataro* because it wasn't initially recognized for what it was. Cline sold his Mourvèdre grapes to BONNY DOON VINEYARD and to Edmunds St. John, early initiators of the RHÔNE-style wines in California. Cline Cellars is now highly regarded for its own Mourvèdre wine along with its ZINFANDEL wines (both regular and reserve). The winery also produces Oakley Cuvée (a blend of Mourvèdre, CARIGNANE, and Zinfandel) and Côtes d'Oakley (mainly Carignane but also Zinfandel, Mourvèdre, and CABERNET SAUVIGNON), SÉMILLON, a LATE HARVEST Zinfandel, and a ROSÉ wine called Angel Rose. Cline Cellars has about 34 acres of vineyard (planted on a 350-acre estate) in the Carneros area and controls another 180 acres of vineyards near Oakley. Annual case production is between 25,000 and 30,000.

Clinet, Château [sha-TOH klee-NAY] As with all CHÂTEAUS in the POMEROL AC in BORDEAUX, Château Clinet is unclassified. It's small, about 17 acres, but the wines are excellent—especially those from 1985 on. The vineyard is planted with about 75 percent MERLOT, 15 percent CABERNET SAUVIGNON, and 10 percent CABERNET FRANC. Only 2,500 to 3,500 cases of red wine are produced each year. Recent vintages have been richer and more full-bodied (*see* BODY), and can age for about 15 to 20 years.

clone; cloning [KLOHN] In vineyard parlance, a clone is a plant that has been propagated asexually, usually by cuttings or by grafting. Cloning is done to reproduce plants with the distinctive traits of its "mother" plant such as high productivity, disease resistance, and/or better adaptability to environmental conditions. *See also* CROSS; HYBRID.

clos [KLOH] The French term for "closed" or "enclosed," usually expanded to mean "enclosed field" or "enclosed vineyard." This term, generally associated with BURGUNDY, may not appear on a French wine label unless a vineyard by that name produces and bottles the wine—for example, CLOS DE LA ROCHE or CLOS DE VOUGEOT.

Le Clos *see* CLOS DU VAL

Les Clos [lay KLOH] Probably the most famous of the seven GRAND CRU vineyards in CHABLIS. Les Clos consists of just over 61 acres and sits between BLANCHOT and VALMUR. Some of the best wines of Chablis come from this vineyard.

Clos Blanc de Vougeot *see* VOUGEOT

Clos de Bèze *see* CHAMBERTIN

Clos de la Gravette *see* VIEUX-CHÂTEAU-CERTAN

Clos de la Maréchale *see* PRÉMEAUX

Clos de la Perrière *see* FIXIN; VOUGEOT

Clos de la Roche AC [kloh duh lah RAWSH] Clos de la Roche is the largest and the best GRAND CRU vineyard in the village of MOREY-SAINT-DENIS in the CÔTE DE NUITS district of France's BURGUNDY region. From its 41.8 acres of PINOT NOIR come some of the longest-lived red wines in Burgundy. Clos de la Roche boasts a cadre of good producers, and their wines are RICH, full-bodied (*see* BODY), and intense. They're best after about 10 years and can AGE for as long as 30 years.

Clos de la Tonnelle *see* SOUTARD, CHÂTEAU

Clos des Chênes *see* VOLNAY

Clos des Ducs *see* VOLNAY

Clos des Jacobins [kloh day zha-koh-BAN] A GRAND CRU CLASSÉ estate located in the SAINT-ÉMILION AC in BORDEAUX. It consists of just over 18 acres and produces about 4,000 to 5,000 cases of high-quality red wine each year. These wines are made from approximately 85 percent MERLOT, 10 percent CABERNET FRANC, and 5 percent CABERNET SAUVIGNON. Most of these wines are less TANNIC and should be consumed in the first 8 to 10 years. Clos des Jacobins is owned by Domaines Cordier, which owns a number of estates including the DEUXIÈME CRU (second growth) Château GRUAUD-LAROSE and a QUATRIÈME CRU (fourth growth) Château TALBOT—both located in the Saint-Julien AC.

Clos des Lambrays AC [kloh day lah*m*-BRAY] Elevated from PREMIER CRU status in 1981, this GRAND CRU vineyard is located in the village of MOREY-SAINT-DENIS in the CÔTE DE NUITS district of France's BURGUNDY region. Planted with PINOT NOIR, this 21.8-acre vineyard is one of the few Burgundian grands crus almost totally owned by one set of owners, the Saier brothers. The vineyards have been extensively replanted over the last few years, and the younger vines are currently producing LIGHT red wines. Older wines from vintages prior to the replanting indicate that this vineyard can produce RICH, full-bodied (*see* BODY) wines with good AGING capabilities.

Clos des Maréchaudes *see* CORTON

Clos des Meix *see* CORTON

Clos des Mouches, Le Clos des Mouches *see* BEAUNE

Clos des Ormes *see* MOREY-SAINT-DENIS

Clos de Tart AC [kloh duh TAHR] An 18.6-acre GRAND CRU vineyard located in the village of MOREY-SAINT-DENIS in the CÔTE DE NUITS district of France's BURGUNDY region. This vineyard is very unusual in that it is totally owned by the Mommessin family who purchased it in 1932 (most Burgundian grand cru vineyards have multiple owners). The vineyard is planted with PINOT NOIR and is capable of producing exceptional red wines.

Clos de Uza *see* SAINT-PIERRE, CHÂTEAU

Clos de Vougeot AC [kloh duh voo-ZHOH] A very famous GRAND CRU vineyard located in the COMMUNE of VOUGEOT in the CÔTE DE NUITS district of France's BURGUNDY region. The Cistercian monks first planted portions of the vineyard in the twelfth century, adding to it during the thirteenth and fourteenth centuries. Its 125 walled acres make it the largest single vineyard in the CÔTE D'OR. Only red wines from PINOT NOIR grapes are produced. Although Clos de Vougeot's reputation has been stellar in the past, today the wines can vary considerably—choosing a wine from this vineyard isn't easy. Clos de Vougeot is often used as the example of Burgundy's fragmented ownership patterns. There are approximately eighty owners of individual parcels within Clos de Vougeot, and the location of the parcels within the vineyard have an impact on the quality of the wine. The upper portion of the vineyard is capable of producing the best wines, followed by the middle section. While the lower portion has poor drainage and is the least effective land, better producers can coax excellent wines out of it. Conversely, there are examples of less-than-impressive wines from the upper section. The bottom line is that choosing a good Clos de Vougeot wine requires knowledge of both the producer and the vineyard parcel.

Clos du Bois [kloh duh BWAH] California winery that was founded in 1976, although partners Frank Woods and Thomas Reed owned acreage and sold grapes prior to that. In 1988 Clos du Bois was sold to Hiram Walker-Allied Lyons' Wine Alliance group, which also owns Callaway Vineyard & Winery near Riverside, California, and WILLIAM HILL WINERY in the NAPA VALLEY. In 1991 Clos du Bois winery moved from the town of Healdsburg to a new facility in the town of Geyserville. This SONOMA COUNTY winery owns nearly 600 acres of vineyard land and annually produces about 350,000 cases of wine, mostly CHARDONNAY. Clos du Bois makes three Chardonnays—one

from ALEXANDER VALLEY and two VINEYARD-DESIGNATED wines, Flintwood and Calcaire. Other white VARIETAL WINES include a SAUVIGNON BLANC and a GEWÜRZTRAMINER. Red wines include a CABERNET SAUVIGNON from Alexander Valley, a MERLOT, a PINOT NOIR from Sonoma County, and two VINEYARD-DESIGNATED wines, Briarcrest Vineyard (100 percent Cabernet Sauvignon) and Marlstone Vineyard (a blend of Cabernet Sauvignon, MALBEC, and Merlot). Clos du Bois wines are all generally well regarded.

Clos du Chapitre *see* FIXIN

Clos du Marquis *see* LÉOVILLE-LAS-CASES

Clos du Roi; Le Clos du Roi *see* BEAUNE; CORTON; LA LOUVIÈRE, CHÂTEAU

Clos du Roy *see* CERTAN-GIRAUD, CHÂTEAU

Clos du Val [kloh deu VAHL] One of the first wineries in what is now the STAGS LEAP AVA, which is a subzone within the larger NAPA VALLEY AVA. It was founded in 1972 by John Goelet under the guidance of French winemaker Bernard Portet. Portet was searching for winery locations when he discovered that this area of the Napa Valley had a cooler microclimate, which he thought was perfect for their needs. (Portet also found an area in the Australian state of Victoria, where Taltarni, another winery, was built and is run now by his younger brother, Dominique Portet.) Winemaking is obviously in the Portet blood—Bernard's and Dominique's father Andre was the RÉGISSEUR of Château LAFITE-ROTHSCHILD. Clos du Val has 140 acres in the Stags Leap area (planted with CABERNET SAUVIGNON, MERLOT, SÉMILLON and ZINFANDEL), 105 acres in the CARNEROS area (planted with CHARDONNAY and PINOT NOIR), and another 20 acres near Yountville in the Napa Valley. Clos du Val puts out a range of ESTATE-BOTTLED wines, as well as the medium-priced label, **Joli Val** and a lower-priced **Le Clos** bottling. Production is about 60,000 cases per year.

closed; closed-in Descriptor for wine that doesn't show its full potential, most likely due to its youth. AGING will usually open up such a wine as it develops CHARACTER and intensity.

Clos Fourtet [kloh foor-TEH] A PREMIER GRAND CRU CLASSÉ estate located in the SAINT-ÉMILION AC in the BORDEAUX region. Clos Fourtet is known for its marvelous underground limestone cellars, which were originally part of a quarry. This estate has been criticized in recent years for not living up to its high classification, although there appears to be attempts to improve the quality. Clos Fourtet consists of about

45 acres and produces between 4,000 and 7,000 cases of red wine each year. The wines use about 70 percent MERLOT, 20 percent CABERNET FRANC, and 10 percent CABERNET SAUVIGNON. Recent VINTAGES have been fruitier and less TANNIC and can AGE for about 8 to 10 years. Clos Fourtet also uses a SECOND LABEL **Domaine de Martialis**.

Clos Haut-Peyraguey *see* LAFAURIE-PEYRAGUEY, CHÂTEAU

Clos J. Kanon *see* CANON, CHÂTEAU

Clos la Gaffelièr *see* LA GAFELIÈRE, CHÂTEAU

Clos l'Eglise [kloh lay-GLEEZ] A small property consisting of about 15 acres located in the POMEROL AC in the BORDEAUX region. The wines are made from about 55 percent MERLOT, 25 percent CABERNET SAUVIGNON, and 20 percent CABERNET FRANC. They're known to be a bit LEAN and AUSTERE due to the high percentage of Cabernet Sauvignon (unusual in a Pomerol wine). About 2,000 to 3,000 cases of red wine are made per year. AGING capability is about 8 to 10 years.

Clos Napoléon *see* FIXIN

Clos Pegase [kloh pay-GAHS] Founded in 1984 by Jan Shrem, this winery is located in the northern part of the NAPA VALLEY between the towns of Calistoga and St. Helena. Clos Pegase is probably as well known for its post-modernist architecture as it is for its wines. Its design is the result of a competition sponsored by the San Francisco Museum of Modern Art and won by architect Michael Graves. Clos Pegase has 50 acres of vineyard adjacent to the winery, 42 acres north of Calistoga, and another 365 acres (70 of which are planted) in the CARNEROS region. CABERNET SAUVIGNON, CHARDONNAY, MERLOT, and SAUVIGNON BLANC grapes are grown at these various sites. The winery produces between 40,000 and 50,000 cases of wine each year.

Clos Saint-Denis AC [kloh sa*n* duh-NEE] A 16-acre GRAND CRU vineyard located in the village of MOREY-SAINT-DENIS in the CÔTE DE NUITS district of France's BURGUNDY region. In 1927 the village of Morey appended the name of this vineyard to its own (a widespread practice among Burgundian villages). The red wines, produced from PINOT NOIR, are not as full-bodied (*see* BODY) as those from the neighboring CLOS DE LA ROCHE grand cru, but they're fruitier and have more delicacy and finesse.

Clos Saint-Jacques *see* GEVRY-CHAMBERTIN AC

Clos Saint-Jean *see* CHASSAGNE-MONTRACHET AC

cloudy; cloudiness Descriptor for a wine that is visually unclear. Cloudiness is considered a defect and is most often due to faulty winemaking. An older wine with SEDIMENT, though not absolutely clear, should not be confused with a cloudy wine.

cloying A descriptor for wine that lacks the balance of ACIDITY to keep it from becoming excessively and unappetizingly sweet.

coarse A winetasting term describing a mediocre or poor-quality wine that may have BODY, but little else. A coarse wine is often the result of inferior grape varieties or growing methods. In SPARKLING WINES, coarseness generally refers to effervescence with large, rough bubbles.

Cockburn-Smithes One of the oldest PORT companies, founded in 1815 by Robert Cockburn. John and Henry Smithes were added as partners in 1848. Descendants of the founders are still involved with running the company, although it's now owned by HARVEYS, which is in turn owned by the English company Allied Lyons. Cockburn makes a full line of port wines but is best known for their *Director's Reserve*—a tawny port—and *Special Reserve*—an AGED ruby port. Cockburn-Smithes is usually ranked as one of the top ten vintage port producers.

cocktail sherry *see* SHERRY

Codorníu [koh-dor-NOO] Codorníu, which is based in northeast Spain, southwest of Barcelona in PENEDÈS, was founded in the sixteenth century. In 1972 it became the first Spanish firm to produce SPARKLING WINE using MÉTHODE CHAMPENOISE. Today it's one of the world's largest sparkling wine companies, producing some 3 million cases each year. The most highly regarded of its CAVA DO wines are the Non Plus Ultra, Gran Codorníu, and the Codorníu Chardonnay. This giant company also owns the wine estates of Masía Bach, also located in Penedès, and RAIMAT, in the DO of COSTERS DEL SEGRE. Both are highly regarded producers of STILL WINES. In addition, Codorníu owns the Cava DO firm of Rondel and has invested in the California sparkling wine industry with their CARNEROS region estate, **Codorníu Napa**.

Cognac [KOHN-yak; KON-yak; Fr. kaw-NYAK] Hailing from the town of Cognac and the surrounding areas in western France, this potent potable is the finest of all BRANDIES. Made primarily from TREBBIANO grapes (known in France as *Ugni Blanc* and *Saint-Émilion*), Cognac is double-DISTILLED immediately after FERMENTATION. Freshly distilled Cognac is strong, sharp, and harsh and needs wood aging (usually in

LIMOUSIN oak) to mellow it and enhance the aroma and flavor. Stars on a Cognac bottle's label vary in meaning from producer to producer although three stars usually indicate longer aging and therefore higher quality than two stars or one star. Older Cognacs are labeled **V.S.** (very superior), **V.S.O.P.** (very superior old pale), and **V.V.S.O.P.** (very, very, superior old pale). A Cognac label can no longer legally claim more than 7 years aging. It has been difficult for authorities to accurately keep track of Cognacs aged longer than this, so they've limited what producers may claim. The label terms **X.O.**, **Extra**, and **Reserve** usually indicate that a Cognac is the oldest put out by a producer. The term **Fine Champagne** on a Cognac label indicates that 60 percent of the grapes came from a superior grape-growing section of Cognac called *Grande Champagne*. A label designating *Grande Fine Champagne* proclaims that all the grapes for that Cognac came from that eminent area.

B. R. Cohn [KOHN] A SONOMA VALLEY winery that is located between the towns of Glen Ellen and Boyes Hot Springs, California. It was founded in 1984 by Bruce Cohn, who'd been a successful rock group manager (his clients included the Doobie Brothers) before establishing the winery. The 65-acre vineyard (called Olive Hill) is now planted with CABERNET SAUVIGNON and MERLOT, which go into the winery's Gold Label ESTATE-BOTTLED wines. A lower-priced, Silver Label line includes Cabernet Sauvignon, CHARDONNAY, and Merlot wines. The Gold Label Olive Hill Cabernet Sauvignon is very well regarded.

Colares DOC [kuh-LAH-rush] A small DENOMINACÃO DE ORIGEM CONTROLADA (DOC) area located northwest of Lisbon on the Atlantic coast. The vineyards are situated on a sandy plateau where the vines must be planted deep into the clay subsoil below. Because of the sandy soil, the vines are free of PHYLLOXERA and, therefore, have never been grafted to a different rootstock. Colares is best known for its red wines, which are made primarily from the Ramisco grape blended with Molar, Parreira Matias, and PERIQUITA. The wines are generally TANNIC and full-bodied (*see* BODY) and require considerable AGING. A small amount of white wine is made from ARINTO, Galego Dourado, and MALVASIA.

cold duck Originating in Germany, this pink sparkling wine is supposedly a mixture of CHAMPAGNE, SPARKLING BURGUNDY, and sugar. In practice, however, cold duck is simply pink and sparkling, and the wines used are often of inferior quality. The resulting potation is quite sweet with few other distinguishable characteristics. Its origin is traced back to the Bavarian practice of mixing bottles of previously opened champagne with cold sparkling Burgundy so that the champagne wouldn't be wasted. This mixture was called *kalte ende* ("cold end"); over the years, *ende* transliterated to *ente* ("duck").

cold maceration *see* MACERATION

cold stabilization *see* STABILIZATION

Cole Ranch AVA A small California AVA located in MENDOCINO COUNTY southwest of the town of Ukiah and northeast of Booneville. There's a single, 61-acre vineyard in this 150-acre viticultural area. CABERNET SAUVIGNON is the dominant variety grown, along with small amounts of RIESLING and CHARDONNAY. FETZER VINEYARDS puchases most of the grapes from this area.

colheita [cuhl-YAY-tah] The Portuguese word for "vintage." On the label of a bottle of PORT, *colheita* indicates that the bottle is not VINTAGE PORT but rather a TAWNY PORT harvested in the indicated year and aged in wood for a minimum of 7 years. Colheita port is sometimes called *dated port*.

Colli Albani [KAWL-lee ahl-BAH-nee] A DOC area located in the Italy's LATIUM region just south of Rome near Lake Albano. The area produces inexpensive white wines that vary in sweetness from DRY to DOLCE (sweet), and they can be STILL or SPUMANTE. The primary grapes used are MALVASIA and TREBBIANO.

Colli Berici DOC [KAWL-lee beh-REE-tchee] DOC located in the central section of the VENETO in northeast Italy. It extends south from the edge of the city of Vicenza to include the vineyards of twenty-eight small villages. Seven VARIETAL WINES are produced—Cabernet from CABERNET SAUVIGNON and CABERNET FRANC, GARGANEGA, MERLOT, Pinot Bianco (PINOT BLANC), Sauvignon (SAUVIGNON BLANC), TOCAI Bianco, and Tocai Rosso. Many of these wines allow for up to 15 percent of other approved varieties to be used.

Colli Bolognesi DOC [KAWL-lee baw-law-NYAY-zee] DOC located in the Appennine foothills southwest of Bologna in Italy's EMILIA-ROMAGNA region. It produces VARIETAL WINES made from BARBERA, CABERNET SAUVIGNON, MERLOT, Pignoletto, Pinot Bianco (PINOT BLANC), Riesling Italico (WELSCHRIESLING) and SAUVIGNON BLANC. Each of these varietals can have up to 15 percent of other approved grapes blended with them. There is also a BIANCO wine that's a blend of ALBANA and TREBBIANO grapes. The Bianco and Pignoletto wines are made in both AMABILE and DRY versions. The wines may have either "Monte San Pietro" or "Castelli Medioevali" added to the label in reference to the two subzones within Colli Bolgnesi. The red Barbera and the white Sauvignon Blanc are more highly regarded than the other wines.

Colli Euganei DOC [KAWL-lee eh-yoo-GAH-neh] A DOC area located southwest of Padova (Padua) in the south central part of Italy's VENETO region. The area produces five VARIETAL WINES plus a ROSSO and a BIANCO. The varietal wines are Cabernet (from CABERNET SAUVIGNON and CABERNET FRANC), MERLOT, Moscato (MUSCAT), Pinot Bianco (PINOT BLANC), and TOCAI Italico. The Rosso is made mainly from the widely planted Merlot but can include up to 40 percent of other approved varieties. The Bianco is made from GARGANEGA, Serprina (PROSECCO), TOCAI FRIULANO, and others.

Colli Fiorentini *see* CHIANTI DOCG

Colli Lanuvini DOC [KAWL-lee lah-noo-VEE-nee] Colli Lanuvini is located in Italy's LATIUM region just south of Lake Albano, which is south of Rome. The DOC zone makes white wines, both DRY and AMABILE, from MALVASIA and TREBBIANO.

Colline Pisane *see* CHIANTI DOCG

Collio DOC; Collio Goriziano DOC [KOH-lee-oh goh-ree-zee-AH-noh] Collio, also known as *Collio Goriziano,* is located in the FRIULI-VENEZIA GIULIA region in northeast Italy. It spreads out north and west of the city of Goriziano and borders the former Yugoslovia on the eastern edge. The area produces ten VARIETAL WINES and Collio Bianco, which is made from Ribolla Gialla (RIBOLLA), MALVASIA, and TOCAI grapes. The varietal wines are CABERNET FRANC, MALVASIA, MERLOT, Pinot Bianco (PINOT BLANC), Pinot Grigio (PINOT GRIS), Pinot Nero (PINOT NOIR), Riesling Italico (WELSCHRIESLING), Sauvignon (SAUVIGNON BLANC), TOCAI FRIULANO, and Traminer (GEWÜRZTRAMINER). The wines from Collio are generally considered the best of the Friuli area.

Colli Orientali del Friuli DOC [KAWL-lee oh-ryayn-TAH-lee free-OO-lee] Colli Orientali del Friuli means "eastern hills of Friuli," which describes this area's location in the FRIULI-VENEZIA GIULIA region in northeast Italy—it's east of Udine and northwest of the COLLIO DOC. Part of the zone borders the former Yugoslavia. The wines are generally well regarded and considered right behind those of the Collio DOC in quality. The DOC covers twenty types of wines, seventeen of which are VARIETALS. These wines include the sweet DESSERT WINES made from the VERDUZZO grape—**Ramandolo** and **Romandolo Classico** (the Classico can come only from the vineyards around the village of Ramandolo). Another of this area's unusual (as well as prized and expensive) dessert wines is the PICOLIT varietal. This DOC is the only one where Picolit is designated. The other varietal wines are Cabernet (from Cabernet Sauvignon and Cabernet Franc), CABERNET SAUVIGNON, CABERNET FRANC, CHARDONNAY, MALVASIA, MERLOT, Pinot Bianco (PINOT BLANC), Pinot Grigio (PINOT GRIS), Pinot Nero (PINOT NOIR), Refosco dal Peducolo Rosso (MONDEUSE), RIBOLLA, Riesling Renano (RIESLING), Sauvignon (SAUVIGNON BLANC), SCHIOPPETTINO, TOCAI, Traminer Aromatico (GEWÜRZTRAMINER), and Verduzzo Friulano. All the varietal wines are required to use a minimum of 90 percent of the named varietal. This DOC also produces a ROSATO, which must be made with 90 percent Merlot.

Colli Piacentini DOC [KAWL-lee pyah-tchen-TEE-nee] In 1984 this DOC combined three previous DOC areas (Gutturnio dei Colli Piacentini, Monterosso Val d'Arda, and Trebbianino Val Trebbia) plus several other areas under this one designation. It's located south of Piacenza in the western part of Italy's EMILIA-ROMAGNA region. This DOC allows VARIETAL WINES made from BARBERA, BONARDA, MALVASIA, Orturgo, Pinot Nero (PINOT NOIR), and SAUVIGNON BLANC. Each of these varietal wines can have up to 15 percent of other approved grapes blended with them. They all have DRY and STILL or FRIZZANTE versions; some can be semisweet or sweet, some SPUMANTE. **Gutturnio** is a blend of Barbera and Bonarda that can be made dry or sweet and also frizzante. Other approved blended wines are **Monterosso Val d'Arda**, **Trebbianino Val Trebbia**, and **Val Nure**—all are made from approved white varieties and can be dry or AMABILE (medium-sweet) and still, frizzante, or spumante.

Colli Senesi *see* CHIANTI DOCG

Collioure AC [kol-YOOR] Small APPELLATION that comprises the vineyards surrounding the villages of Collioure and Port-Vendres in France's LANGUEDOC-ROUSSILLON region along the Mediterranean near the Spanish border. Collioure AC produces full-bodied (*see* BODY) red wines based primarily on GRENACHE and blended with CARIGNAN, CINSAUT, MOURVÈDRE and SYRAH.

Colomba Platino *see* CORVO

Colombar *see* COLOMBARD

Colombard [KAHL-uhm-bahrd (Fr. kaw-law*n*-BAH*R*)] Highly productive white-wine grape that is one of the most widely planted vines in California, where it's called *French Colombard*. The California acreage expanded dramatically (mostly in the SAN JOAQUIN VALLEY) during the 1970s and early 1980s because of this grape's ability to grow in hot climates and still create decent wine. Colombard produces a crisp, moderately DRY, SPICY wine with FLORAL attributes and good ACID-ITY. It's used extensively in blending—usually with CHENIN BLANC—to make JUG WINES and less expensive SPARKLING WINES. The Colombard VA-RIETAL WINES, which are usually produced in cooler growing regions like MENDOCINO COUNTY and LAKE COUNTY, are not as popular as other California whites. In France's Charente district where it originated and was used mainly in the production of COGNAC, Colombard has largely been replaced by the Saint-Émilion (TREBBIANO) variety. It's still grown in parts of BORDEAUX, although the Colombard wines are generally un-interesting. Colombard is, however, making a comeback in France, mainly because French winemakers in some of the hotter growing areas have observed that they can produce quality wines from this grape by adopting some of California's more modern VINIFICATION tech-niques. Colombard is popular in South Africa, where it's called *Colombar,* and is now being grown in the hotter growing regions in Texas.

color The color of a wine is an indicator of its condition, quality, age, and even style. In general, the less intense a wine's color is, the more delicate the flavor and BODY will be. The color of any good wine should be clear. As wines AGE, their colors change—white wines be-come darker, often with traces of amber; red wines begin to fade and often assume a tawny, brick-red cast. A change of color in a young wine signals premature aging. *See also* Winetasting, page 598.

Coltassala [kohl-tahs-SAH-lah] This is the proprietary name for a high-quality VINO DA TAVOLA, one of the so-called super-Tuscans (*see* TUSCANY). Made from SANGIOVESE and Mammolo grapes, Coltassala is aged in small barrels of French oak. This highly regarded red wine is from Castello di Volpaia, a wine estate located in central Tuscany south of Florence.

Columbia Crest Winery is located in the southeast part of Washington, just north of the Oregon border. Columbia Crest owns nearly 2,000 acres near the winery, and is in the COLUMBIA VALLEY AVA. It's part of Stimson Lane, a subsidiary of UST Inc. (owners of U.S. Tobacco), which also owns Washington's CHÂTEAU STE. MICHELLE and the NAPA VALLEY wineries of CONN CREEK and VILLA MT. EDEN. Columbia Crest was started as a SECOND LABEL of Château Ste. Michelle, but it grew so rapidly that it's now run as a separate enterprise. Production, which is nearing 600,000 cases per year, consists mainly of product lines that are lower priced than those of Château Ste. Michelle. Columbia Crest produces a wide variety of wines including CABERNET SAUVIGNON, CHARDONNAY (regular and RESERVE), MERLOT (regular and reserve), SAUVIGNON BLANC, and a SÉMILLON-Chardonnay blend.

Columbia Valley AVA A very large AVA in south-central Washington and northern Oregon. The Columbia Valley AVA contains the smaller VITICULTURAL AREAS of YAKIMA VALLEY and WALLA WALLA. Because it's protected by the Cascade Mountains from the cool weather coming in from the Pacific Ocean, the Columbia Valley is the warmest growing area in the Pacific Northwest. Its growing areas range from Region I to Region III (*see* CLIMATE REGIONS OF CALIFORNIA). Because of the contrasting temperatures throughout the region, different grape varieties do well in various locations. This means that MERLOT, a warm-weather grape, and RIESLING, a cool-weather grape, both can ripen properly here. CABERNET SAUVIGNON, CHENIN BLANC, SAUVIGNON BLANC, and SÉMILLON are also grown, as well as CONCORD and other VITIS LABRUSCA varieties.

La Comarca de Falset *see* TARRAGONA DO

Comb aux Moines *see* GEVREY-CHAMBERTIN

Les Combes *see* CORTON

Comblanchien *see* CÔTE DE NUITS

Commandaria *see* CYPRUS

commerciante [koh-mayr-CHAHN-tay] An Italian term for a producer (merchant) who works primarily with grapes or wines that are purchased before being bottled and sold.

common A descriptor for a wine that, though perfectly drinkable, is rather ordinary and lacks distinction.

commune [KAHM-myoon] A word used to describe a small administrative district, generally comprised of a village and the land (including vineyards) surrounding it.

Compañía Vinícola del Norte de España (CVNE) [kohm-pah-NYEE-ah vihn-ee-KOH-luh dehl NOR-tay day ehs-PAHN-yah] CVNE (pronounced KOO-nay and spelled *Cune* on labels) is an important RIOJA DO estate in Spain. The majority of the wines produced are red, made primarily from the TEMPRANILLO grape. The *Viña Real* brand wines are produced as CRIANZA, RESERVA, and GRAN RESERVA. They're all quite good, but the top of the line is the *Imperial*, which is made in only the best years as either a *reserva* or *gran reserva*. CVNE also produces *Monopole*, a highly regarded white wine made from about 80 percent Viura (MACABEO) and 20 percent MALVASIA.

complex; complexity Complexity is a hallmark of quality in a wine. A complex wine is one with multiple layers and nuances of BOUQUET and flavor. Its myriad elements are perfectly balanced, completely harmonious, and eminently interesting. Such a wine is the diametric opposite of one that is simple and one-dimensional.

Comtes de Champagne *see* CHAMPAGNE

Conca de Barberà DO [KAWN-kuh deh bahr-BEH-rah] A relatively new (1989) DO located north of the PENEDÈS DO in Spain's CATALONIA area. White grapes, mainly MACABEO and PARELLADA, account for 75 to 80 percent of the crop. Much of what is grown is sold off to CAVA producers in the Penedes area. A small amount of red and ROSÉ wine is made from Garnacha Tinta (GRENACHE) and Ull de Lebre (TEMPRANILLO).

Concannon Vineyard *see* WENTE BROS.

concentrate, grape *see* GRAPE CONCENTRATE

Concord [KAHN-kord] Native American variety that is widely grown in the eastern states, particularly in New York, and in Michigan and Washington. Ephraim Bull first planted these native grape seeds in 1843 in his garden in Concord, Massachusetts—hence the name. The vine's beautiful blue-black grapes often appear to have been powdered with silver. They're most often used for jams, jellies, and unfermented juice and as table grapes. Concord wines aren't well regarded by most wine lovers because of their FOXY characteristics, which are often associated with members of this VITIS LABRUSCA species.

Condado de Huelva DO [kohn-DAH-doh day-WAYL-bah] DO located northwest of the JEREZ Y MANZANILLA DO in southern Spain. In the past this area grew grapes that were shipped to the Jerez y Manzanilla area and eventually made into SHERRY; it also produced its own sherrylike wines. Because this style of wine isn't as popular as it once was, the number of vineyard acres has been reduced, and producers have shifted much of their production to DRY white wines. Zalema is the primary grape used, but it's losing ground to higher-quality grapes like Palomino Fino (PALOMINO), Garrido Fino, and Moscatel (MUSCAT). Some sherry-style wines are still produced such as *Condado Palido* (a FINO style) and *Condado Viejo* (an OLOROSO style).

Condrieu AC [kawn-DREE-yuh] An APPELLATION located near the village of Condrieu, south of CÔTE RÔTIE in France's northern RHÔNE region. Condrieu AC produces only white wines made from the rare VIOGNIER variety. These DRY, RICH wines have a perceptible spiciness and aromas and flavors reminiscent of apricots, peaches, and pears. They're very expensive because they're quite good and difficult to find.

Conegliano [koh-nehl-YAH-noh] A small city in the VENETO region and home of Italy's foremost ENOLOGY school and experimental VITICULTURE station (*Istituto Sperimentale per la Viticoltura*). An area around Conegliano, which is located about 35 miles north of Venice, is entitled to the **Prosecco di Conegliano-Valdobbiadene DOC**. This DOC produces FRIZZANTE and SPUMANTE wines (chiefly from PROSECCO grapes) in styles that can range from DRY to AMABILE to DOLCE.

Conero *see* ROSSO CONERO

Conn Creek Winery NAPA VALLEY winery that is owned by Washington State's Stimson Lane, a subsidiary of UST Inc. (owners of U.S. Tobacco), which also owns Washington's CHATEAU STE. MICHELLE and COLUMBIA CREST, and Napa Valley's VILLA MT. EDEN. Conn Creek was founded in 1974 by Bill Collins, who'd already been selling grapes from his vineyards for several years. After building a good reputation, particularly for its CABERNET SAUVIGNON, the Conn Creek Winery was sold to Stimson Lane in 1986. Today this winery owns approximately 145 acres of vineyards. Its annual production is between 30,000 and 35,000 cases of wine including Cabernet Sauvignon, CHARDONNAY, MERLOT, ZINFANDEL and a red MERITAGE called **Triomphe**.

Connétable de Talbot *see* TALBOT, CHÂTEAU

La Conseilante, Château [sha-TOH lah kawn-seh-YAHNT] Highly regarded POMEROL AC chateau that is located between Châteaus PETRUS and CHEVAL BLANC (the latter is actually in SAINT-ÉMILION). The "N" on the label stands for the Nicholas family, who has owned the CHÂTEAU for over a century. Château La Conseilante has produced some excellent wines, particularly during the 1980s. Good VINTAGES can AGE for about 20 years. There are only about 5,000 cases of red wine produced each year from the 31-acre vineyard. The blend for these wines is approximately 45 percent MERLOT (an unusually low percentage for a Pomerol château), 45 percent CABERNET FRANC, and 10 percent MALBEC.

consejo regulador *see* DENOMINACIÓN DE ORIGEN

consorzio [kawn-SOHRD-zyoh] Local growers' associations found throughout Italy that supervise and control wine production, as well as promote and market the wine. Although these consortiums are voluntary, most producers join. The best-known *consorzio* is the GALLO NERO ("black rooster") of the CHIANTI CLASSICO region.

cooked Wine with a heavy, sweet, sometimes caramelly smell and flavor is said to have a *cooked* characteristic. This trait can be due to several causes including an unusually high temperature during VINIFICATION or the addition of some form of sugar.

cooking wine A wine labeled "cooking wine" is generally an inferior wine that would not be drunk on its own. It lacks distinction and flavor, and some have been known to be adulterated with salt. The rule of thumb when cooking with wine is only to use one you'd drink and to be sure the wine's flavor compliments the food with which it's paired.

cooler *see* WINE COOLER

cooling wine *see* TEMPERATURE

Coonawarra An important Australian wine-producing region in the state of South Australia, which is in a rather remote location about 240 miles southeast of the city of Adelaide, near the border of Victoria. The highly regarded red wines from Coonawarra (which means "honeysuckle" in Aborigine) are the result of the cool climate and the terra rosa over limestone soil. CABERNET SAUVIGNON and Shiraz (SYRAH) are the two most popular red grapes and the ones that make this area's reputation. Small amounts of PINOT NOIR, MERLOT, and CABERNET FRANC are also grown. RIESLING is the most popular white variety, followed by CHARDONNAY, Traminer (GEWÜRZTRAMINER), and SAUVIGNON BLANC. Well-known Coonawarra wineries include Brands Laira, Lindermans, Mildara, Rouge Homme, and Wynn's. Among other producers with vineyards here are Penfolds, Rosemount Estate, and Petaluma.

cooperage; cooper [KOO-per-ihj] 1. The work, as well as the place of business of a **cooper**, a craftsman who makes or repairs BARRELS or CASKS. 2. Cooperage also describes the articles (barrels, etc.) made by a cooper. 3. In wineries, cooperage refers to the wine storage capacity in such containers.

cooperative A winery or cellar that's jointly owned and operated by a group of small producers. A cooperative is usually started in an effort to spread the cost of facilities, equipment and marketing among the participants. Europe in particular has hundreds of cooperatives, some of which have grown into huge organizations. For many small producers, these cooperatives continue to be extremely important because it would be prohibitively expensive for each one to upgrade to the latest technology and produce wine that's competitive with the rest of the world. In Italy a cooperative is called a CANTINA SOCIALE or *cantina cooperativa*, in Germany it's called a WEINGÄRTNERGENOSSEN-SCHAFT, WINZERGENOSSENSCHAFT, or ZENTRALKELLEREI. The French term is *cave cooperative*.

copita [koh-PEE-tah] A traditional glass for tasting sherry that originated in Jerez, Spain. *See also* GLASSES; Common Wineglass Shapes, page 593.

Corbières AC [kawr-BYAYR] District located in Frances' LANGUEDOC-ROUSSILLON region that was finally upgraded from VDQS to APPELLATION D'ORIGINE CONTRÔLÉE status in 1986. A huge majority of the wines are red, produced largely from CARIGNAN blended with small amounts of CINSAUT, GRENACHE, MOURVÈDRE and SYRAH. Small quantities of ROSÉ are made from these same red varieties; a miniscule amount of white wine is produced mainly from Bourboulenc, CLAIRETTE, and GRENACHE BLANC. The red wines are considered best and, since the introduction of CARBONIC MACERATION, they're BIG and full-bodied (*see* BODY) yet have a fruitiness that doesn't exist in the older traditionally made wines.

Cordisco *see* MONTEPULCIANO

Corgoloin *see* CÔTE DE NUITS

corkage [CORK-ihj] A fee charged by restaurants to open and serve a bottle of wine brought to the establishment by the patron. A quick call to the restaurant will confirm the amount of the corkage fee. Some restaurants charge a lower fee if the patron's wine is not on the restaurant's wine list, such as might be the case with an older or particularly distinctive wine.

corked; corky Terms used to describe a wine that's been affected by a faulty cork. This characteristic is caused by a chemical compound (2,4,6-Tricloroanisole—246-TCA) that humans can perceive at levels as low as 30 ppt (parts per trillion). High levels of this compound produce an unmistakably putrefying odor and flavor that many compare to that of moldy, wet cardboard or newspapers. At moderate levels, a corked wine takes on a musty quality; at low levels, it seems AUSTERE and lacking in FRUIT. Wine professionals estimate that 3 to 5 percent of wines are ruined because of bad corks, which is why research is proceeding rapidly for an acceptable synthetic cork. *See also* CORKS.

corks Corks are made from the bark of a type of oak tree found in Spain and Portugal known as *Quercus suber*. Once a tree has matured, which takes from 16 to 25 years, the bark can be stripped every 9 years without harming the tree. Once stripped, the bark is processed and graded. Cork lengths generally range from 1¼ to 2¼ inches, although longer corks can be specially ordered. Fine wines with good aging potential are usually sealed with longer, higher-quality corks. Wines made for early consumption generally get shorter, lower-quality corks. Wine should be stored on its side to keep the cork moist and fully expanded, thereby providing an airtight seal. Although corks have long been associated with fine wines (versus screw-top lids for inexpensive wines), much controversy surrounds their use for better wines. Corks have certain desirable attributes—they're very light, they compress enough to be forced into the neck of a wine bottle and then swell back to fill the neck tightly, and their honeycomb texture grips the bottle snugly and forms a tight seal. But corks sometimes leak, spoiling the wine; they can dry out if the wine is not stored correctly. They're also in some way responsible for wines that take on an undesirable musty, moldy character—such wine is referred to as CORKED or corky. Some professional tasters estimate that 3 to 5 percent of wines are ruined because of bad corks, and many feel the problem is escalating. Many leading authorities are suggesting it's time to reconsider the screw-cap, saying it would eliminate the need for corkscrews and many of the problems associated with corks while preserving the wine just as well. The search for an acceptable synthetic "cork" is on. One possibility, **Cellukork**, is made from ethylene vinyl acetate, has the look and feel of natural cork, and costs less than top-quality natural corks. Another synthetic cork called **Supremecorq** comes in vivid shades of blue, green, purple, tangerine, and yellow, making no attempt to hide the fact that it isn't the real thing. Proponents claim that bottles can be stored upright since the synthetic cork does not need to be kept moist. Critics point out that these "plastic corks" still need to prove that they can keep wine properly over the long term.

corkscrew; corkpuller A tool used to withdraw corks from bottles. Typically, a corkscrew has a pointed metal spiral with a transverse handle at one end. There are many varieties of corkscrews, some of which are quite elaborate. The most important part of the corkscrew is the spiral. It needs to be rounded, thin, and tapered, with a sharp point that's not centered but rather keeps in line with the rest of the spiral. The spiral should be about 2½ inches in length because fine wines generally have long corks and the spiral needs to grip most of the cork to ensure that the bottom of an older (possibly fragile) cork doesn't break off. It's also best to have a corkscrew that provides some leverage when pulling the cork. The small, classic **waiter's friend** that folds up like a pocket knife works well, as does the **butterfly**, which contains a center screw and a handle on each side for leverage (the handles move up and down like butterfly wings). There's also the **butler's friend**, a popular corkpuller that consists of two thin parallel prongs connected by a handle. The prongs are pushed down between the inside of the bottle neck and the sides of the cork; then the device is pulled and turned at the same time until the cork comes out. There are also **mounted corkscrews** that insert the metal spiral into the cork and then remove the cork by pulling the attached handle in a single direction (some of these devices will recork the bottle by reversing the motion of the handle). A hand-held device called a **screwpull** works in a similar manner. *See also* Opening and Serving Still Wine, page 590.

Cornas AC [kor-NAH] APPELLATION that sits south of the better-known HERMITAGE AC in Frances' northern RHÔNE region. Fast developing a following of its own, Cornas AC produces only red wines made from the SYRAH variety. These wines are some of the biggest, most full-bodied (*see* BODY) wines made in the region. Other growing districts in the Rhône cut the boldness of their wines by blending in other red or white varieties, but not Cornas. From better vintages, the wines can be dark red, almost black, with an intense fruitiness and plenty of TANNINS. They can require 5 to 10 years of AGING before they SOFTEN and become fully enjoyable.

Corsica [KOHR-sih-kuh] Large Mediterranean island located southwest of the Italian mainland and just north of Sardinia. Corsica is a French DÉPARTEMENT and has three main APPELLATIONS—**Vin de Corse AC**, which covers most of the island's wines; the smaller AJACCIO AC (at the island's north end); and **Patrimonio AC**, which is on the western side. The Vin de Corse AC has five small subzones or CRUS, which can append their name to the label. They are Calvi, Coteaux du Cap Corse, Figari, Porto Vecchio, and Sartène. Most of the wine is red and ROSÉ; the red grapes used include CARIGNAN, CINSAUT, GRENACHE, Nielluccio (which is possibly SANGIOVESE), and Sciacarello. The main white grape is VERMENTINO, which is usually blended with Ugni Blanc (TREBBIANO). Some producers are trying the popular French varieties like CABERNET FRANC, CABERNET SAUVIGNON, CHARDONNAY, CHENIN BLANC, and MERLOT.

Cortese [kohr-TEH-zeh; kohr-TAY-zee] A white-wine grape grown in northwest Italy, mainly in PIEDMONT and parts of LOMBARDY. Cortese generally produces good-quality, high-ACID wines that have a DELICATE, fruity aroma and flavor. Much of this wine is sold as *Cortese del Piemonte*. Higher-quality wines come from the DOC of GAVI, with those known as *Gavi di Gavi* being among the most expensive Italian white wines. Other Cortese wines come from the DOC's of *Colli Tortonesi* and *Cortese dell'Alto Monferrato*.

Cortese di Gavi *see* GAVI DOC

Corton AC [kor-TAWN] A famous GRAND CRU whose vineyards are located on the Montagne de Corton, a vast hill rising above ALOXE-CORTON, an important wine-producing village at the northern end of the CÔTE DE BEAUNE district in France's BURGUNDY region. Although usually associated with Aloxe-Corton, the Corton appellation is also part of the villages of LADOIX-SERRIGNY and PERNAND-VERGELESSES. The Corton grand cru ranking is only for red wines made from PINOT NOIR. Certain vineyards are also permitted to produce white wines made from CHARDONNAY, PINOT BLANC, and PINOT GRIS and to use the name of the other grand cru in this area, CORTON-CHARLEMAGNE. Vineyards not authorized to produce white wines under the Corton-Charlemagne name can produce it under Corton, but the wines are not entitled to grand cru status. There are twenty-eight individually named vineyards that may label their wines with Corton by itself or use Corton followed by the individual vineyard name such as *Corton Bressandes* or *Corton Clos du Roi*. Blended wines using grapes from two or more of these vineyards may only use the designation *Corton*. The twenty-eight vineyards are **En Charlemagne, Les Bressandes, Le Charlemagne, Les Chaumes de la Voirosse, Les Chaumes** (the previous two are usually grouped as one vineyard referred to as Les Chaumes), **Les Combes, Le Corton, Les Fiètres, Les Grèves, Les Languettes, Les Maréchaudes, Clos des Maréchaudes** (usually included with Les Maréchaudes), **Clos des Meix, Les Paulands, Les Perrières, Le Village** (usually included with Les Perrières), **Les Pougets, Les Renardes, Le Clos du Roi, La Vigne au Saint, Les Carriéres, Les Grandes Loliéres, Basses Mourottes, Hautes Mourottes** (the previous two are often referred to as **Les Mourottes**), **Les Moutottes, Le Rognet et Corton, La Toppe au Vert,** and **Les Vergennes**. The Corton AC red wines are usually regarded as the best and the longest-lived of the **Côte** de Beaune.

Corton-Charlemagne AC [kor-TAWN shahr-luh-MAHN-yuh] A celebrated GRAND CRU that produces CHARDONNAY-based white wines, which are considered by many as second only to those from the most famous white-wine grand cru LE MONTRACHET. The Corton-Charlemagne vineyards are located high on the Montagne de Corton, a vast hill ris-

ing above the village of ALOXE-CORTON. Although the individual vineyards of **Les Pouget, Les Languettes, Le Corton, Les Renardes, Basses Mourottes, Hautes Mourottes** (the previous two are often referred to as **Les Mourottes**), and **Le Rognet et Corton** are permitted to produce white wines and use the Corton-Charlemagne AC name, they currently are planted only with PINOT NOIR and produce red wines as part of the grand cru CORTON AC. In actuality, the white wines come from only two vineyards, **En Charlemagne** and **Le Charlemagne**, which make up what is commonly referred to as Corton-Charlemagne. The story goes that these vineyards were planted with red-wine grapes until the eighth century when the Emperor Charlemagne's wife, tired of seeing red stains in his white beard, nagged him until he ripped out the vines and replanted them with white-wine grapes. Although the Corton-Charlemagne AC resides mainly in the village of Aloxe-Corton, it also extends into the villages of LADOIX-SERRIGNY and PERNAND-VERGELESSES. These full-bodied (*see* BODY) white wines are long-lived and thought to be at their best after 7 to 8 years of AGING.

Corvina [kohr-VEE-nuh] This Italian red-wine grape is the principal ingredient in the VALPOLICELLA and BARDOLINO wines of the VENETO region. In both of these wines, Corvina is blended with Rondinella and Molinara to produce light-colored, light-BODIED (*see* BODY) wines that are characterized by a tart, cherry fruit flavor and a slightly bitter almond character. This grape is also called *Corvina Veronese* and *Cruina.*

Corvo [KOHR-voh] SICILY's best known brand, Corvo is used by the Casa Vinicola Duca di Salaparuta, a wine estate based in Casteldaccia, not far from Palermo on the northwest side of the island. Corvo, which means "crow," produces VINI DA TAVOLA, which are popular throughout Italy. It also produces premium wines—a white wine called Colomba Platino and a red one labeled DucaEnrico.

Cos d'Estournel, Château [sha-TOH kaws dehss-toor-NEHL] CHÂTEAU that has risen to become the top estate in the SAINT ESTÈPHE AC (followed closely by Château MONTROSE). It's also one of the top DEUXIÈMES CRUS (second growths) in the MÉDOC area of BORDEAUX. As with many Saint Estèphe wines, those from Cos d'Esournel are full-bodied (*see* BODY) and TANNIC. They require more time to mature, and the best VINTAGES are capable of AGING for 30 years or more. The blend of grape varieties varies, with CABERNET SAUVIGNON making up as much as 68 percent, followed by 30 to 40 percent MERLOT, and occasional use of CABERNET FRANC. The château has about 160 acres and produces 25,000 to 32,000 cases of wine each year, some of it under its SECOND LABEL **de Marbuzet**. In addition to its great wines, the château is noted for its exotic oriental architecture.

cosecha [coh-SEH-chah] The Spanish term for "vintage."

Cos Labory, Château [sha-TOH kaws lah-baw-REE] A CINQUIÈME CRU (fifth growth) of the SAINT-ESTÈPHE AC in BORDEAUX's MÉDOC region. The 37-acre estate produces about 7,000 cases of red wine each year. These wines are made from about 40 percent CABERNET SAUVIGNON, 30 percent MERLOT, 25 percent CABERNET FRANC, and 5 percent PETIT VERDOT. AGING capability for better VINTAGES is about 10 years.

Costers del Segre DO This DO, which was established in 1988, is located in and around the city of Lerida, west of Barcelona in the CATALONIA region in northeastern Spain. The only wines of consistently high quality come from RAIMAT, a wine estate owned by CODORNÍU, the giant SPARKLING WINE firm located in PENEDÈS.

Costières du Gard AC *see* COSTIÈRES DU NÎMES AC

Costières du Nîmes AC [kaws-TYEH*R* duh NEEM] Formerly called **Costières du Gard AC**, this large APPELLATION is located in France's LANGUEDOC-ROUSSILLON region between Nîmes and Montpellier. It produces red, white, and ROSÉ wines. White wines, made mainly from Bourboulenc, CLAIRETTE, GRENACHE BLANC, and Ugni Blanc (TREBBIANO), make up only about 5 percent of the production. A small amount of rosé wine is made, but the majority is red—both are produced from CARIGNAN, CINSAUT, GRENACHE, MOURVÈDRE and SYRAH.

Cot *see* MALBEC

La Côte [lah KOHT] This is one of the three main growing areas in the Swiss canton of VAUD. It's located between Geneva and Lausanne on the sloping northern shore of Lake Geneva. La Côte is chiefly a white-wine area, and CHASSELAS (locally known as Dorin) is the dominant grape. The best wines come from the areas around Féchy, Luins, Perroy, Montsur-Rolle, and Vinzel.

Coteaux Champenois AC *see* CHAMPAGNE

Coteaux d'Aix-en-Provence AC [koh-toh dehks ahn proh-VAH*N*S] APPELLATION, elevated from VDQS in 1985, that is located around the French city of Aix-en-Provence, northeast of Marseille. Red and ROSÉ wines are made from CABERNET SAUVIGNON, CINSAUT, GRENACHE, MOURVÈDRE and SYRAH; white wines are made from CLAIRETTE, GRENACHE BLANC, SAUVIGNON BLANC, SÉMILLON, and Ugni Blanc (TREBBIANO). Because

Coteaux des Baux-en-Provence AC (located around the village of Le Baux, northwest of Aix-en-Provence) is technically a subregion of Coteaux d'Aix-En-Provence, its producers can use both designations. Its red, white, and rosé wines are produced from the same grapes allowed in Coteaux d'Aix-en-Provence. Both areas are viewed as up-and-coming appellations.

Coteaux d'Ancenis VDQS [koh-toh dahn-suh-NEE] VDQS area that encompasses the old fortress town of Ancenis and is located on the Loire River northeast of Nantes in the western part of France's LOIRE region. It makes red and ROSÉ wines from GAMAY and CABERNET FRANC and white wines from CHENIN BLANC or Malvoisie (MALVASIA).

Coteaux de l'Aubance AC [koh-toh duh loh-BAHNS] APPELLATION that is located south of Angers on the river Aubance in the center of France's LOIRE region. It produces limited amounts of white wine, in varying degrees of sweetness, from CHENIN BLANC.

Coteaux des Baux-en-Provence see COTEAUX D'AIX-EN-PROVENCE AC

Les Coteaux du Château L'Arrosée see L'ARROSÉE, CHÂTEAU

Coteaux du Languedoc AC [koh-toh deu LAHNG-dahk] Relatively new (1985) APPELLATION that is quite large. It encompasses the vineyards of over 120 different villages and stretches from near Montpellier to Narbonne in the LANGUEDOC-ROUSSILLON region in southern France. Twelve of the top villages that previously had VDQS status are now designated CRU, and can therefore append their name to the label. They include **Cabrières**, **LA CLAPE**, **Montpeyroux**, **Picpoul de Pinet**, **Pic Saint-Loup**, **Saint-Drézéry**, **Saint-Georges-d'Orques**, and **Saint-Saturnin**. Only red and rosé wines qualify for the Coteaux du Languedoc AC status throughout most of the appellation, and they're made from CARIGNAN, CINSAULT, GRENACHE, MOURVÈDRE and SYRAH. Two of the cru, La Clape and Picpoul de Pinet, are allowed to produce white wines, which are made from BOURBOULENC, CLAIRETTE, Grenache Blanc, MARSANNE, Picpoul, ROLLE, and ROUSSANE. Within Coteaux du Languedoc AC are two smaller appellations—FAUGÈRES AC and SAINT-CHINIAN—whose names also appear on the label.

Coteaux du Layon AC; Coteaux du Layon-Villages AC [koh-toh deu leh-YAWN] APPELLATIONS located south of Angers along the river Layon in the ANJOU district of France's LOIRE region. They produce only white wines (usually semisweet or sweet) from

CHENIN BLANC grapes. The *villages* appellation applies to seven villages—**Beaulieu-sur-Layon, Chaume, Faye-d'Anjou, Rablay-sur-Layon, Rouchefort-sur-Loire, Saint-Aubin-de-Luigné,** and **Saint-Lambert-du-Lattay.** All may append their own name to the label if their wines have at least 1 percent more alcohol that the standard appellation (a minimum of 12 percent versus 11 percent). The grapes in this area are subject to BOTRYTIS CINEREA on occasion. When it strikes, the resulting wines can be RICH, intensely sweet, and luscious. BONNEZEAUX AC and QUARTS DE CHAUME AC are two small appellations located within the Coteaux du Layon area that are noted for their superb DESSERT WINES.

Coteaux du Lyonnais AC [koh-toh deu lee-oh-NAY] APPELLATION that is located around the city of Lyon at the southern end of France's BURGUNDY region just south of the vineyards of BEAUJOLAIS. Upgraded from VDQS status in 1984, it produces mostly light red wines and small amounts of ROSÉ and white wines. The red wines are made from GAMAY and are similiar in style to those from neighboring Beaujolais. The white wines are made from CHARDONNAY, ALIGOTÉ and MUSCADET.

Coteaux du Tricastin AC [koh-toh deu tree-kahss-TAN] Area that is noteworthy because it was established only in the 1960s in an effort to accommodate French winemakers fleeing from North Africa after several nations there gained independence. This fairly large APPELLATION is located in the southern portion of France's RHÔNE region, north of Bollene. It produces mainly red and some ROSÉ wines from CARIGNAN, CINSAUT, GRENACHE, MOUVÈDRE, and SYRAH. The red wines, which have historically been rather light, are gaining BODY as more Syrah is being planted and used in the BLEND. Small amounts of white wine are produced from Bourboulenc and MARSANNE.

Coteaux Varois [koh-toh vah-RWAH] Coteaux Varois is a large VDQS area located west of the CÔTE DE PROVENCE AC in France's Provence region. Standard grapes for making red and ROSÉ wines are CARIGNAN, CINSAUT, GRENACHE and MOUVÈDRE, but recent plantings of CABERNET SAUVIGNON and SYRAH have been improving the quality of the red wines—giving them more BODY and flavor. Minimal amounts of white wine are made from CLAIRETTE, GRENACHE BLANC, and Ugni Blanc (TREBBIANO).

Côte Blonde *see* CÔTE-RÔTIE

Côte Brune *see* CÔTE-RÔTIE

Côte Chalonnaise [koht shah-law-NEHZ] A wine-growing area located just south of the CÔTE D'OR in France's BURGUNDY region. This area has no APPELLATION of its own, and unless the wines are part of one of the five villages entitled to an individual appellation, the wines go into one of the basic Burgundy appellations such as BOURGOGNE AC or BOURGOGNE PASSE-TOUT-GRAIN AC. The five villages with AC status start in the north with Bouzeron and its BOURGOGNE ALIGOTÉ DE BOUZERON AC, which produces white wines from the ALIGOTÉ variety. The rest of the villages—RULLY, MERCUREY, GIVRY, and MONTAGNY—produce red wines from PINOT NOIR and white wines from CHARDONNAY. Mercurey is the largest appellation of the area and has a high enough profile that there is some pressure to formally rename the Côte Chalonnaise to what occasionally is used now, Région de Mercurey. The VINS MOUSSEUX of the Côte Chalonnaise, which fall under the CRÉMANT DE BOURGOGNE AC designation, are a specialty of the area and considered quite good by many sparkling wine enthusiasts.

Côte de Beaune [koht duh BOHN] The southern half of BURGUNDY's famous CÔTE D'OR, which contains the GRAND CRU, PREMIER CRU, and village vineyards responsible for many of the renowned Burgundy wines. The Côte de Beaune includes twenty different villages, seventeen with their own APPELLATIONS—ALOXE-CORTON, AUXEY-DURESSES, BEAUNE, BLAGNY, CHASSAGNE-MONTRACHET, CHOREY-LÈS-BEAUNE, LANDOIX-SERRIGNY, MEURSAULT, MONTHÉLIE, PERNAND-VERGELESSES, POMMARD, PULIGNY-MONTRACHET, SAINT-AUBIN, SAINT-ROMAIN, SANTENEAY, SAVIGNY-LÈS-BEAUNE, and VOLNAY. Three other villages—Cheilly-lès-Maranges, Dezizes-lès-Maranges, and Sampigny-lès-Maragnes—are grouped in a separate appellation **Les Maranges**. The Côte de Beaune area is well known for both its red wines, made from PINOT NOIR grapes, and white wines, made from CHARDONNAY. Even though the Côte de Beaune produces superb red wines, led by the grand cru CORTON, they are somewhat overshadowed by the red wines from the CÔTE DE NUIT in the northern half of the Côte d'Or. However, the white wines from the Côte de Beaune area are considered to be the best in the world. The superstars are the wines from the grands crus of MONTRACHET, BÂTARD-MONTRACHET, BIENVENUE-BÂTARD-MONTRACHET, CHEVALIER-MONTRACHET, CORTON-CHARLEMAGNE, and CRIOTS-BÂTARD-MONTRACHET, and from the numerous outstanding premiers crus vineyards. Wines from individual villages like Meusault also have stellar reputations. In addition to the appellations for grands crus, premiers crus, and the individual villages, there are two others—Côte de Beaune AC and Côte de Beaune-Villages AC. **Côte de Beaune AC** is an appellation for four vineyard sites located on a hill above the town of Beaune that don't qualify for a higher-quality appellations. **Côte de Beaune-Villages AC** is an appellation for wines from sixteen of the area's villages (Aloxe-Corton, Beaune, Pommard, and Volnay are exempted). This appellation applies to wines BLENDED from the various villages, and it's used by villages that are not well known and benefit from using the better-known Côte de Beaune-Villages AC on their labels. The area has a famous vineyard owner HOSPICES DE BEAUNE, a charitable organization that was founded in 1443. *See also* HAUTES-CÔTES DE BEAUNE.

Côte de Brouilly AC [koht duh broo-YEE] This is one of the ten premier growing areas with their own APPELLATION (called CRU), in France's BEAUJOLAIS region. It's located upslope from the BROUILLY AC on Mont de Brouilly, where an annual pilgrimage is made each September to the Notre-Dame du Raisin (Our Lady of the Grape) chapel at the summit to ask protection for the coming harvest. These fruity wines, made from GAMAY grapes that tend to get more sunlight and therefore become riper, are more full-bodied (*see* BODY) and concentrated than those of Brouilly and some of the other Beaujolais cru. They have the highest minimum alcohol level (10.5 percent) in Beaujolais, which isn't hard to achieve because of the high sugar content of the fully ripened grapes. Côte de Brouilly AC wines can AGE well for 2 to 3 years. The acreage of this AC is smaller, making the wines more difficult to find than those from Brouilly.

Côte de Léchet *see* CHABLIS

Côte de Nuits [koht duh NWEE] The Côte de Nuits makes up the northern half of Burgundy's famous CÔTE D'OR and contains the GRAND CRU, PREMIER CRU, and village vineyards responsible for many of the renowned red BURGUNDY wines. PINOT NOIR is the grape of choice in this region, although minute amounts of white wine are produced from CHARDONNAY, PINOT BLANC, and PINOT GRIS. The Côte de Nuits is made up of numerous villages, including eight that have their own AP-PELLATIONS—CHAMBOLLE-MUSIGNY, FIXIN, GEVREY-CHAMBERTIN, MARSANNAY, MOREY-SAINT-DENIS, NUITS SAINT-GEORGE, VOSNE-ROMANÉE, and VOUGEOT. The villages of **Brochon, Comblanchien, Corgoloin, Prémeaux,** and **Fixin** can bottle their wines under the designation **Côte de Nuits-Villages AC**. The quality of the red wines from the seven village appellations and from the Côte de Nuits-Villages AC is generally quite high. However, it's the grand cru and premier cru vineyards that have created this area's esteemed reputation. The grands crus include famous names like BONNES MARES, CHAMBERTIN, CHABERTIN-CLOS DE BÈZE, CLOS DE ROCHE, CLOS DE VOUGEOT, GRANDS ECHÉZEAUX, MUSIGNY, RICHEBOURG, ROMANÉE-CONTI, and LÂ TACHE. Most wine lovers agree that these vineyards produce some of the very best red wines in the world. *See also* HAUTES-CÔTES DE NUITS.

Côte de Sézanne *see* CHAMPAGNE

Côte d'Or [koht DO*R*] The name of this very famous area in France's BURGUNDY region means "slope of gold." It's said that the name comes from the golden color of the vineyard-covered hills during autumn, not from the fact that the wines are so expensive. The Côte d'Or *is* Burgundy to many people. For all its notoriety, the Côte d'Or is rather small—just over 30 miles in length and measuring about 1½ miles at its widest point and only a few hundred yards wide at its narrowest. The Côte d'Or runs from the outskirts of Dijon in the north to just past SANTENAY in the south. It divides neatly into two parts—the CÔTE DE BEAUNE in the south and CÔTE DE NUITS in the north. The Côte de Nuits is famous for its red wines while the Côte de Beaune, although it also produces superb red wines, is more celebrated for its white wines. The area's red wines are based on PINOT NOIR; the white wines are based on CHARDONNAY. The Côte d'Or contains numerous GRAND CRU and PREMIER CRU vineyards that turn out some of the greatest wines in the world which, because of the limited vineyard area, are extremely high priced. This list of famous wines includes BONNES MARES, CHAMBERTIN, CLOS DE VOUGEOT, CORTON-CHARLEMAGNE, MONTRACHET, ROMANÉE-CONTI, LA TÂCHE, and a host of others. These grand cru vineyards are part of the many villages that produce wine in their own right under their village or communal APPELLATIONS such as CHAMBOLLE-MUSIGNY, GEVREY-CHAMBERTIN, MEURSAULT, MOREY-SAINT-DENIS, and PULIGNY-MONTRACHET. Wines that don't qualify for grand cru, premier cru, or the individual village appellations may fit into either the CÔTE DE BEAUNE-VILLAGES AC or the CÔTE DE NUITS-VILLAGES AC. If not, then they may simply fall into one of the general regional appellations such as BOURGOGNE AC or BOURGOGNE PASSE-TOUT-GRAIN AC.

Côte Mignon-La-Gaffelière *see* CANON-LA-GAFFELIÈRE, CHÂTEAU

Côte Roannaises VDQS [koht roh-ah-NEHZ] A French VDQS area located in the upper LOIRE, northwest of the city of Lyon and around the town of Roanne. Côte Roannaises produces LIGHT red and ROSÉ wines made from GAMAY with some PINOT NOIR. The wines are similiar in style to those from Beaujolais.

Côte-Rôtie AC [koht roh-TEE] The most northerly and one of the oldest APPELLATIONS in France's RHÔNE region. Its name means "roasted slope," and it consists of 300 acres of *sunbaked* vineyards, most of which are located on the steep hillside above the village of Ampuis

near the town of Vienne, south of Lyon. The vineyards are built on terraces so narrow and steep that tending and harvesting the vineyards must be done manually. There are two sections that produce the best wines—one with lighter-colored soil called **Côte Blonde** and one with darker soil called **Côte Brune**. Legend has it that Maugiron, a nobleman in this area, gave one of the two sections to his blond daughter and the other section to his brunette daughter and that over time the two sections took on the traits of their perspective owners. Côte-Rôtie produces only red wines made from SYRAH, with up to 20 percent of the white grape VIOGNIER in the blend. The wines are noted for their exotic fragrance, deep color, RICH, spicy flavor, and full BODY. Most of the better Côte-Rôtie wines will age easily for 10 or more years.

Côtes d'Auvergne VDQS [koht doh-VERN-yuh] This VDQS area, which produces red and ROSÉ wines, is located in central France around the village of Clermont-Ferrand in the upper LOIRE (east of the northern RHÔNE region). The wines, which are very BEAUJOLAIS-like, are based on the GAMAY grape blended with a small amount of PINOT NOIR. There are over fifty small villages making these wines, but only the better ones can add their name to the label. They include Boudes, Châteaugay, Chanturgue, Corent, and Médargues.

Côtes de Bergerac *see* BERGERAC

Côtes de Blaye AC *see* BLAYE

Côtes de Bourg AC *see* BOURG

Côtes de Buzet *see* BUZET

Côtes de Castillon AC [koht duh kass-tee-YAWN] APPELLATION that takes its name from the village of Castillon-la-Bataille, which is famous for being the site where the English lost a decisive battle, thus ending the Hundred Years War and England's 300-year control of the Bordeaux region. The area is located east of SAINT-ÉMILION in France's BORDEAUX region. Côtes de Castillon produces red wines from standard Bordeaux grapes but primarily uses MERLOT and CABERNET FRANC. The wines are labeled either Bordeaux Côte de Castillon AC or the higher-quality Bordeaux Supérieur Côtes de Castillon AC.

Côtes de Duras AC [koht duh doo-RAH] APPELLATION that is located east and just outside of the BORDEAUX region in southwest France. It's centered around the town of Duras in the French DÉPARTEMENT of Lot-en-Garonne. White wines dominate the production and are made from the favorite white Bordeaux varieties of SAUVIGNON

BLANC, SÉMILLON, and MUSCADELLE. The red wines are made from CABER-
NET SAUVIGNON, CABERNET FRANC, MERLOT, and MALBEC. Both red and white
wines should be consumed while they're YOUNG.

Côtes de Francs [koht duh frah*n*] A small, obscure APPELLATION
located northeast of SAINT-ÉMILION in France's BORDEAUX region. It produces mainly red wines from CABERNET SAUVIGNON, CABERNET FRANC, MER-
LOT, and MALBEC and a small amount of white wine from SAUVIGNON
BLANC, SÉMILLON, and MUSCADELLE. The wines are labeled **Bordeaux
Côtes de Francs AC**, the higher-quality **Bordeaux Supérieur Côtes
de Francs AC**, or **Côtes de Francs Liquoreux AC** for sweet white
wines. Many feel the Côtes de Francs area has plenty of potential because of its ideal soil and warm weather.

Côtes de Provence AC [koht duh praw-VAH*N*SS] The largest
APPELLATION in France's PROVENCE region, which covers some 45,000
acres. One section stretches from Toulon on the Mediterranean, east-
ward along the coast to above Saint Tropez. Another reaches from
Toulon inland in a northeastern direction, while a third section heads
west from Toulon toward Marseille. ROSÉ is the dominant wine produced in this AC, followed by red wines and a tiny amount of white.
The red and rosé wines are made from CABERNET SAUVIGNON, CINSAUT,
GRENACHE, MOURVÈDRE, SYRAH, and others, while the whites are made
from CLAIRETTE, Rolle, SÉMILLON, and Ugni Blanc (TREBBIANO). Even
though the quality of Côtes de Provence AC wines varies considerably, they appear to be generally improving, primarily because of increased planting of high-quality grape varieties like Cabernet
Sauvignon, Mourvèdre, and Syrah.

Côtes de Saint-Mont VDQS [koht duh sah*n*-MOH*N*] A VDQS
area located in southwest France just south of Armagnac and next to
MADIRAN. Côtes de Saint-Mont produces red and ROSÉ wines from
Tannat, a local variety, blended with CABERNET SAUVIGNON, CABERNET
FRANC, and MERLOT. Small amounts of DRY white wine are produced
from Jurancon, Meslier, Picpoul, and SAUVIGNON BLANC grapes.

Côtes des Blancs *see* CHAMPAGNE

Côtes du Frontonnais AC [koht deu frawn-tawn-NAY] Small
APPELLATION whose vineyards surround the towns of Fronton and
Villaudric just north of the city of Toulouse in southwest France. Côtes
de Frontonnais produces red and ROSÉ wines that must include a minimum of 50 percent of a local grape variety called NÉGRETTE. It's
blended with CABERNET SAUVIGNON, CABERNET FRANC, SYRAH, and
GRENACHE, among others. The wines can be very smooth and supple,

have flavor aspects of strawberry and raspberry, and be capable of medium-term AGING.

Côtes du Jura AC [koht deu zhoo-RAH] Large APPELLATION that covers most of eastern France's Jura region near the Swiss border. The Côtes du Jura AC encompasses red, white, and ROSÉ wine, as well as VIN JAUNE, VIN DE PAILLE, and SPARKLING WINE. The grapes used for the red and rosé wines are PINOT NOIR, Poulsard, and Trousseau; for white wines they're CHARDONNAY, PINOT BLANC, and SAVAGNIN, the Jura specialty. Among the region's vineyards that have their own appellation are ARBOIS AC, CHÂTEAU-CHALON AC, and L'ÉTOILE AC.

Côtes du Lubéron AC [koht deu leu-bay-RAWN] Located in the southern part of France's RHÔNE region, southeast of Avignon and just south of CÔTES DU VENTOUX AC, this APPELLATION was only recently (1988) accorded AC status. A majority of the wine is red and ROSÉ produced from CINSAUT, GRENACHE, MOURVÈDRE, and SYRAH. The white wines are made from CLAIRETTE, CHARDONNAY, SAUVIGNON BLANC, and Ugni Blanc (TREBBIANO). Similar to the lighter-style wines of CÔTES DU RHÔNE AC, those from Côtes du Luberon are generally LIGHT, fruity and made for early consumption.

Côtes du Marmandais VDQS [koht deu mah*r*-mah*n*-DEH] VDQS area that is in southwest France around the town of Marmande, which is on the Garonne River just east of BORDEAUX. The red wines are made from the Bordeaux favorites—CABERNET SAUVIGNON, CABERNET FRANC, and MERLOT—as well as from local varieties of Abouriou and Fer. The Bordeaux varieties of MUSCADELLE, SAUVIGNON BLANC, and SÉMILLON are the main grapes used in the DRY white wines. Generally, the wines from Côtes du Marmandais are meant for early consumption.

Côtes du Rhone [koht deu ROHN] The **Côtes du Rhone AC** is a regional APPELLATION covering various areas throughout France's RHÔNE region. It accounts for about 80 percent of the region's wines, most of which come from a large area north of Avignon in the southern Rhone. Although white wines are made, about 90 percent of Côtes du Rhone wines are red and ROSÉ. The principal red grape is GRENACHE, but CARIGNAN, Counoise, MOURVÈDRE, Terret Noir, and SYRAH are also grown. The white grapes used are Bourboulenc, CLAIRETTE, MARSANNE, Muscardine, Picardan, ROUSSANNE, and Piqupoul (or Picpoule). Though Côtes du Rhone red wines have in the past been rather heavy, the relatively recent implementation of modern winemaking techniques (including CARBONIC MACERATION) has resulted in lighter, fruitier wines. The quality of these wines varies immensely. **Côtes du Rhone-Villages**

AC is a higher-quality appellation that requires lower crop YIELDS and a higher minimum level of ALCOHOL (12½ percent versus 11 percent for Côtes du Rhône AC wines). Seventeen villages are allowed to produce wines under this appellation: **BAUMES DE VENISE**, **CAIRANNE**, **Chusclan**, **LAUDUN**, **RASTEAU**, **Roaix**, **Rochegude**, **Rousset-les-Vignes**, **Sablet**, **Saint Gervais**, **Saint Maurice-sur-Eygues**, **Saint-Pantaléon-les-Vignes**, **Séguret**, **VACQUEYRAS**, **Valréas**, **Vinsobres**, and **Visan**. These wines are generally more full-bodied (*see* BODY) than the regular Côtes du Rhône AC wines, and single estate wines are generally the best. If the wine is from a single village, the label may have the village name appended, as in *Côtes du Rhône-Chusclan*. If the wine is a blend from two or more villages, the designation Côtes du Rhône-Villages must be used.

Côtes du Roussillon [koht deu roo-see-YAW*N*] An area located in southern France's LANGUEDOC-ROUSSILLON region, not far from the Spanish border. The **Côtes du Roussillon AC** is the basic APPELLATION for the area and produces red, white, and ROSÉ wines. The reds and rosés, which constitute about 95 percent of the production, are based on CARIGNAN with some CINSAUT, GRENACHE and MOUVÈDRE. Most red grapes are processed using CARBONIC MACERATION, which results in LIGHT, fruity wines that are best drunk young. The white wines, which are generally DRY and CRISP, are made mostly with MACABEO and MALVOISIE grapes. **Côtes du Roussillon-Villages AC** is an appellation for higher-quality red wines requiring lower YIELDS and a higher minimum ALCOHOL content (12 percent versus 11½ percent for regular Côtes du Roussillon AC). This appellation, which includes the better vineyard areas from twenty-eight villages around the Argly River, is north of Perpignan. The villages of **Caramany** and **Latour-de-France**, which generally produce the best wines, are the only ones allowed to add their name to the label.

Côtes du Ventoux AC [koht deu vaw*n*-TOO] Large APPELLATION located in the southern RHÔNE, east of CHÂTEAUNEUF-DU-PAPE. It produces red, white, and ROSÉ wines from the vineyards planted on the slopes of Mount Ventoux. The red and rosé wines are made from CARIGNAN, CINSAUT, GAMAY, GRENACHE, MOUVÈDRE, and SYRAH. White wines are produced from Bourboulenc, CLAIRETTE, GRENACHE BLANC, and Ugni Blanc (TREBBIANO) grapes. Côtes du Ventoux wines are similar to those from the CÔTES DU RHÔNE AC.

Côtes du Vivarais VDQS [koht deu vee-vah-RAY] A VDQS area that produces LIGHT, easy-to-drink, mostly red wines. Côtes du Vivarais is located in the southern RHÔNE, northeast of CHÂTEAUNEUF-DU-PAPE.

The grape varieties used for red and ROSÉ wines are those popular throughout the Rhône—CARIGNAN, CINSAUT, GAMAY, GRENACHE and SYRAH—as well as CABERNET SAUVIGNON, which is now also being planted. Increasing use of Syrah and Cabernet Sauvignon is resulting in a more full-bodied (*see* BODY), full-flavored style. Bourboulenc, CLAIRETTE, GRENACHE BLANC, and Ugni Blanc (TREBBIANO) go into the area's small amount of white wine.

cotto *see* MARSALA DOC

Coucheray *see* LA LOUVIÈRE, CHÂTEAU

coulure [coo-LYUR] The failure of grapes to develop after flowering. Coulure may occur because of extended rains or very frigid weather during the flowering season. If blossoms are not pollinated, the grape fails to develop and falls off. Other grapes on the same vine may develop, and their quality will not suffer, but the YIELD from a vine with coulure may drop considerably.

Counterpoint *see* LAUREL GLEN VINEYARDS

coupage; coupe [koo-PAHZH; KOOP] *Coupe* is French for the noun form of "cut." *Coupage* refers to a cutting wine or BLENDING WINE. Such wines are added in small quantities to other wines either to correct deficiencies in them or to enhance them.

courtier [koor-TYAY] In the wine world, this French term means "wine broker." Such a person is the middleman between a small producer and a NÉGOCIANT, who bottles and ships the wines. The courtier helps establish the price that a small producer will get from the negociant for his wine.

Coutet, Château [sha-TOH koo-TEE] An excellent PREMIER CRU (first growth) CHÂTEAU located in the BARSAC AC, which is within the larger SAUTERNES AC in France's BORDEAUX region. Many feel that Château Coutet and Château CLIMENS are the two best producers in Barsac. When the right climatic conditions exist, BOTRYTIS CINEREA attacks the grapes, thereby allowing the production of DESSERT WINES. In very special years, Château Coutet produces (in addition to its regular elegant and lighter styled sweet wines) an exceptionally rich, concentrated wine labeled **Cuvée Madame**. This special, difficult-to-find wine compares favorably with Château D'YQUEM. The best vintages of the regular bottling can AGE for 25 years or so, and the Cuvée Madame can age for even longer. This château's nearly 95 acres consist of about 75 percent SÉMILLON, 23 percent SAUVIGNON BLANC, and 2 percent MUSCADELLE. The annual production ranges from 5,500 to 8,000 cases of white wine; some of it is a DRY wine labeled **Vin Sec de Château Coutet**.

Couvent-des-Jacobins, Château [sha-TOH koo-vah*n* day zhah-koh-BA*N*] This 23-acre GRAND CRU CLASSÉ château is located immediately adjacent to the town of SAINT-ÉMILION. It produces 3,500 to 4,000 cases of high-quality red wine using approximately 60 percent MERLOT, 30 percent CABERNET SAUVIGNON, and 10 percent CABERNET FRANC, with occasional use of MALBEC. Depending on the VINTAGE, these wines can AGE from 6 to 12 years. A SECOND LABEL **Beau-Mayne** is used for wines not deemed a high enough quality for the regular Château Couvent-des-Jacobins bottling.

Crabutet *see* MERLOT

crackling Term used in the United States to describe wine that's only slightly SPARKLING, much less so than CHAMPAGNE. Standard champagne is measured at 6 ATMOSPHERES of pressure, whereas crackling wines have only 1 to 2 atmospheres, similar to Italian FRIZZANTE and French PETILLANT wines. Even though a crackling wine's effervescence sometimes occurs naturally, it's often created by pumping in CARBON DIOXIDE. The crackling style is popular with moderately priced red, white, and particularly ROSÉ wines such as Portugal's Lancers and Mateus. Occasionally, the word *crackling* appears in the wine's name, as with Paul Masson Vineyards' Crackling Rosé and Crackling Chablis.

cradle; wine cradle *see* DECANTING

Cramant [kra-MAH*N*] An important wine-producing village located in the Côtes des Blancs area of France's CHAMPAGNE region. Cramant, whose vineyards are planted with CHARDONNAY, is one of only seventeen villages to have obtained a GRAND CRU rating of 100 percent for its vineyards (*see* CHAMPAGNE for explanation of percent system). The grapes from these vineyards are highly regarded, and the resulting champagne, which is often sold unblended, uses the village name on the label.

creaming *see* CREMANT

cream of tartar *see* TARTRATES

cream sherry *see* SHERRY

creamy An adjective sometimes used to describe the creamlike impression left on the palate from a SPARKLING WINE's rich, smooth froth.

crémant [kray-MAH*N*] French for "creaming," which in CHAMPAGNE describes wines that are moderately SPARKLING. This means that they've been made with slightly more than half the pressure of champagne or MOUSSEUX-style sparkling wines, but more pressure than wines described as PÉTILLANT, FRIZZANTE, or CRACKLING. Even though *crémant* is included in the name of three APPELLATION D'ORIGINE CONTRÔLÉES (CRÉMANT D'ALSACE, CRÉMANT DE BOURGOGNE, and CRÉMANT DE LOIRE), their wines are not moderately but rather fully sparkling. The sparkling wines from these three areas are made by the MÉTHODE CHAMPENOISE and have strict regulations regarding their production.

Crémant d'Alsace AC [kray-MAHN dahl-SASS (dahl-SAYSS)]
An APPELLATION in France's ALSACE region that produces dry SPARKLING WINES that must be aged for a minimum of 9 months. The grapes allowed in these wines include AUXERROIS BLANC, PINOT BLANC, PINOT GRIS, PINOT NOIR and RIESLING. The quality of the Crémant d'Alsace wines, which are made using the MÉTHODE CHAMPENOISE, is generally quite good, although they're a bit more expensive than some of the other non-CHAMPAGNE alternatives.

Crémant de Bourgogne AC [kray-MAHN deh boor-GON-yuh]
APPELLATION that covers France's BURGUNDY region and features dry SPARKLING WINES. These wines are made via MÉTHODE CHAMPENOISE from the principal grapes of ALIGOTÉ, CHARDONNAY, PINOT BLANC, and PINOT NOIR. Most of the wines produced are white, with a small amount of ROSÉ. Crémant de Bourgogne wines must be aged for a minimum of 9 months. Their quality is much higher than the wines from the region's older appellation **Bourgogne Mousseux AC**, which is being phased out. Today's Burgundian sparkling wines are viewed very positively and regarded as good, lower-priced alternatives to the wines of CHAMPAGNE.

Crémant de Loire AC [kray-MAHN deh LWAHR]
An APPELLATION covering the ANJOU, SAUMUR, and TOURAINE districts in the LOIRE Valley. It produces dry SPARKLING WINES using the MÉTHODE CHAMPENOISE. CHENIN BLANC is the primary grape, but CABERNET FRANC, CHARDONNAY, GAMAY, and Pineau d'Aunis are also used. Although there's a plentitude of sparkling wine produced in these districts, the quality standards for Crémant de Loire AC are higher. For example, this appellation requires lower yields, a higher proportion of FREE-RUN JUICE, and longer AGING periods (1 year versus 9 months for most others in the area). These higher standards are translating into better sparking wines, which are generally SOFTER and fruitier than those from the ACs of Anjou Mousseux or Saumur Mousseux.

Cremevo *see* MARSALA DOC

Crepy AC [kray-PEE] Crepy is located in eastern France's savoie region very close to the Swiss border, near the south shore of Lake Geneva. This small APPELLATION produces white wines that seem more Swiss than French—they're LIGHT, low-ALCOHOL, and made from one of Switzerland's leading grape varieties, CHASSELAS.

criadera [kree-ah-DEHR-ah] A Spanish term that translates as "nursery." In the sherry-making region around JEREZ DE LA FRONTERA, however, criadera is part of the SOLERA system for aging and ensuring the consistency of SHERRY wines. It is the nursery where young wines are managed, cared for, and evaluated. To be very precise, all levels of wine in the solera system are referred to as criaderas, with the exception of the oldest level, the solera. The next level up (next oldest) from the solera is referred to as the first criadera, the level after that, the second criadera, and so forth. Some producers have up to fourteen levels in their solera systems.

crianza [kree-AHN-zah] The Spanish term meaning "breeding" or "upbringing." "Con crianza" or "vino de crianza" on a wine label refers to the AGING a wine receives. The exact rules are defined by the governing body of each DENOMINACION DE ORIGEN (DO). If a DO has no specific rules, a crianza wine must receive a minimum of 2 years aging either in a tank, an oak barrel, or a bottle. Many of the DOs require that 1 of the 2 years be in oak barrels. By contrast, red RESERVA wines require a minimum of 3 years of aging with at least 1 year in oak barrels; ROSÉ and white RESERVAS require a minimum aging of 2 years with a no less than 6 months in oak barrels. The words **Sin crianza** on a label indicate that the wine did not receive minimum aging and was bottled young.

Criolla *see* MISSION

Criots-Bâtard-Montrachet AC [kree-oh bah-TAHR mohn-rah-SHAY] A 3.9-acre vineyard that is the smallest of the GRANDS CRUS in the CÔTE DE BEAUNE district of France's BURGUNDY region. The vineyard is next to the grand cru BÂTARD-MONTRACHET and is the only grand cru located entirely in the village of CHASSAGNE-MONTRACHET. Considered among the world's best, Criots-Bâtard-Montrachet AC wines are made from CHARDONNAY grapes. They're similar to, although perhaps slightly LIGHTER than, those from the neighboring Bâtard-Montrachet AC.

crisp A descriptor for wine that has a fresh, lively ACIDITY that, although noticeable, doesn't overpower the other components. Crispness is a desirable trait in white wines.

Cristal *see* CHAMPAGNE

Croatina; Croattina [kraw-ah-TEE-nah] Red wine grape that is grown in the southwest area of Italy's LOMBARDY region. The best known Croatina wines are from the OLTREPÒ PAVESE area, where this grape is called *Bonarda* (not to be confused with a different variety, *Bonarda Piemontese*, also called BONARDA). To add to the confusion, Croatina has achieved DOC status in this area under the name *Bonarda dell'Oltrepò Pavese*. These DOC wines are SOFT and ROUND, yet LIVELY and fruity with characteristics of plums and cherries; they generally have a bitter FINISH. Croatina is often BLENDED with terrific results, as in EMILIA-ROMAGNA'S GUTTURNIO, where it's used to soften the BARBERA in this blend. Croatina's also known as *Neretto* and *Uva Vermiglia.*

Croft Founded in 1678 and originally known as Phayre and Bradley, Croft is one of the older PORT firms. The name was changed when the Croft family became involved in 1736. In 1911 the company was purchased by Gilbey's. Both Gilbey's and Croft are now part of International Distillers and Vintners. Croft produces a wide variety of ports including the *Distinction Tawny* and the *Distinction Finest Reserve*, a ruby port. Croft's main vineyards are located at the Quinta da Roeda, and occasionally a single-quinta port is bottled using that name (usually only in years when a traditional vintage port is not declared). Croft also owns two other port firms, Delaforce and Morgan, and is now involved with the production of SHERRY through its sister firm Croft Jerez.

La Croix *see* DUCRU-BEAUCAILLOU, CHÂTEAU

La Croix de Mazerat *see* BEAUSÉJOUR, CHÂTEAU

Croizet-Bages, Château [sha-TOH krwah-zeh BAHZH] CINQUIÈME CRU (fifth growth) CHÂTEAU located in the PAUILLAC AC in the MÉDOC district of France's BORDEAUX region. It consists of approximately 60 acres and annually produces about 8,000 to 10,000 cases of good-quality red wine. The wines are made with around 38 percent CABERNET SAUVIGNON, 30 percent CABERNET FRANC, 30 percent MERLOT, and small amounts of MALBEC and PETIT VERDOT. They're much lighter and not as highly regarded as those from the neighboring Château LYNCH-BAGES. Because they're lighter, these wines will AGE for only about 5 to 6 years. The SECOND LABEL for this château is **Enclos de Moncabon**. This is also the second label for Château RAUZAN-GASSIES—both châteaus are owned by the Quié family.

Cronin Vineyards [KROH-nihn] A home winemaker whose hobby grew into a small business while employed as an IBM executive in California's Silicon Valley, Duane Cronin took early retirement in 1992 to devote more time to his viticultural venture. His winery is located in the ever-expanding basement of his home, which is just above the small town of Woodside in the Santa Cruz Mountains. Although Cronin produces just over 2,000 cases of wine each year, his white wines are considered some of California's best. This esteemed reputation comes from Cronin Vineyards' CHARDONNAY wines, which are made from grapes from four different areas and bottled separately. These four areas are Ventana Vineyards (MONTEREY COUNTY), NAPA VALLEY, ALEXANDER VALLEY, and SANTA CRUZ MOUNTAINS. Cronin Vineyards also produces two red wines, both blends of CABERNET SAUVIGNON and MERLOT. One is from the Santa Cruz Mountains; the other comes from the STAGS LEAP DISTRICT.

Croque-Michotte, Château [sha-TOH krawk mee-SHAWT] CHÂTEAU located in the SAINT-ÉMILION AC right next to POMEROL in the BORDEAUX region. This GRAND CRU CLASSÉ property annually produces about 6,500 to 7,000 cases of good-quality red wine from its nearly 37 acres. The blend of grapes used is approximately 75 percent MERLOT, 20 percent CABERNET FRANC, and 5 percent CABERNET SAUVIGNON. These SUPPLE, full-bodied (*see* BODY) wines mature early. The better VINTAGES can AGE for about 10 years.

cross; crossing *n*. A vine or grape created by breeding two varieties of the same genus (VITIS VINIFERA, for example). Crosses are created in an effort to produce a plant with the best traits of its parents, such as high productivity, disease resistance, and/or better adaptability to environmental conditions. Some of the better-known crosses are Germany's MÜLLER-THURGAU (a RIESLING and SYLVANER cross), California's RUBY CABERNET (a CABERNET SAUVIGNON and CARIGNAN cross) and South Africa's PINOTAGE (a PINOT NOIR and CINSAULT cross). *See also* CLONE; and HYBRID. *v*. The act of creating or breeding a cross from members of the same species. *See also* HYBRIDIZE.

Crouchen [kroo-SHEN] In South Africa, where this white-wine grape is known variously as *South African Riesling, Cape Riesling,* and *Paarl Riesling,* Crouchen has long been thought to be RIESLING. The Australians believed it was SÉMILLON but, strangely, called it *Clare Riesling.* It wasn't until the mid-1970s that this grape was identified as Crouchen, a variety from the Landes region of southwest France (where it's now almost extinct). Crouchen continues to be grown in both South Africa and Australia, where it produces pleasant, lightly AROMATIC wines that are sometimes vinified DRY and other times with a bit of RESIDUAL SUGAR. Other names for Crouchen include *Cruchen Blanc* and *Navarre Blanc*.

crown cap A cap, resembling that on a beer bottle, that is used during BOTTLE FERMENTATION when making SPARKLING WINE via MÉTHODE CHAMPENOISE. The crown cap has a small plastic receptacle attached to it that fits inside the bottle, into which the yeast sediment settles during the RIDDLING process.

Crozes-Hermitage AC [k*r*awz ehr-mee-TAHZH] The largest APPELLATION in France's northern RHÔNE region. The vineyards of the eleven villages that make up Crozes-Hermitage AC surround the more famous HERMITAGE vineyards. Crozes-Hermitage produces red wines from SYRAH and white wines from MARSANNE and ROUSSANNE. The wines from the area vary considerably in quality because some of the vineyards are located in the superior hilly areas, while others are situated on the less-desirable flatlands. The better Crozes-Hermitage wines bear a resemblance to those of the Hermitage AC, but usually without the concentrated flavors and richness.

cru [KROO] A French term for "growth." When related to wine, *cru* is usually combined with another descriptor (as in PREMIER CRU, CRU BOURGEOIS, or CRU CLASSÉ) to indicate a vineyard's ranking. In BEAUJOLAIS the term refers to the top ten villages that have their own APPELLATIONS. In other areas in France, such as the COTEAUX DU LANGUEDOC AC, *cru* identifies villages with exceptional-quality wines that deserve special reference.

cru artisan [kroo AHR-tih-san] Although the term is no longer used, *cru artisan* describes a category for CHÂTEAUS in BORDEAUX that ranks below CRU BOURGEOIS.

cru bourgeois [kroo boor-ZWAH] A category for châteaus of the MÉDOC that ranks just below that of CRU CLASSÉ. When the CLASSIFICATION OF 1855 was completed, thousands of châteaus had been excluded. The cru bourgeois category was created as a means of including the best of these. In 1932 the first list of cru bourgeois châteaus was created by the Bordeaux Chamber of Commerce. It included 444 châteaus classified in three categories. The highest ranking—*cru bourgeois supérieurs exceptionnel* (sometimes called *cru exceptionnel* or *cru bourgeois exceptionnel*)—originally included only six châteaus and was limited to those from the area in the HAUT-MÉDOC where the cru classé châteaus were located. The next category was *cru bourgeois* *supérieurs* with 99 châteaus; the third category was *cru bourgeois* with 339 chateaus. Châteaus in any of these three categories may, however, only use the term "cru bourgeois" on their wine labels. An organization known as *Syndicat des Crus Bourgeois* updated this list in 1966 and again in 1978. However, their list includes only member châteaus, which eliminates many good châteaus who choose not to join. The Syndicat's 1978 list included 127 châteaus, of which only 18 are included in the top category. Ranked below crus bourgeois are two additional categories that are no longer used—CRU ARTISAN and CRU PAYSAN.

cru bourgeois exceptionnel *see* CRU BOURGEOIS

cru bourgeois supérieurs *see* CRU BOURGEOIS

cru bourgeois supérieurs exceptionnel *see* CRU BOURGEOIS

cru classé [kroo klah-SAY] 1. French for "classed growth," indicating that a CHÂTEAU (most often in BORDEAUX) is ranked in the top category. 2. The famous CLASSIFICATION OF 1855 divided the crus classés for Bordeaux's MÉDOC region red wines into five subcategories—PREMIER CRU (first growth) through CINQUIÈME CRU (fifth-growth). The white wines of SAUTERNES were divided into only 2 subcategories—premier cru and DEUXIÈMES CRU (second growth). 3. The term *cru classé* is also used in a similar fashion when referring to other classifications such as the one established in 1953 for the red wines of GRAVES, which didn't create any subcategories but simply listed thirteen cru classé châteaus. In 1959, eight white-wine châteaus in Graves were given cru classé status and—as with the red-wine châteaus—the right to use GRAND CRU CLASSÉ (Great Classed Growth) on their labels. In the SAINT-ÉMILION region there was a 1954 classification (which was revised in 1969 and 1985) that ranked the châteaus in three major categories—PREMIER GRAND CRU CLASSÉ (First Great Growth Class), Grand Cru Classé, and Grand Cru. Saint-Émilion's Premier Grand Cru Classé is similiar to the Médoc's Cru Classé.

cru exceptionnel *see* CRU BOURGEOIS

Cruian *see* CORVINA

cru paysan [kroo peh-SAN] Though no longer used, this term was once applied to CHÂTEAUS in BORDEAUX that were ranked below CRU ARTISAN.

crush A term used in California and other parts of the United States referring to the time when grapes are harvested and crushed to make wine.

crusher; crusher-stemmer A **crusher** is a mechanical device consisting of paddles and rollers that break the grape berries and extract the juice. Crushing must be delicate enough so that the grape seeds are not broken, which would release their bitterness into the wine. With a crusher, a screen is necessary to separate the juice, skins, and seeds from the stems and leaves. With a **crusher-stemmer**, however, the stems and leaves are automatically expelled. Large commercial wineries have continuous-feed crusher-stemmers that can process up to 150 tons of grapes an hour.

crushing The most common way of extracting the juice from grapes (PRESSING is the second most frequent method). At commercial wineries, grape clusters are dumped into a receiving hopper that feeds the recently picked grapes into a CRUSHER (or crusher-stemmer). There the grapes are broken, and the juice, skins, and seeds are separated from any stems and leaves that are attached. White-wine juice is normally separated from the skins and seeds, which are pressed for further juice extraction. For red wines, the juice, skins, and seeds (MUST) are then placed in tanks or vats for FERMENTATION.

crust Another name for the SEDIMENT thrown off by red wines as they age in bottles. The use of the term *crust* is generally associated with vintage port (*see* PORT).

crusted port *see* PORT

cryoextraction [kri-oh-ex-STRAK-shuhn] French term for the practice of subjecting grapes to very low temperatures (around 20°F) so that only the most concentrated grape juice will be extracted during PRESSING. The cryoextraction process begins by putting freshly culled grapes into cold storage until they reach a desired temperature (the temperature can be adjusted upward or downward in accordance with the quality level of the grapes). Because riper, better-quality grapes have a higher concentration of sugars, their freezing point is lower than that of less ripe grapes. Once the grapes reach the proper temperature, they're immediately pressed. As a result of the cryoextraction process, only the premium juice is expressed because the lower-quality (not perfectly ripe) grapes are still frozen. The results are similar to those that occur naturally when frozen grapes are picked to make EISWEIN. Cryoextraction is now being used by some SAUTERNES estates in poorer VINTAGES (particularly wet years) when the quality of individual gapes is inconsistent. With the help of this process, vintners can produce the renowned DESSERT WINES for which Sauternes is famous.

crystals Small, innocuous fragments of tartaric acid found in some wines.

Cugnette *see* JACQUÈRE

cultivars *see* SOUTH AFRICA

Cune *see* COMPAÑÍA VINÍCOLA DEL NORTE DE ESPAÑA

Curé-Bon-la-Madeleine, Château [sha-TOH kyoo-ray bawn lah mad-uh-LEHN] CHÂTEAU that is a small (12-acre) GRAND CRU CLASSÉ located in SAINT-ÉMILION in France's BORDEAUX region. The vineyard is about 12 acres and consists of approximately 90 percent MERLOT, with small amounts of CABERNET SAUVIGNON and MALBEC. Only about 2,000 cases of red wine are produced annually. This difficult-to-find wine is generally described as being powerful and CONCENTRATED. It's capable of AGING for around 15 years.

cutting wine *see* BLENDING WINE

cuvaison [koo-veh-ZOHN] The French term for the period when grape juice is kept in contact with the skins and seeds during both FERMENTATION and MACERATION. Critical in the making of red wines, cuvaison allows color, TANNINS, and AROMA to be transferred from the skins and seeds to the juice. For ROSÉ or BLUSH WINES the cuvaison would be very short (measured in terms of hours) so that not much color or tannin would be extracted from skins and seeds.

Cuvaison Winery [KOO-vay-sawn (Fr. koo-veh-ZOHN)] NAPA VALLEY winery that is located northwest of St. Helena and west of Calistoga on the Silverado Trail. However, the 400 acres (300 of which are planted) it owns are located in the CARNEROS region. Cuvaison Winery, which was founded in 1970, has seen several owners—it's been owned since 1986 by a Swiss family, the Schmidheinys. Early on, this winery was known for its bold, tannic CABERNET SAUVIGNON and ZINFANDEL wines made from hillside grapes. Today it purchases Cabernet grapes from growers in Rutherford and Oakville, and produces a highly regarded Cabernet Sauvignon in a RICH but more elegant style. However, Cuvaison is now better known for its CHARDONNAY wines made from its Carneros vineyard grapes. Cuvaison

Chardonnays are produced in both a regular bottling and a RESERVE. A MERLOT, also from Carneros, also receives high marks; limited quantities of a PINOT NOIR were recently introduced. Cuvaison Winery produces about 50,000 cases a year, with about 70 to 75 percent of that being Chardonnay. A SECOND LABEL, **Calistoga Vineyards**, was introduced in 1992.

cuve [KOOV] The French term for "vat" or "tank," generally associated with a large vat or tank used for fermenting or blending.

cuve-close *see* CHARMAT PROCESS

cuvée [koo-VAY] Term derived from the French CUVE (which means vat) that denotes the "contents of a vat." In France's CHAMPAGNE region it refers to a blended batch of wines. In Champagne the large houses create their traditional (and very secret) house-style cuvées by blending various wines before creating the final product via MÉTHODE CHAMPENOISE. A deluxe version is often referred to as *cuvée speciale*; VIN DE CUVÉE refers to wine from the first pressing. Outside Champagne the term *cuvée* is also used for still wines. It may refer to wines blended from different vineyards, or even different varieties. Occasionally, the word *cuvée* followed by a number is used to identify a specific batch of wines blended separately and distinctly from others. Some French producers, notably those in SAUTERNES, identify their best wines with the term, **Tête de cuvée.**

cuvée de prestige *see* CHAMPAGNE

Cuvée Madame *see* COUTET, CHÂTEAU; SUDUIRAUT, CHÂTEAU

cuvée speciale *see* CHAMPAGNE

CVNE *see* COMPAÑÍA VINÍCOLA DEL NORTE DE ESPAÑA

Cynthiana *see* VITIS AESTIVALIS

Les Cyprès de Climens *see* CLIMENS, CHÂTEAU

Cyprus [SI-pruhs] Independent island republic located south of Turkey in the Mediterranean. Most of the better vineyards are situated in the foothills on the south side of the Troodos Mountains. Because it's a former British colony, Cyprus is, to a degree, still tied to the British idea of wines and winemaking. The best Cypriot wines are their Spanish-style SHERRIES and a DESSERT WINE called **Commandaria**. The latter, which is light red- or amber-colored and can be rich, intense and luscious, is made from various varieties of dried, raisined grapes. The island's primary grape is the red Mavron, which is used in their full-bodied red wines and ROSÉS and for the Commandaria. Small amounts of the red grapes, Opthalmo and Marathefticon, are also grown. The primary white grapes are Xynisteri and Muscat of Alexandria (MUSCAT). Other European varieties are being introduced to Cyprus, but with caution, because the island has never been afflicted with PHYLLOXERA.

La Dame de Montrose *see* MONTROSE, CHÂTEAU

Dame Jeanne *see* DEMIJOHN

Les Damodes *see* NUITS-SAINT-GEORGES

Daniel Estate *see* DOMINUS ESTATE

John Daniel Society *see* DOMINUS ESTATE

Dão DOC [DOWNG] Located in north central Portugal, this well-known wine-producing region's vineyards are situated in the mountainous area surrounding the city of Viseu. Dão, a DENOMINAÇÃO DE ORIGEM CONTROLADA, is best known for BIG, full-bodied (*see* BODY) red wines that require considerable AGING to SOFTEN. Some feel the lengthy aging is a detriment because the wines lose much of their fruitiness. Since Portugal joined the European Economic Community, control has been taken from the local cooperatives that had a monopoly on wine-making. Such changes are allowing independent producers to become more involved, and those who use more modern winemaking techniques are producing fruiter, more youthful wines. The huge SOGRAPE company is leading this new trend with its **Quinta dos Carvalhais** estate. The red wines here are made from a large variety of approved grapes, but mostly from Alfrocheiro Preto, Alvarelhao, Bastardo, Tinta Amarela, and TOURIGA NACIONAL. A small amount of DRY white wine is made from Arinto, Assario, Barcelo, Borrado das Moscas, Branco, Cerceal, Encruzado, and VERDHELO.

dated port *see* COLHEITA

La Dauphin Château Guiraud *see* GUIRAUD, CHÂTEAU

Dauzac, Château [sha-TOH doh-ZAHK] A CINQUIÈME CRU (fifth growth) CHÂTEAU located in the MARGAUX AC in the MÉDOC district of BORDEAUX. It's about 123 acres in size and produces approximately 18,000 to 22,000 cases of good-quality red wine each year. The grapes used are around 60 percent CABERNET SAUVIGNON, 30 percent MERLOT, 5 percent CABERNET FRANC and 5 percent PETIT VERDOT. Most critics think the wines are rather mediocre and that the château would be downgraded to a CRU BOURGEOIS if a reclassification were to take place. AGING capability of these wines is about 10 years.

Davis, University of California The small town of Davis is located in northern California just west of Sacramento. It's home to the University of California, Davis, and its well-known (at least in wine circles) Viticulture and Enology Department. In addition to training a mulitude of today's top winemakers, this Department is a leader in many areas of research and development including grape varieties and their CLONES, ROOTSTOCKS, VINEYARD DISEASES, and winemaking techniques.

deacidification [dee-uh-SIHD-ih-fih-KAY-shuhn] The process of reducing the titratable acidity (*see* ACIDS) in wine, grape juice, or MUST. There are numerous methods for doing this including COLD STABILIZATION and AMELIORATION.

decanter A glass container into which wine is decanted (*see* DECANTING). A decanter can be a simple CARAFE but is generally more elegant and often made of hand-cut crystal.

decanting [dee-KANT-ing] Decanting is done either to separate the wine from any sediment deposited during the AGING process or to allow a wine to BREATHE in order to enhance its flavor. When decanting an older wine, care should be taken not to disturb the sediment. A wine basket (also called *cradle* or *Burgundy basket*) can be used to move the bottle in a horizontal position from where it was stored to where it will be decanted. This position keeps the sediment from disseminating throughout the wine. If such a basket isn't available, stand the bottle upright for an hour so that the sediment can settle to the bottom of the bottle. Once the foil and cork are removed, gently wipe the mouth of the bottle. Then begin slowly pouring the wine into a DECANTER, placing a strong light (a candle is charming, but a flashlight is more practical) behind or below the neck of the bottle. The light lets you see the first signs of sediment, at which point you stop pouring. *See also* Opening and Serving Still Wine, page 590.

Declared Geographical Origin *see* BULGARIA

Decoy *see* DUCKHORN VINEYARDS

deep Many aspects of a wine (its COLOR, flavor or BOUQUET) can be deep which, in the wine world, is a word that signifies intensity. *See also* DEPTH.

dégorgement *see* DISGORGE

degree days *see* CLIMATE REGIONS OF CALIFORNIA

Dehlinger Winery [DAY-leen-ger] RUSSIAN RIVER AVA winery that was started by Tom Dehlinger in 1976. It's become a highly regarded producer of CHARDONNAY and PINOT NOIR wines, both of which are noted for their RICH, COMPLEX styles. This winery annually produces 8,000 to 9,000 cases of wine (all ESTATE BOTTLED) from its 50-acre vineyard. Smaller amounts of CABERNET FRANC, CABERNET SAUVIGNON, and MER-

LOT are also planted. Tiny lots of Cabernet Franc and Merlot VARIETAL WINES are usually made, with the remainder of these two varieties going into Dehlinger's Cabernet Sauvignon wines. Although not as consistent as the Pinot Noir and Chardonnay wines, the Cabernet Sauvignons are also well received.

Deidesheim [DI-duhss-hime] One of several adjoining towns, including FORST, RUPPETSBERG, and WACHENHEM, that produces some of the best wines of Germany's RHEINPFALZ region. This picturesque town has a number of fine estates including BASSERMAN-JORDAN, von Buhl, and Deinhard. Deidesheim is located in the BEREICH Mittelhaardt/Deutsche Weinstrasse and has vineyards located in three of the area's GROSSLAGEN—Hofstück, Mariengarten, and Schnepfenflug. There are a number of excellent EIZELLAGEN including **Grainhübel, Herrgottsacker, Hohenmorgan, Kieselberg, Langenmorgen, Leinhöhle**, and **Paradiesgarten**. Over 50 percent of the vineyards attached to Deidesheim are planted with RIESLING, the variety used to produce Deidesheim's most distinguished wines. The town's reputation for fine wines extends back several centuries.

dekerra *see* BRETTANOMYCES

delicate; delicacy A term used to describe quality wines that are LIGHT, well-BALANCED, and REFINED. It may also apply to a fine wine that's poised to decline.

Del Mar *see* MORGAN WINERY

De Loach Vineyards [deh LOHSH] In 1970 Cecil and Christine De Loach bought their first 24-acre vineyard in California's RUSSIAN RIVER area. They made their first De Loach Vineyards' wines in 1975 and built the original winery building in 1979. Today, De Loach Vineyards owns 200 acres, has a long-term lease on another 75 acres and produces nearly 100,000 cases of wine each year. The initial wines were ZINFANDEL, and today there are five well-made Zins available, three of which are VINEYARD-DESIGNATED (Barbieri Ranch, Papera Ranch, and Pelletti Ranch) and available in limited quantities. The other two are a standard ESTATE-BOTTLED Russian River Zinfandel that's made with grapes from the aforementioned vineyards plus other De Loach vineyards and the O.F.S. Estate-Bottled Zinfandel. O.F.S. is said to stand for "our finest selection," and is similiar to RESERVE wines from other wineries. De Loach production is now dominated by CHARDONNAY and WHITE ZINFANDEL, both of which are highly regarded. In addition, De Loach makes CABERNET SAUVIGNON, PINOT NOIR, SAUVIGNON BLANC, and a LATE HARVEST and regular GEWÜRZTRAMINER. O.F.S. bottlings of Chardonnay and sometimes Cabernet Sauvignon and Pinot Noir are made from selected high-quality batches of grapes.

demi [DEHM-ee] A French term meaning "half" or "lesser," used in combination with other words as a modifier, such as with DEMI-SEC.

demijohn [DEHM-ee-jon] A large squat bottle with a short narrow neck and usually covered in wicker. Demijohns can hold from 1 to 10 gallons. The word is thought to be derived from the French *Dame Jeanne* (Lady Jane), a term which is also still used to describe this bottle.

demi-sec [DEHM-ee sehk] A French term meaning "half dry," used to describe a sweet SPARKLING WINE. *See also* SEC.

Denominação de Origem Controlada (DOC) The highest quality wine category in Portugal. The old term *Região Demarcada* ("Demarcated Region") was replaced by *Denominação de Origem Controlada (DOC)*, which means "Controlled Denomination of Origin." This category is roughly equivalent to the French APPELLATION D'ORIGINE CONTRÔLÉE in that there are rules relating to yields, density of planting, etc. Although Portugal was actually the first country to implement a national APPELLATION system (in 1756), there has been much confusion as the country tries to adjust to its entry into the European Economic Community (1987). Portugal reviewed the structure of the *Região Demarcada* (now DOC) system and added a few regions to increase the number to 14. The fourteen DOCs are: BAIRRADA, known for TANNIC, highly ACIDIC red wine; Bucelas, which produces full-bodied white wines; CARCAVELOS, with its sweet and DRY fortified white wines; COLARES, known for tannic full-bodied red wines; DAO, which makes big, full-bodied red wines; Lagoa; Lagos; MADEIRA, famous for its FORTIFIED wines; PORT and DOURO, which, in addition to the esteemed port wines, produce highly regarded red and white table wines; Portimao; Setubal, with its sweet, fortified white wines; and Travora and VINHO VERDE, known for fresh, fruity red and white "green wines." Of these fourteen DOCS, Langoa, Langos, Protiamo, and Travora have yet to achieve much of a reputation. Officials are also reorganizing a category called *Indicação de Proveniencia Regulamentada (IPR)* for lower-quality wines.

Denominación de Origen (DO) [deh-naw-mee-nah-THYON deh aw-REE-hen] The Spanish system for wine classification that fits the requirments of the European Economic Community's top-quality wine category. This "designation of origin" is similar to France's APPEL-

LATION D'ORIGINE CONTRÔLÉE. Most experts, however, don't think the Spanish standards are as high because approximately 50 percent of the Spanish wines qualify, compared to only about 25 percent of those in France. To qualify for *Denominación de Origen (DO)* status, wines must meet specific requirements including geographic areas where the grapes must be grown and the wines made, grape varieties permitted in that area, vineyard practices, maximum YIELD, minimum ALCOHOL content, and winemaking practices. The first DO—RIOJA—was established in 1926; there are now close to forty areas with DO status. Each DO has its own governing body (*consejo regulador*) that may implement stricter rules for the CRIANZA, RESERVA, and GRAN RESERVA wines than those imposed by federal standards. Spanish officials have recently announced a new higher category, DENOMINACIÓN DE ORIGEN CALIFICADA.

Denominación de Origen Calificada (DOCa) [deh-naw-mee-nah-THYON deh aw-REE-hen kah-lee-fee-KAH-dah] A term meaning "qualified designation of origin," referring to a new top category for Spanish wines. It was presumably introduced as a response to the criticism that many of the holders of DENOMINACIÓN DE ORIGEN (DO) status did not produce wines of acceptably high quality. This new DOCa classification adds the word *calificada* ("qualified"), indicating that it has more exacting standards than those established for DOs. So far, Spain's RIOJA region is the only one that's met the definitive standards of the new DOCa category.

Denominazione di Origine Controllata (DOC) [deh-NAW-mee-nah-TSYAW-neh dee oh-REE-jee-neh con-traw-LAH-tah] Established in 1963 and implemented in 1966, the *Denominazione di Origine Controllata (DOC)* ("Controlled Denomination of Origin") is Italy's equivalent to France's APPELLATION D'ORIGINE CONTRÔLÉE. DOCs are defined by the geographic area of production for each wine, the varieties that can be used, the minimum ALCOHOL content, the maximum YIELD, and specifications for AGING. In 1990 tasting commissions introduced standards for appearance, color, bouquet, and flavor. In addition, chemical analysis is performed to determine alcohol levels, ACIDITY, and RESIDUAL SUGAR content. As with the systems implemented in France, Spain, and other countries, the DOC system doesn't guarantee quality, but it does nudge a majority of the wines in that direction. There are now over 250 DOC zones, including a small group belonging to a new, more elite level called DENOMINAZIONE DI ORIGINE CONTROLLATA E GARANTITA. An issue that many wine experts have with the DOC rules is their strict disposition toward traditional winemaking techniques and grape varieties. They haven't adapted to the many new techniques or the successful production of wines from nontraditional varieties (for each particular growing region). As a result, many excellent wines that are being produced by these modern methods or using nontraditional grapes can't qualify for DOC status. Instead, they must use the lower-ranking VINO DA TAVOLA classification on their labels.

Denominazione di Origine Controllata e Garantita (DOCG)

[deh-NAW-mee-nah-TSYAW-neh dee oh-REE-jee-neh con-traw-LAH-tah eh gah-rahn-TEE-tah] Category that embodies a premier group of growing areas in Italy whose regulations encompass all laws of the DENOMINAZIONE DI ORIGINE CONTROLLATA but are even more demanding. Meaning "Controlled and Guaranteed Denomination of Origin," the *Denominazione di Origine Controllata e Garantita* focuses on the key word *garantita*—the Italian government's quality "guarantee." Government testers examine and taste the wines prior to awarding DOCG status. The producers then bottle the qualifying wines, securing them with a government seal (a colored strip placed over the capsule or cork). The words "Denominazione di Origine Controllata e Garantita" are incorporated into the label. The first five DOCGs were BAROLO and BARBARESCO in the PIEDMONT region and BRUNELLO DI MONTALCINO, VINO NOBILE DI MONTEPULCIANO, and CHIANTI in the TUSCANY region. These five areas all received general approval, but the addition of the sixth area, ALBANA DI ROMAGNA, has been quite controversial. Many experts feel the quality of the wines from this area aren't comparable to the other five DOCGs. Recent DOCG additions include TAURASI Reserve in CAMPANIA, CARMIGNANO and VERNACCIA DI SAN GIMIGNANO in Tuscany, ASTI SPUMANTE, MOSCATO D'ASTI and GATTINARA in Piedmont, and TORGIANO and SAGRANTINO DI MONTEFALCO in UMBRIA. Others appearing to be close to receiving DOCG status include FRASCATI in LATIUM and ORVIETO in Umbria.

département [day-pahr-tehr-MAHN] A French term referring to an administrative area that's similiar to a county within a state in the United States. The French mainland has 95 departements grouped into twenty-two regions.

deposit The SEDIMENT that settles in the bottle as a wine ages. Such deposits occur in many red wines and occasionally in some whites. It's a natural process and doesn't signify that there's anything wrong with the wine.

depth A wine with flavor depth is full-bodied (*see* BODY), INTENSE and has multiple dimensions of flavor and BOUQUET. In this context, depth is similar in meaning to COMPLEXITY. *Depth of color* in a wine refers to the color intensity and is an indicator of quality that, in most instances, accurately predicts (particularly with red wine) how full-bodied a wine will be. The intrinsic degree of color in various grape varieties most certainly influences the depth of a wine's color. The rule of thumb when comparing like wines is that the deeper-colored wines are generally made from higher-quality grapes and will therefore have fuller flavor and body. A pale color intensity, especially in a red wine, can have several meanings—from overplanted vineyards to underripe grapes—any of which diminish a wine's character and flavor. *See also* DEEP.

dessert wine   Generally speaking any of a wide variety of sweet wines (sometimes fortified with brandy), all of which are compatible with desserts. More specifically in the United States, *dessert wine* is a legal term referring to all FORTIFIED wines (whether or not sweet), which typically range from 16 to 21 percent in ALCOHOL BY VOLUME. Some of the more popular dessert wines are LATE HARVEST RIESLING, PORT, SAUTERNES, SHERRY, and AUSLESE.

destemming   [dee-STEHM-ming] The process of removing grape stems from the MUST (juice, pulp, skin, and seeds) prior to FERMENTATION so that, during fermentation, bitter TANNINS in the stems won't transfer to the wine and make it HARSH. During the fermentation of red wines, the juice is in contact with the skins and seeds, which also contain tannins. Destemming is important so that such wines, which obtain enough tannins from the skin and seeds to give them BALANCE, don't become overtly tannic. The French call this process *égrappage.*

Deutscher Sekt   *see* SEKT

Deutscher Tafelwein (DTW)   [DOYT-shur TAH-fuhl-vyn] A phrase indicating that a wine is 100 percent "German TABLE WINE," used to distinguish it from other European countries using German-style labeling. *Deutscher Tafelwein* is Germany's lowest category of wine and must contain a minimum of 8½ percent of ALCOHOL BY VOLUME. The labels for such wine must indicate the name of one of Germany's broad growing regions—Bayern, Neckar, Oberhein, or Rhein-Mosel. The term *Deutscher Tafelwein* is officially recognized by the European Economic Community, meaning other members must abide by the labeling conventions. When used by itself, the word *Tafelwein* on a label indicates that the wine is not German; the label should specify the country of origin. *See also* GERMANY; LANDWEIN; QUALITÄTSWEIN BESTIMMTER ANBAUGEBIETE; QUALITÄTSWEIN MIT PRÄDIKAT.

Deutschherrenberg *see* ZELTINGEN

Deutz *see* CHAMPAGNE

deuxième cru [deu-zyem KROO] French phrase that means "second growth," the second-highest subcategory of the MÉDOC and SAUTERNES area's CRUS CLASSÉS (classed growths). Fifteen of the Médoc's CHÂTEAUS were included in this category when it was established in the CLASSIFICATION OF 1855; that number remains unchanged today.

deuxième taille *see* TAILLE

developed A term that refers to a wine's state of maturity and drinkability. A *well-developed* wine is perfectly matured and ready to drink, while one that's *underdeveloped* needs AGING before being consumed. An *over-developed* wine is just that—over-the-hill and on the decline.

Dézaley [day-zah-LEH] One of the top wine producing COMMUNES in Switzerland's VAUD canton. It's located in the LAVAUX growing zone, where steep vineyards slope down toward Lake Geneva. The primary grape is CHASSELAS, which is generally viewed as producing white wines of neutral character. Here, however, it performs extremely well and produces LIVELY, AROMATIC wines.

Dezizes-lès-Maranges *see* CÔTE DE BEAUNE

DGO *see* BULGARIA

diacetyl *see* MALOLACTIC FERMENTATION

Diamant Bleu *see* CHAMPAGNE

Diamond Creek Vineyards Tiny CABERNET SAUVIGNON specialist situated on Diamond Mountain southwest of Calistoga, California, in the NAPA VALLEY. When the vineyards were first planted by Al Brounstein in the late 1960s, there were three separate blocks, which he named in accordance with their attributes. The three plots are the 8-acre Volcanic Hill (which has volcanic soil), the 7-acre Red Rock Terrace (which has rich, red iron deposits), and the 5-acre Gravelly Meadow (which is noted for its rocky, gravelly soil). These separate vineyards produce distinctively different wines that are bottled separately. Grape juice from a fourth 1-acre block called Winery Lake is usually blended with the Gravelly Meadow output but is occasionally bottled separately. The Diamond Creek wines are generally dense, dark, and somewhat AUSTERE when young but are capable of long AGING. Diamond Creek produces between 2,000 and 3,000 cases of these hard-to-find wines.

Die *see* CLAIRETTE DE DIE

Dienheim [DEEN-hime] An important wine-producing town located just south of OPPENHEIM in the RHEINHESSEN region. Although overshadowed by the reputation of Oppenheim, Dienheim is nonetheless recognized for producing high-quality wines from RIESLING and SYLVANER. Vineyards attached to Dienheim are found in GROSSLAGEN Oppenheimer **Krötenbrunnen** and **Güldenmorgen**. The better EINZELLAGEN associated with Dienheim include **Falkenberg, Herrengarten,** and **Tafelstein**.

Dionysus; Dionysos [di-uh-NI-suhs] The mythical Greek god of wine, fertility, and drama, Dionysus (also called *Bacchos* and known as *Bacchus* by the Romans) was the son of Zeus and Semele. Although known for his following of those who enjoyed licentious binges, it's said that Dionysus also dispersed information about the art of vine cultivation. The *bacchanals* (annual festivals held in his honor) became so outrageously lewd that the Roman Senate finally banned them in 186 A.D.

dirty A term used in the wine world to describe wine with a distinctly disgusting, rank odor.

disgorge; disgorgement [dihs-GORJ] The step where sediment is removed during the MÉTHODE CHAMPENOISE process of making fine SPARKLING WINES. In a prior step called REMUAGE, sediment slowly collects around the cork (the bottle is positioned upside-down). The neck of the bottle is then placed in an icy brine or glycol solution, which causes the neck's contents (mainly sediment) to freeze into a solid plug. During disgorging the cork (or cap) is removed, and the pressure in the bottle causes the frozen plug of sediment to pop out. The procedure is followed by the remaining méthode champenoise steps including adding the DOSAGE, topping off the bottle with additional wine and recorking it. The French term for this process is *dégorgement*. The unofficial term **late disgorged** is used on some wine labels to indicate that a SPARKLING WINE has been AGED longer than normal bottlings and, through this longer aging, absorbed more flavor from the LEES.

distinguished A descriptor for a wine of exceptional CHARACTER, REFINEMENT, and quality.

disulfides [di-SUHL-fides] *see* HYDROGEN SULFIDE

Dizy [dee-ZEE] An important wine-producing village in the Montagne de Reims area of France's Champagne region. It's planted chiefly with PINOT NOIR grapes. Dizy is classified as a PREMIER CRU village; its vineyards have a rating of 95 percent (*see* CHAMPAGNE for explanation of percent system).

DO *see* DENOMINACIÓN DE ORIGEN

DOC The abbreviation for the APPELLATION system of two countries—Italy (DENOMINAZIONE DI ORIGINE CONTROLLATA) and Portugal (DENOMINAÇÃO DE ORIGEM CONTRALADA).

DOCa *see* DENOMINACIÓN DE ORIGEN CALIFICADA

DOCG *see* DENOMINAZIONE DI ORIGINE CONTROLLATA E GARANTITA

Doctor [DAHK-tohr] A world-famous EINZELLAGE located on the steep hills above the town of BERNKASTEL in Germany's MOSEL-SAAR-RUWER region. According to the German laws established in 1971, the minimum size of an Einzellage is 5 HECTARES (12.35 acres) and Bernkasteler Doctor, at about 8 acres, is only one of two vineyards that are given special dispensation. The grapes from this steep vineyard are normally riper than others in this renowned area and possess a slate flavor that's exhibited in the superb wines.

Doisy-Daëne, Château [sha-TOH dwah-zee DAYN] One of the better DEUXIÈMES CRUS (second growths) in the BARSAC AC, which is part of the broader SAUTERNES AC in BORDEAUX. This property was part of a larger estate, Château Doisy, until it was split into three sections in the nineteenth century (the other two parts are Châteaus DOISY-DUBROCA and DOISY-VÉDRINES). In addition to its sweet wines, Château Doisy-Daëne is known for its DRY white wines under the label of **Vin Sec de Doisy-Daëne**. The blend of grapes used is approximately 70 percent SÉMILLON, 20 percent SAUVIGNON BLANC, and 10 percent MUSCADELLE. The CHÂTEAU consists of nearly 35 acres and produces some 4,000 to 5,000 cases of white wine each year. Better VINTAGES can age for 15 to 20 years.

Doisy-Dubroca, Château [sha-TOH dwah-zee doo-broh-KAH] Until the nineteenth century when it was split into three sections, this property (along with Châteaus DOISY-DAËNE and DOISY-VÉDRINES) was part of the larger estate of Château Doisy. Like the other two, Château Doisy-Dubroca is a highly regarded DEUXIÈME CRU (second growth) located in the BARSAC AC. This tiny 10-acre property annually produces only 1,000 to 2,000 cases of 100 percent SÉMILLON white wine, which generally can age for around 20 years. Many ENOPHILES liken these sweet wines to the great wines from Château CLIMENS (the same winemaking team makes both wines).

Doisy-Védrines, Château [sha-TOH dwah-zee vay-DREEN] Along with Châteaus DOISY-DAËNE and DOISY-DUBROCA, this property was part of a larger estate, Château Doisy, until it was split into these three sections in the nineteenth century. This is one of the better DEUXIÈMES CRUS (second growths) in the BARSAC AC, which is part of the broader SAUTERNES AC in BORDEAUX. This estate consists of about 50 acres planted with around 80 percent SÉMILLON and 20 percent SAUVIGNON BLANC. About 2,500 cases of sweet Barsac AC wine is produced, along with an additional 2,000 to 3,000 cases of DRY white wine. This estate also makes some red wine from a 25-acre plot of the property. Both the dry white wine and the red wine are labeled as **Chevalier de Védrines** under the BORDEAUX AC. The sweet wines can AGE for 14 to 15 years.

dolce [DOHL-chay (It. DAWL-cheh)] Italian for "sweet," usually referring to wines with a high degree of RESIDUAL SUGAR.

Dolceacqua *see* ROSSESE DI DOLCEACQUA DOC

Dolcetto [dohl-CHEHT-oh; dohl-CHEHT-uh] Red wine grape, whose name translates to "little sweet one," that is grown mainly in the southwest section of Italy's PIEDMONT region. There are several theories for Dolcetto's name. One suggests that it's because of the sweetness of the grapes and the juice they produce. Another says it's because there's a perception of sweetness in Dolcetto wines, even though they're usually VINIFIED as DRY wines without RESIDUAL SUGAR. Dolcetto wines have high ACIDITY and are usually deep purple in color. They have perfumy BOUQUETS and rich, fruity, ripe-berry flavors, sometimes with a slightly bitter aftertaste. They should be drunk young before the fruit starts to fade. There are seven DOC's for Dolcetto, all in the Piedmont region. They are *Dolcetto d'Aqui, Dolcetto d'Asti, Dolcetto di Diano d'Alba, Dolcetto delle Langhe Monregalesi, Dolcetto di Dogliani, Dolcetto di Ovada,* and, probably the best known, DOLCETTO D'ALBA. This variety's also grown in the Piedmont's neighboring region LIGURIA, where it's known as *Ormeasco.* Other names for Dolcetto include *Dolsin* and *Dolsin Nero.*

Dolcetto d'Alba DOC [dawl-CHEHT-toh DAHL-bah] DOC zone that is considered the best of the seven DOCs in Italy's PIEDMONT region because of the number of high-quality producers making wine. It specializes in wines made with the DOLCETTO grape and the better wines are SMOOTH, with just enough TANNINS to be well BALANCED. This DOC zone encompasses an area around the town of Alba in the southeastern part of Piedmont. Part of the vineyards covered are in the same area as BAROLO and BARBARESCO.

Dôle *see* VALAIS

Dolsin; Dolsin Nero *see* DOLCETTO

domaine [doh-MAYN; Fr. daw-MEHN] French for "estate" or "property." The term is most often used in BURGUNDY where it pertains to a single property, although the property might be made up of several vineyards in different locations. If a wine is ESTATE BOTTLED (made and bottled by the grower), it's labeled MIS AU DOMAINE, MISE DU DOMAINE, MIS EN BOUTEILLE AU DOMAINE, or MIS EN BOUTEILLE A LA PROPRIETE.

Domaine Baury *see* D'ANGLUDET, CHÂTEAU

Domaine Buena Vista *see* BUENA VISTA WINERY

Domaine Carneros [doh-MAYN (Fr. daw-MEHN) kahr-NEH-rohs] Sitting prominently and imposingly on a hillside right off Highway 121 in the CARNEROS region, Domaine Carneros is a partnership in which the the French CHAMPAGNE house TATTINGER is the majority holder. The majestic but controversial château-style winery and visitor's center is modeled after Tattinger's eighteenth-century château, La Marquetterie, in Reims, France. This SPARKLING WINE facility annually produces between 35,000 and 45,000 cases of wine from its nearly 138 adjoining acres. The vineyards are planted mainly with CHARDONNAY and PINOT NOIR, plus small amounts of PINOT BLANC, and Pinot Meunier (*see* MEUNIER). Domaine Carneros primarily produces a light, delicate, non-vintage BRUT, which is a blend of Chardonnay, Pinot Noir, and Pinot Blanc. They also produce a tiny amount of vintage BLANC DE BLANC made from Chardonnay and Pinot Blanc.

Domaine Chandon [doh-MAYN (Fr. daw-MEHN) shahn-DAWN] California SPARKLING WINE facility opened in 1973 by the French company Moet-Hennessy, which has since joined with Louis Vuitton. The combined companies own the CHAMPAGNE houses of MOËT ET CHANDON, Mercier, RUINART, VEUVE CLICQUOT-PONSARDIN, Canard-Duchêne, and Henriot. They also own the COGNAC producers Hennessy and Hine, as well as the SIMI WINERY in the ALEXANDER VALLEY. Domaine Chandon, which is in the NAPA VALLEY, has been extremely successful and now owns about 1,600 acres (1,000 of which are planted with vineyards). The annual production is about 500,000 cases of wine. Domaine Chandon vineyards are variously located on the Napa Valley floor, on Mount Veeder, and in CARNEROS. The winery offers BRUT, Reserve Brut (which has been aged for 4 years), and **Etoile** (its premium CUVÉE made from even older wines). All are made from a blend of PINOT NOIR, CHARDONNAY, and PINOT BLANC. Domaine Chandon also has a BLANC DE

NOIR that's 100 percent Pinot Noir and a Club Cuvée made from Chardonnay and aged for about 5 years. **Panache** is a sweet APÉRITIF wine made by stopping fermentation of Pinot Noir juice with the addition of BRANDY. **Shadow Creek** is a brand owned by Domaine Chandon for sparkling wine produced from non-Napa Valley sources like its own 100-acre vineyard in MENDOCINO COUNTY and another 200 acres in SANTA BARBARA and SONOMA.

Domaine de Chevalier [doh-MAYN duh shuh-vah-LYAY] CRU CLASSÉ château located in the PESSAC-LÉOGNAN AC in the GRAVES area of BORDEAUX. The château has nearly 60 acres and produces mainly red wines (9,000 to 10,000 cases), but also makes a small amount (about 1,500 cases) of DRY white wine. The red wines use approximately 70 percent CABERNET SAUVIGNON, 25 percent MERLOT, and 5 percent CABERNET FRANC; the white wines use nearly 70 percent SAUVIGNON BLANC and 30 percent SÉMILLON. The red wines are compared to the better DEUXIÈME CRU (second growth) châteaus of the MÉDOC. The hard-to-find white wines are considered some of the best produced in Bordeaux. They actually mature more slowly than the red wines and can AGE for up to 30 years compared to about 20 years for the red wines.

Domaine de Curé-Bourse *see* DURFORT-VIVENS, CHÂTEAU

Domaine de Martialis *see* CLOS FOURTET

Domaine de Sainte-Gemme *see* LANESSAN, CHÂTEAU

Domaine des Douves *see* BEAUREGARD, CHÂTEAU

Domaine des Gondats *see* MARQUIS DE TERME, CHÂTEAU

Domaine Drouhin [doh-MAYN (Fr. daw-MEHN) DROO-ah*n*] Located in the Willamette Valley, this Oregon winery was established in 1988 and has quickly attracted some loyal followers for its highly regarded wines. It's owned by Maison Joseph Drouhin, a famous wine firm in France's BURGUNDY region. Domaine Drouhin made wines from purchased grapes starting in 1988. Its vineyards, which were planted in 1987, produced the first ESTATE-BOTTLED wine in 1991. It has 180 acres and currently produces about 3,500 cases each year. Robert Drouhin has installed his ENOLOGIST daughter, Veronique, as winemaker and vineyard manager.

Domaine du Balardin *see* MALESCOT SAINT-EXUPÉRY, CHÂTEAU

Domaine du Grand Archer *see* ARROWOOD VINEYARDS & WINERY

Domaine Montreaux *see* MONTICELLO CELLARS

Domaine Mumm *see* MUMM NAPA VALLEY

Domaine Ste. Michelle *see* CHÂTEAU STE. MICHELLE

Domäne [daw-MEH-nuh] A German word meaning "domain" or "estate" (*see also* WEINGUT). The word domäne generally is used only for state-owned estates or for private estates owned by nobility or other officially recognized family. As is the German habit, Domäne is often combined with others names, such as in *Staatliche Weinbaudomäne* or *Domänenweingut Schloss Schönborn*. The word Domäne may be used on the label only if the wine is made exclusively from grapes grown on the estate's property.

Domdechaney *see* HOCKHEIM

Domecq, Pedro [PAY-droh doh-MAYK] Founded by Irishman Patrick Murphy in 1730, Pedro Domecq is the oldest and largest of the sherry producers. Although large, it produces high-quality sherry wines. Its *La Ina*, a DRY *fino* (*see* SHERRY), is highly regarded and is the second-best selling sherry in the world. Domecq's top-of-the-line wines are *Sibarita Palo Cortado, Pedro Ximénez Venerable,* and the *Amontillado 51 1A* (the number of the SOLERA). Domecq also lays claim to being one of the world's largest brandy producers. Additionally, it's become a primary wine producer in the RIOJA DO, where its over 1300-acre vineyard produces an array of red, white, and ROSÉ wines.

La Dominique, Château [sha-TOH lah daw-mee-NEEK] Sitting next to Château CHEVAL BLANC near the POMEROL AC border, this SAINT-ÉMILION AC CHÂTEAU enjoys the area's great soils. Château La Dominique has produced enough excellent wines in recent VINTAGES that many of its followers think it should be upgraded from its current status of GRAND CRU CLASSÉ to that of a PREMIER GRAND CRU CLASSÉ. The vineyard is around 45 acres in size, and the château produces about 6,000 to 8,000 cases of red wine each year. These wines are made from a blend of approximately 75 percent MERLOT, 15 percent CABERNET FRANC, 5 percent CABERNET SAUVIGNON and 5 percent MALBEC. The AGING capability of these wines is about 20 years. The château uses a SECOND LABEL **Saint-Paul de la Dominque** for its lesser wines.

Dominus Estate [DAHM-ih-nuhs] The label for wines produced by the **John Daniel Society,** a partnership established in 1982 between Christian Moueix, winemaker/director of a number of wine estates in BORDEAUX'S POMEROL district (including the renowned Château PÉTRUS), and the daughters of John Daniel—Robin Lail and Marcia

Smith. John Daniel was the legendary owner of INGLENOOK when it was one of the NAPA VALLEY's premier wineries. The grapes for Dominus Estate wines come from the famous **Napanook Vineyard** (now owned by Lail and Smith), which dates back to the 1880s and was once part of Inglenook Vineyards. Napanook, which is situated in the hills west of Yountville, California, is planted with CABERNET SAUVIGNON, CABERNET FRANC, MERLOT, and CHARDONNAY (the latter not used by Dominus Estate). John Daniel Society produces about 10,000 cases of red wine, some under the SECOND LABEL of **Daniel Estate**. The somewhat controversial Dominus Estate wines are generally intense and TANNIC requiring long AGING before they SOFTEN.

Dom Pérignon *see* CHAMPAGNE

Domprobst *see* GRAACH

Doosberg *see* OESTRICH

Dorado *see* RUEDA DO

Dorin *see* CHASSELAS

dosage [doh-SAHJ] A syrupy mixture of sugar and wine (and sometimes BRANDY and/or citric acid) that's added to CHAMPAGNE and other SPARKLING WINE. A dosage is used in a couple of ways. A **bottling dosage** (*dosage de tirage* or *liqueur de tirage*) plus yeast is added to a CUVÉE (a blend of still wines) in order to cause a SECONDARY FERMENTATION in the bottle. A **shipping dosage** (*dosage d'expédition* or *liqueur d'expédition*)—usually sugar plus some of the same wine that's been reserved for this purpose—is added to a wine immediately prior to final bottling to increase its level of sweetness. The percentage of sugar in the shipping dosage determines the degree of sweetness in the final wine. Depending on this level of sweetness, sparkling wines are described as BRUT, EXTRA DRY or EXTRA-SEC, SEC, DEMI-SEC, or DOUX. *See also* MÉTHODE CHAMPENOISE.

dosage d'expédition *see* DOSAGE

dosage de tirage *see* DOSAGE

double magnum *see* WINE BOTTLES

Douro; Douro DOC [DOO-roh] Douro is a wild mountainous region located around the Douro River starting at the Spanish border and extending west into northern Portugal. The Douro region contains two DENOMINAÇÃO DE ORIGEM CONTROLADA (DOC) areas—Douro DOC for TABLE WINES and PORT DOC (see listing) for port wines.

Although they share much of the same area, the Douro DOC is larger because it includes vineyards that aren't acceptable for the Port DOC because many of the Douro DOC vineyards sit at higher altitudes than are optimum for port vineyards. At the higher altitudes in this hot region, grapes don't ripen quite as fully, which makes them better suited for table wines than for port. The Douro DOC allows a multitude of grapes to be used in the wines. The main varieties for red wines are TOURIGA NACIONAL, TOURIGA FRANCESA, and Tinta Roriz (TEMPRANILLO). The primary white grapes used are Esgana Cão, Folgosão, and VERDELHO. Some of Portugal's best and most sought after wines (like the *Barca Velha* from FERREIRA) come from this region.

Douro bake *see* PORT

doux [DOO] French for "sweet." On a CHAMPAGNE label, *doux* means the wine is very sweet—over 5 percent sugar. *See also* LIQUOREUX; MOELLEUX

Dow *see* SILVA & COSENS

downy mildew *see* MILDEW

Drachenstein *see* RÜDESHEIM

dried out A descriptor for wine that has lost it fruity nuances, which allows the ACID, TANNINS, and ALCOHOL to dominate, throwing the wine out of balance.

dry A term that describes wine that isn't sweet; its French counterpart is SEC. In a fully dry wine, all the sugar has been converted to ALCOHOL during FERMENTATION. A **medium-dry** wine has a small amount of RESIDUAL SUGAR, but not enough to prevent the wine from being enjoyed with a meal. A wine with the barest hint of sweetness is referred to as OFF DRY.

Dry Creek Valley AVA Located in the northern part of SONOMA COUNTY, this APPELLATION runs from north of the town of Geyserville to just south of Healdsburg and spreads west from these towns. Most of the vineyards and wineries are scattered around Dry Creek, a tributary of the Russian River. The warmer northern end of this VITICULTURAL AREA favors ZINFANDEL grapes, which have been planted in this area since the 1880s. Other varieties that do well here include SAUVIGNON BLANC, CHARDONNAY, and CABERNET SAUVIGNON, and in the cooler southern portion (near the RUSSIAN RIVER AVA) even RIESLING does well. There a number of top wineries here including ALDERBROOK, Bellerose, Dry Creek Vineyards, FERRARI-CARANO, LYTTON SPRINGS WINERY, MAZZOCCO VINEYARDS,

Meeker Vineyard, NALLE WINERY, J. Pedroncelli, Preston, QUIVERA VINE-
YARDS, and A. RAFANELLI.

dry sherry *see* SHERRY

DucaEnrico *see* CORVO

Duckhorn Vineyards Established in 1976, this NAPA VALLEY winery is a limited partnership managed by Dan and Margaret Duckhorn.
It has an esteemed reputation for its MERLOT wines, which were first
made in 1978. In addition to its three Merlots (Three Palms Vineyard,
Napa Valley, and Vine Hill Ranch), Duckhorn makes CABERNET SAUVI-
GNON and SAUVIGNON BLANC, both of which are notable. They also make
a small amount of a blended red wine (which they call Claret) from
HOWELL MOUNTAIN grapes. The winery owns about 95 acres and is annually producing close to 30,000 cases of wine, about 75 percent of
which is red. **Decoy** is Duckhorn's SECOND LABEL.

Ducru-Beaucaillou, Château [sha-TOH doo-KROO boh-
kah-YOO] Beaucaillou translates into "beautiful pebbles," which is
what the former owner, Monsieur Ducru, reputedly saw when he
looked at the pebbly soil after which he named this CHÂTEAU, a DEUX-
IÈME CRU (second growth) property located in the SAINT-JULIEN AC of the
BORDEAUX region. Considered one of the top second growths, Château
Ducru-Beaucaillou is constantly challenging the first-growth châteaus
with its outstanding, quality wines. The château, which is beautifully
situated with gorgeous views of the Gironde River, consists of around
123 acres. It produces 16,000 to 20,000 cases of red wine made up of
about 65 percent CABERNET SAUVIGNON, 25 percent MERLOT, 5 percent
CABERNET FRANC, and 5 percent PETIT VERDOT. The best VINTAGES can AGE
for 30 years or more. The SECOND LABEL for this château is **La Croix**.

Duhart-Milon-Rothschild, Château [sha-TOH doo-AHR
mee-LAW*N* rawt-SHEELD (rawth-CHILD)] QUATRIÈME CRU (fourth
growth) CHÂTEAU that was acquired by the Rothschilds, of Château
LAFITE-ROTHSCHILD, in 1962. They instituted a replanting program that
finally began to pay off in the 1980s as the new vines began to mature. Most BORDEAUX fanciers would agree that this château is now producing TROISIÈME CRU (third-growth) quality wines. The property,
which is located in the PAUILLAC, now contains nearly 150 acres and
produces around 20,000 to 25,000 cases of red wine annually. The
mixture of grapes used is about 70 percent CABERNET SAUVIGNON, 20
percent MERLOT, 5 percent CABERNET FRANC, and 5 percent PETIT VERDOT.
The better VINTAGES can age for 20 to 25 years. Their SECOND LABEL is
Moulin de Duhart.

dulce [DOOL-thay; DOOL-say] Spanish for "sweet."

dull Just as it sounds, a dull wine is lackluster and uninteresting. It's devoid of zest and, though drinkable, certainly lacks excitement.

Duluc *see* BRANAIRE-DUCRU, CHÂTEAU

dumb; dumb phase Though the term *dumb* is sometimes used as a synonym for CLOSED, it really has a more complex meaning. The dumb phase of a wine (generally red) is that period of transition from its youth to maturity. Shortly after bottling, a wine may be luscious, with rich, ripe aromas and flavors. However, after a certain period of time (usually several months), such a wine may begin to close down—the fruit begins to decrease before the complexities of maturity have fully developed. The combination of declining fruit and preemergent complexity cancel each other out, creating a wine that simply doesn't taste very good. VINTNERS have no idea what causes this phenomenon but do agree that the time frame for this dumb phase, which can last for several years, is completely unpredictable. The dumb phase of a wine is also referred to as the *flat spot* or the *awkward, transformational,* or *adolescent phase.*

Dunn Vineyards Randy Dunn was the winemaker at CAYMUS from 1975 to 1982 and helped establish that winery's reputation as a producer of premium red wines. In the late 1970s he reestablished a vineyard on HOWELL MOUNTAIN and began to make his own CABERNET SAUVIGNON wines. His first release was a 1979 VINTAGE, and in 1982 he left Caymus to devote his energies to Dunn Vineyards. The Howell Mountain Cabernet Sauvignon is produced from 10 acres (five belonging to Randy Dunn and five to his neighbor) on its namesake mountain. In 1982 Dunn added a NAPA VALLEY Cabernet Sauvignon made from grapes purchased from John Caldwell's vineyard. Today, Dunn Vineyards annually produces about 5,000 cases of highly esteemed red wine. Dunn bought a nearby 47-acre parcel (the old Park-Muscadine vineyard) in 1991. He currently sells the ZINFANDEL and PETITE SIRAH grapes from the 15 acres that are planted there, but plans to eventually convert the land into a Cabernet Sauvignon vineyard.

Duras *see* CÔTES DE DURAS AC

Durfort-Vivens, Château [sha-TOH dyoor-fawr vee-VAHN*S* (vee-VAH*N*)] DEUXIÈME CRU (second growth) CHÂTEAU located in the MARGAUX AC in BORDEAUX. Many critics think the wines are good, but not deserving of the high classification that it has. The estate consists of nearly 74 acres and produces around 6,000 to 8,000 cases of red wine.

Approximately 64 percent CABERNET SAUVIGNON, 21 percent CABERNET FRANC, and 15 percent MERLOT are used in the wines. The better vintages can age for about 14 to 15 years. Château Durfort-Vivens's SECOND LABEL is **Domaine de Curé-Bourse**.

Durif [dyoor-IF; DUR-if] A red wine grape grown in the France's RHÔNE region in the late nineteenth century and up to the middle of the twentieth century. Durif is viewed as a rather common and minor variety and is seldom found in French vineyards today. Some speculate that the variety called PETITE SIRAH in California is actually Durif. Durif is also known as *Pinot de Romans* and *Pinot de l'Ermitage*, although it's not a member of the PINOT NOIR family.

Dürkheim *see* BAD DURKHEIM

dusty Descriptor for wine that gives a palate impression of solid flavor particles. A dusty smell is reminiscent of an earthen-floored cellar.

Dutchess [DUH-chess] A VITUS LABRUSCA and VITIS VINIFERA HYBRID developed in the United States and grown mostly in the eastern states. Even though the white wines it produces have FOXY characteristics, they're generally of good quality. Dutchess is not widely planted so these wines are difficult to find.

arthy; earthiness An aroma or flavor evocative of damp, rich soil. The term is generally used in a positive sense, unless the characteristic is too pronounced.

East India *see* SHERRY

eau de vie; pl. eaux de vie [oh duh VEE] French for "water of life." This term describes any colorless, potent BRANDY or other spirit distilled from fermented fruit juice. Among the grape-based eaux de vie are: *eau de vie de marc* (from MARC), *eau de vie de lie* (from LEES), and *eau de vie de vin* (from wine). Probably the two most popular eaux de vie in the world are Kirsch (from cherries) and Framboise (from raspberries).

Echézeaux AC [ay-shuh-ZOH] A lesser-known GRAND CRU vineyard that is located in the CÔTE DE NUITS area of France's BURGUNDY region. Even though it's located in the village of Flagey-Echézeaux, it is often grouped with the famous grands crus of the neighboring village of VOSNE-ROMANÉE. Echézeaux has 93 acres, all planted with PINOT NOIR grapes, making it the second largest Burgundian grand cru after CLOS DE VOUGEOT. These red wines are generally LIGHTER, more refined, and earlier maturing than those from neighboring grands crus—the acclaimed GRANDS-ECHÉZEAUX in particular, which is recognized as producing superior wines with more depth of aroma and flavor. As a large Burgundian vineyard, Echézeaux has many (80 plus) owners, all of whom produce wines of varying quality, and all using the Echézeaux name.

Edelfäule [ay-duhl-FOY-luh] A German term meaning "noble rot," referring to BOTRYTIS CINEREA, the beneficial mold responsible for the TROCKENBEERNAUSLESE wines.

Edeltraube *see* GEWÜRZTRAMINER

Edelzwicker *see* ALSACE

edes [A-dehsh] The Hungarian term for "sweet."

Edmeades Vineyard & Winery *see* KENDALL-JACKSON VINE-YARDS

Edna Valley AVA Located in SAN LUIS OBISPO COUNTY about halfway between San Francisco and Los Angeles, the Edna Valley AVA runs south and east of San Luis Obispo, California. Ocean breezes sweeping in from Morro Bay give this area a long, cool growing season that's classified as a Region I (*see* CLIMATE REGIONS OF CALIFORNIA).

This environment makes CHARDONNAY the most popular variety by a considerable amount, followed by PINOT NOIR and other grapes like CABERNET SAUVIGNON, SAUVIGNON BLANC, and SÉMILLON. Well-known wineries include Corbett Canyon Vineyards, EDNA VALLEY VINEYARDS, Chamisal Vineyard, and Windemere Wines.

Edna Valley Vineyards Winery located southeast of the town of San Luis Obispo, California, in the EDNA VALLEY AVA. It was formed in 1980 as a joint venture between Chalone Inc. (*see* CHALONE VINEYARD) and Paragon Vineyards. Prior to the partnership, Chalone had made wines under the Edna Valley Vineyards label for several years from grapes purchased from Paragon. Edna Valley Vineyards produces about 55,000 cases of wine from the nearly 700 acres that Paragon owns. Most of their production is a highly regarded CHARDONNAY, plus a small amount of PINOT NOIR. SAUVIGNON BLANC, and SÉMILLON grapes from Paragon are sold to CARMENET VINEYARD, which is also owned by Chalone Inc. **Tiffany Hill** is a label used by Paragon Vineyards for wines produced for it by Edna Valley Vineyards.

eggs *see* SULFUR

L'Eglise-Clinet, Château [sha-TOH leh-GLEEZ klee-NAY] CHÂTEAU located in the POMEROL AC of France's BORDEAUX region that has an excellent reputation. It's small, less than 15 acres, and produces around 2,000 to 2,500 case of RICH, SUPPLE red wine. MERLOT is normally about 80 percent of the blend with CABERNET FRANC making up the rest. Even though it's small, this château uses the SECOND LABEL **La Petite L'Eglise** for wine that doesn't meet its high standards for the Château L'Eglise-Clinet label.

égrappage *see* DESTEMMING

Egri Bikavér [EH-grih BIH-kah-vahr] The town of Eger is located northeast of Budapest in notably mountainous country. Egri Bikavér, which means "bull's blood from Eger," is Hungary's best-known red wine. According to legend, the wine got its name in the sixteenth century after the Eger was attacked by Turkish troops. Fortified with the local wine, the valiant Hungarian soldiers bravely defeated the attacking hoard. Thankfully, there's no bull's blood in the wine, which is made from KADARKA, Kékfrankos, and Médoc Noir (MERLOT) grapes, although other varieties can be used. At one time, Egri Bikavér was a very highly regarded, full-flavored, full-bodied (*see* BODY) wine. It's now considered quite average, which some believe is due to using less of the high-quality Kadarka grapes and more of the rather ordinary Kékfrankos variety.

Ehrenfelser [EHR-en-fehl-zuhr] A good-quality, white-wine, HYBRID grape developed at GEISENHEIM, Germany in the 1920s. Ehrenfelser is a CROSS of RIESLING and SYLVANER that—except for its lower ACID levels—closely resembles Riesling. It has some advantages over Riesling in that Ehrenfelser grows in less desirable locations and ripens earlier, which makes it increasingly popular in some of Germany's northern growing regions.

Einzellage; pl. Einzellagen [I'n-tsuh-lah-guh; I'n-tsuh-lah-gehn] As defined by the German wine laws of 1971, an Einzellage is an individual vineyard site with a minimum size of 5 HECTARES (about 12½ acres). This law caused the absorption of many tiny vineyards into larger ones, reducing the total number of vineyards from approximately 25,000 to about 2,600. The result is a situation similar to France's BURGUNDY region where a vineyard may be divided among many different growers. Nearly all the vineyard sites in Germany are officially registered as Einzellagen, each with their own officially assigned number. Einzellagen are the smallest defined areas under the German system, which includes GROSSLAGEN (general sites), BEREICHE (districts), and ANBAUGEBIETE (growing regions). On labels the name of the Einzellage is most often preceded by the name of village where the vineyard is located. When this is done, the village name has an *er* attached to it. For example, the Einzellage Daubhaus from the village of Oppenheim would appear on the label as "Oppenheimer Daubhaus," the Einzellage Sonnenberg in the village of Eltville appears as "Eltviller Sonnenberg."

Eiswein [ICE-vyn] A German term meaning "ice wine," referring to a rich, flavorful DESSERT WINE. Eiswein is made by picking grapes that are frozen on the vine and then pressing them before they thaw. Because much of the water in the grapes is frozen, the resulting juice is concentrated—rich in flavor and high in sugar and ACID. The resulting wines, although different than Germany's famous BEERENAUSLESEN and TROCKENBEERENAUSLESEN, are similarly extraordinarily sweet, yet balanced by high acidity. Eisweine are candidates for long AGING. In 1982 Eiswein became one of the six subcategories of QUALITÄTSWEIN MIT PRÄDIKAT. In order to qualify, a wine's MUST needs to reach the minimum natural sugar levels of BEERENAUSLESE category wines—110° to 128° OECHSLE (approximately 26 to 30 percent sugar by weight), depending on the region and the variety.

Eitelsbach [I-tls-bahkh] A small village that's part of the city of TRIER in Germany's MOSEL-SAAR-RUWER region. Eitelsbach, which sits on the Ruwer River and is part of the BEREICH SAAR-RUWER, is well known because of one famous wine estate—**Karthäuserhofberg**. This estate's vineyards, which are situated on the steep hills just above Eitelsbach, are considered one of the two best along the Ruwer (the other being MAXIMIN GRÜNHÄUSE). Karthäuserhofberg, which mean "Carthusians' Hill," gets its name from the Carthusian monastery that owned the vineyard for nearly 500 years. Although the estate has five named vineyards—Burgberg, Kronenberg, Orthsberg, Sang, and Stirn—the vineyard names have not been used on labels since 1985, and all wines are labeled Eitelsbacher Karthäuserhofberger.

Elba DOC [EHLL-bah] DOC zone on the island of Elba, which is located off the coast of (and is considered part of) Italy's TUSCANY region. The island is famous as the place where Napoleon was exiled. Elba's BIANCO wines are produced mainly from TREBBIANO and Procanico grapes—a SPUMANTE version may also be made. Their ROSSO wine is made from a blend of at least 75 percent SANGIOVESE, plus CANAIOLO, Trebbiano, and Biancone.

Elbling [EHL-bling] A very productive white-wine grape with origins prior to the Middle Ages—possibly to Roman times. Elbling's grown mainly in Germany's MOSEL region, particularly in environments where RIESLING has trouble ripening. This grape produces rather ordinary wines with neutral flavors and high ACIDITY. Although much of it is made into SPARKLING WINE (called SEKT in Germany), Elbling is occassionally found as either a DRY or medium-dry STILL WINE. This grape is also called *Burger, Grossriesling, Kleinberger,* and *Rheinelbe.*

El Dorado AVA [ehl doh-RAH-doh] APPELLATION that covers the foothills (which range from 1,200 to 3,500 feet in altitude) in El Dorado County, east and slightly north of Sacramento, California. The boundaries of the larger SIERRA FOOTHILLS AVA include the El Dorado AVA. This growing area ranges from a Region II to a Region III (*see* CLIMATE REGIONS OF CALIFORNIA), depending on the location and the year. ZINFANDEL, CABERNET SAUVIGNON, CHARDONNAY, SAUVIGNON BLANC, and a number of other varieties are all grown here. Wineries of note include Boeger Winery, Gold Hill Vineyard, Granite Springs, Lava Cap, and Madrona Vineyards.

elegant; elegance Descriptor for wines that have FINESSE, lightness, and flair. They're gracefully BALANCED and of exceedingly high quality.

éleveur [eh-leh-VUH*R*] A word taken from the French *élevage,* which means "bringing up" or "raising." In the French wine trade, an eleveur is someone who buys recently fermented wine and then "raises" it by performing such functions as BLENDING, FINING, FILTERING, AGING, and bottling. These activities are sometimes performed by a NEGOCIANT, who then labels the wines with the phrase *négociant-eleveur.*

Elysium *see* MUSCAT

embotellado de/en origen [aym-boa-tay-LYAH-doh deh/ehn oh-REE-gehn] A Spanish phrase meaning ESTATE BOTTLED.

Les Embrazées, *see* CHASSAGNE-MONTRACHET AC

Emerald Riesling [EHM-uhr-uhld REEZ-ling; REES-ling] White HYBRID grape that was developed by the University of California at DAVIS in 1948 in an attempt to create high-quality, highly productive grapes for California's hotter growing areas. Emerald Riesling's parents are the highly regarded RIESLING and the rather ordinary MUSCADELLE. The resulting grape produces wines that are fairly AROMATIC, highly ACIDIC, and medium-bodied, but lacking in flavor. These wines are generally used for blending, although there are some medium-dry VARIETAL WINES made, the most famous being Paul Masson's Emerald Dry. Emerald Riesling has never been extremely popular—most of its acreage is in California's CENTRAL VALLEY, with limited amounts in South Africa and Australia.

Emilia-Romagna [eh-MEE-lyah raw-MAH-nyah] Diverse wine-producing region located in northern Italy, north of TUSCANY and south of LOMBARDY and VENETO. Its capital city is Bologna. Emilia-Romagna is renowned for its food and food products and is the home of Parmesan cheese and Parma hams. There are a diverse number of wine-growing areas spread among the plains and the hills of both the Emilia and Romagna sectors. The great flat plain of the Emilia area around Modena produces huge volumes of red wine from the LAMBRUSCO grape and its many subvarieties. In the hilly regions around Colli Bolognesi and Colli Piacentini the principal grapes for red wine are BARBERA and BONARDA. In Romagna, ALBANA and TREBBIANO are the primary white grapes and SANGIOVESE is the primary red grape. Emilia-Romagna has one DOCG, ALBANA DI ROMAGNA, about which there is a great deal of controversy. The general sentiment is that this growing area received DOCG status more through political posturing than through the quality of its wines. Emilia-Romagna also has fourteen DOC areas including COLLI BOLOGNESI, COLLI PIACENTINI, LAMBRUSCO DI SORBARA, Lambrusco Grasparossa di Castelvetro, Lambrusco Salamino di Santa Croces, Sangiovese di Romagna, and Trebbiano di Romagna.

empty *see* HOLLOW

encapsulated yeasts *see* RIDDLING

Enclos de Moncabon *see* CROIZET-BAGES, CHÂTEAU; RAUZAN-GASSIES, CHÂTEAU

engarrafado na origem [ayn-gar-rah-FAH-doh nah oh-REE-zhem] A Portuguese phrase meaning "ESTATE BOTTLED."

Engelsberg *see* NACKENHEIM

Engelsmannberg *see* HATTENHEIM

England The Romans are thought to have been the VITICULTURAL pioneers in England. There were also numerous vineyards producing wine during the Middle Ages, although English rule (through a royal marriage) of France's Bordeaux region from 1152 through 1453 seemed to permanently shift allegiance to the wines of Bordeaux. Most vineyards were associated with monasteries, but when Henry VIII renounced the monasteries, the vineyards were ripped up and the land was planted with other crops. It wasn't until the 1950s that English winemaking began its revival. Britain's northerly climate isn't particularly hospitable for grape growing, but the southern portions of England and Wales contain about 2,000 acres of grapevines. There are over 400 wineries (most are small) producing wine in areas like Essex, Hampshire, Hereford, Kent, Somerset, Suffolk, Sussex, and the Thames Valley. Because of its severe climate, England is white-wine country, with the most popular grapes being MÜLLER-THURGAU, SEYVAL BLAN and the German CROSSES of HUXELREBE, KERNER, ORTEGA, Reichensteiner, Schönburger, and Siegerrebe. Tiny amounts of PINOT NOIR and CHARDONNAY are also planted. English wines are generally DRY, LIGHT, CRISP, and FLOWERY with good ACIDITY. *See also* ENGLISH WINE and BRITISH WINE.

English Wine This term on a label indicates that the wine was produced using grapes grown in England. *See also* BRITISH WINE.

enologist *see* ENOLOGY

enology [ee-NAHL-uh-jee] The science or study of VINICULTURE (making wines). One who is an expert in the science is called an **enologist** or **enologue**. Also spelled *oenology*. *See also* VITICULTURE.

enophile [EE-nuh-file] Someone who enjoys wine, usually referring to a connoisseur. Also spelled *oenophile*.

en tirage *see* TIRAGE

Entre-Deux-Mers [ahn-truh duh MERR] Meaning "between two seas," the area of Entre-Deux-Mers sits between two rivers, the

Dordogne and the Garonne, in the eastern portion of France's BOR-DEAUX region. With approximately 7,400 acres, it's the largest subdistrict within Bordeaux. Its undulating hills make it one of the most beautiful as well. The Entre-Deux-Mers AC applies only to white wines made from MUSCADELLE, SAUVIGNON BLANC, and SÉMILLON. These wines are now made in a CRISP, DRY fashion, a change from the rather bland, semisweet versions made in the past. Within the southern portion of Entre-Deux-Mers is the small **Haut-Benauge AC**, which produces white wines of somewhat higher quality. Red wines produced from the Entre-Deux-Mers region are sold as BORDEAUX AC or Bordeaux Supérieur AC.

Les Epenots *see* POMMARD

Erbach [EHR-bahkh] Located in Germany's RHEINGAU region, this town is known for its esteemed wines, particularly those from **Marcobrunn**, a celebrated EINZELLAGE. Marcobrunn is actually located only partly in the village of Hattenheim, but in 1971 a dispute was settled to the effect that all wines produced in the area are attached to the village of Erbach, and therefore labeled Erbacher Marcobrunn. Wines from the Marcobrunn site are generally full-bodied (*see* BODY) and long-lived. Erbach has also made its mark with wines from other sites including **Hohnenrain**, **Honigberg**, **Michelmark**, **Rheinhell**, **Schlossberg**, **Siegelsberg**, and **Steinmorgen**.

Erbaluce [ehr-bah-LOO-chay] A white-wine grape grown mainly in the northwest area of Italy's PIEDMONT region. Erbaluce yields highly ACIDIC wines of rather ordinary quality. LEAN, DRY wines and SPARKLING WINES are produced under the DOC banner of ERBALUCE DI CALUSO. In the DOC of CALUSO PASSITO, the Erbaluce grapes are laid out in the sun to dry and then FERMENTED into a rich DESSERT WINE that ranges in color from pale yellow to golden. A LIQUOROSO—or FORTIFIED version—of the Caluso Passito is also produced. Erbaluce is most renowned for these PASSITO wines.

Erbaluce di Caluso DOC [ehr-bah-LOO-tchay dee kah-LOO-soh] DOC area located in the northern part of Italy's PIEDMONT region north of Turin. The vineyards are located in thirty-five different villages in and around the town of Caluso. These are ordinary DRY white wines made from the ERBALUCE grape, although a rich, sweet DESSERT WINE called CALUSO PASSITO is also made. A sparkling version called **Caluso Spumante** is produced as well.

Erben [EHR-buhn] German for "heirs" or "successors." Erben is sometimes used on labels much like "& Sons" might be used in England or the United States. Examples include Weingut Bürgermeister Anton Balbach Erben and Weingut Bürgermeister Carl Koch Erben.

Erden [EHR-duhn] A small village located in Germany's MOSEL-SAAR-RUWER region, along the Mosel River downstream from the town of BERNKASTEL in the BEREICH Bernkastel. Erden is surrounded by gently sloping vineyards, but its best vineyards are across the river on the steep hills next to the village of Urzig. The top EINZELLAGEN are **Herrenberg**, **Prälat** (the best known), and **Treppchen**.

Ermitage *See* HERMITAGE; MARSANNE

L'Ermitage de Chasse-Spleen *see* CHASSE-SPLEEN, CHÂTEAU

Erzeugerabfüllung [AYR-tsoy-guhr-AB-few-lung] A German term meaning "producer bottled" and having a meaning somewhat similar to ESTATE BOTTLED. The major difference is that German COOPER-ATIVES, which blend wines from various members, can use the term. The term GUTSABFÜLLUNG is much more restrictive and is much closer to the United States use of the term estate bottled.

erzeugergemeinschaft [AYR-tsoy-guhr-geh-MYN-shawft] German phrase referring to a VITICULTURE producers' association, which is not the same as a winemaking COOPERATIVE.

Escherndorf [ESH-uhrn-dorf] This well-known village produces some of the best wines coming from Germany's FRANKEN region. Escherndorf, which is located on the Main River northeast of Wurzburg, lies at the base of steep hillside vineyards. The best EINZEL-LAGEN are **Berg**, **Fürstenberg**, and **Lump**.

Espagne *see* CINSAUT

Esparte *see* MOURVÈDRE

espumante [ish-poo-MERN-teh] Portuguese term for "sparkling."

espumoso [ehs-poo-MOH-soh] The Spanish term for "sparkling." *See also* CAVA.

Essencia *see* MUSCAT; TOKAY

Est! Est!! Est!!! di Montefiascone DOC [EHST EHST EHST dee mawn-teh-fyahs-KAW-neh] The name of a DOC area located in Italy's LATIUM region, northwest of Rome near Lake Bolsena. According to legend, a twelfth-century German bishop on his way to Rome sent his servant ahead to identify places where wines were particularly good. When the servant found one, he was to identify it by writing the word *Est* (Latin for "it is") on its wall. The servant apparently found the wine at a tavern in Montefiascone to be so fantastic that he enscribed the enthusiastic *Est! Est!! Est!!!* on the wall. According to the story, the bishop (who apparently agreed with his servant's opinion) never left Montefiascone. It produces a light, DRY white wine from TREBBIANO, Procanico, and MALVASIA grapes. The wine is generally viewed as quite ordinary—certainly not worth all the exclamation points.

Estancia Vineyards *see* FRANCISCAN VINEYARDS

estate bottled The words on a wine label indicating that 100 percent of the grapes in the wine were grown in the winery's own vineyards, or from vineyards (in the same APPELLATION) controlled by the winery through a long-term lease. Furthermore, such wines must be VINIFIED and bottled at that winery. The term *château bottled* has a comparable meaning. Both refer to a wine that's considered to be of superior quality and character. European phrases similar to "estate bottled" are: the French MIS EN BOUTEILLE *au Domaine, Mis au Domaine, Mis en Bouteille a la Propriete,* and *Mis en Bouteille du Château;* the Italian IMBOTTIGLIATO ALL'ORIGINE; and the German GUTSABFÜLLUNG and ERZEUGERABFÜLLUNG. *See also* BOTTLED BY; GROWN, PRODUCED AND BOTTLED BY; MADE AND BOTTLED BY; PRODUCED AND BOTTLED BY.

esters [EHS-tuhrs] Compounds produced by the reaction between ACIDS and ALCOHOLS, which happens in wine during FERMENTATION as well as AGING. The contribution of esters (the most prominent of which is ETHYL ACETATE) to wine is an ACETONE smell that's sweet and slightly fruity. Esters also contribute COMPLEXITY to wine.

estufa *see* MADEIRA

estufagem *see* MADEIRA

estufas *see* MADEIRA

ethanol *see* ALCOHOL

ethyl acetate [ETH-uhl ASS-ih-tayt] An ESTER that is a byproduct of FERMENTATION. When ethyl acetate exists in sufficient quantity, it produces a slightly sweet, fruity, vinegary smell. Even though ethyl acetate exists in all wines and can be complementary (especially in rich, sweet wines), noticeable amounts are considered a flaw.

ethyl alcohol *see* ALCOHOL

Etna DOC [EHT-nuh] A DOC area located in eastern SICILY on the eastern slopes of Mount Etna, a famous volcano. It covers ROSSO and ROSATO wines made from Nerello and other grapes (including up to 10 percent white grapes), and white wines made from Carricante, Catarratto, TREBBIANO, and Minnella Bianca. The best Etna wines are the *Bianco Superiore*, which are made predominantly from Carricante grapes.

Etoile *see* DOMAINE CHANDON

L'Étoile AC [lay-TWAHL] French for "the star," L'Étoile is the name of this tiny APPELLATION and the village it encompasses. It's located in eastern France's Jura region, near the Swiss border. This appellation produces white wines made from SAVAGNIN, CHARDONNAY and the red grape Poulsard. L'Étoile AC also covers VIN JAUNE, VIN DE PAILLE, and MOUSSEUX wines.

Etude [ay-TEWD] The label used for wines made by Tony Soter from purchased grapes in rented space. Soter was the winemaker at CHAPELLET VINEYARD and SPOTTSWOODE VINEYARD, where he developed an excellent reputation. He now consults to a number of wineries and annually produces about 3,000 to 4,000 cases of red wine under the Etude label. Etude makes PINOT NOIR from CARNEROS grapes and CABERNET SAUVIGNON from NAPA VALLEY grapes. Both are highly regarded with the Pinot Noir slightly taking the edge.

eucalyptus [yoo-kuh-LIHP-tuhs] In winetasting, this term describes the spicy, aromatic, mintlike aroma of certain red wines, such as Heitz Martha's Vineyard CABERNET SAUVIGNON. Sometimes, the vineyards that produce such wines are surrounded by eucalyptus trees, which some contend contribute their essence to the grapes.

L'Evangile, Château [sha-TOH lay-vah*n*-ZHEEL] Château L'Evangile is nicely situated in the POMEROL AC, where it's surrounded by well-known Pomerol CHÂTEAUS like PETRUS, LA CONSEILLANTE, and VIEUX-CHÂTEAU-CERTAN and CHEVAL-BLANC of SAINT-ÉMILION. Pomerol châteaus have never been ranked, but Château L'Evangile is comparable to a DEUXIÈME CRU (second growth) or TROISIÈME CRU (third growth) château from the MÉDOC. It has around 33 acres planted with around 70 percent MERLOT and 30 percent CABERNET FRANC. There are about 4,500 to 6,000 cases of this RICH, LUSH red wine produced each year. Château L'Evangile wines are age-worthy, capable of lasting for 20 to 25 years.

extended maceration *see* MACERATION

extra brut *see* BRUT

extract [EHKS-trakt] The soluble and nonsoluble substances that contribute to the BODY, flavor, CHARACTER, and color of a wine. Wines made from grapes that provide heavy extract are usually described as full-bodied, and have dense, CONCENTRATED flavors and dark (for the type), opaque colors.

extra dry The term "extra dry" (or *extra sec*) appears on SPARKLING WINE labels to indicate that a wine that is fairly DRY, but with some RESIDUAL SUGAR. Extra dry sparkling wines usually contain 1.2 to 2 percent sugar, making them sweeter than BRUT but drier than SEC, DEMI SEC, or DOUX.

extra sec A French term meaning "EXTRA DRY."

exuberant [ehk-ZOO-buhr-uhnt] Winetasting term that describes LIVELY wines with lavish fruit.

aber [FAH-bur] German HYBRID that was developed in the 1920s, but that wasn't commercially popular until the 1960s. Faber's parents are Weissburgunder (PINOT BLANC) and MÜLLER-THURGAU. It's viewed as a good-quality grape with RIESLING-like characteristics—fruity, SPICY, and, in particular, highly ACIDIC. Although often used for BLENDING, Faber also produces some high-quality, Riesling-style VARIETAL WINES. In addition to its good quality, one of Faber's big advantages is its ability to grow under conditions where Riesling would not properly ripen. The fact that it's not as productive as some of the other varieties is one of its drawbacks. A majority of Faber's acreage is in Germany's RHEINHESSEN region, with some plantings in the NAHE region, as well. This grape is also known as *Faberrebe*.

Factory House A grand mansion in northern Portugal that houses the Association of British Port Shippers. Built during the late eighteenth and early nineteenth centuries, this superb granite structure is the site of some of the world's best PORT tastings. Its dual dining rooms allow attendees to retire after formal dinners to the second dining room in order to enjoy their port properly. The term *factory* refers to an establishment for factors (trading agents) and merchants conducting business in a foreign country.

faded A wine that, through the ravages of age, has lost its COMPLEXITY and CHARACTER, leaving it insipid and lackluster.

Falerian *see* FALERNO DEL MASSICO DOC

Falerno del Massico DOC [fah-LEHR-noh MAHSS-see-koh] Falernian (or Falernum), the most acclaimed wine of ancient Rome, was produced along the northern coast of the CAMPANIA region near Mondragone. Today in that same area (which is northwest of Naples), the modern DOC of Falerno del Massico produces BIANCO made from the Falanghina grape and ROSSO, which is made primarily from AGLIANICO and Piedirosso, although small amounts of Primitivo (*see* ZINFANDEL) and BARBERA can be added. In addition, there is a Primitivo VARIETAL WINE that must contain at least 85 percent Primitivo. Today's wines are promising, but they have little connection to the highly regarded Falernian of Roman times.

Falernum *see* FALERNO DEL MASSICO DOC

Falkenberg *see* DIENHEIM; PIESPORT

false wine *see* SUGAR WINE

farmyard *see* BARNYARD

Gary Farrell Wines Gary Farrell has been the winemaker at Davis Bynum Winery since the late 1970s. He started his own label in 1982 and continues to make Gary Farrell Wines in the Davis Bynum Winery from purchased grapes. These wines have developed a tremendous following and garnered countless high ratings from wine reviewers and in wine competitions. PINOT NOIR is Farrell's focus, with a RUSSIAN RIVER bottling and a VINEYARD-DESIGNATED wine from Allen Vineyard. An excellent Pinot Noir from the Bien Nacido Vineyard in SANTA BARBARA has recently been added to the lineup. His other wines, which are also extremely well regarded, include CABERNET SAUVIGNON and MERLOT, both from Ladi's Vineyard, ZINFANDEL from the Russian River area, and CHARDONNAY. The annual production for Gary Farrell Wines is between 3,500 and 4,000 cases.

fat A positive descriptor sometimes used for wine that, although CONCENTRATED, RICH, and high in GLYCEROL, has low to average ACIDITY. The impression on the palate is full and *fat*. A wine with *almost* the same qualities, but not in the same concentration, might be referred to as **plump**. If a fat wine lacks too much acidity it becomes insipid and is referred to as FLABBY. A sweet wine that's fat can be overwhelmingly unctuous. *See also* LEAN.

fattoria [fah-toh-REE-ah] An Italian term used in and around TUS-CANY to refer to a large farm or estate. Use of the term on a label, however, does not always guarantee that the wine is ESTATE BOTTLED. *See also* MASSERIA.

Faugères AC [foh-ZHEHR] APPELLATION located in the hilly region around the village of Faugères, which is north of Béziers in southern France's LANGUEDOC-ROUSSILLON region. Faugères is known for making good, sturdy red wines. The grapes used are CARIGNAN, CINSAUT, GRENACHE, MOURVÈDRE, and SYRAH.

Faustino Martínez [faws-TEE-noh mahr-TEE-nehz] BODEGA located in the RIOJA DO. It is best known for its RESERVA (*Faustino V*) and GRAN RESERVA (*Faustino I*) wines in their dark, frosted bottles. A broad range of other wines are also produced including BEAUJOLAIS-style reds, fresh, fruity whites, and even SPARKLING WINES—CAVA DO. TEMPRANILLO is the main grape, although Garnacha Tinta (GRENACHE), Mazuelo (CARIG-NAN), and GRACIANO are sometimes used. Faustino Martínez is also experimenting with CABERNET SAUVIGNON and PINOT NOIR.

Favorita *see* VERMENTINO

Faye-d'Anjou *see* COTEAUX DU LAYON

feeble A descriptor for wine that lacks distinction in all respects—flavor, aroma, BODY, CHARACTER, etc.

fehér [FEH-hayr] Hungarian for "white."

Felsenberg *see* SCHLOSSBÖCKELHEIM

Fendant *see* CHASSELAS

fermentation; fermenting [fer-men-TAY-shuhn] The natural process that turns grape juice into wine, fermentation is actually a chain reaction of chemical responses. During this process, technically called the **primary fermentation**, the sugars in the grape juice are converted by the enzymes in yeasts into ALCOHOL (55 to 60 percent) and CARBON DIOXIDE (40 to 45 percent). In addition, fermentation generates minor amounts of numerous incidental by-products that affect the aroma and taste of wine including ACETALDEHYDE, acetic acid (*see* ACIDS), ETHYL ACETATE, GLYCEROL, and alcohols other than ETHANOL. One of the potential problems winemakers must avoid is a **stuck fermentation**. This occurs when the yeast stops converting the sugar into alcohol and carbon dioxide, thereby prematurely leaving undesirable RESIDUAL SUGAR in the wine. As more is learned about fermentation, techniques are evolving to manage the process in order to produce optimum wines. For example, managing the temperature during the fermentation—cooler temperatures (45° to 60°F) for white wines, warmer temperatures (70° to 85°F) for heavier red wines—leads to superior wines. Red wines are usually fermented with their skins, seeds, and pulp to extract color and tannins—something not desirable in white wines. YEAST strains are also being experimented with to determine which ones work best for different wines under various conditions. Many winemakers believe BARREL FERMENTATION adds flavor and complexity to some white wines. CARBONIC MACERATION is a specialized fermentation process for producing light fruity red wines. *See also* BOTTLE FERMENTATION; FERMENTATION CONTAINERS; MALOLACTIC FERMENTATION; WHOLE BERRY FERMENTATION.

fermentation containers A variety of containers have been used over the years for fermenting wine. These include barrels and vats of oak or redwood, concrete vats lined with glass or coated with epoxy, and the huge LAGERS of Spain and Portugal, in which the grapes are stomped and then fermented. Today, most modern wineries use stainless steel tanks with temperature-controlled jackets because they're easy to clean (important in keeping unwanted bacteria out of the wine) and the temperature can be managed throughout the fermentation process. *See also* FERMENTATION.

fermentation lock Also called a *fermentation trap*, this low-pressure valve atop a fermenting vessel allows carbon dioxide gas to escape but inhibits air or bacteria from entering. *See also* FERMENTATION.

fermentation trap *see* FERMENTATION LOCK

fermentation yeasts *see* YEAST

fermentazione [fayr-mayn-tah-TSYOH-nay] The Italian term for "fermentation." On labels of sparkling wines (like SPUMANTE), the term *fermentazione naturale* indicates that carbon dioxide gas has been instilled in the wine through a natural method (usually the CHARMAT PROCESS).

fermentor [fer-MEN-tor] A vessel used to FERMENT grape juice. *See also* FERMENTATION CONTAINERS.

Ferrari-Carano Vineyards [fuh-RAHR-ree kuh-RAH-noh] DRY CREEK VALLEY winery that was founded in 1981 by Don Carano and his wife Rhonda, 2 years after they bought their first vineyard land in the ALEXANDER VALLEY (they also own Reno's El Dorado Hotel). Successive purchases in Dry Creek Valley, Alexander Valley, CARNEROS, and KNIGHTS VALLEY have brought the winery's total vineyard holdings to nearly 500 acres spread over twelve different vineyard sites. The winery established a solid reputation for its CHARDONNAY and FUMÉ BLANC wines before adding a number of red wines to its portfolio. The reds include CABERNET SAUVIGNON, MERLOT, ZINFANDEL, a BORDEAUX BLEND (Cabernet Sauvignon, Petit Verdot, Merlot, Malbec, and Cabernet Franc) called **Reserve Red**, and a SANGIOVESE-Cabernet Sauvignon blend called **Siena**. On occasion, Ferrari-Carano has made a LATE HARVEST Sauvignon Blanc called Eldorado Gold. Production for the winery is around 50,000 cases per year.

Ferreira [feh-RRAY-rah] Old Portuguese wine-producing company that produces not only fine PORT wines but fine TABLE WINES as well. It was founded in 1751 but didn't gain its real fame until the nineteenth century when Dona Antonia Ferreira, wife of the founder's grandson, took over the company's management when her husband died. The company was sold to SOGRAPE, Portugal's largest wine company in 1987; however, family members still own numerous vineyards in the DOURO area. Although Ferreira is well known for its ports, its premium table wine *Barca Velha* attracts tremendous attention and is Portugal's most expensive and sought-after red wine. Barca Velha, which is produced only from better VINTAGES, is made primarily from Tinta Roriz (TEMPRANILLO), along with Tinta Borroca and TOURIGA NACIONAL. It's aged for 18 months in OAK barrels and develops into a RICH, COMPLEX wine. Ferreira also produces a lower-priced, lighter-style table wine called *Esteva,* which has plum and cherry flavors. The best known of their FORTIFIED wines are the Tawny Ports, which include *Dona Antonia's Personal Reserve* (8 years old), *Quinta do Porto Ten-Year Old,* and the *Duque de Braganza 20-Year Old.* Ferreira is considered one of the top fifteen vintage port makers.

Ferrière, Château [sha-TOH feh-*RYEHR*] A TROISIÈME CRU (third growth) CHÂTEAU located in the MARGAUX AC in the MÉDOC district. There are only about 12 acres planted with around 47 percent CABERNET SAUVIGNON, 33 percent MERLOT, 12 percent PETIT VERDOT, and 8 percent CABERNET FRANC. The property has no building, and the wines are actually made at Château LASCOMBES. Many critics feel the LIGHT style of these wines means they're targeted at the restaurant trade and that the château is undeserving of its third-growth ranking. Only about 1,500 to 2,500 cases of red wine are made each year. Better vintages can age for up to about 10 years.

Fetească *see* LEÁNYKA

Fetzer Vineyards [FEHT-zer] Wine-producing firm that was established in 1968 by Barney Fetzer and his sons, although it had been selling grapes from its vineyards for several years prior to that. After growing the production to about 2 million cases per year, the Fetzer family sold the wineries and the brand names in 1992 to Brown-Forman Beverage Company, one of the world's largest companies in the wine and spirit industry. The Fetzer family retained most of the vineyards and continues to sell their grapes to the Fetzer Vineyards wineries. About 25 percent of their volume comes from Fetzer's SECOND LABEL **Bel Arbors**, which produces lower-priced CABERNET SAUVIGNON, CHARDONNAY, MERLOT, SAUVIGNON BLANC, and WHITE ZINFANDEL wines. The Fetzer Vineyards lineup features three levels of wines—the regular bottlings, the Barrel Select, and the Reserve wines. The medium-priced ($10 to $12) Barrel Select wines (Chardonnay, Cabernet Sauvignon, and Zinfandel) are generally highly regarded for wines in this price category. Fetzer's Reserve wines are also considered relatively good values.

feuillette [fuh-YET] A small OAK barrel traditionally used in France's CHABLIS region. The feuillette, which holds approximately 136 liters (36 U.S. gallons), was eventually replaced by the 228-liter (60

U.S. gallons) PIÈCE, which is used primarily in the rest of BURGUNDY. Today, however, most producers in Chablis have eliminated oak barrel aging and instead use stainless steel tanks for storage until bottling.

Les Fêves *see* BEAUNE

Fiano di Avellino DOC [fee-AH-noh dee ah-veh-LEE-noh] Highly regarded, DRY white wines that are made with at least 85 percent of the indigenous Fiano grape. This DOC zone is located in the hills surrounding Avellino and twenty-five other villages, east of Naples in Italy's CAMPANIA region. "Fiano di Lapio" on the label indicates that the wine was made from grapes grown in the classical area just northeast of Avellino near the village of Lapio.

fiasco; pl. fiaschi [fee-YAHS-koh; fee-YAHS-kee] Italian for "flask," the word *fiasco* is most often connected with the squat, round-bottomed, straw-covered bottle containing cheaper wine from the CHIANTI region. The straw covering not only helps the bottle sit upright, but protects the thin, fragile glass. Fiaschi are seldom seen today as the cost of hand-wrapping each flask for cheaper wines has become prohibitive, and the more expensive wines with aging potential need bottles that can be laid on their sides.

Les Fichots *see* PERNAND-VERGELESSES

Fiddletown AVA A small APPELLATION located east of Sacramento in northern California's AMADOR COUNTY. ZINFANDEL is the most popular grape variety here. Eschen Vineyard is a respected Fiddletown grower that sells to both Amador Foothill Winery and Santino Wines.

Les Fiefs de Lagrange *see* LAGRANGE, CHÂTEAU

field blend The practice of planting a single vineyard with several grape varieties that will make up a single wine. Rather than picking and processing each variety separately and then blending them together, the grapes are all picked and crushed together. This method was practiced in Europe and was quite popular in California at one time, although it's not much in evidence today.

field grafting *see* GRAFTING

Les Fiètres *see* CORTON

de Fieuzal, Château [sha-TOH deh fyuh-ZAHL] CRU CLASSÉ property located in the PESSAC-LÉOGNAN AC in the GRAVES district of BORDEAUX. Improvements to the estate in the 1970s have resulted in a string of excellent wines during the 1980s. The wines are thought to be comparable to those from a DEUXIÈME CRU (second growth) or TROISIÈME CRU (third growth) of the MÉDOC. There are about 12,000 to 16,000 cases of red wine and 1,500 to 2,500 cases of white wine produced by the nearly 82-acre château. The grape blend used for the red wines is around 60 percent CABERNET SAUVIGNON, 30 percent MERLOT, 5 percent CABERNET FRANC, and 5 percent PETIT VERDOT. White wines use SAUVIGNON BLANC and SÉMILLON, about evenly proportioned. The white wines, which have developed an excellent reputation since the mid-1980s, can AGE for up to about 10 years. The red wines will last for up to 20 years. **L'Abeille de Fieuzal** is the SECOND LABEL for this château.

fifth growth *see* CINQUIÈME CRU

Figeac, Château [sha-TOH fee-ZHAHK] One of the larger properties of the SAINT-ÉMILION AC. It was even larger prior to 1830, when it included what are now the smaller châteaus of La Tour-Figeac, La Tour-du Pin-Figeac-Giraud-Belivier, and La Tour-du Pin-Figeac-Moueix and the larger, well-known Château CHEVAL BLANC. The current owner, Thierry Manoncourt, likes to point out that at one time Cheval Blanc (which now has a better reputation and receives higher prices for its wine than Figeac) was where the stables of the large Figeac estate were located and that wine produced there was sold as Vin de Figeac. The modern-day Château Figeac, which is still large for Saint-Émilion, consists of nearly 100 acres. The grape variety mix is unusual for the MERLOT-dominated Saint-Émilion area—35 percent CABERNET SAUVIGNON, 35 percent CABERNET FRANC, and 30 percent MERLOT. The CHÂTEAU is a PREMIER GRAND CRU CLASSÉ, and most feel that it's equivalent to a DEUXIÈME CRU (second growth) of the MÉDOC. Production at the château averages about 12,000 cases of red wine each year. The château's SECOND LABEL is called **La Grange Neuve de Figeac**.

fillette *see* WINE BOTTLES

filtering A step used by some winemakers to clarify wine just prior to bottling. The purpose of filtering is to remove yeast cells and other microorganisms that could spoil the wine, as well as any remaining sediment that would keep it from being crystal clear (which is what most of the public expects). The wine is pumped through one or more various filters including those made of cellulose, pads coated with diatomaceous earth, or especially fine membranes. Today's modern winery has filters so fine that they can remove infinitesimal particles. When such fine filters are used, the process is called **sterile filtering**. Some winemakers argue that this precise filtering extracts flavor and character that the sediment lends the wine. *See also* FINING; RACKING; UNFILTERED.

finesse Descriptor for a wine that has distinction and grace—there's perfect harmony among its components.

Finger Lakes AVA APPELLATION located in northern New York State just south of Lake Ontario. Its name comes from its four largest glacial lakes, which look like the fingers of a giant hand. Grape growing survives in this region because the environment around the lakes moderates the temperatures and extends the growing seasons. MICROCLIMATES in this area are extremely important. It's now believed that the areas around the larger lakes of Cayuga (which has it own AVA) and Seneca are best because the lakes are deeper and store more warmth, and because the lower altitude is warmer. About half of all the U.S. wines produced outside of California (about 95 percent of U.S. wine is produced in the Golden State) come from the Finger Lakes area. This AVA still grows mostly native American grapes (CATAWBA, CONCORD, DELAWARE, and NIAGARA) or HYBRIDS (AURORA, BACO NOIR, CHELOIS, DE CHAUNAC, and SEYVAL BLANC). However, some VITIS VINIFERA grapes have been planted including CABERNET SAUVIGNON, CHARDONNAY, PINOT NOIR, and RIESLING. Finger Lake AVA wineries include Bully Hill Vineyards, Glenora, Gold Seal Vineyards and Great Western (both owned by the Taylor Wine Company), Heron Hill, Plane's Cayuga Vineyard, Taylor Wine Company, Vinifera Wine Cellars, Wagner Vineyards, Widmer's Wine Cellars, and Hermann J. Wiemer Vineyard.

fining [FI-ning] A winemaking process that removes microscopic elements such as protein particles that would cloud the wine and PHENOLIC compounds like TANNINS that could cause bitterness and astringency. The most frequently used **fining agents** are activated carbon, activated charcoal, BENTONITE, CASEIN, egg whites, gelatin, ISINGLASS, nylon, and polyvinyl poly-pyrrolidone (PVPP). When added to wine, fining agents capture suspended particles by absorbtion or coagulation, causing them to settle to the bottom of the container. Once the particles sink, the wine can be RACKED, FILTERED, or CENTRIFUGED to separate it from this sediment. In addition to clarifying wines, various fining agents can also be used to remove color from white wines, deodorize wines with an off odor, and reduce acids.

fining agents *see* FINING

finish The final flavor and TEXTURE impression that remains on the palate after a wine is swallowed. The finish is part of a wine's overall balance. A distinctive, lingering (or LONG) finish is the ideal. A wine with a weak or nonexistent finish is considered lacking.

fino *see* SHERRY

Fiorano [fee-oh-RAH-noh] The wine estate of Alberico Boncompagni Ludovisi, the Prince of Verosa. It produces a highly regarded ROSSO from a blend of CABERNET SAUVIGNON and MERLOT, a BIANCO from Malvasia di Candia (MALVASIA), and a white wine made from SÉMILLON. Because of the unauthorized grapes that are used, the wines can only be registered as VINO DA TAVOLA. Fiorano is located south of Rome in Italy's LATIUM region.

firm In winetasting, a positive descriptor for a wine's impression on the palate. Such a wine is fairly high in TANNIN and ACIDITY but still well-BALANCED. Firm is the opposite of FLABBY.

first growth The English translation of the French "PREMIER CRU." The precise meaning of the term *first growth* refers to the original four red-wine CHÂTEAUS ranked in the CLASSIFICATION OF 1855 (LAFITE-ROTHSCHILD, LATOUR, MARGAUX and HAUT-BRION) plus CHÂTEAU MOUTON-ROTHSCHILD, which was added in 1973. Sometimes the meaning of first growth is expanded slightly to include Châteaus AUSONE and CHEVAL BLANC (ranked in a separate classification for SAINT-ÉMILION in 1954) and Château PÉTRUS from POMEROL (which has never been classified but has the status, wine quality, and premium pricing to rank it with the others). Although Château D'YQUEM of SAUTERNES is also a premier cru, it produces white wines, and the narrower use of first growth typically applies only to red wines. Even though BURGUNDY and CHAMPAGNE also have a premier cru class, the first growth designation doesn't usually refer to these areas.

Fisher Vineyards Fred and Juelle Fisher (he's a descendant of the "Body by Fisher" family) planted their first vines high in SONOMA COUNTY's Mayacamas Mountains in 1973. They've developed 25 acres there, plus another 50 acres they purchased later, on two vineyard sites at the northern end of the NAPA VALLEY. The winery was BONDED in 1979 and now produces about 8,000 cases of wine each year. Fisher Vineyards grows CABERNET SAUVIGNON, CHARDONNAY, and MERLOT varieties. The Cabernet Sauvignon and Chardonnay **Coach Insignia** wines are Fisher's equivalent to a RESERVE. Both are viewed favorably, with the Cabernet taking the edge. Fisher also produces Chardonnays with the standard Napa-Sonoma Counties designation, two VINEYARD-DESIGNATED wines—Whitney's Vineyard Chardonnay and Wedding Vineyard Cabernet Sauvignon—and an estate-grown MERLOT.

Fitou AC [fee-TOO] APPELLATION located in the LANGUEDOC-ROUSSILLON region in southern France. It is surrounded by the CÔTES DU ROUSSILLON-VILLAGES AC on one side and on the other side by the large CORBIÈRES AC of which Fitou AC is actually a part. Fitou is split into two sections— one area on the Mediterranean coast between Narbonne and Perpignan and the other inland around the village of Tuchan. Fitou AC makes red wines that are considered some of the best in the Languedoc-Roussillon region. They're made from CARIGNAN, GRENACHE, MOURVÈDRE and SYRAH and require a minimum of 9 months AGING in wooden barrels.

fixed acids *see* ACIDS

Fixin [fee-SAN] One of the most northerly villages in the CÔTE DE NUITS district of France's BURGUNDY region. It's not as well known as some of the neighboring villages in this famous area because it contains no GRAND CRU vineyards. However, Fixin produces some very good PRE-MIER CRU wines, the best of which come from the vineyards of **Les Arvelets**, **Clos de la Perrière**, **Clos du Chapitre**, **Clos Napoléon**, and **Les Hervelets**. Wines from these premier cru vineyards and those from the **Fixin AC** are generally ROBUST, full-bodied (*see* BODY), and re-quire several years of AGING before they're really enjoyable. Fixin AC wines are difficult to find because the total vineyard area isn't that large (320 acres, including premier cru vineyards) and because they can also be bottled as CÔTES DE NUITS-VILLAGES AC wines. A number of producers opt for the latter because they have other acreage entitled only to the Côtes de Nuits-Village AC and its easier to just combine the wines.

flabby In wine parlance, a descriptor for a wine that's heavy on the palate. Such a wine is seriously deficient in ACIDITY, STRUCTURE, and, subsequently, in flavor. *See also* FAT.

Flaccianello [flahk-kee-ah-NEHL-loh] The proprietary name for a highly regarded super-Tuscan (*see* TUSCANY) red wine made by Tenuta Fontodi, a wine estate located near the village of Panzano in the CHI-ANTI CLASSICO area south of Florence. The wine is 100 percent SAN-GIOVESE and is AGED in both large wood casks and small oak BARRIQUES. The wine's full name is *Flaccianello della Pieve.*

Flagey-Echézeaux *see* VOSNE-ROMANÉE

flasche [FLAH-shuh] German word for "bottle."

flat 1. For STILL WINE, the term *flat* describes a dull flavor and CHAR-ACTER due to a lack of ACIDITY. 2. A SPARKLING WINE that has lost its ef-fervescence is *flat.*

fleshy Descriptor for wine with high ALCOHOL, EXTRACT, and, usually, GLYCEROL. It's generally full-bodied (*see* BODY) and smooth. The term *fleshy* is comparable to CHEWY, the opposite of LEAN.

Fleur de Carneros *see* CARNEROS CREEK WINERY

Fleurie AC [fleuh-REE] The third largest of the ten CRUS in France's BEAUJOLAIS region. Made from GAMAY grapes, Fleurie wines are some of the most popular in Beaujolais, which has caused them to become somewhat pricey. These wines are floral-scented and have a fruitiness and richness without the TANNINS of the wines from MOULIN-À-VENT. Although most Fleurie wines are drunk young, they can AGE from 2 to 4 years. Fleurie is sometimes called the "Queen of Beaujolais," while Moulin-à-Vent is referred to as the "King of Beaujolais."

La Fleur-Pétrus, Château [sha-TOH lah fluh*r* pay-T*R*EWSS] CHÂTEAU located in the POMEROL AC between two of the APPELLATION'S best châteaus—PÉTRUS and LAFLEUR. Château La Fleur-Pétrus (sometimes spelled *Lafleur-Pétris*) is owned by the Moueix family, who also owns the famous Château Pétrus and another excellent Pomerol château, TROTANOY. Around 2,500 to 3,500 cases of high-quality red wine are produced from this nearly 20-acre estate. The wines are a blend of about 80 percent MERLOT and 20 percent CABERNET FRANC. They're lighter than those from Pétrus and Trotanoy and can age for 12 to 15 years. The wines of Pomerol are unclassified (*see* CLASSIFICATION OF 1855). If they were, La Fleur-Pétrus would be the equivalent of a TROISIÈME CRU (third growth) in MÉDOC.

fliers Tiny visible but tasteless particles that occasionally appear in wine. Usually caused by a cold environment, fliers generally disappear when the wine is warmed.

flinty A winetasting term used to describe an aroma and flavor reminiscent of flint striking steel. A flinty characteristic, which the French call *pierre-à-fusil*, comes from grapes grown in certain soils. It's found in extremely dry white wines such as certain French CHABLIS and SAUVIGNON BLANCS and is considered a positive trait.

Floc de Gascogne [flawk duh gas-KAW*N*] A FORTIFIED, sweet APÉRITIF made in France's Armagnac region by adding ARMAGNAC to unfermented grape juice to halt any FERMENTATION. Floc de Gascogne is very similar to the much better-known PINEAU DES CHARENTES.

flor [FLAWR] Although this is literally the Spanish word for "flower," in wine terminology *flor* refers to the off-white yeast that develops naturally on certain wines after they're fermented. Usually associated with sherry from the Spanish region of JEREZ DE LA FRONTERA, *flor* is also a factor in Spain's MONTILLA region, as well as France's CHÂTEAU-CHALLON district. In these areas, the wine barrels are not completely filled, so there's enough surface area for air to get to the wine. Assuming reasonable temperature and humidity, this exposure allows flor to grow, creating a gauzy white layer that protects the wine from further air contact and subsequent oxidation (*see* OXIDIZED). Flor also affects the flavor and character of the wine—a sharp pungency or tang is the most notable development. It is this characteristic that's noticeable in the FINO- and AMONTILLADO-style sherries. Flor will not grow on wines FORTIFIED with too much alcohol (above 16.2 percent), as is the case with the OLOROSO-style sherries. In California, Australia, and other areas where flor doesn't grow naturally, flor yeast cultures are introduced to sherry-style wines, thereby creating similar results and improving the quality of such wines.

Flora [FLOR-uh] The fairly rare white-wine grape that is a CROSS of GEWÜRZTRAMINER and SÉMILLON developed in the 1950s by the University of California at DAVIS. As the name suggests, the wines have a floral quality with a high degree of spiciness. They're usually vinified medium-sweet to sweet. One of the more well-known producers is SCHRAMSBERG VINEYARDS, which uses Flora in its Cremant—a medium-sweet SPARKLING WINE. Never very popular, Flora plantings are now under a hundred acres.

floraison *see* FLOWERING

floral; flowery A wine that has an aroma reminiscent of flowers, such as violets, citrus blossoms, or roses. This impression can also be sensed on the palate. Floral characteristics are more likely to be found in white wines like JOHANNISBERG RIESLING and GEWÜRZTRAMINER than in reds, although those made from NEBBIOLO grapes are known to be suggestive of violets.

floral abortion A malady occurring in some grape varieties, such as the Italian PICOLIT, where the flowering buds don't develop properly and often fall off. Floral abortion generally results in a small crop and, therefore, expensive wines.

Flora Springs Winery In 1977 Jerry Komes, former president of Bechtel Corporation, and his wife Flora purchased an old winery and some vineyard land in the western hills of the NAPA VALLEY between St. Helena and Rutherford. They were soon joined by their son and daughter, and the Flora Springs Winery was born. The family members now own almost 400 acres in eight different vineyard sites. The winery produces between 30,000 and 35,000 cases of wine each year represented by two brands—Flora Springs (all ESTATE BOTTLED) and the SECOND LABEL **Floreal**. The lower-priced Floreal offers CABERNET SAUVIGNON, CHARDONNAY, MERLOT, and SAUVIGNON BLANC wines. On the upper end, the Flora Springs line includes **Trilogy** (a blend of equal parts of CABERNET FRANC, Cabernet Sauvignon, and Merlot), **Soliloquy** (BARREL-FERMENTED Sauvignon Blanc), barrel-fermented Chardonnay, and a RESERVE Cabernet Sauvignon. The Chardonnay wines are particularly acclaimed.

Floreal *see* FLORA SPRINGS WINERY

flowering Term that refers to the stage when the vine produces small flowers, a critical time in the development of grapes. Flowering (*floraison* in French) occurs about 2½ months after the first tiny leaf buds burst from the vine. Once flowering is completed, the tiny green berries (that will eventually become mature grapes) begin to form. Warm, dry, sunny weather is critical during flowering because failure to flower properly can result in COULURE, meaning that some or all the grapes may not develop adequately.

flurbereinigung [FLOOR-beh-RINE-ee-goong] A German term that refers to the ongoing process of reconstructing and reallocating vineyards among the growers. The endeavor, which is supported by federal and local governments, is designed to improve the competitiveness of the German wine industry by enhancing vineyard layout and lowering the costs of wine production. Over half of Germany's vineyards have been revamped to allow higher yields with better-suited crops.

flute [FLOOT] 1. In France, a tall, thin, clear glass bottle shaped like the classic green bottle of ALSACE and the brown bottle for RHINE wines. Flutes are also made in clear glass for ROSÉ wines. 2. A stemmed champagne glass with a tall, slender, cone-shaped bowl. *See also* Common Wine Bottle Shapes, page 586.

Thomas Fogarty Winery This SANTA CRUZ MOUNTAINS AVA winery was started in 1981, 3 years after the first vines were planted and 13 years after Dr. Thomas Fogarty first purchased the land. Thomas Fogarty Winery makes between 8,000 and 10,000 cases of wine each year. Among the regular bottlings are three CHARDONNAYS—Edna Valley-Paragon Vineyard, Santa Cruz Mountains, and Ventana Vineyards

(MONTEREY). Other regulars on the roster are PINOT NOIR from the Santa Cruz Mountains, CABERNET SAUVIGNON from the NAPA VALLEY, and GEWÜRZ-TRAMINER from Ventana Vineyards. All the wines receive high marks on occasion, but the Gewürztraminer is consistently the best. Occasionally, this winery also makes SPARKLING WINE.

Folie à Deux Winery [FOH-lee ah doo] This NAPA VALLEY winery is located just northeast of St. Helena, California. Folie à Deux, French for "shared fantasy" (or "lunacy"), was founded by Larry and Evie Dizmang in 1981. The winery garnered praise for its CHARDONNAY wines and grew from about 2,000 to about 20,000 cases per year. Chardonnays comprise about half the production, CABERNET SAUVIGNON about a quarter, and the rest is CHENIN BLANC, with an occasional MER-LOT or MUSCAT wine. Folie à Deux owns about 15 acres next to the winery and another 15 acres near Yountville. **Pas de Deux** is the winery's SECOND LABEL.

Folle Blanche [fawl BLAH*N*SH] A white-wine grape known for its high YIELDS and high ACIDITY, even in hot growing regions. Folle Blanche was once widely planted in France where it was a principal variety in the production of BRANDY from the COGNAC and ARMAGNAC districts. The PHYLLOXERA epidemic changed all that because the remedy for phylloxera was to GRAFT vines to American ROOTSTOCK. Unfortunately, the Folle Blanche vines did not perform well after this process. In addition, Folle Blanche is very susceptible to BLACK ROT and GRAY ROT. These frailties resulted in Folle Blanche being replaced by Ugni Blanc (TREBBIANO) in Cognac and by BACO BLANC in Armagnac. Today, the largest growing region for this grape is centered around the mouth of the LOIRE, where Folle Blanche is called *Gros Plant* and VINI-FIED into the generally highly acidic VDQS wine *Gros Plant du Pays Nantais*. Small amounts of Folle Blanche are grown in California and Argentina. Folle Blanche is also known as *Camobraque* and *Picpoule* (which translates into "lip-stinger," apparently in reference to its mouth-puckering acidity). Folle Blanche is unrelated to the Piquepoul (or Picpoule) grown in the CHÂTEAUNEUF-DU-PAPE area.

Fondillon *see* ALICANTE DO

Fonseca Guimaraens [fawn-SAY-kuh GIH-mah-rah*ns*] A premier PORT producer based in Vila Nova de Gaia, Portugal. When it was founded in the seventeenth century, the firm was called Fonseca, Moneteiro & Company. Its name was changed to Guimaraens Vinhos in 1822 when the Guimaraens family took control; they used Fonseca as a brand name. In 1948 the firm was purchased by the Yeatman family, owners of TAYLOR FLADGATE & YEATMAN, another highly regarded port firm. In 1988 they changed the name of the firm to Fonseca Guimaraens (members of the Guimaraens family are still involved with managment of the firm). The Fonseca vintage port is considered one of the top five vintage ports. The Fonseca-Guimaraens vintage port, which is the firm's SECOND LABEL (made in years when the traditional Fonseca vintage port isn't produced) is ranked in the top twenty. Fonseca Guimaraens produces a wide array of port wines including the well-known *Bin 27*, a vintage character port. Its 40-year-old tawny port is considered one of the best in its class.

de Fontarney *see* BRANE-CANTENAC, CHÂTEAU

Forman Vineyard Small but esteemed winery owned by Ric Forman, a long-time NAPA VALLEY winemaker. His career, which spans 25 years, began at STERLING VINEYARDS where, at age 24, he was the first winemaker. Forman started his winery in 1982 after helping establish NEWTON VINEYARDS with Sterling's founder Peter Newton. Today, Forman Vineyard has about 47 acres on Howell Mountain, planted mainly with CABERNET SAUVIGNON and small amounts of CABERNET FRANC and MERLOT. Grapes for the CHARDONNAY wines come from a vineyard that Forman co-owns with Charles Shaw near Rutherford, California. Forman's highly praised Cabernet Sauvignon and Chardonnay wines have a very limited annual production of about 2,000 cases each. A SECOND LABEL **Chateau La Grande Roche** is used by the winery for GRENACHE or any lesser wines that may be produced.

Forst [FAW*R*ST] Forst, along with the neighboring towns of DEIDESHEIM, RUPPETSBERG, and WACHENHEIM, produce some of the best wines of Germany's RHEINPFALZ region. Located southwest of BAD DÜRKHEIM, Forst is acknowledged for its full-bodied (*see* BODY) yet VELVETY wines, which are said to gain extra character from the vein of black, potassium-rich basalt that runs through the area. The best-known EINZELLAGE is the **Jesuitengarten**, but **Freundstück**, **Kirchenstück**, **Pechsten**, and **Ungeheuer** are all highly regarded as well. RIESLING, the dominant grape here, is the variety used to produce the town's most distinguished wines.

fortified; fortified wine Initially used as a method to preserve some wines, fortification is the addition of brandy or a neutral spirit in order to boost a wine's ALCOHOL content. **Fortified wines** generally have between 17 and 21 percent alcohol. Some of the better-known examples are PORT, SHERRY, MADEIRA, MÁLAGA, and MARSALA.

Les Forts de Latour *see* LATOUR, CHÂTEAU

forward A term used to describe wine that has matured earlier than expected for its age and style. The opposite of BACKWARD.

foudre [FOO-druh] A French term referring to a large wooden cask used for maturing and storing wine. Though the size varies, a *foudre* has a capacity of at least 500 liters.

Fourchaume *see* CHABLIS

Les Fourneaux *see* CHABLIS

Fourtet *see* CLOS FOURTET

fourth growth *see* QUATRIÈME CRU

foxy A term used to describe the pronounced musky, earthy quality found in wines made with grapes from the North American vine species VITIS LABRUSCA.

frais [FRAY] A French word meaning "cool" or "chilly" but also "fresh." When it appears on a French wine label, it means the bottle should be chilled before serving.

Franc-Caillou *see* MAUCAILLOU, CHÂTEAU

France France is definitely a wine-oriented country. It produces over 20 percent of the world's wines, second only to Italy. It's the top per capita consumer of wines—per person, the French population consumes almost nine times that of the U.S. population. But more than that, in its effort to create the best possible wines, France has set the standard for what wines are meant to be. Except for Portugal's PORTS, Germany's RIESLINGS, and Spain's SHERRIES, the wine-producing world primarily uses French wines as benchmarks for excellence in high-quality wines. France's premier wine-growing regions each contribute extraordinary exemplars: BORDEAUX for the red wines made from CABERNET SAUVIGNON, MERLOT, and CABERNET FRANC, for the rich, sweet SAUTERNES wines made from SAUVIGNON BLANC, SÉMILLON, and MUSCADELLE, and even for the DRY white wines of GRAVES made from Sauvignon Blanc and Sémillon; BURGUNDY for the elegant red wines made from PINOT NOIR, the superb white wines made from CHARDONNAY, and the light, fruity red BEAUJOLAIS wines made from GAMAY; CHAMPAGNE for superior SPARKLING WINES made mainly from Pinot Noir and Chardonnay; the RHÔNE region for its red SYRAH wines and white VIOGNIER wines from northern Rhône region; the GRENACHE-based red wines from places like CHÂTEAUNEUF-DU-PAPE from the southern region, and the ROSÉ wines of TAVEL; and the LOIRE for the dry, semisweet, and sweet wines made from CHENIN BLANC and Sauvignon Blanc. The wines of ALSACE, the other premier growing region, are not as widely imitated by the world's wine producers. However, as winemakers continue to make dry wines from GEWÜRZTRAMINER, RIESLING, SYLVANER, PINOT GRIS, PINOT BLANC, and MUSCAT, they're discovering that such wines are Alsacian specialties. Of course, all this doesn't mean that other countries don't produce superior wines. The Italian wines made from NEBBIOLO and SANGIOVESE or the California ZINFANDELS are superb. But no other country's wines are as widely copied as those of France. From South Africa to the United States to Chile to Australia, winemakers are planting French varieties and making French-influenced wines. In addition to their grape varieties and winemaking acumen, the French have contributed their system of quality control to the winemaking world. Their levels of quality—from lowest to highest—are VIN DE TABLE, VIN DE PAYS, VIN DÉLIMITÉ DE QUALITÉ SUPÉRIEURE, and APPELLATION D'ORIGINE CONTRÔLÉE. France did not achieve its esteemed position in the world of wine overnight. Grapes are thought to have been planted in France at least 2,700 years ago, prior to the Roman occupation. The Romans, however, brought many practices with them that improved French wines including planting vineyards on the best slopes, pruning and managing the vineyards, and various winemaking techniques. Over the centuries, the French have learned which grape varieties grow best in which locations and have gradually perfected their winemaking craft. This information has been recorded in detail over time and has been a major factor implementing the Appellation d'Origine Contrôlée system that defines the top quality level for wines. This shouldn't imply that the French drink only top-quality wines. In fact most of the wine consumed is simple *vin de table* that's produced in huge amounts in southwest France, parts of the Rhône region, the LANGUEDOC-ROUSSILLON and PROVENCE, and in smaller amounts throughout the rest of France. But France is continuing to try to improve even these wines by encouraging practices such as the planting of specific higher-quality grape varieties, lowering YIELDS, and modernizing winemaking procedures.

Franciacorta DOC [frahn-shah-KOR-tah] DOC area located northwest of the city of Brescia in the eastern part of Italy's LOMBARDY region. Although it produces a highly regarded white STILL WINE from Pinot Bianco (PINOT BLANC) and CHARDONNAY and a reasonably good red wine from CABERNET FRANC, BARBERA, NEBBIOLO, and MERLOT, it's the Franciacorta SPUMANTE that is widely acclaimed. Both the bianco and ROSATO sparkling wines are made via MÉTHODE CHAMPENOISE and use a combination of Pinot Bianco, Chardonnay, Pinot Grigio (PINOT GRIS), and Pinot Nero (PINOT NOIR).

Franciscan Vineyards [fran-SIHS-kuhn] Founded in 1972, Franciscan Vineyards went through four owners before it found its footing in 1979 under the ownership of the German firm of Peter Eckes. In the mid-1980s, a joint venture between the Eckes Corporation and Augustus Huneus was formed to operate Franciscan and several other wineries owned by it—Estancia Vineyards, Pinnacles Vineyard, and MOUNT VEEDER WINERY. Franciscan Vineyards is located in the center of the NAPA VALLEY between the towns of Rutherford and St. Helena. The winery owns 240 acres just northeast of Oakville and an additional 280 acres (purchased in 1990) near Rutherford. Franciscan produces CABERNET SAUVIGNON, CHARDONNAY (Oakville Estate and Cuvée Sauvage), MERLOT, a red MERITAGE, and ZINFANDEL wines. The winery makes between 50,000 and 60,000 cases of wine per year, a figure that should increase as the acreage near Rutherford begins producing. **Estancia Vineyards** has grown into a sizable operation on its own, making nearly 100,000 cases of white wine. Most of the white wine production is Chardonnay, but there's also SAUVIGNON BLANC and a white Meritage from nearly 500 acres owned in MONTEREY COUNTY. Estancia also makes Cabernet Sauvignon, Merlot, SANGIOVESE, PINOT NOIR, and a red Meritage from vineyards owned in ALEXANDER VALLEY. **Pinnacles Vineyard**, located in Monterey County, specializes in PINOT NOIR and Chardonnay. It makes between 3,000 and 4,000 cases of Pinot Noir (which isn't usually FILTERED or FINED and is sometimes made with 100 percent wild yeast) plus about 4,000 cases of Chardonnay.

Franconia *see* FRANKEN

Franken [FRAHNG-kuhn] One of Germany's thirteen ANBAUGEBIETE (quality wine regions) that lies just east of the city of Frankfort, along the Main River. The river (and the region) follow a large, shaky-W shape in the northern part of Bavaria, around the university city of **Würzburg** (Franken's capital). The climate in Franken (known as **Franconia** in English) can be quite cold, and the vineyards are planted mainly with white grapes. MÜLLER-THURGAU is the primary grape here, followed by silvaner (*see* SYLVANER) and BACCHUS. RIESLING doesn't perform well in Franken's short growing season. Silvaner produces this region's best wines, which are often compared to white wines from France's BURGUNDY region in terms of richness and BODY (although the flavors are quite different). Most Franken wines, which have a slight EARTHY flavor regardless of the grape used, are different from those in other parts of Germany in that they're DRY rather than sweet. Wines with less than 4 grams of sugar per liter (0.4 percent) are identifed by the term *Fränkisch Trocken* (*see* TROCKEN). Franken wines also differ in that many are bottled in unique, flat-sided flagons called BOCKSBEUTEL. Franken wines are sometimes referred to as **Steinwein**, after the region's most famous vineyard **Würzburger Stein** (*see* WÜRZBURGER), a 210-acre EINZELLAGE. The region has three BEREICHS—**Maindreieck**, **Mainviereck**, and **Steigerwald**. The Bereich names are often found on the region's wine bottles since there are no GROSSLAGEN. Franken wines aren't well known outside the region since most of the production is consumed locally.

Franken Riesling *see* SYLVANER

Frankland River *see* LOWER GREAT SOUTHERN REGION

Frascati DOC [frahs-KAH-tee] DOC zone located in the CASTELLI ROMANI area on the southeast edge of Rome in Italy's LATIUM region. It encircles the town of Frascati and neighboring environs. Frascati produces more wine than any other DOC in Latium, most of it DRY white wine (made from MALVASIA, TREBBIANO, and GRECO) that's a favorite in Rome restaurants for HOUSE WINE. Frascati wines can also be AMABILE, DOLCE, or *cannellino*, the latter a special version using very ripe grapes hopefully infected with BOTRYTIS CINEREA. A SPUMANTE version is also produced.

Freemark Abbey Winery The current incarnation of this NAPA VALLEY winery was established in 1967 after the previous Freemark Abbey had closed its doors 5 years earlier after over 25 years in business. The present winery, who is located just north of St. Helena, California, came about through the efforts of seven partners, which included Charles Carpy, Brad Webb, and Bill Jaeger. By the early 1970s, Freemark Abbey was producing highly regarded wines. Particularly notable was the Boché Vineyard CABERNET SAUVIGNON, which Freemark Abbey began bottling in the late 1960s. Today, Freemark Abbey annually produces between 35,000 and 40,000 case of wine, primarily from partner-owned vineyards. The VARIETAL WINES it produces include two CHARDONNAYS (Napa Valley and Carpy Ranch), three Cabernet Sauvignons (Napa Valley, Boché Vineyard, and Sycamore Vineyard), a MERLOT, and a RIESLING. Occasionally, when BOTRYTIS CINEREA attacks the grapes, Freemark Abbey produces a LATE HARVEST RIESLING which they call **Edelwein**.

free-run juice; free-run wine Free-run juice is juice that flows freely from grapes without external pressure, such as that applied by a wine PRESS. This usually occurs simply from the natural weight of the grapes on top of each other or during CRUSHING of the grapes. Free-run juice (usually associated with white-wine grapes) is

considered the best because pressing produces **press juice**, which can contain bitter, sometimes unwanted, compounds that are released from the skins and/or seeds. If not overtly astringent or bitter, press juice is sometimes mixed with free-run juice to give the resulting wine STRUCTURE. Similarly, after the fermentation of red wines, the wine that flows freely (without pressing) from the pulp, skins, and seeds is called **free-run wine** (*vin de goutte* in France). **Press wine**, called *vin de presse* by the French, is then pressed from the MUST. Press wine is darker, more TANNIC, and much coarser than free-run wine. Some winemakers blend some or all of the press wine into the free-run wine to add firmness and structure; those who want more accessible wines don't follow this practice.

free SO₂ *see* SULFUR DIOXIDE

free sulfur dioxide *see* SULFUR DIOXIDE

Freiherrlich Langwerth von Simmern'sches Rentamt
see SIMMERN, FREIHERRLICH LANGWERTH VON

Freisa [FRAY-zah] Italian red-wine grape that has been grown in the PIEDMONT region for centuries. After declining in popularity for several decades, Freisa is enjoying a resurgence of interest. It produces highly ACIDIC, pale cherry-red wines whose AROMA and flavor are reminiscent of raspberries. Freisa is VINIFIED in many styles ranging from DRY to sweet, and STILL to FRIZZANTE (lightly sparkling). Freisa has DOC status in *Freisa di Chieri* and *Freisa d'Asti*. It's also known as *Fresa* or *Fresia*.

Freixenet [fresh-ehn-EHT] With its subsidiaries, Castellblanch and Segura Viudas (large SPARKLING WINE producers based in CATALONIA), Freixenet is the world's largest producer of MÉTHODE CHAMPENOISE wines. Freixenet produces a broad range of sparkling wines, led by its best-selling *Cordon Negro Brut*. It also owns the firms of Conde de Caralt (which produces sparkling and STILL WINES), René Barbier (still wines), Canals and Nubiola (sparkling wines), and the French CHAMPAGNE firm Henri Abelé. Frexinet owners have also joined the California wine industry with its CARNEROS region sparkling-wine estate GLORIA FERRER.

French Colombard *see* COLOMBARD

Fresa *see* FREISA

fresh; freshness A descriptor for a well-balanced wine that's LIVELY, CLEAN, and FRUITY.

Fresia *see* FREISA

Freundstück *see* FORST

Friedrich-Wilhelm-Gymnasium [FREET-rikh VL-hehlm jihm-NAH-zee-uhm] A famous secondary school founded in 1563 in the city of TRIER in Germany's MOSEL-SAAR-RUWER region. Its name is well known in wine circles because its endowments include nearly 90 acres of vineyard land located in some of the best villages in the region. The vineyards are planted with about 85 percent RIESLING, and the wines produced are regarded as some of the best of this region.

Friulara; Friularo *see* RABOSO

Friuli-Venezia Giulia [free-OO-lee veh-NEHT-zee-ah JOO-lee-ah] Wine-producing region located in the northeast corner of Italy, with the former Yugoslavia to the east and Austria to the north. There are seven DOCs here, and the production of DOC wines is about 38 percent of this region's total production, which is one of the highest ratios of Italy's twenty wine-growing regions. The most important DOCs in Friuli-Venezia Giulia are COLLIO, COLLI ORIENTALI DEL FRIULI, and GRAVE DEL FRIULI; the others are AQUILEIA, CARSO, ISONZO, and LATISANA. A wide variety of different grapes are grown in the region including many foreign varieties like CABERNET FRANC, CABERNET SAUVIGNON, MERLOT, Pinot Nero (PINOT NOIR), and CHARDONNAY. White wine DOC production now dominates red wines by two to one. TOCAI is the most populous white grape, but there are many other varieties including Chardonnay, MALVASIA, Pinot Bianco (PINOT BLANC), Pinot Grigio (PINOT GRIS), RIBOLLA, and SAUVIGNON BLANC.

frizzante [freet-TSAHN-teh] An Italian term meaning "lightly sparkling" and referring to wines with light effervescence. Frizzante wines, which are often slightly sweet, are made with less pressure than those described as SPUMANTE. *Pétillant* is the French equivalent to frizzante, while *spritzig* is its German counterpart.

Frog's Leap Winery Winery founded in 1981 by Larry Turley (and his former wife Jeanine Yeomans) and John and Julie Williams. The genesis of Frog's Leap's humorous moniker began several years earlier when they jokingly combined the name of the immensely succesful Stag's Leap Wine Cellars with the fact that Larry's NAPA VALLEY property had once been a frog farm. What started out as a small, part-time venture has grown into a company that's making almost 40,000 cases of wine each year. In 1994 John and Julie Williams bought out Larry Turley, who wanted to return to his original vision of a small,

3,000- to 4,000-case winery. Turley's sister Helen Turley, who's made wine for B.R. COHN and PETER MICHAEL WINERY, will oversee his new venture. The Williamses, who will keep the Frog's Leap label, have moved the operation to another Napa Valley location near Rutherford, California. Frog's Leap produces CABERNET SAUVIGNON, CHARDONNAY, MERLOT, SAUVIGNON BLANC, and ZINFANDEL wines, all of which consistently score high points. Much of Frog's Leap wine is made from purchased fruit.

Fronsac AC [frawn-SAK] APPELLATION centered around the town of Fronsac on the Dordogne River northwest of the SAINT-ÉMILION district in BORDEAUX. Fronsac AC produces only red wines; they're based on CABERNET FRANC plus some CABERNET SAUVIGNON, MERLOT, and small amounts of MALBEC. CANON-FRONSAC AC is a small appellation within Fronsac AC that generally produces better wines, as suggested by its required ½ percent higher minimum ALCOHOL content. Wines from both appellations are known to be BIG and full-flavored (although sometimes somewhat HARD and TANNIC) and require extensive AGING. The improved quality of recent vintages and a new SOFTER style have created renewed interest in the Fronsac area.

Frontignan *see* MUSCAT

fructose [FRUHK-tohs; FROOK-tohs] One of the two main sugars found in grapes (the other being GLUCOSE). Fructose is approximately twice as sweet as glucose.

Früher Roter Malvasier *see* MALVASIA

fruity; fruit Descriptor for a wine that has a characteristic flavor and smell of fresh fruit. Besides grapes, this fruity characteristic can be reminiscent of everything from apples to blackberries to raspberries; it can even resemble cooked fruit. Wines that are high in fruit generally have a FRESH quality and distinctive CHARACTER.

Fuchsberg *see* GEISENHEIM

full-bodied *see* BODY

Fumé Blanc [FOO-may BLAHN; BLAHNGK] Term originally coined by the ROBERT MONDAVI WINERY and another name for SAUVIGNON BLANC. Many feel that Mondavi's extensive marketing campaign for its DRY, oak-aged style of Sauvignon Blanc is what established this variety as California's second most popular white-wine grape after CHARDONNAY.

Furmint [FOOR-mint] White-wine grape most renowned for its contribution to the delicious, sweet wines of Hungary's TOKAY region.

Furmint's thin skin makes it susceptible to BOTRYTIS CINEREA, which causes the famous shriveled ASZÚ berries with their concentrated sugars and flavors. The combination of Furmint and HÁRSLEVELÜ creates the rich sweet Tokay wines that rival—and sometimes surpass—the sweet wines from France's SAUTERNES region. Furmint is also VINIFIED into a strong, high-ALCOHOL, high-ACID, DRY wine, which is widely available throughout Hungary and the rest of eastern Europe. This variety is grown in Hungary and nearby countries. It's thought that *Sipon* and *Posip*, grown in the former Yugoslavia, are actually Furmint. Tokay d'Alsace (PINOT GRIS) and the Italian variety TOCAI are not related to Furmint.

Furstenberg *see* ERSHERNDORF

fut [FEW] One of the French words for "barrel."

"G" *see* GUIRAUD, CHÂTEAU

La Gaffelière, Château [sha-TOH gah-fuh-LYEH*R*] PREMIER GRAND CRU CLASSÉ estate located just outside the walls of SAINT-ÉMILION that has been in the de Malet-Roquefort family for over three centuries. It consists of a formidable four-story château and about 54 acres of vineyards planted with 60 percent MERLOT, 30 percent CABERNET FRANC, and 10 percent CABERNET SAUVIGNON. La Gaffelière produces 7,000 to 9,000 cases of red wine each year. VINTAGES since the early 1980s have been of high quality. This follows a period of 11 to 12 years of mediocre wines that weren't considered premier grand cru classé quality. The château produces wines under the SECOND LABELS of **Clos la Gaffelièr** and **de Rouquefort**. Wines from better VINTAGES can AGE for 15 to 18 years.

Gaillac AC [gah-YAHK] APPELLATION that encircles the town of Gaillac in southwest France, northeast of Toulouse. It produces red, white, and ROSÉ wines that can be sweet or DRY, STILL, or SPARKLING. Much of the production goes into the slightly sweet sparkling wines entitled **Gaillac Mousseux AC**, which are made by the MÉTHODE CHAMPENOISE or RURAL METHOD (locally referred to as **méthode gaillacoise**). A PETILLANT (slightly sparkling) wine called **Gaillac Perle AC** is also produced, but not highly regarded. The white grapes used are Mauzac Blanc, l'El de l'El, SAUVIGNON BLANC and SÉMILLON. Among the many acceptable red varieties are Duras, Fer, GAMAY, NEGRETTE, CABERNET SAUVIGNON, CABERNET FRANC, MERLOT, and SYRAH. The area's red and rosé wines vary greatly in quality, partially due to the number of varieties that can be used.

Gaisböhl *see* RUPPERTSBERG

Galestro [gah-LESS-troh] Name used by a group of CHIANTI producers for a white VINO DA TAVOLA wine made from TREBBIANO, MALVASIA, and VERNACCIA DI SAN GIMIGNANO, plus other varieties such as Pinot Bianco (PINOT BLANC), Pinot Grigio (PINOT GRIS), and CHARDONNAY. Galestro is a LIGHT, CRISP, DRY wine with a maximum of 10½ percent alcohol.

Gallais-Bellevue *see* POTENSAC, CHÂTEAU

E & J Gallo Winery [GA-loh] Company that was started in 1933 by brothers Ernest and Julio Gallo and has grown to become the world's largest wine producer. The brothers began with a borrowed $500 just as PROHIBITION was ending. Today, E & J Gallo Winery sells close to 75 million cases of wine each year. The company is so large that it makes its own bottles, caps, and closures. Gallo, the largest purchaser of grapes in the NORTH COAST AVA, owns over 4,000 acres of vineyards, including about 2,000 in SONOMA COUNTY. This company's long been known as a producer of GENERIC WINES, such as Hearty Burgundy and Chablis Blanc under the Gallo label. What many don't realize, however, is that this gigantic conglomerate also produces myriad other potables including: JUG WINES under the **Carlo Rossi** label; SPARKLING WINES under the labels of **Andre** and **Tott's**; FORTIFIED WINES from **Livingston Cellars**; **E&J Brandy**; WINE COOLERS under the **Bartles & Jaymes** and **Boone's Farm** brands; the infamous **Ripple**; and the high-alcohol **Thunderbird**. Although the bulk of their wines are still generic, Gallo began a series of moves to upgrade their image, starting with the release of its first CORK-closure wines. In 1983 Gallo released its first VINTAGE wine, a 1978 CABERNET SAUVIGNON. In 1993 they released their Northern Sonoma Estate Bottled Cabernet Sauvignon and CHARDONNAY from their SONOMA holdings. The 1991 Chardonnay is made from grapes grown on Gallo's 400-acre Laguna Ranch vineyard in the RUSSIAN RIVER AVA, and the 1990 Cabernet Sauvignon is made from grapes grown on the 600-acre Frei Brothers Ranch in the DRY CREEK VALLEY AVA. These two wines sell in the $30 to $60 range, a significant price jump for the normally price-conscious Gallo products. Huge vineyards have also been planted on other Gallo properties in northern Sonoma near the town of Asti (600 acres) and in the ALEXANDER VALLEY (200 acres).

gallo nero *see* CHIANTI DOCG

Gamay [ga-MAY] The full name of this French red wine grape is *Gamay Noir a'Jus Blanc*. Gamay wines have gained prominence in France's BEAUJOLAIS region where this grape, which represents 98 percent of all vines planted, reigns supreme. They're so associated with Beaujolais that winemakers outside of the region often try to imitate the style of immediately drinkable, light- to medium-weight wines with high ACID and low TANNINS. These light purple, fruity wines suggest flavors of bananas, berries, and peaches. Gamay is grown in other parts of BURGUNDY, such as the CÔTE CHALONNAISE, where a blend of PINOT NOIR and not more than two-thirds Gamay is known as BOURGOGNE PASSE-TOUT-GRAINS. In the LOIRE ANJOU produces **Anjou Gamay**, and from TOURAINE comes **Gamay de Touraine**. There is very little true Gamay cultivated in California. For years California vintners grew what they thought was true *Gamay Noir a'Jus Blanc,* calling the resulting wines GAMAY BEAUJOLAIS. However, this "Gamay" was eventually identified as an unexciting clone of PINOT NOIR. California's NAPA GAMAY is another case of mistaken identity. It too was thought to be a true Gamay, but has since been recognized as *Valdiguie,* a variety from Southern France's LANGUEDOC-ROUSSILLON region. The wines produced from both these grapes are light- to medium-bodied and made in a style similar to true Gamay from Beajolais. Because of historic practice, both California wines are sometimes still called Gamay Beaujolais. BLAUFRÄNKISCH, a variety grown in Austria is also sometimes mistakenly called Gamay. Other names for Gamay include *Bourguignon Noir* and *Petit Gamai.*

Gamay Beaujolais [ga-MAY boh-zhoh-LAY] Grape long thought to be the true GAMAY variety grown in France's BEAUJOLAIS region. Gamay Beaujolais is actually an unexciting clone of PINOT NOIR. The wines produced from this red wine grape are still allowed to be called Gamay Beaujolais, although many wine producers are now labeling them as Pinot Noir. In addition, acreage for this variety has dwindled, making it increasingly difficult to find wines with the Gamay Beaujolais label. These wines are usually light- to medium-bodied (*see* BODY), with pleasantly fruity flavors and fairly high ACIDITY. They should be drunk young. A small amount of this variety is also cultivated in New Zealand. NAPA GAMAY is unrelated to Gamay Beaujolais or France's Gamay.

Gamay Blanc *see* CHARDONNAY

Gambellara DOC [gahm-bell-AH-rah] A DOC area located in Italy's VENETO region southwest of Venice (Vicenze), next to the SOAVE DOC. Like Soave wines, these use GARGANEGA as the main grape, blended with small amounts of TREBBIANO. The regular white wine is LIGHT, CRISP, and DRY. It is similiar to the Soave wines but generally not outstanding. **Recioto di Gambellara**, a sweet white wine that can be STILL, FRIZZANTE, or SPUMANTE is also made. A tiny amount of **Vin Santo di Gambellara**, a golden- to amber-colored DESSERT WINE, is produced as well.

gamey; game A word used to describe a BOUQUET in very old wines that resembles the flesh of game birds or animals, sometimes with a nuance of decay. Though this descriptor is considered positive, wines it applies to can be an acquired taste.

Gamza *see* KADARKA

Gargana *see* GARGANEGA

Garganega [gahr-gah-NEH-gah] Prolific white-wine grape that is the principal variety used in Italy's SOAVE wines. Garganega is widely cultivated in Italy's VENETO region where it's been established for several centuries. It's also grown in neighboring LOMBARDY and farther south in UMBRIA. As with many grapes that are allowed high YIELDS, many Garganega-based wines—such as Soave—are generally bland and unexciting. However, controlled yields and careful winemaking can produce delectable, elegant wines that reveal Garganega's notable almond character. This variety is also used in the wines from the DOC's of BIANCO DI CUSTOZA, COLLI BERICI, and GAMBELLARA. Garganega is also known as *Gargana* and *Lizzana.*

Garnaccia *see* GRENACHE

Garnacha *see* GRENACHE

Garnacha Blanca *see* GRENACHE

Garnacha Tinta *see* GRENACHE

Garnacha Tintorera *see* ALMANSA DO

Garnacho Tinto *see* GRENACHE

garrafeira [gah-rah-FAY-ruh] Portuguese term used on wine labels to suggest a better-quality wine (much like *Reserve* or *Private Reserve* is used in the United States). Red wines using this term must receive 3 years of aging (2 years before bottling and 1 year after). White wines must receive 1 year of aging (6 months before bottling and 6 months after). In addition, these wines must have an alcohol content at least ½ percent higher than the required minimum for regular bottlings.

gassy A negative descriptor for wines with unexpected carbonation produced by bottle FERMENTATION.

Gattinara DOCG [gah-tee-NAH-rah] A small, recently upgraded DOCG zone located in the PIEDMONT region in northwestern Italy, northeast of Turin and northwest of Milan. It's one of the few DOCG areas in Italy and shares this status in the Piedmont region with BARBARESCO and BAROLO . The red wine is made from at least 90 percent Spanna (NEBBIOLO) and the rest BONARDA; it requires 4 years of AGING, two of which must be in wooden barrels. The wines of Gattinara had an excellent reputation from ancient times to the not-so-distant past, but there has been concern about a number of unworthy wines released in more recent VINTAGES. However, there is confidence that the upgrade to DOCG status will force out many second-rate producers and cause a general upgrade in quality. At their best, Gattinara wines can be full-bodied (*see* BODY) and ELEGANT with hints of violets and spice.

Some are also long-lived and capable of aging for 10 to 15 years or more.

Gavi DOC [GAH-vee] DOC area, also referred to as **Cortese di Gavi**, that is located in the southeastern part of Italy's PIEDMONT region. It encompasses an area southeast of Alexandria and directly north of Genoa and includes the town of Gavi and eleven other small villages. Gavi's DRY white wine, which is made from the CORTESE grape, is regarded as one of Italy's best. A SPUMANTE version may be produced as well. **Gavi di Gavi** is produced by La Scolca, a wine estate near the village of Gavi that's given credit for the rise in prestige of the area wines.

Gavilan *see* CHALONE VINEYARDS

Le Gay, Château [sha-TOH luh GAY] A 22-acre property in the POMEROL AC of BORDEAUX that produces about 3,000 cases of high-quality wine each year. Even though it uses a blend of about 70 percent MERLOT and 30 percent CABERNET FRANC, the wines are often COARSE and more TANNIC than most Pomerol wines. They may require 6 to 8 years to SOFTEN and can age for 20 to 25 years. The wines of Pomerol are not classified (*see* CLASSIFICATION OF 1855) as are those from the MÉDOC or SAINT-ÉMILION. If they were, Château Le Gay would most likely be the equivalent of a Médoc QUATRIÈME CRU (fourth growth).

gazeifie *see* CARBONATION

Gazin, Château [sha-TOH gah-ZAN] With almost 50 acres of vineyards, Château Gazin is one of the larger POMEROL AC properties. Its quality record is inconsistent, although the wines from 1988 and 1989 seem to be better. The combination of grapes used is around 80 percent MERLOT, 15 percent CABERNET FRANC, and 5 percent CABERNET SAUVIGNON. Approximately 9,000 to 11,000 cases of red wine are produced each year. AGING capability is variable—the best VINTAGES can go for 14 to 15 years. A SECOND LABEL, **L'Hospitalet**, is used by the château.

gebiet [geh-BEET] A German term meaning "district" or "territory." Gebiet has no official recognition in the European Economic Community designations, but it is sometimes used in place of ANBAUGEBIET, the official designation. *See also* WEINBAUGEBIET.

Gehrn *see* RAUENTHAL

Geisenheim [GI-zuhn-hime] Prominent village located southwest of Wiesbaden in Germany's rheingau region. It is known equally for its top-quality RIESLING wines and its school of VITICULTURE and ENOLOGY.

The best EINZELLAGEN here are **Fuchsberg**, **Mäuerchen**, **Mönchspfad**, and **Rothenberg**. The highly regarded wines from Geisenheim have a distinctively EARTHY flavor.

Gemeinde [ger-MINE-der] A German word for "community" or "village." On German wine labels the name of the Gemeinde (appended with an *er*, which converts it to an adjective) precedes that of the GROSSLAGE or EINZELLAGE. For example, the Einzellage named Mäuerchen associated with the village named Geisenheim appears on the label as *Geisenheimer Mäuerchen*; the Grosslage named Auflangen associated with the town of Nierstein appears as *Niersteiner Auflangen*.

generic wines [jeh-NEHR-ihk] 1. A general category of wine, such as DESSERT WINE, ROSÉ, SPARKLING WINE, SHERRY (when not specifically from Spain's JEREZ DE LA FRONTERA region), and TABLE WINE. 2. On U.S. labels the broad use of European designations (often specific wine regions) in the name, such as Burgundy, Chablis, Champagne, Chianti, Port, Rhine Wine, Sauterne, and Sherry.

generoso [jeh-neh-ROH-soh] Spanish term referring to wines with high ALCOHOL content (above 15 percent). They can be sweet or DRY and are usually served as an APÉRITIF or DESSERT WINE.

Les Genevrières *see* MEURSAULT

geranium A descriptor for the odor of geraniums in a wine, which is a fault caused by sorbic acid degeneration.

Germany Germany's approach to wine is somewhat different from that of other European countries like France and Italy because Germans aren't as focused on wine—the simple fact is that Germans prefer beer. In fact, German per capita wine consumption is less than one-third of either France or Italy. Yet Germany is considered a negative producer because it consumes more wine than it makes, whereas Italy and France produce more wine than they drink. The cool climate in Germany makes it overwhelmingly a white-wine producer (and all their best wines are white) because red grapes don't ripen well under such conditions. The main grape varieties for white wines are MÜLLER-THURGAU, RIESLING, and SYLVANER, which, respectively, represent about 25 percent, 20 percent, and 10 percent of the country's total planted acreage. Other white varieties include BACCHUS, EHRENFELSER, ELBING, FABER, GEWÜRZTRAMINER, Gutedel (CHASSELAS), HUXELREBE, KERNER, MORIO-MUSCAT, OPTIMA, ORTEGA, Rülander (PINOT GRIS), SCHEUREBE, and Weissburgunder (PINOT BLANC). The main red varieties are PORTUGIESER,

Spätburgunder (PINOT NOIR), and Trollinger (SCHIAVA). Riesling is by far the star of the German wines. Germany's approach to promoting wine quality is different from other APPELLATION systems, such as France's APPELLATION D'ORIGINE CONTRÔLÉE and Italy's DENOMINAZIONE DI ORIGINE CONTROLLATA. Appellations in other countries are geographic in nature and have specific regulations controlling each area. Germany, however, chose to base their wine quality on levels of ripeness and sweetness of the grapes. The focus on sugar content embodies the theory that grapes with higher sugar levels are riper and therefore yield richer wines with deep colors, intense flavors, and opulent BOUQUETS. The German wine laws adapted in 1971 set up three categories for defining the quality of German wines. DEUTSCHER TAFELWEIN (DTW) is the lowest-quality level followed by QUALITÄTSWEIN BESTIMMTER ANBAUGEBIET (QbA)—"quality wine from a specified region" and the top level, QUALITÄTSWEIN MIT PRÄDIKAT (QmP)—"quality wine with distinction." Within the premier QmP category, there are six subcategories that ranked from lowest to highest are: KABINETT, SPÄTLESE, AUSLESE, BEERENAUSLESE, EISWEIN, and TROCKENBEERENAUSLESE. CHAPTALIZATION (the addition of sugar) is allowed for DTW and QbA wines but not for QmP wines. It's one of the major differences between the quality levels— most grapes with enough natural sugar are reserved for QmP wines. The addition of sugar, which is converted into alcohol during FERMENTATION, allows producers to reach the required minimum alcohol levels for a DTW or QbA wine. If a quality wine (QbA or QmP) passes all its requirements, an AMTLICHE PRÜFUNGSNUMMER (official test number) is assigned. Abbreviated as A.P.Nr., this number is printed on the label, along with name of the ANBAUGEBIET. Additional information may be printed on a quality-wine label if other requirements are met. For instance, the name of the grape variety can be included if 85 percent of the grapes used in the wine are of one variety. Compared to French and Italian wines, those from Germany are generally lower in ALCOHOL (ranging from about 8½ to 11 percent) and usually contain at least some RESIDUAL SUGAR. The higher-quality wines—such as Auslese, Beerenauslese, Eiswein, and Trockenbeerenauslese—are quite sweet. Recently, there's been a trend toward making more of the DTW, QbA, and Kabinett wines in a less sweet style—either TROCKEN (DRY) or HALBTROCKEN (half-dry). Though Germany's appellation system isn't based on it, geography does come into play. The top two categories, QbA and QmP, must come from specific growing areas. Germany has developed a structure for defining the growing areas—from large general regions to specific vineyard sites. A large general growing region for quality wines is called an ANBAUGEBIET. There are now thirteen of these regions, and their regional name is required on labels of quality wines (QbA and QmP). German law established eleven of these Anbaugebiete in 1971 in an effort to meet European Common Market rules. The original eleven Anbaugebiete are: AHR, BADEN, FRANKEN, HESSISCHE BERGSTRSSE, MITTELRHEIN, MOSEL-SAAR-RUWER, NAHE, RHEINGAU, RHEINHESSEN, RHEINPFALZ, and WÜRTTEMBERG. Two more Anbaugebiete were recently added from the former East Germany—SAALE-UNSTRUT and SACHSEN. Except for Saale-Unstrut and Sachsen, all of Germany's primary growing regions are located along the Rhine River or one of its tributaries. Each Anbaugebiet may be further divided into BEREICHE (districts), GROSSLAGEN (general sites), and EINZELLAGEN (individual sites or vineyards). An Einzellage could be compared to a specific GRAND CRU or PREMIER CRU vineyard site in France's BURGUNDY region that's recognized for a history of producing high-quality wines. There are about 2,600 Einzellagen throughout Germany. The names of specific towns and villages with decade-old reputations for wine-producing prowess are also important in the world of German wines. On German wine labels the name of the town or village (often appended with an *er,* which converts it to an adjective) precedes the name of the GROSSLAGE or EINZELLAGE. For example, the Einzellage named Mäuerchen associated with the village named Geisenheim appears on the label as *Geisenheimer Mäuerchen,* while the Grosslage named Auflangen associated with the town of Nierstein appears as *Niersteiner Auflangen.* If an Einzellage is classified as an ORSTEIL, it doesn't need the nearest village's name.

geropiga [zhih-*r*oo-PEE-guh] Partially fermented grape syrup made by stopping FERMENTATION of grape MUST while it still retains most of the sugar content. It's used in Portugal to sweeten PORT wines during the blending process. It is sometimes spelled *jeropiga.*

Gerümpel *see* WACHENHEIM

Gevrey-Chambertin [zhuh-V*R*UH (zhuh-V*R*AY) shah*m*-beh*r*-TA*N*] Located in France's BURGUNDY region, this famous village is in the northern part (the CÔTE DE NUITS) of the CÔTE D'OR district. It's one of the larger villages in this acclaimed area and contains approximately 1,460 vineyard acres, all focused on producing red wines from PINOT NOIR grapes. At the top quality level are the village's nine GRAND CRU vineyards—CHAMBERTIN, CHAMBERTIN-CLOS DE BÈZE, CHAPPELLE-CHAMBERTIN, CHARMES-CHAMBERTIN, GRIOTTE-CHAMBERTIN, LATRICIÈRES-CHAMBERTIN, MAZIS-CHAMBERTIN, MAZOYÈRES-CHAMBERTIN, and RUCHOTTES-CHAMBERTIN. The Chambertin grand cru is so famous that the village, formerly called simply Gevrey, added Chambertin to its name in 1847. Following the grands crus in descending order of quality are the PREMIER CRU vineyards, which are followed by the Gevry-Chambertin AC and then the Côte de Nuits AC. Several premiers crus are thought to deserve grand cru status (if there's ever a reevaluation) including **Clos Saint-Jacques**, **Combe aux Moines**, **Les Cazetiers**, and **Les Verroilles**. As with much of Burgundy, top producers from premier cru vineyards often turn out better wines than the less accomplished winemakers from grand cru vineyards. In sharp contrast to the highly rated red wines from the large grouping of grands crus and premiers crus, some critics think that, of all the Côte d'Or villages, **Gevrey-Chambertin AC** produces wines that are the most widely varying in quality. Many of their lower-quality wines are pale and flavorless.

Gewürztraminer [guh-VURTS-trah-mee-ner; geh-VEHRTZ-trah-mee-ner] Cultivated for over a thousand years, this white-wine grape (sometimes referred to simply as *Traminer*) is thought to have originated in the village of Tramin (or Temeno) in Italy's ALTO ADIGE region. Although this variety is not now widely planted in Alto Adige, some of the better Gewürztraminer wines still come from that region. Gewürztraminer grapes are planted in ALSACE, a French region between Germany and France that specializes in excellent DRY Gewürztraminer wines. They're also cultivated in Germany, Austria, Hungary, Rumania, Czechoslovakia, and Ukraine. Because they perform better in cooler climates, Gewürztraminer grapes have not done well in many of California's warmer growing regions. However, they thrive in cooler California areas such as CARNEROS, ANDERSON VALLEY, and MONTEREY COUNTY, as well as in parts of Oregon and Washington. Down under, New Zealand's cooler climate is better than Australia's for this grape. The German word *gewürz* means "spiced," and these wines are known for their CRISP, SPICY attributes. They're highly fragrant, with flavor characteristics of litchis, roses (or flowers in general), and spices such as cloves and nutmeg. Gewürztraminer wines are available in varying degrees of sweetness—dry, medium-sweet, and LATE HARVEST. Because of the grape's pinkish (sometimes yellow) pigment, Gewurtztraminer wines are some of the more deeply colored of the whites, many have gold or peach tones. The distinctive color and AROMA of these wines make them easily recognizable by those familiar with this VARIETAL WINE. This is a wine that's best drunk fairly young—even VINTAGE Gewürztraminers rarely age well over 5 years. The Gewurtztraminer grape has myriad names, many beginning or ending with Traminer, such as *Traminer Musqué, Traminer Parfumé, Traminer Aromatique* (or *Aromatico*), and *Rotor Traminer.*

Gewürztraminer is also called *Edeltraube, Rousselet, Savagnin Rosé, Tramini,* and *Traminac.*

Geyser Peak [GI-ser] ALEXANDER VALLEY winery that has an interesting and colorful past. It was founded in 1880, revitalized by the Schlitz Brewing Company in 1972, sold to the Trione family in 1983, and became a joint venture between the Triones and Penfolds (the Australian wine company) in 1989. It was finally bought back by the Trione family in 1992. Geyser Peak has gone from producing bag-in-box GENERIC WINES under the Summit label (which has since been sold off) to producing top-quality premium wines. Today, Geyser Peak produces over 500,000 cases of wine and owns nearly 1,200 acres of vineyard divided between Alexander Valley, RUSSIAN RIVER AVA, and LAKE COUNTY. Geyser Peak produces CABERNET SAUVIGNON, CHARDONNAY, MERLOT, PINOT NOIR, RIESLING, SAUVIGNON BLANC, a Chardonnay-SÉMILLON blend, a red MERITAGE called **Reserve Alexandre**, and a white Meritage called **Château Alexandre**. Recent VINTAGES of red wines have shown marked improvement.

Ghemme DOC [GHEM-meh] A small DOC zone encompassing the town of the same name in the PIEDMONT region in northwestern Italy, northeast of Turin. It's just across the Sesia River from the GATTINARA DOCG. The dominate grape for the red wine made here is Spanna (NEBBIOLO), which must comprise from 65 to 85 percent of the blend. The other grapes used are BONARDA and Vespolina. The wines require 4 years of AGING, three of which must be in wooden barrels. Ghemme wines are considered by some to be as good or better than those of the neighboring Gattinara DOCG. **Collis Breclemae** and **Collis Carellae** are vineyards that belong to one of the high-quality producers, Antichi Vigneti di Cantalupo.

Giaribaldi Dolce (GD) *see* MARSALA DOC

Gigondas AC [zhee-gawn-dah; zhee-gawn-dahss] Gigondas AC was upgraded from CÔTES DU RHÔNE-VILLAGES AC status to its own APPELLATION in 1971. It surrounds the village of the same name, which is located northeast of CHÂTEAUNEUF-DU-PAPE in France's southern RHÔNE region. The wines are mainly red, with a small amount of ROSÉ. The main grape variety is GRENACHE, which is blended with CINSAUT, MOURVÈDRE, and SYRAH. Gigondas wines are generally BIG and ROBUST and require several years of bottle AGING TO SOFTEN.

Girard Winery [zhuhr-AHRD] NAPA VALLEY winery that is situated on the Silverado Trail northeast of Oakville, California, and that produces about 20,000 cases of wine each year from its two vineyards. The first vineyard, which is about 55 acres, sits next to the winery and was purchased in 1974 by Stephen Girard, Sr. The other, purchased in 1982, is located on Mt. Veeder, and about 40 acres are planted. The winery, which is managed by Stephen Girard, Jr., produces regular and RESERVE bottlings of CABERNET SAUVIGNON and CHARDONNAY, plus CHENIN BLANC and SÉMILLON.

girasols *see* RIDDLING

Gironde [zhee-*RAWND*] French DÉPARTEMENT in southwest France that essentially covers the same geographic territory as the BORDEAUX region. Gironde is also the name of the tidal estuary that starts north of the city of Bordeaux where the Garonne and Dordogne rivers join as they make their way through this area to the Atlantic Ocean. Many of the better MÉDOC wine estates sit on the Gironde's west bank.

Giscours, Château [sha-TOH zhees-KOO*R*] A large estate located in the southern part of the MARGAUX AC in the MÉDOC district of BORDEAUX. The 600-acre property includes a grand nineteenth-century CHÂTEAU and about 200 acres of vineyards planted with a mix of about 70 percent CABERNET SAUVIGNON, 21 percent MERLOT, 7 percent CABERNET FRANC, and 2 percent PETIT VERDOT. Château Giscours is a TROISIÈME CRU (third growth) that annually produces between 28,000 to 33,000 cases of high-quality red wine. The wines, which are full-bodied (*see* BODY) and TANNIC, aren't as delicate as many Margaux wines and can AGE for up to about 20 years. The SECOND LABEL for Château Giscours is **Cantelaude**.

Givry AC [zhee-V*REE*] One of the five villages in the CÔTE CHALONNAISE that has APPELLATION status. Located in France's BURGUNDY region, Givry produces about 90 percent red wine from PINOT NOIR grapes and 10 percent white wine from CHARDONNAY. The red wines are generally made in a lighter style with ripe, fruity flavors—they're comparable to a good CÔTE DE BEAUNE AC wine.

glasses, wine In order to enjoy wine fully, proper glassware is required. There are many styles of glassware—some colored, some ornate, and some that are regional in nature in the sense that the glasses were designed to show off the wines of that area. For example, glasses from Germany's RHINE region have colored stems, as do those from ALSACE. Such glasses are designed to reflect the color of the stem into the pale, crystalline wines of these areas. There are distinct sizes and shapes of glasses designed for red, white, DESSERT, and/or

FORTIFIED wines. However, it's difficult and unnecessary for most wine lovers to have a plethora of different glasses to suit the myriad types of available wines. Most needs can be met with just a few sets of glasses. For TABLE WINES a good all-purpose crystal wineglass is adequate. Such a glass should be clear and thin in order to display the wine's color without distractions or obstructions, which colored or cut glass could create. It should have a long enough stem so that one's hand doesn't touch the bowl. The bowl's shape should narrow toward the rim so that the BOUQUET will be captured and not evaporate, but the opening shouldn't be so narrow that it's difficult to drink from. The bowl should be big enough for the wine to be swirled (in order to enhance the bouquet) without spilling, and the bowl's rim should be thin so that the thickness of the glass isn't off-putting while drinking the wine. The recommended size for a table wineglass is about 12 ounces, into which approximately 4 ounces of wine should be poured, leaving plenty of room for swirling the wine. A slightly smaller glass is fine (just serve slightly less wine), and larger bowls are quite good as long as their shape and balance are appropriate. The firms of Riedel and Baccarat both make exceptional wineglasses that hold 28 to 30 ounces. Both red and white table wines can be served in the same style glass. If you have one set of glasses that's smaller than another, however, it's customary to serve white wine in the smaller glasses. Dessert and/or fortified wines can also be served in the same all-purpose glasses, although less wine is usually poured. Smaller glasses with the same shape and recommendations are quite acceptable. The International Standards Organization (ISO) recommends a glass that holds about 7¼ ounces for professional WINE TASTINGS, but then the amount of wine to be served in such glasses is 1½ to 1¾ ounces. The ISO glass is ideal for tasting any type of STILL WINE. SPARKLING WINES are the only wines that should not be served in an all-purpose glass. Such wines should be served in a FLUTE—a stemmed glass with a tall, slender cone- or tulip-shaped bowl. These narrow glasses provide less surface from which the bubbles can escape. Flutes retain a sparkling wine's effervescence much better than all-purpose glasses and markedly better than the shallow, wide-brimmed "champagne" glasses that were once so popular. Like all-purpose wineglasses, flutes should be thin and long stemmed. A flute should hold 6 ounces or more. *See also* Common Wineglass Shapes, page 593.

Glera *see* PROSECCO

glögg [GLUHG; GLOEG] Especially popular during Advent, this Swedish spiced-wine punch gets its *punch* from the addition of Aquavit or Brandy. To take the chill off cold winter nights, it's served hot in cups with several almonds and raisins added to each serving.

Gloria, Château [sha-TOH glaw-*R*YAH] Well-known CHÂTEAU in the SAINT-JULIEN AC that is always used as an example of the need to revise the outdated CLASSIFICATION OF 1855. Château Gloria, which was not in the classification, was created by purchasing parcels from neighboring châteaus—GRUAUD-LAROSE and LÉOVILLE-POYFERRÉ, both DEUXIÈMES CRUS (second growths), and DUHART-MILON and SAINT-PIERRE, both QUATRIÈMES CRUS (fourth growths). The château's nearly 125-acre vineyard annually produces 18,000 to 21,000 cases of red wine that's comparable in quality to that of quatrièmes crus châteaus. The best VINTAGES can age for about 12 to 15 years. The vineyards consist of approximately 65 percent CABERNET SAUVIGNON, 25 percent MERLOT, 5 percent CABERNET FRANC, and 5 percent PETIT VERDOT. Some of the lesser wines are sold under the SECOND LABELS **Haut-Beychevelle Gloria** and **Peymartin**.

glucose [GLOO-kohs] One of the two main sugars found in grapes (the other being FRUCTOSE). Glucose is approximately half as sweet as fructose.

glycerol; glycerine [GLYS-uh-rawl; GLYS-uh-rihn] Also called *glycerine*, glycerol is a colorless, odorless, syrupy substance that, in winemaking, is an incidental by-product of FERMENTATION. It has a slightly sweet taste that gives a palate impression of smoothness in a wine. Although it has long been thought that glycerol contributes VISCOSITY and RICHNESS to wine, many experts say that it exists in such minute amounts as to not have such an effect.

Goldatzel *see* JOHANNISBERG

Goldbächel *see* WACHENHEIM

Golden Chasselas *see* PALOMINO

golden sherry *see* SHERRY

Goldmuskateller *see* MUSCAT

Goldtröpfchen *see* PIESPORT

La Gombaude *see* LASCOMBES, CHÂTEAU

gonci *see* TOKAY

González Byass Large firm based in JEREZ, Spain, that produces the world's best selling fino sherry (*see* SHERRY) Tio Pepe. The name of the firm comes from the original founder, Don Antonio González y Rodriguez, and the London agent who later became his partner, Robert Blake Byass. In addition to the well-known Tio Pepe, González Byass also produces large quantities of La Concha Amontillado, Alfonso Oloroso, and San Domingo Pale Cream. Two of the best wines are the Amontillado del Duque—a DRY, elegant wine—and Matusalem—a slightly sweet *oloroso* (*see* SHERRY). González Byass produces about 2½ million cases of wine each year. It also owns Bodegas Beronia, a wine estate in RIOJA, and Castel de Vilernau, a SPARKLING WINE producer (CAVA DO) in PENEDES.

Gordo Blanco *see* MUSCAT

Goron *see* VALAIS

Goudy-la-Cardonne *see* POTENSAC, CHÂTEAU

Gould-Campbell *see* SMITH WOODHOUSE

goût [GOO] French for "taste." Goût is used in combination with other words to identify a particular flavor in wine. *Goût de terroir* refers to an earthy smell and taste, while *goût de bouchon* refers to a wine that is CORKED. *Goût americain* means "American taste" and refers to a sweet CHAMPAGNE, which isn't logical since these French champagnes aren't usually shipped to the United States. *Goût anglais* means "English taste," referring to the British preference for DRY champagnes.

goût de terroir [GOO duh teh-WAHR] *see* GOÛT

governo [goh-VEHR-noh] A VINIFICATION technique used in Italy's TUSCANY area (primarily CHIANTI) whereby the MUST from grapes previously set aside to dry and shrivel is added to the already-fermented wine. This causes a SECONDARY FERMENTATION, creating wines that are SOFTER, higher in ALCOHOL, more deeply colored, and, sometimes, slightly FRIZZANTE. Although not practiced much anymore, some producers desirous of a smooth-drinking wine still use this technique. The more common practice, however, is to use a GRAPE CONCENTRATE instead of semidried grapes.

Graach [GRAHK] Tiny village located between BERNKASTEL and WEHLEN on the Mosel River in Germany's MOSEL-SAAR-RUWER region. It's famous for its rich, intense, fragrant wines, which are considered some of the best in this region. Key EINZELLAGEN, which are located on the well-situated steep slopes surrounding Graach, include **Domprobst**, **Himmelreich**, and JOSEPHSHÖFER.

Grace Family Vineyard Each year, this tiny winery produces only 250 cases of highly regarded CABERNET SAUVIGNON, which, as a result, is some of the most sought-after wine in the world. Dick Grace planted 1 acre in the mid-1970s and added another acre in the 1980s. The wine, which sells for $65 to $75 a bottle, is primarily sold through a mailing list, with customers being allocated two to four bottles each. Grace Family Vineyard is located just northeast of St. Helena, California, in the NAPA VALLEY.

Graciano [grah-see-YAH-noh (Sp. grah-THYAH-noh)] A high-quality red-wine grape grown in the RIOJA and NAVARRA regions of Spain. Graciano wines are capable of rich color, a lovely fragrant BOUQUET, a hint of spice in the flavor, and long AGING. The high ACIDITY of the Graciano grape makes it a good candidate for blending with low-acid varieties like TEMPRANILLO. Graciano's sparse YIELD is prompting many Spanish growers to replace this quality variety with more productive vines. A similar situation exists in France's LANGUEDOC-ROUSSILLON region where Graciano (known there as *Morrastel*) is also being replaced.

grafting Grafting is a viticultural (*see* VITICULTURE) technique whereby BUDWOOD (a bud-bearing shoot) is secured to the ROOTSTOCK. This technique is critical in most vineyards because the rootstock of VITIS VINIFERA vines (CABERNET SAUVIGNON and CHARDONNAY, for example) aren't resistant to PHYLLOXERA, whereas most NATIVE AMERICAN rootstocks are. Phylloxera has attacked vineyards all over Europe and the United States, and there are few places that haven't been infested (CHILE is one). In order to produce the popular VARIETAL WINES, it's necessary to graft the vitis vinifera vines to the phylloxera-resistant rootstock. Some feel that grapes from ungrafted vineyards produce the best wines. Most grafting is done in a nursery and is called **bench grafting**. When it's done in the vineyard, it's called **field grafting**. *See also* T-BUDDING.

Graham, W. & J. One of the premier PORT firms, W. & J. Graham makes vintage ports that are generally considered among the top four or five. Its SECOND LABEL **Graham's Malvedos** is made in undeclared years (when the top vintage ports are not produced) and is generally also highly regarded. There's some confusion about Malvedos and whether it's a single-quinta port (*see* PORT). It hasn't been in the past because all the wine has not come from a single vineyard. However, the expansion of the Quinta dos Malvedos suggests that in the future there may be a single-quinta port, most likely called Quinta dos Malvedos. W. & J. Graham was run by the Graham family from the early 1800s until 1970, when it was sold to the Symington family (who also own WARRE and Dow (*see* SILVA & COSENS).

Grainhübel *see* DEIDESHEIM

grand cru [grah*n* KROO] 1. The French phrase for "great growth." 2. In BURGUNDY, grand cru is the top ranking a vineyard can receive. It's only bestowed upon a limited number of vineyards in the CÔTE D'OR and CHABLIS. Because the vineyards of Burgundy are divided among many owners, this top ranking doesn't always guarantee that the very best wines will be produced by the various vintners. The rank just below grand cru is PREMIER CRU. 3. In France's CHAMPAGNE region, villages are classified according to wine quality, and a percentage rating is applied, the very best receiving 100 percent. Seventeen villages in Champagne qualify for this highest (grand cru) status, although it's probably less meaningful in Champagne because the house (producer) is generally considered most important. 4. In ALSACE (as of 1983) the grand cru designation is bestowed upon the top vineyards. To date, fifty-one have qualified and are allowed to put "Grand Cru" on their labels. 5. In BORDEAUX the designation grand cru (versus GRAND CRU CLASSÉ) is given to some châteaus (such as those in SAINT-ÉMILION), but it has little real meaning.

grand cru classé [grah*n* kroo klah-SAY] 1. The French phrase for "great classed growth." 2. Grand cru classé is the second highest category for the wines ranked in the SAINT-ÉMILION classification as set forth in 1953 (later revised in 1969 and 1985). As of 1985 the sixty-three CHÂTEAUS with this status may label their wines "Grand Cru Classé." These wines do not have the same prestige as the grand cru classé wines of the MÉDOC. 3. The second- through fifth-growth wines of the MÉDOC and SAUTERNES may use "Grand Cru Classé" on their labels.

Grande Marque [grah*n* MAH*R*K] *see* CHAMPAGNE

Les Grandes Loliéres *see* CORTON

Les Grandes Ruchottes *see* CHASSAGNE-MONTRACHET AC

Grand Parc *see* LÉOVILLE-LAS-CASES, CHÂTEAU

Grand-Mayne, Château [sha-TOH grah*n* MEHN] A 47-acre GRAND CRU CLASSÉ estate located in the SAINT-ÉMILION AC in BORDEAUX. It produces about 10,000 cases of smooth, SUPPLE red wine that's comparable to that from a Médoc CINQUIÈME CRU (fifth growth). These wines can be drunk young but are capable of AGING for 10 to 12 years. The château's SECOND LABEL is **Les Plantes du Mayne.**

Grand-Puy-Ducasse, Château [sha-TOH grah*n* pwee doo-KAHSS] CINQUIÈME CRU (fifth growth) CHÂTEAU located in the PAUILLAC AC in the MÉDOC district. It has nearly 90 acres of vineyards located in three different plots—one near Château GRAND-PUY-LACOSTE, one by Château BATAILLEY, and the third near Château PONTET-CANET. Its wine-making and storage facilities are in Pauillac on the waterfront. The wines, made from approximately 62 percent CABERNET SAUVIGNON and 38 percent MERLOT, are good quality and can AGE for 12 to 14 years. Around 14,000 to 18,000 cases of red wine are produced each year, part of it going into the SECOND LABEL **Artigues-Arnaud.**

Grand-Puy-Lacoste, Château [sha-TOH grah*n* pwee lah-KAWST] A CINQUIÈME CRU (fifth growth) CHÂTEAU located in the PAUILLAC AC in the MÉDOC district, whose excellent wines warrant upgrading. The estate covers nearly 115 acres and produces 13,000 to 17,000 cases of red wine. The wines are a blend of around 70 percent CABERNET SAUVIGNON, 25 percent MERLOT, and 5 percent CABERNET FRANC. They're generally RICH and full-bodied (*see* BODY) and can AGE for up to 18 to 20 years. A SECOND LABEL **Lacosste-Borie** is used by the château.

Grands-Echézeaux AC [grah*n* zay-shuh-ZOH] A prestigious GRAND CRU vineyard located in the CÔTE DE NUITS area of France's BURGUNDY region. Although it's often grouped with the famous grands crus of the neighboring village of VOSNE-ROMANÉE, Grand Echézeaux is physically located in the village of Flagey-Echézeaux. It consists of 22.6 acres, all planted with PINOT NOIR grapes. Grands-Echézeaux red wines don't quite have the acclaim of some of the neighboring grands crus (such as ROMANÉE-CONTI, LA TÂCHE, and RICHEBOURG), but some wine lovers think that makes them a relative bargain. The wines can be very RICH and full-bodied (*see* BODY), with CONCENTRATED aromas and flavors. They're capable of AGING for 10 to 15 years. Grands-Echézeaux AC wines are generally superior to those from the neighboring grand cru, ESCHÉZEAUX.

Grand Siècle *see* CHAMPAGNE

grand vin [grah*n* VA*N*] French for "grand wine." Although used to distinguish a better wine from other "secondary wines," grand vin has no official definition.

Grange Hermitage [GRAH*N*ZH ehr-mee-TAHZH] One of the most famous red wines from Australia. It's made by the wine company Penfolds from Shiraz (SYRAH) grapes and aged in small, American-oak barrels in a BORDEAUX style. Grange Hermitage is a BIG, full-bodied (*see* BODY) wine capable of very long AGING. As it matures, it becomes very much like an older Bordeaux wine. This wine, which Australians sometimes call simply *Hermitage*, was originally made from 100 percent Shiraz, although it now sometimes contains some CABERNET SAUVIGNON. One of the vineyards the grapes come from is called The Grange.

La Grange Neuve de Figeac *see* FIGEAC, CHÂTEAU

gran reserva [grahn ray-SAYR-vah] A Spanish term used for aged, top-quality wines from very good vintages. To use this term on the label, red wines must AGE for 5 years (with 2 of those years in wooden barrels) and white and ROSÉ wines must age for 4 years (6 months in wood).

granvas *see* CHARMAT

grape concentrate Grape juice that's concentrated into a very sweet syrup, usually in the range of 60° to 70° BRIX. In California and Italy, adding sugar to wine (CHAPTALIZATION) is illegal, but grape concentrate may be added to boost the alcohol content or increase the sweetness of the final wine.

grapes Although other fruits are vinified, grapes are the basis for most of the world's wine and all of its fine wines. That's because certain grape species (which today have been refined to deliver the utmost in aroma and flavor) comprise the right properties to produce wine naturally—high amounts of fermentable sugar, strong flavors, color in the skins, and TANNINS in the seeds and skins (to assist AGING). It's surmised that over 5,000 years ago someone discovered a naturally created wine—and that it tasted *good*. That prompted grape cultivation, along with winemaking techniques to help nature along. Today, wine production has become relatively sophisticated, and the wine, presumably, has become much better. Grapes belong to the botanical family *Ampelidaceae*, and of that family's ten genera, the genus *Vitis* is most important to winemakers. There are numerous species within the genus *Vitis*, the most important of which is VITIS VINIFERA, the species that yields over 99 percent of the world's wines. Vitis Vinifera is native to Europe and East and Central Asia, but it has been planted all over the world. There are estimated to be thousands of varieties of this species, some of the best-known being CABERNET SAUVIGNON,

CHARDONNAY, MERLOT, PINOT NOIR, SAUVIGNON BLANC, SYRAH, and ZINFANDEL. Other *Vitis* species that produce grapes suitable for wine include VITIS LABRUSCA, VITIS RIPARIA, and VITIS ROTUNDIFOLIA (all of which are native to the Americas). Even though these species are not the quality of the *vitis vinifera* grapes, some of them have played a critical role in worldwide grape production. That's because the *vitis vinifera* roots are susceptible to PHYLLOXERA, and the native American vines, particularly *vitis riparia*, are resistant to this louse. Most of the world's vineyards now have phylloxera-resistant rootstocks (other than *vitis vinifera*) that have *vitis vinifera* vines grafted to them. This resulting marriage allows the roots to survive while still producing the best wine grapes.

grapey A descriptor for wines with the simple flavors and aromas of raw grapes. A *grapey* characteristic is exemplified in wines made from certain varieties such as the MUSCAT and CONCORD.

Grasevina *see* WELSCHRIESLING

grassy Sensory term used to describe the smell of freshly cut grass or hay, a characteristic found in some SAUVIGNON BLANCS. This quality is sometimes referred to as GREEN. Too much grassiness is considered detrimental.

Grauer Riesling *see* RÜLANDER

Grauvernatsch *see* SCHIAVA

Grave del Friuli DOC [GRAH-veh del free-OO-lee] The largest DOC zone in the FRIULI-VENEZIA GIULIA region in northeastern Italy. It produces over 40 percent of this region's DOC wines. The word *Grave* in the name indicates the presence of gravelly terrain throughout the area. The DOC covers fourteen VARIETAL WINES and a ROSATO. The red varietal wines are Cabernet (made from CABERNET FRANC and CABERNET SAUVIGNON), Cabernet Franc, Cabernet Sauvignon, MERLOT, Pinot Nero (PINOT NOIR), and Refosco del Peduncolo Rosso (MONDEUSE). The white varietals are CHARDONNAY, Pinot Bianco (PINOT BLANC), Pinot Grigio (PINOT GRIS), Riesling Italico (WELSCHRIESLING), Sauvignon (SAUVIGNON BLANC), TOCAI FRIULANO, Traminer Aromatico (GEWÜRZTRAMINER), and VERDUZZO FRIULANO. Varietal wines may contain up to 15 percent of other approved grapes of the same color. The Rosato must be 70 to 80 percent Merlot and 20 to 30 percent other approved red varieties.

gravelly A term that describes wine with a clean, earthy smell. This gravelly characteristic is most often associated with the wines of GRAVES. *See also* EARTHY.

La Grave-Martillac *see* LA TOUR-MARTILLAC, CHÂTEAU

Graves [GRAHV] An important wine-producing area in France's BORDEAUX region. It abuts the MÉDOC in the north just above the city of Bordeaux, extending west and to the south, where it surrounds the appellations of BARSAC, CÉRONS, and SAUTERNES. The Garonne River runs along its eastern border. The word *graves* is French for "gravel," and the area takes its name from its gravelly soil, which is particularly prominent in its northern section. This northern part of Graves contains the best CHÂTEAUS and, in 1987, was given its own appellation—PESSAC-LEOGNAN AC. Since then, the **Graves AC** covers only red and DRY white wines made in Graves' southern area. This AC doesn't have the quality reputation for wines that the Pessac-Leognan AC does. The **Graves Supérieures AC** is an appellation set up for dry, medium-sweet and sweet white wines with a higher minimum ALCOHOL level (12 percent, versus 11 percent for Graves AC). This rarely used appellation produces primarily sweet wines, which come from southern Graves. The entire region of Graves is rather unique for Bordeaux because it's well known for white wines as well as for its reds. In fact, until the mid-1970s the area produced more white wine than red. The white wines, which are made from SAUVIGNON BLANC, SÉMILLON, and MUSCADELLE, have evolved from sweet wines into those with a CRISP, DRY style. One reason the name Graves is often associated with white wines is because white-wine labels specify *Graves AC* (or *Graves Supérieures AC*). Another reason is that the red wines, made predominantly from CABERNET SAUVIGNON, CABERNET FRANC, and MERLOT, are more apt to prominently display the château's name on the label, with the name of the appellation taking a secondary role. The red wines of Graves are generally credited as being of higher quality than whites, particularly in the northern section. They're often equated to those of the Médoc, but they have a distinctively EARTHY quality and are SOFTER because a bit more Merlot is used in the blend. The CLASSIFICATION OF 1855 for Bordeaux wines was limited to wines from the Médoc because those from other areas weren't deemed worthy. The only exception was Graves' Château HAUT-BRION, which received a PREMIER CRU ranking—one of only four Bordeaux châteaus to receive this honor at that time. Today, Haut-Brion is still consistently one of the top estates of Bordeaux. The châteaus of Graves were classified for red wines in 1953, and again in 1959, when white wines were added and selected châteaus were given CRU CLASSÉ status (but no rankings within this category). Thirteen châteaus were deemed *crus classés* for their red wines; six of those thirteen (along with two additional châteaus) also received this honor for their white wines. Some of the other top châteaus of Graves are LA MISSION HAUT-BRION, LAVILLE HAUT-BRION, LES CARMES HAUT-BRION, DOMAIN DE CHEVALIER, PAPE CLÉMENT, and HAUT BAILLY.

Graves de Vayres AC [grahv duh VEH*R*] Located in the northern part of the ENTRE-DEUX-MERS area of France's BORDEAUX region, this small APPELLATION runs along the Dordogne River across from the SAINT-ÉMILION AC. Graves de Vayres AC is unrelated to the GRAVES region, although it has a similar gravelly soil (from which comes its name). Both the white wines (which are DRY) and the red wines are generally satisfactory. The reds are made from CABERNET SAUVIGNON, CABERNET FRANC, and MERLOT; the whites are made from SAUVIGNON BLANC, SÉMILLON, and MUSCADELLE.

Graves-Léognan see PESSAC-LÉOGNAN AC

Graves-Pessac see PESSAC-LÉOGNAN AC

Gray Riesling; Grey Riesling see TROUSSEAU GRIS

gray rot see BOTRYTIS CINEREA

Great Southern Region see LOWER GREAT SOUTHERN REGION

Grechetto [greh-KEH-toh] A white-wine grape grown primarily in Italy's UMBRIA region, where it's a component—along with TREBBIANO TOSCANO and MALVASIA—in the well-known wines of ORVIETO and TORGIANO. Grechetto has gained a much better reputation by itself, where its delightfully rich, nutty character is showcased—as in the Grechetto di Todi wines. This grape is also used to make excellent VIN SANTO. Although Grechetto is also called *Greco Spoletino* and *Greco Bianco di Perugia*, it's unrelated to the GRECO of southwest Italy.

Greco [GREH-koh] 1. White-wine grape grown in southwestern Italy's CAMPANIA and CALABRIA regions. Greco's origins are certainly Greek, although there are numerous theories as to how this ancient variety was introduced into Italy. If cultivated and VINIFIED carefully, Greco is capable of producing high-quality wines with rich, fruity flavors, as well as hints of smoke and toasted nuts. This variety is best known for the GRECO DI TUFO dry wines and the sweet wines of GRECO DI BIANCO. Greco also plays a principal role in the wines from CIRÒ and FIANO DI AVELLINO. This variety goes by other names—most beginning with Greco—including *Greco delle Torre, Greco di Tufo,* and *Greco del Vesuvio.* 2. A name used for the variety ALBANA, which is totally unrelated to the true Greco.

Greco Bianco di Perugia see GRECHETTO

Greco del Vesuvio *see* GRECO

Greco delle Torre *see* GRECO

Greco di Ancona *see* ALBANA

Greco di Tufo DOC [GREH-koh dee TOO-foh] DOC area located east of Naples in Italy's CAMPANIA region that includes the vineyards encompassing the village of Tufo. Greco di Tufo wine is made primarily from the GRECO grape, which is thought to have originated in Greece and is quite popular in this region. In addition to the DRY white wine produced, there is a SPUMANTE version that may be made.

Greco Spoletino *see* GRECHETTO

Greece Although ancient Greeks were renowned winemakers, modern Greeks certainly aren't viewed in the same light. Part of this unenviable contemporary image is attached to Greek RETSINA wines, which for most outsiders is definitely an acquired taste. Greece certainly hasn't kept pace with modern wine-production techniques, but it has made inroads in the last 20 years as it worked to gain European Economic Community (EEC) membership, which was finalized in 1981. Today, the Greeks are implementing an APPELLATION system for their quality wines, and only about 20 percent of the wines produced are of the retsina style. The principal growing regions include: the Peloponnese, the large peninsula in the south of Greece that produces about one-third of the total wines; Macedonia and Epirus in the north; Attica, the second most productive region, which is in the southeastern region around Athens; the Island of Crete, which is south of the mainland; and Cephalonia and other islands west of the mainland. There are also vineyards south and southeast of the mainland on the islands of Rhodes, Samos, and Santorini. The main white grapes of Greece are Savatiano (the most widely planted of all varieties), Assyrtiko, MAVRODAPHNE, Moscophilero, Robola (RIBOLLA), and Rhoditis. Red varieties include Agiorgitiko (also called *St. George* and used in the well-known Neméa wines), Liatiko, Limnio, Mandilaria, Romeiko, and the highly respected Xynomavro—used to make Naoussa. Also planted in large quantities are MALVASIA, used to make a MALMSEY-style wine called Monemvasia, and MUSCAT, which makes a delicious DESSERT WINE.

green Term used in several ways—to describe a very young wine that's not ready to drink, to describe a wine made from underripe grapes, or, sometimes to indicate a grassy quality. It generally suggests a wine with high ACIDITY and a lack of fruity RICHNESS.

green grafting *see* T-BUDDING

Green Grape *see* SÉMILLON

Green Hungarian A white-wine grape grown in limited amounts in California. Green Hungarian's origin is uncertain, although there are suggested connections to AGOSTON HARASZTHY, a Hungarian count often referred to as the father of California VITICULTURE. Green Hungarian grapes produce pleasant but rather nondescript, neutral wines that are now sold by only a handful of VINTNERS. The best known of these is WEIBEL VINEYARDS, where Green Hungarian continues to be one of their leading sellers.

Green Valley-Solano AVA The lesser of two AVA named Green Valley, this one is located in Solano County, California, east of the southern end of NAPA COUNTY. This area doesn't receive the cooling ocean breezes, so it's much hotter and has a shorter growing season than the Napa or Sonoma VITICULTURAL AREAS.

Green Valley-Sonoma AVA APPELLATION that is a subregion within the southwest portion of the larger RUSSIAN RIVER VALLEY AVA. It's located between the towns of Sebastopol and Occidental and extends north of Forestville to the Russian River. Because this area's closer to the ocean, it's cooler than many other parts of the Russian River Valley, making it definitely a Region I growing area (*see* CLIMATE REGIONS OF CALIFORNIA). This makes it ideal for CHARDONNAY and PINOT NOIR, which are used for both STILL and SPARKLING WINES. Gan Eden, IRON HORSE VINEYARDS, and Topolos are three of the better-known wineries in this area.

Grenache [gruh-NAHSH] Grape that comes in both red-wine and white-wine varieties. When used by itself, the word "Grenache" refers to the red version **Grenache Noir**, one of the world's most widely cultivated red grapes. The Grenache grape does well in hot, dry regions, and its strong stalk makes it well suited for windy conditions. It ripens with very high sugar levels and can produce wines with 15 to 16 percent ALCOHOL. Grenache wines are sweet, fruity, and very low in TANNINS. They're usually lacking in color, except in growing areas where YIELDS are low. The vine originated in Spain where it's called *Garnacha; Garnacha Tinta* (or *Garnacho Tinto*) and is the most widely cultivated red-wine grape in Spain. It's widely planted in NAVARRA and in many of the hotter areas of Spain including CARIÑENA, LA MANCHA, PENEDÈS, RIOJA, and UTIEL-REQUENA. In southern France not far from the Spanish border, Grenache is widely cultivated in the areas around LANGUEDOC-ROUSSILLON, PROVENCE, and the southern RHÔNE. It's also extensively grown in Algeria, Australia, Corsica, Israel, Morocco, Sardinia (where it's called *Cannonau*), and California's CENTRAL VALLEY. Red Grenache wines are usually BLENDED with those made from other varieties; 100 percent Grenache wines are rarely found. In Spain Grenache is blended with TEMPRANILLO, and in most of France it's blended with CINSAUT and CARIGNAN. In CHÂTEAUNEUF-DU-PAPE it's used as the primary grape, although it is blended with as many as twelve other VARIETALS including CLAIRETTE, MOURVÈDRE, MUSCADINE, and SYRAH. In ROSÉ wines—particularly those from CÔTES-DU-RHÔNE, CÔTES DU VENTOUX, LIRAC, and TAVEL—Grenache is often the dominant grape used. In California and Australia it's most often used as a blending wine for inexpensive JUG WINES. **Grenache Blanc** (or **Garnacha Blanca**) is the white variety of this grape. Although not as populous as the red, it's still widely planted in both Spain and France. The white wines produced are high in ALCOHOL and low in ACID. Grenache is known by many different monikers including *Alicante, Carignan Rosso, Garnaccia, Roussillon, Tinta,* and *Tinto.*

Grenouilles [gruh-NOO-yuh] One of the seven GRAND CRU vineyards in CHABLIS and, at 23 acres, the smallest. It's situated in the middle of Chablis' *grand cru* slope, between VAUDÉSIR and VALMUR.

Les Grèves *see* BEAUNE; CORTON

Grgich Hills Cellar [GER-gihch] Winery that is a partnership of Mike Grgich, well-known NAPA VALLEY winemaker, and Austin Hills, vineyard owner and part of the Hills Brothers Coffee family. It was established in 1977 just northwest of Rutherford in the Napa Valley. Grgich gained fame at Chateau Montelena for his 1973 CHARDONNAY wine, which won a much publicized Paris winetasting in 1976. His style at Grgich Hills continues to enchant Chardonnay lovers, and these wines are highly regarded. Grgich Hills also produces CABERNET SAUVIGNON, SAUVIGNON BLANC, and ZINFANDEL of very high quality. Case production is between 50,000 and 60,000 per year.

Grifi [GREE-fee] The proprietary name of one of the VINO DA TAVOLA wines that's described as a super-Tuscan (*see* TUSCANY). It's produced by Avignonesi, a highly regarded wine estate located in the Montepulciano, southeast of Siena in Tuscany. Grifi, a blend of SANGIOVESE and CABERNET SAUVIGNON, is AGED in BARRIQUES.

Grignolino [gree-nyoh-LEE-noh] A red-wine grape grown in the southeastern portion of Italy's PIEDMONT region, primarily in the provinces of ASTI and Alessandria. This variety produces unusual wines for this region, which is known for its BIG, bold, long-lived reds.

Conversely, Grignolino wines are rust-colored, delicately scented and flavored, light-bodied (*see* BODY), and best drunk young. These wines have DOC status in Asti and Monferrato Casalese. Grignolino's sporadic YIELDS have caused it to lose popularity with some growers in recent years. Small amounts of this variety are grown in California, where it's turned into light-bodied red or ROSÉ wines, the best known of which are from HEITZ WINE CELLARS.

Grillet *see* CHÂTEAU-GRILLET

Griotte-Chambertin AC [gree-AWT shah*m*-behr-TA*N*] Small (less than 7 acres) GRAND CRU vineyard that produces world-class red wines from PINOT NOIR. It's located in the village of GEVRY-CHAMBERTIN in the CÔTE DE NUITS district of France's BURGUNDY region. Only about 800 cases of this hard-to-find wine are produced, all of it generally of high quality. The wines are RICH, PERFUMED, and COMPLEX, although they won't generally AGE as long as wines from some of the area's other grands crus. *See also* CHAMBERTIN.

grip A descriptor for wine that has a firm (as opposed to FLABBY) TEXTURE, which usually comes from strong TANNINS and ACIDITY.

Gris Meunier *see* MEUNIER

Grolleau *see* GROSLOT

Groppello [groh-PEHL-oh] Good-quality red-wine grape grown in Italy's LOMBARDY region, primarily in the DOC of Riviera del Garda Bresciano, where it's used to create appealing ROSÉ (called CHIARETTO) and red wines. Although Groppello is the principal variety in both the reds and rosés from this area, SANGIOVESE and BARBERA grapes are also used in the blend.

Gros Plant *see* FOLLE BLANCHE

Groslot [groh-LOH] Red-wine grape of rather ordinary quality, grown primarily in the ANJOU district of France's LOIRE region. Groslot is the main component in the semisweet ROSÉ D'ANJOU wines, which are generally low in ALCOHOL, high in ACID, and neutral in flavor. There are, however, some higher-quality Rosé d'Anjou wines that exhibit a wonderful appley flavor with a hint of nuts. Groslot acreage has been declining in France in favor of higher-quality varieties. This grape is also known as *Grolleau.*

Grosse Roussette *see* MARSANNE

Grosse Syrah *see* MONDEUSE

Grosslage; pl. Grosslagen [GROSS-lah-guh; GROSS-lah-gehn] A German term meaning "large vineyard," referring to a collection of individual vineyards (EINZELLAGEN) with similar environmental attributes that produce wines of comparable character and quality. There are about 2,600 Einzellagen and 150 Grosslagen, which are further combined into thirty-four BEREICHE (districts) and thirteen ANBAUGEBIETE (growing regions). Sizes of Grosslagen vary tremendously—from 125 to over 5,000 acres—and contain any number of Einzellagen. The name of an Einselage on a label generally indicates a wine of higher quality than one with the name of a Grosslage. Unfortunately, labels don't indicate whether a name is an Einzellage or a Grosslage, making it difficult to use this information effectively.

Grossriesling *see* ELBLING

Grossvernatsch *see* SCHIAVA

Groth Vineyards & Winery [GRAHTH] NAPA VALLEY winery founded in 1982 by former Atari executive Dennis Groth and his wife Judy. By the time the winery building was finished in 1990, production had risen to nearly 40,000 cases per year. Groth owns the 100-acre Oakcross Vineyard near the town of Oakville, which is planted with CABERNET SAUVIGNON and CHARDONNAY. It also owns a 43-acre Hillview Vineyard south of Yountville, which is planted with CHARDONNAY, MERLOT, and SAUVIGNON BLANC. About half of Groth's production is Cabernet Sauvignon (both a regular and a RESERVE bottling), with the remainder split between Chardonnay and Sauvignon Blanc. The red wines in particular are generally well rated.

grown, produced, and bottled by Label term that is another way of indicating that a wine is ESTATE BOTTLED, meaning that the grapes are grown at the winery's vineyards or vineyards controlled by the winery and that the wine is VINIFIED and bottled at the winery. *See also* BOTTLED BY; MADE AND BOTTLED BY; PRODUCED AND BOTTLED BY.

Gruaud-Larose, Château [sha-TOH groo-oh lah-ROHZ] A highly regarded DEUXIÈME CRU (second growth) located in the SAINT-JULIEN AC of BORDEAUX. With nearly 207 acres, it's one of the largest MÉDOC estates. The CHÂTEAU produces around 29,000 to 35,000 cases of RICH, full-bodied (*see* BODY) fruity red wine that can AGE for 30 to 35 years in the best VINTAGES. It's made from a blend of about 64 percent CABERNET SAUVIGNON, 24 percent MERLOT, 9 percent CABERNET FRANC, and 3 percent PETIT VERDOT. The name was established in the 1700s when a Monsieur Gruaud purchased the estate, which he later sold to his son-in-law, Monsieur de Larose. **Sargent de Gruaud-Larose** is the

SECOND LABEL for this château. The château is owned by Domaines Cordier, which owns a number of estates including Château TALBOT also located in the Saint-Julien AC.

Grüner *see* GRÜNER VELTLINER

Grüner Veltliner [GROO-ner FELT-lih-ner] White-wine grape grown principally in Austria (and that country's most widely planted variety), but also cultivated in Hungary, Czechoslovakia, and Slovenia. This grape produces pale, CRISP, light- to medium-bodied (*see* BODY) slightly SPICY wines of good quality. It's also called *Grünmuskateller* and *Veltlini*, as well as simply *Grüner*.

Grünmuskateller *see* GRÜNER VELTLINER

Guenoc Valley AVA A LAKE COUNTY, California, VITICULTURAL AREA at the northern end of the NAPA VALLEY about 15 miles north of Calistoga. It's unique because it's essentially a single-winery APPELLATION. GUENOC WINERY's owner, Orville Magoon, was the designer of the area, which received AVA status in 1981. The valley's growing season swings from warm days to cool nights, making it a Region III (*see* CLIMATE REGIONS OF CALIFORNIA). The main grape varieties are CABERNET SAUVIGNON and CHARDONNAY, with small amounts of SAUVIGNON BLANC.

Guenoc Winery [GWEN-ahk] Owned by the Magoon family, this winery sits on a 23,000-acre ranch in California's LAKE COUNTY area. The property was acquired by the Magoons through a property swap with the University of Hawaii, which took over 23 acres that they owned in Hawaii. Part of the huge property the Magoons got belonged to actress Lillie Langtry in the late 1800s and early 1900s; her house on the property has been restored. Guenoc wines feature a picture of Lillie Langtry on the label and, in fact, the more expensive wines are produced under the **Langtry** label. Approximately 320 acres are planted in the GUENOC VALLEY AVA and in NAPA COUNTY (all part of the ranch). Planted varieties include CABERNET FRANC, CABERNET SAUVIGNON, CHARDONNAY, CHENIN BLANC, MERLOT, PETITE SIRAH, SAUVIGNON BLANC, and ZINFANDEL. The red wines (Beckstoffer Reserve, Guenoc MERITAGE, Langtry Meritage) have been consistently well regarded the last few VINTAGES. **Le Breton** is the winery's SECOND LABEL.

Aux Guettes *see* SAVIGNY-LÈS-BEAUNE

Guiraud, Château [sha-TOH gee-*R*OH] A PREMIER CRU (first growth) of the SAUTERNES AC in the GRAVES district of BORDEAUX. It's a large estate of about 300 acres, about 60 percent of which is planted in vineyards—part for white wines and a smaller section for reds. It produces some 7,000 to 9,000 cases of SAUTERNES AC sweet wines and 6,000 to 8,000 cases of BORDEAUX SUPÉRIEUR AC red wine called **La Dauphin Château Guiraud**. In addition, a small amount of DRY white wine, called **"G,"** is produced. The mix of white grapes that go into the sweet Sauternes AC wines is about 65 percent SAUVIGNON BLANC and 35 percent SÉMILLON; the DRY white wine is mostly Sauvignon Blanc. The red wines are a blend of about a 55 percent CABERNET SAUVIGNON and 45 percent MERLOT. Château Guiraud's focus is on the sweet white wines, however, and the excellent recent VINTAGES elicit kudos for being made using the techniques of its neighbor, Château D'YQUEM— selective individual berry picking on multiple passes and FERMENTING and AGING in new oak barrels. Vintages of the late 1980s should age for 15 to 25 years.

Güldenmorgen *see* DIENHEIM

Gumpoldskirchen [GOOM-pawlts-ki*r*kh-ehn] Celebrated Austrian wine-producing town located just south of Vienna in an area called the Thermenregion district. Gumpoldskirchen produces highly regarded white wines from Rotgipfler and Zierfandler grapes. The Gumpoldskirchener wines are RICH, DRY, full-bodied (*see* BODY), and HEADY.

Günterslay *see* PIESPORT

Gustave Niebaum Collection *see* INGLENOOK-NAPA VALLEY

Gutedel *see* CHASSELAS

Gutsabfüllung [GOOTS-ab-few-lung] A German term meaning "estate bottled" and comparable to the United States meaning of ESTATE BOTTLED. It has a much more restrictive meaning than the term ERZEUGERABFÜLLUNG.

Gutturnio *see* COLLI PIACENTINI

gyropallets *see* RIDDLING

abzó The Hungarian word for "sparkling."

halbstück [HAHLP-shtook] A round wooden cask holding 600 liters (about 158 U.S. gallons) that's traditionally used by German winemakers along the Rhine River, particularly in the RHEINGAU region. These casks are slowly disappearing because some winemakers no longer use them in wine production for certain grape varieties like MÜLLER-THURGAU.

halbtrocken [HAHLP-trahk-en] The German term for "half-dry" or "medium-dry," pertaining to wines that are sweeter than TROKEN (DRY) wines. In most parts of Germany, halbtrocken applies to wines containing between 9 and 18 grams of RESIDUAL SUGAR per liter (0.9 to 1.8 percent), although the official definition also states that the residual sugar cannot be more than 10 grams greater than the TOTAL ACIDITY. For example, if the residual sugar is 18 grams, then the total acidity must be at least 8 grams; if total acidity is only 6 grams, then the residual sugar can't exceed 16 grams. In Austria, halbtrocken has a slightly different meaning, referring to wines with between 4 and 9 grams of residual sugar per liter.

half bottle *see* WINE BOTTLES

Hallgarten [HAHL-gar-tuhn] An important village situated in the steep slopes above the Rhine River in Germany's RHEINGAU region. The best vineyard sites (EINZELLAGEN) get good exposure to the sun, which results in RIESLING wines that are RICH, full-bodied (*see* BODY), and capable of longer AGING. The primary Einzellagen are **Hendelberg**, **Jungfer**, **Schönhell**, and **Würzgarten**.

Hamptons, The *see* LONG ISLAND

Hanepoot *see* MUSCAT

Hanzell Vineyards [han-ZELL] Winery whose name is a compound of the late Ambassador James Zellerbach's last name and his wife Hana's first name. Hanzell Vineyards is located just north of the town of Sonoma in the SONOMA VALLEY. When Zellerbach built the winery in the mid-1950s, he modeled the winery building after CLOS DE VOUGEOT in France's BURGUNDY region. The equipment he installed was quite modern and innovative for the period. Stainless steel was used throughout, including the first temperature-controlled, glass-lined fermentation tanks. Hanzell Vineyards was also one of the American innovators in using small French oak barrels for AGING wine. Its first CHARDONNAY wines (1956 produced only 5 gallons and 1957 was not widely distributed) were highly regarded and immediately established a name for the winery. Today Hanzell Vineyards produces Chardonnay, PINOT NOIR, and a small amount of CABERNET SAUVIGNON from its 33-acre vineyard. Only about 3,000 cases of these highly regarded wines are produced annually.

Haraszthy, Agoston [AG-goo-stawn HAH-rahs-th'ee] A colorful man who played an important part in California's viticultural history. Agoston Haraszthy, sometimes called Count and other times Colonel, was a Hungarian who arrived in California in the mid-1800s. Although he's often called the father of California viticulture, he wasn't the first to bring the VITIS VINIFERA species to the state. He did, however, significantly influence the course of the California wine industry. In 1851 he successfully planted a small sampling of vitis vinifera vines and cuttings in SONOMA COUNTY. Ten years later, he made a trip to Europe and returned with over 100,000 cuttings of 300 different varieties. Some of them were planted at the BUENA VISTA WINERY that he founded in 1857 in Sonoma; others were sold to growers around the state. The large number of cuttings significantly elevated the state's grape-growing and wine-producing industries. In addition to the grape varieties that he brought back, Haraszthy wrote a book, *Grape Culture, Wines and Wine Making*, which contributed immensely to the local knowledge pool. His Buena Vista Winery is also thought to have produced California's first SPARKLING WINE, called *Eclipse*. Unfortunately, Haraszthy was beset with a string of misfortunes, including the loss of financial backing for his Buena Vista Winery. He eventually moved to Nicaragua where, in 1869, he supposedly was eaten by alligators near the plantation on which he lived.

hard Descriptor for a wine that's young and excessively TANNIC and/or ACIDIC. Such a wine will generally MELLOW and SOFTEN with AGING. *See also* SOFT.

harmonious A winetasting term for a wine that is perfectly BALANCED and ready to drink.

harsh Descriptor for a wine that's HARD in the extreme, usually due to high astringency, which gives it a rough tactile sensation on the palate.

Hárslevelü [HARSH-leh-veh-LOO] A white grape grown mainly in Hungary, with some acreage just across the border in Czechoslovakia. Following FURMINT, Harslevelu is the leading component in Hungary's renowned TOKAY ASZÚ wines, which are made from botrytised grapes. Although the thick-skinned Hárslevelü grapes aren't as susceptible to BOTRYTIS CINEREA as Furmint, they're very AROMATIC and add SUPPLENESS and a strong SPICY, PERFUMED character to Tokay wines. Good Hárslevelü VARIETAL WINES are produced in Hungary around Baja and Villány in the south and Debrö in the north.

Harveys After strictly being shippers for nearly 175 years, Harveys (John Harvey and Sons) began to **buy** vineyards and build production facilities in JEREZ in 1970. Prior to that time, Harveys only blended wines made by other producers, and bottled them under the Harveys label. In the 20 years since it began acquiring vineyards, Harveys has grown to become the largest SHERRY producer; its top seller is *Bristol Cream*. Harveys, which is owned by the huge British firm Allied Lyons, produces a wide variety of moderately priced sherries.

Hasenberg *see* JOHANNISBERG

Hasensprung *see* WINKEL

Hattenheim [HAHT-uhn-hime] A well-known wine-producing village located southwest of the city of Wiesbaden in Germany's RHEINGAU region. This beautiful village comprises a number of well-regarded EINZELLAGEN including the famous STEINBERG, considered one of the best in all of Germany. Even though the Einzellage Marcobrunn is partially in Hattenheim, a dispute settled in 1971 produced the result that all wines are attached to the village of Erbach and therefore labeled Erbacher Marcobrunn. Other notable Einzellagen are **Engelsmannberg**, **Mannberg**, **Nussbrunnen**, **Schützenhaus**, and **Wisselbrunnen**.

haut [OH] French term meaning "high," "higher," or "upper," generally used in a geographical sense—as in HAUT-MÉDOC, which is north of (or above) the MÉDOC. Haut does not refer to a higher quality of wine.

Haut-Bages-Averous *see* LYNCH-BAGES, CHÂTEAU

Haut-Bages-Libéral, Château [sha-TOH oh BAHZH lee-bay-*R*AHL] Located in the PAUILLAC AC of the MÉDOC, this is a CINQUIÈME CRU (fifth growth) CHÂTEAU with nearly 62 acres. It produces about 10,000 to 12,000 cases of good-quality red wine from a mixture of nearly 74 percent CABERNET SAUVIGNON, 23 percent MERLOT, and 3 percent PETIT VERDOT. The better VINTAGES can AGE for 12 to 15 years. The château is now owned by the owners of Château CHASSE-SPLEEN.

Haut-Bailly, Château [sha-TOH oh bah-YEE] A CRU CLASSÉ estate located in the PESSAC-LÉOGNAN AC of the GRAVES district. It produces high-quality red wines but no white wines (as many Graves châteaus do). There are around 69 acres, and the approximate proportion of grapes is 65 percent CABERNET SAUVIGNON, 25 percent MERLOT, and 10 percent CABERNET FRANC. The wines are highly regarded—some compare their quality to those of a TROISIÈME CRU (third growth) from the MÉDOC. The better VINTAGES can AGE from 15 to 20 years. The château's SECOND LABEL is called **La Parde de Haut-Bailly**.

Haut-Batailley, Château [sha-TOH oh bah-tah-YEH] A highly regarded, though not well-known, estate located in the PAUILLAC AC of BORDEAUX'S MÉDOC district. It's classified as a CINQUIÈME CRU (fifth growth) and produces wines consistent with this rating. The property consists of nearly 50 acres but has no château building. The wines are made by the owners of Château DUCRU-BEAUCAILLOU, who are cousins to Madame Brest-Borie, the proprietor of Château Haut-Batailley. Around 7,500 to 10,500 cases of red wine are produced. The wines, which are composed of approximately 65 percent CABERNET SAUVIGNON, 25 percent MERLOT, and 10 percent CABERNET FRANC, are of high quality, but they are rather LIGHT for a Pauillac wine. They usually mature within 10 years but will occasionally AGE for 15 years. **La Tour d'Aspic** is Château Haut-Batailley's SECOND LABEL.

Haut-Benauge AC *see* ENTRE-DEUX-MERS

Haut-Beychevelle Gloria *see* GLORIA, CHÂTEAU

Haut-Brion, Château [sha-TOH oh-bree-OHN] Château Haut-Brion is one of only four CHÂTEAUS (the others being LATOUR, LAFITE-ROTHSCHILD, and MARGAUX) to receive a PREMIER CRU (first-growth) ranking for red wines in the CLASSIFICATION OF 1855. It's the only château outside of the MÉDOC to have been classified at all. Château Haut-Brion is located in the GRAVES district of BORDEAUX in what's now called the PESSAC-LÉOGNAN AC, just outside the city of Bordeaux. The château's history goes back almost 500 years, and it was noted for its outstanding wines even in the fifteenth, sixteenth, and seventeenth centuries. It was visited in 1787 by Thomas Jefferson, reputedly America's first wine connoisseur. Today, the château is owned by the daughter of C. Douglas Dillon (he purchased it in 1935 and was once Secretary of the Treasury of the United States and U.S. ambassador to France). Château Haut-Brion is not only famous for its outstanding red wines, which rank among the world's best, but also for its DRY white wines. The vineyards consist of nearly 108 acres planted mainly with red-wine grapes—about 55 percent CABERNET SAUVIGNON, 25 percent MERLOT, and 20 percent CABERNET FRANC. The small amount of white grapes planted are nearly evenly divided between SAUVIGNON BLANC and SÉMILLON. The red wines are very full-bodied (*see* BODY) and RICH and noted for SMOKY,

MINERAL (imparted by the gravelly soil) characteristics. Those from better VINTAGES can AGE for 25 to 30 years. The better-VINTAGE white wines, labeled Château Haut-Brion Blanc, can also be extremely rich and last for 10 to 15 years. The estate averages around 12,000 to 13,000 cases of red wine each year and only about 700 to 800 cases of white wine. The château's SECOND LABEL **Bahans-Haut-Brion** is generally of high quality and considered one of the best second-label wines.

Hautes-Côtes de Beaune AC [oht koht duh BOHN] A separate APPELLATION located in the beautiful hills behind the famous CÔTE DE BEAUNE area in France's BURGUNDY region. Both red wines, made from PINOT NOIR, and white wines, made from CHARDONNAY, are produced by the twenty villages associated with the appellation. The altitude of these vineyards is higher than that of the Côte de Beaune vineyards, but the exposure to the sun is not as good, so the grapes have a more difficult time ripening. The wines are therefore never quite as FRUITY or full-bodied (*see* BODY) as those from the Côte de Beaune area. There are several producers, however, who keep YIELDS down and use new oak barrels to produce some superb wines.

Hautes-Côtes de Nuits [oht koht duh NWEE] Located in the rugged hills directly behind the famous CÔTE DE NUITS area in France's BURGUNDY region, this APPELLATION encompasses the vineyard areas of fourteen different villages. As with the HAUTES-CÔTES DE BEAUNE AC, higher altitude is a problem for both the PINOT NOIR and CHARDONNAY grapes that are grown there. The grapes have a difficult time ripening, which means that both the red and white wines are never quite as FRUITY or full-bodied (*see* BODY) as those from the Côte de Nuits area.

Hautes Mourottes, *see* CORTON; CORTON-CHARLEMAGNE

Haut-Maurbuzet, Château [sha-TOH oh mar-boo-ZEH] Probably the best GRAND BOURGEOIS EXCEPTIONNEL of the SAINT-ESTÈPHE AC in the MÉDOC. The CHÂTEAU produces a RICH, SPICY red wine that some believe compares favorably with those from TROISIÈME CRU (third-growth) châteaus. The wines, which consist of approximately 50 percent MERLOT, 40 percent CABERNET SAUVIGNON, and 10 percent CABERNET FRANC, display the use of 100 percent new-oak barrels. As evidenced by the 1970 VINTAGE, these wines can AGE for 20 years or more; most are best in the 10- to 15-year range. The estate consists of around 100 acres and averages about 20,000 cases of red wine. The SECOND LABEL of this château is **Tour-de-Marbuzet**.

Haut-Médoc [oh may-DAHK] The southern portion of the MÉDOC district located in France's BORDEAUX region. The Haut-Médoc extends north from the GRAVES area just north of the city of Bordeaux, to just above the village of Saint-Seurin-de-Cardourne north of Saint-Estèphe. The Haut-Médoc is where the best and most famous Médoc CHÂTEAUS are located. The **Haut-Médoc AC** covers all the Haut-Médoc except for the six individual village appellations of LISTRAC, MARGAUX, MOULIS, PAUILLAC, SAINT ESTÈPHE, and SAINT-JULIEN. The Haut-Médoc AC includes five CRU CLASSÉ châteaus not associated with specific village appellations: BELGRAVE, DE CAMENSAC, CANTEMERLE, LA LAGUNE, and LA-TOUR CARNET. In general, wines labeled with the Haut-Médoc AC are much better than those simply labeled Médoc AC, but they are not as good as wines from one of the individual COMMUNE appellations like PAUILLAC AC or MARGAUX AC. The main grapes used throughout the Haut-Médoc are CABERNET FRANC, CABERNET SAUVIGNON, and MERLOT, with occasional use of PETIT VERDOT and minute amounts of MALBEC.

Haut-Poitou VDQS [oh-pwah-TOO] VDQS area located north of the city of Poitiers, southwest of Tours, in the central part of France's LOIRE region. A majority of the wines are red or ROSÉ, made mainly from GAMAY and some CABERNET FRANC and CABERNET SAUVIGNON. The CRISP, DRY white wines are made from SAUVIGNON BLANC, CHARDONNAY, or CHENIN BLANC. Some SPARKLING WINE is made as well.

Les Hauts de Pontet *see* PONTET-CANET, CHÂTEAU

Les Hauts de Smith-Haut-Lafitte *see* SMITH-HAUT-LAFITTE, CHÂTEAU

Hautvillers [oh-vee-LEH*R*] A village on the Marne River just north of Epernay in France's CHAMPAGNE region. Hautvillers is where the Benedictine Abbey of Dom Pérignon fame is located. It's here that Dom Pérignon, the seventeenth-century cellarmaster of the abbey, is credited with developing the art of blending wines to create champagnes with superior flavor. He's also known for his work in preventing champagne bottles and corks from exploding. He did this by using thicker bottles and tying the corks down with string.

Haywood Winery *see* BUENA VISTA

hazy Descriptor for a relatively clear wine that has a moderate amount of suspended particulates. This is common in some UNFILTERED or UNFINED wines. Haziness, however, may be a wine's first step toward CLOUDINESS—a sign of a flawed wine.

heady Descriptor for a wine that's high in ALCOHOL.

hearty Winetasting term generally applied to LIVELY, ROBUST red wines that are high in ALCOHOL.

heat stabilization *see* STABILIZATION

heat summation method *see* CLIMATE REGIONS OF CALIFORNIA

heavy A winetasting term used to describe a wine that's high in AL-COHOL and EXTRACT, combined with a lack of DELICACY.

hectare [HEHK-tahr] Abbreviated as **ha**, a hectare is a unit of surface or land equivalent to 10,000 square meters or 2.471 acres. In countries using the metric system—such as Europe and South America—vineyard area is expressed in hectares. A European vineyard with 50 hectares is equivalent to a U.S. vineyard with just over 123 acres; a 250-acre U.S. vineyard is tantamount to about a 101-hectare European vineyard.

hectoliter [HEHK-tuh-lee-tuhr] A capacity unit equal to 100 liters, or 26.418 U.S. gallons, or 22 Imperial gallons. In European and South American countries, where metric systems are standard, wine production figures are generally expressed in hectoliters. YIELDS in such countries are expressed in terms of hectoliters per HECTARE. In comparing European yields to those of the United States, a hectoliter is approximately equivalent to 0.183 U.S. tons; 40 hectoliter per hectare would be equivalent to 2.96 tons per acre. Two tons per acre would be the equivalent of 27 hecoliters per hectare. **Hecto** is a shortened form of the word; **hl** is the abbreviated form.

Heidsieck, Charles *see* CHAMPAGNE

Heidsieck Monopole *see* CHAMPAGNE

Heitz Wine Cellars Joseph Heitz was one of the winemakers to trigger the revitalization of the NAPA VALLEY when he established Heitz Wine Cellars in 1961. The winery, which was originally located just outside St. Helena, California, is now situated on a site north of Rutherford near the Silverado Trail in the eastern hills of the Napa Valley. The original site is used as a sales office. Heitz rose to fame on the MARTHA'S VINEYARD wines, which he started making in 1965 (although 1966 was the first year for a VINEYARD-DESIGNATED wine). Certain of this wine's VINTAGES (1968 and 1974 in particular) are considered by many to be some of the best California CABERNET SAUVIGNONS ever produced. Heitz Wine Cellars also makes a **Bella Oaks Vineyard** and a **Napa Valley** bottling of Cabernet Sauvignon. CHARDONNAY and ZINFAN-DEL are produced, as well as red and rosé GRIGNOLINO wines. It owns about 115 acres of vineyard, plus a 600-acre site on the lower part of HOWELL MOUNTAIN, which is partially planted at this writing. Though Heitz doesn't own either Martha's Vineyard or Bella Oaks Vineyard, the owners of these vineyards are all stockholders in Heitz Wine Cellars. The winery produces between 35,000 and 40,000 cases of wine each year.

Hendelberg *see* HALLGARTEN

Henriot *see* CHAMPAGNE

L'Hérault [lay-ROH] This is a large DÉPARTEMENT on the Mediterranean in southern France. It's part of the LANGUEDOC-ROUSSILLON region, which is often referred to as the Midi. L'Hérault has more vineyards planted than any other French département, but most of the wines produced are very ordinary and make up part of what some call the "European wine lake"—the huge glut of cheap, lackluster wine coming from the warmer regions of France, Spain, and Italy. L'Hérault is undergoing winemaking improvements including the implementation of stainless steel tanks, using CARBONIC MACERATION, and planting more popular varieties like CABERNET SAUVIGNON, CHARDONNAY, MARSANNE, MERLOT, MOURVÈDRE, SAUVIGNON BLANC, SÉMILLON, and SYRAH. Other grapes grown in the area include BOURBOULENC, CARIGNAN, GRENACH, MACABEO, and MUSCAT. L'Herault has developed popular, quality-winemaking areas in the last 15 years including FAUGERES AC, SAINT CHINIAN AC, and specific villages like LA CLAPE in the CÔTES DU LANGUEDOC.

herbaceous; herbal [hur-BAY-shuhss] A winetasting term for wines that smell of fresh herbs (such as basil, oregano, and rosemary), which can vary, depending on the wine. Sometimes this quality also is sensed on the palate. A herbal characteristic can be a VARIETAL trait in some CABERNET SAUVIGNONS, as well as MERLOTS and SAUVIGNON BLANCS. Unless this quality becomes overpowering or turns VEGETAL, it's considered desirable.

Hermannsberg *see* NIEDERHAUSEN

Hermannshöhle *see* NIEDERHAUSEN

Hermitage *see* CINSAUT

Hermitage AC [ehr-mee-TAHZH] 1. Some of France's greatest wines come from this APPELLATION, which is located in the northern portion of the RHÔNE region south of Lyon. Hermitage, sometimes spelled *Ermitage*, produces both red and white wines, both of excellent repute. The vineyards are thought to have been cultivated as far back as the Roman occupation of this area. The name Hermitage is attributed to a knight, Gaspard de Sterimberg, who, after fighting in the religious wars in the early 1200s, retired to this hill as a *hermit* to tend his vines and meditate. Accolades for Hermitage wines go back centuries, at least to the 1600s, when Louis XIV reigned. The vineyards are planted on the very steep, sun-drenched hillside above the town of Twain-l'Hermitage across the Rhône river from Tournon. The hill itself has three sections, each with a different soil type, and the producers who use grapes from all three of these sections seem to produce the best wines. SYRAH is the red grape of Hermitage. The white varieties MARSANNE and ROUSSANNE are used both in the white wines and in the blend for the robust red wines. Hermitage red wines, which are deep-colored, full-flavored, full-bodied (*see* BODY), and intense, can be brash and TANNIC when young. Those from the best VINTAGES can take up to 15 years to SOFTEN and can AGE for 30 or 40 years or more. The powerful white wines from Hermitage are capable of lengthy aging as well, some as long as the red wines. 2. Hermitage is a name used by South Africans for the grape variety CINSAUT. 3. In Australia, Hermitage is another name for the grape variety Syrah, which is most often called Shiraz.

Hermitage Blanc *see* MARSANNE

Herrenberg *see* ERDEN; KASEL; MAXIMIN GRUNHAUS; OPPENHEIM

Herrengarten *see* DIENHEIM

Herrgottsacker *see* DEIDESHEIM

Les Hervelets *see* FIXIN

Hess Collection, The NAPA VALLEY winery that is located on MOUNT VEDEER in Napa's western hills and that was founded in 1982 by Swiss-born Donald Hess. It's said that Hess, who's still a Swiss resident, was in California searching for new mineral water springs for his Valser mineral water business when California wines caught his attention. In 1978 Hess purchased 550 acres on Mount Veeder and subsequently planted vineyards there. Today, The Hess Collection owns about 900 acres in the Napa Valley with about 285 acres planted primarily with CHARDONNAY and CABERNET SAUVIGNON, plus the other BORDEAUX varieties of CABERNET FRANC, MALBEC, MERLOT, and PETIT VERDOT. The winery produces The Hess Collection line, which includes Chardonnay, Cabernet Sauvignon, and Cabernet Sauvignon Reserve wines, all of which are generally well regarded. The name, The Hess Collection, is derived from Hess' extensive contemporary art collection on display in a two-story gallery in the winery. A SECOND LABEL, called **Hess Select**, produces wines from various sources including vineyards owned by Hess in MONTEREY COUNTY.

Hess Select *see* HESS COLLECTION, THE

Hessische Bergstrasse [HEH-see-shuh BEHRK-strah-suh] The second smallest of the thirteen German ANBAUGEBIETE (quality wine regions), with just over 950 acres of vineyards planted. The region starts just north of the city of Darmstadt and extends south to the city of Heidelberg. RIESLING is the most plentiful variety, covering 50 percent of the acreage. There are two BEREICHE, **Starkenburg** and **Umstadt**. The wines from Hessische Bergstrasse are similar in quality and style to those from the better-known RHEINGAU region, with more BODY and flavor than most German wines. Most wines produced here don't make it outside the region.

heurige; pl. heurigen [HOY-*r*ih-guh] 1. An Austrian term for "new wine," *heurige* refers to wine from the most recent VINTAGE, which is released on November 11. Such wine is officially *heurige* until the following November, when it becomes *alt* wine. Many *heurigen* are produced in the vineyards surrounding Vienna and enjoyed while young by the Viennese. 2. An Austrian wine tavern and cafe that sells these young wines. There are over 1,000 of these *Heurigen* scattered throughout Vienna alone.

William Hill Winery NAPA VALLEY winery that was established in 1976 by William Hill, who has developed and subsequently sold a number of vineyards throughout the Napa Valley. Hill's VITICULTURAL enterprises include Diamond Mountain Ranch (sold to STERLING VINEYARDS), vineyard land on Mount Veeder (sold to THE HESS COLLECTION), and vineyards in Soda Canyon (which now belong to Atlas Peak Vineyards). In 1992 the winery, including the William Hill Winery name, was sold to the Wine Alliance, the wine division of Hiram Walker. This massive conglomerate also owns Callaway Vineyard & Winery near Riverside, California, and CLOS DU BOIS in SONOMA COUNTY. The William Hill Winery, which is located on Atlas Peak just north of the town of Napa, produces between 100,000 and 110,000 cases of wine each year. The wines include CABERNET SAUVIGNON (Reserve or Gold Label, and Napa Valley or Silver Label), CHARDONNAY (Gold and Silver Labels), MERLOT, and SAUVIGNON BLANC.

Himmelreich *see* GRAACH; ZELTINGEN

Hipping *see* NIERSTEIN

hippocras [HIP-uh-kras] A sweet, aromatized wine popular in the Middle Ages. It was made by adding cinnamon, ginger, and other spices and either sugar or honey.

Hitzlay *see* KASEL

hochgewächs [HOHK-guh-veks] A German term referring to a QbA (*see* QUALITÄTSWEIN BESTIMMTER ANBAUGEBIET) wine of superior quality made entirely from RIESLING grapes. To qualify, the grapes must be riper and the wines must pass a more rigorous taste test than those for ordinary QbA wines.

Hochheim [HOHKH-hime] Wine-producing town separated from the rest of Germany's RHEINGAU region by the city of Wiesbaden. Hockheim's vineyards actually are situated along the Main River rather than the Rhine River, as are most of the Rheingau's vineyards. Despite the geographic separation, wines from Hochheim have a distinct Rheingau character. The wines are full-bodied (*see* BODY), yet ELEGANT, with a hint of EARTHINESS. The better EINZELLAGEN include **Domdechaney**, **Hölle**, **Kirchenstuck**, **Königin Victoriaberg**, and **Stein**. SCHLOSS SCHÖNBORN is one of the better Hochheim producers. *See also* HOCK.

hock [HOHKH] A term used by the British to refer to wine from the Rhine regions of Germany. The term's a derivation of HOCKHEIM, a town in the RHEINGAU region. Hocks and Moselles still appear as headings on some English wine merchant lists.

hogshead A cask or barrel of varying capacity used to ship wines (and spirits). A hogshead can vary in size from approixmately 225 liters to about 275 liters (about 60 to 73 U.S. gallons).

Hogue Cellars [HOHG] This Washington State winery is located in the YAKIMA VALLEY AVA, just north of the town of Prosser. The Hogue family started planting VITIS VINIFERA vines in 1974 and made their first wines in 1982. Since then they've expanded the vineyards to nearly 300 acres and produce between 180,000 and 190,000 cases of wine each year. The vineyards are planted with CABERNET SAUVIGNON, CHARDONNAY, CHENIN BLANC, MERLOT, RIESLING, SÉMILLON, and SAUVIGNON BLANC. Hogue supplements its own grapes by purchasing from other growers in the COLUMBIA VALLEY AVA. The wines are consistently good, particularly the RESERVE bottlings.

Hoheburg *see* RUPPERTSBERG

Hohenmorgan *see* DEIDESHEIM

Hohnenrain *see* ERBACH

Hölie *see* HOCKHEIM; JOHANNISBERG; NIERSTEIN; WILTINGEN

hollow Descriptor for a wine that lacks DEPTH. The wine may taste fine going in, but there's usually a lack of BODY, and the flavor isn't sustained. The words *empty* and *shallow* are used synonymously with hollow.

honeyed A term applied to sweet, often BOTRYTISED, wines that have a honeylike fragrance and flavor—SAUTERNES and TROCKENBEERE-NAUSLESEN, just to name two.

Honigberg *see* ERBACH

horizontal tasting *see* WINETASTING

Hospices de Beaune [aws-PEES duh BOHN] A famous charitable organization consisting of the Hôtel-Dieu (a charitable hospital) and the Hospices de la Charité. It's located in the town of Beaune in France's BURGUNDY region and was founded in 1443 by Nicolas Rolin, chancellor to the Duke of Burgundy, and his wife Guigone de Salins. The colorfully tiled Hospices building is one of the landmarks in the town of Beaune, and its medieval architecture is often a focus for photographers. The Hospices de Beaune is subsidized by land endowments including some superior vineyard land in the CÔTE DE BEAUNE and CÔTE DE NUITS districts. The total holdings, which include some GRANDS CRUS and PREMIERS CRUS, consist of about 135 acres of vineyards. This land usually produces 13,000 to 17,000 cases of wine plus 3,000 to 3,500 cases of MARC de Bourgogne, both of which are sold at a famous auction held on the third Sunday in November. Because these wines are the first to be sold from the new VINTAGE, the auction prices are historically a general indicator of projected prices for this vintage in the rest of the region. After taking delivery of the barrels of wine, the auction buyers are responsible for AGING and bottling it. The wines are named after the major benefactors to the Hospices, appended to that of the APPELLATION—for example, *Corton-Docteur Peste, Beaune-Nicolas Rolin,* and *Mazis-Chambertin-Madeleine Collignon.*

Hospices de Nuits [aws-PEES du NWEE] A charitable foundation established in 1692 in NUIT-SAINT-GEORGES in BURGUNDY'S CÔTE DE NUITS district. This is a much smaller version of the more prominent and neighboring HOSPICES DE BEAUNE. Hospices de Nuits has been endowed with about 22 acres and holds an auction each spring, 2 weeks prior to Easter. Although the Hospices de Nuits auction doesn't elicit the same attention as that of the Hospices de Beaune, it does sell off some very good wines.

L'Hospitalet *see* GAZIN, CHÂTEAU

hot A sensory term used to describe wines with excessive ALCOHOL. Unless balanced with strong FRUIT, a high alcohol content creates a burning, prickly sensation in the mouth and throat. Whereas a "hot" sensation may be desirable in FORTIFIED wines such as PORT and SHERRY, it's not acceptable in most wines.

hotte [AWT] A French term for a long basket that's carried on one's back and used to transport grapes during the harvest. The general practice when harvesting grapes manually is to put the freshly cut grapes into hand-held baskets. The grapes are then dumped into the larger hotte, which is then carried to and unloaded into a truck or trailer that will transport the grapes to the winery. A hotte carrier generally works with a group of pickers, taking their grapes from the vineyard to the trailer.

house wine A wine featured by a restaurant and often served in a CARAFE or by the glass. Sometimes a winery does a special bottling and labels the wines for a restaurant. House wines are usually inexpensive wines that offer the diner an economical option to the more pricey, better-known selections on the wine list. Ask the server what the house wine is—he or she should be able to tell you the variety (Chardonnay, Merlot, etc.), brand name, and VINTAGE (if any).

Howell Mountain AVA Located northeast of the town of St. Helena in California's NAPA VALLEY, the hillside vineyards of this AVA range between 1,600 and 2,200 feet in elevation. The lack of fog and subsequent reasonably warm temperatures put Howell Mountain AVA into a Region II category (*see* CLIMATE REGIONS OF CALIFORNIA). The area's plentiful sunshine is perfect for CABERNET SAUVIGNON and ZINFANDEL grapes. Area wineries include DUNN VINEYARDS, CHATEAU WOLTNER, La Jota Vineyard, and Lamborn Family Vineyards.

Hudson River Region AVA; Hudson Valley *see* NEW YORK

Hungary Hungary produces a wide variety of wines from an equally wide assortment of grapes—some familiar, others a specialty of this eastern European country. Some of the more well-known varieties are CABERNET SAUVIGNON, GEWÜRZTRAMINER, Médoc Noir (MERLOT), Szürkebarát (PINOT GRIS), PINOT NOIR, and SYLVANER. However, the most popular varieties in Hungary are the red KADARKA and the white Olasz

Riesling (WELSCHRIESLING). Other white grapes include Ezerjo, FURMINT, HÁRSLEVELÜ, KÉKNYELÜ, and LEÁNYKA. The popular red Kékfrankos is the same as the Blaufränkisch grown in Austria, although not related to GAMAY, as some believe. Hungary has two famous wines—TOKAY, a highly regarded DESSERT WINE, and EGRI BIKAVÉR, the red "bull's blood" wine. Hungary's growing regions include: the Great Plain in the south central part of the country, which produces over half the total production (most of it very ordinary); the Lake Balaton area in the western part of the country, which includes the higher-quality-wine districts of Mount Badacsony (*see* BADACSONYI), Balaton, Balatonfüred-Csopak, Mór, and Somoló; Eger and Tokay, northeast of Budapest, where Egri Bikavér and Tokay are made; and Sopron in the northwestern corner. The labels of Hungarian wines include the name of the producing areas to which an *i* is added, making it a possessive form, as in Soproni Kékfrankos—a wine made in the Sopron area from the Kékfrankos variety—or Badacsonyi Szürkebarát—from the Mount Badacsony area and made with Szürkebarát grapes.

Hunter Valley One of Australia's best wine-producing regions located in the state of New South Wales, about 100 miles northwest of Sydney. It's also one of the oldest, with its first vineyards planted in the early 1800s. Although the outside world knows only of Hunter Valley, winemakers in the area distinguish between the **Upper Hunter Valley** and the **Lower Hunter Valley**. The Lower Hunter Valley, located between Rothbury and Pokolbin, is the older of the two regions and the one most associated with the name. The Upper Hunter Valley, which lies between Denman and Scone, was firmly established in the 1960s when the prestigious wine company Penfolds invested in this area. The most widely planted white variety in Hunter Valley is SÉMILLON followed by CHARDONNAY, GEWÜRTZTRAMINER, RIESLING, and SAUVIGNON BLANC. Shiraz (SYRAH), called *Hermitage* here, is the most popular red grape, although CABERNET SAUVIGNON is the most widely planted in the Upper Hunter Valley. Small amounts of PINOT NOIR are planted as well. Allandale, Brokenwood, Hungerford Hill, Hunter Estate, Lake's Folly, McWilliam's, Richmond Grove, the Rothbury Estate, Tyrrell's, and Wyndham Estate are well-known wineries in the Lower Hunter Valley. In the Upper Hunter Valley, Rosemount Estate is the dominant winery; Mountarrow (formerly Arrowfield) is also there.

Husch Vineyards [HUHSH] Winery that in 1971 was the first to establish itself in the ANDERSON VALLEY since PROHIBITION. The winery, which was founded by Tony Husch, was acquired by the Oswald family in 1979. They also own the 110-acre La Ribera Vineyard near the town of Ukiah, California, and another vineyard in Anderson Valley across from the original Husch vineyards. Nearly 30,000 cases of wine are made each year from the three vineyard sites. Husch Vineyards produces the following VARIETAL WINES: CABERNET SAUVIGNON, CHARDONNAY, CHENIN BLANC, GEWÜRZTRAMINER, PINOT NOIR, and SAUVIGNON BLANC. Although Husch has long had a good reputation for its white wines, the Cabernet Sauvignon identified as **North Field Select** has been generating quite a bit of interest the last few years.

Huxelrebe [HOOK-sehl-reh-buh] A German white-wine grape derived from a CROSS of Weisser Gutedel (CHASSELAS) and Courtillier Musqué. Huxelrebe, grown primarily in the German regions of RHEINHESSEN and RHEINPFALZ, is named after viticulturist Fritz Huxel, who bred this HYBRID extensively in the late 1920s. Huxelrebe is also grown in England. If carefully pruned, these vines can produce grapes with good ACIDITY and high sugar content, which reward the winemaker with very good AUSLESE wines, even in poor VINTAGES. Conversely, uncontained growth and high YIELDS result in lackluster wines. Huxelrebe is often used as a BLENDING WINE.

hybrid; v. hybridize [HI-brihd; HI-brih-dyz] In a pure sense, the word **hybrid** in the wine world refers to a vine or grape created by breeding two varieties from different species or genuses (such as VITIS VINIFERA and VITIS RIPARIA or VITIS LABRUSCA). However, the term sometimes also refers to a CROSS, which is a vine or grape created by breeding two varieties of the same genus (VITIS VINIFERA, for example). BACO NOIR is a red French-American hybrid created by breeding FOLLE BLANCHE (vitis vinifera) with a native American vine (vitis riparia). MÜLLER-THURGAU is an example of a cross between RIESLING and SYLVANER, both of which are vitis vinifera. Hybrids are created in an effort to produce a plant with the best traits of its parents, such as high productivity, disease resistance, and/or better adaptability to environmental conditions. One who creates hybrids is called a *hybridist* or *hybridizer. See also* CLONE.

hydrogen sulfide (H₂S) [HY-druh-jihn SUHL-fyd] Hydrogen sulfide is the result of yeast combining with various forms of SULFUR. It produces an undesirable, rotten-egg smell in wine. Eventually, H_2S in wine transforms into MERCAPTANS (a skunky odor) and disulfides (a sewage smell), both of which ruin a wine.

hydrometer (high-DRAH-mih-ter) Literally meaning "water measurer," a hydrometer is an instrument comprised of a vertical scale inside a sealed glass tube weighted at one end. It's used to measure the ratio (called SPECIFIC GRAVITY) of the density of a liquid (such as grape MUST or wine) to that of pure water. A hydrometer floats upright in liquid—the reading is taken where the liquid's surface hits the scale—and the denser the liquid, the higher it floats. In winemaking, a hydrometer has many uses including: measuring a must's sugar content and calculating its potential ALCOHOL, determining how FERMENTATION is progressing and indicating when it's finished, gauging effervescence in SPARKLING WINES, and measuring a finished wine's alcohol level.

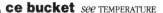

ce bucket *see* TEMPERATURE

ice wine *see* EISWEIN

Idaho Along with Washington and Oregon, Idaho makes up the region called the Pacific Northwest. Its main growing area is in the Snake River Valley in the southwestern part of the state, near Boise, and not far from the Oregon border. Although the climate here is similiar to that of Washington's Columbia Valley, the vineyards are a little higher, the nights are cooler, and the growing season is shorter. All of which makes it difficult for grapes to always fully ripen. At this point the wines that have the most chance of being successful here are CHARDONNAY, RIESLING, and CHENIN BLANC, along with SPARKLING WINE and, occasionally, PINOT NOIR. Idaho wineries include Hell's Canyon, Indian Creek, Pintler, Rose Creek, Ste. Chapelle, and Weston.

Île des Vergelesses *see* PERNAND-VERGELESSES

Imagery *see* BENZIGER OF GLEN ELLEN

imbottigliato [ihm-boh-tee-LYAH-toh] An Italian term meaning "bottled." *Imbottigliato da* means "bottled by;" *Imbottigliato all'origine* means "bottled at the source (or origin)" and is synonymous with ESTATE BOTTLED.

imperial *see* WINE BOTTLES

INAO *see* INSTITUT NATIONALE DES APPELLATIONS D'ORIGINE

Indicação de Proveniencia Regulamentada (IPR) A second-level ranking for Portuguese wines that are striving to achieve Portugal's highest ranking, DENOMINAÇÃO DE ORIGEM CONTROLADA.

Inglenook-Napa Valley Inglenook was established in 1879 by fur trader Gustave Niebaum. It was run by his heirs until it was sold in 1964 to Allied Grape Growers, which was purchased in 1969 by Heublein, the current owner. During Gustave Niebaum's time, and later when John Daniel, Jr. (a grandnephew) was running Inglenook, the winery was known for the high quality of its wines and innovations in winemaking. After the Heublein takeover, Inglenook production was expanded to include: premium wines called **Inglenook-Napa Valley**, a medium-priced line called **Inglenook Vintage** and a low-priced line called **Inglenook Navalle**, which was comprised essentially of JUG WINES made from CENTRAL VALLEY grapes. Today, this latter line has been split—the VARIETAL bottlings are called **Navalle Selections**, while the generic jug wines remain labeled Inglenook Navelle. Nearly 2.5

million cases of the Navelle-labeled wines are sold each year. The medium-priced line (Inglenook Vintage) has been replaced by a SEC-OND LABEL called **Rutherford Estate**. The premium line of Napa Valley varietals is led by RESERVE wines that include a CABERNET SAUVIGNON, MER-LOT, CHARDONNAY, and SAUVIGNON BLANC. Also part of this line is a Cabernet Sauvignon-based wine called **Reunion**, which was intro-duced in 1983. A regular bottling of estate wines is produced as well. Although sales of the Inglenook-Napa Valley line have fallen from more than 150,000 to less than 100,000 cases per year, the reserve wines were well received in the 1980s, particularly the reds—Reserve Cask Cabernet Sauvignon and Reunion. The **Gustave Niebaum Collection** is another product line that was introduced in 1989. It's made up of a number of VINEYARD-DESIGNATED wines, which are pro-duced in limited quantities. The wines offered in this line include Chardonnay (Laird and Bayview Vineyards), Cabernet Sauvignon (Tench, Reference, and Mast Vineyards), and a Sauvignon Blanc-SÉMILLON blend called Chevrier from Herrick Vineyard. This product line, which is nearing 15,000 cases per year, has a separate winemaker but is produced at the Inglenook facility. In 1994 Heublein sold the Inglenook brand (consisting primarily of the jug wine business) to Canandaigua Wine Company of New York. Later that same year, Heublein agreed to sell Francis Ford Coppola (*see* NIEBAUM-COPPOLA ES-TATE) the historic Inglenook winery and its adjacent vineyards, along with the rights to the Gustave Niebaum name. This will allow Coppola to reunite parts of the original Inglenook estate.

inky 1. A winetasting term that is sometimes used to describe an of-fensive metallic flavor that is usually caused by TANNINS coming in con-tact with iron (such as a nail). 2. Inky is also used to indicate the deep, seemingly impenetrable color of some red wines.

insipid Descriptor for a wine that lacks CHARACTER, flavor, BODY, and most other positive attributes.

Institut Nationale des Appellations d'Origine; INAO
[an-stee-tyoo nah-syaw-NAHL dayz ah-pehl-lah-SYOHN daw-ree-ZHEHN] French organization, most often referred to as the INAO, that establishes the broad guidelines for the APPELLATION D'ORIGINE CONTRÔLÉE.

invecchiato [in-veh-chee-YAH-toh] Italian for "aged," *invecchiato* is occasionally used to identify the length of time a DOC wine is aged.

Irancy AC [ee-*rahn*-SEE] A tiny French APPELLATION located around the village of Irancy in northern BURGUNDY just southwest of CHABLIS.

Irancy makes red and ROSÉ wines using mainly PINOT NOIR grapes BLENDED with a small amount of two local varieties, César and Tressot. The wines are generally pleasant, LIGHT, and DELICATE.

Iron Horse Vineyards Property located west of Santa Rosa, California, in the GREEN RIVER AVA (part of the larger RUSSIAN RIVER AVA) that was purchased in 1976 by Audrey and Barry Sterling. Forrest Tracer, who started to develop these vineyards previously for Rodney Strong, was brought on as a partner and winemaker. Vineyards of 110 acres were planted, evenly distributed between CHARDONNAY and PINOT NOIR vines. Iron Horse is best known for its SPARKLING WINES, which include BRUT, BLANC DE BLANCS, BLANC DE NOIRS (called **Wedding Cuvée**), and two LATE DISGORGED wines called **Vrais Amis Brut** and **Late Disgorged Brut**. Iron Horse also has vineyards in the ALEXANDER VALLEY where it grows CABERNET FRANC, CABERNET SAUVIGNON, SANGIOVESE, and SAUVIGNON BLANC grapes for use in STILL WINES. Chardonnay and Pinot Noir VARIETAL WINES are made from the Green River vineyard. **Tiny Pony** is Iron Horse's SECOND LABEL, which is used for lower-quality Pinot Noir wines.

Irouléguy AC [ee-roo-leh-GEE] An obscure APPELLATION encompassing Irouléguy and eight other villages nestled in the Pyrenees Mountains adjacent to the Spanish border in southwestern France. It produces mainly red and ROSÉ wines using the Tannat, CABERNET FRANC, and CABERNET SAUVIGNON varieties. Tiny amounts of white wine are made from Courbu, Gros Manseng, and Petit Manseng.

Isabella [ihz-uh-BELL-uh] HYBRID red wine grape that is the result of a CROSS between VITIS LABRUSCA and VITIS VINIFERA species. Isabella has been essentially replaced by CONCORD in the eastern United States, although small amounts are still grown in New York's FINGER LAKES region, where it's VINIFIED into ROSÉ wine. It's cultivated in areas of the former Soviet Union including Republic of Azerbaijan, Dagestan, Republic of Georgia, Krasnodar, and Republic of Moldavia, as well as in Brazil, Colombia, Madeira, Switzerland, and Uruguay. Isabella has an unattractive FOXY character and is losing its following in most areas. It's also known as *Americano* and *Bellina.*

Ischia DOC [EESS-kyah] DOC located on the island of Ischia in the Bay of Naples that is part of Italy's CAMPANIA region. The island produces a BIANCO made from 65 percent Forastera, 20 percent Biancolella, and 15 percent other white grapes. The *bianco superiore* allows more Biancolella and requires a higher ALCOHOL level. The ROSSO uses 50 percent Guarnaccia, 40 percent Piedirosso, and 10 percent BARBERA.

The wines are generally pretty mediocre but popular with the tourists visiting the island.

isinglass [I-zuhn-glas; Izing-glas] Transparent and pure, this form of gelatin comes from the air bladder of certain fish, especially the sturgeon. It's used as a FINING agent to help clarify wine, although today's modern gelatin (made from beef and veal bones, cartilage, tendons, etc.) has replaced isinglass in most instances.

ISO glass *see* GLASSES; Common Wineglass Shapes, page 593.

Isonzo DOC [ee-ZOHN-tsoh] DOC, which is also called *Isonzo del Friuli*, that is located in the FRIULI-VENEZIA GIULIA region in northeastern Italy. It's just south of the better-known COLLIO DOC. Twenty different wines are authorized, seventeen VARIETALS plus a BIANCO, a ROSSO, and a Pinot Spumante. The varietal wines are Cabernet (from CABERNET SAUVIGNON and CABERNET FRANC), Cabernet Franc, Cabernet Sauvignon, CHARDONNAY, Franconia, MALVASIA, MERLOT, Pinot Bianco (PINOT BLANC), Pinot Grigio (PINOT GRIS), Pinot Nero (PINOT NOIR), Refosco dal Peduncolo Rosso (MONDEUSE), Riesling Italico (WELSCHRIESLING), Riesling Renano (RIESLING), Sauvignon (SAUVIGNON BLANC), TOCAI, Traminer Aromatico (GEWÜRZTRAMINER), and Verduzzo Friulano. The Bianco is made from Tocai, Malvasia, Pinot Bianco, and Chardonnay; the Rosso from mainly Melot, Cabernet Franc, and Cabernet Sauvignon. The Pinot Spumante is made from Pinot Bianco, Pinot Nero, and Chardonnay. The red wines made from Merlot and Cabernet grapes are highly regarded, and the white wines from Chardonnay and Sauvignon Blanc grapes are starting to gain a good reputation.

Israel Despite the fact that winemaking is referred to in the Old Testament, modern winemaking wasn't introduced in Israel until the 1880s. That's when Baron Edmond de Rothschild backed the planting of vineyards and the building of two wineries—one in Richon-le-Zion, southeast of Tel-Aviv, and the other in Zikhron-Jacob on Mount Carmel, south of Haifa. These vineyards and wineries were donated to Israel in 1906, and the Société Cooperative Vigeronne de Grandes Caves was established as a cooperative to produce the wines. The cooperative still produces a majority of Israeli wines under the brand name Carmel. The main winegrowing areas here are: the region around the Sea of Galilee; the Mount Carmel area; the coastal area plains around Tel Aviv; the area around Jerusalem; and the area between Beersheba and Ascalon. The principal grape varieties planted are CARIGNAN and GRENACHE, along with CLAIRETTE, MUSCAT, and SÉMILLON. More recently planted grapes include CABERNET SAUVIGNON, MERLOT,

PINOT NOIR, CHARDONNAY, CHENIN BLANC, RIESLING, and SAUVIGNON BLANC. Israeli wines have shifted from being primarily sweet and FORTIFIED to mostly dry TABLE WINES, many of which are VARIETAL.

d'Issan, Château [sha-TOH dee-SAH*N*] With its fairytale-like castle surrounded by a moat, Château d'Issan is one of the most beautiful estates in the MÉDOC. It's located in the MARGAUX AC and is classified as a TROISIÈME CRU (third-growth) property. Most wine critics, however, don't feel that the wines are in the same class as either the château's ranking or the property's beauty. The wines are viewed as good, but too LIGHT and delicate, especially those from poor VINTAGES. Wines from the best vintages can AGE for around 10 to 12 years. The estate consists of about 79 acres planted with around 75 percent CABERNET SAUVIGNON and 25 percent MERLOT. Between 10,000 to 15,000 cases of red wine are produced each year. This château's SECOND LABEL is **Candel**.

Italy Italy is the world's largest wine producer, with production just under 25 percent of the world's total. It's also the greatest wine consumer, although second to France in per capita consumption (Italy has a larger population). Italy's a land of vast geographic diversity ranging from its northern cool-temperature vineyards in the foothills of the Alps, to the hot southland. Italy's been making wine for at least 3,500 years in a variety of styles (DRY to sweet, STILL to fully SPARKLING) and in a variety of ways, such as the PASSITO method, from many grape varieties not widely grown outside of Italy. The Italian varieties used for red and rosé wines include AGLIANICO, BARBERA, BONARDA, CANAIOLO, DOLCETTO, FREISA, GRIGNOLINO, LAGREIN, LAMBRUSCO, MONTEPULCIANO, NEBBIOLO, RABOSO, Refosco (MONDEUSE), SANGIOVESE, SCHIAVA, and Teroldego. Those used for white wines are ALBANA, BOMBINO BIANCO, CORTESE, GARGANEGA, GRECO, MALVASIA, Moscato (MUSCAT), PICOLIT, PIGATO, PROSECCO, TOCAI FRIULANO, TREBBIANO, VERDICCHIO, VERDUZZO, VERNACCIA DI ORISTANO, and VERNACCIA DI SAN GIMIGNANO. Other European (primarily French and German) varieties grown here are CABERNET FRANC, CABERNET SAUVIGNON, MERLOT, Pinot Nero (PINOT NOIR), SYRAH, CHARDONNAY, GEWÜRZTRAMINER, MÜLLER-THURGAU, Pinot Bianco (PINOT BLANC), Pinot Grigio (PINOT GRIS), Riesling Italico (WELSCHRIESLING), Riesling Renano (RIESLING), SAUVIGNON BLANC, and SYLVANER. The Italians have implemented a system similiar to France's for improving the quality of their wines. At the lowest level of this quality ranking are the VINO DA TAVOLA wines, followed by VINO TIPICO wines and then by the DENOMINAZIONE DI ORIGINE CONTROLLATA (DOC), which is similiar to the French APPELLATION D'ORIGINE CONTRÔLÉE. Parameters for the Italian DOC, however, weren't considered strict enough so another higher level, DENOMINAZIONE DI ORIGINE CONTROLLATA E GARANTITA (DOCG) was added. DOCG status, which requires stricter rules and controls, has been granted to less than fifteen (counting CHIANTI only once) areas since it was implemented in the early 1980s. Italy has twenty large growing regions, the boundaries of which define the area geographically, not by any common wine style, grape variety, or climate. Of these twenty regions, the four largest volume producers are APULIA, SICILY, VENETEO, and EMILIA-ROMAGNA who make over 55 percent of the total wine production. The order of these four regions (as to whose is first, second, etc.) changes depending on the year. The four top regions producing quality wines (those ranked as DOC or DOCG) are VENETO, TUSCANY, PIEDMONT, and TRENTINO-ALTO ADIGE. These four areas produce over 57 percent of the DOC/DOCG wines. Some of the better known of these wines include CHIANTI from the Tuscany region; ASTI SPUMANTE from the Piedmont region; LAMBRUSCO wines from DOC areas like *Lambrusco di Sorbara, Lambrusco Grasparossa di Castelvetro,* and *Lambrusco Salamino di Santa Croce* in the EMILA-ROMAGNA region; and BARDOLINO, VALPOLICELLA, and SOAVE from the Veneto region. High-quality wines also come from DOCG areas like BARBARESCO, BAROLO, and GATTINARA in Piedmont; BRUNELLO DI MONTALCINO and VINO NOBILE DI MONTEPULCIANO in Tuscany; and TORGIANO in UMBRIA.

J *see* JORDAN VINEYARD & WINERY

Jacquère [jah-KEHR] The primary white-wine grape of eastern France's SAVOIE region. Jacquère is the main variety used in the Vin de Savoie APPELLATION wines, which also include ALTESSE grapes. These wines are LIGHT, DRY, and somewhat ACIDIC, with hints of CITRUS and SMOKE. Jacquère is also known as *Buisserate* and *Cugnette.*

jahrgang [YAHR-gahng] The German term for "vintage year."

jammy; jamlike A winetasting term for wine that has an intensely ripe, FRUITY, and CONCENTRATED flavor and aroma.

Jasnières AC [zhah-NYEHR] A tiny APPELLATION located 25 miles north of Tours on the smaller Loir River in the central part of France's LOIRE Valley. Jasnières produces delicious DRY white wines from CHENIN BLANC, but because of this grape's high ACIDITY, the wines seem SHARP and very, very dry. Occasionally, the area produces small amounts of semisweet to sweet wines, which seem to better balance the acidity of the Chenin Blanc grape.

Jerez; Jerez y Manzanilla [heh-RETH; heh-RETH ee mahn-zuh-NEEL-yuh] Shortened versions of the proper name JEREZ-XÉRÈX-SHERRY Y MANZANILLA DE SANLÚCAR DE BARRAMEDA DO. Jerez may also refer to JEREZ DE LA FRONTERA.

Jerez de la Frontera [heh-RETH day lah frawn-TEH-rah] A city in southwestern Spain's Andulusia region, just inland from the Atlantic ocean. Jerez de la Frontera (once known as *Xerex*) is the central city in and birthplace of Spain's SHERRY country. *See also* JEREZ-XÉRÈX-SHERRY Y MANZANILLA DE SANLÚCAR DE BARRAMEDA DO.

Jerez-Xérèx-Sherry y Manzanilla de Sanlúcar de Barrameda DO [heh-RETH seh-REHS sheh-REE ee mahn-zuh-NEEL-yuh day sahn-LOO-kahr day bahr-rah-MEH-thah] The DO in which true sherry is made. It's located in southwest Spain around the city of Jerez de la Frontera. Although the DO zone encompasses a wider area, the core zone, called **Jerez Superior**, forms a rough triangle with Jerez de la Frontera at one corner and the towns of Sanlúcar de Barrameda and El Puerto de Santa Maria at the others. This area is rich with *albariza,* the white, chalky soil that produces the best grapes for fino and manzanilla (*see* SHERRY). This area's clay soil is called *barro,* which isn't quite as good as the albariza for such grapes.

Jeroboam *see* WINE BOTTLES

Jessuitengarten *see* WINKEL

Joannes Seyve 26205 *see* CHAMBOURCIN

João de Santarém *see* PERIQUITA

Johannisberg [yoh-HAHN-ihss-be*r*k] Esteemed name in wine circles that is one of Germany's best and most famous vineyards, SCHLOSS JOHANNISBERG, as well as the famous town where that vineyard is located and the BEREICH covering the entire RHEINGAU region. The town is located in the heart of the Rheingau southwest of the city of Wiesbaden. It's part of a series of towns and villages that are situated in some of Germany's best vineyards. In addition to Schloss Johannisberg, other top EINZELLAGEN include **Goldatzel**, **Hasenberg**, **Hölle**, **Klaus**, and **Vogelsang**. The prestige of the name Johannisberg has crossed the sea where in the United States, the term Johannisberg Riesling is often used for RIESLING wine.

Johannisberg, Schloss *SEE* SCHLOSS JOHANNISBERG

Johannisberger *see* RIESLING

Johannisberg Riesling *See* RIESLING

Joli Val *See* CLOS DU VAL

Jordan Vineyard & Winery Jordan Vineyards is located in the ALEXANDER VALLEY AVA and is part of a 1,500-acre estate that Tom Jordan purchased in 1972. Jordan, who owned an oil and gas exploration company in Colorado, planted about 275 acres, built a magnificent winery and home, and established a migratory bird reserve on the property. A majority of the 60,000 to 70,000 cases produced each year are CABERNET SAUVIGNON, with a smaller amount of CHARDONNAY. A separate concern called Jordan Sparkling Wine Company was established in 1987, with Tom Jordan's daughter Judy at the helm. It produces high-quality SPARKLING WINE labeled simply as "**J.**"

Josephshöf; Josephshöfer [YOH-zehfs-hawf; YOH-zehfs-hawf-uhr] One of Germany's premier EINZELLAGEN, which is located in the township of GRAACH on the Mosel River in Germany's MOSEL-SAAR-RUWER region. The 15-acre RIESLING vineyard, which is situated on a steeply terraced hillside, is owned by Weingut Reichsgraf von KESSEL-STATT, a respected producer in this area. Josephshöf is famous for RICH, ELEGANT wines that AGE well.

Juffer *see* BRAUNEBERG

jug wines A term that originated when consumers used to bring their own jugs to wineries to be filled. Today it applies to inexpensive, usually GENERIC WINES, which are customarily sold in large (1.5- and 3-liter) bottles.

Juliénas AC [zhoo-lyay-NAH] One of the smaller of the ten CRUS in France's BEAUJOLAIS region. Juliénas wines, made from GAMAY grapes, are some of the more substantial of the Beaujolais wines. They have deeper color, richer fruitiness, and more TANNINS than most. Along with the wines from MOULIN-À-VENT, those from Juliénas' steep hillsides are considered capable of the longest AGING of the ten Beaujolais *crus.*

Jumilla DO [khoo-MEE-lyah] DO located in the Levante region in eastern Spain, northeast of the city of Alicante. Jumilla, which has long been associated with BIG, high-ALCOHOL (up to 18 percent) red wines, has been modernizing winemaking techniques in an attempt to produce lower-alcohol wines. In order to achieve a more elegant style of wine, some producers are picking earlier, before grapes get too high in sugar. They're also using modern equipment like cooled, stainless steel tanks. The main grape in this area is the MONASTRELL—there are small amounts of Garnacha (GRENACHE) and Cencibel (TEMPRANILLO).

Jungfer *see* HALLGARTEN

Jurançon AC [zhoo-*rah*n-SAW*N*] APPELLATION located in the foothills of the Pyrenees near the town of Pau in southwest France. It produces only white wines, which are noted for their distinctive FLORAL and spicy (cinnamon and cloves) nuances. The grape varieties used are the local favorites—Courbu, Gros Manseng, and Petite Manseng. The wines can be DRY or sweet, the latter generally only if the grapes are infected with BOTRYTIS CINEREA.

abinett [kah-bih-NEHT] The first (lowest) of the six subcategories of QUALITÄTSWEIN MIT PRÄDIKAT (QmP)—the highest quality-wine category in Germany. Kabinett wines must contain minimum amounts of natural sugar (ranging from 67° to 85° OECHSLE, approximately 17 to 21 percent sugar by weight), depending on the region and the variety. These are the lowest minimums for QmP wines, and these wines are therefore usually the driest (*see* DRY) and least expensive. (QUALITÄTSWEIN BESTIMMTER ANBAUGEBIET and DEUTSCHER TAFELWEIN are the two quality categories lower than QmP wines).

Kadarka [KAH-dahr-kah] Red-wine grape that is Hungary's most widely cultivated variety, although it's thought to have originated in Albania. Kadarka is grown in most other eastern European countries as well, where it's known variously as *Cadarca, Gamza,* and *Skadarska.* This grape produces full-bodied (*see* BODY), TANNIC red wines of medium to deep color. Kadarka wines can be very AROMATIC, with intriguing SPICY characteristics. Along with Kékfrankos and Médoc Noir (MERLOT), Kadarka is one of the varieties used in Hungary's famous EGRI BIKAVÉR.

Kahlenberg *see* BAD KREUZNACH

Kaiserstuhl-Tuniberg [KI-zuhr-shtool TOO-nee-behrg] A prominent BERIECH covering the southern part of Germany's BADEN region, directly across the Rhine River from France's ALSACE region. There are two distinct areas here—Tuniberg and the Kaiserstuhl, which means "emperor's seat." Vineyards for both areas are situated on volcanic hills. The region has undergone FLURBEREINIGUNG, whereby the hillsides have been carefully contoured and replanted into modern, efficient vineyards. The primary grape varieties planted in Beriech Kaiserstuhl-Tuniberg are MÜLLER-THURGAU, Rülander (PINOT GRIS), and SPÄTBURGUNDER (PINOT NOIR).

Kallstadt [KAHL-shtaht] A top German wine-producing village located north of BAD DÜRKHEIM in the middle of the RHEINPFALZ region. The vineyards are planted with a high percentage of RIESLING, along with SYLVANER, and SCHEUREBE. The best EINZELLAGEN include **Annaberg, Kronenberg, Saumagen,** and **Steinacker.**

Kanzem [KAHN-tsuhm] A small, picturesque village located on the Saar River in Germany's MOSEL-SAAR-RUWER region. In good vintages, Kanzem produces top-notch RIESLING wines with EARTHY and SPICY characteristics. The best EINZELLAGEN include **Altenberg, Schlossberg,** and **Sonnenberg.**

Karthäuserhofberg *see* EITELSBACH

Kasel [KAH-zuhl] Ruwer River village that is the largest and most important in this rustic section of Germany's MOSEL-SAAR-RUWER region. Kasel produces high-quality RIESLING wines that are ELEGANT, yet powerfully fragrant. The best EINZELLAGEN here are **Herrenberg**, **Hitzlay**, **Kehrnagel**, and **Nies'chen**.

Kaseler Romerlay *see* RUWER

Robert Keenan Winery A SPRING MOUNTAIN AVA winery that is located high in the western hills of the NAPA VALLEY northwest of the town of St. Helena. There are 47 acres planted with CABERNET SAUVIGNON, CHARDONNAY, and MERLOT and between 10,000 and 11,000 cases of wine produced each year. Since the 1982 vintage, the red wines are generally well regarded.

Kehrnagel *see* KASEL

Kékfrankos *see* BLAUFRÄNKISCH

Kéknyelü [KAYK-nyeh-leu; kayk-NYEL-oo] A well-known Hungarian white-wine grape whose name translates to "blue-stalked." Kéknyelü's fame is belied by the fact that today there are very few acres cultivated, and they're limited to the BADACSONY district. Generally, Kéknyelü is VINIFIED into OFF-DRY wines with SPICY flavors, high ALCOHOL, and a color and aroma reminiscent of new-mown hay.

keller [KEHL-luh*r*] The German term for "cellar." **Kellerei** is a "wine cellar" and implies a merchant's wine cellar as opposed to a producer's cellar, which is included in the meaning of the term WEINGUT. *See also* WEINKELLEREI.

Kendall-Jackson Vineyards LAKE COUNTY winery that was founded in 1982 by Jess Jackson, a San Francisco attorney whose original plan was simply to have a vacation home and grow a few grapes to sell. The success of the first Vintners Reserve Chardonnay was the impetus for a continually expanding and successful wine company. Along the way Kendall-Jackson has acquired over 1,400 acres of vineyard land in various parts of California and established several wineries and brands. In the SANTA MARIA AVA, **Cambria Winery** was established in 1987 after the Tepusquet vineyards were divided and sold to Kendall-Jackson and ROBERT MONDAVI WINERY. In 1988 Kendall-Jackson purchased the former Zellerbach Vineyards, located east of Healdsburg in SONOMA COUNTY, and renamed it **J. Stonestreet Winery**. That same year Kendall-Jackson purchased ANDERSON VALLEY'S **Ed-**

meades Vineyard & Winery, which is being developed into a SPARK-LING WINE facility. In 1993 rights to the name were purchased from faltering **La Crema Winery**, and wines are now being produced under the La Crema label at Kendall-Jackson's facility near Geyserville. Kendall-Jackson Vineyards offers a wide variety of wines including several VINEYARD-DESIGNATED CHARDONNAYS and ZINFANDELS and the esteemed **Cardinale**, a red MERITAGE wine.

Kenwood Vineyards After purchasing the old Pagani Winery in 1970, the Lee family has steadily built Kenwood Vineyards into a premium SONOMA VALLEY winery that annually produces between 170,000 and 180,000 cases of wine. Kenwood is probably best known for its red wines—CABERNET SAUVIGNON (Sonoma Valley, Jack London Vineyard, and Artist Series) and ZINFANDEL (Sonoma Valley and Jack London Vineyard). MERLOT and PINOT NOIR are also produced. Even though its reds are more esteemed, Kenwood actually sells more white wine—three CHARDONNAYS (Sonoma Valley, Beltane Ranch, and Yulpa Vineyard) and a Sauvignon Blanc. Kenwood has about 135 acres of its own vineyards but purchases many of its grapes, including those from Jack London Vineyard.

Kerner [KEHR-nuhr] Developed in the late 1960s, this very successful German white HYBRID is a combination of a red variety, Trollinger (SCHIAVA), and a white grape, RIESLING. It's most heavily planted in Germany's RHEINHESSEN and RHEINPFALZ regions, although it's cultivated to some extent throughout the country. Kerner produces quality, Riesling-like wines with good ACIDITY, FLORAL characteristics, and AGING ability.

Kesselstatt, Weingut Reichsgraf von [KEHSS-uhl-shtaht] The holdings of this large estate in Germany's MOSEL-SAAR-RUWER region include four individually recognized estates—Weingut Domklausenhof, Weingut Der Josephshof (owner of the famous JOSEPH-SHOFER Enzellage), Weingut Oberemmeler Abteihof, and Weingut St. Irminenhof. These properties were purchased in 1978 by the Reh family, who's expanded the estate since then through other purchases. The estate owns over 220 acres spread over numerous prime vineyard sites, all of which are planted with RIESLING. The resulting wines are of consistently high quality.

Kieselberg *see* DEIDESHEIM

kir [KEER] White wine that is flavored with a soupçon of creme de cassis, a black currant-flavored liqueur. Kir is usually served as an APÉRITIF. When made with CHAMPAGNE, it's referred to as **kir royale**.

Kirchenstück *see* FORST; HOCKHEIM

Kirwan, Château [sha-TOH kee*r*-WAH*N*] A TROISIÈME CRU (third growth) CHÂTEAU located in the MARGAUX AC of BORDEAUX'S MÉDOC district. The name refers to an Irishman from Galway, Edward Kirwan, who married into the family owning this property in the late 1700s. The estate, then called Domaine de Lassalle, was later renamed Château Kirwan. Although highly respected during the 1800s, the wines have not been eminently regarded in recent years. Several 1980s VINTAGES show some improvement, which may be related to replanting of the vineyards and improvements in the winery made during the 1960s and 1970s. Most critics think Château Kirwan would be downgraded in any reclassification. The property has about 75 acres planted with around 40 percent CABERNET SAUVIGNON, 30 percent MERLOT, 20 percent CABERNET FRANC, and 10 percent PETIT VERDOT. The château produces from 12,000 to 18,000 cases of red wine, part of which goes into its SECOND LABEL **Margaux Private Reserve**.

Kistler Vineyards Although Kistler Vineyards also produces CABERNET SAUVIGNON and PINOT NOIR, it's their CHARDONNAY wines for which they're best known. Kistler produces five different Chadonnay wines, all highly regarded—Durell Vineyard, Dutton Ranch, McCrea Vineyard, Vine Hill Road, and Kistler Estate. The original Kistler Vineyards property, which was established in 1978, is located high on the Mayacamas Mountains in the SONOMA VALLEY AVA. A new winery has recently been built on their Vine Hill Road property in the RUSSIAN RIVER AVA west of Santa Rosa. Case production is about 12,000 to 14,000 per year. Some wine is produced from grapes grown on Kistler's own 55 acres and the rest from grapes purchased from other Sonoma growers.

Klaus *see* JOHANNISBERG

Kleinberger *see* ELBLING

Kleinvernatsch *see* SCHIAVA

Klingelberger *see* RIESLING

Klosterberg *see* AHR; OESTRICH; RÜDESHEIM

Kloster Eberbach [KLAWS-tuh*r* AY-buh*r*-bahkh] Located in the village of HATTENHEIM in Germany's RHEINGAU region, this renowned, ancient monastery is now the home of the German Wine Academy. Kloster Eberbach was founded in the early 1100s and run by the Cistercian monks for nearly seven centuries. Just as they had at France's CLOS DE VOUGEOT, this order established a splendid vineyard next to their monastery and built a stone wall around it. This 79-acre vineyard, which the monks named **Steinberg**, has become world-famous. Because it's classified as an ORTSTEIL, the wines from this vineyard are not required to have the village name (Hattenheim) on the label—only "Steinberger" appears. The vineyard is planted with about 95 percent RIESLING. The highly regarded wines it produces are full-bodied (*see* BODY), full-flavored, and RICH. Kloster Eberbach and the Steinberg vineyard are now controlled by the Staatsweingüter Eltville (*see* STATE DOMAINS).

Knights Valley AVA APPELLATION located in SONOMA COUNTY, California, just north of NAPA VALLEY, southeast of ALEXANDER VALLEY and directly east of the town of Geyserville. BERINGER VINEYARDS has had vineyards here since the 1970s and has done well with CABERNET SAUVIGNON, SAUVIGNON BLANC, and RIESLING. The PETER MICHAEL WINERY was finished in 1989 and produces an ESTATE-BOTTLED Cabernet Sauvignon wine from the Knights Valley vineyards.

Kocher-Jagst-Tauber, Bereich *see* WÜRTTEMBERG

Königin Victoriaberg *see* HOCKHEIM

Königsfels *see* SCHLOSSBÖCKELHEIM

kosher wine [KOH-sher] Wine made according to Jewish rabbinical law. The word *kosher* is a derivation of the Hebrew *kasher*, meaning "proper" or "pure." Kosher wine production must follow precise standards of purity under the direction of a rabbi and may be handled only by workers who are orthodox Jews. These wines may be red or white, sweet or DRY, STILL or SPARKLING, but most are sweet and red—made from CONCORD grapes.

Kranzberg *see* NIERSTEIN

Kreuz *see* OPPENHEIM

Kreuznach, Bereich *see* NAHE; BAD KREUZNACH

Kronenberg *see* BAD KREUZNACH; KALLSTADT

Krötenbrunnen *see* DIENHEIM

Krötenpfuhl *see* BAD KREUZNACH

Krug [KROOG] One of the great names in champagne, Krug is located in Reims in the northern part of the Champagne district. Although owned by Remy Martin of COGNAC fame, this champagne house is small (producing about ½ million bottles per year) and family-run.

Krug simply doesn't sell inexpensive wines—its Grand Cuvée is a non-VINTAGE (Krug calls it multivintage) champagne, made by blending wines from seven to ten different vintages. It's equivalent to most champagne houses' *cuvée de prestige* (*see* CHAMPAGNE). Krug also makes a small quantity of vintage wine, a ROSÉ, and a single-vineyard, vintage champagne called *Clos de Mesnil.*

Charles Krug Winery [KROOG] Charles Krug, a Prussian emigrant, founded this NAPA VALLEY winery in 1861 and developed it into a fairly large enterprise. After his death in 1892, the estate fell onto hard times due to PHYLLOXERA and old facilities. In 1943 at the urging of his son, Robert, Cesare Mondavi purchased the winery and land from the bankers that controlled it. Soon the winery was revitalized and producing excellent wines. The well-publicized feud between the two Mondavi brothers, Peter and Robert, ended with Robert being forced from the family business in 1965. He subsequently established his own enterprise, ROBERT MONDAVI WINERY. Krug in the meantime was run by Peter and his mother Rosa. A judicial decision a decade later would require the Charles Krug Winery pay Robert Mondavi millions of dollars for his fair share of the winery. The Charles Krug Winery produces some 600,000 to 700,000 cases of wine each year, including those sold under its JUG WINE label, **C.K. Mondavi**. The Charles Krug wines include CABERNET SAUVIGNON, CHARDONNAY, CHENIN BLANC PINOT NOIR, SAUVIGNON BLANC, and ZINFANDEL.

Kürfustlay, Grosslage Bernkasteler *see* BERNKASTEL

Kuhlmann 1882 *see* MARÉCHAL FOCH

Kuhlmann 1942 *see* LEON MILLOT

Kunde Estate Winery [KUHN-dee] Established in 1904, The Kunde Estate Winery and vineyards are located in the hills southeast of Kenwood, California, in the SONOMA VALLEY AVA. Although the Kunde family produced wines prior to 1944, their primary business until the late 1980s was to supply other producers (like SEBASTIANI VINEYARDS) with grapes. In 1989, Kunde started making their own wines again with great success. This winery owns about 650 acres of vineyards and annually produces between 60,000 and 70,000 cases of wine. VARIETAL wines include CABERNET SAUVIGNON, CHARDONNAY, SAUVIGNON BLANC, and ZINFANDEL. The RESERVE wines have been very well received.

Kupfergrube see SCHLOSSBOCKELHEIM

Kupp *see* WILTINGEN

abrusca *see* VITIS LABRUSCA

Lacosste-Borie *see* GRAND-PUY-LACOSTE, CHÂTEAU

La Crema *see* KENDALL-JACKSON VINEYARDS

Lacryma Christi del Vesuvio (LCV) DOC

[LAH-k*r*ee-mah K*R*EESS-tee dehl veh-SOO-vee-oh] Located east of Naples in Italy's CAMPANIA region, this DOC's name means "tears of Christ." Actually, there are two DOCs in the area—this one and **Vesuvio DOC**. Both make BIANCO, ROSSO, and ROSATO and use the same grapes. The difference is that the Lacryma Christi del Vesuvio DOC requires a minimum ALCOHOL level 1 to 1½ percent higher. The varieties used for the red and ROSÉ wines are Piedirosso, Sciascinoso, and AGLIANICO. The white wines are made from Verdeca, Coda di Volpe, Falanghina, and GRECO. There is also an LCV LIQUOROSO, a FORTIFIED white wine made from the same white grapes. Lacryma is sometimes spelled *Lacrima* or *Lachryma*.

lactic acid *see* ACIDS; MALOLACTIC FERMENTATION

Ladoix-Serrigny AC [lah-DWAH seh-*r*ee-NYEE] Little-known APPELLATION that encompasses the villages of Ladoix, Buisson, and Serrigny and is the northernmost in the CÔTE DE BEAUNE district of France's BURGUNDY region. Most of the wine produced by these villages is either entitled to the CORTON GRAND CRU AC, the ALOXE-CORTON PREMIER CRU AC, or the CÔTE DE BEAUNE-VILLAGES AC. This means that only a small amount of wine is actually released as Laoix-Serrigny AC. Wines from this appellation can be red—made with PINOT NOIR grapes, or white, based on CHARDONNAY. They're generally of satisfactory quality and well priced.

Lady Langoa *see* LANGOA-BARTON, CHÂTEAU; LÉOVILLE-BARTON, CHÂTEAU

Lafaurie-Peyraguey, Château [sha-TOH lah-foh-*R*EE peh-rah-GEH] One of the nine PREMIERS CRUS (first growths) noted in the CLASSIFICATION OF 1855 for the SAUTERNES district. The property consists of about 74 acres, which includes a sensational thirteenth century CHÂTEAU. It produces sweet, BOTRYTISED wines from almost 100 percent SÉMILLON, although small amounts of SAUVIGNON BLANC and MUSCADELLE are generally used. These Sauternes AC wines live up to the chateau's ranking, particularly since the 1979 VINTAGE. They're RICH, COMPLEX wines with good ACIDITY and AGING capabilities of 25 years or so. About 4,500 to 5,000 cases of this sweet white wine is produced. Château Lafaurie-Peyraguey also produced about 400 cases of a DRY white wine called **Brut de Lafaurie**, which has also received good reviews. Château Lafaurie-Peyraguey and **Clos Haut-Peyraguey** were both part of the premier cru, Château Peyraguey until it was split in 1879. Both retain this ranking, but Clos Haut-Peyraguey doesn't produce wines of the same high quality as those of Château Lafaurie-Peyraguey.

Lafite-Rothschild, Château [sha-TOH laf-FEET rawt-SHEELD (rawth-CHILD)] The wines of Château Lafite-Rothschild are probably the most famous of BORDEAUX, possibly of all France. This is one of only four CHÂTEAUS (along with HAUT-BRION, LATOUR, and MARGAUX) to receive a PREMIER CRU (first growth) ranking for red wines in the CLASSIFICATION OF 1855 (Château MOUTON-ROTHSCHILD was upgraded to premier cru status in 1973). This estate's beginnings go back some eight centuries; it was famous as far back as the fourteenth century and prominent throughout the eighteenth and nineteenth centuries. It was eventually purchased by Baron James de Rothschild in 1868 and is still owned by the Rothschilds today. Château Lafite-Rothchild is located in the PAUILLAC AC and, with nearly 222 acres, is the largest of the premiers crus. The wines are a blend of approximately 70 percent CABERNET SAUVIGNON, 20 percent MERLOT, 5 percent CABERNET FRANC, and 5 percent PETIT VERDOT. These wines have a reputation for requiring as long as 10 to 15 years before exhibiting their potential; better vintages can easily AGE for 35 years or longer. Although the wines since 1975 have generally been outstanding, wines from the 1960s and early 1970s have a number of critics. The château annually produces between 30,000 and 40,000 cases of red wine, some of which is released under its SECOND LABEL **Les Carruades de Lafite** (previously called **Moulin des Carruades**).

Lafleur, Château [sha-TOH lah-FLEW*R*] A tiny, 10-acre estate located in the POMEROL AC of BORDEAUX. None of the Pomerol properties are classified, but if they were, this one would probably be equal to a Médoc PREMIER CRU (first growth). In some VINTAGES the quality of these wines exceeds even those from Pomerol's most famous château, PÉTRUS. These wines can be DENSE, CONCENTRATED, and full-bodied and can AGE for 30 years or more. Because it's so small, Château Lafleur averages only about 1,000 cases of red wine each year. The wine's a combination of approximately 50 percent CABERNET FRANC and 50 percent MERLOT. For wines that don't meet its high standards, Château Lafleur uses the SECOND LABEL **Les Pensées de Lafleur**.

Lafleur-Pétrus   *see* LA FLEUR-PÉTRUS

Lafon-Rochet, Château [sha-TOH lah-FAW*N* raw-SHAY] A QUATRIÈME CRU (fourth growth) CHÂTEAU located in the SAINT-ESTÈPHE AC of the MÉDOC district in BORDEAUX. The property consists of around 110 acres and produces about 20,000 cases of high-quality red wine, some of it released under the SECOND LABEL **Le Numero 2 de Lafon-Rochet**. The mix of grapes used is approximately 64 percent CABERNET SAUVIGNON, 30 percent MERLOT, and 6 percent CABERNET FRANC.

lagar; pl. lagares [lah-GAHR; lah-GAH-resh] The traditional rectangular stone or cement (occasionally wooden) trough used in the production of SHERRY in and around Spain's JEREZ DE LA FRONTERA and of PORT in Portugal's DOURO region. Lagares, which are 3 to 4 feet high and vary in size, are used for treading grapes and/or for fermentation of the juice. Today, most have been replaced by more modern VINIFICATION equipment.

Lagarino *see* LAGREIN

lage; pl. lagen [LAH-guh] German term for "site," which, in wine parlance, usually refers to a vineyard site. An individual vineyard site is called an EINZELLAGE, an area grouping of einzellagen is called a GROSSLAGE.

Lagrain *see* LAGREIN

Lagrange, Château [sha-TOH la-G*R*AHNZH] A TROISIÈME CRU (third growth) located in the SAINT-JULIEN AC in the MÉDOC. The CHÂTEAU consists of 279 acres, which makes it one of the largest CRU CLASSÉ properties in BORDEAUX. The estate averages about 20,000 cases of red wine, part of which goes into the château's SECOND LABEL **Les Fiefs de Lagrange**. Since the property was taken over by Suntory Company of Japan in 1983, the wines have taken a decided turn for the better. Extensive upgrading has made this château a model of modern winemaking. The percentage of CABERNET SAUVIGNON has increased, making the combination of grape varieties approximately 66 percent Cabernet Sauvignon, 27 percent MERLOT, and 7 percent PETIT VERDOT. Recent vintages have been full-bodied (*see* BODY), fruity and TANNIC, with AGING capabilities of 20 years or longer. This château shouldn't be confused with Château Lagrange of the POMEROL AC, whose wines are not as highly regarded.

Lagrein [lah-GRAYN] A red-wine grape grown mainly in Italy's TRENTINO-ALTO ADIGE region. Lagrein is VINIFIED into deep, dark reds (known as Lagrein Dunkel or Lagrein Scuro) and ROSÉS (called Lagrein Kretzer or Lagrein Rosato). The rosés are considered to be some of

Italy's best; the reds can have wonderful CHOCOLATY nuances and rich fruit flavors. A small amount of Lagrein is used to bolster the SCHIAVA grape in the DOC wines of SANTA MADDALENA. This variety is also known as *Lagrain* and *Lagarino*.

Lairén *see* AIRÉN

Lake County Large California county located north of NAPA COUNTY and east of MENDOCINO COUNTY. The area is dominated by Clear Lake, California's largest lake (which takes up about half of the county's surface area). Lake County is part of the NORTH COAST AVA but has three AVAs of it own—CLEAR LAKE, GUENOC VALLEY, and Benmore Valley, an obscure VITICULTURAL AREA southwest of the town of Lakeport. CABERNET SAUVIGNON, CHARDONNAY, SAUVIGNON BLANC, and ZINFANDEL are the major grape varieties grown in Lake County.

La Lagune, Château [sha-TOH lah lah-GEWN] CHÂTEAU located near the COMMUNE of Ludon, south of MARGAUX in the HAUT-MÉDOC AC. It's only about 10 miles north of the city of Bordeaux. Château La Lagune is a TROISIÈME CRU (third growth) property consisting of nearly 173 acres planted with approximately 55 percent CABERNET SAUVIGNON, 20 percent MERLOT, 20 percent CABERNET FRANC, and 5 percent PETIT VERDOT. About 25,000 cases of high-quality red wine is produced. Some wine reviewers feel that La Lagune's wines consistently match up with those from most DEUXIÈME CRU (second-growth) châteaus and are therefore a relatively good value. These wines can AGE for up to 15 or 20 years. The SECOND LABEL of Château La Lagune is **Ludon-Pomiès-Agassac.**

Lalande-de-Pomerol AC [lah-LAHND duh pawm-uh-RAWL] Although it's considered a lesser-known "satellite" APPELLATION of BORDEAUX'S POMEROL district, Lalande-de-Pomerol actually has more acreage. It encompasses the COMMUNES of Lalande-de-Pomerol and Neac on the northeast edge of Pomerol. Even though MERLOT is the dominant grape in Lalande-de-Pomerol wines, they also include CABERNET FRANC, CABERNET SAUVIGNON, and MALBEC. These wines are usually not as BIG and full-bodied (*see* BODY) as the better Pomerol wines, but then they aren't as expensive, either.

La Louvière, Château [sha-TOH lah loo-VYEHR] A well-known, but unclassified CHÂTEAU located in the PESSAC-LÉOGNAN AC of the GRAVES district of BORDEAUX. The quality of the wines is very high and comparable to many of the CRUS CLASSÉS of this area. There are nearly 116 acres producing about 18,000 cases of high-quality red wine and 5,000 cases of equally impressive white wine. The grape varieties used for red wines are approximately 70 percent CABERNET SAUVIGNON, 20 percent MERLOT, and 10 percent CABERNET FRANC; for white wines, the mix is about 85 percent SAUVIGNON BLANC and 15 percent SÉMILLON. The red wines can AGE for 10 to 12 years; the white wines, for 5 or 6 years. The SECOND LABELS used by Château La Louvière are **Coucheray** and **Clos du Roi**.

Lamartine *see* CANTENAC-BROWN, CHÂTEAU

Lambrusco [lam-BROOS-koh] A red-wine grape that is grown all over Italy, primarily in the EMILIA-ROMAGNA region. The Lambrusco variety has over sixty subvarieties scattered throughout Italy, the most significant being *Lambrusco Grasparossa, Lambrusco Maestri, Lambrusco Marani, Lambrusco Montericco, Lambrusco Salamino,* and *Lambrusco di Sorbara.* There are four Lambrusco wines with DOC status—*Lambrusco di Sorbara, Lambrusco Grasparossa di Castelvetro, Lambrusco Reggiano,* and *Lambrusco Salamino di Santa Croce.* The best of these wines are from the Lambrusco di Sorbara DOC, which come from acreage surrounding the village of Sorbara, believed to be Lambrusco's birthplace. Lambrusco is probably best known, at least by Americans, for the non-DOC, pale red, semisweet, slightly effervescent (FRIZZANTE) wines. It's also made in white (where the skins are quickly separated from the juice) and ROSÉ versions. All three variations are made in two styles—semisweet and DRY, the latter preferred in Italy. Lambrusco wines are not known for their aging capabilities and should be drunk young. This variety is unrelated to the North American vine species VITIS LABRUSCA.

Lamothe, Château [sha-TOH lah-MOTT] The original Château Lamothe was actually split, so there are now two—**Château Lamothe-Despujols** and **Château Lamothe-Guignard**—both with their owner's names appended. Although both estates are entitled to use the SAUTERNES AC and are rated DEUXIÈME CRU (second growth), Château Lamothe-Guignard produces wine that's of higher quality and more befitting of this ranking. Château Lamothe-Despujols consists of about 18 acres and is planted with about 70 percent SÉMILLON, 15 percent SAUVIGNON BLANC, and 15 percent MUSCADELLE. It averages about 1,600 cases of sweet white wine made in a light, early-drinking style. Château Lamothe-Guignard is slightly larger at 37 acres and produces about 2,900 cases each year. The mix of grape varieties is about 90 percent SÉMILLON, 5 percent SAUVIGNON BLANC, and 5 percent MUSCADELLE. These wines, which have steadily improved since the mid-1980s are more intensely flavored and capable of AGING for 15 years or so.

Lamothe-Despujols, Château *See* LAMOTHE, CHÂTEAU

Lamothe-Guignard, Château *See* LAMOTHE, CHÂTEAU

Lamouroux *See* RAUSAN-SÉGLA, CHÂTEAU

Landwein [LAHNT-vyn] A superior subcategory of DEUTSCHER TA-FELWEIN ("German TABLE WINE") that has stricter guidelines than regular Deutscher Tafelwein. For example, the alcohol content must be ½ percent higher and the residual sugar shouldn't be over 1.8 percent (which makes it a TROCKEN or HALBTROCKEN in terms of dryness). There are fifteen areas within Germany's broader growing regions authorized to make these wines and each uses *Landwein* in its name, such as *Ahrtaler Landwein, Landwein der Saar, Frankisher Landwein,* and *Unterbadisher Landwein.* Landweins are equivalent to what the French describe as VIN DE PAYS wines. *See also* QUALITÄTSWEIN BESTIMMTER ANBAUGEBIETE; QUALITÄTSWEIN MIT PRÄDIKAT.

Lanessan, Château [sha-TOH lah-neh-SAHN] A well-known CRU BOURGEOIS château located in the COMMUNE of Cussac-Fort-Médoc, which is part of the SAINT-JULIEN AC in the MÉDOC district. This nearly 100-acre estate makes about 17,000 to 20,000 cases of RICH, flavorful red wine. The vineyards are made up of about 75 percent CABERNET SAUVIGNON, 20 percent MERLOT, and small amounts of CABERNET FRANC and PETIT VERDOT. Even though slightly inconsistent, the wines are generally of CRU CLASSÉ quality and capable of AGING for 15 to 20 years. A SECOND LABEL **Domaine de Sainte-Gemme** is used for the château's lesser wines.

Langenmorgen *See* DEIDESHEIM

Langhorne Creek A small wine-producing area located about 30 miles southeast of Adelaide in the state of South Australia. Langhorne Creek is best known for its full-bodied (*see* BODY) red wines made from Shiraz (SYRAH) and CABERNET SAUVIGNON, as well as limited amounts of FORTIFIED wines. CHARDONNAY, MALBEC, RIESLING, SÉMILLON, SAUVIGNON BLANC, and VERDELHO are also grown here. Langhorne Creek's best-known winery is Bleasdale, which was established in 1850.

Langoa-Barton, Château [sha-TOH lahn-GWAH bahr-TAWN] TROISIÈME CRU (third growth) CHÂTEAU that is one of two that Irishman Hugh Barton bought in the 1820s. Located in the SAINT-JULIEN AC in the MÉDOC district of BORDEAUX, this estate (along with Château LÉOVILLE-BARTON) is still owned by the Barton family. Langoa-Barton consists of about 37 acres and produces around 6,000 to 8,000 cases of high-quality red wine each year. These wines, however, are not as highly regarded as those from Léoville-Barton, a DEUXIÈME CRU (second growth). Interestingly, Léoville-Barton doesn't have its own winemaking facility and makes its wine at Langoa-Barton. The Langoa-Barton wines, which are made up of around 70 percent CABERNET SAUVIGNON, 20 percent MERLOT, 8 percent CABERNET FRANC, and 2 percent PETIT VERDOT, are capable of aging for 20 to 25 years. The SECOND LABEL **Lady Langoa** is used by both Barton properties for wines not reaching the standards of quality for the main châteaus.

Languedoc-Roussillon [lahng-DAWK roo-see-YAWM] Also referred to as the *Midi*, this huge region is located in southern France along the Mediterranean. It consists of the four French DÉPARTEMENTS—Aude, Gard, Hérault, and Pyrénées-Orientales—which produce between 35 and 40 percent of the total French wine-grape crop, and close to 300 million cases of wine. The region is well suited to grape growing, but, unfortunately, the Languedoc-Roussillon growers have been more concerned with quantity than quality, which means most of the wines are very ordinary. The majority (almost 90 percent) of the wine here is red, made primarily from CARIGNAN, CINSAULT, and GRENACHE. To improve quality, MOUVÈDRE, SYRAH, and even CABERNET SAUVIGNON and MERLOT are being used as replacements for high-yielding, lower-quality grapes like Carignan. Improved VINIFICATION techniques are also being encouraged. Although most of the wine produced here is VIN ORDINAIRE, there are numerous VIN DE PAYS wines. There are also a growing number of APPELLATION D'ORIGINE CONTRÔLÉE areas including BANYULS, BLANQUETTE DE LIMOUX, COLLIOURE, CORBIÈRES, COSTIÈRES DU NÎMES, COTEAUX DU LANGUEDOC, CÔTES DU ROUSILLON, FAUGÈRES, FITOU, MAURY, MINERVOIS, MUSCAT DE FRONTIGNAN, MUSCAT DE RIVESALTES, and SAINT-CHINIAN.

Les Languettes *see* CORTON; CORTON-CHARLEMAGNE

Lanson *see* CHAMPAGNE

Lardot *see* MACABEO

Larmande, Château [sha-TOH lahr-MAHND] A highly regarded GRAND CRU CLASSÉ estate located in the SAINT-ÉMILION AC in BORDEAUX. During the 1980s it produced wines considered comparable to a TROISIÈME CRU (third growth) château from the MÉDOC. Château Larmande has about 54 acres planted with about 65 percent MERLOT, 30 percent CABERNET FRANC, and 5 percent CABERNET SAUVIGNON. The château averages about 8,000 cases of red wine. The wines are full-flavored, full-bodied (*see* BODY), and well-STRUCTURED; the better VIN-

TAGES are capable of AGING for 12 to 15 years. **Des Templiers** is Château Larmande's SECOND LABEL.

Lartigue-de-Brochon *see* SOCIANDO-MALLET, CHÂTEAU

Lascombes, Château [sha-TOH lahs-KAW*M*B] Estate that is classified as a DEUXIÈME CRU (second growth) and that is one of the largest properties in the MÉDOC district of BORDEAUX. It consists of 232 acres scattered over forty different parcels located throughout the MAR-GAUX AC. From 1952 to 1971 the CHÂTEAU was owned by the late Alexis Lichine, who undertook a massive effort to renovate the property and restore high winemaking standards. A number of wine reviewers think the quality of wines have been lower since he sold the property. The château produces some 35,000 to 40,000 cases of good-quality red wine from approximately 65 percent CABERNET SAUVIGNON, 30 percent MERLOT, and small amounts of CABERNET FRANC, MALBEC, and PETIT VERDOT. Recent VINTAGES are capable of AGING for about 12 to 15 years. Château Lascombes uses two SECOND LABELS **Segonnes** and **La Gombaude** for its lesser wines. **Chevalier de Lascombes** is a well-regarded, DRY ROSÉ wine produced by the property.

Laskiriesling *see* WELSCHRIESLING

Lassalle *see* POTENSAC, CHÂTEAU

late disgorged *see* DISGORGED

late harvest A wine term referring to wines made from grapes picked toward the end of the harvest (usually late fall) when they are very ripe. Such grapes have a higher sugar content (minimum of 24° BRIX), particularly if they've been infected with BOTRYTIS CINEREA, a desirable fungus that shrivels the grape and thereby concentrates the sugar. The terms **Select Late Harvest** and **Special Select Late Harvest** refer to wines made from grapes picked with higher sugar-content minimums—28° and 35° Brix, respectively. A high Brix measurement can translate to a sweet wine, to a wine that's high in ALCOHOL, or to one with both characteristics. Generally, Select Late Harvest and Special Select Late Harvest wines have a RESIDUAL SUGAR content, some ranging as high as 28 percent. Late harvest wines are noted for their rich, deep, honeyed flavors and are customarily served after the main course, often with dessert or with cheeses such as Roquefort. The most popular grapes used for these DESSERT WINES are GEWÜRZTRAMINER, RIESLING, SAUVIGNON BLANC, and SÉMILLON.

Latisana DOC [lah-tee-ZAH-nah] Small DOC zone that is also known as *Latisana del Friuli* and that is located in the southern part of the FRIULI-VENEZIA GIULIA region in northeast Italy. It covers twelve VA-RIETAL WINES plus a ROSATO, all of which are regarded as fairly ordinary. The varietal wines are Cabernet (from CABERNET SAUVIGNON and CABER-NET FRANC), Caberent Franc, Cabernet Sauvignon, CHARDONNAY, MERLOT, Pinot Bianco (PINOT BLANC), Pinot Grigio (PINOT GRIS), Refosco dal Peduncolo Rosso (MONDEUSE), Sauvignon (SAUVIGNON BLANC), TOCAI, Traminer Aromatico (GEWÜRZTRAMINER), and Verduzzo Friulano. The rosé wine is made mainly from Merlot.

Latium [LAH-tyum] A wine-producing region located on the western coast in central Italy. Rome is the hub of this region, and its vineyard areas spread out in all directions. White wines are dominant in Latium (*Lazio* in Italian) and represent about 90 percent of the total production. The most popular white varieties are TREBBIANO and MAL-VASIA, which are found in some form throughout most of the region. The primary red varieties are Cesanese, SANGIOVESE, MERLOT, and MON-TEPULCIANO. Latium contains sixteen DOC areas including CERVETERI, COLLI ALBANI, COLLI LANUVINI, EST! EST!! EST!!! DI MONTEFIASCONE, FRASCATI, MARINO, MONTECOMPATRI-COLONNA, ORVIETO, and VELLETRI.

Latour, Château [sha-TOH lah-TOO*R*] One of the outstanding CHÂTEAUS of BORDEAUX. It's located in the PAUILLAC AC of the MÉDOC, right on the SAINT-JULIEN AC border. It's one of only four châteaus (along with HAUT-BRION, LAFITE-ROTHSCHILD, and MARGAUX) to receive a PREMIER CRU (first growth) ranking for red wines in the CLASSIFICATION OF 1855 (Château MOUTON-ROTHSCHILD was upgraded to premier cru status in 1973). The wines from the famous property were already highly regarded in the sixteenth century. The name comes from the cream-colored tower (*la tour*) that stands in the center of the 150-acre vineyard. It was erected in the seventeenth century by Louis XIII from the ruins of an old fifteenth century fortress. Château Latour has been under English ownership since 1963, although the de Beaumont family still maintains a minor interest in it. The majority interest was sold to another English buyer in 1989, a transaction that put the property's value at about 100 million dollars. Historically, the wines from this famous estate have been BIG, RICH, and POWERFUL, with plenty of TANNINS. They need 10 to 15 years of AGING to SOFTEN and become more enjoyable—some of the bolder VINTAGES can age 40 to 50 years or longer. The vintages since the late 1970s have been lighter and drinkable earlier, although the 1990 vintage seems to have gone back to the prior, bolder style. Château Latour's wines come from a 125-acre plot just north of Château LÉOVILLE-LAS-CASES; it averages about 20,000 cases per year. The blend of grapes used is approximately 80 percent CABERNET

SAUVIGNON, 15 percent MERLOT, and small amounts of CABERNET FRANC and PETIT VERDOT. Grapes from a separate 25-acre vineyard, along with lesser-quality vats from the main vineyard, go into the wines of the highly regarded SECOND LABEL **Les Forts de Latour**. These second-label wines aren't usually released until they're almost mature, sometimes over 10 years after the vintage.

Latour à Pomerol, Château [sha-TOH lah-TOO*R* ah paw-muh-*R*AWL] A highly regarded estate located in the POMEROL AC of BOR-DEAUX. The property consists of nearly 20 acres planted with 80 to 90 percent MERLOT and the rest CABERNET FRANC. Around 2,500 to 3,500 cases of red wine are produced each year. In the better VINTAGES the wines can be deeply colored, full-bodied (*see* BODY), full of RICH, CON-CENTRATED flavors, and capable of AGING for 15 to 20 years or more.

Latour-de-France *see* CÔTE DU ROUSSILLON

Latricières-Chambertin [lah-t*r*ee-SYEH*R* shah*m*-behr-TA*N*] An 18-acre GRAND CRU vineyard located in the village of GEVRY-CHAMBERTIN in the CÔTE DE NUITS district of France's BURGUNDY region. The note-worthy red wines (which are made with 100 percent PINOT NOIR) from Latricières-Chambertin are similiar to but LIGHTER than the RICH, CON-CENTRATED wines from the adjoining neighbor and well-known grand cru, CHAMBERTIN.

Laudun [loh-DEUH*M*] One of the best of the villages entitled to the CÔTES DE RHONE-VILLAGES AC. Laudun is located northeast of Avignon in the southern portion of France's RHÔNE region. It's known for its white wines, made from Bourboulenc, CLAIRETTE, and ROUSSANE, as well as its GRENACHE-based ROSÉ wines.

Laurel Glen Vineyards Winery located in the SONOMA MOUN-TAIN AVA high on the east side of the mountain. Patrick Campbell, owner and winemaker, planted his first vineyards in 1968 and either sold the grapes or made wine as a home winemaker until the 1981 VINTAGE. Campbell's nearly 40-acre vineyard is devoted mainly to CABERNET SAUVIGNON, although there's a little CABERNET FRANC and MER-LOT (to blend with the Cabernet Sauvignon if need be) and small parcels of MOUVÈDRE, SYRAH, and TEMPRANILLO. Laurel Glen currently produces only Cabernet Sauvignon wines, which are usually very highly regarded. Batches of wine not suited for the primary Laurel Glen label may go into a SECOND LABEL, **Counterpoint**. About 5,000 cases of these two wines are produced. A third, less-expensive Cabernet Sauvignon called **Terra Rose** is made from purchased wines.

Laurent-Perrier [law-RAH*N* pehr-RYAY] One of the medium-sized CHAMPAGNE houses located in Tours-sur-Marne in France's Champagne region. The privately owned firm produces 7 to 7½ million bottles per year, led by the VINTAGE champagne **Millésime Rare** and Laurent-Perrier's premium brand **Cuvée Grand Siècle**. They make an excellent non-vintage BRUT and also produce a fully DRY champagne called Ultra Brut.

Lavaux [lah-VOH] Located east of Lausanne on the north shore of Lake Geneva, Lavaux is one of the three premier growing areas in the Swiss canton of VAUD. It produces primarily white wines (some of Switzerland's best) from CHASSELAS grapes, which grow on the terraced vineyards that make up this area.

Les Lavières *see* SAVIGNY-LÈS-BEAUNE

Laville-Haut-Brion *see* LA MISSION HAUT-BRION, CHÂTEAU

Layon *see* COTEAUX DU LAYON

Lazio *see* LATIUM

LBV *see* PORT

leaf-roll (leafroll) virus A serious grapevine disease that's transmitted by GRAFTING. Some theorize that it may also be disseminated by insects. Leaf-roll virus can be detected visually by downward-curving leaf edges; the leaves of the red-grape varieties turn a brilliant red, while white-grape leaves become golden yellow. The autumnal colors may be wonderful, but this disease is quite the opposite. It impedes the grapes' sugar accumulation, which means that, by the time the grapes reach a sugar level at which they can be harvested, their acid levels (*see* ACIDS) and overall quality is greatly diminished. Such grapes naturally produce wines in which flavor, color and body are attenuated. Leaf-roll virus doesn't kill grapevines but markedly reduces YIELDS. The only treatment currently known for this disease is removal of the vines. Vineyardists can protect against leaf-roll virus by purchasing only vines that are state-certified to be free of known diseases.

leafy A winetasting term for wines that have a quality that smells like leaves, the type of which can vary depending on the wine. Unless this characteristic is overpowering or turns VEGETAL, it's not considered undesirable.

lean The opposite of FLESHY, the term *lean* describes a wine that is somewhat sparse in FRUIT. Some lean wines are also moderately AS-

TRINGENT. Such characteristics, however, don't necessarily translate into an unenjoyable wine. *See also* FAT.

Leányka [LAY-ahn-kyah] White wine grape planted in Hungary, Rumania (where it's known as *Feteasca* and *Mädchentraube*), and surrounding areas. The name translates into something on the order of "young girlish," presumably alluding to the wine's soft, delicate traits. Leanyka wines have AROMATIC, SPICY, and apricot characteristics reminiscent of a GEWÜRZTRAMINER-MUSCAT combination. Most are vinified medium-sweet to medium-DRY. Although viewed as a wine that could be AGED, Leányka's moderate ACIDITY generally limits that time to only 2 to 4 years.

leathery A wine-tasting term used to describe wines, usually BIG, TANNIC reds, that have the rich smell characteristic of a new car's leather interior. This leathery quality is typically the result of the wine's exposure to wooden barrels.

Lebanon *see* MUSAR, CHÂTEAU

Le Cigare Volant *see* BONNY DOON VINEYARD

lees [LEEZ] The heavy, coarse sediment that accumulates during FERMENTATION and aging. Lees primarily consists of dead yeast cells and small grape particles. In most cases this sediment is separated from the wine through RACKING. Sometimes the wine is left in contact with the lees in an attempt to develop more flavor (*see* SUR LIE).

legs After a glass of wine is swirled, it often leaves a coating on the inside of the glass that separates into viscous-looking rivulets called *legs* or *tears*. These legs slowly slide down the glass, returning to the wine's surface. Legs generally indicate a wine that's RICH and full-bodied (*see* BODY). Very wide legs are referred to as *sheets*.

Leinhöhle *see* DEIDESHEIM

Lemberger *see* BLAUFRÄNKISCH

Lenchen *see* OESTRICH

length The length, also known as *persistence*, of a wine is measured (in seconds) by the amount of time its BOUQUET and flavor linger after swallowing. The longer it lingers, the finer the wine.

Leonetti Cellar [lee-oh-NEH-tee] The small Washington State winery that is demonstrating that high-quality red wines can be produced in the state's southwest portion. Leonetti is located in the WALLA

WALLA AVA just north of the Oregon border. The only two wines produced here are CABERNET SAUVIGNON and MERLOT, and the recent VINTAGES of both these wines have been very well received.

León, Jean Wine estate located in the PENEDÈS DO in Spain's CATALONIA region. It is named after its owner, whose story is as interesting as the wine he produces. After immigrating to the United States from Spain as a boy, Jean León had numerous occupations, including serving in the U.S. Army, driving taxis, and waiting tables. Eventually, he opened La Scala, a successful Los Angeles restaurant. After becoming interested in wine, he decided to open his own winery. His quest for a location took him to California, France, and Italy, but he finally chose a 450-acre estate in his native Spain. His wine estate is planted with French varieties—CABERNET SAUVIGNON, CABERNET FRANC, MERLOT, and CHARDONNAY. The wines are made in a California-style (Jean León studied ENOLOGY in California) and are regarded as some of Spain's best from these grape varieties.

Leon Millot [lee-OHN MEE-yoh] A red French-American HYBRID grown in the eastern United States and a few vineyards in England. Officially known as *Kuhlmann 1942*, Leon Millot is the offspring of Goldriesling and an American VITIS RIPARIA-VITIS RUPESTRIS vine—the same parents of the more widely planted MARÉCHAL FOCH. Leon Millot can produce good full-bodied reds with a nuance of chocolate.

Léoville-Barton, Château [sha-TOH lay-aw-VEEL bahr-TAWN] This DEUXIÈME CRU (second growth) CHÂTEAU, located in the SAINT-JULIEN AC, that is one of two that Irishman Hugh Barton bought in the 1820s. At one time it was part of the Léoville estate, which eventually was divided into this vineyard plus those of Châteaus LÉOVILLE-LAS-CASES and LÉOVILLE-POYFERRÉ. This MÉDOC estate, along with Château LANGOA-BARTON, is still owned by the Barton family. The property consists of nearly 100 acres planted with about 70 percent CABERNET SAUVIGNON, 20 percent MERLOT, 8 percent CABERNET FRANC, and 2 percent PETIT VERDOT. The château produces 18,000 to 20,000 cases of high-quality red wine each year. Although both wines are made at the Langoa-Barton estate (Léoville-Barton has no winemaking facilities), the Léoville-Barton wines are the more esteemed of the two. The SECOND LABEL **Lady Langoa** is used by both Barton properties for wines not reaching the standards of quality for the main châteaus.

Léoville-Las-Cases, Château [sha-TOH lay-aw-VEEL lahss KAHZ] This SAINT-JULIAN AC property once comprised half of the Léoville estate, which was broken up into this vineyard plus those of

Châteaus LÉOVILLE-BARTON and LÉOVILLE-POYFERRÉ. Considered the best of the three Léoville estates, Léoville-Las-Cases is classified as a DEUXIÈME CRU (second growth). Some feel, however, that its wine's consistently high quality makes this CHÂTEAU a candidate for a PREMIER CRU (first growth) upgrade. Léoville-Las-Cases now consists of over 200 acres planted with approximately 65 percent CABERNET SAUVIGNON, 20 percent MERLOT, 12 percent CABERNET FRANC, and 3 percent PETIT VERDOT. Approximately 25,000 to 30,000 cases of red wine are produced each year with the best VINTAGES being capable of AGING 25 to 30 years or more. For vats not deemed of high enough quality for the Château Léoville-Las-Cases label, there are two SECOND LABELS—**Clos du Marquis** and **Grand Parc**.

Léoville-Poyferré, Château [sha-TOH lay-aw-VEEL pwah-fuh-*RAY*] A DEUXIÈME CRU (second growth) CHÂTEAU located in the SAINT-JULIAN AC of the MÉDOC district in BORDEAUX. At one time it made up slightly over a quarter of the old Léoville estate, which was broken up into this vineyard plus those of Châteaus LÉOVILLE-LAS-CASES and LÉOVILLE-BARTON. It consists of about 150 acres, the mixture of grape varieties being about 65 percent CABERNET SAUVIGNON, 25 percent MERLOT, 8 percent PETIT VERDOT, and 2 percent CABERNET FRANC. Although there's been some improvement since 1982, the wines of Léoville-Poyferre are the least consistent and the lowest quality of the three Léoville estates. They're capable of AGING for up to 15 to 20 years. **Moulin-Riche** is this château's SECOND LABEL.

Lexia *see* MUSCAT

Liberty School *see* CAYMUS VINEYARDS

Liebfraumilch; Liebfrauenmilch [LEEP-f*r*ow-mihlkh] Germany's most exported wine, which is sweet, inexpensive, and generally looked down upon by connoisseurs. This wine's origins go back to the sixteenth or seventeenth century. The word *Liebfraumilch,* which means "milk of Our Lady," was originally used only for wines produced from the vineyards of the Liebfrauenkirche ("Church of Our Lady"), a church in the city of Worms in Germany's RHEINHESSEN region. Over time, the word *Liebfraumilch* began to be used for any wine made in the Rhine region. In 1971 German law established specifications (which were modified in the 1980s) for calling a wine Liebfraumilch. Today, in order for a wine to be called Liebfraumilch it must meet the following provisions: be a wine "of pleasant character"; contain a minimum of 18 grams of RESIDUAL SUGAR (1.8 percent); be made only from MÜLLER-THURGAU, SYLVANER, KERNER, or RIESLING grapes;

be of QbA quality; not be labeled with Prädikat designations such as SPÄTLESE or AUSLESE; and come from one of the four German regions of RHEINHESSEN, RHEINPFALZ, RHEINGAU, and NAHE (in practice, almost all of it comes from the Rheinhessen and the Rheinpfalz). As with most wines, the quality of Liebfraumilch can vary dramatically from producer to producer.

light In the wine world, the sensory term *light* has several connotations. It can refer to a wine that's light-bodied (*see* BODY), one that's young, fruity, and drinkable, or one that's relatively low in ALCOHOL. None of these meanings are necessarily derogatory. *See also* LIGHT WINE.

light wine 1. In the United States, this legally defined term refers to wine with 14 percent or less alcohol by volume. 2. Light wine has also become a marketing term for wines with a lower alcohol content than regular wines—usually 7 to 10 percent—which translates to fewer calories. These wines are made by decreasing either the sugar (usually by picking the grapes early, before they reach optimum sugar levels) or by using a vacuum distillation process to remove some of the alcohol. Either method lowers the final alcohol content and decreases the caloric content, which generally translates to a lackluster flavor, as well. *See also* the winetasting term LIGHT.

Liguria [lee-GOO-*r*yah] Very small wine-producing region located in northwest Italy on the Ligurian Sea. It touches France's PROVENCE region on the west end and TUSCANY on the east. This area is on the Italian Riviera and includes well-known resorts areas like Potofino and San Remo, as well as the port city of Genoa. Liguria's wine production is one of the smallest of the twenty Italian wine-producing regions, and it contains only four DOCS—CINQUETERRE, Colli di Luni, Riviera Ligure di Ponente, and ROSSESE DI DOLCEACQUA. The main grapes used for white wines are VERMENTINO and PIGATO; red and ROSÉ wines use DOLCETTO (called *Ormeasco* or *Sciacchetra* locally) and Rossese.

Limberger *see* BLAUFRÄNKISCH

limited bottling A wine label term that implies that there's only a small amount of this particular wine. There is no legal definition for this term, however, and it is sometimes misused. Checking the number of cases produced is the only way to determine accurately just how limited a wine really is.

Limousin [lee-moo-ZA*N*] A forest in south-central France near the city of Limoges that produces oak used in barrels. Limousin oak is prized because it is loosely grained and therefore imparts a more obvious oak flavor and stronger TANNINS. There is some evidence, however, that the cooperage treatment may have as much to do with Limousin's esteemed reputation as the wood itself. Limousin barrels are quite popular for use in making COGNAC. They were once very popular with California winemakers, but many have shifted to the tighter-grained oak produced from the French forests of Allier, Nevers, Tronçais, and Vosges. SEE ALSO OAK.

Limoux *see* BLANQUETTE DE LIMOUX

limpid; limpidity In the winetasting world, descriptor for a wine that is crystalline, luminous, and bright. *See also* BRILLIANT.

lingering *see* LONG

Lino Maga *see* BARBACARLO

liqueur de tirage *see* DOSAGE

liqueur d'expédition *see* DOSAGE

liquoreux [lee-koh-REUH] A French winetasting term meaning "rich and sweet," generally used when referring to DESSERT WINES, such as those of SAUTERNES.

liquoroso [lee-kwaw-ROH-soh] An Italian term referring to a wine with a high alcohol content. These wines are usually sweet, and FORTIFIED by the addition of grape alcohol. MARSALA and various wines made from the MALVASIA and MUSCAT (Moscato) varieties are examples of liquoroso-style wines.

Lirac AC [lee-*R*AK] Just north of Tavel in France's southern RHÔNE region is the village of Lirac, surrounded by the vineyards that comprise this APPELLATION. Lirac makes ROSÉ wines similar to those from Tavel. It also produces red wines that are comparable to lighter versions from CHÂTEAUNEUF-DE-PAPE, which is just northeast. These wines are made primarily from GRENACHE, with some CINSAUT and MOURVÈDRE. Tiny amounts of white wine are produced mostly from CLAIRETTE, but Bourboulenc, Picpoul, and others are also used.

Lison-Pramaggiore DOC [LEE-zawn prah-mahd-JAW-ray] Created in 1986, this new DOC includes the old DOCs of Tocai di Lison, Cabernet di Pramaggiore, and Merlot di Pramaggiore. It's located in the eastern part of Italy's VENETO region, right next to the FRIULI-VENEZIA GIULIA region. In creating the new DOC, the authorities included numerous additional wines. The DOC now covers a total of twelve VARIETAL WINES—Cabernet (made from CABERNET SAUVIGNON and CABERNET

FRANC), Cabernet Franc, Cabernet Sauvignon, CHARDONNAY, MERLOT, Pinot Bianco (PINOT BLANC), Pinot Grigio (PINOT GRIS), Refosco dal Peduncolo Rosso (MONDEUSE), Riesling Italico (WELSCHRIESLING), Sauvignon (SAUVIGNON BLANC), TOCAI, and Verduzzo Friulano.

Listán *see* PALOMINO

Listrac AC [lees-TRAHK] One of the lesser-known APPELLATIONS in the MÉDOC district of France's BORDEAUX region. The wines from this area aren't quite as good as those from the neighboring COMMUNES of MARGAUX, PAUILLAC, or SAINT-JULIEN, and the Listrac AC contains no CRUS CLASSÉS (classed growths). The vineyards of this area sit back further from the Gironde estuary and contain less of the desirable gravelly soil than the vineyards of the more famous communes in the area. The area sits northwest of Margaux and southwest of Saint-Julien. The main grapes used are CABERNET FRANC, CABERNET SAUVIGNON, and MERLOT.

liter [LEE-tuhr] A METRIC measure that's equivalent to 33.8 fluid ounces or 0.264 U.S. gallons. *See also* WINE BOTTLES.

lively A descriptor for wine that has fresh, youthful, fruity characteristics, usually the result of good ACIDITY. Even though this term is sometimes applied to red wines, it's more apt for whites.

Livermore Valley AVA One of California's oldest wine districts, which is located in Alameda County, southeast of San Francisco. This AVA, which is about 15 miles long and 10 miles wide, is warm because it is blocked from much of the cooling ocean breezes that some of its neighboring areas receive. For that reason, most of it is ranked a Region III (*see* CLIMATE REGIONS OF CALIFORNIA). SAUVIGNON BLANC and SÉMILLON grapes have always done well here, although CHARDONNAY now accounts for about half the vineyard acreage. CABERNET SAUVIGNON and MERLOT, along with numerous other varieties, are planted here as well. The well-known WENTE BROS. and Concannon wineries are the oldest in the area, both being established in the 1800s.

Livingston Cellars *see* E & J GALLO WINERY

Livingston Vineyards Small CABERNET SAUVIGNON specialist located in the NAPA VALLEY between the towns of Rutherford and St. Helena, California. Randy Dunn of DUNN VINEYARDS is the consultant who supervises the winemaking for owners John and Diane Livingston. Until the mid-1980s, the Livingstons sold off the grapes from their 10-acre estate vineyard, called Moffett (Diane's maiden name) Vineyard. In 1984 the first Livingston Vineyards CABERNET SAUVIGNON wines were produced. Puchased grapes are used for another Cabernet

Sauvignon bottling called Stanley's Selection. Total annual case production for Livingston Vineyards is between 3,500 and 4,500.

Lizzana *see* GARGANEGA

Llords & Elwood *see* MONTICELLO CELLARS

Locorotondo *see* APRILIA DOC

lodge Term that refers to the large warehouses—like those in the town of VILA NOVA DE GAIA in northern Portugal—where PORT matures in wooden vats and barrels. The term was anglicized from the Portuguese word *loja* and is similar to the French CHAI and the Spanish BODEGA.

Lodi AVA [LOH-di] VITICULTURAL AREA in the SAN JOAQUIN VALLEY between Sacramento and Stockton that extends east until it runs into the SIERRA FOOTHILLS AVA. Although this area is part of California's huge, hot CENTRAL VALLEY, San Francisco Bay's cooling breezes can lower temperatures by as much as 10°F compared to areas farther south. Lodi is considered a Region III/Region IV area (*see* CLIMATE REGIONS OF CALIFORNIA), and ZINFANDEL and SAUVIGNON BLANC do well here. There are also increased plantings of CHENIN BLANC, CHARDONNAY, and CABERNET SAUVIGNON. ROBERT MONDAVI's huge Woodbridge Winery is located here, producing some 2,500,000 cases of wine each year. Las Vinas Winery is one of the better-known smaller wineries.

Logan *see* ROBERT TALBOTT VINEYARDS

Loire [LWAH*R*] The meandering region that follows the beautiful Loire River, which begins its nearly 625-mile journey within 30 miles of the RHÔNE region in the southeastern quarter of France. The river flows northward, angling east toward Orleans and then heads in a southwesterly direction towards the Atlantic Ocean. There are a multitude of different wine areas along the Loire producing a number of famous wines. In the upper reaches of the Loire, not too far from its beginning, there are several VDQS areas—CÔTE D'AUVERGNE and CÔTES ROANNAISES and Saint-Pourçain-Sur-Sioule. As the river nears Orleans, it passes the famous POUILLY-FUMÉ and SANCERRE APPELLATIONS, which are known for FRESH, CRISP white wines made from SAUVIGNON BLANC. After Orleans, the river goes by the TOURAINE provence, a region that not only makes white wines from Sauvignon Blanc but also includes two famous areas noted for their CHENIN BLANC wines (VOUVRAY and MONT-LOUIS) and two areas with reputations for the best Loire red wines (CHINON and BOURGUEIL). As the river continues to the Atlantic, it passes through ANJOU, noted for its ROSÉ wines—Rosé d'Anjou and the higher-quality CABERNET D'ANJOU. Finally, as the river nears the ocean, it passes through Nantes where the MUSCADET grape reigns.

Lombardy [LOM-buhr-dee] Lombardy (*Lombardia*, in Italian) is an important wine-producing region in northern Italy. It's located between PIEDMONT on the western edge and TRENTINO-ALTO ADIGE to the east. Milan is the capital city of Lombardy, which is Italy's most populated and industrialized area. Lombardy has thirteen DOC areas that produce around 20 percent of the region's total wine production. The important DOCs include FRANCIACORTA, OLTREPÒ PAVESE, VALCALEPIO, and VALTELLINA. The grape varieties grown in this region include BARBERA, BONARDA, CABERNET FRANC, MERLOT, NEBBIOLO, and Pinot Nero (PINOT NOIR) for red and ROSÉ wines; CHARDONNAY, CORTESE, Pinot Bianco (PINOT BLANC), Pinot Gigio (PINOT GRIS), Riesling Renano (RIESLING), and Riesling Italico (WELSCHRIESLING) for white wines.

London Particular (LP) *see* MARSALA DOC

long In winetasting, a reference to the length of time a wine's presence remains in the mouth after swallowing. A long (or *lingering*) FINISH is generally an indicator of a fine wine. *See also* SHORT.

Long Island Even though vineyards were planted on Long Island in the 1600s, it wasn't until recently that this area started blossoming into a true quality-wine-producing area. Since Alex and Louisa Hargrave started the first winery (in recent history) on the North Fork in the early 1970s, about a dozen wineries have opened. Long Island has a unique microclimate that's warmed by the Atlantic, which produces a longer growing season than might be expected in this part of the United States. In fact, enthusiasts claim that Long Island's climate and well-drained soil is similiar to that of BORDEAUX. With that in mind, wine producers are growing the classic Bordeaux varieties like CABERNET FRANC, CABERNET SAUVIGNON, MERLOT, and SAUVIGNON BLANC, plus other varieties such as CHARDONNAY, PINOT NOIR, RIESLING, and GEWÜRZTRAMINER. There are actually two APPELLATIONS on Long Island, **North Fork of Long Island** and **The Hamptons** (which is the South Fork). Area wineries include Bedell Cellars, Bidwell, Bridgehampton Winery, Gristina Winery, Lenz Vineyards, Long Island Vineyard (which now includes the original Hargrave Vineyard), Palmer Vineyards, Peconic Bay Vineyards, Pindar Vineyards, Schaprio's Winery, and La Reve (a new, very large wine estate in the Hamptons).

López de Heredia [LOH-pehz day ay-ray-DYAH] An old, family-run BODEGA located in the RIOJA DO in northern Spain. It was established in 1877 by Rafael López de Heredia and remains very traditional

in its winemaking approach. Large wooden vats are still used for FER-
MENTING; wines are aged in BARRICAS, FINED with egg whites, and are not
filtered. About 75 percent of the total production is red wine, made
from about 50 percent TEMPRANILLO, 30 percent Garnacha (GRENACHE),
10 percent Mazuelo (CARIGNAN), and 10 percent GRACIANO. Rosé wines
are made from Garnacha (GRENACHE) and Viura (MACABEO). White
wines use Viura (MACABEO) and MALVASIA. The youngest red wine
(which has a minimum of 3 years AGING) made by López de Heredia
is the *Viña Cubillo*, followed by *Viña Tondonia Tinto* and *Viña Bos-
coñia*. Their white wines include the *Viña Tondonia Blanco* and the
Viña Gravonia.

Los Carneros *see* CARNEROS

Los Hermanos *see* BERINGER VINEYARDS

lot # 1. Although it has no legal meaning, a lot # most often is used
to differentiate wine from the same vintage that was bottled at different times. 2. This term is sometimes used to indicate that wine from
the same vintage was processed differently—for instance, part of it
could have been barrel-aged longer, aged in different barrels, etc. 3.
Lot # occasionally means that the bottled wine is a blend either of two
different vintages or possibly of grapes from two different growing regions.

Loupiac AC [loo-PYAHK] Sweet white-wine APPELLATION located in
France's BORDEAUX region, where it sits on the Garonne River inside
the larger PREMIÈRES CÔTES DE BORDEAUX AC, directly across from BARSAC.
Made from SÉMILLON, SAUVIGNON BLANC, and MUSCADELLE, Loupiac wines
are lighter versions of the famous sweet white wines from SAUTERNES
and BARSAC.

Lower Great Southern Region This region, also called the
Great Southern Region, Mount Barker, or *Mount Barker/Frankland
River*, encompasses a huge area in the southern part of the state of
Western Australia. It measures approximately 90 miles by 60 miles and
is broken up into a number of subregions—Albany, Mount Barker,
Frankland River, and Pemberton/Manjimup. The main white grapes
here are RIESLING, CHARDONNAY, and SAUVIGNON BLANC. The primary red
varieties are CABERNET SAUVIGNON, Shiraz (SYRAH), MERLOT, PINOT NOIR,
and MALBEC. Area wineries include Alkoomi, Forest Hill, Galafrey,
Goundrey Wines, and Plantagenet.

Lower Mosel *see* ZELL

de Loyac *see* MALESCOT SAINT-EXUPÉRY, CHÂTEAU

Lubéron *see* CÔTES DU LUBÉRON

Ludon-Pomiès-Agassac *see* LA LAGUNE, CHÂTEAU

Lump *see* ERSHERNDORF

Lunel [lew-NEHL] A little town northeast of Montpellier in southern France that produces FORTIFIED wines (both VIN DOUX NATUREL and VIN DE LIQUEUR) made from the MUSCAT variety. Such wines are entitled to the AC of **Muscat de Lunel**.

luscious *see* LUSH

lush A term applied to wines that are RICH, SOFT, VELVETY, sweet, and FRUITY—in other words, exceedingly drinkable. In winetasting, the term *luscious* is synonymous with lush.

Lussac-Saint-Émilion AC [loo-SAHK sa*n* tay-mee-LYAW*N*] Just northeast of SAINT-ÉMILION sits the village of Lussac and the surrounding vineyards that make up this APPELLATION. It's one of the satellite COMMUNES allowed to append Saint-Émilion to its name. MERLOT dominates the blend, which may also consist of CABERNET FRANC, CABERNET SAUVIGNON, and MALBEC. The wines can be quite good and are best if consumed within 5 to 6 years.

Luxembourg [LUHK-suhm-burg] This tiny country doesn't make much wine, and what is produced is similiar to that of their German neighbors to the east. The vineyards are located along the Moselle River, which forms the border with Germany. The main varieties are AUXERROIS BLANC, ELBLING, Rivaner (MÜLLER-THURGAU, RIESLING, Rülander (PINOT GRIS), and Traminer (GEWÜRZTRAMINER). Only white wines are produced, and, like their German counterparts, Luxembourg wines are light, fruity, and low in ALCOHOL—some are turned into decent SPARKLING WINES. Luxembourg consumes more wine than it produces so few of these wines are found outside of Luxembourg or its neighbor Belgium.

Lynch-Bages, Château [sha-TOH la*n*sh BAZH (lihnsh-BAHZH)] A CINQUIÈME CRU (fifth growth) CHÂTEAU located in the PAUILLAC AC of the MÉDOC district in BORDEAUX. However, its wines are considered the quality of a DEUXIÈME CRU (second growth) château and are priced accordingly. The château's name comes from its location on the Bages plateau and the fact that the Irishman Thomas Lynch, who was once the mayor of Bordeaux, owned the property for a period during the seventeenth and eighteenth centuries. The estate is now owned by the well-known Cazes family. The vineyard area consists of more than 200 acres and produces 35,000 to 45,000 cases of red wine. Wines that don't meet the high quality standards for the Lynch-Bages label are produced under the SECOND LABEL **Haut-Bages-Averous**. The grape varieties used are around 70 percent CABERNET SAUVIGNON, 15 percent MERLOT, 10 percent CABERNET FRANC, and 5 percent PETIT VERDOT. The wines are generally deep colored, RICH, and full-bodied. They can take 6 to 10 years to OPEN but can AGE for 20 to 25 years, and exceptionally intense VINTAGES can last for 40 to 50 years. In 1990 the château produced a small amount of Château Lynch-Bages Blanc, a very good white wine made from about 40 percent SAUVIGNON BLANC, 40 percent SÉMILLON, and 10 percent MUSCADELLE.

Lynch-Moussas, Château [sha-TOH la*n*sh moo-SAH (lihnsh moo-SAH)] A CINQUIEME CRU (fifth growth) CHÂTEAU located in the PAUIL-LAC AC of the MÉDOC district in BORDEAUX. The château's name comes from the same Mr. Lynch who at one time owned Château LYNCH-BAGES and from the nearby tiny village of Moussas. Château Lynch-Moussas wines are not as highly regarded as those from Lynch-Bages, however. They are generally lighter and less complex and have shorter maturation periods—at best they can AGE for about 8 to 10 years. The vineyard area is nearly 100 acres, and the château produces around 12,000 to 15,000 cases of red wine each year. The grapes used are approximately 70 percent CABERNET SAUVIGNON and 30 percent MERLOT, although a small amount of CABERNET FRANC is sometimes used.

Lyonnaise Blanche *see* MELON DE BOURGOGNE

Lytton Springs Winery [LIHT-uhn] From 1976 to 1991 this SONOMA COUNTY winery was known for its big, bold ZINFANDEL wines. Even though the wines were somewhat variable, certain VINTAGES were considered some of the best. The grapes for these heady Zins came from the turn-of-the-century, 50-acre Valley Vista Vineyard, which is north of Healdsburg, California, on the ridge that separates ALEXANDER and DRY CREEK VALLEYS. The Valley Vista Vineyards was once the source of the RIDGE VINEYARDS' Lytton Springs bottling initiated in 1972. Ridge lost this source when Lytton Springs Winery began to produce its own wines. In 1984 Ridge again began to produce a Lytton Springs bottling from other sources. In 1991 the Lytton Springs Winery was purchased by Ridge Vineyards, and Ridge now produces its own Lytton Springs Vineyards bottling (using Lytton Springs Winery grapes), as well as wines under the Lytton Springs Winery label—all at their facility in the Santa Cruz Mountains.

acabeo [mah-kah-BEH-oh] The most widely cultivated white variety in Spain and the most important white grape in the RIOJA region, where it's called *Viura*. It's because of Macabeo's higher yields (and not the quality of its wines) that this variety is pushing out the more traditional white grapes used in Rioja white wines—MALVASIA and Garnacha Blanca (GRENACHE). Macabeo-based wines are generally LIGHT, high in ACID, slightly FLORAL and fairly fruity. Their AROMA and flavor dissipate very early, however, so they should be drunk quite young. Macabeo is often blended with XAREL-LO and PARELLADA to make SPARKLING WINES. Macabeo is also grown in southern France, where it's the sole variety in the CÔTES DE ROUSSILLON Blanc. This grape is also known as *Maccabeu, Lardot,* and *Alcanol.*

Maccabeu *see* MACABEO

maceration [mas-uh-RAY-shun] The period of time grape juice spends in contact with the skins and seeds. *Extended maceration,* which is used only with red wines, takes place after PRIMARY FERMENTATION and prolongs this contact period. The objectives of extended maceration are to increase the wine's depth of color, intensify its aroma, and, according to some winemakers, SOFTEN any harsh, bitter TANNINS so a wine is better suited for aging. In the *cold maceration* process, the grape juice mixture (MUST) is held at a temperature of about 50°F for 5 to 10 days before fermentation is triggered. It's a somewhat controversial procedure—many winemakers want fermentation to start as soon as possible after the grapes are picked, whereas others believe better extraction (*see* EXTRACT) occurs with cold maceration. *See also* CUVAISON; CARBONIC MACERATION.

maceration carbonique *see* CARBONIC MACERATION

Mâcon AC; Mâcon Supérieur AC; Mâcon-Villages AC [mah-KAWN; mah-KAWN suh-pay-YEUR; mah-KAWN vee-LAHZH] These three APPELLATIONS are located in the MÂCONNAIS in the southern portion of France's BURGUNDY region. The **Mâcon AC** is the basic appellation for this area and encompasses red, white, and ROSÉ wines. The main grapes are CHARDONNAY and GAMAY, along with a small amount of PINOT NOIR. The **Mâcon Supérieur AC** indicates that the qualifying wines have reached a minimum alcohol level of 1 percent higher than that for standard Mâcon AC wines. For white wines the minimum is increased from 10 to 11 percent; for red wines, from 9 to 10 percent. The **Mâcon-Villages AC,** which produces the highest-quality wines of the three appellations, is for white wines and encompasses forty-three villages scattered throughout the Mâconnais. These villages are all allowed to use the term "Mâcon-Villages" on the label or append their name to the word Mâcon, as in Mâcon-Lugny. The better villages include Azé, Clessé, Igé, Lugny, Prissé, Viré, and Chardonnay, the latter after which the area's most popular white grape was presumably named.

Maconnais [mah-kawn-NEH] Located in the southern portion of France's BURGUNDY region, this large grape-growing area takes its name from the town of Mâcon. It's positioned between BEAUJOLAIS to the south and the CÔTE CHALONNAISE to the north. White wines, which are made from CHARDONNAY, make up two-thirds of the area's production. Red and ROSÉ wines are made primarily from GAMAY, with some PINOT NOIR. A fair amount of wine is produced under the basic Burgundian APPELLATIONS of BOURGOGNE, BOURGOGNE PASSE TOUT GRAINS, and the sparkling wine appellation CRÉMANT DE BOURGOGNE. Other appellations, in increasing order of quality, are MÂCON AC, MÂCON SUPÉRIEUR AC, and MÂCON-VILLAGES AC. At the top end of the quality spectrum are a number of individual villages with their own appellations—POUILLY FUISSÉ, POUILLY LOCHÉ, POUILLY VINZELLES, and SAINT VÉRAN. Also located in the Mâconnais are the villages of Chardonnay and CHASSELAS, which presumably gave their names to the grape varieties. *See also* ALTESSE.

made and bottled by Term that means a minimum of 10 percent of the wine was FERMENTED at the winery—the other 90 percent can come from other sources. This designation does not generally indicate the quality implied by the phrase PRODUCED AND BOTTLED BY, where at least 75 percent of the wine must be fermented at the winery. *See also* BOTTLED BY; ESTATE BOTTLED; GROWN, PRODUCED AND BOTTLED BY.

Mädchentraube *see* LÉANYKA

Madeira; madeira [muh-DEER-uh] 1. True madeira comes from Portugal's Madeira island, which is located some 530 miles southwest of Lisbon and 360 miles due west of Morocco. It receives Portugal's highest quality ranking—DENOMINAÇÀO DE ORIGEM CONTROLADA (DOC). Madeira is one of the three best-known FORTIFIED WINES, the others being PORT and SHERRY. Madeira is unique in that it gains its flavor from elements that would ruin most other wines—heat and oxidization (*see* OXIDIZED). The first madeiras evolved from the days when wines were transported by ship. It was discovered that during the lengthy voyage, the air circulation (which caused oxidization) and warm temperatures created wonderful wines. Today this activity is emulated through a process called *estufagem*, during which the wines are placed in hot rooms or heated tanks (*estufas*) for a minimum of 90 days where they're allowed to bake slowly. The finer madeiras are stored in wooden casks and left in attics or other extremely warm areas for years. This wood aging slowly develops the tangy, burnt-caramel, slightly bitter flavor that's unique to this wine. Madeira ranges in color from pale blond to deep tawny. It runs the gamut from quite DRY to very sweet and is usually fortified to the 18 to 20 percent alcohol range. There are four distinct styles of madeira. The pale golden SER-CIAL is the lightest, driest style. It's followed by VERDELHO, which is sweeter and stronger, and then by BOAL (or *Bual*), which is fuller and sweeter than either of the previous two. MALMSEY is the richest, darkest, and sweetest of the group. The two lighter wines are generally used as APÉRITIFS, and the heavier, sweeter styles, as DESSERT WINES. **Rainwater** is a SOFT, medium-dry Verdelho. The name, so the story goes, comes from a time when shipments of madeira were left awaiting pickup on one of the island's beaches, during which time the barrels absorbed water during rain showers. This diluted the alcohol and created a less potent wine. While the four styles of madeira were originally made from the classic VARIETALS—Sercial, Verdelho, Boal, and MALVASIA (called *Malmsey* on the island of Madeira)—since the late 1800s, more TINTA NEGRA MOLE grapes have been used, especially in the cheaper versions. In 1986, however, Portugal entered the European Common Market, whose regulations require that by 1993 any madeira wine naming a variety on its label must contain at least 85 percent of that grape. This labeling requirement has caused an upsurge in replanting of the four classic vines. Wines labeled "Boal-style" or "Sercial-style" can contain less than the required 85 percent and most likely are made from Tinta Negra Mole. **2.** A generic name used for dessert wines made in the United States in an attempt to mimic true madeiras. These wines cannot compare with the Portuguese originals, but then they're a fraction of the price.

Mademoiselle de Saint-Marc *see* LA TOUR BLANCHE, CHÂTEAU

Madera AVA [ma-DEHR-uh] Large but obscure APPELLATION in the mid CENTRAL VALLEY, southeast of Merced and northwest of Fresno. The AVA covers most of Madera County and the northern part of Fresno County. Because of the very warm weather, the area is covered with French Colombard (COLOMBARD), followed by CHENIN BLANC and increased planting of CHARDONNAY. The leading red varieties are ZINFAN-DEL, GRENACHE, and BARBERA. Even though this area produces mostly inexpensive JUG WINES, there are two well-known PORT-style winemakers here—Ficklin Vineyards and Quady Winery.

maderisé [mad-DEHR-ee-zay] French for MADERIZED.

maderized [MAD-uh-rized] A winetasting term for an over-the-hill wine that assumes a MADEIRA-like character—an undesirable trait in TABLE WINE. Maderization, which occurs primarily in white and ROSÉ wine, is generally caused by oxidation (exposure to air), often combined with overly warm storage. It's characterized by a heavy, stale smell and flavor reminiscent of overripe apples. The color of maderized wine takes on a brownish tinge. The French term for the same condition is *maderisé*. A comparable English term is SHERRIFIED. Though the term maderized is often used synonymously with that of OXIDIZED, the latter doesn't infer warm storage.

Madiran AC [mah-dee-*R*AH*N*] The AC that encompasses the area around the village of Madiran, which is located in the Pyrenees foothills along the Adour River south of ARMAGNAC in southwestern France. Tannat is the principle grape of this APPELLATION's red wines, which are generally TANNIC and ROUGH. CABERNET FRANC and CABERNET SAUVIGNON are sometimes used to SOFTEN the area's reds. White wines from this same geographic area are labeled with the PACHERENC DU VIC BILH AC.

Madrid *see* VINOS DE MADRID

Magdelaine, Château [sha-TOH mahg-duh-LEHN] A small, 27-acre estate located next to Château BELAIR in the SAINT-ÉMILION AC of BORDEAUX. It's classified as a PREMIER GRAND CRU CLASSÉ and compares favorably with most TROISIÈME CRU (third growth) CHÂTEAUS of the MÉDOC. It's an interesting wine for this area because of the high proportion of MERLOT (about 90 percent plus 10 percent cabernet franc), making it more like a POMEROL AC wine. But this wine isn't as soft as the dominance of Merlot might suggest—primarily due to the château's winemaking style, which gives the wine a solid TANNIC structure to accompany its suppleness. This causes these wines to evolve slowly, with better VINTAGES AGING for 20 to 25 years. The estate averages about 5,000 cases of red wine annually.

magnum; double magnum *see* WINE BOTTLES

Maindreieck, Bereich *see* FRANKEN

Maindviereck, Bereich *see* FRANKEN

maître de chai [MEH-truh duh SHAY] French for "cellarmaster." This term is used in BORDEAUX to refer to the person in charge of the

VINIFICATION and AGING of wines. The *maître de chai* needs to be a proficient winemaker and have a good palate.

Malaga *see* CINSAUT

Málaga DO [MA-luh-guh] DO located in southern Spain, east of JEREZ and south of MONTILLA-MORILES. In the nineteenth century, there was a time that Málaga's sweet, FORTIFIED wines were more famous than the acclaimed SHERRY from Jerez. But in the 1870s, PHYLLOXERA devastated the area, which has never recovered its glorious past. Today, Málaga has less than 1 percent of the vineyard land that it did in the nineteenth century. There are four subzones here, but *Zona Norte*, which is north of the city of Málaga, is the most important. The wines, which are made from PEDRO XIMÉNEZ or Moscatel (MUSCAT) and other white varieties like AIRÉN, come in a variety of styles ranging from DRY to sweet; most are FORTIFIED. Production of the sweeter versions consists of adding various elements such as **arrope** (cooked MUST that's been reduced by about two-thirds), **pantomina** or **vino de color** (an even more concentrated cooked must than arrope), and **vino maestro** and **vino borracho** (differing blends of grape juice and ALCOHOL). The label of a Málaga wine identifies its style—sweetness ranges from SECO to DULCE and colors are *blanco* (white), *dorado* (golden), *rojo-dorado* (tawny), *osuro* (dark), and *negro* (black). Other labeling information may indicate a VARIETAL WINE made entirely from either Pedro Ximénez or Moscatel. The term "Lagrima" on a label specifies a wine made purely from FREE RUN JUICE. Málaga's *Dulce Color* is the most popular style—dark and sweet with about 10 percent arrope added, which gives it a slight molasses characteristic. Better Málaga wines come from a SOLERA system like those used for making the best sherry wines. To qualify as Málaga DO wine, the wine must be shipped to and matured in the city of Málaga.

Malartic-Lagravière, Château [sha-TOH mah-lahr-TEEK lah-gra-VYEHR] A CRU CLASSÉ estate located in the PESSAC-LÉOGNAN AC in the GRAVES district of BORDEAUX. The property consists of about 35 acres. It produces about 7,000 to 8,000 cases of good red wine and 1,000 cases of more highly regarded white wine. The red wines are made from approximately 50 percent CABERNET SAUVIGNON, 25 percent MERLOT, and 25 percent CABERNET FRANC; the whites are made from 100 percent SAUVIGNON BLANC.

Malbec [mahl-BEHK] A French red-wine grape grown in BORDEAUX, in parts of the LOIRE VALLEY, and in CAHORS. In Bordeaux, where Malbec is called *Cot* or *Pressac*, it plays a subordinate role to and is usually BLENDED with CABERNET FRANC, CABERNET SAUVIGNON, and MERLOT. In the Loire Valley Malbec again plays a lesser role as it's blended with GAMAY and Cabernet Franc. However, in Cahors, where dark-colored, full-flavored, TANNIC wines are produced, Malbec is the prominent variety, usually blended with small amounts of Merlot and Tannat. In Cahors, Malbec is called *Auxerrois*, which causes some confusion because it's unrelated to an entirely different variety—AUXERROIS BLANC. Malbec is widely planted in Argentina and Chile but has only modest acreage in Australia and the United States.

Malescot-St. Exupéry, Château [sha-TOH mah-less-KOH san teg-zew-pay-REE] CHÂTEAU located in the MARGAUX AC in the MÉDOC district of BORDEAUX. It was classified as a TROISIÈME CRU (third growth) in the CLASSIFICATION OF 1855. The wines are made from a blend of approximately 50 percent CABERNET SAUVIGNON, 35 percent MERLOT, 10 percent CABERNET FRANC, and 5 percent PETIT VERDOT. The estate consists of about 80 acres and produces about 14,000 to 17,000 cases of good-quality red wine. Older VINTAGES from the 1950s and 1960s are described as being richer and more concentrated than more recent vintages. The latter are capable of AGING for 12 to 15 years. Two SECOND LABELS—**de Loyac** and **Domaine du Balardin**—are used by the château.

malic acid *see* ACIDS; MALOLACTIC FERMENTATION

de Malle, Château [sha-TOH duh MAHL] One of the most beautiful estates in the SAUTERNES AC and, in fact, in all of BORDEAUX. The property consists of about 62 acres and a sensational seventeenth century château. It was classified as a DEUXIÈME CRU (second growth) in the CLASSIFICATION OF 1855 and produces sweet Sauternes wines of this caliber today. The varieties used are about 75 percent SÉMILLON, 23 percent SAUVIGNON BLANC, and 2 percent MUSCADELLE. These sweet wines consistently improved during the late 1980s, and the better VINTAGES are capable of AGING around 15 years. The estate also produces a GRAVES AC, DRY white wine called **Chevalier de Malle** and has a SECOND LABEL **de Sainte-Hélène** for its Sauternes wines. The château also produces two red wines—**de Cardaillan** and **Tours de Malle**—from grapes grown at a different vineyard in Graves.

Malmsey [MAHM-zee] 1. The richest, darkest and sweetest (though rarely cloying) of the MADEIRA wines. Originally made primarily with the MALVASIA grape (called *Malmsey* on the island of Madeira), this style of Madeira has recently included more TINTA NEGRA MOLE (which is con-

sidered a *good,* but not classic grape). This use is particularly prominent in the cheaper versions of Madeira. However, in 1986, Portugal
entered the Common Market, whose regulations required that by 1993
any Madeira wine naming a grape variety on its label must contain at
least 85 percent of that grape. This labeling requirement has caused an
upsurge in replanting of the classic vines like Malvasia. Wines labeled
"Malmsey-style" can contain less than the required 85 percent of
Malvasia grapes, and can be counted on to include more Tinta Negra
Mole. 2. On the island of Madeira, Malmsey is another name for the
Malvasia grape (*see listing*). 3. Extremely sweet, strongly flavored wine
popular in ancient Greece.

malolactic fermentation [ma-loh-LAK-tihk] A biochemical
reaction, sometimes called SECONDARY FERMENTATION, where bacteria
converts malic acid into lactic acid and carbon dioxide—no alcohol is
produced. Because lactic acid is milder than malic acid, wines that undergo this process become softer and smoother. In addition, malolactic fermentation produces diacetyl (or biacetyl), which resembles the
smell of heated butter and adds complexity to wine. Malolactic fermentation is a positive event in some cases, and most high-quality red
wines and some white wines (including white Burgundies and California Chardonnays) undergo it. On the downside, the fruitiness of
wines undergoing this process is diminished, and sometimes off-odors
can result. Many white wines need malic acid's higher acidity to retain
their crisp, lively character, and some are too delicate to withstand the
potential off-odors that might be introduced. Many winemakers now
encourage malolactic fermentation for some batches of their Chardonnay while inhibiting the process in others, thereby giving the final
blend improved complexity while retaining fruitiness and higher
acidity.

La Maltroie *see* CHASSANGE-MONTRACHET AC

Malvasia [mal-vah-SEE-ah; mal-VAH-zha] Grape that has existed
for about 2,000 years. It's believed to have come from the area around
the Aegean Sea, possibly from what is now the southwestern area of
Turkey and the islands between Turkey and Greece. Malvasia is primarily a white-wine grape, but it has many known subvarieties, including a red version called **Malvasia Nera**. The red grape is chiefly
grown in Italy—around Piedmont in the north and Puglia in the south.
It produces very PERFUMY wines and lends a delightful fragrance to
some Italian red wines. The white variations are better known, the
most recognized strains being **Malvasia Bianca del Chianti,
Malvasia del Lazio, Malvasia delle Lipari, Malvasia di Candia,**

Malvasia di Sardegna and **Malvasia Istiana** (or **Malvasia Friulana**). These white varieties are grown all around the Mediterranean in one form or another. They produce golden, perfumy, flavorful wines with hints of apricots, musk, and almonds. Unfortunately, Malvasia is not an extremely high-yielding vine and is being replaced by better-producing but less-flavorful grapes such as TREBBIANO in Italy and Viura (MACABEO) in Spain. Malvasia is made into a variety of finished wines—DRY, sweet, FORTIFIED, and SPARKLING, but probably is best known for its sweet fortified products. On the island of MADEIRA, the Malvasia variety is called *Malmsey* and is combined with TINTA NEGRA MOLE and VERDELHO. The sweetest and richest style of Madeira wine is also often referred to as MALMSEY. In Portugal some port makers use Malvasia grapes in their WHITE PORT. The VERMENTINO grape, grown on CORSICA and SARDINIA, is thought to be related to Malvasia as well. **Malvasia Bianca** is also grown in California, mostly in the CENTRAL VALLEY, and is used primarily in sweet fortified wines. Malvasia is also called *Blanca-Roja, Früher Roter Malvasier,* and *Malvoisie,* as well as a host of other names beginning with "Malvasia."

Malvoisie *see* MALVASIA

La Mancha DO [lah MAHN-chah] DO that is Spain's and Europe's largest designated quality-wine area, with around 420,000 acres of vineyard land. Ninety percent of it is planted with AIRÉN. La Mancha DO has had a reputation for producing dull, yellowish, high-ALCOHOL, somewhat OXIDIZED wines. Thanks to new modern equipment and winemaking techniques, La Mancha is now producing light, crisp, fruity, and slightly aromatic white wines that are gaining a better image. The small amount of red wine from this area comes chiefly from the Cencibel (TEMPRANILLO) grape.

Manchega *see* AIRÉN

Mannberg *see* HATTENHEIM

manzanilla *see* SHERRY

Les Maranges *see* CÔTE DE BEAUNE

de Marbuzet *see* COS D'ESTOURNEL, CHÂTEAU

marc [MARK; MAHR] 1. A French term (known as POMACE in English) for the residue (skins, pips, seeds, etc.) remaining after the juice has been PRESSED from the grapes. 2. A potent *eau de vie* distilled from this mixture. It's the French counterpart to grappa (the name used in Italy and California).

Marches [MAHR-kay] A region in central Italy running along the east coast on the Adriatic Sea between EMILIA-ROMAGNA and ABRUZZI. It contains ten DOC areas that produce about 12 percent of the region's total wine. The DOCs include ROSSO CONERO, ROSSO PICERNO, VERDICCHIO DEI CASTELLI DI JESI, and VERDICCHIO DI MATELICA. MONTEPULCIANO and SAN-GIOVESE are the primary red grapes and MALVASIA, TREBBIANO, and VERDIC-CHIO are the main white varieties.

Marchigiano *see* VERDICCHIO

Marcobrunn [MAHR-koh-bruhn] A famous EINZELLAGEN located in Germany's RHEINGAU region between the villages of ERBACH and HAT-TENHEIM. Marcobrunn's 13 acres are actually situated partly in both of these villages. In 1971, however, a dispute was settled to the effect that all wines produced are attached to the village of Erbach and therefore labeled "Erbacher Marcobrunn." Wines from the Marco-brunn site are generally full-bodied (*see* BODY), fragrant, and long-lived.

Les Marconnets *see* BEAUNE

Maréchal Foch [MAH-ray-shahl FOHSH] This red grape, offi-cially known as *Kuhlmann 1882*, is a widely grown French-American HYBRID. It's a CROSS of Goldriesling and an American VITIS RIPARIA-VITIS RUPESTRIS vine, the same parents of LEON MILLOT. Maréchal Foch is cul-tivated in the eastern United States and Canada, but it is rarely found in France today. It produces light, BEAUJOLAIS-like red wines.

Les Maréchaudes *see* CORTON

Margaret River Area located about 200 miles south of the city of Perth in the state of Western Australia. Although vineyards were first planted in the nineteenth century, this is considered a relatively new area because major vineyards weren't reestablished until the late 1960s. The red wines, which attracted considerable attention, didn't reach the market until the mid-1970s. Grape varieties grown in this region include CABERNET SAUVIGNON, Shiraz (SYRAH, which is usually la-beled *Hermitage* in this area), MERLOT, PINOT NOIR, CHARDONNAY, SÉMIL-LON, SAUVIGNON BLANC, CHENIN BLANC, and RIESLING. Area wineries include Ashbrook Estate, Cape Mentelle, Château Xanadu, Cullens, Evans and Tate, Happ's, Leeuwin, Moss Wood, Sandalford, and Vasse Felix.

Margaux AC [mah*r*-GOH] APPELLATION considered one of the best areas within the MÉDOC district of France's BORDEAUX region. It not only encompasses vineyards around the village of Margaux but also includes those of the villages of Arsac, Cantenac, Issan, Labarde and Soussans. The Margaux AC has twenty-one CRU CLASSÉ châteaus, more than any of the other Médoc COMMUNE appellations. Heading the list is the PREMIER CRU CHÂTEAU MARGAUX, followed by other top châteaus including BRANE-CANTENAC, DURFORT-VIVENS, GISCOURS, PALMER, and RAUSAN-SEGLA. The wines from the Margaux AC can be very PERFUMY and exhibit a wonderful silkiness (*see* SILKY) and ELEGANCE. They're made from CABERNET FRANC, CABERNET SAUVIGNON, MERLOT, and PETIT VERDOT.

Margaux, Château [sha-TOH mahr-GOH] Château Margaux is one of only four CHÂTEAUS (along with HAUT-BRION, LAFITE-ROTHSCHILD, and LATOUR) to receive a PREMIER CRU (first growth) ranking in the CLASSIFICATION OF 1855 (Château MOUTON-ROTHSCHILD was upgraded to *premier cru* status in 1973). It's also the only premier cru in the MARGAUX AC. This estate's exalted reputation dates back many centuries. In the fifteenth century the highly regarded wine from this estate was known as *Margou* or *Margous*. In the eighteenth century, Thomas Jefferson stated that the 1784 vintage from Château Margaux was one of BORDEAUX's best. In 1978 Château Margaux emerged from over a decade of mediocre wines to reestablish itself as one of the premier Bordeaux châteaus—a result of new ownership (the Mentzelopoulos family) and extensive renovation. As a whole, the wines from Margaux during the 1980s might be considered the best of any château in Bordeaux. These wines are known for their magnificent perfumed BOUQUETS and for being RICH and full-bodied (*see* BODY). The best VINTAGES, such as the 1986, can last for 40 to 50 years. The estate consists of nearly 210 acres and annually produces about 25,000 to 30,000 cases of red wine and another 3,000 to 5,000 cases of DRY white wine. Red wine is made from about 75 percent CABERNET SAUVIGNON, 20 percent MERLOT, and small amounts of CABERNET FRANC and PETIT VERDOT. The white wine called **Pavillon Blanc du Château Margaux** is made from 100 percent SAUVIGNON BLANC grown on a small parcel to the north near the COMMUNE of Soussans. The château uses a SECOND LABEL for red wines called **Pavillon Rouge du Château Margaux**.

Margaux Private Reserve *see* KIRWAN, CHÂTEAU

Marino DOC [mah-REE-noh] DOC area that sits in the CASTELLI ROMANI area southeast of Rome in Italy's LATIUM region. The wines are made from MALVASI, TREBBIANO, Bonvino, and Cacchione. Most of the wines produced are STILL and DRY, although AMABILE and SPUMANTE are also permitted. Marino's wines are very similiar to those from its better-known neighbor FRASCATI DOC.

Markgräflerland, Bereich [MARK-grehf-luhr-lahnt] A large BEREICH (subregion) located in the southern part of Germany's BADEN region. It runs along the Rhine River, south from the University city of Freiburg to Basel on the Swiss border. The wines from this area are generally mild and rather neutral but quite pleasant. Gutedel (CHASSE-LAS) is the most popular grape variety, along with MÜLLER-THURGAU and Spätburgunder (PINOT NOIR).

Markham Vineyards NAPA VALLEY winery founded by Bruce Markham in 1978. He sold it to Mercian a decade later after building the business to about 18,000 cases a year. Mercian (formerly known as Sanraku), Japan's largest wine-producing company, has invested millions of dollars expanding the Markham facility and vineyards. Today, Markham Vineyards annually produces over 110,000 cases, including over 40,000 under its SECOND LABEL **Glass Mountain Quarry**. Despite the rapid expansion, Markham continues to produce high-quality wines. It favors CABERNET SAUVIGNON, CHARDONNAY, and MERLOT, although smaller amounts of SAUVIGNON BLANC and Muscat Frontignan (MUSCAT) are also available. The Glass Mountain Quarry label produces other VARIETAL wines like PETITE SIRAH and CHARBONNO. Markham, which is located just northwest of the town of St. Helena, owns three desirable Napa Valley vineyards, which total nearly 250 acres.

Marqués de Cáceres [mahr-KAYSS deh kah-THAY-rehs] Large wine estate located in the RIOJA DO in northern Spain that produces nearly 600,000 cases of wine each year. It makes fresh, fruity white wines (and was one of the first BODEGAS to use modern winemaking techniques to achieve this style) mainly from Viura (MACABEO grapes). Red wines, which make up about 70 percent of the total, are made from TEMPRANILLO, Garnacha (GRENACHE), Mazuelo (CARIGNAN), and GRACIANO. A small amount of ROSÉ wine, made from Tempranillo and Garnacha, is also made. The best wines are sold under the Marqués de Cáceres name, offered in CRIANZA, RESERVA, and GRAN RESERVA styles. Marqués de Cáceres was founded by Enrique Forner, a Spaniard raised in BORDEAUX, who, along with his brother, owns Château DE CAMENSAC in Bordeaux's HAUT-MÉDOC AC.

Marqués de Murrieta [mahr-KAYSS deh myoor-ree-EHT-uh] The second oldest BODEGA in the RIOJA DO that is considered one of the aristocrats of the region, along with the oldest bodega, MARQUÉS DE RISCAL. Founded in 1872, Marqués de Murrieta makes wines using traditional Rioja ways—fermenting in cement vats and AGING for long periods of time in OAK BARRICAS. The youngest wines, the *Etiqueta Blanc*, spend at least 2 years (usually three) in oak barrels, but the *Castillo de*

Ygay GRAN RESERVA wines, produced only in very exceptional years, can spend 30 to 40 years in oak. The red wines here are made from TEMPRANILLO, Garnacha Tinta (GRENACHE), Mazuelo (CARIGNAN), and GRACIANO; ROSÉS are made from these same grapes plus the white Viura (MACABEO). White wines are made from Viura, MALVASIA, and Garnacha Blanc (GRENACHE).

Marqués de Riscal [mahr-KAYSS deh rees-KAHL] RIOJA DO estate established in 1860 and the oldest BODEGA in this area. The founder, Camilo Hurtado de Amazaga, the Marqués de Riscal, had spent considerable time in BORDEAUX and had help from a French VIGNERON in establishing the bodega. Along with implementing French winemaking techniques, a small amount of CABERNET SAUVIGNON was planted in addition to native Spanish varieties. The main grape used in the red wines is TEMPRANILLO, but GRACIANO and Mazuelo (CARIGNAN) are also used. Cabernet Sauvignon is generally used in all red wines but especially in the RESERVAS. Marqués de Riscal is the only bodega allowed to use Cabernet Sauvignon in their Rioja DO wines. The wines are AGED in oak barrels, and the youngest wines aren't released until their fourth year after the VINTAGE date.

Marqués de Villamagne *see* CAMPO VIEJO

Marquis d'Alesme-Becker, Château [sha-TOH mahr-KEE dah-lehm beh-KEHR] A small, obscure CHÂTEAU located in the MARGAUX AC in the MÉDOC district of BORDEAUX. Château Marquis d'Alesme-Becker was classified as a TROISIÈME CRU (third growth) in the CLASSIFICATION OF 1855, but some wine reviewers feel it hardly warrants that ranking today. The estate has nearly 23 acres and averages about 5,000 cases of red wine each year. The mix of grape VARIETIES used for these wines is about 30 percent CABERNET SAUVIGNON, 30 percent MERLOT, 30 percent CABERNET FRANC, and 10 percent PETIT VERDOT. These wines can AGE for about 8 to 10 years.

Marquis de Terme, Château [sha-TOH mahr-KEE duh TEHRM] A 94-acre estate located in the MARGAUX AC of the MÉDOC district of BORDEAUX. The château is ranked as a QUATRIÈME CRU (fourth growth), and VINTAGES since 1983 have been at a quality level that would warrant this classification. The estate produces around 12,000 to 14,000 cases of high-quality red wine, which is made with about 60 percent CABERNET SAUVIGNON, 30 percent MERLOT, 7 percent PETIT VERDOT, and 3 percent CABERNET FRANC. Wines from the better vintages are capable of AGING for 20 to 25 years. The château has added a SECOND LABEL **Domaine des Gondats** for lower-quality wine.

Marsala DOC [mahr-SAH-lah] DOC that produces Italy's most famous FORTIFIED wines. The DOC vineyards are located around the old seaside port city of Marsala on the western tip of SICILY. This area has a long history of making this style of fortified wine, going back to Roman times and later, during Spanish rule, when sherrylike wines were made here. In the late 1700s, however, an Englishman by the name of John Woodhouse devised today's conventional techniques for making Marsala and subsequently developed its following in England. As with other fortified wines, like SHERRY and MADEIRA, much of a Marsala's flavor comes from OXIDATION during aging. Marsala wines come in various styles—secco (DRY), semisecco (semisweet), and dolce (sweet). The wines are initially VINIFIED completely dry and must reach a minimum of 12 percent ALCOHOL. Depending on the quality level, this dry wine may be supplemented with a concentrated MUST, a cooked, reduced must (called **cotto** or **musto cotto**) that acquires a carmelized flavor, and/or a mixture of grape alcohol and sweet must known as **sifone** (sometimes called **mistella** and similar to the French MISTELLE). The various quality levels for Marsala are *Fine, Superiore, Superiore Riserva, Vergine,* and *Vergine Stravecchio* or *Vergine Riserva.* **Fine,** which is the lowest level and the most commonly found, has a minimum alcohol level of 17 percent and requires 1 year of AGING. **Superiore** must have a minimum of 18 percent alcohol and 2 years aging in wood, and **Superiore Riserva** must have a minimum of 4 years of wood aging. Superiore may also be called *Giaribaldi Dolce (GD), London Particular (LP),* or *Superior Old Marsala (SOM).* The highest-quality Marsala is **Vergine,** which may be fortified with grape alcohol but cannot have any concentrated must, cotto, or sifone added; it requires aging in wood for a minimum of 5 years. Vergine can be **stravecchio** or RISERVA, which must be aged in wood for a minimum of 10 years. Vergine wines are dry and austere with a distinctive caramel or toffee flavor and hints of smoked wood. Dry Marsalas, especially the Vergine styles, are best served as APÉRITIFS, whereas many of the semisweet and sweet styles are best as DESSERT WINES. In 1984 the official terms of **ambra** (amber), **oro** (gold), and **rubino** (ruby) became optional additional descriptions for any of the Marsala wine's quality levels. Ambra and oro describe Marsala wines made from white grapes—Catarratto, Inzolia, Grillo, and Damaschino. The addition of cotto is not allowed in the ambra versions. Ambra wines darken as they age, turning from the paler yellowish hues, to gold, to amber. The term rubino describes Marsala wines made from red grapes—Perricone, Calabrese, and Nerello (though up to 30 percent of any of the aforementioned white grapes can also be used).

Cremevo (*Cremevo Zabaione Vino Aromatizzato*) is a wine made from 80 percent Marsala and other flavorings like coffee or egg and was once called **Marsala Speciali**.

Marsannay AC [mahr-sah-NAY] In 1987 this became the first new village APPELLATION to be established in the CÔTE D'OR area since the 1930s. The village of Marsannay, also called Marsannay-la-Côte, is located at the northern end of the CÔTE DE NUITS (the northern portion of the Côte d'Or) in France's BURGUNDY region. The Marsannay AC covers all three categories of wine (red, white, and ROSÉ), which is unique for this area. Prior to receiving their own AC status, red wines from this area were sold as **Bourgogne Marsannay-la-Côte AC** and rosé wines as **Bourgogne Marsannay-la-Côte Rosé AC**. Marsanny AC wines are generally considered comparable to those from the CÔTE DE NUITS-VILLAGES.

Marsanne [mahr-SAN] White-wine grape that is widely grown in France's northern RHÔNE region and that is the principal grape in the white wines of CROZES-HERMITAGE, HERMITAGE, and SAINT JOSEPH. Small amounts of Marsanne are also grown in Australia, Switzerland, and the United States. Marsanne, which is usually BLENDED with ROUSSANNE in the Rhône whites, is also officially sanctioned in the Hermitage red wines as well. Traditionally made white wines can be full-bodied (*see* BODY), heavy, and somewhat dull when young, but can develop magnificently with age. Wines made with more modern methods can be lighter and fruitier, with a perfumy fragrance; they should be drunk young. Marsanne is also known as *Ermitage, Hermitage Blanc,* and *Grosse Roussette.*

Martha's Vineyard 1. A famous 40-acre vineyard located south of the town of Oakville in the western part of California's NAPA VALLEY. The vineyard is planted with CABERNET SAUVIGNON and produces (under the Heitz Cellars label) one of the most sought-after California red wines. These RICH, full-bodied (*see* BODY), long-lived wines are known for their minty/eucalyptus character, noticeable in most VINTAGES. The eucalyptus flavor is thought by some to come from the grove of eucalyptus trees that surround the vineyard. 2. Also a Massachusetts' AVA area covering the island of Martha's Vineyard. It has only one winery, Chicama Vineyards, which grows CABERNET SAUVIGNON, CHARDONNAY, CHENIN BLANC, GEWÜRZTRAMINER, MERLOT, PINOT NOIR, and RIESLING.

Martina Franca *see* APRILIA DOC

Louis M. Martini Winery [LOO-ee mahr-TEE-nee] Family-owned winery founded in 1922 by Louis M. Martini. In 1957 it was taken over by his son Louis P. Martini and today is run by his grandchildren—Carolyn, who is president, and Michael, who's the wine-maker. Louis M. Martini Winery owns nearly 1,000 acres of vineyard scattered throughout the NAPA VALLEY, SONOMA COUNTY, LAKE COUNTY, and CARNEROS. In 1937 Louis M. Martini had the foresight to buy the 250-acre Monte Rosso Vineyard in the SONOMA VALLEY hills and added the Carneros area's 200-acre La Loma Vineyard in 1942—all long before these areas became so immensely popular as prime grape-growing lo-cations. Throughout the 1940s, 1950s, and 1960s Louis M. Martini Winery developed a prominent position in the Napa Valley wine world and produced well-respected wines, particularly reds. The win-ery's lighter more elegant style lost support during the 1970s and 1980s, however, causing the winery to change some of its winemaking approaches. Today, the winery annually produces between 225,000 and 250,000 cases of wine, with essentially three different lines of TABLE WINE. The least expensive line supplies as many as twelve differ-ent VARIETAL WINES. The RESERVE bottlings are the next level, followed by the VINEYARD-DESIGNATED wines, which are the best and most expensive (although all Martini wines are compartively moderately priced). The vineyard-designated wines include CABERNET SAUVIGNON from the Monte Rosso Vineyard (Sonoma Valley), CHARDONNAY from the Las Amigas Vineyard (Carneros), GEWÜRZTRAMINER and MERLOT from the Los Vinedos del Rio Vineyard (RUSSIAN RIVER AVA), and PINOT NOIR from both the Las Amigas Vineyard and the La Loma Vineyard.

Marzemina Bianca *see* CHASSELAS

masculine *see* MUSCULAR

masseria [mahs-suh-REE-uh] A term used mainly in southern Italy, referring to a wine-producing farm or estate. *See also* FATTORIA.

massive *see* BIG

Master of Wine A title earned by passing extensive tasting and written examinations given by the Institute of Masters of Wine, a British organization established in 1953. The examinations include BLIND TAST-INGS of about three dozen wines and written tests on VITICULTURE, VINIFI-CATION, and various aspects of the wine trade. The Master of Wine title was available only to British citizens until 1988, when non-British citi-zens were allowed to apply. Taking and passing the test culminates in-tensive schooling and at least 5 years experience working in the wine trade. A Master of Wine may put the initials M. W. after his or her name.

Matanzas Creek Winery [muh-TAN-zuhs] SONOMA VALLEY AVA winery that was founded in 1977 by Sandra and Bill MacIver, although they first planted grapes on the estate vineyards in 1974. Nearly 45 acres of vineyard are planted near the winery, which is located southeast of Santa Rosa, California. Matanzas Creek Winery produces three wines—CHARDONNAY, MERLOT, and SAUVIGNON BLANC, all of which are well regarded. The Merlot is usually blended with small amounts of CABERNET FRANC and CABERNET SAUVIGNON, and the Sauvignon Blanc has some SÉMILLON included. The winery's output has increased from about 3,000 cases of wine in 1977, to a current annual production of between 25,000 and 30,000 cases.

Mataro *see* MOURVÈDRE

Mateus Rosé *see* SOGRAPE

Matrix *see* MAZZOCCO VINEYARDS

mature; maturity A term for wine that is perfectly DEVELOPED and AGED and ready to drink.

Maucaillou, Château [sha-TOH mow-kah-YOO] A highly regarded CRU BOURGEOIS located in the MOULIS AC in the MÉDOC district of BORDEAUX. The estate consists of about 135 acres and averages 25,000 to 30,000 cases of high-quality red wine each year. The mix of grape varieties used is around 58 percent CABERNET SAUVIGNON, 35 percent MERLOT, and 7 percent PETIT VERDOT although a small amount of CABERNET FRANC is used in some VINTAGES. The wines can be drunk fairly young but can also AGE for 10 to 12 years. Two SECOND LABELS are used by the château—**Cap de Haut** and **Franc-Caillou**.

Mäuerchen *see* GEISENHEIM

Maury AC [moh-REE] A little village located northwest of Perpignan in the southern part of France's vast LANGUEDOC-ROUSSILLON region. The vineyards surrounding Maury make up this AC, which makes both ROSÉ and red VIN DOUX NATUREL from the GRENACHE grape. The wines are available in both a young, fresh style as well as a RANCIO style, which has an OXIDIZED character.

Mavrodaphne [mahv-rroh-DAHF-nee] Popular Greek red-wine grape grown along the Gulf of Corinth. It is generally made into a sweet, full-bodied, AROMATIC, lightly FORTIFIED wine. The name, which translates to "black laurel," comes from the resemblance this grape has to the laurel berry. The celebrated Mavrodaphne wines spend their first summer in oak barrels outside, basking in the sunshine. This technique allows the wine to SOFTEN into a pleasant DESSERT WINE.

Maximin Grünhäus [MAHK-sih-mihn GRYOON-howss] A tiny village located on the Ruwer River in Germany's MOSEL-SAAR-RUWER region. It's actually classified as an ORSTEIL that's part of the village of Mertesdorf. Maximin Grünhaus has approximately 80 acres that have been owned by the von Schubert family since 1882. The vineyards are broken into three EINZELLAGEN (individual vineyard sites)—**Bruderberg** at the bottom, **Herrenberg** in the upper section, and **Abtsberg**, the steep middle section that produces the best grapes. The wines from each Einzellagen are labeled separately, using the village's name—for example, Maximin Grünhäuser Bruderberg. The wines are highly regarded, and those from good VINTAGES are capable of AGING for around 20 years.

May wine Originally a German specialty, this is a punch made from sweet, light wine infused with aromatic woodruff leaves. It's served cold with fruit (usually strawberries) floating in it.

Mayacamas Vineyards [mi-yuh-KAH-muhs] Resurrection of this small winery, which is located high on Mt. Veeder (part of the Mayacamas mountain range), was started in 1941 by Jack and Mary Taylor. The site contained an abandoned winery (the Fisher Winery, founded by John Fisher) that had been established in the late 1800s. In 1968 Mayacamas Vineyards was sold to Bob and Elinor Travers. The wines of Mayacamas are controversial in that the CABERNET SAUVIGNONS are always BIG and TANNIC, requiring lengthy AGING to SOFTEN and become drinkable. Critics feel they're too tannic, while proponents say they're some of California's longest aging reds. Mayacamas CHARDONNAYS are also known for the long aging capability. Only about 5,000 cases of wine are produced each year.

Mazis-Chambertin AC [mah-ZEE shah*m*-behr-TAN] A 22½-acre GRAND CRU vineyard that adjoins that of the better-known CHAMBERTIN-CLOS DE BÈZE. Mazis-Chambertin is located in the village of GEVREY-CHAMBERTIN in the CÔTE DE NUITS district of France's BURGUNDY region. The general quality of its red (PINOT NOIR) wines is extremely high, and they're considered some of the best in the world. These wines are deep-colored, RICH, CONCENTRATED, and TANNIC, which makes them prime candidates for long aging (15 to 25 years for the best ones). *See also* CHAMBERTIN.

Mazoyères-Chambertin AC *see* CHARMES-CHAMBERTIN

Mazuelo *see* CARIGNAN

Mazzocco Vineyards [muh-ZAH-koh] A DRY CREEK VALLEY AVA winery that was established in 1984 by the famous eye surgeon Dr. Thomas Mazzocco. It got off to a good start with its 1985 CHARDONNAYS, followed in 1986 and 1987 with equally successful CABERNET SAUVIGNON and ZINFANDEL wines. After building annual sales to between 30,000 and 35,000 cases of wine, Mazzocco sold his winery to Vintech in 1990. In 1991 Vintech experienced severe financial problems, and Dr. Mazzocco got his winery back. Production is now about 15,000 cases a year, with the River Lane Chardonnay leading the way. Mazzocco Vineyards also makes Cabernet Sauvignon, Zinfandel, a small amount of MERLOT, and a red Bordeaux blend called **Matrix**.

McDowell Valley AVA Small California VITICULTURAL AREA in MENDOCINO COUNTY between the town of Hopland on the west and the large CLEAR LAKE AVA on the east. It's a subregion of the larger MENDO-CINO AVA. There's only one winery, McDowell Valley Vineyards, but several growers have vineyards and sell their grapes to wineries outside the area. CABERNET SAUVIGNON and CHARDONNAY are the main varieties, but the climate seems to do well with ZINFANDEL and some RHÔNE varieties like SYRAH, GRENACHE, MOURVÈDRE, CINSAULT, and VIOGNIER.

McLaren Vale *see* SOUTHERN VALES

mead [MEED] A beverage made by fermenting honey, water, and yeast with flavorings such as herbs, spices, or flowers. Mead dates back to Biblical times and was popular in early England. Although not widely distributed today, it is still bottled.

meaty A term used to describe wine (primarily red) that's so RICH and full-bodied (*see* BODY) that it gives the sense of being *chewable*. A synonym for CHEWY.

medium-bodied *see* BODY

medium-dry *see* DRY

Médoc [may-DAWK] BORDEAUX'S largest and best-known wine region. It's located on the triangular piece of land between the Atlantic Ocean and the Gironde estuary in western France. It stretches some 50 miles, from just below the Pointe de Grave at the peninsula's northern point, to south of the village of Blanquefort just outside the northern suburbs of the city of Bordeaux. The Médoc region is broken into the Bas-Médoc ("lower" Médoc) and the HAUT-MÉDOC ("upper" Médoc) and, in addition to the standard Bordeaux APPELLATIONS, includes two area and six village appellations. The **Bas-Médoc** is the area from the northern point down to just above the village of Saint-Seurin-de-Cardourne north of SAINT-ESTÈPHE. This area, which has the least desirable soil, produces good-quality wines but generally not great ones. The Bas-Médoc red wines are covered under the **Médoc AC**, one of the two area appellations—the other being the **Haut-Médoc AC**, which is also only for red wines. (White wines throughout the Médoc are simply labeled BORDEAUX AC or BORDEAUX SUPÉRIEUR AC.) The **Haut-Médoc** area, which covers the southern portion of the Médoc, extending from just north of the city of Bordeaux to the Bas-Médoc, is where the best and most famous Médoc CHÂTEAUS are located. The Haut-Médoc AC encompasses all of this area except for the six village appellations of LISTRAC, MARGAUX, MOULIS, PAUILLAC, Saint-Estèphe, and SAINT-JULIEN. In general, wines labeled with the individual village appellations are better than those with the Haut-Médoc AC, which are better than those labeled Médoc AC. The main red grapes used throughout the Médoc are CABERNET FRANC, CABERNET SAUVIGNON, and MERLOT, with occasional use of PETIT VERDOT and minute amounts of MALBEC. The CLASSIFICATION OF 1855, which created five tiers of CRUS CLASSÉS (Classed Growths) for red wines, was limited to 61 châteaus— all in the Médoc with the exception of GRAVES' Château HAUT-BRION. Included in this classification's top category of PREMIER CRU (first growth) are the châteaus of LAFITE-ROTHSCHILD, LATOUR, and MOUTON-ROTHSCHILD (all from Pauillac AC), MARGAUX from Margaux AC, and Haut-Brion from Graves. Just below the cru classé category is that of CRU BOURGEOIS, which was established for the better châteaus that didn't qualify for the top grouping. There are numerous cru bourgeois châteaus in the Médoc, and a majority of these are in the Haut-Médoc area. The classification system provides some guidance to the quality of wines from the Médoc, although many feel it's outdated and needs revision.

Médoc Noir *see* MERLOT

Mélinots *see* CHABLIS

mellow A descriptor for a MATURE, well-AGED wine that's SOFT (but not FLABBY) and pleasant.

Melon d'Arbois *see* CHARDONNAY

Melon de Bourgogne [meh-loh*n* duh boor-GAWN-yuh] Although this French white wine grape originated in BURGUNDY, it has now all but vanished from that region. Those that are still grown in Burgundy go into the BOURGOGNE GRAND ORDINAIRE wines. Melon de Bourgogne, however, is widely planted in the LOIRE, particularly in the Pays Nantais region where the grape and the wine is known as **Muscadet**. The grape's popularity in this part of the Loire is related to its ability to withstand cold weather, and its tendency to ripen early and produce a large crop. Unfortunately, most wines produced from this grape are viewed as insipid in flavor. The best wines are those from the APPELLATION of MUSCADET DE SÈVRE-ET-MAINE and are labeled *mise en bouteille sur lie,* which means they're bottled directly off the LEES without filtering. This process can produce flavorful wines that are SOFT and CREAMY with hints of CITRUS. It was discovered that a variety growing on the grounds of the University of California at DAVIS that was thought to be PINOT BLANC was actually Melon de Bourgogne. It's now believed that many of the wines called Pinot Blanc in California are really Melon de Bourgogne. This grape is also known as *Lyonnaise Blanche* and *Weisserburgunder.*

Mendocino County; Mendocino AVA [mihn-doh-SEE-noh] **Mendocino County** is north of San Francisco and is the northernmost county in the NORTH COAST AVA. In addition to the non-AVA areas like Redwood Valley and Talmage, the county contains five AVAs—MENDOCINO, ANDERSON VALLEY, COLE RANCH, MCDOWELL VALLEY, and POTTER VALLEY. The **Mendocino AVA** is situated in the county's southern portion and encompasses all the other AVAs as well as Redwood Valley and Talmage. The climate varies throughout this area, ranging from a cool Region I (*see* CLIMATE REGIONS OF CALIFORNIA) rating for the Anderson Valley to a Region III for most other parts of Mendocino. CHARDONNAY is the most widely planted variety, followed by ZINFANDEL, CABERNET SAUVIGNON, CARIGNANE, and SAUVIGNON BLANC. COLOMBARD, RIESLING, GEWÜRZTRAMINER, PINOT NOIR, and PETITE SIRAH are also grown here.

Mendoza *see* ARGENTINA

Menetou-Salon AC [meh-neh-TOO sah-LOHN] APPELLATION located near the more famous SANCERRE AC in western France's upper LOIRE Valley. There are 10 small villages whose wines are covered by this appellation. Although the white wines, which are made from SAUVIGNON BLANC, are compared to those of Sancerre, they're not equal to Sancerre's best. On the other hand, the red and ROSÉ wines, made from PINOT NOIR, are as good or better than Sancerre's.

meniscus [mih-NIHS-kuhs] The rim of a wine in a glass is called the meniscus. The COLOR intensity of the meniscus is an indicator of several of the wine's characteristics including concentration, maturity, and richness.

Méntrida DO [mayn-TRREE-dah] This is a large but obscure DO area located southwest of Madrid in Spain's CASTILLA-LA MANCHA region. Because most of the wine produced is sold in bulk, not much of what is bottled is seen outside of central Spain. This DO produces red and ROSÉ wines. The main grape used is Garnacha Tinta (GRENACHE), along with some Cencibel (TEMPRANILLO) and Tinto Madrid. Most of these wines are mediocre in quality and high in ALCOHOL (ranging from 13 to 18 percent).

mercaptans [mer-KAP-tuhns] Mercaptans are the result of HYDROGEN SULFIDE combining with wine components, the result of which is a pungently offensive, sour odor that can smell like garlic, stale sweat, skunk, or rubber. Mercaptan characteristics in a wine are a sign of careless winemaking and signal the wine's deterioration.

Mercier *see* CHAMPAGNE

Mercurey AC [mehr-kyoo-REH] The biggest and the most important of the five villages with individual APPELLATION status in the CÔTE CHALONNAISE in France's BURGUNDY region. About 95 percent of the wine produced is red, made from PINOT NOIR. The red wines are thought to be the best of the Côte Chalonnaise, comparable to a good CÔTE-DE-BEAUNE-VILLAGES AC wine from the better-known neighboring area to the north. The area produces a small amount of white wine, made from CHARDONNAY. These flavorful, LIGHT, CRISP white wines are meant to be drunk young. There are a number of major wine firms from other parts of Burgundy who own land in Mercurey. This gives these wines better representation than other Côte Chalonnaise wines, both in France and internationally. The Mercurey wines have such presence that the Côte Chalonnaise is occasionally referred to as *Région de Mercurey,* and there is pressure to change the name formally.

Meritage [MEHR-ih-tihj] Instituted in 1989, the term *Meritage* is a certification mark registered with the U.S. Department of Trademarks and Patents. It was coined in 1988 by a group of vintners who sought to establish standards of identification for a category of American blended wines made with traditional BORDEAUX grape varieties. The name Meritage (a compound of the words *merit* and *heritage*) was chosen from over 6,000 entries in an international contest held by these vintners. The purpose of The Meritage Association is to help identify quality American wine blends that, because they're not made with at least 75 percent of a single variety, can't use the variety name on the label. This forced many producers of excellent wines to either use generic names (like CLARET or Red TABLE WINE) or proprietary names (like *Insignia* from JOSEPH PHELPS VINEYARDS). Both practices caused great confusion in the marketplace. To be designated as Meritage, a wine must meet the following standards: 1. It must be a blend of two or more Bordeaux grape varieties—for red wines these

are CABERNET FRANC, CABERNET SAUVIGNON, Carmenere, Gros Verdot, MAL-
BEC, MERLOT, PETITE VERDOT, and St. Macaire, and for whites they're
SAUVIGNON BLANC, MUSCADELLE, and SÉMILLON (no more than 90 percent of
any single variety may go into a Meritage wine); 2. It must be the winery's best wine of its type; 3. It must be produced and bottled by a U.S.
winery from grapes that carry a U.S. APPELLATION; and 4. Its production
is limited to a maximum 25,000 cases per VINTAGE. Wineries that are
approved for the Meritage designation may use it in various ways on
the label. They may simply use the term *Meritage* or use *Meritage* in
conjunction with their own proprietary name (as with *Cardinale* from
KENDALL-JACKSON VINEYARDS), or they may use only their proprietary
name. At this writing The Meritage Association is petitioning the
Bureau of Alcohol, Tobacco, and Firearms (BATF) for approval of
Meritage as a class and type of wine.

Merlau *see* MERLOT

Merlau Blanc *see* MERLOT BLANC

Merlot [mehr-LOH; mer-LOH] Though commonly referrred to as
simply *Merlot*, this red-wine grape is really **Merlot Noir** (there's also
a MERLOT BLANC variety). Merlot is the primary grape in SAINT-ÉMILION
and POMEROL, and one of two primaries (the other being CABERNET
SAUVIGNON) of BORDEAUX. Merlot acreage in the DÉPARTEMENT of
GIRONDE, which encompasses most of Bordeaux, is almost twice that
of Cabernet Sauvignon. However, Merlot has never been as highly regarded as Cabernet Sauvignon, which dominates in the MÉDOC and
GRAVES—growing areas that produce wines traditionally viewed as
Bordeaux's most important. Much of the wine world views Merlot as
simply a grape to be blended with Cabernet Sauvignon or CABERNET
FRANC. Still, Merlot can produce great wines like those of Pomerol's
CHÂTEAU PÉTRUS, which makes one of the world's most expensive red
wines, most of which are 100 percent Merlot. Merlot is also widely
planted in other areas of France. Growers in the LANGUEDOC-ROUSSIL-
LON region, for instance, are being encouraged to plant this grape in
order to improve the vast quantities of wine produced there. Merlot
is extensively grown throughout the world but has developed a tarnished reputation from overproduction in areas like northeastern
Italy. It's an extremely important grape in Italy's FRIULI-VENEZIA GIULIA
and VENETO regions, which produce some great Merlots. This grape is
widely grown in eastern Europe with sizable plantings in Bulgaria,
Hungary, and Rumania. Australians have been slow to adopt Merlot,
since their dominate grape SHIRAZ is often used for blending with
Cabernet Sauvignon. In California and Washington, Merlot was ini-

tially planted as a blending grape, but in the late 1970s it began to stand on its own as a variety and has been continually gaining popularity. California Merlot acreage has continued to increase, as have the number of wineries producing Merlot wines. California's DUCK-HORN VINEYARDS, generally regarded as a leading producer of quality Merlot wines, has been producing them since the late 1970s. In French the word *Merlot* means "young blackbird," probably alluding to the grape's beautiful dark-blue color. Compared to Cabernet Sauvignon, Merlot grapes ripen fairly early and have lower TANNINS and higher sugar levels. They produce wines that are generally SOFTER and with slightly higher ALCOHOL content. High-quality Merlot wines are medium to dark red in color, rich, and FRUITY, with characteristics of black currant, cherry, and mint. Merlot wines are ROUNDER and more SUPPLE than Cabernet Sauvignons and usually can be enjoyed much earlier. Generally, Merlot wines do not AGE as long as Cabernet Sauvignons. A small amount of Cabernet Sauvignon or Cabernet Franc is often blended with Merlot grapes to give the wine a bit more STRUCTURE. Merlot is also called *Bigney, Crabutet, Médoc Noir,* and *Merlau.*

Merlot Blanc [mehr-LOH BLAHN; mer-LOH BLAHNGK] Also called *Merlau Blanc,* this white-wine grape is not related to MERLOT (Noir). It's presumed that the name comes from the simple fact that the leaves of this variety resemble those of Merlot Noir. Merlot Blanc is an unimportant variety grown mainly in France's districts of Blaye, Bourg, and Fronsac, northeast of the city of Bordeaux. It generally produces low-quality wines.

Merritt Island AVA [MEHR-riht] Tiny VITICULTURAL AREA that is a subzone to the CLARKSBURG AVA and home of Bogle Vineyards and Winery. Merritt Island, a 5,000-acre, man-made island, is south of Clarksburg in Yolo County. It's cooled by San Francisco Bay breezes and is generally considered a Region II growing area (*see* CLIMATE REGIONS OF CALIFORNIA). The variety that's done the best here is CHENIN BLANC.

Merryvale Vineyards Established in 1983 by five partners, Merryvale Vineyards is located in St. Helena, California. This winery actually has no vineyards of its own and purchases its grapes from NAPA VALLEY sources, some of which are partners in the winery like Robin Lail, owner of the famous Napanook Vineyard and also a partner in DOMINUS ESTATE. Merryvale Vineyards uses the Sunny St. Helena Winery in St. Helena as its wine-producing facility. It makes two CHARDONNAY wines—Napa Valley (now Starmont Vineyard) and Napa

Valley Reserve, although previous VINTAGES included Chardonnay from the STAGS LEAP DISTRICT. It also produces CABERNET SAUVIGNON, a red MERITAGE called Profile, and a white Meritage made from SAUVIGNON BLANC and SÉMILLON. Recent vintages have been well received. Merryvale's SECOND LABEL is **Sunny St. Helena Winery**.

meta *see* POTASSIUM METABISULFITE

metallic A winetasting term describing an unpleasant tinny characteristic, which is generally the result of a wine's contact with metal.

méthode ancestrale *see* RURAL METHOD

méthode artisnale *see* RURAL METHOD

méthode champenoise [may-TOHD shahm-peh-NWAHZ; may-TOD shahm-peh-NWAHZ] The traditional method of making SPARKLING WINE developed in France's CHAMPAGNE region. This process consists of taking various STILL WINES and blending them to make a CUVÉE that represents the style of a winery or champagne house. A complex cuvée can consist of as many as thirty to forty different wines. Once the various wines are blended in large blending vats, a bottling DOSAGE (also known as *dosage d'tirage* or *liqueur d'tirage*), a syrupy mixture of sugar and wine (and sometimes BRANDY and/or citric acid), is added along with special yeasts. The cuvée is then immediately bottled and corked. The sugar (in the bottling dosage) and the yeast cells cause a SECONDARY FERMENTATION to take place in the bottle. This results in the creation of additional alcohol and CARBON DIOXIDE gas, which gives the wine its effervescence or "sparkle." During this secondary fermentation, pressure in the bottle builds up to 90 to 110 pounds per square inch (psi). If less bottling dosage is used in the cuvée, there will be less pressure, which will result in a lightly sparkling wine style called CRÉMANT. Such wines have slightly more than half the pressure of a regular bottling. SEDIMENT is also thrown off during the second fermentation and is removed through the steps of RIDDLING (or *rémuage*) and DISGORGING (or *dégorgement*). Just before final bottling, a shipping dosage (*dosage d'expédition* or *liqueur d'expédition*), sugar, and some of the same cuvée (reserved for this purpose) is added. The percentage of sugar in the shipping dosage determines the degree of sweetness in the final wine. From dryest to sweetest, sparkling wines are classified as BRUT, EXTRA DRY (or *extra-sec*), SEC, DEMI-SEC, or DOUX. Once the final handling is complete and the bottles are recorked, the final pressure in a standard bottle ranges from 60 to 90 psi (approximately 6 ATMOSPHERES). The words "méthode champenoise" are used only on labels of wines that use this method. *See also* CHARMAT.

méthode dioise *see* CLAIRETTE DE DIE

méthode gaillaçoise *see* GAILLAC; RURAL METHOD

méthode rurale *see* RURAL METHOD

méthode tradition *see* CLAIRETTE DE DIE

Methuselah *see* WINE BOTTLES

metodo champenois [MEH-toh-doh shahm-peh-NWAHZ] Italian phrase that means the same as the French MÉTHODE CHAMPENOISE. However, *metodo classico* or *metodo tradizionale* are generally used in its place because EEC regulations restrict the term *méthode champenoise* and its translations to French sparkling wines.

metodo charmat [MEH-toh-doh shar-MAHT] An Italian phrase for the CHARMAT PROCESS.

metodo classico [MEH-toh-doh CLAH-see-coh] *See* MÉTODO CHAMPENOIS; MÉTHODE CHAMPENOISE

método continuo *see* CHARMAT

metodo tradizionale *see* METODO CHAMPENOIS; MÉTHODE CHAMPENOISE

metric A decimal-based measurement system used throughout much of the world. For volume, the **liter** is the standard measurement and is equivalent to 33.8 fluid ounces. A **milliliter** is equal to one-thousandth of a liter or 0.338 ounces; a **centiliter** is equal to one-hundredth of a liter. A HECTOLITER is equal to 100 liters and is a common measurement of wine production in most European and South American countries. In the United States, the Bureau of Alcohol, Tobacco, and Firearms (BATF) implemented the metric system for wine bottles in 1975, with mandatory compliance beginning in January of 1979. The size of a standard wine bottle is 750 milliliters or 75 centiliters or 0.75 liters. Other bottles both larger and smaller are based on this metric measurement. *See also* WINE BOTTLES.

Meunier [muh-NYAY] French red grape that is the most widely cultivated variety in France's CHAMPAGNE region, even though its relative, PINOT NOIR, and CHARDONNAY get most of the attention. Meunier is used extensively in the region's SPARKLING WINES, usually blended with these other two varieties. The name for this grape is French for "miller," derived from the fact that the white underside of its leaves looks like sifted flour. This variety's positive properties include more fruitiness and higher ACIDITY than Pinot Noir or Chardonnay, an ability to better survive in the coolest areas of the Champagne region, and higher yields than Pinot Noir. Australia, which produces limited amounts of 100-percent Meunier STILL WINE, and Germany are the only other areas to grow Meunier in any quantity. Meunier is also known as *Gris Meunier, Plant Meunier, Pinot Meunier, Müllerrebe,* and *Schwarzriesling.*

Meursault AC [meh*r*-SOH] APPELLATION that surrounds the village of Meursault, which is one of the largest of the CÔTE DE BEAUNE. Although it has no GRAND CRU vineyards, Meursault is quite famous for its white wines. Its reputation comes from its PREMIER CRU vineyards, the best known of which are **Les Charmes**, **Les Genevrières**, and **Les Perrières**. This last vineyard is often touted as a grand cru candidate, and its wines are favorably compared to those of LE MONTRACHET, considered by many as the very best white-wine grand cru vineyard. The *premier cru* vineyards can append their name on the label, as in Meursault-Perriers or Mersault-Charmes.

Mexico Even though vineyards were planted as early as the 1500s, Mexico does not produce much TABLE WINE, mainly because its climate isn't particularly suited for wine grapes. Nor do Mexicans drink much wine—beer is the beverage of choice. Most Mexico-made wine is usually FORTIFIED or further distilled and turned into brandy. Some European grape varieties are grown for table wines, and are planted in the northern part of the country in areas like Baja California.

Meyney, Château [sha-TOH may-NAY] A highly regarded CRU BOURGEOIS EXCEPTIONNEL located in the SAINT-ESTÈPHE AC in the MÉDOC district of BORDEAUX. The estate consists of about 125 acres located just north of Château MONTROSE with beautiful views of the Gironde River. The wines—made from around 70 percent CABERNET SAUVIGNON, 24 percent MERLOT, 4 percent CABERNET FRANC, and 2 percent PETIT VERDOT—are generally BIG and full-bodied (*see* BODY) and capable of AGING for 20 to 25 years. Around 25,000 to 30,000 cases of this high-quality red wine are produced annually. **Prieuré de Meyney** is the SECOND LABEL.

Peter Michael Winery Although other wineries own vineyard land in the KNIGHTS VALLEY AVA, Peter Michael Winery is the only one with a winery physically located there. The English-born Peter Michael purchased the property in 1980, planted grapes in 1984, and completed the winery in 1989. Several CHARDONNAY wines are produced, including Mon Plaisir and Howell Mountain. There's also a CABERNET SAUVIGNON wine called Les Pavots, which is made from estate-grown grapes. Peter Michael Winery has about 60 vineyard acres planted and produces nearly 10,000 cases of wine a year.

Michelmark *see* ERBACH

microclimate Term used in the wine world to describe the environmental factors affecting the quality of grapes. The factors, which aren't fully understood yet, include the type of soil, drainage, slope angle, bearing of the sun and amount of sun received by the growing area, altitude, both day and night temperature of the area, wind, and amount of rainfall and time when rainfall occurs. Each of these factors affect grape quality to some degree. They can even create circumstances whereby a small vineyard (or plot within a vineyard) can produce superb grapes while the immediate neighboring land never achieves the same quality. In BURGUNDY the term CLIMAT is used to encompass these same factors, while in other parts of France the term TERROIR is used.

Midi *see* LANGUEDOC-ROUSSILLON

mildew Various vineyard fungi that can cause severe damage if not treated for prevention. There are two main types—powdery mildew and downy mildew. **Powdery mildew**, also known as *oidium*, isn't dependent on moisture like other fungi and is found in the dryer California climate where most fungi don't do well. It attacks most parts of the vine including the fruit, leaves, shoots, and tendrils. Powdery mildew can affect the smell, taste, and color of wines made from infected grapes. **Downy mildew**, also called *peronospera*, likes wet, humid areas. It's not a problem in California but is found east of the Rocky Mountains, where VITIS VINIFERA vines are susceptible to it. Downy mildew produces a white fuzzy growth on the underside of the leaves and attacks the flowers and the fruit. Mildew is of American origin but has been exported to most other winegrowing regions. Powdery mildew was introduced to Europe in the 1850s and caused widespread damage, almost as serious as the PHYLLOXERA epidimic that followed shortly thereafter. Most mildews can be controlled by using copper sulfate sprays (*see* BORDEAUX MIXTURE) or ground or powdered sulfur.

Les Millandes *see* MOREY-SAINT-DENIS

millésime [mee-lay-ZEEM] French term for "vintage" or "year."

milliliter *see* METRIC

Minervois AC [mee-nehr-VWAH] APPELLATION that produces some of the best red wines in France's LANGUEDOC-ROUSSILON region. It's located north of CORBIÈRS, inland from the Mediterranean coast. The vineyards begin around the village of Minerve on a high plateau and run south and west down to the river Aude. Minervois wines, which are generally good and fairly full-bodied (*see* BODY), are made from CARIGNAN, CINSAUT, GRENACHE, and, in an effort to improve quality, increasingly from MOURVÈDRE and SYRAH. Most of the production comes from area cooperatives, which generally produce agreeable wines.

Mineur J. J. de Bethmann *see* OLIVIER, CHÂTEAU

minty; mint A descriptor for an appealing mintlike characteristic found in some California CABERNETS and ZINFANDELS. As long as it isn't predominant, this is considered a desirable trait. Mint and EUCALYPTUS have a similar sensory appeal.

Mireval *see* MUSCAT DE MIREVAL

mirin *see* SAKE

Mis au Domaine *see* MIS EN BOUTEILLE

Mis en Bouteille [mee zahn boo-TEH-yuh (boo-TAY)] A French phrase meaning "bottled." *Mis en Bouteille au Domaine* (or *Mis au Domaine*) means "bottled at the estate" (ESTATE BOTTLED); *Mis en Bouteille au Château* (or *Mis du Château*) means "bottled at the château" (CHÂTEAU BOTTLED). *Mis en Bouteille a la Propriete* ("bottled at the property") and *Mis par le Propriétaire* ("bottled by the proprietor") have the same meaning as estate bottled. *Mis en Bouteille dans nos Caves* and *Mis en Bouteille dans nos Chais* mean "bottled in our cellars," and usually suggest that the grapes were grown elsewhere and that the wine is not the quality of one that is estate bottled.

Mis par le Propriétaire *see* MIS EN BOUTEILLE

Mission [MISH-uhn] The red-wine grape that the Franciscan missionaries planted during the eighteenth century as they migrated from Mexico up through southern and northern California. Although Mission was California's prevailing grape through the 1870s, its popularity and acreage has since diminished. Most of the remaining plantings are in the CENTRAL VALLEY and southern California. The Mission grape, which is closely related (some think the same grape) to Chile's *Pais* variety and Argentina's *Criolla*, is still extensively grown in Argentina as well as Mexico. Although definitely a VITIS VINIFERA grape, its European connection has never been established.

Mission wines are generally poor to medium quality; they're primarily used in BLENDING.

La Mission-Haut-Brion, Château [sha-TOH lah mee-SYAW*N* oh-bree-OH*N*] The wines from this CRU CLASSÉ CHÂTEAU are viewed as some of the best in all of BORDEAUX and are favorably compared to the PREMIERS CRUS (first growths) of the MÉDOC. La Mission Haut-Brion is located in the PESSAC-LÉOGNAN AC, just a few miles outside of the city of Bordeaux. It sits across the road from the only GRAVES premier cru, Château HAUT BRION, and for many years the two have been rivals. This rivalry ended in 1983 when the owners of Haut-Brion purchased La Mission Haut-Brion, along with adjoining properties La Tour-Haut-Brion and Laville-Haut-Brion. For many years **La Tour-Haut-Brion** was essentially the SECOND LABEL of La Mission Haut-Brion. The best barrels of wine from both vineyards were used for La Mission Haut-Brion's wines and the remaining were used in La Tour-Haut-Brion's wines. This changed in 1983, as well, and the wines of the two vineyards are no longer combined in any way. La Tour-Haut-Brion now produces about 2,000 cases of good-quality red wine on its own. **Laville-Haut-Brion** was formerly a section of La Tour-Haut-Brion that was planted with about 60 percent SÉMILLON and 40 percent SAUVIGNON BLANC. It produces about 2,000 cases of very highly regarded white wine. Laville-Haut-Brion and La Tour-Haut-Brion are both ranked as cru classé vineyards. La Mission Haut-Brion consists of nearly 50 acres and produces about 7,000 to 8,000 cases of top-quality red wine each year. These wines are made from approximately 50 percent CABERNET SAUVIGNON, 40 percent MERLOT, and 10 percent CABERNET FRANC, and the best VINTAGES are capable of AGING for 35 or 40 years.

mistella *see* MARSALA DOC

mistelle [mees-TEHL] Grape juice in which FERMENTATION has been stopped by the addition of ALCOHOL. Because only small amounts of the grape sugars have usually been converted to alcohol, mistelle is very sweet. It's used mainly as a base for APÉRITIFS, particularly VERMOUTH.

Mittelhaardt/Deutsche Weinstrasse, Bereich *see* RHEINPFALZ

Mittelmosel [MIHT-uhl-MOH-zuhl] One of Germany's best wine-producing areas. Its name, which means "middle Mosel," refers to its location in the central portion of German's MOSEL-SAAR-RUWER region. Its boundaries closely approximate those of the BEREICH BERNKASTEL and include villages such as BRAUNEBERG, BERNKASTEL, GRAACH, PIESPORT,

WEHLEN, and ZELTINGEN. The RIESLINGS of Mittelmosel are highly regarded.

Mittelrhein [MIHT-uhl-rine] With less than 2,000 acres of vineyards planted, Mittelrhein is the fifth smallest of the thirteen German ANBAUGEBIETE (quality-wine regions). The region follows the path of the Rhine River from the bend in the river near the villages of Lorch and Bingen stretching northward about 60 miles to Konigswinter, just south of Bonn. RIESLING grapevines cover nearly 75 percent of the thin strand of vineyards running along both sides of the Rhine. The wines are of high quality, and most are consumed within the region. High-quality SEKT is made as well. The Mittelrhein region is noted for its spectacular, picturesque scenery as the Rhine twists and turns its way north. There are three BEREICHS—**Siebengebirge**, **Rheinburgengau**, and **Bacharach**—and eleven GROSSLAGEN in the region.

Mittervernatsch *see* SCHIAVA

moelleux [mwah-LEUH] A French sensory term used to describe white wines that have at least some RESIDUAL SUGAR. A single-word translation is difficult because the meaning for *moelleux* is a complex compound meaning "soft-smooth-mellow-velvety-lush."

Moët et Chandon [moh-EHT ay Shahn-DAWN] The largest CHAMPAGNE house in France, founded in 1743 by Claude Moët. Located in Epernay, Moët et Chandon is part of the huge Moët-Hennessy group, which also has holdings in Argentina, Australia, Austria, Brazil, Germany, and Spain. Moët et Chandon produces over 18 million bottles of wine a year and owns over 2,000 acres throughout the Champagne region. Fruit from these vineyards also helps supply the smaller champagne houses of Mercier and Ruinart, which are also owned by Moët-Hennessy. Moët et Chandon produces large volumes of non-vintage wine under the *White Star* and *Brut Imperial* designations. It is best known, however, for its premium brand DOM PÉRIGNON, named after the famous monk credited with enhancing the MÉTHODE CHAMPENOISE process. Moët et Chandon produces a variety of other wines including VINTAGE champagnes under the *Brut Imperial* and *Brut Rosé* designations. It was one of the first French companies to invest in the California SPARKLING WINE industry with the creation of DOMAINE CHANDON; it also owns the SIMI WINERY.

moldy If a moldy smell and flavor can be detected in a wine, it's generally a signal that it was made from moldy grapes or stored in improperly cleaned or deteriorating barrels.

Molette Noire *see* MONDEUSE

Monastrell [maw-nahs-TRRELL] After Garnacha Tinta (GRENACHE), this grape is Spain's second most widely planted red variety. It's grown in Spain's RIOJA and PENEDÈS regions and is extensively planted in the ALICANTE region. Monastrell wines are moderately colored, high in ALCOHOL, and low in ACID. They're heavier and drier than the Garnacha Tinta with which they're usually BLENDED. Monastrell is sometimes processed similarly to SHERRY to produce FORTIFIED, RANCIO-style wines. This variety is also called *Alcayata, Valcarcelia,* and *Morastel* (or *Morrastal*), although it's unrelated to the *Morrastel* of southern France (which is actually GRACIANO).

Monbazillac AC [mawn-bah-zee-YAHK] APPELLATION for semisweet and sweet wines that is located in France's BERGERAC area, east of the city of Bordeaux. The wines, made mainly from SÉMILLON with some MUSCADELLE and SAUVIGNON BLANC, rely on BOTRYTIS CINEREA-infected grapes. This infection is important for the grapes to have the concentrated sweetness and flavor necessary for the best DESSERT WINES. If botrytis doesn't set in, some growers—not wanting to risk losing their crop to the late autumn weather—get nervous and pick the grapes before it does. Those who lack tenacity for the waiting game produce LIGHT, semisweet wines of average quality. In good years, however, the wines can assume the character of a SAUTERNES, although usually not with the same richness and finesse. Wines not qualifying for Monbazillac AC status may be downgraded to Côtes de Bergerac AC (*see* BERGERAC) status.

Monbrison, Château [sha-TOH mawn-bree-SAW*N*] A highly regarded CRU BOURGEOIS located in the MARGAUX AC. It produces excellent wines from the low-yielding vines on its 35 acres. The varieties used are approximately 35 percent MERLOT, 30 percent CABERNET SAUVIGNON, 30 percent CABERNET FRANC, and 5 percent PETIT VERDOT. The estate produces around 5,000 to 6,000 cases of red wine, which is capable of AGING for 12 to 15 years. A SECOND LABEL **Cordat** is used for lower-quality wine.

Mönchspfad *see* GEISENHEIM

Mondavi, C.K. *see* CHARLES KRUG WINERY

Robert Mondavi Winery [mawn-DAH-vee] The well-publicized feud between the two Mondavi brothers, Robert and Peter, ended with Robert being forced from the family business (Charles Krug Winery) in 1965. In 1966 he established his own wine business, Robert Mondavi Winery. Over the years, Robert vigorously promoted both his winery and the NAPA VALLEY, and both he and his winery have become some of the valley's most visible elements. Today, the Robert Mondavi Winery, which is located on Highway 29 between Oakville and Rutherford, produces over 650,000 cases of wine each year. Production is led by CHARDONNAY and CABERNET SAUVIGNON, although the winery also produces FUMÉ BLANC (a term coined by Mondavi for DRY, oak-aged SAUVIGNON BLANCS), CHENIN BLANC, MERLOT, PINOT NOIR, RIESLING, and SPARKLING WINES. Mondavi RESERVE wines, which are consistently praised for high quality, are produced from many of the varieties. In 1979 Mondavi started the Woodbridge wine-producing facility near the town of Lodi, just north of Stockton in the CENTRAL VALLEY. Today this facility annually produces over 2 million cases of lower-priced wine. Robert Mondavi Winery owns about 1,500 acres in the Napa Valley and another 500 acres in the SANTA BARBARA area. Mondavi is also in partnership with the Baron Phillipe de Rothschild family (owners of Château MOUTON-ROTHSCHILD) in the Napa Valley winery OPUS ONE. In addition, the winery or family members own or have interests in BYRON VINEYARD & WINERY, Montpellier Vineyards, and VICHON WINERY. In 1993 the winery raised additional funds through a public stock offering. It's now publicly traded, although the family has controlling interest.

Mondeuse [mohn-DEUHZ] Although commonly referrred to as Mondeuse, this red-wine grape is really **Mondeuse Noir**. There's also an obscure white variety called **Mondeuse Blanche**. Mondeuse is primarily grown in France's SAVOIE and Italy's FRIULI-VENEZIA GIULIA region, where it's known as *Refosco*. It can produce high-quality, deeply colored wines with concentrated flavors reminiscent of tart plums and a FINISH that's slightly bitter. In France the MUSCULAR Mondeuse is often lightened slightly by BLENDING in PINOT NOIR and/or GAMAY. Italy has several Mondeuse CLONES, with the one known as *Refosco del Peduncolo Rosso* considered superior to the *Refosco Nostrano*. Small amounts of Mondeuse are grown in Argentina, Australia, and California (where its called *Refosco*). Other names for Mondeuse Noire include *Grosse Syrah, Molette Noire, Savoyance,* and *Terrano*.

Mondot   *see* TROPLONG-MONDOT, CHÂTEAU

Monestel   *see* CARIGNAN

monopole [maw-naw-PAWL] French for "monopoly," this word on a French wine label refers to a proprietary name that's trademarked or owned exclusively by the producer.

Mont de Milieu   *see* CHABLIS

Montagne de Reims *see* CHAMPAGNE

Montagne-Saint-Émilion **AC** [mawn-TAHN-yuh sa*n* tay-mee-LYAW*N*] APPELLATION that is considered a satellite of and is located northeast of the better-known SAINT-ÉMILION AC in the eastern part of France's BORDEAUX region. As in Saint-Émilion and neighboring POM-EROL, MERLOT is the dominant grape. It's usually blended with CABERNET FRANC, CABERNET SAUVIGNON, and MALBEC. Montagne-Saint-Émilion AC wines are generally quite good, with the top ones compared to better Saint-Émilion wines.

Montagny AC [maw*n*-tah-NYEE] One of the five villages in the CÔTE CHALONNAISE in France's BURGUNDY region that has an individual APPELLATION. It produces only white wines from CHARDONNAY. Unlike the rest of Burgundy, where only specific vineyards are designated PREMIER CRU, Montagny AC allows any wine with a minimum of 11½ percent ALCOHOL to be labeled premier cru.

Montalbano *see* CHIANTI DOCG

Montalcino *see* BRUNELLO DI MONTALCINO DOCG; ROSSO DI MONTALCINO DOC

Montecarlo DOC [mawn-teh-KA*R*-loh] A DOC zone surrounding the hilltop town of Montecarlo, west of Florence in the northwest part of Italy's TUSCANY region. Montecarlo DOC makes only a BIANCO and a ROSSO, the former with the best reputation. The white wine uses mainly TREBBIANO, but a host of other grapes are allowed—Pinot Bianco (PINOT BLANC), Pinot Grigio (PINOT GRIS), ROUSSANE, Sauvignon (SAUVIGNON BLANC), SÉMILLON, and VERMENTINO. The red wine uses from 50 to 75 percent SANGIOVESE, plus CANAIOLO, Cilegiolo, Colorino, MALVASIA, and SYRAH.

Montecompatri-Colonna **DOC** [mawn-teh-kawm-PAH-tree koh-LOHN-uh] DOC that encompasses vineyards surrounding the villages of Montecompatri and Colonna and that is located in the CASTELLI ROMANI area southeast of Rome in Italy's LATIUM region. The DRY white wine is made from MALVASI, TREBBIANO, Bonvino, and Bellone. Montecompatri-Colonna DOC wines are very similiar to those from its better-known neighbor FRASCATI DOC. An AMABILE version is also allowed. Labels may contain both village names or either one individually.

Montée de Tonnerre *see* CHABLIS

Montefalco DOC [mawn-teh-FAHL-koh] A small hilltop town lo-cated southeast of Perugia in Italy's UMBRIA region. The DOC zone cov-ers the vineyards on the slopes around Montefalco, plus those of several neighboring villages. Montefalco makes a good-quality, full-flavored ROSSO out of SANGIOVESE, TREBBIANO, and Sagrantino plus small amounts of BARBERA, Ciliegiolo, MERLOT, MALVASIA, and MONTEPULCIANO. However, it's the *Sagrantino di Montefalco* wines—made in both DRY and PASSITO versions from Sagrantino grapes—that are creating this area's reputation. These wines are RICH and full-bodied (*see* BODY) with adequate TANNINS to let them AGE for a while. In recognition of its high-quality wines, the Sagrantino di Montefalco zone was upgraded to DOCG status in the mid-1990s.

Montefiascone *see* EST! EST!! EST!!! DI MONTEFIASCONE DOC

Montepulciano [mohn-teh-pool-CHAH-noh; mawn-teh-pool-CHAH-naw] 1. A red-wine grape widely cultivated throughout Italy, with the most concentrated plantings in the southeastern regions from the MARCHES down to APULIA. Some argue that Montepulciano orginated in the ABRUZZI region, with which it's still most closely associated, mainly because of the DOC wines of MONTEPULCIANO D'ABRUSSO. This grape variety is capable of creating deeply colored, rich red wines with blackberry fruit flavors and SPICY, PEPPERY qualities. Because of its moderate ACID levels, Montepulciano generally produces wines that are smooth and MELLOW, but sometimes TANNIC enough to be AGED. This variety is also made into a cherry-pink ROSÉ called CERASUOLO. Other red wines based on Montepulciano grapes (but usually blended with local grapes) include the ROSSO CONERO DOC wines from the Marches region and the DOC wines of CERVETERI and VELLETRI from the LATIUM region. Montepulciano is also known as *Cordisco, Morellone, Primaticcio,* and *Uva Abruzzi.* 2. A town in western Italy's TUSCANY region that lends its name to VINO NOBILE DI MONTEPULCIANO, a wine based on the SANGIOVESE, not the Montepulciano, grape.

Montepulciano d'Abruzzo DOC [mawn-teh-pool-CHAH-noh dah-BROOD-dzoh] DOC that is located in central Italy's ABRUZZI region and that isn't related to the VINO NOBILE DI MONTEPULCIANO DOCG, which is named after a town in the TUSCANY region. Montepulciano d'Abruzzo is named after the grape variety MONTEPULCIANO, which must make up at least 85 percent of this DOC's wine (the rest is SANGIOVESE). Montepulciano d'Abruzzo DOC wines are generally ordinary, although several producers who keep YIELDS low take care to produce good, full-bodied (*see* BODY) wines capable of long AGING. Wines with "VECCHIO" on the label have been AGED for a minimum of 2 years. The same grapes go into a CERASUOLO (dry ROSATO), which is considered quite good.

Monterey County; Monterey AVA Located on the California coast south of San Francisco. Most of the growing area is centered in the 84-mile long Salinas Valley which, though inland, is subject to cooling breezes off Monterey Bay and the Pacific Ocean. The climate, which is very cool at the northern end of the valley, is ranked a Region I growing area (*see* CLIMATE REGIONS OF CALIFORNIA). Heading south, it gets warmer, changing to a Region II, then a Region III, and finally a Region IV around San Lucas at the valley's southern end. CHARDONNAY is by far the most widely planted variety in Monterey County. CABERNET SAUVIGNON is second, followed by RIESLING (over half of California's Riesling is grown here), CHENIN BLANC, ZINFANDEL, PINOT NOIR, SAUVIGNON BLANC, PINOT BLANC (also over half of California's total crop), and others. The **Monterey AVA** covers all but a few hundred acres of the county's total wine-grape acreage. Other Monterey County APPELLATIONS are ARROYO SECO, CARMEL VALLEY, CHALONE, and SAN LUCAS.

Monterey Riesling *see* SYLVANER

Monterosso Val d'Arda *see* COLLI PIACENTINI

Monthélie AC [mawn-tay-LEE] Small APPELLATION that surrounds the tiny, picturesque village of Monthélie, located in the CÔTE DE BEAUNE district of France's BURGUNDY region. It's situated on a hill just north of MEURSAULT and southwest of VOLNAY. The wines, predominantly red and made from PINOT NOIR, used to be sold under the better-known Volnay AC label. They're similar in style to the Volnay wines but not as well known, which means that they're not as expensive and therefore a good value. The best wines usually come from the two PREMIER CRU vineyards closest to Volnay, **Les Champs Fulliot** and **Sur la Velle**. Small amounts of CHARDONNAY-based white wines are also produced.

Monticello Cellars [mawn-tih-CHEHL-oh] In the early 1970s real estate-insurance executive Jay Corley bought this 125-acre NAPA VALLEY site, which is just north of the city of Napa, California. He proceeded to plant vines and subsequently sold the grapes for a number of years. In 1980 Corley ventured into winemaking, completing the winery building in 1982. His admiration for Thomas Jefferson led Corley to name his wine estate after Jefferson's home, and the Monticello Cellars visitor's center and administrative offices are in a building modeled after this famous residence. Today Monticello Cellars annually produces between 25,000 and 30,000 cases of wine. About half the production is CABERNET SAUVIGNON, which is offered as

Jefferson Cuvée, a SOFTER style, and Corley Reserve, a longer AGING version. CHARDONNAY is also produced in Jefferson Cuvée and Corley Reserve bottlings. The RESERVE wines are both well regarded. In addition, Monticello Cellars produced GEWÜRZTRAMINER, PINOT NOIR, and SAUVIGNON BLANC. Corely is also active in running **Domaine Montreaux**, a SPARKLING WINE producer located nearby, and **Llords & Elwood**, a FORTIFIED wine producer now making a moderately priced line of VARIETAL WINES.

Montillia-Moriles DO [mawn-TEE-lyah maw-REE-lehs] DO area located northeast of JEREZ in southern Spain. The designated area includes vineyards around the town of Montillia and the village of Moriles. The dominant grape is the PEDRO XIMÉNEZ, which develops best when grown in the white chalky soil that's similiar to Jerez's better vineyard areas. The Montillia-Moriles DO produces wines similiar to the sherry wines made in Jerez. Until the 1960s large amounts of BULK WINE were shipped from Montillia and Moriles to Jerez to be used for blending. Today, the sherrylike wines are FERMENTED in stainless steel tanks, although some of the large earthenware vessels called *tinjas* are still used. The wines are then matured in a SOLERA system like that used in sherrymaking. Unlike sherry, not all Montillia-Moriles wines need to be FORTIFIED. That's because the high natural sugar levels of the grapes can usually produce wines with 15 percent or more ALCOHOL. Although there are some excellent wines from this DO, most of what's available are blends of *finos* and *olerosos* (*see* SHERRY) with sweet concentrated MUST added. Due to legal hassles with the Jerez producers, the terms *fino, oloroso,* and *amontillado* couldn't be used by Montilla-Moriles for a period of time (even though *amontillado* means "made in the style of Montilla"). Many of the wines are simply labeled Dry, Medium, Cream, or Sweet. Today, *fino* wines with over 15 percent alcohol and *oloroso* and *amontillado* wines with over 16 percent can use these terms on the labels.

Montlouis AC [mawn-LWEE] APPELLATION that surrounds the village of Montlouis, which is located in the TOURAINE area of France's LOIRE region, directly across the Loire River from VOUVRAY. The wines are similar to those from Vouvray, although usually not quite as rich. CHENIN BLANC is the only grape allowed in the wines of this AC. The wines can range from DRY to sweet, and be STILL, PÉTILLANT, or SPARKLING (MOUSSEUX).

Montmains *see* CHABLIS

Montonec *see* PARELLADA

Montpeyroux *see* CÔTEAUX DU LANGUEDOC

Montrachet AC (Le Montrachet) [luh mawn-rah-SHAY] Famous GRAND CRU vineyard that produces one of the most sought after and expensive white wines in the world. The 20 acres of CHARDONNAY grapes are situated on a slope in the CÔTE D'BEAUNE district in France's BURGUNDY region. Half the acreage is in the village of PULIGNY-MONTRACHET, the other half in CHASSAGNE-MONTRACHET. The vineyard is so famous that both villages added its name to their own, as did several adjacent *grand cru* vineyards—BÂTARD-MONTRACHET, BIEN-VENUES-BÂTARD-MONTRACHET, CHEVALIER-MONTRACHET, and CRIOTS-BÂTARD-MONTRACHET. There are various theories on why this particular vineyard is so special including the angle of the slope, the chalky soil on top of a bed of limestone, the excellent drainage, the just-right, maximum sun exposure, or the combination of all these. The result is a RICH, luscious wine that, though DRY, seems to be full of sweet, HONEYED fruit. All these qualities produce another result—Montrachet wines are among the most expensive white wines in the world. These wonderful wines are generally best when aged for 10 years or longer.

Montravel [mawn-rah-VEHL] Located on the west side of the BERGERAC area close to France's BORDEAUX region, Montravel produces white wines from SÉMILLON, SAUVIGNON BLANC, and MUSCADELLE. Wines labeled **Montravel AC** are almost DRY, whereas those designated **Côtes de Montravel AC** or **Haut-Montravel AC** are semisweet to sweet. The wines are not outstanding, and, because they don't fall into today's popular catagories of fully dry or richly sweet, they're declining in popularity.

Montrose, Château [sha-TOH mawn-ROHZ] A DEUXIÈME CRU (second-growth) CHÂTEAU located in the SAINT-ESTÈPHE AC in the MÉDOC district of BORDEAUX. Historically, Château Montrose is known for its FIRM, TANNIC, and powerfully flavored wines that can take 10 to 12 years to SOFTEN and can AGE for 30 to 35 years. However, in the 1980s several VINTAGES were of a lighter style, suggesting a change of winemaking philosophy. There are about 168 acres planted with around 65 percent CABERNET SAUVIGNON, 25 percent MERLOT, and 10 percent CABERNET FRANC. The château averages about 25,000 cases of high-quality red wine each year. The SECOND LABEL is called **La Dame de Montrose**.

Les Monts Luisants *see* MOREY-SAINT-DENIS

Morastel *see* MONASTRELL

Morellino di Scansano DOC [maw-reh-LEE-noh dee skahn-SAH-noh] DOC zone located in the southern portion of Italy's TUSCANY region southeast of Grosseto. It encompasses the vineyards around the hilltop town of Scansano. The wine, which is developing a good reputation among Sangiovese fans, is made from at least 85 percent SANGIOVESE grapes. This DOC is one of only a few that may use 100 percent of this grape. "Riserva" on the label means that the wine's been AGED for 2 years, one of which must be in wooden barrels.

Morellone *see* MONTEPULCIANO

Morey-Saint-Denis [maw-*r*ay sa*n* duh-NEE] The vineyards surrounding the small village of Morey-Saint-Denis include all or part of five GRAND CRU vineyards and twenty PREMIER CRU vineyards. Even so, this village is not as well known as its neighboring villages, GEVRY-CHAMBERTIN and CHAMBOLLE-MUSIGNY, in the CÔTE DE NUITS area of France's BURGUNDY region. This is largely because, until the 1950s, most wines were sold under the labels of these two neighboring villages. The grands crus located in Morey-Saint-Denis are BONNES-MARES, CLOS DE LA ROCHE, CLOS DE TART, CLOS DES LAMBRAYS, and CLOS SAINT-DENIS. The village of Morey added the name of this last grand cru to its own in 1927. The better premier cru vineyards include **Clos des Ormes**, **Les Monts Luisants**, **Les Millandes**, and **La Bussière**. Because of the high number of quality producers, the village wines (labeled **Morey-Saint-Denis AC**) can generally be relied on to be of very high quality. Almost all the Morey-Saint-Denis wines are red and made from PINOT NOIR, although a few hundred cases of white wine are produced each year.

Morgan Winery Winery that was founded on a part-time basis by winemaker Dan Lee in 1982 and expanded into a full-time endeavor in 1986. Initially just a CHARDONNAY producer (both regular and RESERVE bottlings), Morgan Winery gradually expanded to include SAUVIGNON BLANC, CABERNET SAUVIGNON, and PINOT NOIR. Although the Chardonnay wines seem to attract most of the attention, the other three VARIETAL WINES are also highly regarded. The winery is located in a warehouse in the town of Salinas in MONTEREY COUNTY, California. Grapes are purchased from various growers to meet the annual production of 20,000 to 25,000 cases. **Del Mar** is Morgan Winery's SECOND LABEL.

Morgeot *see* CHASSAGNE-MONTRACHET AC

Morgon AC [maw*r*-GAW*N*] One of the best of the ten CRUS in France's BEAUJOLAIS region. These GAMAY-based wines are full-bodied and CONCENTRATED. They have a more intense color but less fruitiness than wines from other crus. Their flavors are reminiscent of cherries and plums, as opposed to the lighter, fresher, strawberry nuances of the other cru wines. Unlike most Beaujolais wines, those from Morgon AC are generally bottled later. They're better after a little BOTTLE AGING and do well for 2 to 5 years. The best wines come from the slopes of Mont du Py, whereas those from the flatlands have a much lighter style

Morio-Muskat [MOH-ree-oh MEWS-kat] German white-wine grape—a CROSS of SYLVANER and Weissburgunder (PINOT BLANC)—that was created by Peter Morio. Morio-Muskat produces such exotically perfumed wines that only small amounts are needed to enrich the flavor and aroma of a blander wine. It's grown mostly in Germany's RHEINPFALZ and RHEINHESSEN regions and is used mainly in the production of less-expensive wines.

Morocco [muh-RAHK-oh] The population of this North African country is predominately Muslim, a religion that prohibits the consumption of alcoholic beverages. It wasn't until the French took control and French settlers began arriving in the late 1920s and early 1930s that vineyards were planted in large numbers. As a French protectorate, Morocco produced substantial quantities of wine. When Morocco regained its independence in 1956, however, wine production began to decline. Although the wines don't compare with the quality of the French wines, Morocco has a quality system, *appellation d'origine garantie*, that is similiar to the French AC system. Most Moroccan wines are red, and are usually ROUGH and ALCOHOLIC. They're generally exported in bulk to be used as BLENDING WINES by European countries. Morocco's main grape varieties are ALICANTE BOUSHET, CARIGNAN, CINSAUT, and GRENACHE. MOURVÈDRE and SYRAH are grown in small quantites for higher-quality wines. Some ROSÉ wines and a small amount of white wine are also made. The main growing areas are near the coastal cities of Casablanca and Rabat and inland around Meknès and Fes at the base of the Atlas Mountains.

Morrastal *see* MONASTRELL; GRACIANO

Mortágua *see* TOURIGA NACIONAL

Moscadello di Montalcino DOC [moss-kah-DELL-oh dee mawn-tahl-TCHEE-noh] DOC zone that is in the southern portion of Italy's TUSCANY region and is exactly the same zone as that for the BRUNELLO DI MONTALCINO DOCG. Moscadello di Montalcino DOC produces a sweet white wine, made mainly from Moscato Bianco (MUSCAT), which can be STILL or FRIZZANTE. There's also a LIQUOROSO, which is a FORTIFIED version. There was a similiar wine made in the Middle Ages, but the grape used is thought to have been the Moscadelletto, a Muscat mutant not quite the same as today's variety.

Moscatel *see* MUSCAT

Moscatel de Málaga *see* MUSCAT

Moscatel de Setúbal DOC [maws-kah-TEHL deh sih-TOO-bawl] Area that is located south of Lisbon on the Setúbal peninsula and that has had RD (now called DOC) status since 1907. Muscat of Alexandria (MUSCAT) grapes are used for the area's strong, FORTIFIED wines, which are produced by halting FERMENTATION partway through the process by adding grape alcohol. The fortified wine then goes through a period of MACERATION where it's left in contact with the skins for 5 or 6 months. The wines are then AGED for 5 or 6 years in large vats and small barrels. The result is a deep golden colored, grapey-flavored, high-ALCOHOL wine capable of aging for many years.

Moscatel Gordo *see* MUSCAT

Moscatello *see* ALEATICO

Moscatel Rosé *see* MUSCAT

Moscato Bianco *see* MUSCAT

Moscato d'Asti DOCG *see* ASTI SPUMANTE DOCG

Moscato di Amburgo *see* MUSCAT

Moscato di Pantelleria DOC; Moscato Passito di Pantelleria [maws-KAH-toh dee pahn-tehl-LEH-ryah] Two DOCs that are located on the small Italian island of Pantelleria, which is southwest of Sicily, close to North Africa. They produce sweet wines of varying styles—PASSITO and non-passito, some are FORTIFIED and some are SPARKLING. The variety used is the Zibibbo, one of the muscat grapes. The best Moscato di Pantelleria wines make lusciously sweet dessert wines.

Moscato Giallo *see* MUSCAT

Moscato Rosa *see* MUSCAT

Mosel; Moselle [MOH-zuhl; moh-ZELL] A famous river that winds through one of Germany's important ANBAUGEBIETE (quality wine regions), MOSEL-SAAR-RUWER. The river actually starts in eastern France's Vosges mountains, flows along the Luxembourg border into western Germany, and finally joins the Rhine River in western Germany at the city of Koblenz. There are vineyards along the river in France and Luxembourg, but wines from the German vineyards are the most widely recognized. *Mosel* is the German spelling; *Moselle* is the English and French spelling.

Mosel-Saar-Ruwer [MOH-zuhl sahr ROO-vay*r*] The official all-encompassing name of the German ANBAUGEBIET (quality-wine region) that encompasses the vineyards surrounding the Mosel River and its two tributaries, the Saar and the Ruwer. The region stretches from the French border to the point where the Mosel joins with the Rhine. Internationally, this Anbaugebiete is the best known of the thirteen German regions. RIESLING grapes cover over 50 percent of the planted acreage, followed by MÜLLER-THURGAU and ELBLING. Many of the vineyards are on steep, difficult, slate-based terrain, which produces excellent, STEELY Riesling wines, the best of which are capable of AGING for many years. The region consists of 4 BEREICHE—ZELL/MOSEL, BERNKASTEL, SAAR-RUWER, and **Obermosel**—19 GROSSLAGEN, and 525 EINZELLAGEN. The Zell/Mosel is the northernmost part of this Anbaugebiet. Bernkastel, the most prolific of the Bereiche, covers the midsection of the Mosel River called the MITTELMOSEL. Saar-Ruwer covers the two tributaries, and Obermosel, which means "Upper Mosel," is the farthest south. Well-known Grosslagen include Bernkasteler Badstube, Bernkasteler Kurfustlay, Kröver Nacktarsch, Michelsberg, Piesporter, Wiltinger Scharzberg, and Zeller Schwarze Katz.

Moseltaler [MOH-zuhl-TAH-luh*r*] Created in 1986, Moseltaler is a new category for wines produced in Germany's MOSEL-SAAR-RUWER region. These wines are similar to the LIEBFRAUMILCH wines produced along the Rhine. Moseltaler must be made from ELBLING, KERN, MÜLLER-THURGAU, or RIESLING grapes, contain between 1.5 and 3 percent RESIDUAL SUGAR and a minimum of 0.7 percent total acidity (*see* ACIDS), and be of QUALITÄTSWEIN BESTIMMTER ANBAUGEBIET (QbA) quality.

mosto [MAWSH-toh] Italian term for "MUST" or "grape juice."

Moulin-à-Vent AC [moo-la*n*-nah-VAH*N*] APPELLATION that gets its name from the windmill (moulin-à-vent) that sits in the area's vineyards. Moulin-à-Vent is considered by many as the best of the ten CRUS in France's BEAUJOLAIS region and is sometimes called the King of Beaujolais wines. The full-bodied (*see* BODY), concentrated wines—some of Beaujolais' most expensive—are made from GAMAY and have abundant TANNINS. Unlike the common perception of Beaujolais wines, these should not be drunk young but rather AGED—some can last ten years or more. Moulin-à-Vent AC wines are so uncharacteristic of the region that many wine aficionados compare them to the lighter style, PINOT NOIR-based red Burgundies from the CÔTE D'OR.

Moulin de Duhart *see* DUHART-MILON-ROTHSCHILD, CHÂTEAU

Moulin des Carruades *see* LAFITE-ROTHSCHILD, CHÂTEAU

Moulin-Riche   *see* LÉOVILLE-POYFERRÉ

Moulis AC [moo-LEE] The smallest of the village APPELLATIONS in the HAUT-MÉDOC area. Its center is the village of Moulis, which is located a few miles northwest of the Margaux AC. None of the Moulis AC CHÂTEAUS were included in the CLASSIFICATION OF 1855, which helps explain why it's not as well known as other village appellations such as MARGAUX, PAUILLAC, SAINT-ESTÈPHE, and SAINT-JULIEN. There are some excellent red wines (made with the BORDEAUX varieties) produced in the Moulis AC, however, and they've proven to be some of the longest lived. The best wines usually come from Château CHASSE-SPLEEN, followed by those from Châteaus Gressier Grand-Poujeaux, MAUCAILLOU, and POUJEAUX.

Mount Barker   *see* LOWER GREAT SOUTHERN REGION

Mount Eden Vineyards The estate vineyards for this winery started out as part of Martin Ray Vineyards in the early 1940s. A struggle between Martin Ray and his investors resulted in this hilltop property going to the investors and the formation of Mount Eden Vineyards in 1972. The winery and vineyards are located high in the SANTA CRUZ MOUNTAINS, overlooking the Santa Clara Valley. The estate-grown grapes produce tiny quantities of CHARDONNAY (800 cases), CABERNET SAUVIGNON (600 cases each of Lathweisen Ridge and Estate), and PINOT NOIR (200 cases). Chardonnay grapes purchased from the MacGregor Vineyard in the EDNA VALLEY AVA add another 4,000 cases of wine annually. Although the wines have changed style over the years, they're customarily highly regarded. In fact, the estate-bottled wines are in such demand that they're generally allocated.

Mount Veeder AVA APPELLATION that encompasses Mount Veeder, which is west of the town of Yountville and is part of the Mayacamas Mountains that divide NAPA VALLEY and SONOMA VALLEY. The climate in this area differs from the floor of the Napa Valley because of the fog on the valley floor, the thermal layers created, and the altitude of the vineyards. The result is more sunshine but generally cooler daytime temperatures and warmer nighttime conditions. Mount Veeder AVA straddles the Region I/Region II growing areas (*see* CLIMATE REGIONS OF CALIFORNIA), depending on the atmospheric conditions of a particular year. CABERNET SAUVIGNON and CHARDONNAY do well and are widely planted, along with small amounts of ZINFANDEL, SAUVIGNON BLANC, MERLOT, SYRAH, and VIOGNIER. Top wineries include Château Potelle, HESS COLLECTION, MAYACAMAS, MOUNT VEEDER, and Sky.

Mount Veeder Winery Located on Mount Veeder in the western hills of the NAPA VALLEY, this winery was established in 1972 by Mike and Arlene Berstein. It was sold to the Matheson family in 1982 and to its current owner, FRANCISCAN VINEYARDS, in 1989. The vineyards, which have doubled to about 40 acres, are planted mainly with red varieties—CABERNET FRANC, CABERNET SAUVIGNON, MALBEC, MERLOT, and PETIT VERDOT—plus a small amount of CHARDONNAY. The winery produces Chardonnay, Cabernet Sauvignon, and a red MERITAGE wine. Annual case production is between 10,000 and 12,000 and is headed toward a peak of about 15,000.

Les Mourottes *see* CORTON; CORTON-CHARLEMAGNE

Mourvèdre [moor-VEH-druh] Though best known today for its presence in southern France, this red-wine grape is thought to have originated in Spain's CATALONIA region. Mourvèdre produces good-quality, garnet-colored wines with SPICY, PEPPERY characteristics. They can, however, be a bit TANNIC and HARD and are at their best when blended with other grape varieties. Mourvèdre is the principal component in the BANDOL red and ROSÉ wines of France's PROVENCE region. In other red wines—such as those from CÔTES DU RHÔNE, CHÂTEAUNEUF-DE-PAPE, and CÔTES DE PROVENCE—Mourvèdre is used to improve color and STRUCTURE. Although there's recently been renewed interest in California, only small amounts of this variety are currently grown in California and Australia; it's known in both places as *Mataro*. Mourvèdre is sometimes called *Balzac* or *Esparte*.

mousse [MOOSS] A French term meaning "froth" or "foam," which, when applied to wine, refers to the foam that forms on the surface of SPARKLING WINE when it's first poured. Mousse is analogous to the term "head," which is the foam on a freshly poured glass of beer.

mousseux [moo-SEUHR; moo-SUR] A French term that means "sparkling" or "frothy." It's used to refer to all SPARKLING WINES except those produced in the CHAMPAGNE region, which are the only ones allowed to be called *champagne*. Sometimes referred to as *vins mousseux*, these sparkling wines are produced all over France, and there are some twenty that have achieved AC status. The ACs of BLANQUETTE DE LIMOUX, CLAIRETTE DE DIE TRADITION, CRÉMANT D'ALSACE, CRÉMANT DE BOURGOGNE, CREMANT DE LOIRE, GAILLAC, MONTLOUIS, SEYSSEL, and VOUVRAY all produce good vins mousseux. Most of these sparkling wines are made by MÉTHODE CHAMPENOISE, although some are still made by *méthode rurale* (RURAL METHOD).

mousy; mousey [MOW-see] A winetasting term describing an ACETIC, though flat smell and flavor caused by bacterial contamination.

mouth-filling A winetasting term used to describe wines that seem to fill the mouth with textural tactile impressions. Such wines are generally BIG, RICH, and CHEWY, with intense flavors and a high ALCOHOL and GLYCEROL content.

Mouton-Baronne-Philippe, Château *see* MOUTON D'AR-MAILHACQ, CHÂTEAU

Mouton-Cadet [moo-TAW*N* kah-DAY] The brand name of one of the top-selling BORDEAUX wines. It was created by Baron Philippe de Rothschild in the 1930s when a series of poor vintages produced some lower-quality wines that he didn't want sold under his CHÂTEAU MOUTON-ROTHSCHILD label. Mouton-Cadet isn't, as some people think, a SECOND LABEL of Château Mouton-Rothschild. In fact, the grapes might not necessarily come from Château Mouton-Rothschild but rather from all over Bordeaux, as evidenced by the use of the term "Bordeaux AC" on the label. Mouton-Cadet has become immensely popular, although some feel the quality is not as high as it once was.

Mouton d'Armailhacq, Château [sha-TOH moo-TAW*N* dah*r*-mah-YAK] A CINQUIÈME CRU (fifth growth) purchased by Baron Philippe de Rothschild in 1933. The name was changed from Mouton d'Armailhacq to **Château Mouton-Baron-Philippe** in 1956 and changed again in 1975 to **Château Mouton-Baronne-Philippe**, in honor of the Baron's late wife. The CHÂTEAU's name reverted back to Mouton d'Armailhacq with the 1989 VINTAGE. The property consists of 125 acres and adjoins the Baron's most famous property, Château MOUTON-ROTHSCHILD. At one time both châteaus were part of the same estate. Mouton d'Armailhacq produces around 15,000 to 18,000 cases of good-quality red wine. The blend of grapes used is approximately 70 percent CABERNET SAUVIGNON, 20 percent MERLOT, and 10 percent CABERNET FRANC. The wines are lighter than those from either Mouton-Rothschild or the Baron's third property Château CLERC-MILON and are capable of AGING for up to 12 to 14 years.

Mouton-Rothschild, Château [sha-TOH moo-TAW*N* rawt-SHEELD (rawth-CHILD)] Château Mouton-Rothschild has been owned by the Barons de Rothschild for over 100 years. It was the tireless effort of Baron Philippe de Rothschild that resulted in the château's historical upgrade to PREMIER CRU (first-growth) status in 1973. The Baron began his odyssey to modify the classification in the early 1920s, when he took over the château's administration and eventual ownership.

This landmark upgrade (the only change ever made to the famous CLASSIFICATION OF 1855) made Château Mouton-Rothschild one of only four premiers crus (the others being LAFITE-ROTHSCHILD, LATOUR, and MARGAUX) in the MÉDOC district. (The premier cru, Château HAUT-BRION, is in GRAVES.) Prior to the original classification, the château's wine labels declared, *Premier ne puis, Second ne daigne, Mouton suis* ("First I cannot be, Second I do not deign to be, I am Mouton"). After the upgrade, the motto was changed to *Premier je suis, second je fus, Mouton ne change* ("First I am, second I was, Mouton does not change"). The Mouton-Rothschild estate includes about 185 acres planted with around 85 percent CABERNET SAUVIGNON, 8 percent MERLOT, and 7 percent CABERNET FRANC. There are 20,000 to 30,000 cases of red wine produced annually. These wines are generally BIG and full-bodied (*see* BODY) and the best VINTAGES can AGE 40 to 50 years or more. In addition to producing marvelous wines, Baron Philippe, who died in 1988, was immensely succesful at marketing. In 1945, he began a series of artistic labels featuring a different world-renowned artist (such as Chagall, Miro, Picasso, and Warhol) each year. The family of Baron Philippe de Rothschild also owns Châteaus MOUTON D'ARMAILHACQ and CLERC-MILON, as well as the proprietary brand MOUTON-CADET.

Mudgee A small Australian wine-producing area located about 160 miles northwest of Sydney and 100 miles west of the better-known HUNTER VALLEY region. CHARDONNAY and CABERNET SAUVIGNON do well in the area and are the most widely planted varieties. SÉMILLON, RIESLING, Shiraz (SYRAH), and PINOT NOIR are also grown here. Area producers include Amberton, Botobolar, Craigmoor, Huntington Estate, Miramar, and Montrose.

muffa nobile [MOOF-fah NAW-bee-lay] Italian for "noble mold," which in the wine world refers to BOTRYTIS CINEREA, the beneficial mold that contributes to some of the world's great DESSERT WINES.

mulled wine Red or white wine that's heated with various citrus fruits and spices such as cinnamon, cloves, allspice, or nutmeg. Mulled wine is generally sweetened with sugar and often FORTIFIED with a spirit, usually BRANDY. Some recipes call for stirring the hot wine mixture into beaten eggs, which gives the beverage flavor and body.

Müller-Burggraef *see* THANISCH, WWE, DR. H

Müllerrebe *see* MEUNIER

Müller-Thurgau [MEW-luhr TOOR-gow; MOO-lehr TOOR-gow] Even though some ENOLOGISTS believe this grape is a CROSS of two strains of RIESLING, the Müller-Thurgau grape is widely known to be a Riesling-SYLVANER hybrid. It was named for its breeder, Dr. Hermann Müller-Thurgau, who created it in the late 1800s. Regardless of its beginnings, this white-wine grape is now the most widely cultivated grape in Germany, especially in the regions of BADEN, RHEINHESSEN, and RHEINPFALZ. Although not extensively grown in the United States, this prolific vine is planted in Austria, Switzerland, England, New Zealand, Italy's northern mountain regions, and Hungary (the world's second largest grower after Germany). Müller-Thurgau grapes produce smooth, low-ACID, medium-sweet wines with a hint of MUSCAT character. Unfortunately, because of high YIELDS, these wines generally lack flavor, and most don't age well. The best wines come from Germany's MOSEL region and Italy's ALTO ADIGE. They're made with grapes grown in yield-restricted vineyards, which produce grapes with concentrated flavor. Müller-Thurgau is also a heavy contributor to the flood of inexpensive LIEBFRAUMILCH coming out of Germany. In New Zealand, the wines—often referred to as *Riesling-Sylvaner*—have higher acids and are more flavorful than most German examples. Müller-Thurgau is also known as *Rivaner* and *Rizlingszilvani.*

multivintage *see* VINTAGE

Mumm [MUHM] Located in Reims in France's Champagne region, Mumms is a large CHAMPAGNE house whose majority owner is the Canadian firm Seagrams. It produces between 9 and 10 million bottles annually. Its best-known brand is the non-VINTAGE **Cordon Rouge**; its premium brand is **Réné Lalou**. Another of its top wines is **Crémant de Cramant**, a lightly sparkling wine (*see* CRÉMANT) produced from CHARDONNAY grapes grown in the village of Cramant. Mumm also owns the champagne houses of JOSEPH PERRIER and Heidsieck Monopole. California's Domaine Mumm, now called MUMM NAPA VALLEY, was established to produce SPARKLING WINE in a joint venture with Seagram.

Mumm Napa Valley SPARKLING WINE concern that is a joint venture between MUMM, the French CHAMPAGNE house, and Seagram, the giant Canadian firm that also owns STERLING VINEYARDS. The winery is located just off the Silverado Trail, northeast of the town of Rutherford, California. The first wines were released in 1986 from grapes picked in the 1984 VINTAGE. Earlier vintages were labeled **Domaine Mumm**. Mumm Napa Valley now produces between 65,000 and 75,000 cases of wine each year and is capable of about 150,000. It owns about 50 acres, utilizes about 200 acres owned by Sterling, and still buys grapes from as many as fifty to sixty other growers in areas as far south as the SANTA MARIA AVA. Mumm produces four high-quality, MÉTHODE CHAMPENOISE sparkling wines—Brut Prestige, Vintage Reserve, Blanc de Noirs, and Winery Lake.

Aux Murgers *see* NUITS-SAINT-GEORGES

Murphy-Goode Estate Vineyards Winery located in the ALEXANDER VALLEY AVA, north and slightly east of Healdsburg, California. It was formed by three partners—Tim Murphy, Dale Goode, and Dave Ready. Murphy and Goode are both growers and vineyard managers with acreage in the Alexander Valley. The partners own or control over 300 acres of vineyard land. This winery produced its first wine, a FUMÉ BLANC, from the 1985 VINTAGE. Production has steadily climbed to between 40,000 and 45,000 cases per year. Four additional VARIETAL WINES are now produced—CABERNET SAUVIGNON, CHARDONNAY, MERLOT, and PINOT BLANC.

Murrieta's Wells *see* WENTE BROS.

Musar, Château [sha-TOH moo-SAHR] Unique Lebanese wine estate that has its winery situated about 16 miles north of Beirut and its Bekaa Valley vineyards located about 40 miles south of Beirut. In order to keep producing wine, Château Muscar has endured the trials of the Lebanese civil war, including armored tanks in its vineyards. Established by Gaston Hochar in the 1930s, Château Musar is still owned by the Hochar family. The founder's son, Serge Hochar, was trained in BORDEAUX, and the château's wines are VINIFIED and AGED following traditional Bordeaux methods. The winery uses CABERNET SAUVIGNON, CINSAUT, and SYRAH grapes to produce highly regarded red wines that are long-lived and very Bordeaux-like. The white wines, made from CHARDONNAY, SAUVIGNON BLANC, and MUSCAT, do not have the same fine reputation.

Muscadelle [mus-kuh-DEHL] A highly productive white-wine grape grown in France's BORDEAUX region, mostly in sweet wine-producing areas such as BARSAC, SAUTERNES, and PREMIERES CÔTES DE BORDEAUX. Muscadelle has an intense, perfumy character and is used in small quantities to add bouquet to sweet wines, usually those based on SÉMILLON and/or SAUVIGNON BLANC grapes. Because of Muscadelle's intensity, no more than 5 percent is added to the higher-quality wines of Barsac and Sauternes. A larger percentage often finds its way into the wines of Premieres Côtes de Bordeaux. Some Muscadelle is grown in Australia, where it's known as *Tokay* and often used in DESSERT WINES called *liqueur Tokays*. Small amounts of it are grown in California, where it's known as *Sauvignon Vert*; it was long mistakenly thought to be a Sauvignon Blanc relative. Muscadelle is also called *Musquette, Muscadet Doux,* and *Raisinotte.*

Muscadet [meuhs-kah-DAY] A popular LIGHT, DRY wine produced in western portion of France's LOIRE region. Unlike most other wines in France, the name is not taken from a town or geographic area but rather from a grape known locally as Muscadet (although its proper name is MELON DE BOURGOGNE). The area where Muscadet is produced is centered around Nantes, not far from where the Loire River empties into the Atlantic Ocean. There are three APPELLATIONS that produce these wines—Muscadet AC, Muscadet de Sèvre-et-Maine AC, and Muscadet des Côteaux de la Loire AC. The **Muscadet AC** produces the lowest-quality wines, which are usually inexpensive and ordinary. One unusual requirement of this appellation is that the ALCOHOL level has a *maximum* (rather than minimum) strength of 12.3 percent. The best Muscadet wines come from **Muscadet de Sèvre-et-Maine AC**, an area southeast of Nantes that produces 85 percent of the Muscadet wines. Because of the large amount produced, some of these wines are also fairly ordinary. Wines labeled *mise en bouteille sur lie,* meaning they're bottled directly off their LEES without filtering, are considered best. This process produces more flavorful wines that are SOFT, CREAMY and have citrus nuances. Only a small amount of wine is produced in the third appellation, **Muscadet des Côteaux de la Loire AC**, which is located northeast of Nantes. Most Muscadet should be drunk young although the SUR LIE versions can sometimes AGE for several years.

Muscadet Doux *see* MUSCADELLE

Muscadine [MUHS-kuh-dihn] Found in the southeastern United States, the Muscadine grape family has at least eleven important varieties. The best-known species of this family is VITIS ROTUNDIFOLIA, a name attributed to the vines' round leaves. The thick-skinned Muscadine grapes have a strong, musky flavor and can range in color from bronze to deep purple. Even though these native American grapes are primarily grown for table grapes, they're also used to make limited quantities of wine. In fact, some of the very first American wines were made from Muscadine grapes. One variety—the bronze-colored SCUPPERNONG—is used to make sweet wines that are still popular in some parts of the South.

Muscat [MUHS-kat; MUHS-kuht] Grape family used for winemaking, table grapes, and raisins. It is comprised of hundreds of varieties that range in color from white to almost black. Muscat grapes are grown in temperate climates around the world in Italy, France, Greece, Spain, Australia, and California. This category of grapes has existed for centuries and is one of the oldest known to man. Muscat wines are noted for their musky, fresh-grape flavors and range from fine, light whites (often SPARKLING) to sweet, dark versions (often FORTIFIED). **Muscat Blanc à Petits Grains** ("white Muscat with little berries") is generally regarded as the best of the Muscat grape family. It varies in color from white to pink to dark reddish-brown. This grape has a limited YIELD, which produces concentrated flavors. It's responsible for the lovely, sweet, fortified MUSCAT DE BEAUMES-DE-VENISE wines from the southern RHÔNE. It also makes the dark, fortified liqueur wines of Australia, where their Muscat Blanc à Petits Grains is called *Brown Muscat* or *Frontignan*. In the northern Rhône, this grape is blended with CLAIRETTE to produce the CLAIRETTE DE DIE wines. In Italy it forms the basis for the sparkling ASTI SPUMANTE wines. In California Muscat Blanc à Petits Grains is called *Muscat Blanc, Muscat Canelli,* or *Muscat Frontignan. Moscato Giallo* (or *Goldmuskateller*) and *Moscato Rosa* (or *Rosenmuskateller*) are thought to be colored versions of Muscat Blanc à Petits Grains. Although also VINIFIED dry, these colored grapes are best known for making the fragrant sweet wines from Italy's ALTO ADIGE region. Regardless of where Muscat grapes are grown or what types of wines they're used to produce, the PERFUMY, MUSKY, ripe-grape characteristics persist. Muscat Blanc à Petits Grains has many names around the world including *Moscato Bianco, Muscat de Frontignan, Muscat d'Alsace, Muskateller, Muscatel de Grano Menudo,* and *Moscatel Rosé.* Although not as well regarded as the Muscat Blanc à Petits Grains, another strain—**Muscat of Alexandria** (also known as *Moscatel Romano*)—is very ancient and thought to go back to Egyptian times. These high-yield grapes have low ACID and high sugar content, which generally produces low-quality wines with raisiny characteristics. A majority of the cultivated Muscat of Alexandria end up as table grapes or raisins. This grape is grown in warmer climates throughout the world. It's most widely cultivated in Spain, where it's known as *Moscatel de Málaga,* and made into heavy, sweet, golden- to dark-brown wines. In Portugal it's the basis for the sweet, fortified MOSCATEL DE SETÚBAL wines. Muscat of Alexandria is also known as *Gordo Blanco, Hanepoot, Lexia, Moscatel, Moscatel Gordo,* and *Zibibbo.* Another variety is **Muscat Ottonel**, which is thought to be a cross between an unknown strain of Muscat and CHASSELAS. This much lighter flavored grape is not as overpoweringly "Muscat" as the other variations. It grows in cooler climates, and its most notable wines come from ALSACE, which produces DRY, perfumy wines, and Austria, where rich DESSERT WINES are the result. Muscat Ottonel is also known as *Muskotaly.* The dark-colored **Muscat Hamburg** variety is used mainly as a table grape but also produces thin, red wines—

mainly from eastern European countries. In Australia, where its called *Black Muscat,* this grape seldom finds its way into wine. Muscat Hamburg is called *Moscato di Amburgo* in Italy. The perfumy **Orange Muscat** variety has gained a following in California, pioneered by Quady Winery and its proprietary brands *Essencia* and *Elysium.*

Muscat Blanc *see* MUSCAT

Muscat Blanc à Petits Grains *see* MUSCAT

Muscat Canelli *see* MUSCAT

Muscat d'Alsace *see* MUSCAT

Muscat de Beaumes-de-Venise AC [mews-KAH (muhs-KAT) duh bohm duh vuh-NEEZ] APPELLATION located in France's southern RHÔNE region. The wine, made from Muscat à Petits Grains (MUSCAT) grapes, is a VIN DOUX NATUREL. This is a category of sweet, FORTIFIED wine made from grapes that are high in natural sugar (capable of reaching 15 percent ALCOHOL) and whose FERMENTATION is stopped by the addition of alcohol (no more than 10 percent of the volume). Muscat de Beaumes-de-Venise has blossomed from a little-known local potable enjoyed by BEAUMES-DE-VENISE residents to an extremely popular, high-priced wine. It's rich, honeyed, and full of floral and fruit aromas and flavors like peaches, apples, oranges, roses, and the ever-present GRAPEY character of Muscat. Good ACIDITY stops it from being CLOYING.

Muscat de Frontignan AC [mews-KAH (muhs-KAT) duh fraw*n*-tee-NYAHN] APPELLATION that is centered around the town of Frontignan, southwest of Monpellier on the Mediterranean in France's LANGUEDOC-ROUSSILLON region. It produces a well-known VIN DOUX NATUREL (sweet, FORTIFIED wine) made from the Muscat Blanc à Petits Grains variety, also referred to locally as Muscat de Frontignan (*see* MUSCAT). These wines are deep golden to almost orange in color and have a distinctive Muscat aroma and flavor.

Muscat de Lunel *see* LUNEL

Muscat de Mireval AC [mews-KAH (muhs-KAT) duh mee-ray-VAHL] APPELLATION centered around the town of Mireval, southwest of Monpellier on the Mediterranean in France's LANGUEDOC-ROUSSILLON region. It produces a well-known VIN DOUX NATUREL (sweet FORTIFIED wine) made from the Muscat Blanc à Petits Grains variety (*see* MUSCAT). The wines from Mireval are similar to those from the neighboring Frontignan (*see* MUSCAT DE FRONTIGNAN), although slightly BIGGER and RICHER.

Muscat de Rivesaltes AC [mews-KAH (muhs-KAT) reev-SAHLT] APPELLATION that surrounds the small town of Rivesaltes, which is located north of Perpignan in France's LANGUEDOC-ROUSSILLON region. It produces a well-known VIN DOUX NATUREL (sweet FORTIFIED wine) using the primary grapes of Muscat Blanc à Petits Grains and Muscat of Alexandria (*see* MUSCAT). The resulting wines are deep colored, alcoholic, and sweet. The RIVESALTES AC also produces Vin Doux Naturel in which GRENACHE, MALVOISIE, MACABEO, and Muscat grapes can be used.

Muscatel de Grano Menudo *see* MUSCAT

Muscateller *see* ALEATICO

Muscat Frontignan *see* MUSCAT

Muscat Hamburg *see* MUSCAT

Muscat of Alexandria *see* MUSCAT

Muscat Ottenel *see* MUSCAT

muscular A descriptor applied to wine (almost always red) that's BIG, bold, and full-bodied (*see* BODY). Also referred to as *masculine.*

Musigny AC [myoo-zee-NYEE] A distinguished GRAND CRU vineyard located in the village of CHAMBOLLE-MUSIGNY in the CÔTE DE NUITS district of France's BURGUNDY region. The 26½-acre site, which sits just above the famous CLOS DE VOUGEOT *grand cru* vineyard, is planted entirely with PINOT NOIR grapes (except for a small ¾-acre plot that grows CHARDONNAY). Known for their magnificent PERFUMED fragrance, Musigny red wines are LIGHTER and have more ELEGANCE and FINESSE than many of the other grands crus (such as CHAMBERTIN or BONNES MARES). They generally MATURE more quickly and can be drunk relatively YOUNG. Even though the small plot of Chardonnay produces very good white wines, their quantity is limited, which makes them very expensive. They're generally not deemed as good as white wines from other top grands crus, nor are they as highly regarded as the Musigny red wines.

Muskateller *see* MUSCAT

Muskotaly *see* MUSCAT

musky A winetasting term to describe an earthy-spicy characteristic.

Musquette *see* MUSCADELLE

must The juice of freshly crushed grapes that will be FERMENTED into wine. Must can include pulp, skins, and seeds.

musto cotto *see* MARSALA DOC

musty A winetasting term for an undesirable damp, moldy smell and flavor in a wine, usually due to its being stored in unclean barrels. A musty characteristic can also sometimes be attributed to a faulty cork, in which case it may disappear on aeration.

mutage [meu-TAZH] A French term for the process of stopping FERMENTATION either by using sulfur dioxide (*see* SULFITES) and sterile FILTERING or by adding grape alcohol or brandy. The latter technique is how PORT wines or VINS DOUX NATURELS are made.

muté [mew-TAY] Completely unfermented or partially fermented grape juice whose FERMENTATION was stopped. This can happen either by the addition of sulfur dioxide (*see* SULFITES), followed by sterile FILTERING to extract any yeast, or by adding grape alcohol or brandy. The resulting juice retains all or most of its natural grape sugars and is used to blend with other wines that need BODY or sweetness or to make APÉRITIFS.

mycoderma [my-koh-DER-muh] A class of bacteria that converts ethyl alcohol (*see* ALCOHOL) into acetic acid (*see* ACIDS) and ETHYL ACETATE and spoils wine with a vinegary flavor and odor. Wine affected by mycoderma is sometimes referred to as PIQUE.

Myrat, Château [sha-TOH mee-RAH] DEUXIÈME CRU (second growth) located in the SAUTERNES AC. It was uprooted in 1976, and part of the 54-acre parcel was replanted with approximately 85 percent SÉMILLON, 10 percent SAUVIGNON BLANC, and 5 percent MUSCADELLE. The first Sauternes AC wines were released with the 1990 VINTAGE.

ackenheim [NAHK-ehn-hime] One of the better wine-producing villages in Germany's RHEINHESSE region. It's located in the area of excellent vineyards known as the RHEINTERRASSE, which is south of the city of Mainz. The red sandstone, which runs through the area, yields grapes that produce high-quality wines with unique CHARACTER. RIESLING and SYLVANER grapes can both produce great wines. **Engelsberg** and **Rothenberg** are the top EINZELLAGEN.

Nagyburgundi *see* PINOT NOIR

Nahe [NAH-uh] Although the Nahe is one of the smaller of Germany's ANBAUGEBIETE (quality-wine regions), it's well-known to connoisseurs as a producer of high-quality RIESLING wines. The Nahe River is a tributary of the Rhine River, flowing into it at Bingen. The vineyards here, which are spread out along both banks and part of the surrounding areas, are planted primarily with white varieties. MÜLLER-THURGAU is the most widely planted grape, followed by Riesling and SYLVANER. Riesling grapes, however, occupy most of the prime vineyard sites. The Nahe is divided into two BEREICHE, **Kreuznach** and SCHLOSS-BÖCKELHEIM, and has seven GROSSLAGEN. Of the Grosslagen, **Burgweg** is considered the best, but the best known is **Rüdesheim Rosengarten** (not to be confused with the more famous village of RÜDESHEIM in the RHEINGAU region).

Nairac, Château [sha-TOH neh-RAK] Château located in the SAUTERNES AC in BORDEAUX. It's classified as a DEUXIÈME CRU (second growth) in the CLASSIFICATION OF 1855. The estate produces about 2,000 cases of high-quality sweet Sauternes AC wine each year. Wines from the best VINTAGES are capable of AGING for 15 to 20 years. The estate contains nearly 40 acres planted with almost 90 percent SÉMILLON, along with small amounts of SAUVIGNON BLANC and MUSCADELLE.

Nalle Winery [NAHL] Doug Nalle, former winemaker at Chateau Soverain, JORDAN VINEYARDS, and QUIVERA VINEYARDS, started Nalle Winery on a part-time basis in 1984 and finally put all his energies into it in 1989. It's Nalle's ZINFANDEL from the DRY CREEK AVA that consistently gets high ratings from reviewers. This Zin is usually blended with a small amount of PETITE SIRAH. Nalle Winery also produces a small amount of CABERNET SAUVIGNON. Between 3,000 and 4,000 cases of wine are made each year, all from purchased grapes. The winery is located on Dry Creek Road northwest of the town of Healdsburg, California.

Napa County; Napa Valley AVA The Napa Valley is the most famous wine region in California and the United States. Its winemaking history started in 1838 when MISSION grapes were planted by George C. Yount, who made his first wines in the early 1840s. The earliest commercial winery was established by CHARLES KRUG in 1861. This was followed by SCHRAMSBERG (1862), BERINGER (1876), INGLENOOK (1879) and BEAULIEU VINEYARD (1900). After growing to over 160 wineries in the 1880s, the Napa Valley was devastated by PHYLLOXERA, which had attacked vineyards in Europe and now began to ravage the Napa vineyards. Napa's next major setback was PROHIBITION, instituted from 1920 to 1933, which severely curtailed the growth of the winemaking industry. A few wineries survived Prohibition by making sacramental wines and selling grapes to home winemakers. By the end of the 1950s, there were only a dozen or so wineries that had survived the dual devastation of phylloxera and Prohibition. Viticultural activity began to revive in the 1960s when Joe Heitz started HEITZ WINE CELLARS in 1961, the Davies' reestablished Schramsberg in 1966, and ROBERT MONDAVI left the family winery (Charles Krug Winery) and established his own winery in 1966. Others were getting the same idea, and wineries began appearing in quick succession all over the Napa Valley. Today there are almost 200 wineries and over 34,000 acres of vineyards. The terms *Napa County* and *Napa Valley* are almost synonymous because the Napa Valley APPELLATION includes all Napa County except for a small portion northeast of Lake Berryessa. The **Napa Valley AVA** is located northeast of San Francisco, beginning on the south end at San Pablo Bay, which is connected to and just north of San Francisco Bay. The Napa Valley ranges in width from about 1 to 4 miles and extends north and slightly west for just over 30 miles to Mount St. Helena. From south to north, it encompasses the towns of Napa, Yountville, Oakville, Rutherford, St. Helena, and Calistoga. The Napa Valley AVA climate changes from a cool Region I (*see* CLIMATE REGIONS OF CALIFORNIA) in the south to a warm Region III in the north. This VITICULTURAL AREA also encompasses several smaller subzones that must use "Napa Valley" on the label as well. Wines from the CARNEROS AVA, which is partly in the Napa Valley and partly in SONOMA COUNTY, do not have to use Napa Valley on the label. Some of the notable growing areas within the Napa Valley are CHILES VALLEY, Diamond Mountain, HOWELL MOUNTAIN AVA, Spring Mountain, the RUTHERFORD BENCH, Pope Valley, and STAGS LEAP DISTRICT AVA. About 65 percent of the white grapes planted in Napa are CHARDONNAY. Other white varieties in order of popularity include SAUVIGNON BLANC, CHENIN BLANC, RIESLING, SÉMILLON, and GEWÜRTZTRAMINER. CABERNET SAUVIGNON, with over 50 percent of the vineyard acreage, is the dominant red variety. Other red varieties include PINOT NOIR, MERLOT, ZINFANDEL, CABERNET FRANC, and PE-

TITE SIRAH. Among the numerous well-known wineries producing high-quality wine in the Napa Valley are ACACIA, BEAULIEU VINEYARD, BERINGER VINEYARDS, BURGESS, CAFARO CELLARS, CAKEBREAD CELLARS, CAYMUS VINEYARDS, CHÂTEAU MONTELENA, CLOS DU VAL, CUVAISON WINERY, DOMAINE CHANDON, DUCKHORN VINEYARDS, DUNN VINEYARDS, FORMAN WINERY, FREEMARK ABBEY, GRGICH HILLS CELLARS, Heitz Wine Cellars, INGLENOOK, LOUIS MARTINI, MAYACAMAS, Robert Mondavi, MUMM NAPA VALLEY, JOSEPH PHELPS, RAYMOND, SAINTSBURY, Schramsberg, SHAFER VINEYARD, SPOTTSWOODE VINEYARD, STAG'S LEAP WINE CELLARS, STERLING, and TREFETHEN.

Napa Gamay *see* GAMAY

Napanook Vineyard *see* DOMINUS ESTATE

Napa Ridge *see* BERINGER VINEYARDS

native American grapes A term used for grape varieties indigenous to the Americas. There are four main species that are related to wine production—VITIS AESTIVALIS, VITIS LABRUSCA, VITIS RIPARIA, and VITIS ROTUNDIFOLIA—none of which produce grapes used to make the world's fine wines. That honor goes to VITIS VINIFERA (which includes CABERNET SAUVIGNON, CHARDONNAY, and SAUVIGNON BLANC grapes), an Asian and European species used in over 99 percent of the world's wines. Native American varieties have made an important contribution to the wine world in that they are PHYLLOXERA-resistant, particularly the *vitis riparia* species. After European vineyards were devastated by the phylloxera infestation in the 1800s, it was discovered that grafting *vitis vinifera* BUDWOOD to native American ROOTSTOCKS produced phylloxera-resistant *vitis vinifera* grapes.

native yeast fermentation *see* YEAST

natur; naturrein; naturwein [nah-TOOR] Old German terms referring to wines that don't have added sugar. These terms have been outdated by the QUALITÄTSWEIN MIT PRADIKÄT (QmP) category, established in 1971, which defines the finest German wines.

nature; naturel [nah-TEWR; nah-tew-REHL] 1. French words meaning "nature" and "natural," referring to wine to which nothing (usually meaning sugar or ALCOHOL) has been added. 2. On CHAMPAGNE or SPARKLING WINE labels, these terms typically refer to wines that don't have *liqueur d'expédition* (DOSAGE) added, which would contribute to sweetness. Such wines are sometimes called *Brut Nature*. 3. On some sparkling wine labels, *naturel* may mean that the wine is not totally DRY but simply the driest style of that producer. 4. In the Champagne region, the terms *Vin Nature* or *Vin Nature de la Champagne* were once used when referring to still wines from this area. Since 1974, however, the CÔTEAUX CHAMPENOIS AC name appears on the labels of these wines.

naturrein; naturwein *see* NATUR

Navalle Selections *see* INGLENOOK-NAPA VALLEY

Navarra DO [nah-VAH*R*-*R*AH] DO located south of Pamplona in the southern part of the Navarra province in north central Spain. The dominant grape is Garnacha (GRENACHE), although TEMPRANILLO is gaining in popularity. Navarra is best known for its *rosado* (ROSÉ) wines, although it now produces more red wine than rosé. The area also makes a small amount of white wine from MACABEO, MALVASIA, and Garnach Blanca (GRENACHE). The Navarra DO is going through a modernization program, which includes not only adding new equipment and implementing modern winemaking techniques but also experimenting with different varieties like CABERNET SAUVIGNON and CHARDONNAY.

Néac *see* LALANDE-DE-POMEROL

Nebbiolo [neh-b'YOH-loh] The fog (*nebbia* in Italian) that rolls over the hills of northern PIEDMONT and the regions nearby, helps the Nebbiolo grape ripen properly, thereby creating some of Italy's finest red wines. Wines made from Nebbiolo grapes are known by a variety of names including BAROLO, BARBARESCO, GATTINARA, GHEMME, and SPANNA. They're characterized as being rich, full-bodied, and CHEWY. These wines often have a high ALCOHOL content (13 percent and above), as well as fairly substantial TANNINS, both of which are easily supported by the wine's hefty fruit flavors. The aroma and flavor of these dark-colored wines are suggestive of chocolate, licorice, raspberries, truffles, and violets. Nebbiolo wines generally require significant aging to develop and SOFTEN. Although recognized as one of the world's great wine grapes, Nebbiolo has not been planted in significant amounts outside of northwest Italy. Very little has been planted in California or other U.S. growing regions. The Nebbiolo grape is also known as *Chiavennasca, Picotener, Pugent,* and *Spanna* or *Spana.*

Nebbiolo d'Alba DOC [nehb-BYOH-loh DAHL-bah] DOC zone that covers a large area around the town of Alba extending on both sides of the Tanaro River in the southeastern part of Italy's PIEDMONT region. These wines are made from the NEBBIOLO grape, which is the same one used in the famous neighboring DOCGs of BAROLO and BARBERESCO. Nebbiolo d'Alba DOC red wines, however, require only 1 year of AGING, compared to a minimum of 3 years for Barolo and 2 years for Barbersco wines. Nebbiolo d'Alba wines are well-regarded and viewed as lighter versions of those from Barolo and Barbersco. Although most of the wines produced here are STILL and DRY, DOC rules permit sweet and SPUMANTE versions as well.

Nebuchadnezzar *see* WINE BOTTLES

négociant [nay-goh-SYAH*N*] French for "merchant" or "dealer," used in the wine world to refer to a person or firm that sells and ships wine as a wholesaler. The extent of the role played by this middleman has expanded over time. Traditionally, négociants bought, matured, sometimes blended, and then bottled and shipped wine. Over time, the role expanded to include purchasing grapes and making wine. Some labels may contain the phrase *négociant-éleveur* (*see* ÉLEVEUR), indicating the merchant played a more extensive role in producing the wine. In some transactions there is another middleman—a COURTIER or "wine broker," who helps establish the price paid by a *négociant* to a small producer. Some of the better-known French négociants are Barton & Guestier, Calvet, Cordier, Moueix, and Sichel.

Negra Mole; Tinta Negra Mole [NAY-gruh MOH-leh; TEEN-tuh NAY-gruh MOH-leh] A red-wine grape grown on the island of MADEIRA and in the Portuguese regions of Algrave and CARCAVELOS. After the PHYLLOXERA invasion in the 1870s, Negra Mole replaced many of Madeira's classic varieties including BOAL, MALVASIA, SERCIAL, and VERDELHO. Although Negra Mole is considered only a *good* variety, it's important today in the production of the long-lived FORTIFIED wines of Madeira. In 1986 Portugal entered the Common Market, whose regulations stipulate that by 1993 any Madeira wine naming a variety on its label will have to contain at least 85 percent of that grape. This new requirement has already stimulated replanting of the more classic varieties as already mentioned and will probably lessen the importance of Negra Mole in the future. In Spain, this variety is called *Negramoll*.

Negramoll *see* NEGRA MOLE

Négrette [neh-GREHT] A red-wine grape cultivated mainly in southwestern France. Négrette is the main grape in the wines of CÔTES DU FRONTONNAIS, which can be very SMOOTH and SUPPLE, have flavor aspects of strawberry and raspberry, and be capable of medium-term AGING. Limited amounts of this variety are grown in California, where it's known as *Pinot St. George* because it was long thought to be a member of the Pinot family. Negrette is also known as *Petit Noir*.

Negron *see* RABOSO

Nenin, Château [sha-TOH neh-NAN] At nearly 70 acres, this is one of the larger POMEROL AC properties. The wines are regarded as good but not great. The grapes used are a blend of around 50 percent CABERNET SAUVIGNON, 30 percent MERLOT, and 20 percent CABERNET FRANC. Around 10,000 to 12,000 cases of red wine are produced each year.

Neretto *see* CROATINA

nerveux [nehr-VEUH] French term that literally means "nervous," "energetic," or "vigorous." In winetasting circles it describes wines that are full-bodied (*see* BODY), lively, and well-BALANCED, with excellent AGING qualities.

Neuburger *see* AUSTRIA

Neuchâtel [neuh-shah-TEHL] Located north of Geneva, this Swiss canton is well known for its white wines made from CHASSELAS grapes. These Chasselas wines are LIGHT and DRY, with a touch of effervescence, the latter due to being bottled SUR LIE, which results in a second fermentation in the bottle. The vineyards, which are located on the north shore of Lake Neuchâtel, are planted mainly with Chasselas, although some PINOT NOIR is grown as well. The Pinot Noir wines, which are considered some of the best Swiss reds, are often produced in a pale ROSÉ style known as OEIL DE PERDRIX ("eye of the partridge").

neutral A term used to describe wine that, although perfectly acceptable, is somewhat ordinary and lacks distinction.

Newton Vineyard Peter Newton founded Newton Vineyard after selling STERLING VINEYARDS (of which he was the founding partner) to Coca-Cola in 1977. He purchased 650 acres on SPRING MOUNTAIN, planting 62 of them with CABERNET SAUVIGNON, MERLOT, and SAUVIGNON BLANC (the latter was eventually dropped). The winery now annually produces between 25,000 and 35,000 cases of wine—Cabernet Sauvginon, Merlot, a red BORDEAUX BLEND, and a regular and a Reserve CHARDONNAY, the latter from purchased grapes.

New York New York State is the United States' second largest wine-producing state after California. A majority of the state's vineyards, however, are planted with native VITIS LABRUSCA or HYBRID vines and few of the VITIS VINIFERA species. Because of this, New York hasn't been considered a producer of high-quality wines until recently. Vitis vinifera grapes like CABERNET SAUVIGNON, CHARDONNAY, PINOT NOIR, and RIESLING account for less than 6 percent of New York's vineyard acreage. Native American grapes like CATAWBA, CONCORD, DELAWARE, and NIAGARA comprise 80 percent of the vineyard acreage. HYBRIDS like AURORA, BACO NOIR, CHELOIS, DE CHAUNAC, and SEYVAL BLANC account for the remaining vineyard acreage. New York's most important growing region is the FINGER LAKE AVA and its subzone Cayuga Lake AVA. Other regions include the Hudson River Valley Region AVA, Lake Erie AVA, and LONG ISLAND, with its VITICULTURAL AREAS of North Fork of Long Island and The Hamptons. The Hamptons leads the way in new vitis vinifera planting. Much of New York's production goes into GENERIC WINES labeled BURGUNDY, CHABLIS, RHINE WINE or SAUTERNE or into SPARKLING WINES. Wines with an AVA designation on the label must contain a minimum of 85 percent of that viticultural area's wine. Wines labeled "New York State" must contain a minimum of 75 percent of the state's wine. Those labeled with a vitis labrusca grape must contain 51 percent of that grape in the wine's makeup. Other VARIETAL WINES must contain 75 percent of a particular grape. New York wineries (other than those mentioned in the Long Island and Finger Lake listings) include Benmarl Wine Company, Clinton Vineyards, Cascade Mountain, Eaton, Royal Kedem, Walker Valley, and Woodbury.

New Zealand   Although New Zealand had vineyards and produced wines as far back as 1819, it didn't have a reputation for making high-quality TABLE WINES until recently. It's essentially been a nation of beer drinkers, and the wine it did produce was usually FORTIFIED. Many of New Zealand's grapes were HYBRIDS but, starting in the mid-1960s, winemakers gradually began to experiment with European varieties like CABERNET SAUVIGNON. What resulted was a rapid expansion of vineyards producing VITIS VINIFERA wines, with New Zealand winemakers determining they had better success with white wines. Today MÜLLER-THURGAU is the most widely planted white grape, followed by CHARDONNAY. Other popular white varieties include SAUVIGNON BLANC, RIESLING, MUSCAT, CHENIN BLANC, and SÉMILLON. New Zealand's most highly regarded wines are their Chardonnays, Sauvignon Blancs, and sweet DESSERT WINES made from BOTRITISED Riesling grapes. Cabernet Sauvignon is the top red variety, followed by PINOT NOIR, MERLOT, and PINOTAGE. Because of New Zealand's cool climate, Cabernet Sauvignon and Cabernet Sauvignon/Merlot blends lean toward being slightly HERBACEOUS. Pinot Noir is gaining ground as producers discover it's doing better than expected in New Zealand, particularly when used for SPARKLING WINES. New Zealand's North Island—with growing areas in Auckland, Gisborne/Poverty Bay, Hawkes Bay, and the Wairarapa/Martinborough area—was the first of the islands to start producing wines. The South Island subsequently followed and now has growing areas in Marlborough, Caterbury, and Central Otago. New Zealand wineries include Babich, Cloudy Bay, Collards, Cooks, Hunters, Montana, Morton Estate, Nobilo Te Mata, Vidal, and Villa Maria.

Niagara [ni-AG-ruh] An American white-wine grape created by CROSSING the CONCORD and Cassady varieties. Niagara is grown primarily in the eastern United States (with the heaviest concentration in New York) and, to some extent, in the Midwest. It's also found in Canada, Brazil, and New Zealand. Niagara is generally vinified into sweet or medium-sweet wines that have GRAPEY and FOXY properties.

Niebaum-Coppola Estate [NEE-bowm KOH-puh-luh] Moviemaker Francis Ford Coppola purchased this NAPA VALLEY estate in 1975. It had been the home of Gustave Niebaum, founder of INGLENOOK, and the site included over 80 acres of what was once some of the prime Inglenook vineyards in the RUTHERFORD BENCH area. Coppola added adjoining acreage, bringing the total up to about 120 acres planted primarily with CABERNET SAUVIGNON, plus some CABERNET FRANC and MERLOT. Niebaum-Coppola Estate is famous for **Rubicon**, a blend of the three aforementioned grapes. Because Rubicon is aged for about 3 years in oak barrels and another 2 to 3 years in the bottle, it's sometimes 6 years or more after the VINTAGE date before a wine is released. The inaugural vintage of 1978 wasn't released until 1985. These wines are designed to AGE and are generally full-bodied (*see* BODY) and quite TANNIC upon release. This winery also produces a rich, fruity ZINFANDEL called **Edizione Pennino** and, occasionally, a Cabernet Franc wine under the label of Francis Coppola Family Wines. About 4,000 to 5,000 cases of wine are produced each year. *See also* INGLENOOK-NAPA VALLEY.

Nies'chen, *see* KASEL

Niederhausen [NEE-duhr-how-zuhn] A small, highly regarded wine-producing village located southwest of BAD KREUZNACH in Germany's NAHE region. It has a reputation for producing some of the region's finest RIESLING wines. The top EINZELLAGEN are **Hermannshöhle** and **Hermannsberg**.

Nierstein [NEER-SHTINE] The premier wine-producing village of Germany's RHEINHESSE region. It's located in an area of excellent vineyards known as the RHEINTERRASSE, south of the city of Mainz. Nierstein also lends its name to the BEREICH that covers this area and to the three GROSSLAGEN that cover its vineyards—Niersteiner **Auflangen**, Niersteiner **Rehbach**, and Niersteiner **Spiegelberg**. In addition, it's used in the name of the Grosslage Niersteiner Gutes Domtal, which covers

N

vineyards for other area villages. Nierstein has many fine vineyards including **Bildstock, Hipping, Hölle, Kranzberg, Ölberg, Paterberg,** and **Pettenthal**. The finest wines generally come from vineyard sites (EINZELLAGEN) like these and, because the Bereich Nierstein annually produces a tremendous amount of wine (12 million cases in some years), it's important for consumers to check the label for the Einzellagen name (such as Niersteiner *Olberg*). Many estates also produce fine wines under the three Niersteiner Grosslagen.

Nightingale *see* BERINGER VINEYARDS

noble A winetasting term used to describe a superior wine of remarkable CHARACTER and great BREED. The word *noble* may also be used to describe an eminent vineyard or grape variety known for producing superlative wines.

noble mold *see* BOTRYTIS CINEREA

noble rot *see* BOTRYTIS CINEREA

Nonnenberg *see* RAUENTHAL

Non Plus Ultra *see* CODORNIU

non-vintage *see* VINTAGE

North Coast AVA APPELLATION comprised of the counties north of San Franciso including LAKE, Marin, MENDOCINO, NAPA, SONOMA, and Solano. Previously, the North Coast region included counties south of San Francisco, which are now in the CENTRAL COAST region. The North Coast AVA is a leader in acreage producing high-quality wine grapes including CABERNET FRANC, CABERNET SAUVIGNON, CHARDONNAY, MERLOT, PINOT NOIR, and SAUVIGNON BLANC.

North Fork *see* LONG ISLAND

North Yuba AVA Small California AVA located in the larger Sierra Foothills AVA, northwest of the towns of Grass Valley and Nevada City. Small amounts of CABERNET SAUVIGNON, RIESLING, and SAUVIGNON BLANC are planted here. The Renaissance Vineyard and Winery is the only winery.

Norton *see* VITIS AESTIVALIS

nose A general term referring to the olfactory sense of wine. Some wine experts use the word *nose* to describe an extremely intense BOUQUET, although common usage doesn't generally connote quality. *See also* AROMA.

Nostrano *see* TICINO

Notton *see* BRANE-CANTENAC, CHÂTEAU

nouveau; pl. nouveaux [noo-VOH] The French term for "new" that, when applied to wine, refers to one that is very young. Because of the influence of France's BEAUJOLAIS NOUVEAU wines, this word has taken on a meaning relating to this particular wine's style— light, fruity, youthful, and lacking aging potential. These nouveau wines are almost always released shortly after harvest. Many of them are made using CARBONIC MACERATION, a FERMENTATION technique designed to enhance their intensely fruity yet light-bodied (*see* BODY) characteristics. The term *nouveau* is also used in the United States. Italians call this style of wine *novello* or VINO NOVELLO.

novello *see* NOUVEAU; VINO NOVELLO

nu [NEUH] The French word for "naked," which in the wine trade refers to the price of wine without cask or bottles.

Nuits-Saint-Georges AC [nwee sa*n* ZHAW*R*ZH] After BEAUNE, the town of Nuits-Saint-Georges is the second most important commercial center in France's CÔTE D'OR section of BURGUNDY. The town contains a significant number of NÉGOCIANTS and has given its name to the northern half of the Côte d'Or—the CÔTE DE NUITS. The town is the center of the Nuits-Saint-Georges AC, which lies between the villages of VOSNE-ROMANÉE and Prémeaux-Prissey. Prémeaux-Prissey wines are allowed to use the Nuits-Saint-Georges AC and usually do. There are no GRAND CRU vineyards in this APPELLATION, but there are thirty-eight PREMIERS CRUS—more than any other appellation. The best of these are **Les Saint-Georges**, **Les Vaucrains**, and **Les Cailles**, followed by **Les Damodes**, **Aux Boudots**, **Aux Murgers**, **Les Pruliers**, and **Les Perrières**. Red wines made from PINOT NOIR grapes dominate the production, although tiny amounts of white wine are also made. The wines from the best producers can be quite good with richly CONCENTRATED flavors and good TANNIC structure. Current critiques indicate that the presence of many mediocre producers results in varying levels of quality, which makes the selection of Nuits-Saint-Georges AC wines difficult.

Le Numero 2 de Lafon-Rochet *see* LAFON-ROCHET, CHÂTEAU

Nuragus di Cagliari DOC [noo-RAH-goos dee kah-LYAH-ree] The largest DOC on the island of SARDINIA. It covers the southern third of the island and is centered in the province of Cagliari. The wines, which are made mainly from Nuragus grapes, are DRY, LIGHT, and CRISP thirst quenchers that are mediocre, at best. AMABILE and FRIZZANTE versions are also permitted.

Nussbien *see* RUPPERTSBERG

Nussbrunnen *see* HATTENHEIM

nutty A term used for some wines, such as SHERRY or tawny PORT, that have a crisp, nutty (usually hazelnut or walnut) characteristic. Full-bodied (*see* BODY) Chardonnays sometimes also have a very subtle nutty trait. An overt nutty trait in TABLE WINE is considered a flaw.

NV *see* VINTAGE

ak The preferred wood for making the barrels and casks in which wine is AGED. Oak barrels impart flavors and TAN-NINS, both of which are desirable for most red wine as well as some white wines. Oak is slightly porous, which creates an environment ideal for aging wines. Redwood and chestnut are distant second choices to oak, and neither do the job as well. Sometimes these woods are used for larger casks because the expense of using oak is a luxury. Despite oak's unique capabilities, more delicate wines do not do well with oak aging of any length, and some wines can easily become over-oaked. In either case, oak flavors and tannins can overpower a wine's VARIETAL CHARACTER, which results in a poorly BALANCED wine. Oak is also a matter of personal taste. For instance, some wine lovers prefer big, oaky CHARDONNAYS, while others prefer leaner, cleaner styles where the oak character isn't so prominent. Choosing the right barrel requires some knowledge of and experience with various types of oak, as well as the COOPERS who make the barrels. The favorite wood for wine barrels is **white oak** (red oak is too porous), with the U.S. species differing slightly from European. In Europe, the primary sources of oak are France and the former Yugoslavia. The best-known French sources are: LIMOUSIN, a forest in south-central France; central France's forests of Allier, Nevers, and Troncais; and Vosges, a forest in northeastern France. The leading sources of white oak in the United States are Kentucky, Minnesota, Missouri, Ohio, Tennessee, and Wisconsin. There's a great deal of discussion about how the oak from different locations affects various types of wines. Some feel that Limousin oak, which has a looser grain, imparts more oak flavor, while others say it delivers less. Most agree that American oak imparts a slightly sweeter character than European oak. However, it's also argued that the cooper's barrel-making technique has as much to do with the barrel's effect on wine as the wood from which it's made. Barrel making in America (which was primarily for the distilled spirit industry) was much different than that found in Europe. This is now changing, with many European barrel makers opening COOPERAGES in California to handle the expanded demand from California winemakers. Oak barrels loose their ability to impart flavor in 4 to 5 years, and most high-quality wine estates and CHÂTEAUS replace all or part of their oak barrels with new ones each year so a high level of new oak character is imparted to each new VINTAGE.

Oakville AVA VITICULTURAL AREA located in the center of the NAPA VALLEY. It begins north of the town of Yountville and extends northwest about a mile past the town of Oakville just before CAKEBREAD CELLARS. It abuts the RUTHERFORD AVA on its northwest boundary. The

Oakville AVA extends across the valley floor and includes many es-teemed Napa Valley wineries including GROTH VINEYARDS AND WINERY, ROBERT MONDAVI WINERY, OPUS ONE, SILVER OAK CELLARS, and VILLA MT. EDEN. It also encompasses the famous MARTHA'S VINEYARD, whose CABERNET SAUVIGNON grapes go into the VINEYARD-DESIGNATED bottling by HEITZ WINE CELLARS.

oaky; oakiness A wine tasting term describing a TOASTY, VANILLA flavor and fragrance in wines that have been aged in new OAK barrels. An oaky characteristic is wonderful in the proper balance. Exagger-ated oakiness, however, can overwhelm a wine's other components and is considered undesirable.

Obermosel, Bereich *see* MOSEL-SAAR-RUWER

Ockfen [AWK-fuhn] A highly regarded wine-producing village lo-cated south of Konz along the Saar River in Germany's MOSEL-SAAR-RUWEN region. The village owes its reputation to the extremely steep hillside vineyards, which include the well-known EINZELLAGE **Bockstein**. In good growing years, Ockfen's STEELY, yet ELEGANT and intensely fragrant RIESLING wines can rival any produced in Germany.

Oechsle [UHK-sluh] A German method of measuring the SPECIFIC GRAVITY (therefore, the sugar content) of MUST or grape juice prior to FERMENTATION. Developed in the nineteenth century by Germany's Christian Ferdinand Oechsle, this method is similar to the BRIX system used in the United States and the BAUMÉ scale used in France. Germany employs the Oechsle scale to establish the quality levels of wines (*see* QUALITÄTSWEIN BESTIMMTER ANBAUGEBIET (QbA) and QUALITÄTSWEIN MIT PRÄDIKAT (QmP). The required Oechsle reading varies for a given qual-ity level, depending on the grape varieties and the German region. For example, KABINETT wines (the lowest quality level within QmP—the highest quality category) require an Oechsle reading of 73° for RIESLING in the RHEINGAU region, but only 67 in Germany's AHR region. TROCKEN-BEERENAUSLESE, the highest quality level of all German wine, requires an Oechsle reading of 150° (equivalent to a 35° Brix reading) for Riesling in all regions.

oeil de perdrix [uh-yuh deuh pehr-DREE] A French term mean-ing "partridge eye," used in the past to describe white wines made from red grapes and having a pinkish hue—similar to the pinkish tint of a partridge's eye. Today the terms VIN GRIS or VIN ROSÉ usually ap-pear on labels of such wines.

Oeillade *see* CINSAUT

oenologist *see* ENOLOGY

oenology *see* ENOLOGY

oenophile *see* ENOPHILE

Oestrich [UH-st*r*ihch] A large village located along the Rhine River southwest of the city of Wiesbaden in Germany's RHEINGAU region. The wines from this area are generally of high quality and occasionally superior. RIESLING is the grape of choice and it produces FIRM, full-bodied (*see* BODY) wines. The best EINZELLAGEN include **Doosberg**, **Klosterberg**, **Lenchen**, and **Schloss Reichartshausen** (the latter, which is classified as an ORTSEIL, isn't required to use Oestrich's name on the label).

off A term used for wine that's obviously spoiled or seriously flawed. Some winetasters also use the term to describe a wine that's not true to CHARACTER.

off dry A tasting term for a wine that has the barest hint of sweetness.

Ohio The third largest wine-producing state after California and New York. There was a period during the 1800s when Ohio was the largest wine producer in the nation, but vine diseases and PROHIBITION impeded industry growth. Today, most vineyards are planted around Lake Erie in the northeast section of Ohio. The vineyards contain mostly native vines like CATAWBA, CONCORD, and NIAGARA. HYBRIDS like SEYVAL BLANC and VIDAL BLANC are also very popular. VITIS VINIFERA vines, which are planted in very small numbers, include CABERNET SAUVIGNON, CHARDONNAY, GEWÜRZTRAMINER, MERLOT, PINOT NOIR, and RIESLING. Ohio wineries include Meier's Wine Cellars (the state's largest), Colonial Vineyards, Firelands Winery, Grand River Winery, and Markko Vineyard.

oidium *see* MILDEW

oily Winetasting term that can refer to either texture or flavor, although it's more commonly applied to the former. A wine described as having an oily texture will produce a smooth, slightly slippery impression in the mouth, and is usually the result of relatively high GLYCEROL, often combined with low ACIDITY. This tactile characteristic is often found in FAT wines. The term oily is used sometimes to describe the BOUQUET of a wine, such as a mature RIESLING, although the term PETROL is more appropriate in this instance.

Ojo de Liebre *see* TEMPRANILLO

Olaszriesling *see* WELSCHRIESLING

Ölberg *see* NIERSTEIN

Old Telegram *see* BONNY DOON VINEYARD

Olivier, Château [sha-TOH aw-lee-VYAY] Estate that contains a picturesque, moat-encircled, turreted castle built in the twelfth century and modified in the fourteenth. This property, which is located in the PESSAC-LÉOGNAN AC in GRAVES, has a CRU CLASSÉ rating, but its wines are not that highly regarded. The white wines generally receive the best reviews, although red wines from the VINTAGES of the late 1980s show some improvement. The red wines are made from around 65 percent CABERNET SAUVIGNON and 35 percent MERLOT, and the white wines are made from about 65 percent SAUVIGNON BLANC, 30 percent SÉMILLON, and 5 percent MUSCADELLE. The château averages about 12,000 cases of red wine and 10,000 cases of white wine a year. Both wines seem to mature very quickly. A SECOND LABEL **Mineur J.J. de Bethmann** is used by the estate.

oloroso *see* SHERRY

Oltrepò Pavese DOC [ohl-TRAY-poh pah-VEH-zuh] Large DOC that makes about two-thirds of the DOC wine produced in Italy's LOMBARDY region. It's located in the southwestern corner of Lombardy, south of Pavia. Two of the designated wines—**Buttafuoco** (which means "sparks like fire") and **Sangue di Giuda** ("blood of Judas")—can only be produced in a smaller subzone. These two red wines are made from BARBERA, CROATINA, Pinot Nero (PINOT NOIR), Uva Rara and Ughetta (Vespolina). They both can be STILL but are usually FRIZZANTE. The Buttafuoco is DRY; the Sangue di Giuda ranges from dry to sweet. These same grapes are used for the ROSSO and ROSATO. Other wines made include the red VARIETALS Barbera, BONARDA, and Pinot Nero and the white varietals CORTESE, Moscato (MUSCAT), Pinot Grigio (PINOT GRIS), Riesling Italico (WELSHRIESLING), and Riesling Renano (RIESLING). Many of these are allowed to be frizzante (some SPUMANTE) and can range from dry to sweet.

open; opened A winetasting term that describes a wine that's accessible or ready to drink.

opening The opening of a wine is the first impression it gives and can apply to smell, flavor, or both. The characteristic of a wine can change between the opening (or first taste) to one a few minutes later. For instance, the smell of SULFUR on the opening may blow off and be entirely indistinguishable on subsequent tastes.

Oporto *see* PORT; PORTUGIESER

Oppenheim [AHP-uhn-hime] An important wine-producing village in Germany's RHEINHESSEN region, south of the city of Mainz near NIERSTEIN. Oppenheim, along with towns like Nierstein, NACKEHHEIM, and DIENHEIM, is part of area of excellent vineyards known as the RHEINTERRASSE. Its wines, which are generally rated just a fraction below Nierstein in terms of overall quality, are some of the Rheinhessen's finest. RIESLING, which is planted on over half of the available vineyard land, produces the best wines—ELEGANT, with concentrated flavors. The best Oppenheimer wines come from EINZELLAGEN such as **Herrenberg**, **Kreuz**, and **Sackträger**.

Optima [OP-tee-muh] German white-wine variety created in the 1970s that is a cross of MÜLLER-THURGAU and a SYLVANER-RIESLING hybrid. Optima grapes, which tend to grow in less than choice conditions, are low in ACID and high in sugar. The wines they produce can be very sweet and are generally used to boost the sugar content of other wines.

Opus One [OH-puhs] Well-known NAPA VALLEY winery that is the joint enterprise established by Robert Mondavi and Baron Phillipe de Rothschild. After much discussion, the venture began with the first wines (1979) produced from grapes from selected sections of Mondavi vineyards and made in Mondavi's Napa facility. Opus One proceeded to purchase its own vineyards and began planting in 1981. Its striking winery building was completed in 1991. Unfortunately, PHYLLOXERA struck the estate vineyards in the early 1990s, which necessitated extensive replanting. Opus One makes only one wine—a highly regarded and expensive red made primarily of CABERNET SAUVIGNON with small amounts of CABERNET FRANC and MERLOT. Annual production is currently close to 15,000 cases.

Orange Muscat *see* MUSCAT

ordinaire [ohr-dee-NAYR] French term meaning "plain" or "ordinary." *Vin ordinaire* is used to refer to inexpensive, everyday wines.

Oregon Along with Washington and Idaho, Oregon makes up the region known as the Pacific Northwest. Although grapes were planted here in the nineteenth century, most of the vineyards were abandoned during PROHIBITION. It wasn't until the early 1960s that Oregon was viewed as a promising site for vineyards, particularly for cooler climate varieties like RIESLING, which Richard Sommer planted at his Hillcrest Vineyard in 1961, and PINOT NOIR, which has become this state's most celebrated grape. David Lett of Eyrie Vineyard first demonstrated the promising marriage of Oregon and Pinot Noir with his 1975 vintage, which showed extremely well in a 1979 BLIND TASTING with a number of wines from BURGUNDY. Today, Pinot Noir, Riesling, and CHARDONNAY are Oregon's most popular grape varieties, followed by PINOT GRIS. Other grapes planted in small amounts include CABERNET SAUVIGNON, GEWÜRZTRAMINER, MÜLLER-THURGAU, SÉMILLON, and ZINFANDEL. The best growing areas are located between the coastal range to the west and the Cascade Mountains to the east, running from north of the city of Portland to the south. The WILLAMETTE VALLEY AVA is in the northern portion, starting north of Portland and stretching to just south of Eugene. The UMPQUA VALLEY AVA is just south of the Willamette Valley and encompasses the towns of Umpqua and Roseburg. There's a smaller area, ROGUE VALLEY AVA, just before the California border and west of the towns of Medford and Ashland. Although primarily associated with the state of Washington, parts of both the COLUMBIA VALLEY AVA and WALLA WALLA AVA extend into northern Oregon. Other Oregeon wineries (there are over seventy) include Adelsheim, Amity, Bethel Heights, DOMAINE DROUHIN (by the Drouhins of Burgundy), Elk Cover, Henry Estate, Knudsen-Erath Winery, Laurel Ridge, Montinore Vineyards, PANTHER CREEK, Ponzoi, Rex Hill, Sokal Blosser Winery, Tualatin Vineyards, and Yamhill Valley Vineyards. In Oregon a VARIETAL WINE must contain at least 90 percent of the named variety, except for Cabernet Sauvignon, which needs only 75 percent. Wines labeled with a named region must contain 100 percent of the wine from that region.

Oremasco *see* DOLCETTO

organic [or-GAN-ihk] The definition of an organic wine changes as various organizations study the subject in detail. In the United States these organizations include the Bureau of Alcohol, Tobacco and Firearms (BATF) and the California Certified Organic Farmers (CCOF). The phrase **organically grown grapes** refers to grapes that have been grown without the use of synthetic or chemically altered pesticides or fertilizers. **Organically processed wines** cannot contain any sulfur dioxide (SULFITES) added during winemaking. If a wine contains less than 10 parts per million (ppm) of sulfur dioxide, it's not required to print the "Contains Sulfites" warning on the label. The BATF does not allow the term *organic wine* to be used on wine labels, so the label must carry phrases such as "grapes organically grown" and "wine organically processed." The Organic Grapes Into Wine Alliance (OGWA) is also looking into other winemaking aspects such as FINING, FILTERING, and clarifying materials, storage tanks, barrel sterilizing materials, bottle CAPSULE materials, and CORKS (chemicals used to bleach them) to determine how these elements fit into the concept of organic winemaking.

organoleptic [or-guh-nl-EHP-tihk; or-ga-nl-EHP-tihk] In the wine world, this term—which fundamentally means "perceived by a sense organ"—is used in relation to evaluating wine with the senses of sight, smell, and taste, rather than by a scientific or chemical examination. Although winemakers rely on precise technical evaluations of their wines, the final outcome usually depends on an expert's organoleptic determination.

originalabfüllung [oh-RIHG-ih-nahl-AHB-foo-lung] A German term once used to indicate that a wine was ESTATE BOTTLED. In 1971 the term Originalabfüllung was legally replaced by ERZEUGERABFÜLLUNG, which means "bottled by the proprietor" and has a denotation similar to estate bottled. More recently, the term GUTSABFÜLLUNG was introduced—it's more restrictive and even closer to the United States definition of estate bottled.

oro *see* MARSALA DOC

Ortega [or-TAY-guh] White-wine grape named after the Spanish philosopher José Ortega y Gasset. It is a cross of MÜLLER-THURGAU and Siegerrebe (which is a GEWÜRZTRAMINER-Madeleine Angevine hybrid). The low-ACID, high-sugar Ortega grape produces wines with delightful FLORAL characteristics and hints of peach in both aroma and flavor. Ortega VARIETAL WINES are popular in Germany where they've won numerous medals in wine competitions. Ortega is primarily used for BLENDING, however, usually combined with grapes that have lower sugar content and higher acid.

Ortsteil [OHRTS-tile] A German term referring to an area that's part of a larger commuity (as a suburb is of a city), yet is independent of that larger community. For example, the village of ERBACH is an *Ortsteil* of Eltville. Esteemed vineyards, like SCHLOSS JOHANNISBERG and STEINBERG, are classified as Ortsteile and, therefore, unlike other vineyards, aren't required to put the name of their village (the larger community) on bottle labels. For example, wines from the Steinberg vineyard, which is part of HATTENHEIM, are labeled simply "Steinberg," whereas wines from the neighboring Schützenhaus vineyard are labeled "Hattenheimer Schützenhaus."

Orvieto DOC [ohr-VYAY-toh] Well-known DOC area that is located in the southwestern part of Italy's UMBRIA region and that produces about two-thirds of Umbria's DOC wines. It covers a large area surrounding the hilltop town of Orvieto, with a Classico zone covering a smaller area at the center. Wines from this Classico area are generally better. Orvieto produces mostly DRY, ordinary white wines from TREBBIANO, MALVASIA, Verdello, GRECHETTO, and Drupeggio grapes. The sweeter wines of this DOC (ABBOCCATO, AMABILE, or DOLCE) are better, especially those made from grapes infected with BOTRYTIS CINEREA, which engenders a RICH, honeyed flavor. It's thought that Orvieto's *abboccato*-style wines were favored in the Middle Ages; they were also prized by Pope Gregory XVI in the nineteenth century.

Osiris   *see* LA TOUR BLANCHE, CHÂTEAU

Ottaianello   *see* CINSAUT

ouillage   *see* TOPPING

ouvrée   [OO-vray] An old French measure used in Burgundy for area. An ouvrée is equal to about one-tenth of an acre.

overripe   Descriptor for a wine that usually has been made from grapes that have remained on the vine too long before being picked. Such grapes are generally high in sugar and low in ACID. In some wines, such as ZINFANDELS, slightly overripe grapes can be desirable; a CHARDONNAY made with such grapes, however, can be HEAVY and out of BALANCE. *See also* PRUNEY.

oxidation   *see* OXIDIZED

oxidized   A term used to describe wine that has undergone *oxidation* (exposure to air), which causes chemical changes and deterioration. Oxidized wines have a stale, sherrylike smell and flavor, and their color takes on a brownish cast. Although this trait is considered undesirable in a TABLE WINE and can render it undrinkable, it's deemed an asset in wines like SHERRY and MADEIRA. Even though the term oxidized is often used synonymously with that of MADERIZED, the latter infers that, in addition to air exposure, the wine has also endured storage in an overly warm environment.

aarl Riesling *see* CROUCHEN

Pacherenc du Vic Bilh AC [pah-shuh-RAHNK doo veek BEEL] In this part of southwest France, the local dialect uses the word *pacherenc* for "posts in a row." This refers to the modern method of planting vineyards in regular rows, using a post to support each vine. Vic Bilh is the name for the local hills in this area, which are part the Pyrenees foothills, along the Adour River south of ARMAGNAC. This APPELLATION produces only white wines and shares the same geographic area as the MADIRAN AC, which produces only red wines. The grapes used for these white wines are Arrufiat (or *Ruffiac*), Gros Manseng, and Petit Manseng, with some SAUVIGNON BLANC and SÉMILLON. These wines are similiar to those from the JURANCON AC (SPICY and FLORAL) and should be drunk young.

Padthaway [PAD-thuh-way] An Australian wine-producing area in the southeastern corner of South Australia near the New South Wales border. Early on it was called Keppoch, but after a struggle over the name it was changed to Padthaway. This is predominately white wine country. Rhine Riesling (RIESLING) is the most popular grape, followed by CHARDONNAY, and Traminer (GEWÜRZTRAMINER). Shiraz (SYRAH) is the most widely planted red variety.

Pais *see* MISSION

Palatinate *see* RHEINPFALZ

Palazzo Altesi [pah-LAHT-tsoh ahl-TAY-see] The proprietary name for a high-quality VINO DA TAVOLA made by Altesino, a wine estate in the Montalcino that also makes highly regarded BRUNELLO DI MONTALCINO DOCG wines. Palazzo Altesi is made from Brunello (SANGIOVESE), with part of the grapes going through CARBONIC MACERATION and the rest FERMENTED normally. The wines are combined and then AGED in BARRIQUES. The resulting super-Tuscan (*see* TUSCANY) wine is highly regarded.

pale cream *see* SHERRY

Palette AC [pah-LEHT] A tiny APPELLATION located east of AIX-EN-PROVENCE in the western part of France's PROVENCE region. The majority of the wines are red and ROSÉ, produced from CINSAUT, GRENACHE, MOURVÈDRE, and SYRAH. White wines use CLAIRETTE, Grenache Blanc, MUSCAT, Picpoul, and Ugni Blanc (TREBBIANO). The dominant producer is **Château Simone**.

Pálido *see* RUEDA DO

Palmer, Château [sha-TOH pahl-MEH*R* (PAHL-muhr)] Although ranked as a TROISIÈME CRU (third growth) in the CLASSIFICATION OF 1855, many wine fanciers feel that this CHÂTEAU is a candidate for upgrading to PREMIER CRU (first growth) status. Located in the MARGAUX AC in BORDEAUX, Château Palmer gets its name from the Englishman General Palmer, who owned the property in the nineteenth century. It consists of nearly 111 acres and produces 12,000 to 15,000 cases of superior-quality wine each year. The wines, which are a blend of about 55 percent CABERNET SAUVIGNON, 40 percent MERLOT, and small amounts of CABERNET FRANC and PETIT VERDOT, are generally RICH and SUPPLE and have a marvelous perfumed BOUQUET. The best VINTAGES are capable of AGING for 20 to 30 years. A SECOND LABEL **Réserve du Général** is in honor of the General.

palo cortado [PAH-loh koh-TAH-doh] *see* SHERRY

Palomino [pah-loh-MEE-noh] The grape that makes the great Spanish SHERRIES. Palomino is not distinctive when used to make standard white TABLE WINES, but when it's processed to make sherry it can turn into something special. It's heavily grown in and around JEREZ DE LA FRONTERA in the ANDALUCIA region of Spain. *Palomino Fino* is actually the strain that now represents about 90 percent of the planting in the Jerez area, as opposed to the previously favored *Palomino Basto* (or *Palomino de Jerez*) grape. Palomino is also cultivated in the hotter growing areas of Australia, California, France, and South Africa. Attempts to make sherry in these regions has produced some good versions of this FORTIFIED wine, but they're not the quality of the top Spanish wines. Palomino is also called *Ablan, Listán,* and *Tempranilla*; in California it's mistakenly call *Golden Chasselas.* Australia's *Common Palomino* is not the same grape as Palomino.

Panache *see* DOMAINE CHANDON

pantomina *see* MÁLAGA DO

Pape-Clément, Château [sha-TOH pahp klay-MAH*N*] A CRU CLASSÉ château located in the PESSAC-LÉOGNAN AC of BORDEAUX. This estate's name is associated with Bertrand de Goth, who purchased the property in 1300 as the Archbishop of Bordeaux and later became Pope Clement V. He's the same pope who moved the papacy to the city of Avignon in southern France and produced wines in the nearby wine-growing area that's become known as CHÂTEAUNEUF-DU-PAPE. Château Pape-Clement has around 86 acres that annually produce about 11,000 cases of red wine and 1,000 cases of white wine. The quality of the CHÂTEAU'S wines have been somewhat inconsistent, although VINTAGES since 1984 show definite signs of improvement. Some of the better vintages are capable of AGING for 18 to 20 years. The red wines are made with about 60 percent CABERNET SAUVIGNON and 40 percent MERLOT and the white wines with about equal parts SÉMILLON and SAUVIGNON BLANC. The château's SECOND LABEL is called **Le Clémentin du Pape-Clément**.

Paradiesgarten *see* DEIDESHEIM

La Parde de Haut-Bailly *see* HAUT-BAILLY, CHÂTEAU

Parellada [par-eh-LYAH-duh] Spanish white-wine grape that is one of the main varieties in Spain's CATALONIA region. Parellada produces light, fruity, good-quality STILL wines with floral BOUQUETS. These wines don't AGE well, however, and should be drunk young. The best known single-variety Parellada wine is the Vina Sol from TORRES. This producer also blends Parellada with CHARDONNAY to produce Gran Vina Sol and with SAUVIGNON BLANC to produce Fransola. Parellada is one of the three main varieties used in SPARKLING WINE production as well. It's also known as *Montonec*.

Parsac *see* PUISSEGUIN-SAINT-ÉMILION AC

Pas de Deux *see* FOLIE À DEUX WINERY

Paso Robles AVA [PAH-soh ROH-blays] A large APPELLATION located around the town of Paso Robles in California's SAN LUIS OBISPO COUNTY. Its northern boundary is the MONTEREY COUNTY line, and it extends south of the town of Santa Margarita. The eastern boundary is parallel to the Kern County line, and the western boundary is the San Lucia Mountains, west of Paso Robles. Most of the growing area is classified as Region III (*see* CLIMATE REGIONS OF CALIFORNIA), although portions in the east are hotter and fall into Region IV. Some microclimates that receive more cooling ocean breezes fall into the cooler Region II category. CABERNET SAUVIGNON, CHARDONNAY, ZINFANDEL, and SAUVIGNON BLANC are the top four grape varieties grown in the Paso Robles AVA. Other red varieties include MERLOT, PETITE SIRAH, PINOT NOIR, SYRAH, GAMAY, and CABERNET FRANC. Other whites grapes are CHENIN BLANC, MUSCAT, and SÉMILLON. The area's best known for its red wines such as Cabernet Sauvignon and Zinfandel. Area wineries include Castoro Cellars, Creston Vineyards, Eberle, Meridian, Martin Brothers, Peachy Canyon, and Wild Horse Winery. J. Lohr Winery, located in

Santa Clara, California, produces VINEYARD-DESIGNATED Cabernet Sauvignon from here as well.

passe-tout-grains *see* BOURGOGNE PASSE-TOUT-GRAIN AC

passito [pah-SEE-toh] An Italian term used both for a method of making sweet wines and for the sweet wines made this way. Passito wines begin by laying freshly picked grapes on mats (or hanging them in bunches) so that they can partially dry. This process eliminates much of the grape's water and concentrates its sugar and flavor components. Depending on the technique used, the drying time can vary from several weeks (in the hot sun) to several months (in a cool ventilated room). When the grapes are crushed and FERMENTATION begins, the sugar content is usually high enough to take the wine to a reasonable alcohol level (*see* ALCOHOL BY VOLUME) and still end up with enough RESIDUAL SUGAR to make these wines fairly sweet.

pasteurize [PAS-chuh-rize; PAS-tuh-rize] To kill bacteria by heating wine or other liquid to moderately high temperatures for a short period of time and then rapidly cooling it to 40°F or lower. The process was discovered by the famous French scientist Louis Pasteur while he was researching the cause of beer and wine spoilage. Although pasteurization is used in beer processing and for some wines meant for early consumption, it's not used for fine wines because it kills off the bacteria that contribute to AGING.

Paterberg *see* NIERSTEIN

Patrimonio AC *see* CORSICA

Pauillac AC [poh-YAK] The town of Pauillac, located in HAUT-MÉDOC that is probably the most noteworthy in France's BORDEAUX region. The APPELLATION surrounding Pauillac contains three of the five PREMIER CRU (first growth) Châteaus—LATOUR, LAFITE-ROTHSCHILD, and MOUTON-ROTHSCHILD—along with fifteen other CRU CLASSÉ châteaus including LYNCH-BAGES, PICHON-LONGUEVILLE-BARON, and PICHON-LALANDE. Because cru classé châteaus own much of the approximately 2,400 acres in the appellation, there are few well-known CRU BOURGEOIS châteaus. The dominant grape in Pauillac is CABERNET SAUVIGNON, which is blended with CABERNET FRANC, MERLOT, and, occasionally, small amounts of MALBEC and PETIT VERDOT. Pauillac AC wines from the best VINTAGES are generally powerful, full-flavored, and ELEGANT. When young, they're a bit ROUGH, but they AGE magnificently.

Les Paulands *see* CORTON

Pavie, Château [sha-TOH pah-VEE] The largest of the PREMIERS GRANDS CRUS CLASSÉS in SAINT-ÉMILION AC. Château Pavie has nearly 92 acres planted with about 55 percent MERLOT, 25 percent CABERNET FRANC, and 20 percent CABERNET SAUVIGNON. It averages about 15,000 cases of red wine each year. The wines during the 1980s have been of consistently better quality than those from preceding years. They're deep-colored, full-bodied, and TANNIC. They generally require 5 to 6 years to SOFTEN and are capable of AGING for 18 to 20 years. **Château Pavie-Decesse** is owned by the proprietors of Château Pavie. It also produced good red wines throughout the 1980s, although they're a different style—more tannic and AUSTERE.

Pavie-Decesse, Château *see* PAVIE, CHÂTEAU

Pavie-Macquin, Château [sha-TOH pah-vee mah-KEE*N*] A GRAND CRU CLASSÉ estate located in the SAINT-ÉMILION AC in BORDEAUX. Château Pavie-Macquin has nearly 35 acres planted with about 80 percent MERLOT and the rest CABERNET FRANC and CABERNET SAUVIGNON. The high-quality 1988, 1989, and 1990 VINTAGES are comparable to a CINQUIÈME CRU (fifth growth) of the MÉDOC district. This CHÂTEAU produces about 4,000 cases of red wine each year.

Pavillon Blanc du Château Margaux *see* MARGAUX, CHÂTEAU

Pavillon Rouge du Château Margaux *see* MARGAUX, CHÂTEAU

pays *see* VIN DE PAYS

Pécharmant AC [pay-sha*r*-MAH*N*] A small area east of the town of BERGERAC that produces red wines from MERLOT, CABERNET SAUVIGNON, CABERNET FRANC, and MALBEC. The wines, which are some of the better ones in the Bergerac region, resemble those from nearby SAINT-ÉMILION in the BORDEAUX region.

Pechsten *see* FORST

Robert Pecota Winery [peh-KOH-tuh] Robert Pecota learned the wine business during his stint at BERINGER VINEYARDS in a variety of capacities. He bought a 35-acre PETITE SIRAH vineyard in 1978 and built a small winery on the property. Pecota now owns 50 acres of vineyards planted with CABERNET SAUVIGNON, MERLOT, and SAUVIGNON BLANC (the Petite Sirah is gone). Robert Pecota Winery produces all three varieties as VARIETAL WINES. It also makes GAMAY, CHARDONNAY, and a sweet

MUSCAT called Muscato di Andrea, after Pecota's daughter. About 20,000 cases of wine are produced each year.

Pedernão *see* ARINTO

Pedesclaux, Château [sha-TOH pay-dehs-KLOH] An obscure CINQUIÈME CRU (fifth growth) CHÂTEAU located in the PAUILLAC AC in the MÉDOC district of BORDEAUX. Its nearly 44 acres produce about 8,000 cases of average-quality red wine each year. The château's main customers are in Belgium and France, and not much is sold to other countries. The grape varieties are approximately 65 percent CABERNET SAUVIGNON and 20 percent MERLOT, along with small amounts of CABERNET FRANC, MALBEC, and PETIT VERDOT.

Pedro Domecq *see* DOMECQ, PEDRO

Pedro Jiménez *see* PEDRO XIMÉNEZ

Pedro Ximénez [PEH-droh hee-MEH-nihs; PAY-droh hee-MAY-nays] A white-wine grape grown in southern Spain whose name is the Hispanic transliteration of Peter Siemens, the man who brought the vine from Germany to Spain's SHERRY-making region, Jerez (JEREZ Y MANZANILLA). Although usually associated with sherry, Pedro Ximénez (or *PX,* as it's commonly called) has been heavily supplanted by PALOMINO in Jerez and is now used mainly for sweetening and darkening the Palomino-based blends. Pedro Ximénez is still widely planted in Spain's MONTILLA-MORILES area where it's often processed to make a sherry-style wine. It's also a major grape of Spain's MÁLAGA region where it's made into high-ALCOHOL, medium- to very-sweet wines. In much of Spain, a light, rather bland, DRY white TABLE WINE is also made from this variety. Pedro Ximénez is the most widely planted white variety in Argentina and is widely grown in Australia as well. In the United States, small amounts of sherry-style PX wines are used to soften blended whiskeys. Pedro Ximénez is also known as *Pedro Jiménez* and *Pero Ximen.*

pelure d'oignon [peh-LEWR dohn-YAWN] A French term for "onion skin." In wine parlance it refers to the brownish-orange tint that some older red wines develop as they age. The term is also sometimes used with light red or ROSÉ wines.

Penedès DO [pay-NAY-dahss] DO area located southwest of the city of Barcelona in northeast Spain's CATALONIA region. The area is the center of the SPARKLING WINE industry, which has its own DO, CAVA. There are three subzones—Bajo Penedès, Medio Penedès, and Penedès Superior—all with different growing conditions. Because of this, the subzones are each best for specific kinds of grapes. The Penedès DO makes STILL WINES, which are predominantly white because of the large amount of white varieties planted for the sparkling wine industry. The predominant grapes are PARELLADA, MACABEO, and XAREL-LO, although there is a growing interest in CHARDONNAY. The smaller amount of red and ROSÉ wine that's produced here is made primarily from Garnacha Tinta (GRENACHE), Carinena (CARIGNAN), and TEMPRANILLO. CABERNET SAUVIGNON is an approved variety and the best red wines are made from it. Compared to most of Spain's wine industry, the Penedès DO is very modern. It's a leader in still-wine innovations—led by the wine estates of TORRES, JEAN LEÓN, and Masía Bach.

penetrating A wine described as penetrating, or having a penetrating NOSE, is one with an intense, almost tactile aroma, generally the result of high ALCOHOL and overt ESTERS.

Les Pensées de Lafleur *see* LAFLEUR, CHÂTEAU

peppery A winetasting term for wines with spicy, black-pepper characteristics, sometimes accompanied by high ALCOHOL. A peppery trait is often found in RHÔNE wines and some vintage PORTS.

perfume; perfumed The perfume of a wine is its smell—a perfumed wine has an intensely fragrant aroma, which is usually representative of the grapes from which it was made. *See also* BOUQUET.

Le Pergole Torte The proprietary name for a super-Tuscan (*see* TUSCANY) made by the CHIANTI CLASSICO estate of Monte Vertine. Le Pergole Torte was the first wine from this area to use only SANGIOVESE and to be AGED in BARRIQUES. The first release was in 1977. IL SODACCIO is produced by the same firm.

Periquita [peh-ree-KEE-tah] A red-wine grape grown throughout southern Portugal, especially in the coastal areas. Periquita produces full-bodied (*see* BODY) wines that can be quite HARSH when young. They AGE well, however, and SOFTEN in the bottle, developing into firm-STRUCTURED wines with a hint of fig in the flavor. In Portugal's Algrave region, Periquita is often BLENDED with TINTA NEGRA MOLE, producing a much lighter style of wine. Periquita is also known as *Castellhão Frances* and *João de Santarém.*

Perlan *see* CHASSELAS

perlant [PEHR-law*n*] A French tasting term referring to a wine with an extremely slight sparkle—so slight that it feels more like a tickle on the palate.

perlwein [PEH*R*L-vine] A German term for a slightly SPARKLING WINE, usually artificially carbonated and of TAFELWEIN (the lowest) quality. SEKT is a finer-quality German sparkling wine.

Pernand-Vergelesses [peh*r*-NAH*N* veh*r*-zhuh-LEHSS] A lesser-known wine-producing village at the northern end of the CÔTE DE BEAUNE district in France's BURGUNDY region. The most celebrated wines come from the vineyards on Montagne de Corton, a vast hill rising above the village. The area's red wines, made from PINOT NOIR grapes, and white wines, made from CHARDONNAY grapes (and a small amount from ALIGOTÉ grapes), are both highly regarded—the reds slightly more than the whites. Pernand-Vergelesses shares two GRANDS CRUS—CORTON (red wines) and CORTON-CHARLEMAGNE (white wines)— with the villages of ALOXE-CORTON and LADOIX-SERRIGNY. Wines from these two grands crus are ranked among the world's finest. The red wines from Corton are considered some of the best and longest aging in Burgundy, and Corton-Charlemagne's whites are compared to other top white wines from the region. Pernand Vergelesses also has a number of fine PREMIER CRU vineyards including **En Caradeux, Île des Vergelesses, Les Vergeless,** and **Les Fichots**. The wines produced under the general village appellation of **Pernand Vergelesses AC** are generally of good quality and usually less expensive than some of Burgundy's other village wines.

peronospera *see* MILDEW

Pero Ximen *see* PEDRO XIMÉNEZ

Perrier, Joseph [peh-RYAY] A small CHAMPAGNE house located in Chalons-sur-Marne in France's Champagne region. It produces only about 650,000 bottles annually. The premium brand is Cuvée du Cent-Cinquantenaire, made entirely from CHARDONNAY grapes. Their non-VINTAGE wines like the Cuvée Royale Brut and Brut Blanc de Blancs are usually of a LIGHT, FRESH style.

Les Perrières *see* CORTON; MEURSAULT; NUITS-SAINT-GEORGES

Perrier-Jouët [peh-RYAY zhoo-AY] Located in Epernay, France, this medium-sized CHAMPAGNE house is owned by the larger house MUMM. Perrier-Jouët produces about 3 million bottles annually, led by its premium brand *Belle Epoque* in its distinctive painted bottle. Perrier-Jouët is also well-known for its *Blason de France.*

persistence *see* LENGTH

Pesquera *see* RIBERA DEL DUERO DO

Pessac-Léognan AC [peh-SAK leh-oh-NYAH*N*] A new APPELLA-TION created in 1987 out of the northern part of the GRAVES area in France's BORDEAUX region. Wines in this area were formerly part of the Graves AC, although the use of **Graves-Pessac** or **Graves-Léognan** had been allowed on labels for several years prior to the new appellation's approval. This northern part of Graves contains more of the desirable gravelly soil than the southern portion and generally makes superior wines. The Pessac-Léognan AC takes in all the CRU CLASSÉ châteaus of Graves. It encompasses ten northerly COMMUNES, two of which—Pessac and Léognan—contribute to the appellation's name. This appellation's roster of CHÂTEAUS is led by HAUT-BRION, the only non-MÉDOC château to be included in the CLASSIFICATION OF 1855, and one of only four Bordeaux châteaus to receive a PREMIER CRU ranking at that time. Other noteworthy châteaus include LA MISSION HAUT-BRION, LAVILLE HAUT-BRION, LES CARMES HAUT-BRION, DOMAIN DE CHEVALIER, PAPE CLÉ-MENT, and HAUT BAILLY. The area's white wines, which are produced from SAUVIGNON BLANC, SÉMILLON and MUSCADELLE, are made in a CRISP, DRY style. Pessac-Léognan AC's distinctive, EARTHY red wines—made predominantly from CABERNET SAUVIGNON, CABERNET FRANC, and MERLOT—have a reputation for being of higher quality than the whites.

pétillant; pétillance [pay-tee-YAW*N*] A French wine-tasting term meaning "slightly sparkling," referring to wines with light effervescence. *Pétillance* is the noun form. The Italian equivalent of pétillant is *frizzante*; the German is *spritzig*.

petit [puh-TEE] French word meaning "small" or "little." When used as a wine descriptor, petit refers to a rather ordinary, lesser-quality wine that lacks BODY and ALCOHOL.

Petit Chablis AC *see* CHABLIS

Le Petit Cheval *see* CHEVAL BLANC, CHÂTEAU

Petite-Cabernet *see* CABERNET SAUVIGNON

La Petite L'Eglise *see* L'EGLISE-CLINET, CHÂTEAU

Petite Sirah; Petite Syrah [peh-TEET sih-RAH; peh-TEET see-RAH] Grown mainly in California, this red-wine grape was initially thought to be related to the renowned SYRAH of France's RHÔNE region. Some, however, believe it is actually a variety called DURIF, which was also grown in the Rhone but is now almost extinct. Petite Sirah produces a deep-colored, ROBUST, and PEPPERY wine that packs plenty of TANNINS and has good AGING ability. Although not as popular as CABERNET SAUVIGNON, PINOT NOIR, or ZINFANDEL, Petite Sirah does much better in California than in France and has a following among those who like BIG, full-bodied wines. Although in vogue during the 1970s, Petite Sirah's popularity has since diminished somewhat, and acreage throughout the state has subsequently declined. In addition to being bottled as a VARIETAL WINE, Petite Sirah is often blended with other varietals (ZINFANDEL, for example) to give them zest and complexity.

Petit Gamai *see* GAMAY

Petit Gris *see* PINOT GRIS

Petit-Mayne *see* LE CAILLOU, CHÂTEAU

Petit Noir *see* NEGRETTE

Les Petits Vougeots *see* VOUGEOT

Petit Verdau *see* PETIT VERDOT

Petit Verdot [puh-TEE veh*r*-DOH] A high-quality red-wine grape grown mainly in France's BORDEAUX region. Petit Verdot produces full-bodied, extremely deep-colored wines with peppery, spicy flavor characteristics, and high TANNINS and ALCOHOL. It's traditionally been used to add flavor, color, and tannins to the BORDEAUX blend. This is particularly true in the southern MÉDOC where, because of the soils, lighter wines are generally produced from the basic grapes CABERNET SAUVIGNON, MERLOT, and CABERNET FRANC. Petit Verdot ripens very late and sometimes doesn't mature at all, a trait that's prompted a number of CHÂTEAUS in Bordeaux to eliminate it from their vineyards. Recently, there's been a minor planting revival by some of the more quality-conscious producers. Small amounts of Petit Verdot are planted in Chile and California. It's also called *Carmelin, Petit Verdau,* and *Verdot Rouge.*

Petit-Village, Château [sha-TOH puh-TEE vee-LAHZH] A 27-acre estate located in the POMEROL AC of BORDEAUX. The quality of the wines continued to improve throughout the 1980s, and recent VINTAGES make it one of the better Pomerol estates. Annual production is around 5,000 cases of red wine, made with 70 to 80 percent MERLOT and the rest CABERNET FRANC and CABERNET SAUVIGNON. Although wines from recent vintages are mature and drinkable within 5 to 6 years, they can AGE for up to 12 to 15 years.

petrol; petroleum A sensory term used to describe the faint smell of petroleum found in some wines, such as mature RIESLINGS. This term is generally considered positive.

Pétrus, Château [sha-TOH pay-TREWSS] Although the CHÂ-TEAUS of the POMEROL AC have never been classified, that hardly matters to Château Pétrus. It's considered an equal of the Médoc PREMIERS CRUS (first growths) and has become the most expensive wine in BORDEAUX, with recent VINTAGES ranging from $250 to $400 or more per bottle. Château Pétrus is a small, 28-acre estate that averages around 4,000 cases of red wine each year. Although the vineyards are planted with about 95 percent MERLOT and 5 percent CABERNET FRANC, the grapes selected for many VINTAGES are 100 percent MERLOT. Although Merlot is generally viewed as producing less TANNIC wines that are SOFTER and more SUPPLE (than CABERNET SAUVIGNON, for example), those from Château Pétrus are often BIG and full-bodied, with plenty of concentrated fruit and tannins. Wines from years like 1964, 1970, and 1975 are demonstrating that they can AGE for 40 to 50 years or more.

Pettenthal *see* NIERSTEIN

Peymartin *see* GLORIA, CHÂTEAU

Pfalz *see* RHEINPFALZ

pH A standard used to measure the ACIDITY or alkalinity of a liquid on a scale of 0 to 14. A pH greater than 7 represents alkalinity, 7 denotes neutrality, and less than 7 indicates acidity (the lower the number, the higher the acidity). The pH measurement represents the *intensity* of the acid, whereas titratable (total) acidity measures the *volume* of acid. The desirable pH range for TABLE WINES is approximately 3.0 to 3.6. As the pH level drops below 3.0, the wine becomes unpleasantly SHARP; above 3.6 and it becomes FLAT and FLABBY. Even though the volume of acidity might be in the proper range, if the pH is too high or too low, the wine won't be well BALANCED. Low pH also deters bacterial growth (which translates to better AGING) and helps wine keep its color. Winemakers use pH, along with other factors such as grape ripeness and volume of acid, to help determine the resulting wine's potential quality. *See also* ACIDS; MALOLACTIC FERMENTATION.

Joseph Phelps Vineyards In the early 1970s, Joseph Phelps visited California planning to expand his succesful Colorado construction business. He ended up building a few wineries and buying a 670-acre NAPA VALLEY ranch east of St. Helena and the Silverado Trail. Phelps then proceeded to plant his own vineyards and build his own winery. After an initial start with white VARIETALS like RIESLING, GEWÜRZ-TRAMINER, and SAUVIGNON BLANC, the winery began producing red wines. These included Insignia (a CABERNET SAUVIGNON-CABERNET FRANC-MERLOT blend), a Backus Vineyard Cabernet Sauvignon, an Eisele

Vineyard Cabernet Sauvignon, and a Napa Valley Cabernet Sauvignon. The earlier white wines had drawn a great deal of favorable attention, but the red wines elicited even more notice. Phelps continues to experiment with different grape varieties and styles of wine. The **Vin du Mistral** line features RHÔNE-region grapes such as GRENACHE, MOURVÈDRE, SYRAH, and VIOGNIER. The winery also produces CHARDONNAY, MERLOT, and ZINFANDEL wines. About 80,000 cases per year are produced from over 300 acres of estate-owned vineyards.

phenolic compounds [fee-NAHL-ihk] Naturally occurring compounds present in grape skins and seeds and extracted from oak barrels. Phenolic compounds include TANNINS and pigments and are responsible for ASTRINGENCY, bitterness, color, some flavors and odors (like VANILLIN), and antioxidant activity (which helps wines AGE). These compounds are present in all wine in small amounts, with red wines containing more because of the extended contact with skins and seeds and, in many cases, longer oak barrel aging.

phylloxera [fihl-LOX-er-uh] A tiny aphidlike insect that attacks the roots of grapevines. Phylloxera sucks the nutrients from the roots and slowly starves the vine, creating a dramatic decrease in fruit. It doesn't affect the taste of the resulting wine but, eventually, replanting is required. Unfortunately, new vines do not produce the same quality fruit until they mature, which can take 8 to 10 years or more. *Phylloxera vastatrix* (its Latin name) is thought to be indigenous to the eastern United States and the thick, strong, native American ROOTSTOCKS are reasonably resistant to this parasite. Much more vulnerable to phylloxera is the VITIS VINIFERA rootstock—a species native to Europe and Central Asia and responsible for a majority of the world's wine production. In the 1860s vine cuttings from the eastern United States transmitted phylloxera to Europe, and eventually most of the vineyards in France and many in other parts of Europe were totally devastated. The parasite eventually spread, causing grave problems in California and other parts of the world including Australia, New Zealand, and South Africa. The solution was to graft vitis vinifera vines to native American rootstocks, a remedy that worked for the better part of a century. However, in the early 1980s a new strain of phylloxera—Biotype B—attacked California vineyards. It appears that a rootstock called AxR #1, used primarily throughout California's NAPA and SONOMA COUNTIES (and in other parts of California) wasn't resistant to this new phylloxera strain. Although AxR #1 had some vitis vinifera in its makeup, experts at the University of California at DAVIS originally recommended it because it produced much higher yields than other rootstocks and appeared to be phylloxera resistant. Chile is one of the few places that phylloxera has never invaded, and many of the vineyards are planted on vitis vinifera rootstock. At this writing, extensive replanting of more resistant rootstock is taking place throughout northern California.

Picardan Noir *see* CINSAUT

Pichon-Lalande, Château *see* PICHON-LONGUEVILLE-COMTESSE DE LALANDE, CHÂTEAU

Pichon-Longueville Baron, Château [sha-TOH pee-SHAW*N* law*ng*-VEEL beh*r*-ON] The full name of this estate is **Château Pichon-Longueville au Baron de Pichon-Longueville**, although it's more often referred to as *Pichon-Longueville Baron* or sometimes simply as *Pichon-Longueville* or *Pichon-Baron*. The estate was once part of a larger property (Pichon-Longueville) that was divided between the Baron de Pichon-Longueville and his three sisters. The other Pichon property (Château PICHON-LONGUEVILLE-COMTESSE DE LALANDE) bears the name of Virginie, the sister who became the Comtesse de Lalande. Château Pichon-Longueville Baron is located in the PAUILLAC AC of the MÉDOC district of BORDEAUX. It was ranked as a DEUXIÈME CRU (second growth) in the CLASSIFICATION OF 1855. The property consists of nearly 77 acres and produces some 14,000 to 20,000 cases of red wine. The quality of the wines has improved throughout the 1980s, especially since Jean-Michel Cazes of Château LYNCH-BAGES took over in 1987. The château now merits its second-growth rating and compares favorably with the neighboring Château Pichon-Longueville-Comtesse de Lalande. The wines, which are made using approximately 75 percent CABERNET SAUVIGNON and 25 percent MERLOT, are now deeply-colored, full-bodied (*see* BODY), richly flavored, and capable of AGING for 20 to 30 years. A SECOND LABEL **Les Tourelles de Pichon** is now being used.

Pichon-Longueville-Comtesse de Lalande, Château [sha-TOH pee-SHAW*N* law*ng*-VEEL koh*m*-TEHSS duh lah-LAH*N*D] Highly regarded estate, which is also known simply as **Pichon-Lalande** or **Pichon-Comtesse**, that was once part of a larger property named Pichon-Longueville. It was divided in 1850 between the Baron de Pichon-Longueville (*see* Château PICHON-LONGUEVILLE BARON) and his three sisters. This CHÂTEAU was named after one sister, Virginie, who became the Comtesse de Lalande. It's located in the PAUILLAC AC (although part of the vineyards are actually in the SAINT-JULIAN AC) of the MÉDOC district of BORDEAUX. It's classified as DEUXIÈME CRU (second growth), but the quality of its wines—particularly since the early 1960s—has been more like that of a PREMIER CRU (first growth). The estate consists of 185 acres planted with about 45 percent CABERNET SAUVIGNON, 35 percent MERLOT, 12 percent CABERNET FRANC, and 8 percent PETIT VERDOT. This is a high percentage of Merlot for this area and results in wines that are PERFUMED, SOFT, and FLESHY. The château averages about 30,000 cases of red wine per year plus an additional 6,000 cases under its SECOND LABEL **Réserve de la Comtesse**.

Picolit [PEEK-oh-lee] Thought to have been cultivated since Roman times, Picolit is a rather scarce and unique white-wine grape found in Italy's FRIULI-VENEZIA GIULIA region. The only DOC in which it is designated is COLLI ORIENTALI DEL FRIULI. Picolit was once more widely planted than it is now and had gained a reputation as this region's most exalted DESSERT WINE. However, because of FLORAL ABORTION, Picolit is an extremely low-yielding vine, and plantings are very limited today. The historic reputation and the scarce supply has created exorbitant prices for these sweet, flowery wines.

Picotener *see* NEBBIOLO

Picpoul de Pinet VDQS *see* COTEAUX DU LANGUEDOC

Picpoule *see* FOLLE BLANCHE

Pic Saint-Loup *see* COTEAUX DU LANGUEDOC

pièce [pee-YESS] The French name for an oak barrel used in the CÔTE D'OR, BEAUJOLAIS, and MACON regions of BURGUNDY to age and store wine. A pièce can vary in size from 215 to 228 liters (approximately 56 to 60 U.S. gallons). It's similar in size to the BARRIQUE used in BORDEAUX.

Piedmont; It. Piemonte [PEED-mawnt (It. pay-MAWN-tay)] An important wine-producing region in northwestern Italy. Its name, which means "foot of the mountain," refers to its place at the base of the Alps, which create the natural boundary between Italy and its two neighbors France and Switzerland. A majority of the region's vineyards are southeast of Turin, the capital of Piedmont, although there are a few to the north and northeast. Piedmont contains four DOCG areas—ASTI SPUMANTE, BAROLO, BARBARESCO, and GATTINARA—and over thirty-four DOCS including BARBERA D'ALBA, BARBERA D'ASTI, DOLCETTO D'ALBA, ERBULANCE DI CALUSO, GAVI, GHEMME, and NEBBIOLO D'ALBA. Red wines are the favorites in this region, and the premier grape variety is NEBBIOLO, which is used in three of the DOCG wines and in a number of the DOC wines. BARBERA is the most widely planted variety, however, taking up over half the available vineyard space. Other popular red varieties include DOLCETTO, BONARDA, FREISA, GRIGNOLINO, CROATINA, and Vespolina. White wines are made from CORTESE, Moscato Bianco, Moscato di Caneli (*see* MUSCAT), ARNEIS, ERBALUCE, and Favorita. Also very popular in this region are the Muscat-based SPUMANTE (sparkling) wines from the DOCGs of ASTI SPUMANTE and MOSCATO D'ASTI (*see* ASTI SPUMANTE).

pierre-à-fusil [pee-AIR ah FOO-zee] French for FLINTY.

Piesport [PEEZ-port] A famous wine-producing village located along the Mosel River southwest of BERNKASTEL in Germany's MOSEL-SAAR-RUWER region. It's situated in the middle of a huge horseshoe-shaped bend in the river, where its steep hillside vineyards get the best southerly exposure. Piesporter wines, which are usually RIPE yet ELEGANT, with powerful BOUQUETS, can be some of the best of this region. The most famous EINZELLAGE is the 300-acre **Goldtröpfchen**, followed by **Falkenberg**, **Günterslay**, and **Treppchen**.

Pigato [pee-GAH-toh] A white-wine grape grown primarily in Italy's LIGURIA region. Pigato, whose name refers to its blotchy (oddly pigmented) skin, is thought to have originated in Greece. It produces attractive, full-bodied dry wines with floral and peach characteristics.

Pineau *see* PINOT NOIR

Pineau d'Anjou *see* CHENIN BLANC

Pineau de la Loire *see* CHENIN BLANC

Pineau des Charentes [pee-NOH day shah-RAHNT] A sweet, FORTIFIED apéritif made in France's Cognac region by adding COGNAC to unfermented grape juice to halt any FERMENTATION activity. The result is sweet (12 to 15 percent RESIDUAL SUGAR) and potent (from 16 to 22 percent ALCOHOL). Pineau des Charentes can be found in white, ROSÉ, and red versions. Because it's made with cognac instead of a neutral alcoholic spirit it's not classified as a VIN DOUX NATUREL but rather as a VIN DE LIQUEUR. Pineau des Charentes is similar to the RATAFIA from the CHAMPAGNE region and the FLOC DE GASCOGNE from the ARMAGNAC region, although it is better known than either. All are drunk chilled or on ice.

Pine Ridge Winery Winery that is located in the STAGS LEAP DISTRICT AVA in the NAPA VALLEY and that was started on a 50-acre site in 1978 by Gary Andrus and his partners. Pine Ridge Winery's holdings have now grown to nearly 150 acres of vineyards scattered throughout the Napa Valley. These vineyards are planted with CHARDONNAY, CHENIN BLANC, CABERNET SAUVIGNON, CABERNET FRANC, MALBEC, MERLOT, and

PETIT VERDOT. The Cabernet Sauvignon wines come in four different bottlings—Rutherford Cuvée, Stags Leap District, Diamond Mountain, and Andrus Reserve. A joint venture with Château LYNCH BAGES that produced a red wine called Cuvée Duet from the 1985 VINTAGE was short lived. Chardonnay is produced in two bottlings—Oak Knoll Cuvée and Stags Leap District. Pine Ridge Winery also makes a Merlot, called Selected Cuvée, and a Chenin Blanc, called Yountville Cuvée. The winery produces between 65,000 and 75,000 cases of wine each year.

pink champagne A generic term used in the United States for inexpensive, pink-hued, usually sweet, SPARKLING WINE. Pink champagne is generally made via the CHARMAT process or with artificially induced CARBONATION. *See also* CHAMPAGNE.

Pinnacles Vineyard *see* FRANCISCAN VINEYARDS

Pinotage [pee-noh-TAHJ] A South African CROSS of PINOT NOIR and CINSAUT (which the South Africans call *Hermitage,* thus the derived name Pinotage). This red-wine grape was bred in 1925, but it wasn't until wines made from Pinotage won awards in 1959 that it became popular. Pinotage is now extensively grown in South Africa with small amounts in California and New Zealand. The best examples of Pinotage wines are medium-bodied and subtly flavored—better than most Cinsaut wines but not as good as Pinot Noir.

Pinot Beurot *see* PINOT GRIS

Pinot Bianco *see* PINOT BLANC

Pinot Blanc [PEE-noh BLAH*N* (BLAH*N*GK)] There is much confusion about this white-wine grape. Pinot Blanc is not related to CHARDONNAY as once believed—it is part of the Pinot family of grapes, but Chardonnay is not. Adding to the confusion about Pinot Blanc is that much of what is called Pinot Blanc in Australia is really Chardonnay, and some of the Pinot Blanc vines in California have been identified as MELON DE BOURGOGNE. Pinot Blanc grapes produce comely DRY, white wines that are often compared to Chardonnay. They are, however, generally not as COMPLEX or flavorful as Chardonnay. Pinot Blanc's most noted growing area is the ALSACE region in France. However, some of the best Pinot Blanc wines come from California (CHALONE VINEYARDS does an excellent job) and the ALTO ADIGE region in Italy. Pinot Blanc wines are noted for their FRESH, YEASTY, appley aroma, sometimes with hints of spice. Although not considered to AGE as well as Chardonnay, better Pinot Blancs that are aged for a few years take on delicious honey overtones. Because of the crisp fresh flavors and the grape's high ACIDITY, Pinot Blanc is finding its way into more and more SPARKLING WINE. Pinot Blanc is also known as *Beli Pinot, Clevner, Pinot Bianco, Weissburgunder, Weisserburgunder,* and *Weisser Klevner.*

Pinot Buot *see* PINOT GRIS

Pinot Chardonnay *see* CHARDONNAY

Pinot de l'Ermitage *see* DURIF

Pinot de Romans *see* DURIF

Pinot Grigio *see* PINOT GRIS

Pinot Gris [PEE-noh GREE] French for "gray," which presumably refers to the grayish hue of this member of the Pinot family. The color of this grape can vary substantially, producing wines that range from white to slightly pink. The style of wines ranges from CRISP, LIGHT, and DRY—such as those produced in northern Italy (where Pinot Gris is called *Pinot Grigio*), to the RICH, FAT, HONEYED versions from France's ALSACE region (where Pinot Gris is called *Tokay d'Alsace*). Limited amounts of this grape are grown in other parts of France, as well as in Austria, Germany, Hungary, and Rumania. Other than a small group of producers in Oregon, there aren't substantial Pinot Gris plantings in the United States. Pinot Gris is also known as *Auxerrois Gris, Petit Gris, Pinot Beurot, Pinot Buot, Rülander,* and *Szükerbarát.*

Pinot Meunier *see* MEUNIER

Pinot Nero *see* PINOT NOIR

Pinot Noir [PEE-noh NWAHR] *The* red grape of France's BURGUNDY region. It's responsible for the great (and expensive) red wines from Burgundy's CÔTE D'OR region, which include those from BEAUNE, BONNES MARES, CHAMBERTIN, CORTON, MUSIGNY, POMMARD, RICHEBOURG, ROMANÉE-CONTI, and VOLNAY. Pinot Noir is thought to have been grown in France for over 2,000 years, perhaps even prior to the Roman invasion of this area. The Pinot vine is described as "genetically unstable," meaning that it mutates very easily, which makes consistency from this vine extremely difficult. There are estimates of over 1,000 different types or clones belonging to the Pinot family. Some, such as PINOT BLANC, PINOT GRIS, and PINOT MEUNIER, have become well-known varieties on their own. The combination of Pinot Noir's mutating characteristic and difficult growing requirements (a long, cool growing season) makes this variety a frustrating grape from which to make wine (even for the

Burgundians). This situation is aggravating for Pinot Noir lovers as well, because the gap between the high and low quality of this wine is broader than any of the other important reds. The flavor of Pinot Noir is chameleonlike. When young, good wines exhibit the simpler fruity characteristics of cherries, plums, raspberries, and strawberries. As these wines mature, they display a variety of COMPLEX characteristics including chocolate, game, figs, prunes, SMOKINESS, truffles, and violets. France is the largest cultivator of the Pinot Noir grape, but few areas outside of Burgundy make really *great* Pinot Noir wines. ALSACE, IRANCY, Jura, Lorraine, SANCERRE, and SAVOIE produce lighter red and rosé wines. In the CHAMPAGNE region Pinot Noir is one of the three grape varieties (along with CHARDONNAY and MEUNIER) allowed in the region's sparkling wine. Here, care must be taken in pressing the grapes so that the juice does not pick up the indigo color of the grape's skin. Pinot Noir is also an important red grape in Germany (where it's known as *Spätburgunder*), but it has a hard time fully ripening there and produces pale, light-bodied wines. In northern Italy, Pinot Noir is known as *Blauburgunder* in some areas and *Pinot Nero* in others. There are some very good Pinot Noir wines that come out of Italy's mountainous areas. Pinot Noir is also grown in Switzerland, as well as some of the eastern European countries. There's been a great deal of effort in the United States to emulate the great Burgundy Pinots, but vintners are still experimenting to come up with the right formula. Some of California's better Pinot Noir wines come from the state's cooler regions such as CARNEROS, the RUSSIAN RIVER VALLEY, and parts of MONTEREY, SAN LUIS OBISPO, and SANTA BARBARA counties. Oregon's long, cool growing season is conducive to the production of some delightful Pinot Noir wines. In various parts of the world Pinot Noir is also known as *Blauer Klevner, Blauer Spätburgunder, Burgundac Crni, Nagyburgundi, Pineau,* and *Savagnin Noir.*

pipe The Portuguese word for barrel is *pipa*. A pipe is, in fact, a large, lengthy barrel or cask with tapered ends. It's used for aging and shipping wine—extensively for PORT and also for MARSALA and MADEIRA. Pipes range in capacity from 418 to 630 liters (110½ to 166½ U.S. gallons). In Portugal's DOURO region where most port is made, the standard pipe measures 550 liters (145 U.S. gallons). In VILA NOVA DE GAIA where much of the port wine is aged pipes vary in size, although the standard pipe measure is 534 liters (141 U.S. gallons). For madeira wines, the standard is 418 liters (110½ U.S. gallons).

Piper Heidsieck [PIPE-er HIDE-sehk] A medium-size CHAMPAGNE house located in Reims in France's Champagne region. Piper

Heidsieck, which is owned by Rémy Martin, produces about 5 million bottles a year. Their premium brand is *Florens Louis,* and they produce a fully DRY premium champagne called *Brut Sauvage.* Piper Heidsieck invested in the California SPARKLING WINE industry with the creation of PIPER-SONOMA CELLARS.

Piper-Sonoma Cellars The French CHAMPAGNE house PIPER HEID-SIECK initially established Piper-Sonoma Cellars in 1980 as a joint venture with the Renfield Corporation and Sonoma Vineyards; it took over full ownership in 1988. The SPARKLING WINE facility is in the RUSSIAN RIVER AVA, between the towns of Windsor and Healdsburg in SONOMA COUNTY. Piper-Sonoma owns only 40 acres of its own and purchases most of its grapes from growers tied to the winery through long-term contracts. Between 140,000 and 150,00 cases of wine are produced each year. Four styles of MÉTHODE CHAMPENOISE sparkling wine, all VINTAGE dated, are produced—BLANC DE NOIRS, BRUT, Brut Reserve, and Tête de Cuvée.

pips Another term for grapeseeds that, if broken during CRUSHING, can impart a bitterness to the wine.

piqué [pee-KAY] A French term referring to wine that has gone sour and is turning vinegary. The English synonym is PRICKED.

Piqupoul de Pays *see* BACO BLANC

Pisse-vin *see* ARAMON

Plante Riche *see* ARAMON

Les Plantes du Mayne *see* GRAND-MAYNE, CHÂTEAU

Plant Gris *see* ALIGOTÉ

Plant Meunier *see* MEUNIER

plastering In winemaking this term refers to an archaic practice of adding gypsum or calcium sulfate (plaster of Paris) to improve the ACID level of a low-acid grape juice. As a side benefit, plastering also helps to clarify the wine. In Spain, where gypsum is called *yeso,* plastering has been popular in the making of SHERRY. In recent years, however, the addition of tartaric acid is replacing this process. Today, plastering is not used in making most higher-quality wines.

plonk [PLONGK] A slang term used in Britain to describe ordinary low-quality wines.

plump *see* FAT

podere [poh-DAY-reh] Italian for a "farm" or "estate."

pointe [PWANT] A French word synonymous with PUNT, the indentation in the bottom of a wine or CHAMPAGNE bottle.

La Pointe, Château [sha-TOH lah PWAHNT] With just over 61 acres, Château La Pointe is one of the larger POMEROL AC estates. Because of its size, it's also quite well known. The estate produces about 8,000 to 10,000 cases of red wine annually. MERLOT is the dominant variety, making up about 80 percent of the blend, the remainder of which is CABERNET FRANC and MALBEC. The quality of these wines is inconsistent, however, and, with AGING capabilities of 8 to 10 years at the most, not extremely long lived.

Pol Roger [pawl roh-ZHAY] Small CHAMPAGNE house that was Winston Churchill's favorite. In honor of him, they named their premium brand *Cuvée Sir Winston Churchill.* Upon his death, they gave the label a black border. Pol Roger is known for producing fresh, YEASTY, non-VINTAGE wines. Based in Epernay, France, Pol Roger produces approximately 1.4 million bottles annually.

pomace [PAH-muss] Called MARC in France, pomace is the residue (skins, pips, seeds, and pulp) that remains after the juice has been PRESSED from the grapes. Sometimes the pomace is further processed to make a brandy variously known as pomace brandy, EAU DE VIE, marc, grappa, or SUGAR WINE.

Pomerol AC [paw-muh-RAWL] Located on the east side of France's Dordogne River, this is the smallest of the fine-wine-producing districts of the BORDEAUX region. It's also the only district not to have rated its CHÂTEAUS in some official classification. Because it's not near the better-known districts of MÉDOC and GRAVES, Pomerol didn't gain much of an international following until the 1960s. Now its wines, led by those from the famous CHÂTEAU PÉTRUS, bring some of the highest prices in all of Bordeaux. The Pomerol area's 1,800 acres are planted predominantly with MERLOT, which does extremely well in the region's clay soil. Merlot, blended with some CABERNET FRANC and small amounts of CABERNET SAUVIGNON, produces wines that are generally SOFTER and less TANNIC than those from the Cabernet Sauvignon-dominated Médoc, yet Pomerol wines are still RICH and LUSH. The general perception is that these wines don't AGE as well as those from the Médoc, but there are great Pomerol wines from outstanding VINTAGES that have aged beautifully for 40 years and more. Château Pétrus, which is favorably compared to the PREMIERS CRUS (first growths) of the Médoc, is first among many superb châteaus including CERTAN DE MAY, LA CONSEILLANTE, L'EGLISE-CLINET, L'EVANGILE,

LAFEUR, LATOUR-POMEROL, PETIT-VILLAGE, TROTANOY, and VIEUX-CHÂTEAU-CERTAN.

Pomino DOC [paw-MEE-noh] A small DOC area located east of Florence in Italy's TUSCANY region. The area encircles the town of Pomino and includes some vineyards that are within the CHIANTI Rufina subzone as well. Pomino produces BIANCO, ROSSO, VIN SANTO Bianco, and Vin Santo Rosso. The BIANCO wines are made mainly from Pinot Bianco (PINOT BLANC), CHARDONNAY, and TREBBIANO but can also include up to 15 percent of other white grapes. SANGIOVESE is the dominant grape in the ROSSO wines, which can also include CANAIOLO, CABERNET FRANC, CABERNET SAUVIGNON, MERLOT, and others. Standard Rosso must be AGED for 1 year, the RISERVA for 3 years. The *vin santo* wines can range from DRY to sweet and must be aged for 3 years in small oak barrels called *caratelli*. The wine estate of Marchesi de'Frescobaldi dominates the area's production.

Pommard AC [paw-MAH*R*] The vineyards of this APPELLATION encircle the village of Pommard, which sits between BEAUNE and VOLNEY in the CÔTE DE BEAUNE area of France's BURGUNDY region. The fact that the wines are quite well known is due somewhat to the pronounceability of its name. In fact, it's well known enough for unscrupulous producers to pass non-area wines off as Pommard. Even though this deceitful practice is seemingly over, it's still best to know the producer for any wines bearing Pommard AC on the label. Although this AC has no GRAND CRU vineyards, there are two excellent PREMIER CRU vineyards that many feel are of grand cru caliber—**Les Epenots** (also spelled *Epeneaux*) and **Les Rugiens**. The better wines from this appellation can be ROBUST and full-bodied (*see* BODY), with perfumed BOUQUETS.

Pommery and Greno *see* CHAMPAGNE

Pontet-Canet, Château [sha-TOH paw*n*-teh kah-NEH] A large well-known estate located in the PAUILLAC AC of the BORDEAUX region. Although it's classified as a CINQUIÈME CRU (fifth growth) and historically has had a reputation for producing high-quality wines, its stature suffered during the 1960s and 1970s. In 1975 the estate was purchased by new owners, whose subsequent investment and improvements began paying dividends with the VINTAGES of the late 1980s. The best vintages are capable of AGING for 30 years or more. There are about 185 acres planted with around 70 percent CABERNET SAUVIGNON, 26 percent MERLOT, and 4 percent CABERNET FRANC. The château produces from 30,000 to 40,000 cases of red wines each year, some of them under its SECOND LABEL **Les Hauts de Pontet**.

Pope Valley AVA Located east of Calistoga, California, this small Napa County growing area is somewhat hotter than the Napa Valley. The grape it does best with is SAUVIGNON BLANC, with SANGIOVESE on the rise. Other varieties planted here are CHARDONNAY, CABERNET SAUVIGNON, and MERLOT. Pope Valley wines are entitled to use the NAPA VALLEY AVA on their labels.

porron [pawr-*RAWN*] A Spanish glass wine container with a narrow, pointed spout that shoots a stream of wine directly into a drinker's mouth. The concept is similar to that of the goatskin BOTA bag from Spain. The use of a *porron* takes skill and good guzzling ability to keep up with the steady stream of wine.

port; Porto; Port DOC A sweet FORTIFIED WINE most often served after a meal. Port originated in northern Portugal's Douro Valley and the best ports still come from that area. The name port derives from the fact that these wines are shipped out of the Portugese city of Oporto and, in fact, such wines (true ports) are labeled *Porto* rather than *port*. Today there's a specific demarcated region (*Port DOC*) in the Douro Valley. This region has established rules for producing quality port wines. To make port, a neutral grape alcohol is added to the wine partway through FERMENTATION. This stops the fermentation process while the wine still has plenty of natural sweetness (9 to 10 percent RESIDUAL SUGAR) and boosts the alcohol level to 18 to 20 percent. The wines are then generally shipped from the Douro Valley across the river to the town of Vila Nova de Gaia, which is replete with LODGES (warehouses) for AGING the wines. Wines left to age in the Douro often develop what's called the *Douro bake*, a baked character that's a result of the hotter climate there. Although there are many types of port wine (which can make labels confusing), there are four basic categories—vintage, ruby, tawny, and white. **Vintage ports** are regarded by many as the best; they're also the most expensive. They are made from grapes of a single VINTAGE and bottled within 2 years. Vintage ports are made only with grapes from the best sites and from the best vintages, and not every year is *declared*—a port firm won't produce a traditional vintage port in undeclared years (those not considered the best). Wines from years that aren't declared go into other types of port wine. The very best vintage ports can age 50 years or more. **Ruby ports** are made from lower-quality batches of wine, which are aged in wood for about 2 years. The wine is bottled while it still exhibits youth, fruitiness, and a bright red color. Ruby ports are generally the least expensive. **Tawny ports** are made from a blend of grapes from several different years; they can be aged in wood for as long as 40 years. They're tawny in color and ready to drink when bottled. The labels on the best tawny ports stipulate the time that they've matured—10, 20, 30, or 40 years. Inexpensive tawny ports are created by blending white port and ruby port. Ruby and tawny ports are sometimes called *wood ports* or *wood-aged ports*. There are many grapes that can be used for red (vintage, ruby, and tawny) ports, but the main ones are Tinta Barroca, Tinta Cão, Tinta Roriz (TEMPRANILLO), TOURIGA FRANCESA, and TOURIGA NACIONAL. **White ports** are produced the same way that red ports are produced except that they use white grapes—Esgana-Cão, Folgasão, MALVASIA, Rabigato, VERDELHO, and Viosinho. If the producer wants a drier (*see* DRY) style of white port, a longer fermentation is allowed. The subsequent wine is generally consumed as an APÉRITIF. Within the four basic categories of port are many types. **Single-quinta ports** are essentially vintage ports produced from a single high-quality wine estate. They're usually made in years when a port firm doesn't declare a traditional vintage port; however, some port producers have started to make them in declared years. In many cases, these single-quinta ports are not quite as rich or intense as the standard vintage ports. On the other hand, some port firms feel single-quinta bottlings should be even better and consider them comparable to RESERVE wines. Taylor's Quinta de Vargellas (*see* TAYLOR, FLADGATE & YEATMAN) is an example of a single-quinta port. **Second label vintage ports** are produced when a port firm feels that a traditional vintage port should not be declared but that the vintage is still quite good. A second label vintage port, like a traditional one, is made from the better wines from various sites. GRAHAM'S Malvedos is an example of a second label vintage port. **Late-Bottled Vintage ports (LBV)** and **colheita ports** (also called *single-vintage ports* or *dated ports*) are made from grapes of a single vintage, even though the quality of the grapes is not as high as that for vintage ports. LBVs are aged in wood from 4 to 6 years and are considered high-quality ruby ports; colheita ports have been wood-aged at least 7 years and fall into the tawny port category. Both are ready to drink when bottled and do not have the aging potential of vintage ports. **Crusted ports**—a blend of two or three wines from different vintages—are aged for 3 or 4 years before being bottled. Like vintage port, crusted port improves with age in the bottle. It derives its name from the deposit or CRUST that is thrown during this aging process. Crusted port is not often made today and has been replaced primarily by late-bottled vintage port. **Vintage character ports** are essentially high-quality ruby ports. They're blended from several vintages and wood-aged, but not nearly as long as tawny port. They're the lightest and fruitiest in flavor and are ready to drink when bottled. In countries outside of Portugal, port is a generic name for wines modeled after the Portuguese originals. Inexpensive "ports" will usually simply use names like Ruby or Tawny. The better ones will be vintage ports and may possibly be a VARIETAL WINE either made from native Portuguese varieties or perhaps ZINFANDEL or CABERNET SAUVIGNON.

porto *see* PORT

Portugais Bleu *see* PORTUGIESER

Portugal Although Portugal may be best known internationally for its two FORTIFIED wines (PORT and MADEIRA) and its ROSÉS (such as Lancer's and Mateus), it produces a large amount of red and white TABLE WINE. In fact, it's the world's seventh largest wine-producing nation. Most of Portugal's wine is consumed within its borders—it ranks third in the world for per capita consumption. As a wine-producing country, Portugal's somewhat of an enigma. In one sense it's innovative—it was the first country to implement an APPELLATION system with its REGIÃO DEMARCADA (RD), now called DENOMINAÇÃO DE ORIGEM CONTROLADA (DOC). It instituted this "demarcated region" system in 1756, almost 180 years before the French adopted their APPELLATION D'ORIGINE CONTRÔLÉE system. Yet Portugal has been so steeped in tradition that, in general, its winemaking techniques are far from progressive by today's standards. Those producers who have kept up with modern methods have done so outside Portugal's appellation system. To do so, they've adopted proprietary brand names and dropped the use of regional names. This means, of course, that there's no sense of regional identification as there is with French and Italian wines. Neither do the Portuguese have a labeling procedure to identify their wines by grape varieties, as is popular in some countries like Australia, Chile, and the United States. Portugal began to sharpen its image only after joining the European Economic Community in 1987 (which made European countries more accessible) and realizing that their table wines have tremendous export potential. It reviewed the structure of the *Região Demarcada* (now DOC) system, adding a few regions to increase the number to fourteen. These DOCs are: BAIRRADA, known for TANNIC, highly ACIDIC red wine; Bucelas, which produces full-bodied white wines; CARCAVELOS, with its sweet and DRY fortified white wines; COLARES, known for tannic, full-bodied red wines; DÃO, which makes big, full-bodied red wines; Lagoa; Lagos; MADEIRA, with its famous fortified wines; PORT and DOURO which, in addition to their esteemed port wines, produce highly regarded red and white table wines; Portimão; Setúbal, with its sweet, fortified white wines; Travora and VINHO VERDE, known for "green wines"—fresh, fruity red and white wines. Of these fourteen DOCs, Langoa, Langos, Protiamo, and Travora have yet to achieve much of a reputation. Portugal has also established INDICAÇÃO DE PROVE-NIENCIA REGULAMENTADA system to denote regions (of which there are currently twenty-eight) that are striving to become DOCs. A big problem for Portuguese DOC wines is the continued requirement for extensive AGING, which causes some of the wines to become dull and lifeless. In addition, cooperatives, many of which lack the modern equipment necessary to produce fresh fruity wines, make almost 70 percent of the Portuguese wines. However, many other producers are updating their winemaking equipment and methods and are producing good high-quality wines. As Portugal continues to make improvements, their wines will gain further acceptance and offer international markets new and interesting wines made from the many local varieties. Portuguese white wines are made from a wide variety of grapes including ARINTO, Assario, Barcelo, Bical, Boais, BOAL, Borrado das Moscas, Branco, Cerceal do Douro, Encruzado, Esgana Cão, Fernão Pires, Folgosão, Galego Dourado, Loureiro, MALVASIA, Maria Gomez, Moscatel (MUSCAT), Rabo de Ovelha, Roupeiro (also called Codega), SER-CIAL, TREBBIANO, and VERDELHO. Red wines are made from Alfrocheiro Preto, Alvarelhão, Azal Tinto, Tinta Bairrada (BAGA), Bastardo, Borracal, Espadeiro, Molar, NEGRA MOLE (or *Tinta Negra Mole*), *Parreira Matias*, PERIQUITA, Ramisco, Tinta Amarela, Tinta Pinheira, Tinta Roriz (TEM-PRANILLO), TOURIGA FRANCESA, TOURIGA NACIONAL, and Trajadura. Some of the better-known Portuguese producers of table wines are CAVES ALIANÇA, FERREIRA, and SOGRAPE and for Port, COCKBURN-SMITHES, CROFT, FONSECA GUIMARAENS, W. & J. GRAHAM, QUITA DO NOVAL, SANDMAN, SMITH WOODHOUSE, TAYLOR FLADGATE & YEATMAN, and WARRE.

Portugieser [por-chuh-GHEE-zer; por-too-GHEE-zer] This variety (whose full name is *Blauer Portugieser*) is the most widely planted red wine grape in Austria, and second behind Spätburgunder (PINOT NOIR) in Germany. Despite its name, Portugieser seems to have no connection to Portugal and appears, in fact, to have originated in Austria. It is a high-yielding vine that produces slightly sweet but rather ordinary light red and ROSÉ wines. Moderate amounts are planted in France, where it's called *Portugais Bleu*. Small quantities are also grown in Hungary, where it's known as *Oporto* and used as a minor component in their "bull's blood" (EGRI BIKAVÉR) wines.

pot [POH] A small French bottle that holds about 50 centiliters (500 milliliters or just under 17 ounces), used in and around BEAUJOLAIS for serving wine in restaurants and cafés. This size bottle is slowly beginning to make an appearance in the U.S. market. A *pot* is generally filled from a cask.

potassium bitartrate *see* TARTRATES

potassium metabisulfite [puh-TAS-ee-uhm meht-uh-bi-SUHL-fite] A white powder or salt containing approximately 57 percent SULFUR DIOXIDE. Potassium metabisulfite also comes in tablet form, known as **Campden tablets.** *Meta*, as it's also called, is dissolved in warm water before being used. When stirred into wine or MUST, it reacts with natural acids to release sulfur dioxide, which protects wines from unwanted bacteria and OXIDATION.

Potensac, Château [sha-TOH poh-tahn-SAK] A highly regarded CRU BOURGEOIS estate, which is owned by the proprietors of Château LÉOVILLE-LAS-CASES. It's located in the MÉDOC AC near the COMMUNE of Saint-Yzans-de-Médoc and produces very high quality wines for a château from that area. The full-flavored wines have good STRUCTURE, which allows better VINTAGES to AGE for 10 to 12 years. The property consists of nearly 99 acres and produces about 20,000 cases of red wines each year. Several SECOND LABELS are used by the château— **Gallais-Bellevue, Lassalle,** and **Goudy-la-Cardonne**.

potential alcohol *see* BRIX

Potter Valley AVA Small AVA that is part of California's larger MENDOCINO AVA. It's located on the eastern side of Mendocino County, northeast of CLEAR LAKE AVA. The growing season here is characterized by warm days and cool nights. SAUVIGNON BLANC, SÉMILLON, and RIESLING do well in this climate; CHARDONNAY and PINOT NOIR are also grown. There are no wineries here, only vineyards.

Pouget, Château [sha-TOH poo-ZHEH] A QUATRIÈME CRU (fourth growth) estate located in the MARGAUX AC in the MÉDOC district of BORDEAUX. The château is small, only 25 acres, and not very well known. It's owned by Pierre Guillemet, who is also Château BOYD-CANTENAC'S proprietor. The wines from both properties are produced at Château Pouget and are similar in style. Château Pouget uses about 66 percent CABERNET SAUVIGNON, 30 percent MERLOT, and 4 percent CABERNET FRANC in their wines. Production averages around 4,500 cases each year.

Les Pougets *see* CORTON; CORTON-CHARLEMAGNE

Pouilly-Fuissé AC [poo-yee fwee-SAY] Located in the MÂCONNAIS area of France's BURGUNDY region, this well-known APPELLATION controls the white wines from five villages—Chaintré, Fuissé, Pouilly,

Solutré, and Vergisson. The CHARDONNAY wines can be quite good when made by diligent producers. Unfortunately, much of the Pouilly-Fuissé wine is made by the large cooperative in Chaintré from grapes picked from vineyards that are allowed huge YIELDS. Although these wines have a large international audience, many wine reviewers think they're mediocre and overpriced. Pouilly-Fuissé should not be confused with POUILLY-FUMÉ wines from the LOIRE region, which are made from SAUVIGNON BLANC grapes. As an historical note, the rock of Solutré, which towers over the scenic Pouilly-Fuissé area, is commemorated as the site where early man drove thousands of wild horses off the cliffs to their deaths.

Pouilly-Fumé AC [poo-yee few-MAY] APPELLATION that produces some of the better-known wines in the central part of France's LOIRE region. The vineyards are scattered around seven villages including Pouilly-Sur-Loire, which lends its name to the appellation. The word *fumée* is French for "smoke," and it's said the name comes from the SMOKY or FLINTY quality of these wines. The only grape allowed in the Pouilly-Fumé AC is SAUVIGNON BLANC, which produces wines that are generally CRISP, TART, and somewhat GRASSY. The best wines have either *Les Berthiers* or *Les Loges* (two of the area's villages) on the label. There's some criticism that Pouilly-Fumé wines have become too well known and are now overpriced. Occasionally, Pouilly-Fumé wines also are labeled **Pouilly-Blanc-Fumé AC** or **Blanc Fumé de Pouilly AC**. Pouilly-Fumé wines should not be confused with the BURGUNDY region's POUILLY-FUISSÉ wines, which are made from CHARDONNAY. *See also* POUILLY-SUR-LOIRE-AC.

Pouilly-Loché AC [poo-yee law-SHAY] APPELLATION that is located next to the better-known POUILLY-FUISSÉ AC in the MÂCONNAIS area of France's BURGUNDY region. Its vineyards surround the village of Loché, which is near the village of Fuissé. Much of the Pouilly-Loché AC CHARDONNAY-based wine is produced by the cooperative at Loché. It's considered a cheaper alternative to Pouilly-Fuissé wine, although some wine critics believe that the use of Pouilly in its name allows Pouilly-Loché to be a bit overpriced. Pouilly-Loché wines may also be sold under the better-known POUILLY-VINZELLES AC label.

Pouilly-Sur-Loire AC [poo-yee syoor LWAHR] The small French town of Pouilly-Sur-Loire is the center not only for the APPELLATION of the same name, but also for POUILLY-FUMÉ AC wines. The Pouilly-Sur-Loire AC produces white wines from the area's traditional grape, CHASSELAS. Because Chasselas is considered a better table grape than a winemaking grape, its allotted acreage has dwindled tremendously. SAUVIGNON BLANC is now planted everywhere possible, leaving Chasselas only with whatever acreage is least desirable for Sauvignon Blanc. Pouilly-Sur-Loire AC wines are considered fairly mediocre and should be drunk young.

Pouilly-Vinzelles AC [poo-yee va*n*-ZEHL] APPELLATION that adjoins the better-known POUILLY-FUISSÉ AC in the MÂCONNAIS area of France's BURGUNDY region. Its vineyards encompass the village of Vinzelles, which is southeast of the village of Fuissé. The wines are similar to but a bit LIGHTER (and less expensive than) those from the neighboring Pouilly-Fuissé AC. The nearby POUILLY-LOCHÉ AC may also sell its wines under the Pouilly-Vinzelles AC label.

Poujeaux, Château [sha-TOH poo-ZHOH] A highly regarded CRU BOURGEOIS château located in the MOULIS AC in the MÉDOC district of BORDEAUX. It consists of about 123 acres and produces about 20,000 cases of high-quality red wine each year. The wines, made with approximately 40 percent CABERNET SAUVIGNON, 36 percent MERLOT, 12 percent CABERNET FRANC, and 12 percent PETIT VERDOT, can be a bit HARD when young and may require 5 to 6 years to SOFTEN. They're capable of AGING for 15 to 20 years.

pourriture gris [poo-ree-TYUR GREE] The French term for "gray rot." *See also* BOTRYTIS CINEREA.

pourriture noble [poo-ree-TYUR NOH-bl] French term for "noble rot." *See also* BOTRYTIS CINEREA.

powdery mildew *see* MILDEW

powerful BOLD, high-ALCOHOL, full-flavored wines can be referred to as powerful or *strong*. This term is more likely to be used with red wines than with white.

Prädikat *see* QUALITÄTSWEIN MIT PRÄDIKAT

Pralat *see* ERDEN

Pramaggiore *see* LISON-PRAMAGGIORE

Prémeaux [pray-MOH] A small village just south of NUITS-SAINT-GEORGES in the CÔTE DE NUITS area of France's BURGUNDY region. The PINOT NOIR-based red wines produced here are entitled to be bottled as NUITS-SAINT-GEORGES AC or Côte de Nuits-Villages AC. There are several PREMIER CRU vineyards, the best known being **Clos de la Maréchale**.

premier cru [preh-MYAY (preh-MEER) KROO] 1. A French phrase meaning "first growth." 2. In BORDEAUX'S regions of the MÉDOC and SAUTERNES, premier cru is the highest subcategory of CRU CLASSÉ (classed growth), which was established in the CLASSIFICATION OF 1855. Bordeaux wines that achieve this ultimate ranking may put "Premier Grand Cru Classé" on their labels. In 1855 four red-wine-producing châteaus were given this top ranking: LAFITE-ROTHSCHILD, LATOUR, MARGAUX, and HAUT-BRION. In 1973 CHÂTEAU MOUTON-ROTHSCHILD was upgraded to *premier cru* status. There are eleven châteaus in Sauternes with the premier cru designation, plus CHÂTEAU D'YQUEM, with its elevated status of premier grand cru (first great growth). *See also* PREMIER GRAND CRU CLASSÉ; FIRST GROWTH. 3. In BURGUNDY, where premier cru vineyards are some of the best, there is one higher category—GRAND CRU.

premier grand cru [preh-MYAY (preh-MEER) grah*n* KROO] The French phrase for "first great growth."

premier grand cru classé [preh-MYAY (preh-MEER) grah*n* kroo klah-SAY] 1. The French phrase for "first great classed growth." 2. Premier grand cru classé is the highest category for French wines classified in the APPELLATION of SAINT-ÉMILION as set forth in the 1953 classification (and later revised in 1969 and 1985). As of 1985, this status was given to eleven châteaus, which may label their wines "Premier Grand Cru Classé." 3. France's first growth (PREMIER CRU) wines of the MÉDOC and SAUTERNES may use "Premier Grand Cru Classé" on their label.

Premières Côtes de Blaye AC *see* BLAYE

Premierès Côtes de Bordeaux AC [pruh-MYEH*R* koht duh bohr-DOH] Located in France's BORDEAUX region, this AC extends for about 38 miles along the right bank of the Garonne River, across from the better-known APPELLATIONS of GRAVES and SAUTERNES. The Premières Côtes de Bordeaux AC applies to red, ROSÉ, and slightly sweet white wines. Because slightly sweet wines are no longer popular, the white wines are moving toward a drier style, but DRY wines can qualify only as BORDEAUX AC or BORDEAUX SUPÉRIEUR AC wines. The area is shifting to more red wine production, which now accounts for about two-thirds of the total. Generally, red wines come from the appellation's northern portion, and whites come from the southern part (particularly around the sweet-wine villages of CADILLAC and LOUPIAC). As with the rest of Bordeaux, the white-wine grapes are MUSCADELLE, SAUVIGNON BLANC, and SÉMILLON; red-wine grapes are primarily CABERNET FRANC, CABERNET SAUVIGNON, and MERLOT. Premières Côtes de Bordeaux AC wines are considered to be of good quality and improving as recently planted vineyards mature. Prices for these wines are relatively inexpensive.

première taille *see* TAILLE

press *n.* A device used to squeeze juice from grapes. Of the many types of presses in use today, the **basket press**, designed to squeeze out as much juice as possible, is one of the earliest. It uses a plate to push down on the grapes in the basket, forcing out juice through small slots. Numerous versions of this press have evolved over time and many are still used today. A **bladder press** uses an inflatable bladder that forces the grapes against a perforated outer shell through which the juice drains into a container. The most recent generation is the **tank press**, which uses an airtight tank lined with a membrane that lightly presses the grapes. The tank press is currently thought to be one of the best because the gentle pressure and lack of air exposure produces high-quality juice *v.* press. To extract juice from grapes using one of several various presses. Pressing usually follows CRUSHING and precedes FERMENTATION of white wines, but follows the fermenting of red wines.

Pressac *see* MALBEC

press juice; press wine *see* FREE-RUN JUICE

Preuses, Les [lay PREWZ] One of the seven GRAND CRU vineyards in CHABLIS. Positioned between BOUGROS and VAUDÉSIR, Les Preuses consists of just under 29 acres. The land benefits from being higher up the grand cru slope and therefore receiving more sun.

pricked A pricked wine is one that has an off-putting sharpness caused by VOLATILE ACIDITY. In an extreme state, such wines have almost turned to vinegar.

Prieuré de Meyney *see* MEYNEY, CHÂTEAU

Prieuré-Lichine,   Château [sha-TOH   pree-uh-RAY   lee-SHEEN] This CHÂTEAU was purchased in 1951 by the famous wine authority and writer Alexis Lichine. The name was changed from Château Prieuré-Cantenac in 1953. Lichene, who died in 1989, increased the acreage and improved the facilities of this QUATRIÈME CRU (fourth growth) estate. Now run by Alexis' son Sacha, Prieuré-Lichine currently owns about 150 acres consisting of numerous parcels scattered around the MARGAUX AC in BORDEAUX. The château annually produces about 25,000 cases of red wines from a grape blend of 58 percent CABERNET SAUVIGNON, 34 percent MERLOT, and 4 percent *each*

CABERNET FRANC and PETIT VERDOT. The wines, which have received mixed reviews in the past, have become increasingly better during the VINTAGES of the 1980s. Recent vintages are capable of AGING for 10 to 15 years. The SECOND LABEL for Château Prieuré-Lichine is **de Clairefont**.

primary fermentation *see* FERMENTATION

Primaticcio *see* MONTEPULCIANO

Primitivo *see* ZINFANDEL

Primitivo di Manduria DOC [pree-mee-TEE-voh dee mahn-doo-REE-uh] DOC located in the APULIA region in southern Italy. It's part way down the Salento peninsula, which is the "heel" on the Italian boot. The wines are made from Primitivo, a variety that's related to California's ZINFANDEL grape. In addition to making a DRY red wine, producers make other styles including AMABILE, DOLCE NATURALE (a sweet wine with a minimum of 16 percent ALCOHOL), LIQUOROSO SECCO (a dry FORTIFIED wine with a minimum of 18 percent alcohol), and *liquoroso secco naturale* (a sweet, fortified wine with a minimum of 17½ percent alcohol).

Prinz von Preussen *see* SCHLOSS REINHARTSHAUSEN

Priorato DO [pryaw-RAW-tah] DO located within the larger Tarragona DO in the southern part of Spain's CATALONIA region. The mountainous region in which the area is situated has created terraced vineyards clinging to steep hillsides. It also produces low YIELDS, which allows Priorato winemakers to create intense, full-flavored, full-bodied (*see* BODY) wines that are generally high in ALCOHOL (13.5 percent is the minimum, 18 percent the maximum). Most of the wines are red, made from Garnacha Tinta (GRENACHE), Carinena (CARIGNAN), and a variant of Garnacha Tinta called Garnacha Peluda. A small amount of white wine is made from Garnacha Blanca (Grenache), MACABEO, and PEDRO XIMÉNEZ. FORTIFIED wines ranging from DRY to sweet are also produced.

Private Reserve *see* RESERVE

produced and bottled by This phrase indicates that the named winery CRUSHED, FERMENTED, and bottled a minimum of 75 percent of the wine in that particular bottling. The phrase, however, does not mean that the winery *grew* the grapes. *See also* BOTTLED BY; ESTATE BOTTLED; GROWN, PRODUCED AND BOTTLED BY; MADE AND BOTTLED BY.

Prohibition In January 1920, the U.S. Federal Prohibition Law was enacted through the Eighteenth Amendment to the Constitution. This law prohibited the manufacture, transportation, or sale of alcoholic beverages. It wasn't until almost 14 years later, in December 1933, that Prohibition was repealed by the Twenty-first Amendment. During Prohibition, certain activities were sanctioned, including home wine-making and wineries being allowed to make sacramental wines. During this period, wine consumption actually increased. Many wineries did not survive Prohibition, however. Those that did had converted their vineyards from high-quality wine grapes to varieties like THOMPSON SEEDLESS (which could be used for table grapes, raisins, or very ordinary wines) or ALICANTE BOUSCHET (which could survive the cross-country trip for home winemakers in the east). As the close of Prohibition drew near, resourceful wineries stockpiled wines and had ample stocks to sell a thirsty nation. The conversion of vineyards back to high-quality grapes happened slowly over the next several decades.

propriétaire [proh-pree-ay-TEHR]   French   for   "proprietor," "owner," or "grower." *See also* MIS EN BOUTEILLE.

Proprietor's Reserve *see* RESERVE

Prosecco [praw-SEHK-koh; proh-SEHK-koh] A white-wine grape that's grown primarily in the eastern part of Italy's VENETO region. Prosecco's made into lightly sparkling (FRIZZANTE), fully sparkling (SPUMANTE), and STILL WINES. Its fine reputation, however, comes from the sparkling versions. The wines are CRISP and appley and, though they can be sweet, are more often found DRY. The best-known wines made principally from Prosecco come from the DOC of Prosecco di Conegliano-Valdobbiadene and are generally sold with either the name of Conegliano or Valdobbiadene attached. The very best Prosecco wines are labeled "Superiore di Cartizze" and come from a subzone within Valdobbiadene. Prosecco is also known as *Balbi, Glera, Serprina,* and *Tondo.*

Prosecco di Conegliano-Valdobbiadene DOC *see* CONEGLIANO

Provence [praw-VAHNSS] It's thought that winemaking has existed in this beautiful area of southern France since about 600 B.C. Although Provence, which sits on the Mediterranean just east of the RHÔNE region, has never been known for fine wine, it's now undergoing an upgrading process. The largest APPELLATION in this area is CÔTES DE PROVENCE. Other appellations are BANDOL, BELLET, CASSIS, PALETTE, COTEAUX D'AIX-EN-PROVENCE, and its subregion, CÔTEAUX DES BAUX-EN-

PROVENCE. Red-wine grapes grown in this area include CARIGNAN, CIN-SAUT, GRENACHE, MOURVÈDRE, SYRAH, and, increasingly, CABERNET SAUVI-GNON. Bourboulenc, CLAIRETTE, SAUVIGNON BLANC, SÉMILION, and Ugni Blanc (TREBBIANO) are some of the white-wine grapes used.

Provence *see* CÔTES DE PROVENCE

Prugnolo *see* SANGIOVESE

Les Pruliers *see* NUITS-SAINT-GEORGES

Prüm [PROOM] A very important family of wine producers who reside in Germany's MOSEL-SAAR-RUWER region. They have lived in this region since the sixteenth century and began to make their name in the wine world in the eighteenth century when they were able to buy prime vineyards after Napoleon invaded the area and subsequently sold off land belonging to the churches. Over the years the original estate has been broken up through inheritance. There are now numerous Prüm estates, the best known of which is **Joh. Jos. Prüm**, which produces exceptionally long-lived wines from the famous Sonnenuhr vineyard in WEHLEN. Other Prüm estates include Dr. Weins-Prüm (Selbach), S. A. Prüm Erben, and Dr. Zach. Bergweiler-Prüm Erben.

Prunella *see* CINSAUT

pruney Negative winetasting term that is sometimes applied to wines made from extremely overripe grapes, which give the wine an undesirable pungent characteristic.

pruning A critical viticultural practice involving the cutting back of the grape vines, usually during the dormant season. Pruning helps maintain the vines properly so that the grower produces a good crop of high-quality grapes. It's done for any of several objectives including controlling the YIELD, strengthening the vines, improving the quality of the grapes, or making the grapes easier to harvest. The generally agreed upon wisdom is that superior wines come from vines that don't overproduce because the grape's flavor is diluted if the vine's productivity exceeds its optimum level. In the past, most pruning has been done by hand by skilled pruners. Today, some areas are utilizing **mechanical pruning**, which consists of a group of small circular power saws that encircle the upper part of the vine and cut all wood extending beyond the perimeter of the saws. Although this mechanical method isn't particularly aesthetic and may require some secondary hand pruning, it costs a fraction of hand pruning. Initial results indicate that it's just about as successful.

puckery Descriptor for wines that are so high in TANNINS that they make the mouth and teeth feel extremely dry. The term ASTRINGENT is more appropriately used for the same sensation.

Pugent *see* NEBBIOLO

Puglia *see* APULIA

Puisseguin-Saint-Émilion AC [pwees-GAN san tay-mee-LYAWN] The easternmost of the six small APPELLATIONS surrounding the famous SAINT-ÉMILION AC in France's BORDEAUX region. Its vineyards encompass the village of Puisseguin and the neighboring village of **Parsac**. (Parsac essentially disolved its appellation, preferring to market its wines as Puisseguin-Saint-Émilion AC.) It's said that the word Puisseguin is Celtic in origin and means "hill with the powerful wine." The red wines, made primarily from MERLOT and CABERNET FRANC, with some CABERNET SAUVIGNON and MALBEC, are generally SOFT yet full-bodied (*see* BODY) and can represent good values for Bordeaux wines.

Puligny-Montrachet [pew-lee-NYEH (pew-lee-NYEE) mawn-rah-SHAY] A famous village in the CÔTE DE BEAUNE section of the CÔTE D'OR in France's BURGUNDY region. The village itself is rather unexciting, but it is regarded as *the* home of CHARDONNAY, a reputation based on the general consensus that the world's best DRY white wines are produced here. Puligny-Montrachet AC contains two GRAND CRU vineyards—CHEVALIER-MONTRACHET and BIENVENUES-BÂTARD-MONTRACHET—and nearly half of each of two others—LE MONTRACHET and BÂTARD-MONTRACHET. The best wines from Le Montrachet are viewed by many as the best DRY white wines in the world, although the wines from Chevalier-Montrachet have supporters who feel the same. The other two grand cru aren't far behind, and the village's fourteen PREMIER CRU vineyards also produce superb wines. The best of these premier cru vineyards are **Le Cailleret**, **Les Combettes**, **Les Folatières**, **Les Pucelles**, and **Les Referts**. Wines from other vineyards are bottled under the designation of **Puligny-Montrachet AC** or CÔTE-DE-BEAUNE VILLAGES AC. This area produces small amounts of red wine (from PINOT NOIR), which don't have the stature of the great whites.

pulp The soft, fleshy, juice-laden part of the grape.

pumping over A process of pumping juice over the CAP during FERMENTATION to expedite extraction of color, flavor, and TANNINS and to ensure that the cap doesn't dry out and develop unwanted bacteria.

puncheon [PUNCH-uhn] A large oak barrel that can vary in capacity from about 80 to about 133 gallons.

punching down A process of pushing the CAP down into the juice during FERMENTATION to facilitate extraction of color, flavor, and TANNINS and to ensure that the cap doesn't dry out and develop unwanted bacteria. Workers use a long paddle to punch the cap down.

punt The indentation in the bottom of a wine or champagne bottle. The punt's design serves two purposes—catching sediment and reinforcing the bottle.

pupitres *see* RIDDLING

puttonyos *see* TOKAY

PX *see* PEDRO XIMÉNEZ

bA *see* QUALITÄTSWEIN BESTIMMTER ANBAUGEBIET

Q. C. Fly *see* BOUCHAINE

QmP *see* QUALITÄTSWEIN MIT PRÄDIKAT

Qualitätschaumwein *see* SEKT

Qualitätswein bestimmter Anbaugebiet (QbA) [kvah-lih-TAYTS-vine behr-SHTIHMT-tuhr ahn-BOW-geh-beet]

The German wine laws adapted in 1971 set up three categories defining the quality of German wines. Qualitätswein bestimmter Anbaugebiet ("quality wine from a specified region") is the middle quality category in between DEUTSCHER TAFELWEIN (DTW), the lowest quality, and QUALITÄTSWEIN MIT PRÄDIKAT (QmP), the highest. To qualify for Qualitätswein bestimmter Anbaugebiet (QbA) status, a wine is tested by a local panel to ensure that it shows the typical character of an approved grape variety and of the region. In addition, the MUST (unfermented grape juice) needs to be a certain sugar level, and the wine must have a minimum ALCOHOL content. The required sugar and alcohol levels vary from region to region and from variety to variety. QbA wines must come from one of the thirteen ANBAUGEBIETE (quality wine regions) and can not contain wine from any other region. The thirteen Anbaugebiete are AHR, BADEN, FRANKEN, HESSISCHE BERGSTRASSE, MITTELRHEIN, MOSEL-SAAR-RUWER, NAHE, RHEINGAU, RHEINHESSEN, RHEINPFALZ, and WÜRTTEMBERG—plus SAALE-UNSTRUT and SACHSEN, recent additions from the former East Germany. CHAPTALIZATION (the addition of sugar) is allowed for QbA wines and is one of the major differences between these wines and higher quality QmP wines (most grapes with enough natural sugar go into QmP wines). The addition of sugar, which is converted into alcohol during fermentation, allows producers to reach the required minimum alcohol levels for a QbA wine. If a wine passes all the QbA requirements, an AMTLICHE PRÜFUNGSNUMMER (official test number) is assigned. Abbreviated as A.P.Nr., this number is printed on the label, along with name of the Anbaugebiet. Additional information may be printed on a QbA wine label if other requirements are met. For instance, the name of the grape variety can be included if 85 percent of the grapes used to make the wine are that variety.

Qualitätswein mit Prädikat (QmP) [kvah-lih-TAYTS-vine mitt PRAY-dee-kaht]

Qualitätswein mit Prädikat (QmP) is the highest quality category defined by the German wine laws adapted in 1971. DEUTSCHER TAFELWEIN (DTW) and QUALITÄTSWEIN BESTIMMTER ANBAUGEBIET (QbA) are the two lower-quality categories. Qualitätswein mit Prädikat translates crudely to "quality wine with distinction" or "quality wine with special attributes." In addition to meeting the rules for QbA wines, QmP wines cannot have any sugar added (*see* CHAPTALIZATION), must be ESTATE BOTTLED (*erzeugerabfüllung*), and come from a defined BEREICH (district). There are six subcategories within the QmP category, ranked from lowest to highest they are: KABINETT, SPÄTLESE, AUSLESE, BEERENAUSLESE, EISWEIN, and TROCKENBEERENAUSLESE. Each category is defined by a minimum sugar content of the grapes, which varies from region to region and from variety to variety. The focus on sugar content embodies the theory that grapes with higher sugar levels are riper and therefore yield richer wines with deep colors, intense flavors, and opulent BOUQUETS.

Quarts de Chaume AC [kah*r* duh SHOHM] This APPELLATION, which received GRAND CRU status in 1954, encompasses the village of Chaume in the ANJOU area of France's LOIRE region. As the story goes, its name stems from the fact that a former landowner required a quarter (*quart*) of the vintage be turned over to him as a form of payment. The MICROCLIMATE in this area is perfect for CHENIN BLANC grapes to ripen to their fullest. The environment also creates the conditions necessary to attract the desirable mold BOTRYTIS CINEREA, which shrivels the grapes and concentrates the flavors and sugar. The YIELDS from the Quarts de Chaume AC vineyards are some of the lowest in France, and the crop is harvested several times so that individual grapes are picked at their ripest. The combination of microclimate and low yields produces RICH, HONEYED, golden wines that, thanks to the ACIDITY of the Chenin Blanc grape, can AGE for 30 to 40 years or more. These wines are generally at their best after 10 years of bottle aging.

quatrième cru [kah-tryehm KROO] A French phrase meaning "fourth growth," referring to the fourth-highest subcategory of the MÉDOC area's CRUS CLASSÉS (classed growths), which were established in the CLASSIFICATION OF 1855. Ten châteaus were ranked as quatrième cru in 1855, and this hasn't changed.

Quincy AC [ka*n*-SEE] A tiny APPELLATION surrounding the village of Quincy in the central LOIRE region southwest of SANCERRE AC and POUILLY-FUMÉ AC. Quincy produces white wines from the SAUVIGNON BLANC grape that are similar in style to those from these other two appellations—generally CRISP and TART, with a somewhat GRASSY characteristic.

quinta [KEEN-tah] Portuguese for "farm," used to refer to a vineyard site or estate. Quintas, which are similar in connotation to the CHÂTEAUS of BORDEAUX, grow grapes for port, as well as for other wines.

They're often connected with one of the well-known port houses, such as DOW, FONSECA, or GRAHAM. Many of the wines end up in house blends, but the concept of single-quinta wine, including single-quinta vintage port (*see* PORT), is becoming more popular.

Quinta do Noval [KEEN-tah doh NOH-vahl] Highly regarded PORT company that produces what some believe is the very best vintage port, **Quinta do Noval Nacional**, which comes from a section of vineyard with ungrafted (*see* GRAFTING) vines. The Nacional is produced in small quantities (around 250 cases) and is very expensive— purportedly, a bottle of the legendary 1931 vintage recently sold for over $7,000. The regular Quinta do Noval vintage port is also highly regarded but usually isn't as rich and concentrated as the Nacional. Quinta do Noval, which was known as A. J. da Silva until 1973, is also noted for introducing Late Bottled Vintage (LBV) port.

Quivira Vineyards [kee-VEER-uh] DRY CREEK VALLEY AVA winery located northwest of Healdsburg, California, in SONOMA COUNTY. It was founded in 1981 by Henry and Holly Wendt and has grown to an annual production of between 20,000 and 25,000 cases of wine. The winery owns nearly 90 acres and produces three VARIETAL WINES—SAUVIGNON BLANC, ZINFANDEL, and CABERNET SAUVIGNON (which is blended with MERLOT and CABERNET FRANC). There's also a new arrival called Dry Creek Cuvée, a blend of GRENACHE, MOURVÈDRE, and SYRAH. The Zinfandel is usually considered the best of Quivira's wines.

"R" *see* RIEUSSEC, CHÂTEAU

Rabaud-Promis, Château [sha-TOH ra-BOH praw-mee] A PREMIER CRU (first growth) located in the SAUTERNES AC in BORDEAUX. It was part of larger property named Rabaud, which was split into Rabaud-Promis and Château SIGALAS RABAUD in 1903. Château Rabaud-Promis consists of nearly 79 acres planted with about 80 percent SÉMILLON, 18 percent SAUVIGNON BLANC, and 2 percent MUSCADELLE. It produces 4,000 to 5,000 cases of sweet white wine each year. After a long period of mediocrity, the quality of the wine improved markedly in the 1980s. Recent VINTAGES are capable of AGING for 20 to 25 years. The château uses the SECOND LABEL **Domaine de l'Estremade** for wines that don't meet the standard of the Rabaud-Promis-labeled wines.

Rablay-sur-Layon *see* COTEAUX DU LAYON

Raboso [ruh-BOH-soh] A red-wine grape grown primarily in Italy's VENETO region, where it's thought to have originated. Raboso's known for its heavy TANNINS, high ACIDITY, and deep color. There are two distinct clones of this variety—*Raboso Veronese* and *Raboso del Piave.* Raboso Veronese produces greater YIELDS and is more widely planted. Raboso del Piave, also known as *Friularo* or *Friulara,* produces a more AUSTERE wine than does the Raboso Veronese grape. Raboso is often BLENDED with much softer wines to improve their STRUCTURE, COMPLEXITY, and smoothness. The Raboso VARIETAL WINES from the Piave DOC are usually HARSH and austere in their youth but can SOFTEN nicely with AGE. This variety is also called *Negron.*

race [*R*AHSS] The French term for BREED.

racking The process of siphoning off the clear juice from the SEDIMENT that has fallen to the bottom of the container either naturally or with the help of FINING agents. During the winemaking process, racking can occur three or four times before the wine is clear. After racking, some wines are also FILTERED prior to bottling to remove any remaining miniscule particles.

A. Rafanelli Winery [ra-fuh-NEHL-lee] Although the winery was founded in 1974, the Rafanelli family had been selling grapes from their vineyards for 20 years before that. They have 50 acres planted mainly with CABERNET SAUVIGNON and ZINFANDEL. Rafanelli annually produces between 6,000 and 8,000 cases of these two VARIETAL WINES, both of which are very highly respected. A. Rafanelli Winery is located northwest of the town of Healdsburg in SONOMA COUNTY'S DRY CREEK VALLEY AVA.

Rainwater *see* MADEIRA

Raisinotte *see* MUSCADELLE

raisiny A sensory term that, in some LATE HARVEST and FORTIFIED WINES, is used in a positive sense to describe a rich, concentrated, almost caramelly flavor. However, this trait is considered a fault in DRY wines and is usually because they were made with dried-out grapes grown in an excessively hot climate.

rancio [Fr. *rahn*-SYOH; Sp. *R*AHN-thyoh] A style of wine made by purposefully OXIDIZING or MADERIZING it by placing small barrels of wine in the hot summer sun. This procedure gives the wine a tawny color and a rich, unique flavor. Rancio wines are usually either naturally very high in alcohol or FORTIFIED. The results are similar to MADEIRA, tawny PORT, or MARSALA. Rancio wines are made throughout Spain, as well as in southern France. They're usually sipped as an APÉRITIF.

Rasteau [rass-TOH] A village in the southern portion of France's RHÔNE region, northeast of CHÂTEAUNEUF-DU-PAPE. It's one of the seventeen villages entitled to use the CÔTES DU RHÔNE-VILLAGES AC, and the label usually also includes the village's name. These wines generally exhibit dark color, spicy fruit, and enough TANNINS to age well. The main grapes used for red wines are GRENACHE, SYRAH, CINSAUT, and MOURVÈDRE. A specialty of Rasteau is a VIN DOUX NATUREL, a category of sweet, FORTIFIED red or white wine made from Grenache grapes.

ratafia [rat-uh-FEE-uh] A sweet French APÉRITIF´ made from a mixture of unfermented grape juice and BRANDY. The best known are Ratafia de Bourgogne and Ratafia de Champagne. Ratafia is similar to the better-known PINEAU DES CHARENTES.

Rauenthal [*R*OW-uhn-tahl] A small wine-producing village situated in the foothills of the Taunas Mountains, set back from the Rhine River in Germany's RHEINGAU region. Rauenthal produces highly regarded wines that are known for their spiciness, excellent ACIDITY, and age-worthiness. **Steinmächer** is the GROSSLAGE that covers Rauenthal's vineyards, but the better wines are labeled with the names of the individual EINZELLAGEN—**Baiken, Gehrn, Nonnenberg, Rothenberg,** and **Wülfen.**

Rausan-Ségla, Château [sha-TOH roh-ZAH*N* say-GLAH] A DEUXIÈME CRU (second growth) CHÂTEAU located in the MARGAUX AC of BORDEAUX. Historically, the wines from this property were highly regarded, but they went through a very poor period during the 1960s and 1970s. Since 1983, however, the château has received very favorable reviews that suggest the wines are living up to their second-growth classification. Recent VINTAGES are darker colored and more full-bodied (*see* BODY) and CONCENTRATED than their predessors and are capable of AGING for 20 years or more. The château has slightly over 100 acres planted with about 67 percent CABERNET SAUVIGNON, 30 percent MERLOT, and small amounts of CABERNET FRANC and PETIT VERDOT. Around 12,000 to 14,000 cases of red wine are produced each year. The château's SECOND LABEL is **Lamouroux**.

Rauzan-Gassies, Château [sha-TOH roh-ZAH*N* gah-SEE (gah-SEES)] A DEUXIÈME CRU (second growth) CHÂTEAU located in the MARGAUX AC in BORDEAUX. Rauzan-Gassies, once part of a larger estate that included RAUSAN-SÉGLA, has been heavily criticized in the past for the quality of its wines. Some improvements were made in the 1980s, but the wines are still receiving mixed reviews. The vineyard consists of nearly 75 acres planted with about 40 percent CABERNET SAUVIGNON, 35 percent MERLOT, 23 percent CABERNET FRANC, and 2 percent PETIT VERDOT. This estate produces around 10,000 to 11,000 cases of red wines each year. Its SECOND LABEL is **Enclos de Moncabon**, which is also the second label for Château CROIZET-BAGES (both estates are owned by Quié family).

Ravat [ra-VA] In the late nineteenth century, J. F. Ravat, a French HYBRIDIZER, created numerous successful HYBRIDS by combining VITUS VINIFERA vines with NATIVE AMERICAN VINES. The best known of these are: *Ravat 262* (popularly known as *Ravat Noir*), which produces light fruity red wines; *Ravat 6* (better known as *Ravat Blanc*), which produces good-quality white wines; and *Ravat 51* (or *Vignoles*), another white-wine grape. The latter has become the more widely planted of the Ravats, with acreage in New York, Pennsylvania, and Michigan. BOTRYTIS CINEREA sometimes forms on the highly acidic Vignoles grapes, which subsequently produce a rich, HONEYED wine. Vignoles grapes are also made into DRY and semisweet wines.

Ravenswood Joel Peterson, Ravenswood co-owner and winemaker, began his viticultural career as an apprentice to ZINFANDEL expert Joseph Swan in the early 1970s. In 1976 Peterson graduated by making his first wines (327 cases) in a rented portion of JOSEPH SWAN VINEYARD'S winery. In 1981 he and his new partner W. Reed Foster moved to their own facility just south of the town of Sonoma, California. Today, Ravenswood's annual production is between 50,000 and 60,000 cases of wine, most of it red—primarily Zinfandel. The extraordinary Ravenswood Zin comes in six different bottlings—Vintner's Blend,

Sonoma County, Napa Valley, Dickerson Vineyard, Old Hill Ranch, and Cooke's Vineyard. The last three wines are low-quantity, VINEYARD-DESIGNATED, and highly sought after. Although most famous for its superb Zinfandel wines, Ravenswood also produces other VARIETALS including three bottlings of MERLOT (Vintner's Blend, Sonoma County, and Sangiacomo Vineyard) and several CABERNET SAUVIGNON wines from SONOMA COUNTY, SONOMA VALLEY, and the Gregory Vineyard. Small amounts of CHARDONNAY are produced and labeled either "Estate Bottled" or "Sangiacomo Vineyard." Ravenswood also makes Pickberry, a Cabernet Sauvignon-CABERNET FRANC-Merlot blend from Sonoma Valley.

raw A winetasting term for wine that is usually young and undeveloped. Such a wine is often HARSH because of unbalanced ALCOHOL, TANNINS, and ACIDITY. With time, raw wines will usually become BALANCED and quite drinkable.

Martin Ray A legendary winemaker who purchased the original Paul Masson Winery in 1936 and then sold it in 1942 to Seagram. Ray then established his own winery high in the SANTA CRUZ MOUNTAINS and was known for producing some of California's best wines from the late 1940s through the 1960s. In 1971, after numerous squabbles and a court battle, Ray lost control of 23 acres of historically significant mountaintop vineyards to his investment partners. This prime property and the winery became MOUNT EDEN VINEYARDS. Martin Ray continued to make wine from the bottom portion of his vineyard under the designation of Martin Ray Vineyard until shortly before he died in 1983.

Raymond Vineyard In 1970 Roy Raymond and his wife, the former Mary Jane Beringer, sold BERINGER VINEYARDS to Nestlé. The Raymonds and their two sons began developing Raymond Vineyard in 1971, choosing an 80-acre site in the center of the NAPA VALLEY between the towns of Rutherford and St. Helena. The sons' involvement include Roy Jr. as vineyard manager and Walt as winemaker. In 1989 a majority interest in the winery was sold to the Kirin Brewing Company of Japan, with the Raymonds continuing to manage the enterprise. This transfusion of capital allowed a major expansion in both the vineyard holdings and the winery. Today, Raymond Vineyards annually produces between 130,000 and 140,000 cases of wine, focusing on CHARDONNAY, CABERNET SAUVIGNON, and SAUVIGNON BLANC. The Chardonnay comes in three types—California, Napa Valley, and Reserve (ESTATE BOTTLED)—and the Cabernet Sauvignon is produced as Napa Valley or Reserve. A small amount of a red BORDEAUX BLEND is produced as well.

La Belle is the SECOND LABEL used for a lower-priced line of VARIETAL WINES.

Raymond-Lafon, Château [sha-TOH ray-MAW*N* lah-FAW*N*] A highly regarded CRU BOURGEOIS estate located in the SAUTERNES AC in BORDEAUX. Although not a CRU CLASSÉ château, Raymond-Lafon consistently produces high-quality wines equal to those of many of the Sauternes AC PREMIERS CRUS (first growths). This sweet Sauternes wine is extremely difficult to find because there are less than 2,000 cases produced annually from the 49-acre vineyard. These RICH, CONCENTRATED wines are capable of AGING for 20 to 25 years. They're made from about 80 percent SÉMILLON and 20 percent SAUVIGNON BLANC.

Rayne-Vigneau, Château [sha-TOH rayn vee-NYOH] A SAUTERNES AC estate that was ranked as a PREMIER CRU (first growth) in the CLASSIFICATION OF 1855. Not only has this CHÂTEAU'S soil produced excellent wines in the past, but it has also yielded numerous precious and semiprecious stones like amethysts, opals, onyx, sapphires, and topaz. Although the château developed a reputation for mediocre wines over most of the last few decades, the wines made in the last half of the 1980s show immense improvement. The estate consists of 168 acres, which are planted mainly with SÉMILLON and a small amount of SAUVIGNON BLANC. It annually produces 16,000 to 17,000 cases of white wine, less than half of which is sweet Sauternes AC wine. The rest of the production is a DRY white wine distributed under the Le Sec de Rayne-Vigneau label.

RD *see* DENOMINAÇÃO DE ORIGEM CONTROLADA

rebêche *see* VIN DE CUVÉE

Rebula *see* RIBOLLA

Rechbächel *see* WACHENHEIM

recioto [*r*eh-CHAW-toh] An Italian wine made in the VENETO region using the PASSITO method. In this method, grapes are dried in a cool, airy room for up to 4 months until semi-dry, which produces concentrated sugars and flavors. Occasionally, the grapes develop BOTRYTIS CINEREA, which gives them added richness. If during VINIFICATION, FERMENTATION stops either naturally or because of human intervention, the wine's left with RESIDUAL SUGAR and it's simply a *recioto*. If fermentation continues until the wine is completely DRY, then the term *amarone,* which means "strongly bitter," is added to the name. RECIOTO DELLA VALPOLICELLA and RECIOTO DELLA VALPOLICELLA AMARONE are examples of these two different types of wines. Recioto's name is derived from a local dialect term *recie* meaning "ears." A grape bunch often has two small clusters—called ears—branching out of the main bunch. The ears are thought to be of better quality because they stick out and catch more sun. Because of this, ears were always used in recioto wines. Today, although this approach isn't consistently employed, the grapes used are always of high quality. *See also* RECIOTO DI SOAVE DOC.

Recioto della Valpolicella DOC; Recioto della Valpolicella Amarone DOC [reh-CHAW-toh deh-lah vahl-paw-lee-CHEHL-lah (ah-mah-ROH-neh)] These wines are made primarily from the red CORVINA grape, but also with Rondinella, Molinara, and others. They are not like other VALPOLICELLA wines because of the special process that RECIOTO wines go through, such as the use of semi-dried grapes. The *Recioto della Valpolicella,* with its cherry and plum flavors, can be sweet and quite pleasant. The *Recioto della Valpolicella Amarone* (also called *Amarone della Valpolicella*) is the DRY version, which is essentially the same as the sweet except that it's allowed to FERMENT fully. It too can be quite good, with similar flavors but a bittersweet essence. There are FORTIFIED and SPARKLING versions also, although they're not as highly regarded.

Recioto di Gambellara *see* GAMBELLARA DOC

Recioto di Soave DOC [reh-CHAW-toh dee SWAH-veh] A sweet wine made using the PASSITO process whereby grapes are dried to concentrate the sugar and flavors. Made from GARGANEGA and TREBBIANO grapes, in the same designated area as SOAVE DOC wines, *Recioto di Soave* can be an excellent ABBOCCATO (lightly sweet) wine, with more richness and lushness than most Soave wines. It can be found in SPUMANTE and LIQUOROSO styles as well.

recólte [ray-KAWLT] French for "harvest," "crop," or "vintage."

red wine A wine made from dark-skinned grapes (red, purple, black, blue), which remains in contact with the grape skins (from which color is extracted) during FERMENTATION. The pulp or flesh isn't generally red, the rare exceptions being TEINTURIER grapes like ALICANTE BOUSCHET. BLUSH and ROSÉ wines are a lighter color because they're not kept in contact with the skins as long.

reducing sugar *see* RESIDUAL SUGAR

refined; refinement In winetasting vernacular, a refined wine (or one of refinement) is one that's high in quality, as well as being in perfect CHARACTER and BALANCE for its origin and style.

Refosco *see* MONDEUSE

Refosco del Peduncolo Rosso *see* MONDEUSE

Refosco Nostrano *see* MONDEUSE

refractometer [ree-frak-TOM-ih-tuhr] An instrument used in winemaking to measure the sugar content of grapes and MUST. A refractometer, which can be used right in the vineyard, works by placing a drop of juice between the refractometer's prisms and reading the angle at which the light bends. The angle will vary depending on the juice's sugar content. This refractometer reading is described in terms of BRIX in the United States, BAUMÉ in France, and OECHSLE in Germany.

Regaleali [reh-gah-leh-AH-lee] Located in the middle of Sicily, this wine-producing estate is owned by the Conte Tasca d'Almerita. The estate consists of several thousand acres of which about 700 are planted with grapevines. Regaleali produces high-quality VINO DA TAVOLA wines. These fresh dry white wines are made from Catarratto, Inzolia, and SAUVIGNON BLANC grapes. The best is *Nozze d'Oro* ("golden wedding"), which was first released in 1985 on the Conte's fiftieth wedding anniversary. The red and ROSÉ wines are made from Nero d'Avola, Nerello, and Perricone grapes. Rosso del Conte and the Rosso del Conte Riserva are the best reds.

Região Demarcada (RD) *see* DENOMINAÇÃO DE ORIGEM CONTROLADA

regional A regional wine is generally one that's a blend of several wines from different parts of a region or district instead of from a single vineyard or proximate vineyards. The use of a term such as NAPA VALLEY, SONOMA VALLEY, CALIFORNIA, MÉDOC, BORDEAUX, or RIOJA indicates that the wine is regional.

Regions I–V *see* CLIMATE REGIONS OF CALIFORNIA

régisseur [ray-zhee-SEUR] The manager in charge of a CHÂTEAU's vineyard and cellar operations in France's BORDEAUX region.

Régnié AC [ray-NYAY] The newest of the ten CRUS in France's BEAUJOLAIS region. In 1988 its status was upgraded from BEAUJOLAIS-VILLAGES AC. Régnié AC wines, which are made from GAMAY grapes, vary depending on the locale. The northern and eastern portions of the APPELLATION abut the MORGON AC, and the Régnié AC wines there are similar—BIG and RICH. In the southern portion, the wines are much more like its southern neighbors, the BROUILLY AC and the CÔTES DE BROUILLY AC—LIGHT and FRUITY.

Rehbach *see* NIERSTEIN

Rehoboam *see* WINE BOTTLES

reid Austrian term meaning "vineyard." When the name of a reid is used on a label, 100 percent of the wine must be from the named site.

Reiterpfad *see* RUPPERTSBERG

Remstal-Stuttgart, Bereich *see* WÜRTTEMBERG

remuage *see* RIDDLING

remuer *see* RIDDLING

Les Renardes *see* CORTON; CORTON-CHARLEMAGNE

reserva [ray-ZEHR-vah] A Spanish term referring to quality wine from a good VINTAGE that has satisfied specific AGING requirements. To be labeled "reserva," red wines must have a minimum of 3 years of aging with at least 1 year in OAK barrels; ROSÉ and white reservas require a minimum aging of 2 years with no less than 6 months in oak. *See also* GRAN RESERVA.

reserve Even though this term is found on U.S. wine labels, it has no legal definition, which means it can't be relied on to have any special meaning. Reserve appears on labels in a number of ways—*Private Reserve, Proprietor's Reserve, Special Reserve, Vintner's Reserve*, or simply *Reserve*. For some producers—like BEAULIEU VINEYARDS and BERINGER VINEYARDS—the term *Private Reserve* means the wines are their top quality. These wines are either produced from grapes coming from special vineyards or blended from superior batches of grapes. But the terms do not always indicate high quality and are often used simply for as a marketing ploy. The bottom line is that wines using any of these terms should be judged on their own merit and not on the labeling.

Réserve de la Comtesse *see* PICHON-LONGUEVILLE-COMTESSE DE LALANDE, CHÂTEAU

Réserve du Général *see* PALMER, CHÂTEAU

residual sugar The natural grape sugar that is either unfermented at the end of the FERMENTATION process or added back into the wine, as with a DOSAGE added to a SPARKLING WINE. In some cases there is so much natural sugar that fermentation can't complete its process, as is the case with some DESSERT WINES like Germany's TROKENBEER-ENAUSLESE. In other instances, fermentation is purposefully arrested by adding a soupçon of SULFUR DIOXIDE, which inhibits the yeast, or by adding ALCOHOL (as is done with FORTIFIED wines), which raises the alcohol to a level (15 to 16 percent) above which the YEAST cannot work. DRY wines may have little residual sugar (0.1 to 0.2 percent), semisweet wines usually range from 1 to 3 percent, and LATE HARVEST wines may range as high as 28 to 30 percent. Residual sugar is sometimes referred to as **reducing sugar**.

residuo [ray-SEE-dwoh] The Italian term used for RESIDUAL SUGAR.

resinous [REH-sihn-uhs] A winetasting term for a characteristic found in wines, predominantly Greek, that have been treated with pine-tree resin, which gives them a distinctive turpentinelike flavor and smell. *See also* RETSINA.

restzucker [REHST-tsoo-kehr] German for "RESIDUAL SUGAR." *Restsüsse* means "residual sweetness" and is also used to refer to residual sugar.

retsina [reht-SEE-nah] Made for more than 3,000 years, this traditional Greek wine is resinated—treated with pine-tree resin. This process gives the wine a distinctively sappy, turpentinelike flavor which, according to most non-Greeks, is an acquired taste. In Greece the word *retsina* (Greek for "resin") is synonymous with wine. Retsinas can be either white (labeled "Retsina") or ROSÉ (labeled "Kokineli"); both should be served very cold. The Savatiano grape is the main variety used in retsina, although it's usually blended with either Rhoditis or Assyrtiko grapes.

Reuilly AC [reuh-YEE] Located southwest of the SANCERRE AC and POUILLY-FUMÉ AC, this tiny APPELLATION surrounds the village of Reuilly near the QUINCY AC in the central LOIRE region. Reuilly produces white wines from the SAUVIGNON BLANC grape that are similar in style to those from these three neighboring appellations—generally CRISP and TART with a somewhat GRASSY characteristic. It also produces light red wines from PINOT NOIR and ROSÉ wines from Pinot Noir and PINOT GRIS.

Rex Hill Vineyards Hilltop winery located in Oregon's WILLAMETTE VALLEY just northeast of the town of Newberg and southwest of Portland. It was established in 1983 by Paul Hart and has grown to about 15,000 cases of wine each year. Rex Hill is best known for its PINOT NOIR wines, which make up a majority of the production. Other VARIETAL WINES include CHARDONNAY, PINOT GRIS, RIESLING, and SYMPHONY.

Reynella *see* SOUTHERN VALES

Rhein [RINE] The German name for the Rhine River, which appears in many of the country's regional names.

Rheinburgengau, Bereich *see* MITTELRHEIN

Rheinelbe *see* ELBLING

Rheingau [RINE-gow] The wines of this German ANBAUGEBIET (quality wine region) are considered by many to be some of the finest in Germany and therefore among the world's great wines. Over 80 percent of the vineyards are planted with RIESLING, Germany's premier variety. The Rheingau, whose vineyards cover the right or northerly bank of the Rhine River, starts just east of Hochheim and extends north to Lorch, with the principal portion situated between the villages of RAUENTHAL and RÜDESHEIM. The climate and soil of this stretch of vineyards is ideal for Riesling. It's from this area that the Rheingau gets its reputation for wines that are generally RICH, FRUITY, and full-bodied (*see* BODY) with a STEELY character. The better VINTAGES can produce AUSLESE, BEERENAUSLESE, and occasionally TROCKENBEERENAUSLESE wines of remarkable quality. Even though these wines are very RICH, they're balanced with good ACIDITY and are capable of very long AGING. The Rheingau's only BEREICH is JOHANNISBERG, which covers the entire region and includes ten GROSSLAGEN—Burgweg, Daubhaus, Deutelsberg, Erntebringer, Gottesthal, Heiligensotck, Honigberg, Mehrhölzchen, Steil, and Steinmächer. Some of Germany's best-known wine estates are located here including SCHLOSS JOHANNISBERG, SCHLOSS SCHÖNBORN, SCHLOSS RHEINHARTSHAUSEN, and SCHLOSS VOLLRADS.

Rheinhell *see* ERBACH

Rheinhessen [RINE-hehs-uhn] With nearly 62,000 acres of vineyards, this is the largest of Germany's thirteen ANBAUGEBIETE (quality wine regions). It's in the center of the wine-growing regions located along the Rhine, with RHEINGAU to the north, RHEINPFALZ to the south, NAHE to the west, and HESSISCHE BERGSTRASSE to the east. Rheinhessen is divided into just three BEREICHE—BINGEN, NIERSTEIN, and Wonnegau—and twenty-four GROSSLAGEN. Despite the large number of vineyards, only a small percentage produce high-quality wines. Many of the vineyards in the fertile land away from the Rhine have large YIELDS and are major providers of vast quantities of LIEBFRAUMILCH. In fact, over 50 percent of Germany's production of this simple, inexpensive wine come from Rheinhessen. The best wines come from the vineyards located closest to the Rhine, starting near Bingen in the north, east to Mainz, and then south to around Worms. In particular, the vineyards near Bingen and Ingelheim and the RHEINTERRASE near Nierstein produce excellent wines. MÜLLER-THURGAU, which accounts for about 25 percent of Rheinhessen's total planted acreage, is the most widely planted variety. It's followed by SYLVANER and SCHEUREBE, as well as myriad others like BACCHUS, Faberebe (FABER), HUXELREBE, and KERNER.

Rheinpfalz [RINE-fahlts] The second largest of Germany's thirteen ANBAUGEBIETE (quality wine regions). However, it's often the largest volume producer, averaging nearly 28 million cases of wine annually, or over 25 percent of Germany's total production. The region's English name, *Palatinate,* is derived from the Latin *palatium* meaning "palace." It refers to the first palace built by the Holy Roman Empire for its governors, who became known as Counts Palatine. The region is also simply called the **Pfalz**, which is the German transliteration of *palatium*. Rheinpfalz borders France's ALSACE region in the south and RHEINHESSEN in the north, with the Rhine River forming its eastern boundary. There are two BEREICHE covering the Rheinpfalz—**Südliche Weinstrasse**, which is the southern half of the region, and **Mittelhaardt/Deutsche Weinstrasse**, which takes in the north. The southern half is extremely fertile and sunny and produces large quantities of wine—almost as much inexpensive LIEBFRAUMILCH as the Rheinhessen region. Most of the best wines produced in the Bereich Südliche Weinstrasse are consumed locally. It's the northern section that produces the better wines, and the best of that section is called the Mittelhaardt, which lies between Neustadt and Bad Dürkheim. Great wines, primarily RIESLING, are made in the villages of Deidesheim, Forst, Ruppertsberg, and Wachenhem. MÜLLER-THURGAU is the most widely planted variety, followed by Riesling and a host of others including GEWÜRZTRAMINER, KERNER, MARIO-MUSKAT, Rülander (PINOT GRIS), SCHEUREBE, SYLVANER, and the red PORTUGIESER.

Rheinterrasse [RINE-tehr-ah-suh] This German term, which means "Rhine terrace," refers to a strip of vineyards situated along Rhine River from the village of Bodenheim south to the village of Mettenheim. These vineyards are part of the RHEINHESSEN region and are noted for producing superb wines, particularly those made from RIESLING, but also SYLVANER. The very best of the Rheinterrasse vineyards are around the villages of NACKENHEIM, NIERSTEIN, and OPPENHEIM.

Rhine Riesling *see* RIESLING

Rhine wine [RINE] A generic name in the United States for white, usually somewhat sweet, TABLE WINES. Such wines shouldn't be confused with German wines from the Rhine region.

Rhône [*R*OHN] The Rhône River actually starts high in the Swiss Alps, tumbling down the mountains into Lake Geneva and then exiting the lake to begin its journey through France. The vineyards of the Rhône form one of France's great wine regions, which follows the river for approximately 125 miles from just below Vienne in the north, to south of Avignon. The Rhône region breaks up into two distinct north and south portions. The northern part contains many great individual APPELLATIONS like CÔTE RÔTIE, CONDRIEU, CHÂTEAU GRILLET, SAINT-JOSEPH, and HERMITAGE. Many of these vineyards are planted on small steep terraces with breathtaking views of the Rhône River. The dominant grapes here are SYRAH for red wines and MARSANNE, ROUSSANNE, and VIOGNIER for whites. As one heads south, there is a gap in the vineyards around Montélimar and then the valley widens to form the southern portion. The most famous appellation in the south is CHÂTEAUNEUF-DU-PAPE. Other well-known ACs are GIGONDAS, LIRAC, MUSCAT DE BEAUMES-DE-VENISE, and TAVEL. Most of the vineyards in the southern Rhône produce wines covered by the ACs of CÔTES DU RHÔNE and CÔTES DU RHÔNE-VILLAGES. In the southern Rhône the principal red grape is GRENACHE, but others include CARIGNAN, Counoise, MOURVÈDRE, Terret Noir and SYRAH. The white grapes used include Bourboulenc, CLAIRETTE, Marsanne, Muscardine, Picardan, Roussanne, and Piquepoul (or *Picpoule*). More blends of different grapes are used in the south than in the north.

Rias Baixas DO; Rias Bajas DO [REE-ahs bi-SHAHS (BAH-hahs)]

New DO area that is in northwest Spain's Galicia region, adjacent to Portugal's northern border. The word *Rias* refers to this region's numerous wide channels, similiar to fjords, that reach inland from the Atlantic Ocean. Rias Baixas (also called *Rias Bajas*) refers to the lower or southern part of the region. The white wines made from Albariño (ALVARINHO) are the best known here, although there are other grapes used as well. The Albariño vines are low yielding; the grapes are thick skinned and don't produce a lot of juice. This combination results in wines that are somewhat expensive and highly sought after by Spaniards. The red wines, made from a variety of local grapes, are not at all highly regarded.

Ribeiro DO [ree-BAY-roh]

DO area located in the Galicia region in northwest Spain, inland from the RIAS BAIXAS DO. Two-thirds of the wines produced are white. The primary grape here is PALOMINO, the principal variety used in making Spanish SHERRY. Because it's too neutral for the DRY, fresh wine that the area produces, Palomino is being replaced with local varieties like Godello, Loureiro, Treixadura, and Torrontés. These grapes are known to produce more exciting wines, similiar to the fresh, crisp wines from Portugal's VINHO VERDE DOC. Red wines, made from Garnacha (GRENACHE) and local varieties like Caiño, Ferrón, and Mencía, are generally undistinguished.

Ribera del Duero DO [ree-BEHR-ah del DWAY-roh] DO area located along the Duero River in northern Spain, halfway between Madrid and the Atlantic Ocean (Bay of Biscay). The Duero River becomes the Douro (the famous PORT river) in Portugal. Ribera del Duero is famous for its red wines, principally because of VEGA SICILIA, a premier wine estate that's been around for over a century, and also the more recent discoveries in the 1980s of wine estates like Alejandro Fernandez and its Tinto Pesquera wines. Several other wine estates in this area have sparked a trend of attracting producers interested in producing high-quality red wines. However, much of the wine is still made by the Cooperative de Ribera del Duero, which, although it can produce very good wines, is rather inconsistent. The primary grape here is Tinta del Pais (TEMPRANILLO), but numerous other red grapes are grown as well. Vega Sicilia use about 60 percent Tinta del Pais blended with CABERNET SAUVIGNON, MERLOT, and MALBEC. Alejandro Fernandez, however, uses mainly Tinta del Pais with some Garnacha (GRENACHE). A small amount of ROSÉ wine is made in this area, but white wines are not included as part of the DO.

La Ribera d'Erbe *see* TARRAGONA DO

Ribolla [ree-BOH-lah] White wine grape, whose full name is *Ribolla Gialla,* that is grown in Italy's FRIULI-VENEZIA GIULIA in Slovenia, where it's known as *Rebula,* and in Greece, where it's called *Robola*. Ribolla's been grown in Friuli since the twelfth century and is thought to be a native of this region, although there's some speculation that it has Greek origins. This variety produces DRY, CRISP, citrus-flavored wines that are medium-bodied and deeply colored. Ribolla will stand some aging, during which time it becomes richer and SOFTER. There's also a red version, *Ribolla Nera,* more popularly known as SCHIOPPETTINO.

rice wine A sweet, golden wine made from fermenting freshly steamed glutinous rice. Most rice wines are low in alcohol. The most well-known Japanese rice wines are SAKE and MIRIN, while Chinese renditions include Chia Fan, Hsiang Hsueh, Shan Niang, and Yen Hung.

rich A winetasting term depicting wines that have an opulently full and balanced complement of intense flavor, FRUIT, ALCOHOL, and EXTRACT.

Richebourg AC [reesh-BOOR] Located at the northern end of the village of VOSNE-ROMANÉE in the CÔTE DE NUITS, Richebourg is one of the great Burgundian GRAND CRU vineyards. Its 19.8 acres are planted with PINOT NOIR, and the red wines that are produced here are some of the best in the world. The largest and most famous of the twelve different parcel owners is the Domaine de la Romanée-Conti. The wines from the Richebourg vineyards are said to be richer and deeper colored than those from the famous neighboring vineyards ROMANÉE-CONTI and LA TÂCHE, although not quite as PERFUMED or elegant.

riddling [RIHD-ling] Madame Clicquot, a young French widow who took over her dead husband's CHAMPAGNE house in 1805, was the visionary who developed the important riddling procedure—a way to remove dead yeast cells from bottles of SPARKLING WINE made by the MÉTHODE CHAMPENOISE. In the step just before riddling, a BOTTLING DOSAGE (*dosage de tirage* or *liqueur de tirage*) and yeast are added to a CUVÉE (a blend of still wines) in order to produce a SECONDARY FERMENTATION in the bottle. The SEDIMENT that forms during this secondary fermentation is maneuvered into the neck of the bottle and up against the cork through riddling (called *remuage* in France). The riddling process consists of positioning the bottles upside down at a 45° angle in specially built racks called *pupitres*. Every 3 or 4 days, a trained workman (called a *remuer* in France) gives the bottles a shake and a slight turn, gradually increasing the angle of tilt and dropping the bottle back in the rack with a slight whack. In 6 to 8 weeks, all the bottles are positioned straight downward and the sediment has collected in the neck. The sediment is then removed by another step called DISGORGEMENT. A skilled *remuer* can handle over 30,000 bottles per day. Although riddling was once done entirely by hand, today many winemakers are employing large metal racks (pioneered in Spain) that hold over 500 bottles. These racks—called *girasols* in Spain, *gyropallets* in France, and *VLMs* (very large machines) in the United States—mechanically perform the riddling process and have dramatically shortened the procedure. Another process being tried is the placement of yeast in **calcium alginate beads** (also called **encapsulated yeasts**), which fall to the neck of the bottle immediately when it is turned upside down. If successful, this technique could eliminate the need for riddling altogether.

Ridge Vineyards A winery located in the SANTA CRUZ MOUNTAINS AVA near the top of Monte Bello Ridge, looking down on the Santa Clara Valley. Although the property was purchased in 1959 by three Stanford Research Institute engineers and their families for recreational purposes, the discovery of the historically famous Monte Bello Winery facility (with its three-level cellar built into the mountainside) proved to be an irresistible stroke of kismet. The renowned Monte Bello Winery and vineyard had been abandoned during PROHIBITION, but the partners set about bringing both the facility and vineyards back to life. Ridge Vineyards was officially started in 1962 when a small amount of outstanding CABERNET SAUVIGNON wine was produced from the Monte Bello Vineyard. The endeavor grew slowly but steadily until 1967, when partner Dave Bennion left the Research Institute to become Ridge's full-time winemaker. After that, production rapidly increased, and the winery began buying grapes from vineyards throughout California, a practice that continues today. In 1986 the extremely successful Ridge Vineyards was sold to Akihito Otsuka, owner of Japan's Otsuka Pharmaceutical Company. The winery continues to produce some of the finest wines in California. It's best known for its Monte Bello Cabernet Sauvignon and the ZINFANDEL wines labeled Lytton Springs and Geyserville. It makes other Cabernet Sauvignons from York Creek Vineyard (NAPA VALLEY) and the Santa Cruz Mountains. Several other Zinfandels are offered, as well as MERLOT, PETITE SIRAH, and CHARDONNAYS from HOWELL MOUNTAIN and the Santa Cruz Mountains. In 1991 Ridge purchased the **Lytton Springs Winery**, a respected producer of Zinfandel wines that's situated in the DRY CREEK VALLEY AVA in SONOMA COUNTY.

Riesling [REEZ-ling; REES-ling] Riesling is considered to be one of the world's great white-wine grapes and produces some of the very best white wines. It's a native of Germany, where it's believed to have been cultivated for at least 500—and possibly as long as 2,000—years. The Riesling grape's ability to retain its acidity while achieving high sugar levels is what creates wines with considerable aging potential. Riesling wines are DELICATE but COMPLEX and are characterized by a SPICY, FRUITY flavor (that's sometimes reminiscent of peaches and apricots), a flower-scented BOUQUET, and a long FINISH. Riesling is vinified in a variety of styles ranging from DRY to very sweet. In Germany, these sweet wines—which are usually affected by BOTRYTIS CINEREA—are graded in ascending order of sweetness as AUSLESE, BEERENAUSLESE, and TROCKENBEERENAUSLESE. There are extensive Riesling plantings in California where early wines were made in a DRY, OAKY style. California winemakers now produce high-quality, German-style Rieslings, which are lighter, more delicate, and slightly to medium sweet. They also make some excellent LATE HARVEST wines from botrytis-infected grapes. Other states that have had success with Riesling wines include Oregon, Washington, and New York. Australia has extensive plantings of this grape and produces high-quality Riesling wines, particularly from the Eden and Clare Valleys. France's ALSACE region and Italy's ALTO ADIGE also produce excellent Rieslings. Because the name "Riesling" is used in many ways, it's sometimes difficult to find wines truly made from this variety. In California, for instance, **Johannisberg Riesling** is the true Riesling, whereas GRAY RIESLING and EMERALD RIESLING are actually other varieties. Californians also call the variety SYLVANER such names as *Sylvaner Riesling, Franken Riesling, Monterey Riesling,* and *Sonoma Riesling*. A bottle of California wine labeled simply "Riesling" usually means that the wine's made from one of the lesser varieties, not Johannisberg Riesling. In parts of Europe, there is also WELSCHRIESLING (or Italian Riesling), which is a different variety. In Australia, the word *Riesling* often refers to any type of white wine, whereas **Rhine Riesling** refers to the real thing. South Africans have *Cape Riesling, Clare Riesling, Paarl Riesling,* and *South African Riesling,* all of which refer to a variety officially known as CRUCHEN BLANC. **Weisser Riesling** is the name South Africans (and some Germans) use for the true Riesling. The confusion is perpetuated even in Germany, where the variety Müllerrebe (MEUNIER) is called *Schwarzriesling* and the variety RÜLANDER is called *Grauer Riesling*. The Germans have also bred a number of Riesling hybrids, the most famous being the MÜLLER-THURGAU, a cross between Riesling and SYLVANER. Riesling is also known as *Johannisberger, Klingelberger, Riesling Renano,* and *White Riesling*.

Riesling Italico *see* WELSCHRIESLING

Riesling Renano *see* RIESLING

Riesling-Sylvaner *see* MÜLLER-THURGAU

Rieussec, Château [sha-TOH ree-uh-SEHK] A PREMIER CRU (first growth) CHÂTEAU located in the SAUTERNES AC in BORDEAUX. It was acquired in 1984 by the Domaines Rothschild, owners of Château LAFITE-ROTHSCHILD. The quality of the wine, which has been improving since the early 1970s, continues to elevate under the Rothschilds. In fact, Château Rieussec is now viewed as one of the top half-dozen Sauternes AC producers. There are about 163 acres planted with about 80 percent SÉMILLON and small amounts of SAUVIGNON BLANC and MUSCADELLE. This estate produces 6,000 to 8,000 cases of white wine a year. In addition to sweet Sauternes AC wines, the château produces a DRY white wine called simply **"R."**

Rioja DOCa [ree-OH-hah] DOCA area that is in northern Spain around the town of Logroño and along the Ebro River. The name comes from Río Oja, a tributary of the Ebro. Established in 1926, Rioja was the first DO, and in 1991 it became the first (and so far only)

Spanish DOCa. Wine has been made in this region for over 2,500 years—prior to the Roman occupation. Rioja DOCa TABLE WINES are the most famous and some of the best in Spain. Rioja's vineyards are situated in the provinces of Alava and Navarra, as well as La Rioja. This DOCa is divided into three subzones—**La Rioja Alavesa** is the northwestern portion, **La Rioja Alta** in the southwestern section, and **La Rioja Baja** in the eastern segment. The cooler, wetter climate of the two western subzones produces more delicate wines. The hotter, drier eastern section, La Rioja Baja, produces bigger, more ALCOHOLIC wines. La Rioja Alta generally produces the best wines, followed by those from La Rioja Alavesa. Rioja wines, which tend to be made very much in a BORDEAUX style, are greatly influenced by winemaking practices introduced by French families who migrated to Rioja in the late 1800s after PHYLLOXERA struck the Bordeaux vineyards. The extensive use of oak BARRIQUES (called *barricas* locally) for AGING wines still exists, although somewhat less aggressively than in the past. The OAK imparts the familiar vanilla characteristic that's associated with Rioja wines. Red wines make up 75 to 80 percent of the total production, and TEMPRANILLO is the primary red grape used. Garnacha Tinta (GRENACHE), Mazuelo (CARIGNAN), and GRACIANO are also allowed. There's a small quantity of ROSÉ wine made from these same grapes. A limited amount of white wine is made from Viura (MACABEO), Garnacha Blanca (GRENACHE) and MALVASIA. In the past, the white wines from Rioja have also been heavily oaked, but fresher, crisper wines are now the style.

riparia *see* VITIS RIPARIA

ripasso process [ree-PAH-soh] A process used in producing some VALPOLICELLA wines to give them richness and BODY. After the wine is FERMENTED in the usual way, it's placed in casks containing the LEES from a prior batch of RECIOTO or RECIOTO AMARONE, a concentrated wine made from PASSITO grapes. This process, which lasts from 2 to 3 weeks, adds color, TANNINS, and complex flavors. Unfortunately, the term *ripasso* is not allowed on the label, so you need to know producers who make this style of wine. Boscaini's Le Canne, Masi's CAMPO FIORIN, and Santi's Castello are some of the wines made this way.

ripe Winetasting term that describes a wine made from perfectly ripened grapes, which contribute RICH, ROUND, naturally sweet, FRUITY characteristics. *See also* UNRIPE.

Ripple *see* E & J GALLO WINERY

riserva [ree-ZEHR-vah] Italian for "reserve," which in the wine world can be applied only to DOC or DOCG wines that have been AGED longer than regular wines. The better wines are usually chosen to become riservas. The total aging time varies from wine to wine. For instance, CHIANTI Riserva receives 3 years aging, BARBARESCO Riserva gets 4 years, and BAROLO and BRUNELLO DI MONTALCINO Riservas each get 5 years of aging. Sometimes, but not always, part of the additional aging time occurs in wood. *Riserva speciale* denotes even longer aging, usually an additional year.

riserva speciale *see* RISERVA

Rivaner *see* MÜLLER-THURGAU

River Break *see* BABCOCK VINEYARDS

Rivesaltes AC [reev-ZALT] Small town located just north of Perpignan in France's LANGEUDOC-ROUSSILLON region. The APPELLATION that surrounds the town produces VIN DOUX NATUREL (VDN), a category of sweet, FORTIFIED wine. Rivesaltes AC produces red, white, and ROSÉ wines from GRENACHE, MALVOISIE, MACABEO, and MUSCAT. A more celebrated VDN from this same area is MUSCAT DE RIVESALTES AC, which is made from 100 percent MUSCAT.

Riviera Ligure di Ponente *see* VERMENTINO

Rizlingszilvani *see* MÜLLER-THURGAU

Rkatsiteli [ruh-KAT-see-TELL-ee] White-wine grape that is the most widely planted variety in what was formerly the Soviet Union—it's extensively grown in Russia and Georgia. Rkatsiteli is also widely grown in Bulgaria and is now thought to be the world's second most planted white grape after Spain's AIRÉN. There are even a few acres in California and New York. Rkatsiteli produces good-quality wines that have high ACIDITY, good sugar levels, and pleasant SPICY, FLORAL characteristics. It's vinified in a variety of styles ranging from DRY to very sweet, used in sparkling wine production, and is even processed into SHERRY-like wines and COGNAC-style spirits.

Roaix *see* CÔTES DU RHÔNE

Robola *see* RIBOLLA

robust A winetasting term similar in meaning to BIG, describing wine that's full-bodied (*see* BODY), ROUND, and full of FRUIT—in short, a big mouthful. This term is more apt for red wines than for white.

Roc-Blanquant *see* BELAIR, CHÂTEAU

Rochegude *see* CÔTES DU RHÔNE

J. Rochioli Vineyards [roh-kee-OH-lee] A top-notch grower and winery located in the RUSSIAN RIVER AVA. The Rochioli family has been selling grapes since the late 1930s, but winemaking didn't become a serious consideration until 1982. There are now 95 acres planted with CABERNET SAUVIGNON, CHARDONNAY, PINOT NOIR, SAUVIGNON BLANC, and ZINFANDEL. In addition to being a desirable source of PINOT NOIR grapes (Gary Allen Vineyards and Williams Selyem Winery both produce top-quality wines from Rochioli grapes), Rochioli has been producing superb Pinot Noir wines of its own. The winery also produces high-caliber Chardonnays and Sauvignon Blancs, particularly the RESERVE wines.

Roederer, Louis [loo-EE ROH-duh-rer] Small privately owned CHAMPAGNE house that produces about 2 million bottles annually. The Louis Roederer premium brand is the well-known and highly regarded **Cristal**. This champagne house is also known for its full-bodied non-vintage champagnes. Roederer has invested in California's SPARKLING WINE industry by purchasing 500 acres in MENDOCINO COUNTY, California, and creating the ANDERSON VALLEY sparkling wine facility, ROEDERER ESTATE.

Roederer Estate [ROH-duh-rer] The French CHAMPAGNE house LOUIS ROEDERER started this California SPARKLING WINE effort in 1982 with the purchase of over 500 acres in the ANDERSON VALLEY AVA. It's since built a marvelous production facility and purchased three other sizable sites in the valley. Now over 400 acres are planted with CHARDONNAY and PINOT NOIR vines, which allows Roederer to make all their wines without buying grapes from other growers. Between 40,000 and 50,000 cases of wine a year are now being produced. A non-vintage BRUT was the first offering in 1988, followed by a non-vintage ROSÉ and a VINTAGE brut. A premium-priced, vintage brut (the 1989 vintage) called L'Ermitage was released in 1993 to excellent reviews.

Roero DOC; Roero Arneis DOC [roh-EHR-oh ahr-NAYZ] DOC located in the Roero hills north and east of Alba in southeastern PIEDMONT. This zone lies within the larger NEBBIOLO D'ALBA DOC and was granted its own DOC designation in 1985 at the request of the area's producers. The wines from the two DOCs are similiar. **Roero** makes red wine primarily from NEBBIOLO grapes, although small amounts of ARNEIS and other grapes are allowed. The *Roero Superiore* has a higher ALCOHOL content and is AGED for 8 months. The right to make DOC white wine was granted in 1989. The white wine called **Roero Arneis** (or *Arneis di Roero*) is made from 100 percent Arneis grapes. The *Superiore* version has a higher alcohol content and is aged for 1 year. A SPUMANTE rendition of the Roero Arneis may be made as well.

Le Rognet et Corton *see* CORTON; CORTON-CHARLEMAGNE

Rogue River Valley AVA AVA that is located in southern Oregon near the California border and encompasses the towns of Medford and Ashland. This area is warmer than most parts of Oregon and is best known for its CABERNET SAUVIGNON and CHARDONNAY. Valley View Winery in the Applegate Valley section is the best-known winery.

La Romanée AC [lah raw-ma-NAY] The tiniest GRAND CRU vineyard in France's BURGUNDY region and also the smallest APPELLATION in France (not CHÂTEAU-GRILLET, as is often indicated). La Romanée is located in the village VOSNE-ROMANÉE next to two other famous grands crus of this village—ROMANÉE-CONTI AC and RICHEBOURG AC. La Romanée consists of slightly more than two acres planted in PINOT NOIR. The miniscule amount of red wine that it produces is ranked as some of the best in the world, as is that of its neighbors. These wines are usually considered more like those from Richebourg AC than Romanée-Conti, which is deeper colored and more intense but not as elegant or PERFUMED as Romanée-Conti.

Romanée-Conti AC [raw-ma-NAY kaw*n*-TEE] The red wines from this 4½-acre GRAND CRU vineyard are destined only for the very rich. The vineyard, wholly owned by the Domaine de la Romanée-Conti, is located in the village of VOSNE-ROMANÉE in CÔTE DE NUITS area of France's BURGUNDY region. The wines are thought to be the ultimate in PINOT NOIRS. They're so sought after, in fact, that recent vintages have been priced at $500 to $650 *per bottle*. Romanée-Conti wines, although usually not as RICH and intense as those from the neighboring RICHEBOURG AC and LA TÂCHE AC, are considered to be the perfect example of what a red Burgundy should be. They're RICH, with a seeming sweetness and enough TANNINS to AGE gracefully. Their most distinguishing trademark is an exotic spiciness reminiscent of cinnamon and cloves.

Romanée-Saint-Vivant AC [raw-ma-NAY sa*n* vee-VAH*N*] The largest of the five GRAND CRU vineyards located in the village of VOSNE ROMANÉE in the CÔTE DE NUITS. It consists of slightly over 23 acres planted with PINOT NOIR. Although the wines from this vineyard are some of the world's best and most expensive, they're often overshadowed by those from the neighboring and more famous grand cru vineyards of ROMANÉE-CONTI, RICHEBOURG, and LA TÂCHE. The Romanée-Saint-Vivant AC wines are somewhat lighter in style than the wines from these other famous vineyards, but they possess much of the elegance and spiciness found in the celebrated Romanée-Conti AC wines.

Romania *see* RUMANIA

römer [RUH-muhr] A traditional German wine glass with a long green or amber stem. The bowl, which is made of clear glass and is sometimes engraved, holds from 6½ to 8½ ounces.

Romer du Hayot, Château [sha-TOH raw-MEHR doo hay-OH] A small, 37-acre DEUXIÈME CRU (second growth) CHÂTEAU located in the SAUTERNES AC in BORDEAUX. It produces about 4,000 cases of good-quality, lighter-styled sweet white wine that's capable of AGING for 10 to 12 years. The grapes used are about 70 percent SÉMILLON, 25 percent SAUVIGNON BLANC, and 5 percent MUSCADELLE.

Romondolo Classico *see* VERDUZZO

room temperature *see* CHAMBRER

rootstock The lower portion of a root and its corresponding growth buds, used for plant propagation. In grape growing, the root-stock should be PHYLLOXERA-resistant. American rootstock often has European (VITIS VINIFERA) vines GRAFTED to it.

rosado [roh-SAH-thoh] Spanish for ROSÉ.

rosato; Rosato [roh-ZAH-toh] 1. Italian for ROSÉ. 2. In Italy the term *Rosato* is also used to indicate a rosé wine that's made from spe-cific, approved grape varieties, which can differ depending on the DOC and region.

rosé [roh-ZAY] French for "pink" or "rose-colored," used in the wine world to refer to wines of this color. Except for rosé CHAMPAGNES, rosé wines are usually (always in France) made from red grapes. However, contrary to the normal process of making red wine, the skins are re-moved almost immediately, generally within 2 to 3 days. This brief skin contact gives the wine its light pink color. However, it's also the reason that rosés lack the body and character of most red wines. In addition to being very light-bodied (*see* BODY), most rosés are generally slightly sweet. In France, rosé champagnes can be made with a little red wine added to the white-wine CUVÉE prior to the SECONDARY FERMENTATION—an exception to the red-grape-only rule. Excellent French rosé wines come from TAVEL and ANJOU. In the United States the term BLUSH WINE has all but replaced that of "rosé." *See also* BLANC DE NOIR.

Rosé d'Anjou AC [roh-ZAY dah*n*-ZHOO] An APPELLATION for ROSÉ wines from the ANJOU region, which is in the central part of France's LOIRE Valley. These sweetish, pale pink wines are produced from the Cot (MALBEC), GAMAY, GROSLOT, and Pineau d'Aunis grapes.

Although this appellation's production is one of the largest in the region, the wines don't have a great reputation. The CABERNET FRANC-based rosé wines of the CABERNET D'ANJOU AC from this same geographic area are more highly regarded.

Rosé de Loire AC [ro-ZAY duh LWAH*R*] An APPELLATION that covers a wide area in France's LOIRE Valley including the subregions of ANJOU, SAUMUR, and TOURAINE. The Rosé de Loir AC is for wines made from a minimum of 30 percent Cabernet (usually CABERNET FRANC) blended with GAMAY, GROSLOT, Pineau d'Aunis, and PINOT NOIR. The wines are drier (*see* DRY) than the ROSÉ D'ANJOU AC wines produced throughout much of the same region.

Rosé des Riceys AC *see* CHAMPAGNE

Rosenberg *see* WILTINGEN

Rosenblum Cellars [ROH-suhn-bloom] Kent Rosenblum established his winery in 1978 after operating as a home winemaker for about 5 years. Since then he's expanded Rosenblum Cellars to an annual production of between 20,000 and 25,000 cases. The Rosenblum Cellars facility is located in an industrial section of Alameda, California, just across the bay from San Francisco. Rosenblum, who's a full-time veterinarian, produces myriad wines from purchased grapes he selects from numerous growers throughout California. The selection of wine varies and is continually expanding as new sources of grapes are discovered. Many of Rosenblum's best wines are from specific vineyards and are so labeled. The highly regarded ZINFANDELS are Rosenblum's specialty, and there are as many as eight or nine different bottlings from various sources. The winery also produces CABERNET SAUVIGNON, MERLOT, PETITE SIRAH, PINOT NOIR, and a red BORDEAUX BLEND called Holbrook Mitchell Trio.

Roseneck *see* RÜDESHEIM

Rosengarten *see* RÜDESHEIM

Rosenmuskateller *see* MUSCAT

Rosette AC [raw-ZEHT] A tiny APPELLATION in the BERGERAC area, located in southwestern France not far from BORDEAUX. It produces semisweet white wines of mediocre quality from MUSCADELLE, SAUVIGNON BLANC, and SÉMILLON. As the popularity of semisweet wines has dwindled, so has this appellation's production.

Rossese di Dolceacqua DOC [raw-SEH-zeh dee dawl-cheh-AHK-wah] Small DOC zone, also known simply as *Dolceacqua,* located in the western part of Italy's LIGURIA region, close to the French border. The area, which encircles the town of Dolceacqua, overlaps in some areas with the recently established **Riviera Ligure di Ponente DOC**. The Rossese di Dolceacqua wines must include 95 percent of the Rossese grape. These red wines are very fruity and reminiscent of French BEAUJOLAIS wines. The *superiore* has 1 percent higher ALCOHOL (13 percent) and is AGED for 1 year.

Rossi, Carlo *see* E & J GALLO WINERY

rosso; Rosso [RAWS-soh] 1. Italian for "red." 2. In Italy the term *Rosso* is also used to indicate a red wine that's made from specific, approved grape varieties, which can differ depending on the DOC and region. *Rosso* is added to the name of several Italian DOC wines including ROSSO CONERO, ROSSO DI MONTALCINO, ROSSO DI MONTEPULCIANO, and ROSSO PICENO. 3. *Vino rosso* is usually a DRY wine in Italy, whereas in the United States it's often an inexpensive sweet wine.

Rosso Conero DOC [RAWS-soh KAW-neh-roh] The full-flavored red wines from this area are considered the best from central Italy's MARCHES region. Rosso Conero is a small zone located on the Adriatic Sea surrounding the seaside town of Ancona. The wines are made from at least 85 percent MONTEPULCIANO and the rest SANGIOVESE.

Rosso di Montalcino DOC [RAWS-soh dee mawn-tahl-CHEE-noh] DOC that was established after BRUNELLO DI MONTALCINO was upgraded to DOCG status. Rosso di Montalcino encompasses the same area as Brunello di Montalcino (around the town of Montalcino in southern TUSCANY) and uses the same SANGIOVESE clone, Brunello. Rosso di Montalcino wines require only 1 year of AGING, compared to the 4 years necessary for Brunello di Montalcino. The reduced aging time allows this area's producers to release a less-expensive version of the Brunello di Montalcino, which is lighter and less intense, but has a younger, fresher character to it. It also enables producers to make better Brunello di Montalcino wines because the best grapes can be selected for them, with the rest of the grapes going into the Rosso di Montalcino.

Rosso di Montepulciano DOC [RAWS-soh dee mohn-teh-pool-CHAH-noh] DOC located in the hilly area around the town of Montepulciano, southeast of Siena in the eastern portion of Italy's TUSCANY region. Its designated zone is precisely the same as the one for VINO NOBILE DI MONTEPULCIANO DOCG. The exact same grapes are used as well—60 to 80 percent Prugnolo (SANGIOVESE), 10 to 20 percent CANAIOLO, and up to 20 percent of other varieties, although no more than

10 percent white grapes. One of the other red varieties most often used is the Mammolo, which contributes the fragrance of violets to the BOUQUET. The AGING requirement is only 1 year instead of the 2 years required for Vino Nobile di Montepulciano wines. The result is that Rosso di Montepulciano wines are fruitier, less intense mimics of their big brothers.

Rosso Piceno DOC [RAWS-soh pee-CHEH-noh] Rosso Piceno is located in the southern half of (and is the largest DOC in) the MARCHES region. This DOC's DRY red wines are made from a minimum of 60 percent SANGIOVESE with up to 40 percent MONTEPULCIANO and up to 15 percent of Passerina and TREBBIANO. The wines labeled "Superiore" (which are usually the best) are from a special area at this region's southern end around Ascoli Piceno. They're more like a CLASSICO and require an additional ½ percent minimum ALCOHOL and 1 year of AGING.

Rothenberg *see* GESENHEIM; NACKENHEIM; RAUENTHAL

rotling [ROHT-ling] A rose-colored wine made from a mixture of red and white grapes (not wines). *Rotling* is produced in limited quantities in Germany.

Rotor Traminer *see* GEWÜRZTRAMINER

rotten eggs *see* SULFUR

Rottland *see* RÜDESHEIM

rotundifolia *see* VITIS ROTUNDIFOLIA

rotwein [RAWT-vine] A German word for "red wine."

Rouchefort-sur-Loire *see* CÔTEAUX DU LAYON

rouge [ROOZH] French for "red."

rough; roughness A winetasting term used for COARSE, generally ordinary wines that are overly TANNIC and/or ACIDIC. However, some wines that exhibit roughness eventually mature and become full-bodied (*see* BODY) and well-BALANCED.

round; rounded In the world of winetasting, a well-BALANCED, MELLOW, full-bodied (*see* BODY) wine is sometimes referred to as *round,* its flavor *rounded.* The term is similar to FAT.

Round Hill Winery Winery established in 1977 to blend and bottle wine purchased from other sources. In 1987, having outgrown its original NAPA VALLEY facility, Round Hill Winery moved into its present location, which is northeast of Rutherford, California, just east of the Silverado Trail. Today, Round Hill produces over 300,000 cases of wine each year through four product lines. The lowest-priced line is the House designation, which features CABERNET SAUVIGNON, CHARDONNAY, WHITE ZINFANDEL, and ZINFANDEL, plus some GENERIC WINES. The next step up are wines produced with a Napa Valley AVA designation, consisting of Cabernet Sauvignon, Chardonnay, GEWÜRZTRAMINER, and Zinfandel. The high end of the Round Hill labeled wines are the RESERVES—Cabernet Sauvignon, Chardonnay, and Merlot. The fourth product line is bottled under the label **Rutherford Ranch** and consists of a small number of cases of high-quality Cabernet Sauvignon, Cabernet Franc, Chardonnay, and Merlot.

de Rouquefort *see* LA GAFFELIÈRE, CHÂTEAU

Roussanne [roo-SAHN] A white-wine grape grown mainly in the northern portion of France's RHÔNE region. Roussanne can produce delicate, refined wines and is best known for its use in the white wines of CHÂTEAUNEUF-DU-PAPE, CROZES-HERMITAGE, HERMITAGE, and SAINT-JOSEPH. It's also one of the four white grapes allowed in the red wines of Châteauneuf-du-Pape. Since the 1950s, Roussanne has been steadily replaced by the more productive MARSANNE, which produces full-bodied (*see* BODY), somewhat FAT wines. Small amounts of Roussanne are also grown in Italy's TUSCANY region and are allowed in the white wines of the MONTECARLO DOC. There's also a pink variation known as *Roussanne du Var* that's used in many of the Rhône's lesser wines.

Rousselet *see* GEWÜRZTRAMINER

Rousset-les-Vignes *see* CÔTES DU RHÔNE

Roussette [roo-SEHT] Another name for the ALTESSE grape that's cultivated in northeastern France, particularly in the SAVOIE and BUGEY districts where the wines are respectively entitled to the APPELLATIONS Rousette de Savoie and Rousette de Bugey. Roussette is unrelated to ROUSSANE with which it's sometimes erroneously associated.

Roussette de Savoie AC *see* SAVOIE

Roussillon *see* CÔTES DU ROUSSILLON; GRENACHE

Roussillonen *see* CARIGNAN

Royalty Created from the varieties Trousseau and Alicante Ganzin, this HYBRID is a red grape that yields red juice (instead of white). It's used mainly to add color to BLENDS. Royalty was developed by the University of California at DAVIS and released in 1958. It's grown primarily in California's CENTRAL VALLEY, although its acreage is declining due to lack of popularity.

rubbery A negative sensory term describing the odor of rubber in wine, which is caused by the presence of MERCAPTANS.

Rubesco *see* TORGIANO DOC

Rubicon *see* NIEBAUM-COPPOLA ESTATE

rubino *see* MARSALA DOC

Rubired [ROO-bee-red] Introduced in 1958, this HYBRID was developed by the University of California at DAVIS by crossing Alicante Ganzin and Tinta Cão. *Alicante Ganzin* is also a hybrid, whose parentage is traceable to ALICANTE BOUSHCHET; *Tinta Cão* is a good-quality PORT variety. Rubired is an easy-to-grow, prolific red grape that produces red juice instead of white. Grown primarily in California's CENTRAL VALLEY, it's used to add color to port-style and JUG WINES.

Ruby Cabernet [ROO-bee ka-behr-NAY] This CROSS between CARIGNAN and CABERNET SAUVIGNON was developed in the 1940s by Dr. Harold Olmo at the University of California at DAVIS. His goal was to combine the Carignan's ability to withstand hot weather and produce high YIELDS, with the excellent quality of Cabernet Sauvignon. Disappointingly, Ruby Cabernet takes on Cabernet Sauvignon characteristics only in the very best of its wines. Even then, the flavor of these wines tends to be flat and, in general, lacking the structure of good Cabernet Sauvignons. Most Ruby Cabernet grapes are grown in California's hot CENTRAL VALLEY. The wines from this area have few Cabernet Sauvignon characteristics and are used mainly in JUG WINES.

ruby port *see* PORT

Ruchottes-Chambertin AC [ryoo-SHAWT shah*m*-behr-TA*N*] A small, 8-acre GRAND CRU vineyard that adjoins the grand cru MAZIS-CHAMBERTIN in the village of GEVREY-CHAMBERTIN. It's located in the CÔTE DE NUITS district of France's BURGUNDY region. These PINOT NOIR-based wines are deeply colored, RICH, intense, TANNIC, and generally good candidates for long AGING. They're considered to be some of the best red wines in the world and, with production of only about 1,000 cases per year, very difficult to find. *See also* CHAMBERTIN.

Rüdesheim [*R*OO-duhs-hime] An important wine-producing village located in Germany's RHEINGAU region, southwest of the city of Wiesbaden and across the Rhine River from BINGEN (which is in the NAHE region). Rüdesheim is the last of a string of villages (including

ERBACH, OESTRICH, WINKEL, and GEISENHEIM) that have some of the best vineyards in the Rheingau. Of the numerous good EINZELLAGEN (vineyard sites), those carrying the designation **Berg** as well as the site name are generally the best. Rüdesheimer Berg **Roseneck**, Rüdesheimer Berg **Rottland**, and Rüdesheimer Berg **Schlossberg**, for example, are all situated on the prime steepest section called the Rüdesheimer Berg. Other quality vineyard sites are **Bischofsberg**, **Drachenstein**, **Klosterberg**, and **Rosengarten**. The wines of Rüdesheim are generally full-bodied (*see* BODY) and rich with RIPE, concentrated flavors. In years with exceptionally good weather, however, these wines can become a bit too BIG and ALCOHOLIC. This famous Rüdesheim shouldn't be confused with the small village of Rüdesheim in the Nahe region, the wines of which are not in the same class.

Rüdesheim Rosengarten *see* NAHE

Rueda DO [roo-AY-dah] A DO northwest of Madrid near Portugal's northeast corner, not far from the city of Valladolid. This area is known for its high-quality white wines made from VERDEJO, although other varieties like Viaura (MACABEO) and PALOMINO are used. Rueda's climate and altitude create an environment that enables the Verdejo grapes to develop favorably and allows the area producers to make AROMATIC, FRESH, yet full-bodied (*see* BODY) wines. Basic Rueda wines require a minimum of 25 percent Verdejo. **Rueda Superior** wines require a minimum of 60 percent Verdejo; SAUVIGNON BLANC is also allowed in the Superiors. There are also sherrylike wines being produced in this DO—**Pálido**, which is like a fino (*see* SHERRY), and **Dorado**, which is like an amontillado (*see* SHERRY). Red and ROSÉ wines are not currently allowed under DO rules, but producers are experimenting with TEMPRANILLO as well as CABERNET SAUVIGNON and MERLOT, which will be categorized as VINOS DE MESA until approved for DO status.

Rufina *see* CHIANTI DOCG

Les Rugiens *see* POMMARD

Ruinart [rwee-NAHR] A small CHAMPAGNE house located in Reims and owned by Moët-Hennessy. It receives about 20 percent of its grapes from MOËT-CHANDON (also owned by Moët-Hennessy). The premium brand is Dom Ruinart, which comes in both BLANC DE BLANCS and ROSÉ. Founded in 1729, Ruinart is one of the older firms but has remained small, producing about 1.4 million bottles annually. Their non-VINTAGE champagnes are a lighter style but very high quality.

Rulander *see* PINOT GRIS

Rully AC [ryoo-YEE] One of the five villages in the CÔTE CHALON-NAISE in France's BURGUNDY region that has APPELLATION status. It produces FRESH, CRISP white wines from CHARDONNAY and LIGHT, fruity reds from PINOT NOIR. Production is about equally divided between the red and white wines.

Rumania Rumania ranks as one of the top ten wine-producing countries, yet few Rumanian wines are seen in Western countries. With the fall of the communist regime, however, this is slowly changing. Rumania grows many international as well local grape varieties and produces a wide assortment of wines. In general, the white wines are better than the reds. Some of the white grapes grown here are Banat Riesling, CHARDONNAY, Fetească Albă, GEWÜRZTRAMINER, Grasă, MUSCAT, RIESLING, Rülander (PINOT GRIS), and Tămîîoasă Romaneasca. The red varieties used include CABERNET SAUVIGNON, Babeasca Neagra, Fetească Negră, MERLOT, and PINOT NOIR. The Tîrnave area in the northern part of the country (Transylvania) is thought to produce Rumania's best wines. By most accounts, however, the sweet SAUTERNES-style wines from Cotnari in the northeast (Moldavia) are really the only ones worth seeking. Other growing areas include: Stefănesti, Dragăsăni, and Segarcea, all in the southern part of the country; Odo bești, Nicorești and Cotești in the eastern portion; Murfatlar near the Black Sea; the Banat Plain in the west; and Dealul Mare in the southeast where Pinot Noir and other international varieties are grown.

Ruppertsberg [ROOP-uhrts-berk] One of several adjoining towns, including DEIDESHEIM, FORST, and WACHENHEIM, that produce some of the best wines of Germany's RHEINPFALZ region. These appealing wines are made from RIESLING, SCHEUREBE, and SYLVANER. The top wines come from the EINZELLAGEN of **Gaisböhl, Hoheburg, Nussbien, Reiterpfad**, and **Spiess**.

rural method Known in France as *méthode rurale,* méthode artisnale, méthode ancestrale, or *méthode gaillacois,* the rural method is an old technique for making SPARKLING WINE. It's generally been replaced by MÉTHODE CHAMPENOISE for higher-quality wines or by the CHARMAT PROCESS for less-expensive wines. To create effervescence using the rural method, FERMENTATION is slowed or stopped, sometimes by chilling the MUST to a very cold temperature. The must is then bottled and the fermentation process restarted, often by warming the bottles. As with the *méthode champenoise,* the by-product of this fermentation is carbon dioxide, which creates bubbles in the bottled wine. Sparkling wines produced by the rural method are often cloudy unless they undergo a filtering process. Only a few wines are still made this way, including some from the GAILLAC AC and Limoux. The CLAIRETTE DE DIE TRADITION AC uses a variation of the rural method called *méthode dioise,* which is unique to this APPELLATION. This technique removes sediment by RACKING and FILTERING the wines under pressure, which eliminates the sediment while retaining as much effervescence as possible. The wines are then rebottled.

Russia There are three main wine-producing regions in Russia: the area along the Caspian Sea just north of Azerbaijan, which is known for its DESSERT WINES; the area south of the city of Krasnodar, along the Black Sea and somewhat inland; and the area surrounding the city of Rostov, north of the Black Sea on the Sea of Azov. The two latter regions make red, white, and SPARKLING WINES. Although most Russian wines are made from indigenous grape varieties like RKATSITELI, Black Tsimlyansky, Pletchistik, and Saperavi, some western European grapes are now being cultivated.

Russian River Valley; Russian River Valley AVA
The Russian River basin starts in MENDOCINO COUNTY, runs south into SONOMA COUNTY, and then west as the river turns toward the Pacific Ocean just north of Forestville, California. Along the way it encompasses the Ukiah and Alexander Valleys. The area comprising the **Russian River AVA** starts around Healdsburg (in Sonoma County) and goes in a southerly direction toward Sebastopol. The eastern section includes the CHALK HILL AVA, which is located just east of the town of Windsor; the western section extends to the coastal hills and includes the GREEN VALLEY-SONOMA AVA. The climate is quite cool, mostly Region I (*see* CLIMATE REGIONS OF CALIFORNIA), and does well with CHARDONNAY, GEWÜRZTRAMINER, PINOT NOIR and SAUVIGNON BLANC grapes. Occasionally, good ZINFANDEL grapes are produced as well. Cabernet Sauvignon doesn't usually peform too well here, although in the warmer growing areas it can produce good wines. Among the more than fifty wineries in the Russian River AVA are DE LOACH, DEHLINGER, Hanna Winery, IRON HORSE, KISTLER VINEYARDS, PIPER SONOMA, SONOMA-CUTRER, J. ROCHIOLI VINEYARDS, and JOSEPH SWAN.

Rutherford AVA VITICULTURAL AREA located in the central part of the NAPA VALLEY. Its southeastern boundary is adjacent to that of the OAKVILLE AVA (just south of CAKEBREAD CELLARS), and its northwestern boundary parallels Zinfandel Lane. The Rutherford AVA extends from the foothills of the western hills across the valley floor to just the other side of the Silverado Trail. Well-known wineries located within this

AVA include BEAULIEU VINEYARDS, CAYMUS VINEYARDS, FRANCISCAN VINEYARDS, GRIGICH HILLS CELLAR, MUMM NAPA VALLEY, NIEBAUM-COPPOLA ESTATE, RAYMOND VINEYARD, SEQUOIA GROVE, and WHITEHALL LANE.

Rutherford Bench A California growing area with a reputation for producing some of the best CABERNET SAUVIGNON grapes in the world. At this writing, the Rutherford Bench is not an official AMERICAN VITICULTURAL AREA (AVA), and the area it covers isn't fully defined. However, the term generally refers to about a 6-mile stretch of land in the NAPA VALLEY that runs along the west side of Highway 29 from just north of Yountville to north of Rutherford and includes a small section east of the freeway between Oakville and Rutherford. Some argue, however, that the term Rutherford Bench should also include the land between Highway 29 and the Napa River, a mile or so to the east. Whatever the final resolution (if there is one) for a designated Rutherford Bench AVA, the bottom line is that this area contains deep, alluvial soils that drain well and are capable of producing remarkable Cabernet Sauvignon grapes (some CHARDONNAY grapes also grow here). Producers who use Rutherford Bench grapes include BEAULIEU VINEYARDS, CAKEBREAD CELLARS, Far Niente, FREEMARK ABBEY (Bosché Vineyard), GRGICH HILLS, HEITZ WINE CELLARS (Martha's Vineyard and Bella Oaks Vineyard), INGLENOOK, JOSEPH PHELPS, OPUS ONE, ROBERT MONDAVI, Sequoia Grove, and WHITEHALL LANE.

Rutherford Estate *see* INGLENOOK-NAPA VALLEY

Ruwer [*R*OO-vay*r*] Located in Germany's MOSEL-SAAR-RUWER region, Ruwer is a small tributary of the Mosel River and host to a number of fine vineyards in the surrounding valley. Although the wines from this area aren't considered quite as superb as those from the SAAR River area, they can rank as some of Germany's best. The main wine-producing villages are EITELSBACH, KASEL, and Waldrach. The GROSSLAGE **Kaseler Römerlay** covers this area.

Saale-Unstrut [ZAHL oon-sht*r*uht] With less than 1,000 acres of vineyards, this is the third smallest of Germany's thirteen ANBAUGEBIETE (quality-wine regions). Its vineyards are situated around the Saale and Unstrut Rivers in eastern Germany. Naumburg and Weissenfels are the main towns in the region. Because Saale-Unstrut was part of the former East Germany, wine producers are still in the process of working their way out from under the problems left by the former communist regime. The wines are similar to those of FRANKEN, but the true quality potential won't be known for several more years until vineyards and winemaking facilities are upgraded. The main variety planted in this region is MÜLLER-THURGAU, with 37 percent of the total acreage, followed by SYLVANER, with about 28 percent. Other varieties include BACCHUS, Gutedel (CHASSELAS), PORTUGIESER, and Spätburgunder (PINOT NOIR).

Saar [ZAHR; SAHR] Starting high in the Vosges Mountains in France, this tributary of the Mosel River joins the Mosel at the German town of Konz, southwest of the city of Trier. The vineyards, which begin around the tiny German village of Serrig in the south, are part of the Bereich SAAR-RUWER and Germany's MOSEL-SAAR-RUWER region. This is a cold growing region, and in good growing years, the wines of the Saar area can be magnificent—some of Germany's best. In the cooler years when grapes don't fully ripen, much of the crop is used in SEKT. The main villages are Ayl, Seerig, Ockfen, and WILTINGEN, which has SCHARZHOFBERG, the best vineyard in the area. The GROSSLAGE **Wiltinger Scharzberg** covers the vineyards in this area.

Saar-Ruwer, Bereich [ZAHR (SAHR) *R*OO-vay*r*] One of four BEREICHE (subregions) in Germany's MOSEL-SAAR-RUWER region. It covers all the vineyards surrounding the two tributaries of the MOSEL, the RUWER River, and the SAAR River. The Bereich has two GROSSLAGEN—Wiltinger Scharzberg for the Saar area and Kaseler Römerlay for the Ruwer area.

Sablet *see* CÔTES DU RHÔNE

Sachsen [ZAHKH-zuhn] The smallest of Germany's thirteen AN-BAUGEBIETE (quality wine regions), with less than 800 acres of vineyards. Its vineyards are situated around the Elbe River area in eastern Germany; Dresden is the region's main city. The primary variety planted in this region is MÜLLER-THURGAU, which has 38 percent of the total acreage. Traminer (GEWÜRZTRAMINER) and Weissburgunder (PINOT BLANC) follow, each with about 15 percent of the acreage. Other varieties include Gutedel (CHASSELAS), RIESLING, and PORTUGIESER. Like SAALE-

UNSTRUT, the Sachsen region was part of the former East Germany, which means its area producers are still in the process of working out from under the problems left by the former communist regime. The true potential quality of this region's wines won't be known for several more years as vineyards and winemaking facilities are upgraded.

sack The name used in the sixteenth century during the reign of Elizabeth I for SHERRY or other FORTIFIED wines from MÁLAGA or the Canary Islands. Such wines were known as Málaga Sack and Canary Sack. The word comes from the Spanish *sacar,* meaning "to take out" or "to export."

Sackträger *see* OPPENHEIM

Sacramento Valley *see* CENTRAL VALLEY

Sagrantino di Montefalco DOCG *see* MONTEFALCO DOC

Saint-Amour AC [san tah-MOOR] The northernmost of the ten CRUS in France's BEAUJOLAIS region. Saint-Amour sits far enough north that it's the only Beaujolais cru extending into the MÂCONNAIS area. White wines from this area are entitled to the SAINT-VÉRAN AC, a Mâconnais APPELLATION. Saint-Amour is one of the smaller Beaujolais crus, making its wines more difficult to find. The wines, made from GAMAY grapes, are LIGHT, delicate, and fruity (strawberries, bananas, and peaches).

Saint-Aubin AC [san toh-BAN] APPELLATION that consists of the vineyards surrounding the villages of Gamay (the village that gave its name to the grape variety) and Saint-Aubin. It's located in the CÔTE DE BEAUNE section of France's BURGUNDY region. The Saint-Aubin AC sits between CHASSAGNE-MONTRACHET AC and PULIGNY-MONTRACHET AC, wedged into a small valley higher up the hill. Although there are a fair amount of GAMAY grapes grown in this geographic area, only PINOT NOIR can go into this appellation's red wines. Compared to many of the neighboring villages, Saint-Aubin AC reds are of a lighter, more elegant style. The white wines, which make up about one-third of the production, are considered better than the reds. The best of these CHARDONNAY wines are often compared to good-quality Chassagne-Montrachet or MEURSAULT AC wines. The Saint-Aubin AC wines are regarded as relatively good values.

Saint-Aubin-de-Luigné *see* CÔTEAUX DU LAYON

Saint-Bris *see* SAUVIGNON DE SAINT BRIS VDQS

Saint-Chinian AC [san shee-NYAHN] The village of Saint-Chinian is located in the hills above Beziers, southwest of FAUGÈRES AC in France's LANGUEDOC-ROUSSILLON region. Like the Faugères AC, the Saint-Chinian AC makes red wines of a much higher quality than most of the rest of this huge region. The grapes used are CARIGNAN, CINSAUT, GRENACHE, and, recently, increasing amounts of MOURVÈDRE and SYRAH. The wines, which are full-bodied (*see* BODY) and SPICY, are generally slightly lighter than those from the Faugères AC.

St. Clement Vineyards [saynt KLIH-muhnt] Winery located just northwest of St. Helena, California, in the NAPA VALLEY. The site, which has only about 2 acres of vineyard, was home to Spring Mountain Winery in the late 1960s and early 1970s. In 1975 it was purchased by Dr. William Casey, who renamed it St. Clement Vineyards. Casey maintained ownership until 1987, when he sold the winery to Sapporo Limited of Japan. The new owners purchased the 22-acre Abbott's Vineyard in the CARNEROS AVA, which is planted with CHARDON-NAY and PINOT NOIR. St. Clement Vineyards now produces CABERNET SAUVIGNON, CHARDONNAY, MERLOT, SAUVIGNON BLANC, and a small amout of sparkling wine (BLANC DE NOIRS). Annual production of these high-quality wines is between 12,000 and 14,000 cases.

Saint-Drézéry *see* CÔTEAUX DU LANGUEDOC

de Sainte-Hélène *see* DE MALL, CHÂTEAU

Saint-Émilion [sah*n* tay-mee-LYAW*N*] The village of Saint-Émilion is quite picturesque and beautiful with its medieval walls and buildings, its undulating hills, and the fields of vines that grow right up to the ancient walls. Saint-Émilion is northeast of the city of Bordeaux and sits on the east side of the Dordogne River next to the smaller, but well-known, POMEROL AC. Grapes have been cultivated here since at least the second century. Saint-Émilion is the second most important growing area in BORDEAUX after the MÉDOC, and because it's not broken up into smaller APPELLATIONS like the Médoc (such as MARGAUX AC, PAUILLAC AC, SAINT-ESTÈPHE AC, and SAINT-JULIEN AC), more fine wine is sold under the Saint-Émilion appellation than any other. Unlike the Médoc where CABERNET SAUVIGNON reigns, MERLOT is the dominant grape in Saint-Émilion because of the clay soil. CABERNET FRANC is the next most popular grape, followed by Cabernet Sauvignon and some MALBEC, Because of the prevalent use of Merlot, the Saint-Émilion wines are generally SOFTER and more drinkable at an earlier age than those from the Médoc. However, wines from good VINTAGES of top CHÂTEAUS like AUSONE and CHEVAL BLANC have considerable AGING ability. Saint-Émilion was passed over in the CLASSIFICATION OF 1855, which established the CRU CLASSÉ châteaus of the Médoc, and it wasn't until 1954 that an official classification for Saint-Émilion estates was developed. Unlike the Médoc, Saint-Émilion's classification system was set up so that it could be revised every 10 years, at which time châteaus could be elevated or downgraded. Revisions were done in 1969 and 1985, and another is scheduled in the 1994 timeframe. The 1985 classification lists eleven châteaus as PREMIERS GRANDS CRUS CLASSÉS, the highest level. Two of the eleven, Château Ausone and Château Cheval Blanc, were set above all the rest into Category A; they're both generally considered comparable in quality to the Médoc FIRST GROWTHS. The other nine châteaus, which are in Category B, are BEAUSÉJOUR-DUFFAU-LAGARROSSE, BELAIR, CANON, CLOS FOURTET, FIGEAC, LA GAFFELIÈRE, MAGDELAINE, PAVIE, and TROTTEVIEILLE. Sixty-four estates are classified at the next level, GRANDS CRUS CLASSÉS, and there is a third level called simply GRANDS CRUS. The number in this last category (usually 150 to 200) varies because châteaus must apply each year and qualify by submitting their wines for tastings. The aforementioned three levels of châteaus receive the **Saint-Émilion Grand Cru AC**. Other wines in the area may qualify for the simpler **Saint-Émilion AC**, while those below that may receive the designation BORDEAUX SUPÉRIEUR AC or BORDEAUX AC. Saint-Émilion is surrounded by six "satellite" COMMUNES, which once sold their wines as Saint-Émilion AC but now are part of separate appellations that may append the name Saint-Émilion to their own (as in PUISSEGUIN-SAINT-ÉMILION AC). The communes are LUSSAC, MONTAGNE, Parsac, Puisseguin, Sables and SAINT-GEORGES, although separate appellations for Parsac and Sables no longer exist.

Saint-Émilion   *see* TREBBIANO

Saint-Estèphe AC [sa*n* teh-STEHF] The northernmost of the communal APPELLATIONS in the HAUT-MÉDOC area of France's BORDEAUX region. Of the wines from the well-known COMMUNES in the Haut-Médoc, those from Saint-Estèphe AC are usually ranked fourth in quality after those of MARGAUX, PAUILLAC, and SAINT-JULIEN. This ranking is because Saint-Estèphe contains fewer (only five) GRAND CRU CLASSÉ châteaus and more CRUS BOURGEOIS. The grand cru classé CHÂTEAUS are CALON-SÉGUR, COS D'ESTOURNEL, COS LABORY, LAFON-ROCHET, and MONTROSE. Saint-Estèphe AC wines are made from CABERNET SAUVIGNON, MERLOT, CABERNET FRANC, and PETIT VERDOT. They're often described as being full-bodied (*see* BODY), the most TANNIC, and requiring the longest period to mature. Many producers are now using more Merlot to produce suppler (*see* SUPPLE), SOFTER wines.

St. Francis Vineyards   Small amounts of CABERNET SAUVIGNON, GEWÜRZTRAMINER, and ZINFANDEL are made by St. Francis Vineyards, but

CHARDONNAY and MERLOT wines are this winery's focus. St. Francis is one of the early proponents of Merlot as a stand-alone VARIETAL WINE. This winery, which is located in the SONOMA VALLEY AVA northwest of the town of Kenwood, owns about 90 acres planted with its two primary varieties, Chardonnay and Merlot. The consensus is, however, that the Merlot and Cabernet Sauvignon (particularly the RESERVE bottlings) are the best. St. Francis Vineyards produces over 45,000 cases of wine a year.

Les Saint-Georges *see* NUITS-SAINT-GEORGES

Saint-Georges-d'Orques *see* CÔTEAUX DU LANGUEDOC

Saint-Georges-Saint-Émilion AC [sa*n* ZHOR*R*ZH ay-mee-LYAW*N*] One of the SAINT-ÉMILION AC satellite APPELLATIONS that's allowed to append the name Saint-Émilion to its own. Some feel that the wines from this AC are the best of those from the appellations surrounding Saint-Émilion. Like Saint-Émilion itself, the dominant grape here is MERLOT. Since 1972, wines from this appellation have been allowed to be labeled with the MONTAGNE-SAINT ÉMILION AC—the larger, neighboring appellation. Some producers still prefer to use the Saint-Georges-Saint-Émilion AC, however.

Saint Gervais *see* CÔTES DU RHÔNE

Saint-Joseph AC [sa*n* zhoh-ZEHF] Located south of CHÂTEAU-GRILLET in the northern portion of France's RHÔNE Valley, this APPELLATION was established in 1956. It ecompasses six villages clustered around the village of Mauves. In 1969 the Saint-Joseph AC was expanded to include another twenty small COMMUNES farther south, creating an appellation that extends for over 35 miles along the west bank of the Rhône River, stopping in the south at the CORNAS AC. The Saint-Joseph AC produces both red and white wines. White wines are made from MARSANNE and ROUSSANNE grapes; reds use mainly SYRAH, sometimes blended with a small amount of the two white grapes. The red wines are said to be similar to but lighter than those from neighboring appellations of HERMITAGE and Cornas—deep-colored, full-flavored, full-bodied (*see* BODY), and intense. White wines are usually described as lighter versions of the powerful, long-aging whites from Hermitage AC.

Saint-Julien AC [sa*n* zhoo-LYA*N*] Many people think that the Saint-Julien AC produces the most consistently high-quality wines of any APPELLATION in France's BORDEAUX region. It's the smallest of four main COMMUNES in the MÉDOC and is located just south of PAUILLAC. It contains eleven CRU CLASSÉ châteaus (which use about 75 percent of the available vineyard land) and a number of very good CRU BOURGEOIS châteaus. This leaves very little land for low-quality wine producers. Heading the list of cru classé CHÂTEAUS are DUCRU-BEAUCAILLOU, GRUAUD-LAROSE, and LÉOVILLE-LAS CASES—DEUXIÈMES CRUS (second growths). They're followed by other excellent châteaus like BEYCHEVELLE, BRANAIRE-DUCRU, LÉOVILLE-BARTON, and TALBOT. CABERNET SAUVIGNON is the dominant grape, which is blended with CABERNET FRANC, MERLOT, and, occasionally, small amounts of PETIT VERDOT.

Saint-Lambert-du-Lattay *see* COTEAUX DU LAYON

Saint Louis-le-Bosq *see* SAINT-PIERRE, CHÂTEAU

Saint Maurice-sur-Eygues *see* CÔTES DU RHÔNE

Saint-Nicolas-de-Bourgueil AC [san nee-koh-lah duh boor-GUH-yuh] A village located in the TOURAINE region of France's LOIRE Valley. Like its neighbors the CHINON AC and the BOURGUEIL AC, the Saint-Nicolas-de-Bourgueil AC is one of the few village APPELLATIONS in the area focused on red wines. Its dry climate allows it to grow CABERNET FRANC and limited quantities of CABERNET SAUVIGNON. Generally, the wines are light and fruity, with raspberry overtones. Better vintages can be AGED for 8 to 10 years.

Saint-Pantaléon-les-Vignes *see* CÔTES DU RHÔNE

Saint-Paul de la Dominque *see* LA DOMINIQUE, CHÂTEAU

Saint-Péray [san pay-REH] The village that lies just below the CORNAS AC and that is the farthest south of the wine-producing villages in the northern RHÔNE. There are two APPELLATIONS here—**Saint-Péray AC** for white STILL WINES and **Saint-Péray Mousseux AC** for SPARKLING WINES. In both types of wine, MARSANNE is the dominant grape, usually blended with some ROUSSANNE. The sparkling wines make up about 75 to 80 percent of the production.

Saint-Pierre, Château [sha-TOH san PYEHR] A somewhat unknown CHÂTEAU located in the SAINT-JULIEN AC in the MÉDOC district in BORDEAUX. The château was classified as a QUATRIÈME CRU (fourth growth) in the CLASSIFICATION OF 1855 and produces high-quality wines deserving of the rank. It's small (only 44 acres) and produces between 5,000 and 8,000 cases of red wine. These wines are generally deep-colored, full-bodied (*see* BODY), and BIG—many VINTAGES are capable of AGING for 15 to 20 years. The blend of grapes used is about 70 percent CABERNET SAUVIGNON, 20 percent MERLOT, and 10 percent CABERNET

FRANC. Saint-Pierre uses two SECOND LABELS—**Clos de Uza** and **Saint Louis-le-Bosq**.

Saint-Romain AC [san raw-MAN] Tiny APPELLATION that surrounds the village of Saint-Romain, which is located in the CÔTE DE BEAUNE area of France's BURGUNDY region. It consists of only 350 acres and is wedged in a valley up behind the better-known villages of MEURSAULT and AUXEY-DURESSES. Saint-Roman AC produces both red wines from PINOT NOIR and white wines from CHARDONNAY.

Saintsbury Cellars [SAYNTS-behry] Winery situated in the NAPA VALLEY side of the CARNEROS AVA, southwest of the city of Napa. It annually produces over 40,000 cases of CHARDONNAY and PINOT NOIR made from grapes grown only in the Carneros area. There are three Pinot Noir wines—Garnet, Carneros, and Reserve—and two Chardonnays—Carneros and Reserve. All five wines regularly win enthusiastic support from reviewers.

Saint-Véran AC [san vay-RAHN] This APPELLATION, which surrounds the village of Saint-Vérand (the *d* is correct) and five other villages, is located in the MÂCONNAIS subregion in BURGUNDY. The Saint-Véran AC is located next to the well-known POUILLY-FUISSÉ AC and produces white CHARDONNAY wines of a similar style. Although it only received appellation status in 1971, the wines have long been thought to be the equal of those from Pouilly-Fuissé, and because they're not as well known, they're available at much lower prices.

sake [SAH-kee; SAH-kay] Although sake is often called Japanese rice wine, it's difficult to categorize as wine because it's not made from fruit—in fact, some consider it a beer because it's made from grain. The U.S. Bureau of Alcohol, Tobacco, and Firearms (BATF), however, settles any dispute by categorizing sake in Class 6—wine from other agricultural products. Sake is made in several steps, during which the starch of specially selected, steamed rice is converted to sugar and then to ALCOHOL and CARBON DIOXIDE through FERMENTATION. Once fermentation is complete, the liquid is drawn off, filtered, heated, and placed in casks for maturing. None of the carbon dioxide is retained so there's no effervescence. Sake's alcohol ranges from 12 to 16 percent—high for beer, low for most grain-based spirits, but in the range for most wines. Sake, which is colorless (or very pale yellow) and slightly sweet, is traditionally served warm in small porcelain cups called *sakazuki*. Another popular Japanese rice wine is *Mirin*.

Salice Salentino *see* APRILIA DOC

Salmanazar *see* WINE BOTTLES

Salon *see* CHAMPAGNE

Salvagnin *see* VAUD

Sampigny-les-Maragnes *see* CÔTE DE BEAUNE

San Benito County; San Benito AVA [san beh-NEE-toh] California's San Benito County lies just east of MONTEREY COUNTY and is known for the vineyards planted by Almaden Vineyards. Most of the vineyard area is covered by the **San Benito AVA**, which encompasses three smaller AVAs—Cienega Valley, Lime Kiln Valley, and Paicines, each of which has only a single vineyard. Because it's positioned in one of the openings that draws air off the Pacific through the mountain ranges into the CENTRAL VALLEY, the San Benito AVA is fairly cool and is classified as a Region II (*see* CLIMATE REGIONS OF CALIFORNIA). CALERA WINE COMPANY is the best-known winery in the area.

Sancerre AC [sahn-SEHR] The Sancerre AC surrounds the village of Sancerre and thirteen others in the upper portion of France's LOIRE Valley. It's located 120 miles south and slightly west of Paris, where Sancerre white wines first gained a huge following before becoming international favorites. SAUVIGNON BLANC is the grape used for the white wines, which are generally produced in a CRISP, highly ACIDIC style with herb and gooseberry characteristics—very similar to those from the neighboring POUILLY-FUMÉ AC. The best white Sancerre AC wines come from the better producers in the villages of Bué, Chavigno, Ménétréol, and Verdigny and not from the village of Sancerre itself. Small amounts of red and ROSÉ wines are made from PINOT NOIR grapes, but most of these are rather LIGHT and not nearly as highly regarded as the white wines.

Sandeman This large producer of both PORT and SHERRY was founded in 1970 by George Sandeman. Sandeman is now owned by Seagrams, but descendants of the founder are still involved with the management. The facility in Jerez produces fine sherries including Fino Apitiv, Dry Don Amontillado, Armada Cream, and the premium brands of Royal Corregidor and Imperial Correidor. The Portuguese facility produces a broad range of port wines including very good, aged tawny ports—the 10-year-old Royal and the 20-year-old Imperial. The vintage ports have not been as highly regarded since the 1970s when Sandeman lost some of the QUINTAS that were supplying them with grapes. The last really great Sandeman vintage port was the 1967. Sandeman, which previously hadn't owned any of its own vineyards, began to buy them in the 1970s to ensure a steady supply of grapes.

Sanford Winery California winery that was established in 1981 after the breakup of the partnership that had owned Sanford and Benedict Vineyards. Using rented space, Richard Sanford has built the production of his new winery to over 30,000 cases per year. In 1991 Sanford regained access to the vineyards that had been part of the orignal Sanford & Benedict partnership. A new winery was completed in 1993 on a 738-acre property near the town of Buellton in the SANTA YNEZ VALLEY (SANTA BARBARA COUNTY). Sanford Winery focuses on CHARDONNAY, SAUVIGNON BLANC, and PINOT NOIR. Even though the Chardonnay wines are generally highly regarded, it's the Pinot Noirs for which Sanford Winery is most admired.

Sangiovese [san-joh-VAY-zeh; san-jaw-VAY-zeh] Etymologists believe this red grape's name is derived from *sanguis Jovis* meaning "the blood of Jove (Jupiter)." Its beginnings are thought to predate Roman times. Sangiovese is one of the top two red grapes (the other being NEBBIOLO) in Italy, where it's extensively planted—particularly in the central and southern regions. It's believed to have originated in TUSCANY, where it dominates today. Sangiovese wines vary immensely depending on where the grapes are grown, how they're grown (the YIELD allowed), and which of the many subvarieties they're made from. Generally, Sangiovese wines are high in ACID, with moderate to high TANNINS, and medium levels of ALCOHOL. The flavors have a hint of EARTHINESS and are usually not boldly FRUITY. Sangiovese wines are not deeply colored and often have a slightly orange tint around the edges. Most are not long-lived and will last for less than 10 years. Of the numerous strains of this grape, *Sangiovese Grosso* and *Sangiovese Piccolo* have taken the lead. Compared to Sangiovese Piccolo's smaller grape clusters, Sangiovese Grosso has larger, more loosely bunched grapes. It's also more widely cultivated and yields a larger crop. One strain of Sangiovese Grosso is *Brunello* ("little dark one"), so named for the brown hue of its skin. It's the grape responsible for the potent and long-lived BRUNELLO DI MONTALCINO wines, which are made totally from this variety. *Prugnolo* is MONTEPULCIANO'S local name for the Sangiovese Grosso grape, which produces the VINO NOBILE DI MONTEPULCIANO wines. Though Sangiovese is the dominant grape in Italy's well-known CHIANTI wines, it must officially (for DOC qualification) be BLENDED with other varieties, including a percentage of white grapes. Fortunately, the maximum allowable Sangiovese (also known as *Sangioveto* in Chianti) went from 80 to 90 percent in 1984, which allows Chianti wines to have a more robust character. Some producers, particularly in Tuscany, are now making non-DOC wines either using only Sangiovese grapes or blending them with small amounts of CABERNET SAUVIGNON. Cabernet is a particularly complimentary partner that lends BOUQUET, STRUCTURE, and longevity. The CARMIGNANO DOCG officially allows 10 percent Cabernet Sauvignon to be blended with their elegant Sangiovese-based wines. Outside of Italy, Sangiovese is almost a stranger to the vineyard. California has very little acreage of Sangiovese planted—the best-known producer is Napa Valley's Atlas Peak Vineyards, which drew attention when it released its 1989 Sangiovese. Sangiovese is known by several different names including *Calabrese, Sanvicetro,* and *San Gioveto,* as well as many beginning with "Sangiovese," such as *Sangiovese di Romagna* and *Sangiovese Dolce.*

Sangioveto; San Gioveto *see* SANGIOVESE

sangria [san-GREE-uh] The blood-red color of this beverage inspired its name, which is Spanish for "bleeding." Sangria is made with red wine, fruit juices, soda water, fruit, and sometimes liqueurs, and BRANDY or COGNAC. Sangria *blanco* (white sangria) is made with white wine. Both are served cold over ice.

Sangue di Giuda *see* OLTREPO PAVESE DOC

San Joaquin Valley *see* CENTRAL VALLEY

Sanlúcar de Barramdea *see* SHERRY; JEREZ-XÉRÈX-SHERRY Y MANZANILLA DE SANLÚCAR DE BARRAMEDA DO

San Luis Obispo County [san LOO-ihs uh-BIHS-poh] Located just south of MONTEREY COUNTY, this area is part of California's CENTRAL COAST AVA. San Luis Obispo County has over twenty-five wineries centered in the three main growing areas—PASO ROBLES AVA, EDNA VALLEY AVA, and ARROYO GRANDE AVA. The YORK MOUNTAIN AVA is also located in the county. The most popular varieties grown in this county are CHARDONNAY, CABERNET SAUVIGNON, ZINFANDEL, MERLOT, SAUVIGNON BLANC, and CHENIN BLANC.

San Severo *see* APRILIA DOC

Santa Barbara County California area just south of SAN LUIS OBISPO COUNTY and north of Ventura County. This county's vineyard land has grown enormously during the last two decades. There are now over twenty-five wineries, located in the two major growing areas—SANTA MARIA VALLEY AVA and SANTA YNEZ VALLEY AVA, both of which are north of Santa Barbara. The Santa Maria Valley AVA is the farthest north and actually starts in San Luis Obispo County. The dominant variety is CHARDONNAY, which takes up over 50 percent of the planted vineyard land. It's followed by CABERNET SAUVIGNON, PINOT NOIR, RIESING, SAUVIGNON BLANC, and CHENIN BLANC. Some of this county's wineries are AU BON CLIMAT, Brander, BYRON VINEYARD AND WINERY, Cambria (part of KENDALL-JACKSON), Firestone, Qupe, SANFORD, and Zaca Mesa.

Santa Barbara Winery When it was established in downtown Santa Barbara in 1962, this was the first winery since PROHIBITION to produce wine in SANTA BARBARA COUNTY. It produced a variety of wines from purchased grapes until the early 1970s, when a 70-acre vineyard was developed in the SANTA YNEZ VALLEY. The winery now produces CABERNET SAUVIGNON, CHARDONNAY, CHENIN BLANC, PINOT NOIR, RIESLING, SAUVIGNON BLANC, and ZINFANDEL wines. Although the Riesling wines are often very good, it's the RESERVE bottlings of Chardonnay and Pinot Noir that draw the most attention. Santa Barbara Winery is producing around 30,000 cases of wine each year.

Santa Clara County; Santa Clara Valley AVA County located at the south end of the San Francisco Bay that includes the cities of San Jose, Sunnyvale, and Santa Clara. The population expansion has pushed out most of the vineyard area, and the majority of what's left is in the **Santa Clara Valley AVA**. This AVA includes the southern end of Alameda County around Pleasanton plus the vineyard areas in the Santa Clara Valley—those around Gilroy, Hecker Pass, and Morgan Hill. The western boundary runs along the SANTA CRUZ MOUNTAINS AVA. The dominant variety in the Santa Clara area is CHARDONNAY followed by CABERNET SAUVIGNON, MERLOT, and ZINFANDEL. There are over twenty-five wineries in Santa Clara County, but most get their grapes from other areas. County wineries include Fortino, Jory, J. Lohr, and Mirassou.

Santa Cruz Mountains AVA A region in California's Santa Cruz mountains, starting in northern San Mateo County and extending south to about the MONTEREY COUNTY line. To the east, the AVA extends down to the lower levels of the foothills; to the west, some portions reach almost to the Pacific Ocean. A majority of this area is cool and therefore classified as a Region I (*see* CLIMATE REGIONS OF CALIFORNIA). Portions on the inland valley side are warmer and classified as Region II areas. The primary grapes grown in this VITICULTURAL AREA are CHARDONNAY, CABERNET SAUVIGNON, and PINOT NOIR. Area wineries include Bargetto's Santa Cruz Winery, BONNY DOON VINEYARD, DAVID BRUCE, Byington Winery & Vineyards, Cinnabar Vineyard and Winery, CRONIN

VINEYARDS, THOMAS FOGARTY WINERY, Hallcrest Vineyards, MOUNT EDEN VINEYARDS, RIDGE VINEYARDS, Roudon-Smith Vineyards, and SANTA CRUZ MOUNTAIN VINEYARD.

Santa Maddalena DOC [SAHN-tah mahd-dah-LEH-nah] A DOC located in the Alto Adige area of Italy's TRENTINO-ALTO ADIGE region. The vineyards are located just minutes above the city of Bolzano, the capital city of the Alto Adige area. Santa Maddalena DOC wine has had an excellent reputation since the 1920s and was considered one of the top three or four wines by Mussolini's regime. These red wines are made primarily from SCHIAVA grapes, although small amounts of LA-GREIN and Pinot Nero (PINOT NOIR) may be added. The result is a light red wine with fresh, fruity flavors and a slightly smoky character—it's not TANNIC and should be drunk young.

Santa Maria Valley AVA APPELLATION located in SANTA BARBARA COUNTY, except for a tiny northern section in SAN LUIS OBISPO COUNTY. It's situated east of the town of Santa Maria in both northerly and southerly directions. Its cool climate is classified mostly as Region I, although there are a few warmer Region II areas (*see* CLIMATE REGIONS OF CALIFORNIA). CHARDONNAY is the dominant variety followed by PINOT NOIR, CABERNET SAUVIGNON, SAUVIGNON BLANC, RIESLING, CHENIN BLANC, and MERLOT. The area's wineries include AU BON CLIMAT, BYRON VINEYARD AND WINERY, Cambria (part of KENDALL-JACKSON), Foxen, Qupé, and Rancho Sisquoc.

Santa Ynez Valley AVA [SAN-tuh ee-NEHZ] A VITICULTURAL AREA located in California's SANTA BARBARA COUNTY, north of the city of Santa Barbara and south of the SANTA MARIA VALLEY AVA. Its bounded on the east by Los Padres National Forest and on the west by the Pacific Ocean. The AVA is cooled by the ocean breezes and is considered a Region II (*see* CLIMATE REGIONS OF CALIFORNIA) area. CHARDONNAY is by far the dominant grape variety, followed by CABERNET SAUVIGNON, RIESLING, PINOT NOIR, CHENIN BLANC, SAUVIGNON BLANC, and GEWÜRTRAMINER. This area produces very good wines from the white varieties and Pinot Noir. Santa Ynez Valley wineries include Austin Cellars, Babcock Vineyards, Brander Vineyard, J. Carey Cellars, Fess Parker Winery, Firestone Vineyard, Gainey Vineyard, SANFORD WINERY, Santa Barbara Winery, and Zaca Mesa Winery.

Santenay AC [sah*n*-tuh-NEH] The last major village in the southern part of the famous CÔTE D'OR in BURGUNDY. It's just north of the next major Burgundian subregion, the CÔTE CHALONNAIS. Because the Santenay AC is not nearly as well known as most of the neighboring village

APPELLATIONS to the north (CHASSAGNE-MONTRACHET, PULIGNY-MONTRACHET, and MEURSAULT), the prices of the wines are usually lower. Almost all the wines produced are red, made from PINOT NOIR. The red wines are similar in style to those from CHASSAGNE-MONTRACHET but usually not quite as good. Miniscule amounts of white wines are produced from CHARDONNAY. There are no GRAND CRU vineyards, but there are several fine PREMIER CRU vineyards including **Clos de Tavannes**, **La Comme**, **Les Gravières**, and **Le Passe Temps**.

Sanvicetro *see* SANGIOVESE

Sardinia; It. Sardegna [sahr-DIHN-ee-uh (It. sahr-DIHN-yuh)] An Italian island and wine-producing region located off the west coast of Italy just south the French island of CORSICA. Sardinia (*Sardegna* in Italian) makes a wide variety of wines, most of them quite mediocre. There are eighteen DOCs and only about 5 percent of Sardinia's total production is DOC wine. Even though the main DOC is NURAGUS DI CAGLIARI, other popular DOCs include Cannonau di Sardegna, Monica di Sardegna, and Vermentino di Gallura. The principal red grape varieties are Cannonau (GRENACHE), Monica, Carignano (CARIGNAN), and Giro. White wines are made from the widely planted Nuragus plus VERMENTINO, Torbato, and VERNACCIA DI ORISTANO.

Sargent de Gruaud-Larose *see* GRUAUD-LAROSE, CHÂTEAU

Sassella *see* VALTELLINA DOC

Sassicaia DOC [sahs-see-KAH-yah] The proprietary name for a CABERNET SAUVIGNON/CABERNET FRANC blend that led to the current trend in Italy's Tuscany region toward non-DOC wines called super-Tuscans (*see* TUSCANY). In 1994 the Italian government granted Sassicaia the right to carry the DOC certification mark. This wine is made by the wine estate of Marchesi Incisa della Rocchetta, which is located in Bolgheri not far from the Tuscan coast. It's made in a BORDEAUX style from vines planted originally with cuttings from the CHÂTEAU LAFITE-ROTHSCHILD estate. The first release of Sassicaia occurred in 1968, although the wine had been made (but not released) for numerous vintages before that. Sassicaia is AGED in BARRIQUES for 18 to 24 months prior to release. It's often confused for a fine Bordeaux or California wine made from Cabernet grapes.

Saumagen *see* KALLSTADT

Saumur [soh-MYOO*R*] An attractive town located on the LOIRE River not far from the city of Angers in the central Loire. The surrounding area is part of a larger growing region known as Anjou-Saumur.

There are a number of APPELLATIONS in the area including Saumur, Cabernet de Saumur, Saumur Mousseux, and Saumur- Champigny. The **Saumur AC** is for red, white, and ROSÉ wines. The white wines are made mainly from CHENIN BLANC, although some CHARDONNAY and SAUVIGNON BLANC is sometimes added. The wines are usually quite ACIDIC and many of them end up in the SPARKLING WINES of the **Saumur Mousseux AC**. These sparkling wines, which are made via MÉTHODE CHAMPENOISE, have been produced in this area since 1811. They're allowed to use Chenin Blanc, Chardonnay, and Sauvignon Blanc, as well as other varieties like CABERNET FRANC, CABERNET SAUVIGNON, GAMAY, and PINOT NOIR. Some of the area producers are shifting production to a higher-quality CRÉMANT DE LOIRE AC sparkling wine. **Saumur AC** red and rosé wines are made mainly from Cabernet Franc, occasionally with the addition of Cabernet Sauvignon and Pineau d'Aunis. The **Saumur-Champigny AC** is an appellation with higher standards for red wines made from these same grapes. Qualifying rosé wines from this area can also, and usually do, use the **Cabernet de Saumur AC**.

sauterne [soh-TERN; saw-TERN] A generic name used in the United States for inexpensive white wines ranging from DRY to semi-sweet. Such wines aren't anything like the famous French SAUTERNES (spelled with a final *s*) and are often simply JUG WINES made from a variety of mediocre grapes.

Sauternes AC [soh-TEH*R*N] Famous APPELLATION that produces some of the most outstanding sweet wines in the world. The Sauternes AC lies within the GRAVES district of France's BORDEAUX region, approximately 25 miles southeast of the city of Bordeaux. The designated area includes the five COMMUNES of Barsac, Bommes, Fargues, Preignac, and Sauternes. Barsac is unusual in that it has its own appellation and its wines can be labeled either BARSAC AC or Sauternes AC; however, none of the other wines can be labeled Barsac AC. The dominant grape in Sauternes is SÉMILLON, although the final blend generally includes some SAUVIGNON BLANC and, occasionally, small amounts of MUSCADELLE. In good VINTAGES, this appellation is the lucky recipient of the right climatic conditions to infect the grapes with BOTRYTIS CINEREA. This beneficial mold causes the grapes to shrivel, leaving sugar-laden fruit full of rich, concentrated flavors. Botrytis cinerea doesn't always develop and, when it does, it's sometimes very late, rewarding only those daring vineyard owners who haven't picked their grapes (but who have risked losing the entire crop due to inclement weather). The best Sauternes wines come from low-yielding vines that have been hand-picked (some as many as twelve separate times) to ensure that the grapes are not culled before reaching the perfect degree of required ripeness. The resulting classic Sauternes wine is rich and sweet—the botrytis cinerea contributes a desirable HONEYED and COMPLEX nature to both the aroma and flavor. Châteaus don't produce sweet Sauternes AC wines every vintage. If the grapes do not progress properly—through suitable ripening and botrytis infection—a château may make fully DRY wines and sell them as BORDEAUX AC or BORDEAUX SUPÉRIER AC wines. Some Sauternes properties started using CRYOEXTRACTION in the late 1980s in an effort to produce good sweet wines from poorer vintages. The Sauternes châteaus were ranked in the CLASSIFICATION OF 1855. Château D'YQUEM was elevated to a class all by itself—known variously as PREMIER GRAND CRU, grand premier cru, and premier cru superieur—and is allowed to put PREMIER GRAND CRU CLASSÉ on its label (although it doesn't). It undisputedly makes the best wines in the area and some feel they're the best in all Bordeaux. The classification also named eleven PREMIERS CRUS and fifteen DEUXIÈMES CRUS. Some of the other châteaus producing marvelous wines are CLIMENS, COUTET, GUIRAUD, LAFAURIE-PEYRAGUEY, RABAUD-PROMIS, RAYNE-VIGNEAU, RAYMOND-LAFON, RIEUSSEC, SUDUIRAUT, and LA TOUR BLANCE. *See also* SAUTERNE.

Sauvignon *see* TOCAI FRIULANO

Sauvignonasse *see* TOCAI FRIULANO

Sauvignon Blanc [SOH-vihn-yoh*n* BLAH*N*; SOH-vee-nyaw*n* BLAH*N*GK] White wine grape that is widely cultivated in France and California. It's also grown in Italy, eastern Europe, Australia, New Zealand, and South America. Sauvignon Blanc wines have noticeable ACIDITY and a GRASSY, HERBACEOUS aroma and flavor. They are CRISP, flavorful wines that generally should be drunk young. The best of the French wines made from 100 percent Sauvignon Blanc grapes are produced in the LOIRE Valley at SANCERRE and POUILLY-FUMÉ. They are crisp and TART, sometimes with a noticeable FLINTY characteristic. The elegant DRY wines from BORDEAUX—primarily from GRAVES—are a blend of Sauvignon Blanc and SÉMILLON that's been AGED in oak barrels. The Sémillon rounds out the flavor and provides additional STRUCTURE, enabling these wines to age for decades. Some of the best and most expensive of these Bordeaux wines come from Château HAUT-BRION and DOMAINE DE CHEVALIER. Although not the primary grape used in the great SAUTERNES wines (Sémillon is, in most cases), Sauvignon Blanc plays an important role in these rich, sweet wines. In California, Robert Mondavi gave this VARIETY a push when he introduced an oaky-styled Sauvignon Blanc VARIETAL WINE he called FUMÉ BLANC. Now the second best-selling varietal in California after CHARDONNAY, Sauvignon Blanc wines are made in a variety of additional styles—from those that are crisp and unoaked to Sémillon blends. Steps have been taken over the last decade to lessen the pronounced grassy characteristic of California's Sauvignon Blancs. This grape is also known as *Blanc Fumé, Sauvignon Jaune,* and *Sauvignon Musqué.*

Sauvignon Jaune *see* SAUVIGNON BLANC

Sauvignon Musqué *see* SAUVIGNON BLANC

Sauvignon Rouge *see* CABERNET SAUVIGNON

Sauvignon Vert *see* MUSCADELLE

Savagnin [sah-vah-NYA*N*] A rather rare, high-quality white-wine grape grown primarily in France's Jura region. Savagnin is best known as the variety used in the VIN JAUNE (yellow wine) of CHÂTEAU-CHALON. AGED for 6 years, vin jaune undergoes a process similar to SHERRY, whereby a film of YEAST covers the surface, thereby preventing OXIDATION but allowing evaporation and the subsequent concentration of the wine. The result is a sherrylike wine with a delicate, nutty richness that can age for decades. Savagnin is also blended—most often with CHARDONNAY—as in the white wines of ARBOIS, CÔTES DU JURA, and L'ETOILE. It's also known as *Savagnin Blanc* and *Savagnin Jaune.* The term *Savagnin Noir* is a synonym for PINOT NOIR.

Savagnin Noir *see* PINOT NOIR

Savagnin Rosé *see* GEWÜRZTRAMINER

Savennières AC [sa-veh-NYEH*R*] Consisting of only 150 acres, Savennières AC is one of the smallest APPELLATIONS in the Anjou area of France's LOIRE region. The grape used is CHENIN BLANC, and the white wines produced are thought to be some of the best in the area. Because of Chenin Blanc's high ACIDITY, the wines are capable of long AGING; in their youth they can be quite ROUGH. The wines of this appellation are required to have an unusually high minimum ALCOHOL content of 12 percent. There are two GRAND CRU vineyards with their own appellations—**Coulée de Serrant** and **LaRoche aux Moines**.

Savigny-Lès-Beaune AC [sa-vee-nyee lay BOH*N*] The village of Savigny-Lès-Beaune is located between BEAUNE and ALOXE-CORTON. The Savigny-Lès-Beaune AC, which surrounds this village, is the third largest producing APPELLATION in the CÔTE DE BEAUNE section of BURGUNDY. Red wines are made from PINOT NOIR, and white wines are made from CHARDONNAY. The reputation of the wines from Savigny-Lès-Beaune is that they're generally LIGHTER and less full-bodied (and therefore not considered as good) as that of many of its neighbors, which means prices are lower. **Aux Vergelesses, Aux Guettes, Les Lavières**, and **Aux Serpentières** are some of the better PREMIER CRU vineyards.

Savoie [sa-VWAH] Wine district located in eastern France very close to the Swiss border near Lake Geneva. Vineyards are scattered throughout the area, stretching south toward Grenoble. The main APPELLATIONS in the area are Vin de Savoie, Vin de Savoie Mousseux, CRÉPY, Roussette de Savoie, and SEYSSEL. **Vin de Savoie**, the area's main appellation, is for DRY wines—white, red, and ROSÉ. The grapes for red wines are GAMAY, MONDEUSE, and PINOT NOIR. Many wine aficionados prefer the Mondeuse-based wines. White wines make up 75 percent of the production. They're made primarily from JACQUÈRE, but ALIGOTÉ, ALTESSE, CHARDONNAY, and CHASSELAS are also used. The **Vin de Savoie Mousseux AC** is for SPARKLING WINES made from Altesse, Molette, and Chardonnay. The **Roussette de Savoie AC** is for dry white wines made mainly from the Altesse variety (locally called *Roussette*), with small amounts of Chardonnay and Mondeuse Blanche. There are sixteen CRU villages in the Savoie, all of which have higher standards than those of the Vin de Savoie AC and Roussette de Savoie AC and may append their name to either of these appellations if their wines meet these higher criteria.

savory A general descriptor for wines that are RICH, full-bodied (*see* BODY), SPICY, and all-around wonderful.

Savoyance *see* MONDEUSE

Scharlachberg *see* BINGEN

Scharzhofberg [SHAHRTS-hoff-berk] One of Germany's premier vineyards, which is located near the village of Wiltingen along the SAAR River in the MOSEL-SAAR-RUWER region. RIESLING wines from this vineyard are often rated in the top echelon of all German wines. The Scharzhofberg vineyard consists of approximately 67 acres planted almost entirely with Riesling vines. There are a half-dozen growers, but the largest and best parcel is owned by the Müller family. Scharzhofberg is classified as an ORTSTEIL, which means its wines don't use Wiltingen in the name—they're simply labeled Scharzhofberg. Wines from the GROSSLAGE that covers this area are labeled Wiltinger Scharzberg, which can cause some confusion.

Schaumwein [SHOUM-vine] *Schaum* means "froth" or "foam," and *Schaumwein* refers to the lowest category of SPARKLING WINE in

Germany. The highest category is called *Qualitätschaumwein* and is popularly known as SEKT.

Scheurebe [SHEWR-uhb] The most widely grown in Germany's RHEINHESSEN and RHEINPFALZ regions, this CROSS of RIESLING and SYLVANER was created in 1916 by botanist George Scheu (*Rebe* means "vine"). Even though this white-wine grape is one of the higher-quality Riesling crossings, it must be fully ripe to achieve its potential. This feature is a drawback for Scheurebe because it requires this variety to be planted on prime vineyard land, which is most often reserved for Riesling. This grape is susceptible to BOTRYTIS CINEREA, making it attractive for the production of DESSERT WINES. Compared to Riesling, Scheurebe produces higher sugar levels, greater YIELDS, and comparable ACID levels. Scheurebe wines can be similiar to Rieslings, with an added black currant characteristic. Small amounts of this grape are cultivated in California where it's used to make VARIETAL WINES.

Schiava [SKYAH-vah] A red-wine grape thought to be native to Italy's ALTO ADIGE region, where it's extensively grown. It's also widely cultivated in neighboring TRENTINO. These regions are heavily populated with German-speaking citizens who call this grape *Vernatsch*. This variety produces light-colored, fruity wines that are low in ACID, TANNINS, and ALCOHOL; they should be drunk young. There are several varieties of Schiava: *Schiava Grossa* (in German, *Grossvernatsch*), which is the most common; *Schiava Grigia* (or *Grauvernatsch*), which is more difficult to grow but produces better wines; and the low-yielding *Schiava Gentile* (also called *Kleinvernatsch* and *Mittervernatsch*). Another clone called *Tschaggel* (or *Tschaggelevernatsch*) produces good wines but isn't widely planted because it's an inconsistent ripener. The best Schiava-based wines come from the DOC's LAGO DI CALDARO (*Kalterersee,* in German) and SANTA MADDALENA (or *St. Magdalener*). This variety is also cultivated in Germany's WÜRTTEMBERG region where its called *Trollinger.*

Schillerwein [SHIHL-uh*r*-vine] A ROSÉ wine that's a specialty in Germany's WÜRTTEMBERG region. It's made from a mix of red and white grapes that are FERMENTED together. In the past these grapes were also sometimes planted and harvested together. *Schillern* means "to change color" and refers to the varying shades of pink found in the wines.

Schioppettino [skyaw-peh-TEE-noh] A red-wine grape grown in Italy's FRIULI-VENEZIA GIULIA region, particularly in the DOC of COLLI ORIENTALI DEL FRIULI. Schioppettino, also known as *Ribolla Nera,* was on the verge of extinction when it was resurrected by the Ronchi di Cialla estate. Since then other producers have followed suit, and this variety has slowly been gaining a following. Schioppettino produces DRY, intense wines with a flavor suggestive of wild blackberries.

schloss [SHLAWSS] The German word for "castle." When the name of a schloss is used on a wine label, the meaning is similar to ESTATE GROWN, meaning the wine must be made from grapes grown in its own vineyards. The word *schloss* can also appear as part of the name of a BEREICH—as in Bereich Schloss Bockelheim—or of a GROSSLAGE—as in Grosslage Schloss Rodeck.

Schlossberg *see* ERBACH; KANZEM; RÜDESHEIM; ZELTINGEN

Schlossböckelheim [SHLAWSS BUH-kuhl-hime] A prime wine-producing village located southwest of BAD KREUZNACH in Germany's NAHE region. The village produces top-quality RIESLINGS from its top vineyard sites, which include **Kupfergrube, Felsenberg**, and **Königsfels**. The name Schlossböckelheim is also used in the name of the BEREICH that covers this area (the southern part of the Nahe region), in which case it's usually split into two words—Beriech Shloss Böckelheim. The area's GROSSLAGE, which covers other surrounding villages as well, also uses this village's name—Grosslage Schlossböckelheimer Burweg.

Schloss Groenesteyn [SHLAWSS GRUH-nuh-shtine] Located in Germany's RHEINGAU region, this important estate dates back to the fourteenth century. It's been owned by the Barons von Ritter zu Groenesteyn since 1640. It consists of nearly 80 acres comprised of numerous sections of various EINZELLAGEN scattered throughout the region. Schloss Groenesteyn's vineyards are planted with about 92 percent RIESLING, plus small amounts of MÜLLER-THURGAU and Spätburgunder (PINOT NOIR). The wines from the various vineyards are kept and bottled separately and are generally highly regarded.

Schloss Johannisberg [SHLAWSS yoh-HAHN-ihss-berk] One of Germany's great estates, and probably its most famous. Its origin goes back to a twelfth century abbey dedicated to St. John the Baptist and the sloping hills below, which were planted with vines. It was at this time that the estate became known as Johannisberg ("John's mountain"). In 1716 Schloss Johannisberg was the first recorded estate to plant entirely with RIESLING. It's said that in 1775 permission to pick the crop was mistakenly delayed, and this accidental circumstance resulted in the discovery of the positive effects of BOTRYTIS CINEREA on grapes and the subsequent coining of the term SPÄTLESE ("late picking"). The 87-acre estate became the property of Prince Metternich in 1816. It was awarded to him by the emperor of Austria, for whom the prince had been Chancellor. The prince's descendants still retain part ownership today. The wines, which are matured in oak, are often depicted as classic Rieslings, with concentrated flavors and considerable AGING ability. Schloss Johannisberg is classified as an ORSTEIL and, as such, is allowed to use only its name on the label (a village name is not required). It also uses differing labels and color-coded CAPSULES to identify the quality of the wines (in addition to the standard terminology).

Schloss Reichartshausen *see* OESTRICH

Schloss Reinhartshausen [SHLAWSS RINE-harts-how-zuhn]
An important German wine estate previously belonging to the princes of Prussia, descendants of Kaiser Wilhelm. It consists of about 170 acres planted with about 80 percent RIESLING, plus GEWÜRZTRAMINER, KERNER, Spätburgunder (PINOT NOIR), and Weissburgunder (PINOT BLANC). Schloss Reicharthausen, located between ERBACH and HATTENHEIM, has vineyards scattered throughout top vineyard sites in Germany's RHEINGAU region, including part of MARCOBRUNN, the famous vineyard in Erbach. Schloss Reinhartshausen produces wines that are generally RICH and full-bodied (*see* BODY). **Prinz von Preussen** is the SECOND LABEL used by the estate.

Schloss Schönborn [SHLAWSS SHOEN-born] With over 185 acres, Schloss Schönborn is the largest privately held estate in Germany's RHEINGAU region. It's located in HATTENHEIM but owns prime vineyards throughout the Rheingau, including sites in ERBACH, HALLGARTEN, HOCKHEIM, JOHANNISBERG, RAUENTHAL, and RÜDESHEIM. The vineyards are planted with over 85 percent RIESLING, plus small amounts of other varieties including MÜLLER-THURGAU, Spätburgunder (PINOT NOIR), and Wiessburgunder (PINOT BLANC). The top wines of this estate are some of the Rheingau's best. The von Schönborn family has owned the estate since 1349.

Schloss Vollrads [SHLAWSS FAWL-rahts] One of Germany's most famous wine estates, built in the fourteenth century by the Greiffenclau family, who still retain ownership. It's situated in the hills above the village of WINKEL in the RHEINGAU region. The nearly 125-acre estate is planted with 98 percent RIESLING and a tiny amount of EHRENFELSER. Schloss Vollrads is classified as an ORTSTEIL and, therefore, simply uses its name on labels. The estate's wines are highly sought after and have a good international following. Because the current policy

of Schloss Vollrads is to produce drier (*see* DRY) wines, they produce a larger percentage of TROCKEN and HALBTROCKEN wines than is usual for other German producers. Like another famous estate, SCHLOSS JOHANNISBERG, Schloss Vollrads uses different colored CAPSULES to distinguish the various quality levels of their wines (QUALITÄTSWEIN BESTIMMTER ANBAUGEBIET, KABINETT, SPÄTLESE, AUSLESE, etc.).

Schönhell *see* HALLGARTEN

Schramsberg Vineyards [SHRAMS-berg] The original Schramsberg Vineyards was established in 1862 by Jacob Schram, but PHYLLOXERA and PROHIBITION stopped all wineproducing activity for decades. The modern Schramsberg Vineyards was started in 1965, when Jack and Jamie Davies purchased the defunct winery and began its revitalization. From those first SPARKLING WINES produced in 1965 from purchased grapes, production has grown to about 45,000 cases per year. Today, the winery produces six MÉTHODE CHAMPENOISE-style SPARKLING WINES—BLANC DE BLANCS, BLANC DE NOIRS, Cuvée de Pinot, Cremant Demi-Sec, RESERVE, and the premium label J. Schram. All are high quality and rank as some of California's best sparkling wines.

Schützenhaus *see* HATTENHEIM

Schwarze Katz *see* ZELL

Schwarzriesling *see* MEUNIER

Sciacchetra *see* CINQUETERRE DOC

Scuppernong [SKUHP-uhr-nawng] White-wine grape that is indigenous to the southeastern United States and is probably the most important member of the MUSCADINE family. Scuppernong is one of the first grapes the colonists used to make wine. It's now cultivated primarily in the southeastern United States and is well known for its high YIELD. Scuppernong produces an unusual, rather sweet, aromatic wine that takes some getting used to by those more familiar with wines made from European-type (VITIS VINIFERA) grapes.

Sebastiani Vineyards [seh-bas-tee-YAH-nee] Winery located on the edge of the town of Sonoma, California, in the SONOMA VALLEY AVA. It was founded in 1904 by Samuele Sebastiani and taken over by his son August in 1944. Upon August's death in 1980, his son Sam assumed responsibilities and began to transform the large (4 million cases per year) enterprise by thinning the line of generic JUG WINES it made and adding some higher-quality VARIETAL WINES. These seemingly bold moves caused immense family unrest, and in 1986 Sam was ousted in a family dispute similar to that of the Mondavis in the mid-1960s. Sam left to found his own winery Viansa, and his brother Don began running Sebastiani Vineyards. Ironically, the winery today produces several higher-quality varietal bottlings, including its VINEYARD-DESIGNATED wines and its Sonoma County line, which includes BARBERA, CABERNET FRANC, CABERNET SAUVIGNON, CHARDONNAY, MERLOT, and ZINFANDEL. Sebastiani Vineyards continues to produce GENERIC WINES and other lower-priced wines through its various lines including Eye of the Swan, August Sebastiani Country Wines, Oakbrook, and Vendange. After a dip in production during the transition between brothers, Sebastiani is now producing over 4 million cases each year. Although the winery owns about 300 acres of vineyards in Sonoma County it purchases most of its grapes from other growers.

sec [SEHK] This French word literally means "DRY," which in the wine world means "not sweet." When used to describe STILL (non-SPARKLING) wines, *sec* indicates that the wine has little if any RESIDUAL SUGAR left after FERMENTATION. In sparkling wines like CHAMPAGNE, however, the word takes on quite another meaning: "sec" indicates a relatively sweet wine, whereas DEMI-SEC is even sweeter. Drier sparkling wines are referred to as BRUT and the very driest as *Extra Brut* or *Brut Nature.*

secco [SAY-koh] Italian for DRY.

Le Sec de la Tour Blanche *see* LA TOUR BLANCHE, CHÂTEAU

Le Sec de Rayne-Vigneau *see* RAYNE-VIGNEAU, CHÂTEAU

seco [SEH-koh] Spanish for DRY.

secondary fermentation 1. When making SPARKLING WINE via MÉTHODE CHAMPENOISE, the FERMENTATION that takes place in the bottle once the *liqueur d'tirage* (*see* DOSAGE) is added is called the secondary (or second) fermentation. 2. When making still wines, MALOLACTIC FERMENTATION is sometimes called secondary fermentation.

second growth *see* DEUXIÈME CRU

second label A term used for winery- or CHÂTEAU-produced wines that aren't the quality necessary to be bottled under the primary label. Such wines are generally made from grapes that are either from new vineyards or below top quality because of a substandard growing season. Although not usually as wonderful as primary-label wines, second-labels can be surprisingly good. Some examples of second labels in California include Liberty School from CAYMUS VINEYARDS and

Hawk Crest from STAG'S LEAP WINE CELLARS. Examples in BORDEAUX, where such wines are sometimes referred to as **second wines**, are Les Forts de Latour from CHÂTEAU LATOUR and Moulin-des-Carruades from CHÂTEAU LAFITE-ROTHSCHILD.

second wine *see* SECOND LABEL; SUGAR WINE

sediment The grainy, bitter-tasting deposit sometimes found in wine bottles, most often with older wines. Sediment is not a bad sign but in fact may indicate a superior wine. It's the natural separation of bitartrates (*see* TARTARIC ACID), TANNINS, and color pigments that occurs as wines AGE. Although generally associated with finer red wines, sediment occasionally appears in white wines, usually in the form of nearly colorless crystals. For PORT drinkers the term CRUST, synonymous with sediment, is often used. Sediment should be allowed to settle completely before the wine is DECANTED into another container so that when the wine is served none of the deposit will transfer to the glass.

Segonnes *see* LASCOMBES, CHÂTEAU

de Ségur *see* BROUSTET, CHÂTEAU

Séguret *see* CÔTES DU RHÔNE

Seibel, Albert A well-known French hybridist (*see* HYBRID) who lived from 1844 to 1936. Albert Seibel was responsible for creating numerous new grape varieties including Plantet and Rayon d'Or and the French-American hybrids—AURORA, Cascade, CHANCELLOR, CHELOIS, Colobel, DE CHAUNAC, Rougeon, and Verdelet.

Seibel 5279 *see* AURORA

Seibel 7053 *see* CHANCELLOR

Seibel 9549 *see* DE CHAUNAC

Seibel 10878 *see* CHELOIS

Sekt [ZEHKT] A German term that's the popular shortened substitute for *Qualitätschaumwein*—"quality sparkling wine." It's the top-quality category for sparkling wine, the lowest being SCHAUMWEIN. The term **Deutscher Sekt** may be used for sparkling wine made entirely from grapes cultivated in Germany, whereas other countries simply use *Sekt* in their German-speaking regions. If a wine is from one of Germany's thirteen ANBAUGEBIETE (official growing regions), its label can state "Deutscher Sekt bA" and may contain the name of a BEREICH (district) and GROSSLAGE (general site). The label may also include the

EINZELLAGE (individual site or vineyard) if 85 percent of the grapes are from the named vineyard and the rest of the grapes are from the Anbaugebiet. If a Sekt is made from a single variety (usually RIESLING), the label may include the name of the variety and would read *Rieslingsekt*. Sekt is fruity and traditionally somewhat sweeter than the better sparkling wines from France, Spain, and the United States.

select A label term that, though not legally defined, is used often as a marketing term to infer there's something special about the wine. Such a conclusion, however, may not be true.

Sélection de Grains Nobles *see* ALSACE

Select Late Harvest *see* LATE HARVEST

Sémillon [say-mee-YOH*N*; seh-mee-YOH*N* (Fr. say-mee-YAW*N*)] White-wine grape that is planted around the world—Argentina, Australia, Chile, France, South Africa, eastern Europe, and the United States—and, in most cases, turns out neutral-flavored, mediocre wines. By itself, Sémillon generally produces wines that are not well-ROUNDED. Combine Sémillon with SAUVIGNON BLANC, however, and the resulting wines can be quite extraordinary. Sémillon marries well with oak and tends to produce high-ALCOHOL wines that have good EXTRACT and TEXTURE but what are often low in ACID and on AROMA. Sauvignon Blanc adds the missing acidity and aroma while Sémillon tempers Sauvignon Blanc's tendency toward GRASSINESS. Blending the two grapes creates a richer, more COMPLEX wine than either can create alone. Indicative of this style are the white wines from BORDEAUX, which often use from 50 to 80 percent Sémillon in the BLEND, producing dry, marvelously complex wines with great AGING ability. Bordeaux also produces the world-famous sweet wines from SAUTERNES, which capitalize on Sémillon's susceptibility to BOTRYTIS CINEREA, a mold that shrivels the grapes, intensifying the acid and sugar levels. The resulting wines are RICH, HONEYED, concentrated, and expensive. In Australia, the image of this grape's inability to stand alone is blurred by the world-class, dry Sémillon wines from HUNTER VALLEY (which are sometimes called *Hunter Valley Riesling*) and—to some extent—the dry, oaked wines produced in the Barossa Valley. Tremendous recognition is also going to Australia's De Bortoli Wines for their botrytised, Sauternes-style Sémillon wine. In the United States, Sémillon grapes have not been extensively grown. There are elegant Sémillon wines coming out of the Pacific Northwest (like those from Washington's Hogue Cellars), but much of the west coast Sémillon is used simply for blending. In the United States and Australia there are now Sémillon/Chardonnay blends appearing on retail shelves. Sémillon is also known as *Chevrier, Green Grape,* and *Wyndruif.*

Sequoia Grove [sih-KWOY-uh] Situated between the towns of Oakville and Rutherford, California, this NAPA VALLEY winery was established in 1980 by brothers Jim and Steve Allen. In addition to the 25-acre vineyard next to the winery, the Allens purchased a 138-acre vineyard in the CARNEROS AVA in 1981. This property eventually became part of DOMAINE CARNEROS but still provides the Allens with CHARDONNAY grapes. Sequoia Grove focuses on CABERNET SAUVIGNON and CHARDONNAY wines. The Chardonnay comes in estate and Carneros bottlings and the Cabernet Sauvigon as Napa Valley and Estate Reserve. So far, the red wines have developed the best reputation. Annual production is between 20,000 and 25,000 cases.

Sercial [SER-shuhl] 1. A white-wine grape grown mainly in Portugal's DAO region. Although associated historically with the island of MADEIRA, Sercial is now found there only in limited quantities. When PHYLLOXERA attacked the Madeira vineyards in the 1870s, the vineyards were eventually replanted, replacing the classic Madeira varieties like Sercial with TINTA NEGRA MOLE. Because of Common Market labeling regulations (see the following discussion), Sercial is making a comeback. These wines are very PERFUMY, yet SO ASTRINGENT that they take 6–8 years to mellow into drinkability. 2. The driest and lightest style of the Madeira wines. Although originally associated with the Sercial grape, a lot of Tinta Negra Mole has been used in this style of Madeira in the recent past (especially in the cheaper versions). However, in 1986 Portugal entered the Common Market, whose regulations required that by 1993 any Madeira wine naming a variety on its label must contain at least 85 percent of that grape. This labeling requirement caused an upsurge in replanting the classic vines such as Sercial. Wines labeled "Sercial-style" can contain less than the required 85 percent, and most likely contain more Tinta Negra Mole.

Aux Serpentières *see* SAVIGNY-LÈS-BEAUNE

Serprina *see* PROSECCO

serre *see* VIN DE CUVÉE

Setúbal *see* MOSCATEL DE SETÚBAL

Sèvre-et-Maine *see* MUSCADET

Seyre-Villard 5276 *see* SEYVAL BLANC

Seyssel [seh-SEHL] One of the best-known villages in France's SAVOIE region, Seyssel is located just southwest of Lake Geneva on the Rhône River, not far from the Swiss border. Seyssel produces white STILL WINES under the **Seyssel AC** and SPARKLING WINES under the **Seyssel Mousseux AC**. The grapes used are ALTESSE (locally called *Roussette*) and a local variety Molette, which lends an interesting peppery character. Most of these wines should be drunk young.

Seyval Blanc [say-vahl BLAH*N*; BLAH*N*GK] A French-American HYBRID created by the French hybridizer Seyve-Villard by crossing two other hybrids—Seibel 5656 and Seibel 4986 (Rayon d'Or). Officially known as *Seyre-Villard 5276,* Seyval Blanc is widely grown in the eastern United States, England, and parts of northern France. Wines produced from this variety are high in acidity and therefore CRISP and LEAN, with a hint of grapefruit in the flavor. This is particularly characteristic of the wines from the northern areas like Michigan and New York. Wines produced from the more southern areas such as Virginia and Maryland are somewhat softer and fuller. Some producers are aging their Seyval Blanc wines in oak barrels to SOFTEN and enrich the wine, as well as increase the bottle life.

Seyve Villard 12.375 *see* VILLARD BLANC

Seyve Villard 18.315 *see* VILLARD NOIR

Shadow Creek *see* DOMAINE CHANDON

Shafer Vineyards Winery that was established in 1979, 7 years after the Shafers had purchased their 210-acre property in the STAGS LEAP DISTRICT of the NAPA VALLEY. They sold grapes for several years before building their own winery. Today, Shafer Vineyards has 50 acres planted with CABERNET FRANC, CABERNET SAUVIGNON, and MERLOT on the original site, plus an additional 17-acre plot about 6 miles away near the town of Oak Knoll and an 83-acre site in the CARNEROS AVA. The winery focuses on CHARDONNAY, Merlot, and Cabernet Sauvignon wines, the latter made in two versions—Stags Leap District and Hillside Select. All of Shafer Vineyards wines are considered very high quality.

shallow *see* HOLLOW

sharp A winetasting term for a wine that has a biting sensation due to excess ACIDITY or ACETIC ACID. Some sharp wines will mellow with age.

sheets *see* LEGS

Shenandoah Valley AVA [shen-uhn-DOH-uh] A VITICULTURAL AREA located east of Sacramento, California, in AMADOR COUNTY. It's part of the large SIERRA FOOTHILLS AVA. ZINFANDEL and SAUVIGNON BLANC are the two most popular varieties here. Shenandoah Valley wineries include Amador Foothill, Baldinelli, Karly, Montevina, Santino, and Shenandoah.

sherrified [SHEHR-rih-fide] A winetasting term for a TABLE WINE that assumes a SHERRYlike character, which is generally caused by oxidation (*see* OXIDIZED). Such wines are characterized by a heavy, stale smell and flavor; the color takes on a brownish tinge. This term is comparable to MADERIZED. A wine that is sherrified is a faulty wine unless it was specifically produced to achieve this character.

sherry A FORTIFIED wine made in the JEREZ-XÉRÈX-SHERRY Y MANZANILLA DE SANLÚCAR DE BARRAMEDA DO, a designated area located around the town of JEREZ DE LA FRONTERA in southern Spain's Andalusia region. Along with PORT and MADEIRA, sherry is considered one of the three great FORTIFIED wines. Sherries range broadly in color, flavor, and sweetness, but there are fundamentally only two types—*fino* and *oloroso*. The difference between these two originates with a peculiar yeast called FLOR and relates to the level of ALCOHOL. Flor develops only on fino-type wines and imparts a sharp, tangy characteristic. It also forms an insulating layer on the wine's surface that protects the wine from oxidation (*see* OXIDIZED) and keeps the wine's pale color. Flor won't develop in wines with over 15½ percent alcohol, so *fino*-style wines are generally lower in alcohol than olorosos, which are fortified up to 18 percent alcohol. **Oloroso:** Since all sherry barrels are only filled about five-sixths full, air gets to the *olorosos* and—because they're not protected by a layer of flor—causes them to oxidize. This oxidation turns the wine's color from deep gold to deep brown and endows the aroma and flavor with rich, nutty-raisiny characteristics. Because olorosos are usually aged longer than most sherries, they're also more expensive. In Spain, most olorosos are DRY. **Cream sherries** are usually lower-grade olorosos that have been heavily sweetened. **Amoroso** (also called *East India*) is also a sweetened oloroso, as is the very dark, extremely sweet **brown sherry**. **Rayas** are also lower-grade olorosos. Because of their color, lighter olorosos are sometimes called **golden sherries**. There are several different variations of fino-style sherries. **Fino:** This pale, delicate, very dry, tangy wine is considered by many to be the world's finest sherry. Finos are excellent when young and should not be aged because they don't improve and may lose some of their vitality. A **fino amontillado** occurs when a fino has lost its flor (at about 6 years) and begins to turn amber-colored and gain a little of the nutty flavor found in an oloroso.

Amontillado, still a fino-style wine, is aged longer and is darker and softer than a fino amontillado. It should have a distinctively nutty flavor and retain some of the pungent tang. **Manzanilla** is the lightest, most delicate, and most pungent of the fino-style sherries. It's made in Sanlúcar de Barrameda, a seaside town whose location is said to give the wine a hint of saltiness. A **manzanilla pasada** occurs when the flor fades (at about 7 years) and the wine takes on some of the characteristics of an amontillado—nutty flavor and darker color—while still retaining its pungent character. **Pale cream sherry** is a fino that has been sweetened. **Palo cortado** is a cross between an oloroso and a fino and varies from producer to producer. Supposedly, a palo cortado starts life as a fino—developing and gaining a tangy character from flor. At some point in its evolution, it deviates and evolves as an oloroso would by oxidizing and developing rich, nutty characteristics and a darker color—all while retaining some of a fino's tanginess. This style is very rare and greatly sought after by sherry connoisseurs. Generally sherries are non-vintage (*see* VINTAGE) and the quality is consistent year after year because the Spanish use the SOLERA system of topping off older wines with the more recently made sherry. Simply described, the solera system consists of a number of tiers of sherry casks from oldest to the most recently made. Usually one-quarter to one-third of the oldest wine is drawn off for bottling and then replaced by wine from the next oldest tier and so on up through the solera system. This process lets the old wines infuse the younger wines with character while the younger wines give their nutrients to the older wines. In fino-style wines this latter activity gives the flor something to live on. In 1994 GONZALES BYPASS introduced two unusual vintage-dated sherries, a 1963 and a 1966. Both sherries bypassed the normal solera system aging process and were aged separately in their own oak casks. Spanish sherry is made primarily from the PALAMINO grape along with small amounts of PEDRO XIMÉNEZ and Moscatel (MUSCAT). Sherry-style wines are now also made in the United States, as well as in other parts of the world including Australia and South Africa. Many wines that call themselves sherry are inexpensive potables that aren't produced anything like the Spanish originals. A few, however, attain a close approximation by using flor innoculations and the solera system. Sherries can be drunk before or after dinner. Dry sherries are usually served chilled; sweet sherries are served at room temperature.

shipping dosage *see* DOSAGE

shiraz *see* SYRAH

short In winetasting terminology, a wine that's short has an abrupt FINISH, not an admirable quality. *See also* LONG.

Sicily [SIHS-uh-lee] Sicily (*Sicilia* in Italian) is located right off the tip of the "toe" of Italy's boot-shaped land mass. It's the biggest island in the Mediterranean and Italy's largest wine-producing region (both in vineyard acreage and overall size). Sicily usually competes with APULIA for the largest production out of Italy's twenty wine regions. As with Apulia's production, much of Sicily's wine is distilled into spirits. Even though there are ten DOC areas in Sicily, less than 2½ percent of the total wine production is covered by DOCs. Some of the better-known DOCs are ALCAMO, ETNA, MOSCATO DI PANTELLERIA, and the best-known historically, MARSALA. Many of the best wines are VINO DA TAVOLA (VdT), made by better producers like CORVO and REGALEALI. Sicily has developed its own regional method of identifying quality wines, establishing its own standards and allowing wines that qualify to place a "Q" (for quality) on the label or CAPSULE. The most widely planted white grape is Catarratto Bianco, followed by TREBBIANO. Other white grapes include Grillo, Inzolia, Carricante (also called Catanese Bianco), and MUSCAT (the local subvariety is called *Zibibbo*). The most widely planted red grape is Nero d'Avola (also called Calabrese), followed by Nerello Mascalse, Nerello Cappuccio, and Perricone (also called Pignatello). The red varieties, BARBERA and SANGIOVESE, are starting to make some inroads.

Siebengebirge, Bereich *see* MITTELRHEIN

Siegelsberg *see* ERBACH

Sierra Foothills AVA [see-EHR-ruh] Large APPELLATION that runs through California's "gold country." It's about 160 miles long and includes parts of Yuba, Nevada, Placer, EL DORADO, AMADOR, Calaveras, Tuolumne, and Mariposa Counties. There are more than thirty wineries scattered throughout the region, mostly in El Dorado and Amador Counties. The Sierra Foothills AVA includes the smaller AVAs of El Dorado, FIDDLETOWN, and SHENANDOAH VALLEY. The most widely planted grape variety by a very wide margin is ZINFANDEL. It's followed by SAUVIGNON BLANC, CABERNET SAUVIGNON, CHARDONNAY, and an assortment of other grapes. Some of the wineries located in this VITICULTURAL AREA are Amador Foothill, Boeger Winery, Gold Hill Vineyard, Granite Springs, Lava Cap, Madrona Vineyards, Montevina, Santino, and Shenandoah.

sifone *see* MARSALA DOC

Sigalas Rabaud, Château [sha-TOH see-gah-LAH *r*ah-BOH]
A PREMIER CRU (first growth) located in the SAUTERNES AC in BORDEAUX. It
was once part of a larger property named Rabaud, which was split in
1903 into Château RABAUD-PROMIS and Château Sigalas Rabaud. This estate consists of 35 acres, planted with 90 percent SÉMILLON and 10 percent SAUVIGNON BLANC. It produces about 2,500 cases of high-quality,
sweet Sauternes AC wine. The style of these wines is lighter and fruiter
than many of the Sauternes AC wines, partially because oak barrels
aren't used for AGING. They should be drunk young, but some vintages
are capable of bottle aging for 12 to 14 years.

silky A winetasting term for wines that are incredibly smooth, LUSH,
and finely TEXTURED. Its synonym is VELVETY.

Silva & Cosens The owner of the Dow-branded PORT wines.
The firm was started in 1862 by the Silva family. In 1877 it added a
partner, James Ramsey Dow, who had his own shipping firm—Dow &
Co. Over time, Silva & Cosens formed a relationship with WARRE. Both
were later absorbed by the Symington family, which also owns Gould-
Campbell, GRAHAM, Quarles Harris, and SMITH WOODHOUSE. Dow vintage
port is generally regarded as one of the top six produced. Silva &
Cosens makes a single-quinta port from their primary QUINTA, Quinta
do Bomfim, in some years when there is not a declared vintage for the
Dow brand. It's usually quite good. The firm also produces various
white and ruby ports as well as a 30-year-old tawny.

Silvaner *see* SYLVANER

Silverado Vineyards [sihl-vuh-RAH-doh] This winery, which is
located in the STAGS LEAP DISTRICT of NAPA VALLEY, is owned by members
of Walt Disney's family—his widow Lillian and his daugther and son-
in-law Diane and Ronald Miller. The group began their viticultural venture by selling grapes from vineyards they had purchased in
1976. In 1981 the winery was built, and the first wines were made.
Silverado-owned vineyards now total nearly 350 acres situated in four
different sites—in Stags Leap District, one near Yountville, another in
CARNEROS, and one in Soda Canyon. The winery produces CABERNET
SAUVIGNON (regular and RESERVE), CHARDONNAY (regular and reserve),
MERLOT, and, most recently, SANGIOVESE and ZINFANDEL. All the wines are
of high quality, and the Cabernet Sauvignon and Merlot in particular have consistently received high ratings from reviewers. Between
90,000 and 100,000 cases are produced each year.

Silver Oak Cellars Winery that was founded in 1972 by former
Christian Brothers priest Justin Meyer and his partner Colorado oil

man Ray Duncan. Silver Oak focuses on only one grape variety, CABER-NET SAUVIGNON. It offers three different Cabernet Sauvignon bottlings—Alexander Valley, Napa Valley, and Bonny's Vineyard. The wines, which are known for their lavish American oak characteristics, are highly acclaimed and have a large following. The winery annually produces between 25,000 and 30,000 cases of wine, most of which is the Alexander Valley Cabernet. Production may increase because Silver Oak purchased the former Lyeth Winery, which is near the town of Geyserville in the Alexander Valley.

Simi Winery [SEE-mee] This winery, which was founded in 1876, is one of the few to survive PROHIBITION. It was run by Isabel Simi, daughter of one of the founders, from 1904 to 1969, when she finally sold it. In 1981 it was sold again, this time to Moët-Hennessy of France, which has since joined with the Louis Vuitton Group. (The combined companies own DOMAINE CHANDON in the NAPA VALLEY, the CHAMPAGNE houses of MOËT ET CHANDON, Mercier, RUINART, VEUVE CLICQUOT-PONSARDIN, Canard-Duchene and Henriot, and the COGNAC producers Hennessy and Hine.) With Zelma Long guiding Simi Winery first as winemaker and now as president, this winery has increased its production to about 150,000 cases per year. It owns 175 acres in the ALEXANDER VALLEY AVA, where the winery is located, and another 100 acres in the RUSSIAN RIVER AVA. The winery produces CABERNET SAUVIGNON (regular bottling and a RESERVE), CHARDONNAY (regular and reserve), CHENIN BLANC, SAUVIGNON BLANC, Sendal (a blend of Sauvignon Blanc and SÉMILLON), and a Cabernet Sauvignon ROSÉ.

Simmern, Langwerth von [LAHNG-vayrt fuhn ZIHM-uhrn] Comprising nearly 110 acres, this important estate is located in the village of Eltville in Germany's RHEINGAU region. Its full title is Freiherrlich Langwerth von Simmern'sches Rentamt. The estate's acreage is spread out over a number of superb vineyard sites in the villages of Eltville, ERBACH, HATTENHEIM, and RAUENTHAL. The von Simmern family has owned the estate since 1464. It has a reputation for consistently producing fine RIESLING wines.

Simone, Château *see* PALETTE

simple A winetasting term for wine that, though not COMPLEX, is forthright and quite good.

Robert Sinskey Vineyards [SIHN-skee] Founded by Dr. Robert Sinskey in 1988, this NAPA VALLEY winery is situated just off the Silverado Trail in the STAGS LEAP AVA. It has a small 5-acre vineyard around the winery, plus two sites in Carneros—one 35 acres and the other 72 acres. Robert Sinskey Vineyards annually produces about 8,000 cases of high-quality wines including CABERNET SAUVIGNON, MERLOT, PINOT NOIR, CHARDONNAY, and a red blend called Carneros Claret made from CABERNET FRANC, Cabernet Sauvignon, and primarily Merlot. There are several RESERVE bottlings, which are labeled RSV.

Skadarska *see* KADARKA

skin contact; skin contact time A process associated with making white wines that is the step between CRUSHING and FERMENTATION. Unlike red wine, white wine isn't fermented with the skins and seeds so it doesn't extract any of the skins' flavors and aromas. However, winemakers get favorable results by leaving the freshly expressed juice in contact with the skins and seeds for a short period— 2 hours to 2 days. The major concerns are that the white wine would extract too much color from the grape skins and/or extract some bitterness from the skins or seeds. These factors can be controlled by keeping the juice at a cooler temperature during the skin contact time. *See also* MACERATION.

skunky A winetasting term for the analogous smell, which is caused by MERCAPTANS. *See also* SULFUR.

Smith-Haut-Lafitte, Château [sha-TOH smeet oh lah-FEET] A CRU CLASSÉ estate located in the PESSAC-LÉOGNAN AC in the GRAVES district in BORDEAUX. The Smith in the name comes from Scotsman George Smith, who owned the property in the eighteenth century. The château consists of about 135 acres, all but about 15 of which are planted with red grapes—65 percent CABERNET SAUVIGNON, 25 percent MERLOT, and 10 percent CABERNET FRANC. Annual production is about 23,000 cases of red wine and 2,200 cases of white wine, made from 100 percent SAUVIGNON BLANC. Château Smith-Haut-Lafitte's red wines have received mixed reviews, causing many to believe this estate is undeserving of its cru classé ranking. However, new ownership has produced a highly regarded 1990 VINTAGE. Although the white wines are not included in the cru classé rating, they're more esteemed than the red wines. Neither the red nor the white wines are considered long-lived—from the best vintages, the reds can AGE for 8 to 10 years; the whites, for 4 to 5 years. The château's SECOND LABEL is **Les Hauts-de-Smith-Haut-Laffite**.

Smith Woodhouse PORT company that was founded in 1784 by Christopher Smith, who added the Woodhouse brothers as partners. In 1970 Smith Woodhouse was purchased by the Symington family who also owns Dow (*see* SILVA & COSENS), GRAHAM, and WARRE. Smith Woodhouse produces a wide variety of port wines including some highly regarded older tawny ports like the 29-year-old His Majesty's Choice. In addition to their vintage ports, Smith Woodhouse produces a Late Bottled Vintage port (LBV), which is unfined and unfiltered and produces more flavor (closer to vintage port) than most producer's LBVs. Smith Woodhouse also makes the **Gould Campbell** port wines, which are highly regarded in their own right.

smoky A winetasting term for a smoky character found in some wines—usually the result of the soil in which the grapes were grown or the barrels in which the wine was aged.

smooth In winetasting, this self-explanatory term can be used to describe a variety of things including a wine's TEXTURE, FINISH, and the tactile impression of FLAVOR and BODY.

soapy A descriptor sometimes used to describe a wine with a dull, disagreeable flavor, generally due to a lack of ACIDITY.

Soave DOC [SWAH-veh] Located in the western part of Italy's VENETO area east of Verona around the town of Soave, this DOC zone produces Italy's most popular DRY white wine. There's a smaller CLASSICO zone that encompasses the hilly areas that are mostly north and east of the town. Soave wines are made from GARGANEGA and TREBBIANO grapes. Most Soave wine is regarded as undistinguished, but the wines from the Classico area are generally of higher quality. There are also a few producers that make single-vineyard wines that are of very high quality. SUPERIORE on the label indicates that the wine is 1 percent higher in ALCOHOL and is AGED for a minimum of 8 months. A SPUMANTE version and a RECIOTO DI SOAVE (a sweet wine) is also made in this same area. Bolla, the Verona-based wine firm, is closely associated with Soave—so much so that many consumers think that Soave is a proprietary brand name of Bolla.

Sociando-Mallet, Château [sha-TOH soh-syahn-DOH mah-LAY] A highly regarded CRU BOURGEOIS estate located in the COMMUNE of Saint-Seurin-de-Cadourne in the HAUT-MÉDOC AC. It has a reputation for producing wines the quality of many QUATRIÈMES CRUS (fourth growths) of the MÉDOC. Château Sociando-Mallet consists of almost 100 acres and produces about 13,000 to 16,000 cases of red wine each year. These wines are deeply colored, full of concentrated flavors, full-bodied (*see* BODY) and TANNIC—some VINTAGES are capable of AGING for 25 years or more. The mix of grape varieties used is about 60 percent CABERNET SAUVIGNON, 25 percent MERLOT, 10 percent CABERNET FRANC, and 5 percent PETIT VERDOT. **Lartigue-de-Brochon** is the château's SECOND LABEL.

Il Sodaccio [eel soh-DAH-tchoh] The proprietary name for one of the super-Tuscan wines (*see* TUSCANY) produced by the CHIANTI CLASSICO estate of Monte Vertine. The wine, which is actually classified as a VINO DA TAVOLA, is made from SANGIOVESE and CANAIOLO and AGED in large oak barrels (rather than the smaller BARRIQUES used for many super-Tuscans). It was first released in 1980. LE PERGOLE TORTE is another super-Tuscan made by the same firm.

I Sodi di San Niccolo [ee SOH-dee dee sahn nee-KOH-loh] The proprietary name for a VINO DA TAVOLA wine made by the CHIANTI Classico estate of Castellare di Castellina. It's a super-Tuscan wine (*see* TUSCANY) made mainly from SANGIOVESE grapes, with a small amount MALVASIA Nera.

soft A descriptor for a wine that's well BALANCED, fruity, mellow and pleasant, which is generally the result of lower ACIDITY and/or TANNINS (or the perfect fusion of the two). The term *soft* is the antonym for HARD. *See also* SOFTEN.

soften A term used to describe the mellowing process of a wine that's young, TANNIC, and/or ACIDIC. Such a wine generally will soften during AGING. *See also* SOFT.

Sogrape The largest wine company in Portugal, Sogrape produces Mateus Rosé, which accounts for over 90 percent of their sales. **Mateus Rosé** is a semisweet, slightly effervescent ROSÉ wine produced from a variety of grapes (including BAGA, Bastardo, and Tinta Pinheira) grown all over northern Portugal. Sogrape has invested in a number of properties to produce higher-quality wine, as well. These properties include Solar Honra de Azevedo in the VINHO VERDE DOC, Vinicola do Vale do Dao in the DAO DOC, and the STILL and PORT wine maker, FERREIRA, in the DOURO DOC.

Solaia [soh-LEH-yuh] The proprietary name for one of the better-known super-Tuscan wines (*see* TUSCANY). It's made from a blend of CABERNET SAUVIGNON (and usually some SANGIOVESE) by the famous Tuscan wine firm Marchesi Antinori (who also makes TIGNANELLO). Solaia, which comes from a single vineyard in the CHIANTI Classico area, is AGED in BARRIQUES for about 2 years.

solera [soh-LEH-rah] Spain's age-old blending and maturation system, used to maintain quality and style consistency in some FORTIFIED wines. It's used most notably for Spain's SHERRY, although producers of such wines in other countries have also established soleras. The solera system is based on the maturity levels of several wines, ranging in tiers from the oldest to the most recently produced. It consists of drawing off one-quarter to one-third of the oldest wine for bottling. The wine that was drawn off is replaced with wine from the next oldest tier, which is replaced with a younger wine from the next level, and so on up through the levels of the solera. With this process, the old wines infuse the younger ones with character, while the youngsters endow their older counterparts with nutrients, which—in *fino*-style sherries—gives the FLOR something to live on. A solera is generally pictured as tiers of wine casks stacked on top of each other—the oldest wines being the bottom level, the next oldest on the tier above that, and on up, with the youngest wine at the top. In actuality, however, the various age levels or scales (*escalas*) of wine may be kept in separate BODEGAS (storage areas). The oldest wines in a solera depend on when it was established—some are 40 to 50 years old. In practice, soleras are very complex, with numerous casks and levels involved. Young wines are managed in a CRIADERA (nursery) prior to being selected to go into a particular solera. To be precise, only the oldest level of wines is referred to as the solera; the successive (next oldest) tier up is referred to as the **first criadera**, followed by the **second criadera**, and so forth. Some producers have up to fourteen levels in their solera systems. The final wine that's bottled is often a blend of the output of various soleras—the result of the integrated solera system.

solid A descriptor for wine that is full-bodied (*see* BODY) and loaded with ACIDITY, ALCOHOL, FRUIT, and TANNINS. The term sometimes refers to youthful wines that will develop well with AGING.

sommelier [saw-muh-LYAY] The French term for a steward or waiter in charge of wine. For hundreds of years, sommeliers were responsible for the cellaring and serving of wines for royalty. Eventually, the tradition of the sommelier spread to restaurants, where such an individual is expected to have extensive knowledge of wines and their suitability with various dishes.

Sonnenberg *see* KANZEM

Sonnenuhr *see* WEHLEN; ZELTINGEN

Sonoma Coast AVA A large AVA designed to identify specific SONOMA COUNTY, cooler-climate areas, which can be classified as Region I or Region II (*see* CLIMATE REGIONS OF CALIFORNIA). This APPELLATION is thus an odd-shaped area that runs from near the Mendocino County line in the north to the Marin County border in the south. It includes part of other AVAs like CHALK HILL, GREEN VALLEY-SONOMA, LOS CARNEROS,

SONOMA VALLEY, and RUSSIAN RIVER, while excluding warmer areas like the ALEXANDER VALLEY AVA and the DRY CREEK AVA.

Sonoma County; Sonoma County AVA; Northern Sonoma AVA
A very important California wine-producing county situated north of San Francisco and west of the NAPA VALLEY. Although the neighboring Napa Valley has dominated the region as far as recognition and in attracting many major wineries, Sonoma has made tremendous progress since the early 1970s and has now carved out significant recognition in its own right. Sonoma's winemaking history goes back to the 1820s, when the Sonoma Mission's vineyards were planted by Franciscan monks. Unfortunately, they planted MISSION grapes, which don't produce high-quality TABLE WINES. In the 1850s and 1860s, AGOSTON HARASZTHY (who established the original BUENA VISTA WINERY in 1857) expanded the effort by trying to determine which varieties did best in various California areas. To this end, he imported thousands of cuttings of about 300 different grape varieties. He planted many of these in SONOMA COUNTY and sold the rest to others around the state. Like much of California, the influx of PHYLLOXERA in the 1890s and PROHIBITION from 1920 to 1933 severely curtailed the growth of Sonoma County's wine business. It wasn't until the Napa Valley boom started in the mid- to late-1960s that Sonoma County was reenergized as a top winemaking region. It began converting from grapes that had been used primarily for JUG WINES—like ALICANTE BOUSCHET, CARIGNANE, and PETITE SIRAH—and now leads Napa County in acreage for CHARDONNAY, PINOT NOIR, and ZINFANDEL. Sonoma has built a solid reputation for wines made from CABERNET SAUVIGNON, Chardonnay, GEWÜRZTRAMINER, Pinot Noir, SAUVIGNON BLANC, and Zinfandel. Sonoma County is quite large and has diverse climate areas ranging from Region I to Region III (see CLIMATE REGIONS OF CALIFORNIA). Numerous AVAs have been established here since 1978, some sharing the same geographic area. In addition to belonging to the huge NORTH COAST AVA and having its own APPELLATION, Sonoma County contains the following AVAs: ALEXANDER VALLEY, CHALK HILL, DRY CREEK, GREEN VALLEY-SONOMA, KNIGHTS VALLEY, LOS CARNEROS, Northern Sonoma, RUSSIAN RIVER VALLEY, SONOMA COAST, SONOMA MOUNTAIN, and SONOMA VALLEY. A number of wineries are permitted to use any of five or six different AVA designations for the same wine. The **Sonoma County AVA** covers the whole county while the **Northern Sonoma AVA** covers the smaller VITICULTURAL AREAS of Alexander Valley, Chalk Hill, Dry Creek, Green Valley-Sonoma, Knight's Valley, and Russian River Valley. Sonoma County has over 175 wineries, which ranks it second only to Napa County in the United States for number of wineries.

Sonoma-Cutrer [soh-NOH-muh koo-TREHR] This state-of-the-art winery is located in the RUSSIAN RIVER AVA northwest of Santa Rosa, California. It was established in 1981 by Brice Jones to focus on CHARDONNAY wines. Today, the winery produces three different Chardonnays—Russian River Ranches, Les Pierres, and Cutrer Vineyard—the last two are both VINEYARD DESIGNATED. Sonoma-Cutrer owns a total of about 410 acres of vineyards. The Russian River Ranches consists of three vineyards totalling about 210 acres and Cutrer Vineyard with about 100 acres—all located in the Russian River AVA. Les Pierres, located in the SONOMA VALLEY, also consists of 100 acres. The winery produces between 70,000 and 75,000 cases of wine each year. Their wines are always of high quality and sometimes exceptional.

Sonoma Mountain AVA A small subzone of the SONOMA VALLEY AVA in SONOMA COUNTY, California. The Sonoma Mountain AVA is situated in the Sonoma Mountain range, west of the town of Glen Ellen. The vineyards are located on both the east and west sides of the mountains, with the majority on the eastern side. Elevation levels for Sonoma Mountain vineyards are 400 to 600 feet on the east and 1,200 to 1,600 feet on the west. At these elevations, the vineyards receive more precipitation. They're also warmer and less susceptible to temperature changes than the valley floor because they're above the fog line. CABERNET SAUVIGNON and ZINFANDEL do very well in this area. Sonoma Mountain AVA wineries are BENZIGER OF GLEN ELLEN, LAUREL GLEN VINEYARDS, and H. Coturri & Sons. The Jack London Vineyard, which supplies grapes to KENWOOD VINEYARDS, and LOUIS M. MARTINI'S Monte Rosso Vineyard are also located here.

Sonoma Riesling *see* SYLVANER

Sonoma Valley AVA California's Sonoma Valley, also known as *Valley of the Moon,* is situated between the Mayacamas Mountains (which separate it from the NAPA VALLEY to the east) and the Sonoma Mountain range on the west. The northern end of the Sonoma Valley AVA starts just southeast of Santa Rosa and extends in a southeasterly direction to San Pablo Bay; it includes the Sonoma portion of the CARNEROS AVA. The smaller SONOMA MOUNTAIN AVA is part of the Sonoma Valley AVA. The southern end of the valley (Carneros) is cooler and CHARDONNAY, GEWÜRZTRAMINER, PINOT NOIR, and MERLOT do better there. CABERNET SAUVIGNON and ZINFANDEL do well in various warmer locations around the valley and in the mountains. There are about 30 wineries in the Sonoma Valley AVA including Adler Fels, ARROWOOD VINEYARDS AND WINERY, BENZIGER AT GLEN ELLEN, the original BUENA VISTA WINERY (the valley's first winery, established by AGOSTON HARASZTHY), CHATEAU ST.

JEAN, Cline Cellars, B. R. Cohn Winery, Gundlach Bundschu Winery, HANZELL VINEYARDS, KENWOOD VINEYARDS, Landmark Vineyards, LAUREL GLEN VINEYARD, MANTANZAS CREEK WINERY, RAVENSWOOD, ST. FRANCIS VINE-YARDS & WINERY, SEBASTIANI VINEYARDS, and Viansa Winery.

Le Sophiste *see* BONNY DOON VINEYARD

sori [SOHR-ree] Piedmontese for a hill or slope that has the best exposure to the sun and therefore produces riper grapes and the best wines. Sori is often used with the vineyard names, like *Sori San Lorenzo* and *Sori Vigna Riunda*.

sound A term describing wine that's without faults in clarity, color, aroma, or flavor.

sour A winetasting term for a spoiled wine that's making its turn toward vinegar. A wine with high acidity is more aptly referred to as ACIDIC or TART than sour.

Soutard, Château [sha-TOH soo-TAHR] A GRAND CRU CLASSÉ estate located in the SAINT-ÉMILION AC in BORDEAUX. Its wines are highly regarded and are thought to be the equivalent of at least a QUATRIÈME CRU (fourth growth) of the MÉDOC. The 55-acre CHÂTEAU produces about 8,000 to 10,000 cases of red wine each year. These well-made wines, which are about 60 percent MERLOT and 40 percent CABERNET FRANC, are BIG and capable of AGING for 20 to 25 years. Château Soutard's SECOND LABEL is **Clos de la Tonnelle**.

South Africa South Africa's wine industry began in the mid-1600s when Jan van Riebeck first planted vines there. In 1679 Simon van der Stel established Groot Constantia, which developed a worldwide reputation for its DESSERT WINES (called *Constantia*). In 1688 the wine industry here was given a boost with the arrival of the French Huguenots, who brought many winemaking skills with them. South African wines had many ups and downs over the years, including serious problems with overproduction in the early 1900s. This dilemma resulted in the formation of the Cooperative Wine Growers' Association (known as the KWV—Kooperatiewe Wijnbouwers Vereniging van Zuid-Africa). The KWV, which controls the supply and demand of grapes and establishes consistent pricing, remains a powerful force today. In addition to KWV, which markets a wide range of wines and distilled spirits, the other two major producers are Oude Meester and the Stellenbosch Farmers' Winery (known as *SFW* or *Farmers*). Other important producers include Blacksberg, Boschendal, Delheim, Groot Constantia, Hamilton Russell, Meerlust, Montpellier, Simonsig, Spier, and Twee

Jonge Gezellen. The primary South Africa growing areas are all in the southwestern part of the country near the Cape of Good Hope. In 1973 an APPELLATION system, *Wine of Origin,* was established along the lines of the European Economic Community rules. The best known of these appellations are Paarl and Stellenbosch. Other Wine of Origin areas are Analusia, Benede-Orange, Boberg, Constantia, Douglas, Durbanvielle, Klein Karoo, Olifantsriver, Overberg, Piketberg, Robertson, Swarland, Swellendam, Tulbagh, and Worcester. The most widely planted grape in South Africa is CHENIN BLANC (called *Steen* locally) followed by other white VARIETIES (called *cultivars* here) including Cape Riesling (CROUCHEN), Clairette Blanche (CLAIRETTE), Colombar (COLOMBARD), Green Grape (SÉMILLON), Hanepoot (MUSCAT), and PALOMINO. CHARDONNAY, RIESLING, and SAUVIGNON are also becoming more popular. The leading red grape is CINSAUT (called *Hermitage* locally), although most agree that CABERNET SAUVIGNON produces the best wines. PINOTAGE, a South African specialty that's declining in popularity, is a CROSS of Hermitage (Cinsaut) and PINOT NOIR. Red varieties growing in popularity include CABERNET FRANC, MERLOT, PINOT NOIR, and Shiraz (SYRAH). During much of this century, FORTIFIED wines (SHERRY and PORT styles) dominated South African wine production. In the 1970s semisweet white TABLE WINES, influenced by Germany, became popular. Now South Africa is producing a wide range of red and white DRY table wines and SPARKLING WINES. The popularity of dry table wines has only become fashionable in South Africa during the last 10 to 15 years.

South African Riesling   *see* CROUCHEN

South Coast AVA   California VITICULTURAL AREA that includes parts of Orange, Riverside, and San Diego counties. There are two smaller AVAS (subzones) here—TEMECULA and San Pasqual. The main grape varieties are CHARDONNAY and SAUVIGNON BLANC. Other varieties are CHENIN BLANC, CABERNET SAUVIGNON, RIESLING, ZINFANDEL, PINOT BLANC, and MERLOT. There are almost twenty-five wineries in this area. Callaway Vineyard & Winery is the largest producer; others include Maurice Car'rie Vineyards & Winery, Culbertson Winery, and Mount Palomar.

Southern Vales   An Australian wine-producing region located southeast of Adelaide in the state of South Australia. It includes the districts of **McLaren Vale** and **Reynella**, among others. The red varieties of CABERNET SAUVIGNON, Shiraz (SYRAH), and GRENACHE are the most widely planted grapes, followed by the white varieties CHARDONNAY and RIESLING. Others grown in the Southern Vales include PINOT NOIR, MERLOT, PALOMINO, PEDRO XIMÉNEZ, SAUVIGNON BLANC, and SÉMILLON. The red wines, particularly Cabernet Sauvignon and Shiraz are best known, but McLaren Vale's Chardonnay and Sauvignon Blanc wines have a wide following. Well-known Southern Vales wineries include Andrew Garret, Coolawin, D'arenberg, A. Norman and Sons, Pirramimma, Château Reynella (headquarters for the giant Thomas Hardy & Sons), Ryecroft, Seaview, Wirra Wirra, and Woodstock.

South Tyrol *see* TRENTINO-ALTO ADIGE

Souzão; Sousão [suh-ZAH-oh; shuh-ZAH-oh] Although this red-wine grape is indigenous to northern Portugal, it's not widely grown there. Souzão has met with greater success in California and South Africa, where it's more highly regarded for PORT production. This variety produces deep-colored wines with concentrated ripe and raisiny flavors.

Spain Spain has more vineyard acreage (over 4 million acres) than any other country, but comes in third behind Italy and France in terms of volume of wine produced. The vineyard land is extremely arid in many areas and can't be densely planted because the vines won't get enough moisture. This, plus rather antiquated viticultural practices, limits YIELDS in most parts of the country. The exception is the area around JEREZ where yields are very high. Aside from SHERRY, the RIOJA DO red wines, and the SPARKLING WINES from the CAVA DO (mainly from Penedès in CATALONIA), most of Spain's wines are not well known outside of this country. This is partially because the style of many Spanish wines—such as high-ALCOHOL, full-bodied (*see* BODY) reds and neutral, low-ACID whites—aren't popular internationally. But Spain is trying to change this image. It began by revamping its APPELLATION system, DENOMINACIÓN DE ORIGEN (DO), after criticism that many areas with DO status did not produce wines of acceptably high quality. A new higher classification, DENOMINACIÓN DE ORIGEN CALIFICADA (DOCa), has more exacting standards than those established for DOs. While there are almost forty regions with DO status, only one—RIOJA—is classified as DOCa. New, tighter DO regulations, plus planting in cooler regions, modernizing winery equipment, and improving winemaking techniques have all contributed to improving the overall quality of Spain's wines. Additionally, both red and white wines have benefited because long AGING requirements have been lowered, or eliminated altogether in the case of white wines. Extensive oak aging tended to eliminate the freshness in these wines and make many seem dull. (Conversely, some aged red Riojas are quite highly regarded.) Many DOs throughout Spain are notable in their own right. SHERRY, by far Spain's most famous wine and one of the world's classic FORTIFIED wines, is produced in the

JEREZ-XÉRÈX-SHERRY Y MANZANILLA DE SANLÚCAR DE BARRAMEDA DO (Jerez, for short) in a variety of styles. The nearby DOs of MÁLAGA and MONTILLA-MORILES also produce fortified wines of a similar style and usually at lower prices. The Rioja DO is still best known for its red wines but is now producing improved white wines, for which it's gaining a good reputation. The white wines from the RUEDA DO are also winning stature. Spain's Catalonia area—particularly the PENEDÈS DO—is gaining a reputation for high-quality red and white STILL WINES, in addition to their MÉTHODE CHAMPENOISE sparkling wines. The red wines from the RIBERA DEL DUERO DO are gaining a solid reputation based on the historically renowned VEGA SICILIA wine estate and the more recently acclaimed Tinto Pesquera wines from Alejandro Fernandez. Other high-quality wine estates are now showing up in this region as well. Although improvements are underway, large amounts of ordinary wine are still produced from the vast central plains south of Madrid. This includes the wine-producing region of LA MANCHA and the neighboring ALICANTE, JUMILLA, UTIEL-REQUENA, and YECLA regions, as well as CARIÑENA further north. Some of the other Spanish DOs are ALELLA, ALMANSA, AMPPURDÁN-COSTA BRAVA, CAMPO DE BORJA, CONCA DE BARBERÀ, CONDADO DE HUELVA, COSTERS DEL SEGRE, MENTRIDA, NAVARRA, PRIORATO, RIAS BAIXAS, RIBEIRO, TARRAGONA, TERRA ALTA, VALDEORRAS, VALDEPEÑAS, VALENCIA, and VINOS DE MADRID. A large number of grape varieties are used throughout Spain for the diverse styles of wine. Red varieties include Azal Tinto, Baga, Borracal, Caiño, Cariñena (CARIGNAN), Espadeiro, Ferron, Garnacha Tinta (GRENACHE), GRACIANO, Mazuelo (Carignan), Mencía, MONASTRELL, Moreto, Pansá Rosado, TEMPRANILLO (also called *Cencibel, Ull de Llebre,* and *Tinto del Pais*), and Tinta Pinheira. The most widely planted white variety in Spain and, in fact, the world is AIRÉN. Other white varieties include Albariño (ALVARINHO), Garnacha Blanca (Grenache), Godello, Loureiro, Malvar, MALVASIA, Merseguera, Moscatel (MUSCAT), PALOMINO, PARELLADA, PEDRO XIMÉNEZ, Planta Nova, Torrontés, Trajadura, Treixadura, Verdil, Viura (MACABEO), XAREL-LO (also called *Pansá Blanca*). In addition, there are some plantings of French favorites including CABERNET SAUVIGNON, CABERNET FRANC, CHARDONNAY, MALBEC, MERLOT, PINOT NOIR, and SAUVIGNON BLANC.

Spanna *see* NEBBIOLO

sparkling *see* SPARKLING WINE

sparkling Burgundy In France, sparkling Burgundies are always the lower-quality wines—red, white or rosé—that are processed by either MÉTHODE CHAMPENOISE or the CHARMAT PROCESS. In the United

States, this term usually describes an inexpensive, lower-quality red wine made by the charmat process.

sparkling wine A term used to describe wine that contains bubbles of CARBON DIOXIDE gas. There are generally four methods to infuse wine with gas. MÉTHODE CHAMPENOISE is the traditional method used in France's CHAMPAGNE region and other countries that make fine sparkling wine. With this method, a second fermentation takes place in the bottle, thereby creating carbon dioxide that permeates the wine. The TRANSFER METHOD is similar to *méthode champenoise* except the RIDDLING and DISGORGEMENT processes are replaced by conveying the wine through a pressurized filtration system and then rebottling it. The CHARMAT PROCESS, also called *bulk process* or *cuve close,* uses large pressurized tanks throughout production. These interconnecting tanks retain the pressure created during a second fermentation throughout the entire process. A fourth method, called CARBONATION, injects carbon dioxide directly into the wine. This last method is the least successful in creating effervescence and is used only for very inexpensive wines. Sparkling wines are measured for pressure in ATMOSPHERES (atms). Technically, an atm is the normal air pressure at sea level, approximately 14.7 pounds per square inch. Sparkling wines such as champagne or SPUMANTE should have 6 atms of pressure. A CRÉMANT-style sparkling wine has about half that pressure, and some FRIZZANTE-style Italian wines may have only 2 atms of pressure. *See also* Opening and Serving Champagne and Sparkling Wines, page 591.

Spätburgunder *see* PINOT NOIR

Spätlese [SHPAYT-lay-zuh] German for "late picking," this wine term refers to grapes that are selectively picked at least 7 days after the main harvest starts for that specific variety. Because such fruit is riper than the grapes from the main harvest, it contains more sugar and produces wines that are rich and sweet. Spätlese is one of the six subcategories of QUALITÄTSWEIN MIT PRÄDIKAT (QmP) and ranks above KABINETT but below AUSLESE, BEERENAUSLESE, EISWEIN, and TROCKENBEERENAUSLESE. To attain the Spätlese category, the natural sugar content of the grapes must reach a certain minimum—76° to 95° OECHSLE, approximately 19 to 23 percent sugar by weight, depending on the region and the variety. The selective picking process makes Spätlese wines quite expensive.

Special Reserve *see* RESERVE

specific gravity The ratio of the density of a substance (such as MUST or wine) to the density of pure water, measured by an instrument called a HYDROMETER. A liquid with precisely the same density as water has a specific gravity (s.g.) reading of 1.000. If it's denser than water (as would be the case if sugar is added), its reading will be over 1.000. When grape juice begins to ferment—converting the sugar into alcohol—the specific gravity drops because the s.g. of pure ALCOHOL is 0.792—lower than that of water. Therefore, a DRY wine, which contains little or no sugar, would have a specific gravity reading below 1.000. In the United States, specific gravity is measured on the BRIX scale, in Germany on the OECHSLE scale, and in France on the BAUMÉ scale.

spicy A analogous winetasting term for the lively, fragrant aroma and flavor of some wines. It's an umbrella term that may cover any of many spices including allspice, cinnamon, cloves, mace, nutmeg, and pepper. This spicy characteristic is usually related to the grape (GEWÜRZTRAMINER has a lot of spiciness) but can also come from the wine's contact with new oak barrels.

Spiegelberg *see* NIERSTEIN

Spielberg *see* BAD DÜRKHEIM

Spiess *see* RUPPERTSBERG

spitzenwein [SHPIHTS-ehn-vine] The Austrian term for "top-quality wine."

split *see* WINE BOTTLES

Spottswoode Vineyard [SPOTS-wood] Premier producer of CABERNET SAUVIGNON and SAUVIGNON BLANC located within the town of St. Helena in the NAPA VALLEY. The Victorian house and land surrounding it were purchased in 1972 by Mary and Jack Novak. Shortly thereafter, about 35 acres were planted with Cabernet Sauvignon, CABERNET FRANC, MERLOT, Sauvignon Blanc, and SÉMILLON. The grapes were sold off until 1982, when Spottswoode Vineyard began making their own wines. About 6,500 cases of wine are made each year, a majority of it Cabernet Sauvignon. Both the Cabernet Sauvignon and Sauvignon Blanc generally receive very good ratings from reviewers. PHYLLOXERA infested the vineyard during the early 1990s, and the Sauvignon Blanc vines have been eliminated in the subsequent replanting. Sauvignon Blanc wines will continue to be made, but from purchased grapes.

Spring Mountain AVA A new AVA situated on Spring Mountain in NAPA VALLEY just west of the town of St. Helena. Although Spring Mountain was a fashionable growing area prior to PROHIBITION, it's only been in the last 20 years that some of these vineyards and wineries have been reestablished. The area has a diversity of microclimates, which allow CABERNET SAUVIGNON, CHARDONNAY, PETITE SIRAH, PINOT NOIR, and ZINFANDEL to do well here. Area wineries include CAIN CELLARS, ROBERT KEENAN, NEWTON VINEYARD, Ritchie Creek, Smith-Madrone, Spring Mountain, STONY HILL VINEYARD, and Philp Togni.

spritzer [SPRIHT-ser] A tall, chilled drink, customarily made with wine and soda water.

spritzig [SHPRIH-tsihg] A German term used to describe slightly SPARKLING WINES that produce a gentle prickling sensation on the tongue. Spritzig is the German equivalent to the French *pétillant* and the Italian *frizzante*.

spritzy [SPRIHT-see] A tasting term for wine with a tiny degree of pinpoint effervescence, just enough to make it seem refreshing. In French, spritzy's counterpart is *perlant*.

spumante; pl. spumanti [spoo-MAHN-tay; spoo-MAHN-tee] Italian for "sparkling," "foamy," or "frothy," referring to fully sparkling wines, as opposed to those that are slightly sparkling (FRIZZANTE). Spumante is made throughout Italy from a variety of different grapes either by the Metodo Classico (MÉTHODE CHAMPENOISE) or by using an AUTOCLAVE (sealed tanks). The most renowned of the spumanti is the sweet ASTI SPUMANTE from the PIEDMONT region, which is made from the MUSCAT grape.

staatliche weinbaudomänen *see* STATE DOMAINS

staatsweingüter *see* STATE DOMAINS

stabilization A process that clears a wine of tartrates (*see* TARTARIC ACID) and small protein particles that might cause it to be cloudy or contain small crystals. **Heat stabilization** is a process for ensuring that wine doesn't develop a haziness or cloudiness when stored at warm temperatures. It's usually accomplished by FINING with an agent such as BENTONITE just prior to bottling. Fining collects the minute particles that cause cloudiness and settles them to the bottom of the storage vessel. The wine is then RACKED to separate the clear wine from the SEDIMENT. **Cold stabilization** is a method of removing tartrates by storing wine at a very low temperature (26° to 32°F) for up to 3 weeks. The flavorless tartrates, which are removed only for aesthetic purposes, fall to the bottom at such cool temperatures, leaving the wine clear.

Stags Leap District AVA California AVA located in the NAPA VALLEY, north of the town of Napa along the Silverado Trail. It runs from the Yountville Crossing south for about 3 miles. Its name comes from an outcropping of red rocks at the area's eastern end, where a stag supposedly escaped his pursuers by leaping across the treacherous gap. This area comprises the right soil and climate to make superb CABERNET SAUVIGNON wines. MERLOT is planted here as well, but CHARDONNAY is losing acreage as growers increasingly turn to Cabernet Sauvignon. The superb grouping of wineries in the area include S. ANDERSON, Chimney Rock, CLOS DU VAL, PINE RIDGE WINERY, SHAFER VINEYARDS, SILVERADO VINEYARDS, ROBERT SINSKEY, STAG'S LEAP WINE CELLARS, Stags' Leap Winery, and STELTZNER VINEYARDS.

Stag's Leap Wine Cellars In 1972 Warren Winiarski established this winery in the STAGS LEAP DISTRICT AVA in the NAPA VALLEY. In 1976 his wines and winery attracted worldwide attention when his 1973 CABERNET SAUVIGNON finished ahead of some well-known French wines and took first place in a Paris tasting organized by Steve Spurrier. Stag's Leap Wine Cellars' original vineyard near the winery consists of about 44 acres. These holdings were expanded in 1986 with the purchase of the adjacent 70-acre Fay Vineyard. These estate-owned vineyards are planted with Cabernet Sauvignon, MERLOT, and PETITE VERDOT. Stag's Leap Wine Cellars (which shouldn't be confused with neighboring Stags' Leap Winery) produces several different Cabernet Sauvignon wines: Napa Valley, made from purchased grapes; SLV, made from estate-grown grapes; and Cask 23, made with grapes from a prime section of the estate's vineyards. In addition, three styles of CHARDONNAY wines are made—Napa Valley, Beckstoffer Vineyard, and RESERVE. RIESLING, SAUVIGNON BLANC, and an occasional Merlot complete the list. **Hawk Crest** is the winery's SECOND LABEL.

stale A winetasting term that describes wines that have lost their vitality and freshness, the result of which is a dull flavor and BOUQUET.

stalky *see* STEMMY

Starkenburg, Bereich *see* HESSISCHE BERGSTRASSE

starter A term used for a YEAST culture added to fresh grape MUST to "start" the FERMENTATION process. Many winemakers use commercially developed yeast cultures with specific characteristics to ensure that fermentation proceeds in a desired fashion.

state domains Scattered throughout Germany are a number of state-owned wine estates which, in addition to conducting research, produce commerically available wines. State domains (called a *Staatsweingüter* or *Staatlichen Weinbaudomänen*) were established by the King of Prussia in the late 1800s and early 1900s. The best known are **Staatsweingüter Eltville** (with acreage in the RHEINGAU and HES-SICHE BERGSTRASSE regions), **Staatliche Weinbaudomäne Trier** (which owns vineyards in the MOSEL-SAAR-RUWER region), and **Staatliche Weinbaudomäne Niderhausen-Schlossböckelheim** (which is in the NAHE region). The quality of the wines from the state domains is quite high, a surprise to those wary of government-run opera-tions. The gold-rimmed state-domain labels display a black and gold eagle.

steely Winetasting term that describes white wines that are LEAN but well BALANCED and quite high in ACIDITY.

Steen *see* CHENIN BLANC

Steigerwald, Bereich *see* FRANKEN

Stein *see* CHENIN BLANC; HOCKHEIM; WÜRZBURG

Steinacker *see* KALLSTADT

Steinberg *see* KLOSTER EBERBACH

Steinmächer *see* RAUENTHAL

Steinmorgen *see* ERBACH

Steinweg *see* BAD KREUZNACH

Steinwein *see* FRANKEN

Steltzner Vineyards [STEHLT-sner] Although Steltzner Vine-yards didn't produce wine until 1977, the vineyards were planted by Dick Steltzner in 1966, and the grapes were sold to others for many years. The winery facility itself wasn't finished until 1983. The winery and vineyard, consisting of 54 acres planted with CABERNET SAUVIGNON, CABERNET FRANC, and MERLOT, are located in the STAGS LEAP DISTRICT AVA in the NAPA VALLEY. Grapes from the estate vineyard go into the pro-duction of the winery's Stags Leap District Cabernet Sauvignon and Merlot wines. SAUVIGNON BLANC is also produced from a vineyard in which Dick Steltzner is a partner. The winery is best known for its high-quality Cabernet Sauvignon wines. Production is between 7,500 and 9,500 cases each year.

stemmer A device for separating grape stems from the crushed grapes. *See also* CRUSHER.

stemmy Also called *stalky,* this winetasting term describes wines that have an astringently harsh, "green" flavor, usually due to pro-longed contact of the juice with grape stems during winemaking.

stem retention A technique used by some winemakers in the making of red wine (particularly PINOT NOIR) where some of the grape stems are added back into the MUST in order to make the wine richer, as well as more TANNIC and VISCOUS. The risk with this process is in making the wine too ASTRINGENT.

sterile filtering *see* FILTERING

Sterling Vineyards The impressive Mediterranean-style sparkling white Sterling Vineyards winery sits prominently on a hill at the northern end of the NAPA VALLEY between St. Helena and Calistoga. The winery, started in 1969 by four partners of the Sterling International Paper Group, was sold to Coca-Cola in 1977 and then to Seagram in 1983. Sterling Vineyards has numerous vineyard holdings throughout the Napa Valley, totaling nearly 1,200 acres. Some of the better-known sites are Diamond Creek Ranch, Winery Lake Vineyard, and Three Palms. Grapes from these vineyards are used in various VINEYARD-DES-IGNATED wines like CABERNET SAUVIGNON and CHARDONNAY from Diamond Creek Ranch, Chardonnay and PINOT NOIR from Winery Lake Vineyard, and a Cabernet Sauvignon and MERLOT blend from Three Palms. Grapes from Three Palms Vineyard are also sold to DUCKHORN VINE-YARDS. Sterling Vineyards' annual production is now over 200,000 cases, with SAUVIGNON BLANC the volume leader. Of all the high-quality wines produced by this winery, the Sterling Reserve, a blend of Cabernet Sauvignon, Merlot, CABERNET FRANC, and PETITE VERDOT, seems to be the most consistent.

still wine A descriptor for wine that contains no CARBON DIOXIDE, which would make it sparkling or effervescent.

J. Stonestreet Winery *see* KENDALL-JACKSON VINEYARDS

Stony Hill Vineyard In 1943, long before Robert Mondavi, Joseph Heitz, or the Davies (SCHRAMSBERG VINEYARDS) led NAPA VALLEY's resurgence in the mid-1960s, Eleanor and Fred McCrea bought land on SPRING MOUNTAIN. They planted 35 acres and sold grapes until the early 1950s, when they built a small winery and began to make and sell wine. Although the vineyard was planted with CHARDONNAY, GEWÜRZTRAMINER, RIESLING, and SÉMILLON, it's the graceful, long-aging Chardonnay wines that have attracted devoted followers for four decades. The annual production here is limited to 4,000 cases, making Stony Hill wines difficult to find.

storing wine *see* WINE CELLAR

Storybook Mountain Vineyard This ZINFANDEL specialist is located in the mountains northwest of the town of Calistoga in the northern part of the NAPA VALLEY. Jerry Seps, a former Stanford University history professor, purchased this 90-acre site in 1976, planted about 36 acres of vines, and produced his first wines in 1980. Storybook Mountain Vineyard now annually produces between 8,000 and 9,000 cases of high-quality Zinfandel—a RESERVE and a regular ESTATE-BOTTLED wine. A previously offered SONOMA COUNTY bottling has been discontinued.

Stravecchia *see* MARSALA DOC

straw wine *see* VIN DE PAILLE

strong *see* POWERFUL

structure In winetasting, the term *structure* refers to a wine's architecture—its plan—which includes all the main building blocks of ACID, ALCOHOL, FRUIT, GLYCEROL, and TANNINS. It's not enough, however, to say that a wine simply has "structure" (which all do). The term should be clarified with adjectives such as *inadequate* or *strong;* one can also refer to a wine as *well structured.*

stuck fermentation *see* FERMENTATION

sturdy Descriptor for a wine that is generally substantial, powerful, and assertive.

Suau, Château [sha-TOH soo-OH] A DEUXIÈME CRU (second growth) located in the SAUTERNES AC in BORDEAUX. It consists of about 20 acres and produces about 1,500 cases of sweet Sauternes AC wine. The wines aren't highly regarded or long-lived and should usually be consumed within the first 5 years. The varieties used are about 85 percent SÉMILLON and 15 percent SAUVIGNON BLANC.

Südlich Weinstrasse *see* RHEINPFALZ

Südtirol *see* ALTO ADIGE

Suduiraut, Château [sha-TOH soo-dwee-ROH] Located in the SAUTERNES AC in BORDEAUX, this extremely large, beautiful estate has about 187 acres set aside for vineyards. This PREMIER CRU (first-growth) property is planted with about 80 percent SÉMILLON and 20 percent SAUVIGNON BLANC. The CHÂTEAU averages 8,000 to 10,000 cases of sweet Sauternes AC wines each year. In the past, there were some problems with consistent quality, but this has improved since the mid-1970s. Suduiraut's best wines, which are very RICH and unctuous, bear a striking resemblance to those of its famous neighbor, Château D'YQUEM, and are capable of AGING for 20 to 25 years. In very rare years, a luxuriously sweet wine, **Cuvée Madame**, is produced.

sugaring *see* CHAPTALIZATION

sugar wine A "wine"—sometimes called **false** or **second wine**—made by adding sugar, water, and TARTARIC ACID to the POMACE after the true wine has all been PRESSED from it. The pomace still contains yeasts, which cause FERMENTATION to begin. The result is a much lighter version of the real wine. It's illegal for commercial wineries to make and sell sugar wines.

sulfites; sulfiting [SUHL-fites] Sulfites are the salts of sulfurous acid. The words "Contains Sulfites" are mandatory on labels of wine sold in the United States if the wine contains 10 ppm or more of sulfites. They're a signal that *sulfur dioxide* (SO_2)—a colorless, water-soluble, nonflammable gas—was used somewhere in the grape-growing or winemaking process. This practice is called **sulfiting** and is utilized by winemakers in a variety of ways. Before harvest, sulfur is often sprayed directly on the vines in an effort to deter many insects and diseases. Once the grapes are crushed, sulfur dioxide is used to inhibit the growth of bacteria, mold, and wild yeasts in MUST, as well as to prevent spoilage or OXIDATION in the finished wine. After the must is treated with sulfur dioxide, the winemaker inoculates it with a YEAST culture that's been selected specifically for that wine. Sulfur dioxide can be added to wine as a gas or as POTASSIUM METABISULFITE, often in the form of Campden tablets. It reacts with the natural acids in grapes to create sulfur dioxide gas. **Sulfur wicks** are sometimes burned to create sulfur dioxide in empty or partially filled wine barrels to prevent the growth of mold. During these processes, some sulfur dioxide combines with the wine, in which case it's called **fixed** or **bound sulfur dioxide;** it has no odor so isn't noticeable. Free sulfur dioxide is that which doesn't combine with wine. Excessive amounts of it produce an undesirable trait indicated by a slight biting sensation at the back of the throat and in the upper part of the nose. **Total sulfur dioxide** includes all bound and free sulfur dioxide in wine, the allowed amounts of which are regulated by law. Sulfites can cause severe allergic reactions in certain sulfite-sensitive individuals. *See also* HYDROGEN SULFIDE; ORGANIC.

sulfur dioxide (SO_2) *see* SULFITES

sulfur; sulphur There are two distinct sulfurous characteristics that affect a wine's smell. One, which occurs when there are excessive amounts of sulfur dioxide (*see* SULFITES), has the smell of a burnt matchstick just after it's lit. This pungent odor is often accompanied by a prickling sensation in the back of the throat and upper part of the nose. A sulphur dioxide characteristic will generally dissipate through aeration, either by DECANTING the wine or swirling it in the glass. The other form of sulfur that can negatively influence wine is HYDROGEN SULFIDE (H_2S), which creates the distinctively foul odor of rotten eggs, sometimes rubber. H_2S that stays too long in wine combines with other constituents to form MERCAPTANS (which smell skunky) and, eventually, DISULFIDES, which reek of sewage.

Sultana [suhl-TAN-uh] Originating in Smyrna, Turkey, this small, pale golden-green grape is the most widely planted variety in California. There it's known as *Thompson Seedless,* after William Thompson, the first commercial Sultana grower in California. In the United States, during the white-wine boom of the 1970s, Sultana was widely used for winemaking. Today, however, varieties like FRENCH COLOMBARD and CHENIN BLANC have diminished Sultana's role. In California, Sultana's use for winemaking ranks third behind its demand first as a raisin and then as a table grape. Sultana is also widely grown in Australia and Chile. It produces a neutral-flavored wine used in JUG WINES and inexpensive SPARKLING WINES.

Sumarello *see* UVA DI TROIA

Sunny St. Helena Winery *see* MERRYVALE VINEYARDS

super-Tuscan *see* TUSCANY

supérieur [soo-pehr-YUR] A French term indicating a somewhat higher-quality wine than the standard. This ranking is generally expressed as a requirement for a slightly higher ALCOHOL content and slightly lower maximum vineyard YIELDS (the latter produces more intense flavors). For example, the BORDEAUX SUPÉRIEUR AC requires a minimum alcohol level of 10½ percent, versus 10 percent for BORDEAUX AC, and BEAJOLAIS-SUPÉRIEUR AC wines must be 1 percent higher in alcohol than those of BEAJOLAIS AC. The maximum vineyard yield for Bordeaux Supérieur AC is set about 20 percent lower than that for the Bordeaux AC.

Superior Old Marsala (SOM) *see* MARSALA DOC

superiore [soo-payr-YOH-reh] The Italian word for "superior." On an Italian wine label, superiore indicates a DOC wine that has a slightly higher alcoholic strength and, sometimes, longer aging capabilities than other DOC wines. The higher alcohol content is due to riper grapes, which results in a fuller flavored and, therefore, superior wine.

supple A winetasting term for well-STRUCTURED wines that are HARMONIOUS, SOFT, and VELVETY—in short, extremely pleasing.

surdo [SOOR-dhoo] Surdo, sometimes called *vinho surdo,* is the Portuguese term for grape juice that has been prevented from FERMENTING by the addition of ALCOHOL. None of the grape sugar has been converted to alcohol, so surdo is very sweet. It's used to sweeten other wines, particularly MADEIRA. The French MISTELLE is a similar solution.

Sur la Velle *see* MONTHÉLIE

sur lie [soor LEE] The French expression for "on the lees." LEES is the coarse sediment, which consists mainly of dead yeast cells and small grape particles that accumulate during fermentation. Winemakers believe that certain wines benefit from being aged *sur lie.* CHARDONNAY or SAUVIGNON BLANC wines are thought to gain complexity if aged in this way for a few months. This happens as a matter of course with SPARKLING WINES made via MÉTHODE CHAMPENOISE because the second fermentation occurs in the bottle where the wine is aged (sometimes for up to 10 years) until the lees are DISGORGED. MUSCADET wines from France's LOIRE region occasionally have the phrase *mis en bouteille sur lie* on the label, which means the wine was bottled from barrels where the lees were not drained (although the sediment has fallen to the bottom of the barrel). These wines have a creamy, yeasty flavor and a touch of CARBON DIOXIDE, which gives a slight prickling sensation on the tongue. *Also see* AUTOLYSIS.

Süssreserve [sooss-ray-ZEHR-veh] German for "sweet reserve," referring to unfermented grape juice that's set aside to be added later to fully fermented (DRY) wines in order to achieve the desired level of sweetness. The Germans developed this technique so that winemakers don't have to be so exacting about arresting FERMENTATION in order to control RESIDUAL SUGAR. The procedure also lowers the use of sulfur dioxide (*see* SULFITES), which is often employed to stop fermentation. There are strict rules about using *Süssreserve,* including limiting its volume to 15 percent of the final wine and ensuring that its origin and quality are the same as the wine to which it's added.

Joseph Swan Vineyards After retiring early from his career as an airline pilot, Joseph Swan purchased a small property in the RUSSIAN RIVER area near the town of Forestville in 1967. Although he planted CHARDONNAY and PINOT NOIR grapes, it was his ZINFANDEL wines, made with grapes purchased from Teldeschi Vineyard, for which he really became famous. The Zinfandels made in the late 1960s and in the 1970s were highly acclaimed and sought after. The Pinot Noir wines were also admired, even though quality was less consistent. Unfortunately, wines produced from Joseph Swan Vineyards in the 1980s and 1990s have not been as well regarded. Joseph Swan died in 1988, and winemaking has been continued by son-in-law Rod Berglund. About 13 acres of vineyard are planted, and about 4,000 cases of wine are produced each year—much of it in small lots from various designated vineyards.

sweet Sweetness is detected on the very tip of the tongue and, in wine, comes from RESIDUAL SUGAR or, occasionally, from GLYCEROL, a byproduct of FERMENTATION. The sugar may be intrinsic (from the grapes) or supplemental (as by adding GRAPE CONCENTRATE) or both. Some fine sweet wines (such as BEERENAUSLESE) are made from grapes that have been left on the vine until they're so overripe that the fruit is sugar-laden and full of rich, concentrated flavors. The juice from such grapes contains more sugar than can be fermented out. Whether or not sweetness in a wine is pleasant or cloying depends on the balance between ACID and sugar. Though the term *sweet* generally applies to the sense of taste, certain components—such as oakiness, which contributes a sweet vanilla essence, or intense fruitiness—can give wine a seemingly sweet smell. Winetasters may therefore use the term *sweet* for both flavor and BOUQUET.

Switzerland Although Switzerland produces a reasonable amount of wine and ranks as one of the top 20 wine-producing countries, few Swiss wines are seen outside the country. There are several reasons for this including the fact that the Swiss consume between 2½ and 3 times what they produce. Their wines are also generally expensive by international standards, and they produce many wines that are specialized for the Swiss market and not widely accepted elsewhere. Like its culture, Switzerland's growing areas can be segmented into French-, German-, and Italian-speaking cantons. The French-speaking cantons include the primary vineyard areas of VAUD and VALAIS, and Geneva, the only canton to introduce a comprehensive APPELLATION system. (Vaud has introduced a less strict version.) The most productive German-speaking cantons are Zürich and Schaffhausen. The most notable Italian-speaking canton is the TICINO or *Tessin*. CHASSELAS (also known as *Dorin, Fendant,* and *Perlan* in various parts of Switzerland) is Switzerland's most widely planted white grape. Generally, it produces neutral, low-ACID, low-ALCOHOL wines that reflect the flavor of the soil in which they're grown. The Swiss like Chasselas wines, although they're not popular outside the country. Red wines are made predominantly with PINOT NOIR and GAMAY grapes, which are often blended together into a wine called Dôle (*see* VALAIS). In the Italian areas, MERLOT is the most popular red grape. Other varieties grown in Switzerland include Amigne, Arvine, BARBERA, FREISA, Johannisberger (RIESLING), Humagne, Malvoisie de Valais (PINOT GRIS), PINOT BLANC, and Riesling-Sylvaner (MÜLLER-THURGAU).

Sylvaner; Silvaner [sihl-VAN-uhr; sihl-VAH-ner; Ger. zihl-vah-nehr] Even though this productive white-wine grape was once the most widely planted vine in Germany (where it's spelled *Silvaner*), it's now been replaced by its more prolific offspring, MÜLLER-THURGAU—a Riesling/Sylvaner HYBRID. Sylvaner, however, is still extensively culti-vated in Germany, particularly in RHEINHESSEN, RHEINPFALZ, and FRANKEN. Although this grape is believed to have originated in Austria, very lit-tle is planted there now. The extensive plantings once found in France's ALSACE region have now also dwindled, and only small amounts of Sylvaner come out of Switzerland and northern Italy. California—where Sylvaner is called *Sylvaner Riesling, Franken Ries-ling, Monterey Riesling,* and *Sonoma Riesling*—has all but abandoned this variety. Sylvaner grapes generally produce LIGHT, SOFT wines with noticeable ACIDITY and pleasant—but not very pronounced—AROMA and flavor. Some of today's best Sylvaner wines come out of Alsace, Franken (where this variety is often called *Franken Riesling*), northern Italy, and Switzerland (where it's frequently called *Johannisberger*). The correct name for this grape is actually *Grüner Sylvaner,* differen-tiating it from the rarely grown, pale-red strain called *Blauer Sylvaner.* Other names for Sylvaner include *Osterreicher* and *Gentil Vert.*

Symphony [SIHM-fuh-nee] A CROSS between Muscat of Alexandria (MUSCAT) and Grenache Gris, developed by the University of California at DAVIS, and introduced in 1981. Symphony has met with limited ac-ceptance and is therefore planted in limited amounts. Symphony wines have a hint of spiceness and sometimes show apricot and peach characteristics. Château de Baun in SONOMA is the best-known pro-ducer of a variety of Symphony wines—from DRY to sweet and from STILL to SPARKLING. This winery's known for the musical names of their various Symphony wines such as *Finale, Rhapsody Rosé,* and *Jazz.*

Syrah [see-RAH] This high-quality red-wine grape gained its repu-tation in France's RHÔNE region. Thought to have originated in the Middle East, the ancient Syrah grape has been grown in the Rhône valley at least since Roman times. In the northern Rhône, Syrah is the principal grape of the esteemed wines from CORNAS, CÔTE-RÔTIE,

CROZES-HERMITAGE, HERMITAGE, and SAINT-JOSEPH. When young, these wines are deep-colored and TANNIC, with strong TAR, SPICE, and PEPPER qualities. Syrahs are long-lived, and as they slowly mature, they take on characteristics of sweet blackberries, black currants, and plums, with hints of SMOKINESS. In the southern Rhône, Syrah is used to contribute flavor and STRUCTURE to the multi-variety WINES from CHÂTEAUNEUF-DU-PAPE and CÔTES-DU-RHÔNE. France's LANGUEDOC ROUSSILLON region has been planting large amounts of new Syrah acreage because it's one of the grapes recommended for improving the quality of that region's wines. *Shiraz,* as Syrah is called in Australia, made its way there in the 1830s and is now that country's most widely planted red grape. Because this grape's so widely cultivated in Australia, an extensive variety of wine styles are produced there—from JUG WINES to very serious wines of international renown. The best of these auspicious wines come from COONAWARRA and the BAROSSA and HUNTER VALLEYS. The most famous Shiraz is the incredibly rich and complex GRANGE HERMITAGE, produced by Penfolds. In California the PETITE SIRAH grape was long thought to be Syrah, but some ENOLOGISTS now believe it actually may be the DURIF variety. True Syrah has been increasingly planted in California over the years, and there are now many more Syrah wines and Rhône-style blends appearing on retail shelves. The ranks of long-time, prominent Syrah producers like JOSEPH PHELPS VINEYARDS and MCDOWELL VALLEY VINEYARDS have been joined by relative newcomers BONNY DOON, EDMUNDS ST. JOHN, and Qupé. Syrah has not significantly established itself in other parts of the world. It's also known as *Hermitage, Marsanne Noir, Petite Syrah,* and *Sirac.*

syrupy A winetasting term generally used to describe RICH, almost thick sweet wines such as a TROCKENBEERENAUSLESE.

szamorodni [sah-moh-RAHD-nee] Hungarian label term meaning "as it comes." It refers to the fact that nothing is added to the wine— usually only ASZÚ paste (*see* TOKAY) is used for sweetening. These wines are therefore generally DRY or semisweet rather than sweet.

száras [sah-RAHSS] The Hungarian word meaning "DRY."

Szükerbarát *see* PINOT GRIS

able wine 1. Any wine that is not FORTIFIED or SPARKLING. 2. In the United States the official definition is a wine that contains a minimum of 7 percent alcohol and a maximum of 14 percent. This definition does not define quality in any way, although some connote table wine with lower-quality, inexpensive wine. That's a mistake because many wines that simply say "Red Table Wine" or "White Table Wine" are excellent and not at all inexpensive. 3. European synonyms for table wine include Germany's DEUTSHER TAFELWEIN, France's VIN DE TABLE, and Italy's VINO DA TAVOLA. Each country has its own definition for table wine.

La Tâche AC [lah TAHSH] A GRAND CRU vineyard that produces what some consider to be the epitome of a red BURGUNDY wine, even ranking it ahead of neighboring grand cru ROMANÉE-CONTI. The nearly 15-acre vineyard is located in the village of VOSNE-ROMANÉE in the CÔTE DE NUITS. It produces more wine than the 4½-acre Romanée-Conti, and its prices are not quite as high (in the $200 to $300 range per bottle for recent VINTAGES). Like Romanée-Conti, La Tâche is wholly owned by the Domaine de la Romanée-Conti. La Tâche AC wines are said to be RICHER and more intense and with a deeper color than those from the Romanée-Conti vineyard, and they possess some of the latter's exotic spiciness.

Tafelstein *see* DIENHEIM

Tafelwein *see* DEUTSHER TAFELWEIN

taglio [TAH-lyoh] The Italian word for "cut." A *vino da taglio* is a "cutting wine"—one with high ALCOHOL, deep color, and/or good BODY. Such wines are added in small quantities to other wines either to correct their deficiencies or to enhance them in some way.

taille [TI] A term used in France's CHAMPAGNE region to describe the juice produced from the second and third PRESSING of the grapes. The juice from the second pressing is called *premiere taille;* the third pressing is *deuxieme taille.* Both are considered lower quality than VIN DE CUVÉE (the juice from the first pressing) and are either used in lower-quality wines or sold off.

Taittinger [taht-teen-ZHEHR] Established in 1734, Taittinger is one of France's important CHAMPAGNE houses. It's located in Reims, in the Champagne region, and produces about 4 million bottles annually. Taittinger's premium brand champagne, Comtes de Champagne, is made in both a BLANC DE BLANCS and a ROSÉ.

Talbot, Château [sha-TOH tahl-BOH] A highly regarded QUA-TRIÈME CRU (fourth growth) CHÂTEAU located in the SAINT-JULIEN AC in the MÉDOC district in BORDEAUX. Although it doesn't appear that he ever owned this château, it was named after John Talbot, the Earl of Shrewbury. He was the English commander who was defeated and killed in the battle at Castillon-la-Bataille, which ended the Hundred Years War and England's 300-year control of the Bordeaux region. Château Talbot includes nearly 250 acres of vineyard planted with about 70 percent CABERNET SAUVIGNON, 20 percent MERLOT, 5 percent CABERNET FRANC, and 5 percent PETIT VERDOT. A small 15-acre plot is planted with SAUVIGNON BLANC. Annual production ranges from 37,000 to 45,000 cases of red wine, as well as a small amount of white wine, which is labeled Caillou Blanc du Château Talbot. The red wines are generally full-flavored, full-bodied (*see* BODY), and TANNIC and can AGE for 20 to 25 years. The white wines are regarded as some of the better examples produced in the Médoc. Château Talbot's SECOND LABEL is **Connétable de Talbot**. The château is owned by Domaines Cordier, which owns a number of estates including the DEUXIÈME CRU (second growth) Château GRUAUD-LAROSE, which is also located in the Saint-Julien AC.

Robert Talbott Vineyard This premier CHARDONNAY producer was founded in 1983. Originally housed in a winery in the CARMEL VALLEY AVA, it has since built a larger facility near the town of Gonzales in the San Lucia Highlands AVA. The new site is planted with about 60 acres of Chardonnay grapes, and the original site has nearly 32 acres. Talbott produces two wines—Monterey County and Diamond T Estate—as well as a SECOND LABEL **Logan**. All three wines are well regarded.

tannic *see* TANNINS

tannins [TAN-ihns] Any of a group of astringent substances found in the seeds, skins, and stems of grapes, as well as in oak barrels, particularly new ones. Tannins are part of a grouping technically called PHENOLIC COMPOUNDS. They are important in the production of good red wines because they provide flavor, STRUCTURE, and TEXTURE and, because of their antioxidant traits, contribute to long and graceful AGING. Tannins often give young wines a noticeable astringency, a quality that diminishes as the wine ages, mellows, and develops character. Wines with noticeable tannins are referred to as *tannic*. Tannins are detectable by a dry, sometimes puckery, sensation in the mouth and back of the throat.

tar A positive winetasting term sometimes used to describe the smell of hot tar occasionally found in some CABERNETS and ZINFANDELS.

Tarragona DO [tah-rah-GAW-nuh] A large DO located in the southern part of Spain's CATALONIA region. The area has three sub-zones—**El Campo de Tarragona**, **La Comarca de Falset**, and **La Ribera d'Erbe**. El Campo de Tarragona is the largest of these sub-zones. It produces mainly white wines from MACABEO, PARELLADA, and XAREL-LO grapes. La Comarca de Falset adjoins the Priorato DO to the north and produces intense red wines from Garnacha Tinta (GRENACHE) and Cariñena (CARIGNAN). La Ribera d'Erbe produces both red and white wines using the aforementioned grapes. Most of the area's wine, much of which is mediocre, is produced by the numerous coopera-tives in the region. *Tarragona Clasico* is a rich, sweet DESSERT WINE that is sometimes FORTIFIED up to 23 percent ALCOHOL.

tart A term used to describe wines that are high in ACID, which pro-duces a harsh, sharp impression on the palate.

tartar *see* TARTRATES

tartaric acid *see* ACIDS

tartrates [TAR-trayts] One of the by-products of tartaric acid (*see* ACIDS) is tartrates, also called *potassium bitartrate, cream of tartar,* and *tartar.* These small, innocuous crystals can appear in wine unless re-moved through the COLD STABILIZATION process. Tartrates aren't harmful and only impact the wine visually.

tastevin [taht-VAH*N*; tahst-VAH*N*] Used in Burgundian cellars for analyzing and tasting wine, a tastevin is a small, shallow silver cup with raised indentations that help reflect the wine's color and exhibit its clarity. It's become customary for a SOMMELIER to wear a tastevin on a chain or ribbon around his or her neck. The Burgundian wine tast-ing fraternity, Chevaliers du Tastevin, was named after the tasting cup.

tasting *see* WINETASTING

tasting terms *see* Winetasting Terms, page 605.

Taurasi DOC; Taurasi Reserve DOCG [tow-RAH-zee] Located east and slightly north of Naples in Italy's CAMPANIA region, this is a highly regarded DOC situated in the hilly area surrounding the vil-lage of Taurasi, northeast of Avellino. The red wine is made primarily from AGLIANCO grapes, although up to 30 percent of BARBERA, Piediroso, and SANGIOVESE can be used. When young, Taurasi wines are noted for their ROUGHNESS due to high TANNINS, noticeable ACIDITY, and a dense concentration of flavors; they're definitely built for AGING. As these wines mature, they can show great BALANCE, with subtle fruit flavors and EARTHY, TARRY, and CHOCOLATY characteristics. Prior to release, Taurasi wines are aged for a minimum of 3 years, one of which must be in wood barrels. The RISERVA, which was upgraded to DOCG status in 1993, has been aged for 4 years. Mastroberardino is the dominant producer in this area.

Tavel AC [ta-VEHL] An AC located just southwest of CHÂTEAUNEUF-DU-PAPE in the southern part of France's RHÔNE region. It makes only ROSÉ wines, which some feel are France's best. Tavel wines, which are generally DRY and more full-bodied (*see* BODY) than most rosés, have an international reputation and are probably the best known rosés from France. They're made primarily from GRENACHE (although this variety can't comprise more than 60 percent of the total) and CINSAUT, even though seven other grapes are allowed.

Tavernelle [tah-vehr-NEHL] The proprietary name for the super-Tuscan (*see* TUSCANY) produced by Villa Banfi, the large American-owned wine estate. Tavernelle is made from 100 percent CABERNET SAUVIGNON and AGED in French oak barrels. It's similar to California-style Cabernets. Tavernelle is produced from vineyards in the Montalcino area, which is south and slightly east of Siena in the southern portion of Tuscany.

tawny port *see* PORT

Taylor, Fladgate & Yeatman One of the premier PORT producers. Its vintage port (considered one of the top three or four) and single-quinta port from Quinta de Vargellas are both very highly regarded. The company was founded in 1692 by Job Bearsley. The company's name comes from John Taylor who joined it in 1816, John Fladgate who came aboard in 1837, and Morgan Yeatman who joined in 1844. The company is still controlled by the Yeatman family, who also own FONSECA GUIMARAENS, another premier port producer. Taylor, Fladgate & Yeatman produces a full line of port wines including tawny and Late Bottled Vintage ports.

T-budding A technique for converting a vine from one specific variety to another, such as from ZINFANDEL to SAUVIGNON BLANC. This comparatively new process is done by cutting off the fruit-bearing part of the vine and grafting the new variety to a T-shaped incision made in the top portion of the ROOTSTOCK. This process speeds up the time in which the new variety is productive by 2 to 3 years. A newly planted vine might take 3 years or more to become fully productive, whereas a variety created by T-budding can be fully productive in the second year. This process is widely used in California and Australia, where it's called *green grafting*.

tears *see* LEGS

Teinturier [ta*n*-tew*r*-EH*R*] Dark-skinned grapes that have red (rather than white) pulp and juice. (Most grapes have white pulp and juice and get their coloring from being in contact with the skins during FERMENTATION.) Teinturier grapes are often planted to be used as a BLENDING WINE to add color to such wines. Examples of Teinturier grapes are ALICANTE BOUSCHET, ROYALTY, and RUBIRED. Most Teinturier grapes have some connection to Alicante Bouschet.

Temecula AVA [teh-MEH-kyoo-luh] AVA located in southern California's Riverside County between the cities of Riverside and San Diego. The main grape varieties here are CHARDONNAY, SAUVIGNON BLANC, CHENIN BLANC, and CABERNET SAUVIGNON. There are about twelve wineries in the area, with Callaway Vineyard & Winery being the largest producer. Others include Maurice Car'rie Vineyards & Winery, Culbertson Winery, and Mount Palomar.

temperature There are two important temperatures to consider with wine—storage and serving. The ideal **storage temperature** is 50° to 55°F, but a range of 45° to 70°F is completely acceptable. What's important is that the storage temperature remain constant or, if it changes, that the change not be drastic. Warmer storage temperatures make stored wines age faster but, unless the temperature is excessively hot, don't damage wine. The **serving temperature** for wine varies depending on the style of wine and one's personal preference. Serving wine too cold masks its aroma and flavor and highlights any bitterness. Serving it too warm can make the flavors unpleasantly FLAT and DULL and the wine seem harshly ALCOHOLIC. White wines are served cold, but how cold is a matter of individual taste. Generally, SPARKLING WINES, CHAMPAGNE, and young, sweet white wines are served colder, about 40° to 50°F. On the other hand, RICH, full-bodied whites like California and Australian CHARDONNAYS and French white BURGUNDIES are better served at around 50° to 55°F. Other white wines should be served somewhere in the 43° to 53°F range, depending on the complexity of their flavor. More intricately flavored wines should be served on the warmer side of this range in order to fully reveal their full scope of aromas and flavors. Because cold masks flavor, flawed or less expensive wines (except those with a bitter characteristic) should be served slightly cooler so detriments aren't so glaringly obvious. Lighter red wines like BEAU-

JOLAIS or VALPOLICELLA are best served at 50° to 60°F, whereas bolder reds like BORDEAUX, RHÔNE, BAROLO, CHIANTI, and California CABERNET SAUVIGNON and ZINFANDEL are best at about 62° to 67°F. Other red wines, such as California PINOT NOIR and red Burgundies, are best served in the 55° to 65°F range, depending how rich and full-bodied they are. The cellar temperature dictates how a wine should be handled before serving. Some will require chilling (if the cellar's not cool enough), while others should be removed from the cellar early so that they can gradually warm to the proper temperature. A cautionary note about serving a wine at "room temperature": today's centrally heated homes can be warmer than the maximum temperature (62° to 67°F) suggested for the bigger red wines. Remember that wine will warm up a little through the natural effects of air, swirling the wine in the glass, and the heat of one's hands. **Chilling or cooling wine** can be accomplished by placing the bottle in a refrigerator for 1 to 2 hours, depending on the desired final temperature. Or wine can be chilled in about 20 minutes by submerging the bottle in an ice (or wine) bucket filled with half cold water and half ice. If the bucket isn't tall enough for the ice and water to cover the bottle's neck, invert the bottle for the last 5 minutes. Invert a bottle only if sediment isn't a problem. In warm environments the ice bucket should be brought to the table to keep the wine cool. Conversely, wines that are too cold can be quickly but gently warmed by placing the bottle in a bucket of warm (70°F) water for about 5 minutes.

Des Templiers *see* LARMANDE, CHÂTEAU

Tempranilla *see* TEMPRANILLO

Tempranillo [tem-prah-NEE-yoh; tem-prah-NEE-lyoh] An important red wine grape native to northern Spain and widely cultivated in the northern and central parts of that country. Tempranillo produces its best results in the cooler growing regions of Rioja Alavesa, Rioja Alta, RIBERA DEL DUERO, and parts of PENÈDES. In these areas, Tempranillo can generate deep-colored wines with characteristics of strawberry, SPICE, and fresh TOBACCO. Because of its lower ACID and ALCOHOL levels, Tempranillo is usually blended with other grape varieties. It's a principal component in the famous RIOJA wines, which are usually blended with Garnacha (GRENACHE), Mazuelo, and GRACIANO. It's also the dominant red variety of VALDEPEÑAS and LA MANCHA; both areas call the grape *Cencibel*. In different regions of Spain, Tempranillo goes by various names including *Ojo de Liebre, Tinto Fino, Tinto del Pais, Tinto de Toro,* and *Ull de Llebre.* Argentina is one of the few places outside of Spain where Tempranillo is widely planted. In the Portugese regions of Alentejo (where this grape's called *Aragonez*) and DOURO (where it's known as *Tinta Roriz*), Tempranillo's a minor grape used in PORT production. There's speculation that *Valdepeñas,* a secondary grape used for JUG WINES in California, might actually be Tempranillo.

tent An old English word (probably derived from the Spanish word TINTO, which means "red") that referred to POWERFUL red wines from Spain, particularly from the area in and around ALICANTE.

tenuta [teh-NOO-tah] An Italian term meaning "holding," which applies to land, and in wine parlance refers to an estate which grows its own grapes and bottles the wine.

Teroldego Rotaliano DOC [teh-*r*awl-DEH-goh roh-tahl-YAH-noh] DOC located in the Campo Rotaliano area in the Trentino province, which is part of the TRENTINO-ALTO ADIGE region in northeastern Italy. Its specialties are ROSSO and ROSATO wines produced in a DRY style from Teroldego grapes.

Terra Alta DO [TEHR-ruh AHL-tah] A new, obscure DO located west of the TARRAGONA DO in southwestern portion of Spain's CATALONIA region. The area is hilly and hot, and the grape YIELDS are low. About 75 percent of the wine produced is white, made from Garnacha Blanc (GRENACHE) and MACABEO. The red and ROSÉ wines are made from Cariñena (CARIGNAN) and Garnacha Tinta (Grenache). Most of the wines are processed by the local cooperatives and are generally high in ALCOHOL and of mediocre quality.

Terrano *see* MONDEUSE

terroir [teh-*R*WAH*R*] French for "soil" and used in the phrase *gout de terroir* ("taste of the soil") to refer to the EARTHY flavor of some wines. When French wine producers use the term *terroir,* it not only includes reference to the type of soil (chalky, claylike, gravelly, sandy), but also to other geographic factors that might influence the quality of the finished wine like altitude, position relative to the sun, angle of incline, and water drainage. In the United States, wine producers use the term MICROCLIMATE to encompass the same considerations. *See also* CLIMAT.

du Tertre, Château [sha-TOH doo teh*r*-T*R*UH] A highly regarded CINQUIÈME CRU (fifth growth) located in the MARGAUX AC in the MÉDOC district in BORDEAUX. It has about about 124 acres of vineyards and produces around 16,000 to 20,000 cases of red wine each year. The SOFT, SUPPLE wines, which are produced from about 85 percent CABERNET SAUVIGNON and small amounts of MERLOT and PETIT VERDOT, generally have a floral BOUQUET (violets) and deep color. Although many VINTAGES can be drunk young, some of the more TANNIC versions can AGE for 15 or more years.

Le Tertre-Roteboeuf, Château [sha-TOH luh tehr-TRUH roht-BURF] The strange name of this CHÂTEAU translates to "the hill of burping beef," apparently in reference to the oxen that used to work the vineyards. This small 11-acre estate averages only about 2,000 cases of red wine each year. Although it's now a GRAND CRU château, experts agree that the wines it produced in the 1980s are good enough to elevate it to a GRAND CRU CLASSÉ or PREMIER GRAND CRU CLASSÉ at the next SAINT-ÉMILION AC reclassification. Château le Tertre-Roteboeuf wines are RICH, CONCENTRATED, and well-STRUCTURED. The bigger (*see* BIG) VINTAGES are capable of AGING for 20 years or more.

Tessin *see* TICINO

Les Teurons *see* BEAUNE

Texas In the last 20 years, this state has gone from one winery to over twenty-five, even though growth slowed during the economic trials of the late 1980s. The history of Texas grape growing goes back at least to the 1660s, when Franciscan monks planted MISSION grapes adjacent to their missions. In the 1880s a Texan by the name of Thomas Volney Munson became a hero to the French when he shipped thousands of ROOTSTOCKS to European vineyards after they'd been attacked by PHYLLOXERA. Texan vineyards initially used native American varieties and HYBRIDS like CHANCELLOR, CHAMBOURCIN, and VIDAL BLANC. In the late 1970s, however, wineries began to move toward European varieties. Today a majority of Texan vineyards grow VITIS VINIFERA grapes including CABERNET FRANC, CABERNET SAUVIGNON, CHARDONNAY, CHENIN BLANC, COLOMBARD, GEWÜRZTRAMINER, MERLOT, MUSCAT, PINOT NOIR, RIESLING, RUBY CABERNET, SAUVIGNON BLANC, and SÉMILLON. Wineries are scattered throughout the state, but the biggest concentrations are around the city of Lubbock in northwest Texas and west of Austin in central Texas. There are also wineries near Fort Stockton in west Texas and some north of the Dallas-Fort Worth area. Texas now has a number of AVAS including Bell Mountain, Escondido Valley, Mesilla Valley, Fredericksberg, and Texas Hill Country. Among the Texas wineries are Bell Mountain, Cordier (formerly Ste. Genevieve), Fall Creek Vineyard, Llano Estacado, Messina Hof Wine Cellars, Moyer Champagne, Pheasant Hill, and Teysha.

texture A winetasting term used for wines that are DENSE, INTENSE, and full-bodied (*see* BODY). Such wines produce a weighty, mouth-filling impression on the palate that makes them seem almost thick.

Thalia *see* TREBBIANO

Thanisch, Wwe, Dr. H. [TAH-nihsh] A famous wine estate in the village of BERNKASTEL in Germany's MOSEL-SAAR-RUWER region. Established in 1650, it developed a worldwide reputation for its wines, particularly those produced from the famous DOCTOR vineyard located in Bernkastel. The estate owns numerous other vineyard sites in the villages of Bernkastel and GRAACH. The vineyards are planted almost entirely with RIESLING, Germany's best grape. The estate was split in 1988, with one section now known as **Thanisch-Knabben** and the other as **Müller-Burggraef**.

thick A winetasting term used for wines that are extremely RICH, almost HEAVY, combined with a lack of ACIDITY.

thief *see* WINE THIEF

thin *see* BODY

third growth *see* TROISIÈME CRU

Thompson Seedless *see* SULTANA

Thunderbird *see* E & J GALLO WINERY

Ticino [tee-CHEE-noh] This Italian-speaking Swiss canton is located in the southern Alps. There are four main wine-producing areas in Ticino—around Lake Lugano, Mendrisiotto, and in the areas north and south of Monte Céneri, Sopraceneri, and Sottoceneri. Ticino produces mostly red wines, with MERLOT the dominant variety. These wines are usually labeled *Merlot del Ticino*. Lower-quality wines made from a mix of red grapes such as BARBERA and FREISA are often labeled *Nostrano* (Italian for "ours"). The word *Nostrano* was once used for VITIS VINIFERA grapes to set them apart from Americano grapes, the latter alluding to NATIVE AMERICAN vines used in this area after PHYLLOXERA wiped out most of the European varieties.

Tierra de Madrid *see* VINOS DE MADRID

Tiffany Hill *see* EDNA VALLEY VINEYARDS

tight; tightly knit A young, undeveloped wine that seems HARD on the palate is sometimes referred to as tight or tightly knit. Such a wine will generally MELLOW with AGING.

Tignanello [tee-nyah-NELL-oh] The proprietary name of the first super-Tuscan wine (*see* TUSCANY) to be commercially successful using a SANGIOVESE/Cabernet blend. It was introduced in 1971 by the famous Tuscan wine firm, Marchesi Antinori (who also makes SOLAIA). At that time, Tuscany's CHIANTI DOCG wines required the use of a small amount of white grapes and AGING in large OAK barrels. Those requirements were ignored with Tignanello, which generally uses about 80 percent Sangiovese and 20 percent CABERNET SAUVIGNON and is AGED in BAR-RIQUES for about 18 months. The resulting BORDEAUX-style red wine is ELEGANT, well-structured, and long-lived. Such admirable qualities encouraged expanded development of this style of wine. Soon following the Tignanello lead were COLTASSALA, FLACCIANELLO, GRIFI, SAMMARCO, I SO-DIDI SAN NICCOLO, and Solaia wines. Departure from Chianti DOCG parameters means Tignanello and other super-Tuscans can be classified only as VINI DA TAVOLA.

Tindilloro *see* CANAIOLO

Tinta *see* GRENACHE

Tinta Cão *see* RUBIRED

Tinta Madeira [TEEN-tuh muh-DEH-ruh] A minor red-wine grape grown in limited amounts on the Portuguese island of MADEIRA, where plantings are now slightly on the increase. In California a small amount of Tinta Madeira is grown (mostly in the CENTRAL VALLEY) and used in the production of PORT.

Tinta Negra Mole *see* NEGRA MOLE

Tinta Roriz *See* TEMPRANILLO

tinto [TEEN-toh] A Spanish word meaning "red" when used to describe wine, as in *vino tinto* ("red wine").

Tinto *see* GRENACHE

Tinto del Pais *see* TEMPRANILLO

Tinto de Toro *see* TEMPRANILLO

Tinto Fino *see* TEMPRANILLO

Tiny Pony *See* IRON HORSE VINEYARDS

tirage [tee-RAHZH] French for "to pull" or "to draw." In France's wine industry, it means "to draw from the barrel," referring to bottling wine; a **tireuse** is a bottling machine. In the CHAMPAGNE region a *liqueur de tirage* (*see* DOSAGE) is added when the wine is bottled to cause a SECONDARY FERMENTATION in the bottle. *En tirage* refers to the time SPARKLING WINE stays in the bottle to AGE, both during this secondary fermentation and after it's complete.

tired A winetasting term for a wine that's DULL, past its prime, and generally uninteresting.

tireuse *see* TIRAGE

tischwein [TIHSH-vine] German for TABLE WINE, but referring to common, ordinary wine. It shouldn't be confused with DEUTSCHER TAFELWEIN, which has certain quality requirements. *Tischwein* is similar to France's VIN ORDINAIRE.

titratable acidity *see* ACIDS

titration *see* ACIDS

toasty In winetasting parlance, a descriptor that refers to the appealing smell of toasted bread, which is particularly desirable in some CHARDONNAYS and SPARKLING WINES. This characteristic is the result of the wine being stored in oak barrels that have charred (or toasted) interiors.

tobacco A descriptor for the BOUQUET of some wines, such as many reds from GRAVES, which is uniquely similar to that of freshly lit tobacco. Such a characteristic is considered desirable.

Tocai; Tocai Friulano A white-wine grape widely grown in and around Italy's FRIULI-VENEZIA GIULIA region. When Tocai (also called *Tocai Friulano*) vines are pruned back and the YIELDS held down, this variety can produce ELEGANT yet LIVELY, full-bodied (*see* BODY) wines. Otherwise, Tocai produces rather bland juice, most of which finds its way into JUG WINES. Tocai is unrelated to Tokay d'Alsace (which is actually PINOT GRIS) or to Hungary's famous TOKAY wines (which are made primarily from the FURMINT grape). *Tocai Italico* is a related clone, but *Tocai Rosso*—a minor red variety—is not. Tocai is also called *Sauvignonasse, Sauvignon,* and *Tokai*.

Tocai Italico *see* TOCAI

Tokai *see* TOCAI

Tokaji Aszú *see* TOKAY

Tokay; Tokay Aszú; Tokay Essencia [toh-KAY ah-SOO; ehs-SIHN-see-uh] 1. This esteemed Hungarian wine ranks as one of the world's best sweet white wines. It comes from the area around the town of Tokay, which Hungarians call *Tokaj*. Hungarian wine labels include the name of the originating area by adding an *i*, which makes it a possessive form. Therefore, labels for this wine display *Tokaji* or *Tokaji Aszú*, though the wines are commonly referred to as Tokay or Tokay Aszú. Tokay-area wines are made primarily from FURMINT grapes, although a small amount of HÁRSLEVELÜ is used and, occasionally, some MUSCAT. The Tokay area is located in the foothills of the Carpathian Mountains in northeastern Hungary. Warm summers combined with the humidity from the area's streams and rivers can create an environment where BOTRYTIS CINEREA (which Hungarians call ASZÚ) develops. The shriveled, botrytis-infected grapes are picked separately and set aside in large vats. **Tokay Essencia**, the rarest and most expensive of the Tokay wines, is made from the small amount of juice that is squeezed out naturally by the weight of the grapes on top of each other. Over a period of years, this syrupy juice slowly ferments in casks called *gönci* (which are approximately 140 liters or 37 gallons in size). This extremely slow process produces a liquid so sweet that the ALCOHOL level rarely exceeds 2 percent. There are numerous stories of the restorative powers of Tokay Essencia, including the fact that it was once reserved principally for dying monarchs. **Tokay Aszú** is made from those same botrytis-infected grapes that gave up much of their juice to make Tokay Essencia. These grapes are kneaded into a paste, which is measured in traditional *puttonyos* (baskets or hods that hold about 25 kilos or 55 pounds). The sweetness and RICHNESS of a Tokay Aszú depends on how many puttonyos go into a gönci (along with regular MUST from uninfected grapes). The more puttonyos, the sweeter and richer the wine. Tokay Aszú labels indicate how many puttonyos have been used—three, four, or five are the norm, and six on rare occasions. Even sweeter and richer than a six-puttonyos Tokay Aszú is the **Tokay Aszú Essencia**, which is made without any regular must. A Tokay Aszú Essencia is not too far removed from a Tokay Essensia and is likened to a German TROKENBEERENAUSLESE. The sugar content of a Tokay Aszú Essencia is so high that it takes several years and the use of a special yeast for it to ferment. **Tokay Szamorodni**, which means "as it comes," is a basic wine made from uninfected grapes without the intentional addition of any aszú grapes. It can range from sweet (*édes*) to DRY (*száraz*), depending on whether or not and, if so, how many aszú grapes were picked along with the uninfected grapes. 2. In Australia, the MUSCADELLE grape is called Tokay.

Tokay d'Alsace *see* PINOT GRIS

Tondo *see* PROSECCO

tonneau [taw-NOH] A volume measurement that was once used in BORDEAUX for selling wine. A *tonneau* is equal to 900 liters (about 238 gallons), which represents the capacity of four French BARRIQUES (225 liters each). Although the tonneau isn't a real barrel or container, it was an old method for pricing wine. It was intially equivalent to 96 cases of wine, a figure that was adjusted to 100 cases in 1977. Today, however, most Bordeaux CHÂTEAUS price their wine by the bottle, not the tonneau.

La Toppe au Vert *see* CORTON

topping; topping-up A term that refers to adding wine to containers, such as oak barrels, to replace liquid that has evaporated. Topping is necessary to ensure there's no airspace (ULLAGE) that would allow air contact with the wine (*see* OXIDIZED). The French term for this procedure is *ouillage*.

Torbato di Alghero [tohr-BAH-toh dee ahl-GEH-roh] The proprietary name for a VINO DA TAVOLA wine produced by Sella & Mosca, a large wine estate on the island of SARDINIA. The highly regarded, DRY white wine, which is made from the Torbato grape, comes in STILL and SPUMANTE versions. Wines labeled Terre Bianche are made from grapes grown in a special vineyard and are considered the best.

Torcolato [tohr-koh-LAH-toh] A proprietary sweet white wine made from Vespaiolo, TOCAI, and GARGANEGA grapes in a RECIOTO style. It's made by Maculan, a highly regarded wine estate in the Breganze district of Italy's VENETO region.

Torgiano DOCG [tohr-jee-AH-noh] DOCG that encircles the town of Torgiano, which is located just south of Perugia in the center of Italy's UMBRIA region. Torgiano covers ROSSO wines made from SANGIOVESE, CANAIOLO, TREBBIANO, Ciliegiolo, and MONTEPULCIANO grapes and BIANCO wines made from Trebbiano, GRECHETTO, MALVASIA, and Verdello. The ROSSO RISERVA has a higher ALCOHOL content and 3 years of AGING. This area's production is so dominated by the Lungarotti firm's production that the DOCG is closely associated with Lungarotti's proprietary brand names—**Rubesco** for the red wines and **Torre di Giano** for the whites. The quality of this firm's wines are so high that recently the area in which it's located was upgraded to DOCG status and is one of the small number throughout Italy to achieve this ranking. The very best wines are the Rubesco Riserva from the Monticchio vineyard and the Torre di Giano Riserva from the Il Pino vineyard.

Torre di Giano *see* TORGIANO DOC

Torres [TAWR-rehs] A highly respected, family-run wine firm based in the PENEDÈS DO in northeastern Spain's CATALONIA region. Miguel Torres, president of the company until his death in 1991, was the consummate salesman, continually opening up new export markets for his company's wines. His son, Miguel A. Torres, a French-trained winemaker with extraordinary talent, took over as president upon his death. A wide variety of wines are produced, some from local grapes and some from European varieties that were planted in the 1960s. The highly regarded white wines include: Viña Sol, a light, fruity wine made from the PARELLADA grape; Gran Viña Sol, a full-bodied (*see* BODY) and complex white wine made with Parellada and CHARDONNAY; Viña Esmeralda, a fragrant, fruity wine made from MUSCAT and GEWÜRZTRAMINER; Waltraud, a RIESLING wine; Fransola (formerly called Gran Viña Sol Green Label), made from Parellada and SAUVIGNON BLANC; and the rare Milmanda, made from select Chardonnay grapes from the Milmanda vineyard in the CONCA DE BARBERÀ DO area. Red wines include the Tres Torres and Gran Sangre de Toro, full-bodied wines made from Garnacha (GRENACHE) and Carinena (CARIGNAN). The Coronas is made from TEMPRANILLO, and the Gran Coronas is made from Tempranillo and CABERNET SAUVIGNON. The Viña Magdala is made from Tempranillo and PINOT NOIR, whereas the Mas Borras is pure Pinot Noir. The premier Torres red wine is the Mas La Plana (formerly called Gran Coronas Black Label), made from 100 percent Cabernet Sauvignon from the Milmanda vineyard.

total acidity *see* ACIDS

total SO$_2$ *see* SULFITES

Tott's Sparkling Wine *see* E & J GALLO WINERY

tough A winetasting term used to describe a full-bodied (*see* BODY), excessively TANNIC wine. Such a wine will often mellow with proper AGING.

Touraine [too-REHN] A large, picturesque, wine-producing provence surrounding the city of Tours in the middle of France's LOIRE Valley, an area commonly known as the château country. Red, white, and ROSÉ wines are produced throughout the region. The grapes used for red wines include CABERNET SAUVIGNON, CABERNET FRANC, GAMAY, MALBEC, and PINOT NOIR. These grapes, plus the local grapes of Grolleau and Pineau d'Aunis, are also used for rosé wines. The two white-wine grapes are CHENIN BLANC and SAUVIGNON BLANC—wines made from this latter grape are usually the best. **Touraine AC** is a general APPELLATION that encompasses most of the surrounding region. There are three villages—Amboise, Azay-le-Rideau, and Mesland—that make higher-quality wines and can therefore append their name to the Touraine AC. In addition, there are a number of smaller appellations scattered throughout the area, some of which are quite well known. These include BOURGUEIL, CHINON, and SAINT-NICOLAS DE BOURGUEIL (all known for their red wines), and JASNIÈRES, MONTLOUIS, and VOUVRAY, which are known for their white wines. Appellations making fully SPARKLING WINES include **Touraine Mousseux AC, Montlouis Mousseux AC,** and **Vouvray Mousseux AC.** Those making lightly sparkling wine include **Touraine Pétillant AC, Montlouis Pétillant AC,** and **Vouvray Pétillant AC.**

La Tour Blanche, Château [sha-TOH lah toor BLAH/\SH] In the CLASSIFICATION OF 1855, this CHÂTEAU was ranked right after the famous Château D'YQUEM for SAUTERNES wines. In 1910 the property was donated to the French government and has become a college of VITICULTURE. The château has about 74 acres and annually produces about 4,000 cases of sweet SAUTERNES AC wine. The blend of grapes used is about 75 percent SÉMILLON, 20 percent SAUVIGNON BLANC, and 5 percent MUSCADELLE. Although many VINTAGES have been mediocre, significant improvement began in 1985. Some wines are now capable of AGING for 15 to 30 years. The château also makes two DRY white wines, **Osiris** and **Le Sec de la Tour Blanche.** Its SECOND LABEL wine, made from lower-quality batches, is **Mademoiselle de Saint-Marc.**

La Tour-Carnet, Château [sha-TOH lah toor kah*r*-nay] A QUATRIÈME CRU (fourth growth) located in Saint-Laurent-et-Benon, part of the HAUT-MÉDOC AC in France's BORDEAUX region. It's a beautiful, moated estate with a thirteenth century tower (*la tour*) and about 77 acres of vineyards. The property was neglected until the 1960s, when new owners took over and replanted the vineyards. Château La Tour-Carnet wines are considered average and not of fourth-growth quality, although certain of the 1980s VINTAGES show promise. The blend of grapes used is about 53 percent CABERNET SAUVIGNON, 33 percent MERLOT, 10 percent CABERNET FRANC, and 4 percent PETIT VERDOT. The best vintages can AGE for up to 10 or 12 years.

La Tour d'Aspic *see* HAUT-BATAILLEY, CHÂTEAU

Tour-de-Marbuzet *see* HAUT-MARBUZET, CHÂTEAU

Tour du Haut-Moulin, Château [sha-TOH toor doo oh moo-LAH/\] A highly regarded CRU BOURGEOIS château located near the COMMUNE of Cussac in the HAUT-MÉDOC AC in BORDEAUX. The CHÂTEAU consists of nearly 86 acres planted with about 55 percent CABERNET SAUVIGNON, 40 percent MERLOT, and 5 percent PETIT VERDOT. The annual production is from 17,000 to 20,000 cases of red wine. These RICH, full-flavored wines are comparable to many CRUS CLASSÉS (classed growths). The bigger (*see* BIG) VINTAGES are capable of aging for 12 to 14 years.

Les Tourelles de Balestard *see* BALESTARD-LA-TONNELLE, CHÂTEAU

Les Tourelles de Pichon *see* PICHON-LONGUEVILLE BARON, CHÂTEAU

La Tour-Haut-Brion *see* LA MISSION HAUT-BRION, CHÂTEAU

Touriga Francesa [too-REE-gah fran-SAYS-kuh] Portuguese red-wine grape that is important in the production of PORT. Although Touriga Francesa is lighter and more delicate in body, color, and flavor than TOURIGA NACIONAL, it has a wonderful perfumy character that makes it perfect for port blends.

Touriga Nacional [too-REE-gah nah-syoo-NAHL] This high-quality Portuguese red-wine grape is thought to be the preeminent variety for making PORT. The very best VINTAGE ports are based on this grape. Touriga Nacional is widely grown in Portugal's DOURO region. It's also highly prized in the DÃO region, where it's known simply as *Touriga,* and where it must represent 20 percent of that region's red-wine blends. This vine yields very small, concentrated berries that produce wines that are very dark, fruity, aromatic, and TANNIC. Touriga Nacional is also known as *Mortagua.* Related subvarieties include *Touriga Fina, Touriga Foiufeira,* and *Touriga Macho.*

La Tour-Léognan, Château *see* CARBONNIEUX, CHÂTEAU

La Tour-Martillac, Château [sha-TOH lah toor mahr-tee-YAHK] Located in the PESSAC-LÉOGNAN AC, this CHÂTEAU is a well-known CRU CLASSÉ of the GRAVES district. The estate consists of just over 60 acres, 75 percent of which is planted with red varieties—approximately 60 percent CABERNET SAUVIGNON, 30 percent MERLOT, and small amounts of CABERNET FRANC, MALBEC, and PETIT VERDOT. The white grapes used are about 55 percent SÉMILLON, 40 percent SAUVIGNON BLANC, and 5 percent MUSCADELLE. Annual production is about 10,000 cases of red wine and about 2,000 cases of white wine. The red wines are viewed as average, but the white wines are considered worthy of the *cru class* ranking. The château's SECOND LABEL is **La Grave-Martillac**.

Tournelle des Moines *see* BEAU-SÉJOUR-BÉCOT, CHÂTEAU

Tours de Malle *see* DE MALLE, CHÂTEAU

Traisen [TRI-zen] A small wine-producing village located southwest of BAD KREUZNACH in Germany's NAHE region. It's best known for superb RIESLING wines produced from two EINZELLAGEN—**Bastei** and **Rotenfels**.

Traminac *see* GEWÜRZTRAMINER

Traminer *see* GEWÜRZTRAMINER

Traminer Aromatico *see* GEWÜRZTRAMINER

Traminer Aromatique *see* GEWÜRZTRAMINER

Traminer Musqué *see* GEWÜRZTRAMINER

Traminer Parfumé *see* GEWÜRZTRAMINER

Tramini *see* GEWÜRZTRAMINER

transfer method A method of making SPARKLING WINE that's similar to MÉTHODE CHAMPENOISE. The major difference is that—instead of the RIDDLING and DISGORGEMENT steps—the wine, after a second fermentation in the bottle, is transferred to a pressurized tank where it passes through a filtration system to remove sediment. Sparkling wines made this way may be labeled "bottle fermented," "fermented in the bottle," or "transfer method."

Trebbianino Val d'Arda *see* COLLI PIACENTINI

Trebbiano [treb-BYAH-noh; treh-bee-AH-noh] A very important white-wine grape, not because it produces great wines, but because it's so extensively planted. Estimates indicate that Trebbiano produces more wine than any other variety in the world even though the AIRÉN is planted on more acreage. However, these rather neutral wines have high ACID, medium ALCOHOL, and very little discernible aroma or flavor. The Trebbiano grape is most often blended with varieties exhibiting more dominant traits. Originating in central Italy, Trebbiano spread throughout that country and across the border to become France's most important white variety as well. In Italy it's so extensively grown that in some areas it's difficult to find a bottle of white wine that doesn't contain some Trebbiano. In TUSCANY, the laws controlling wine production specify that a certain amount of Trebbiano and MALVASIA (another white-wine grape) be blended into their red wine CHIANTI. There are many different Trebbiano clones, *Trebbiano Toscano* and *Trebbiano Romagnolo* being the most important. *Trebbiano Abruzzo,* however, is actually a different variety— BOMBINO BIANCO. In France, where this grape is known by various names including *Ugni Blanc* and *Saint-Émilion,* large amounts of Trebbiano wine is processed into brandy, including the finest from COGNAC and ARMAGNAC. Other French names for this grape include *Clairette Ronde* and *Clairette Rose*—sometimes confusing because there's an entirely different variety called CLAIRETTE. Trebbiano is also planted in eastern Europe, Australia, South America, and Portugal, where it's called *Thalia*. It's known as *Saint-Emilion* in California and planted mainly in the SAN JOAQUIN VALLEY, where it's primary use is in the production of brandy.

Trebbiano Abruzzo *see* BOMBINO BIANCO

Trebbiano d'Abruzzo *see* BOMBINO BIANCO

Trebbiano d'Abruzzo DOC [treh-BYAH-noh dah-BROOD-zoh] DOC located in Italy's ABRUZZI region and covering a number of vineyard areas throughout the region. It's one of the two DOCs to use the name of the TREBBIANO grape (the other is *Trebbiano di Romagna* in Italy's EMILIA-ROMAGNA region). The odd thing is that this DOC adopted this name because the main grape variety used is the *Trebbiano Abruzzo,* which actually appears not to be Trebbiano, but an entirely different variety—BOMBINO BIANCO. The wines of this DOC can use Trebbiano Toscano (*see* TREBBIANO) grapes instead, but the better wines generally come from Bombino Bianco grapes. Up to 15 percent of other white grapes can be used as well. Generally the quality of the Trebbiano d'Abruzzo DOC wines is not very high, but there are a few producers who keep YIELDS down and produce some very good wines.

Trebbiano Romagnolo *see* TREBBIANO

Trebbiano Toscano *see* TREBBIANO

Trefethen Vineyards [treh-FEH-thihn] This 600-acre vineyard and century-old winery are situated in the center of the NAPA VALLEY, just north of the city of Napa, California. In 1968 the property was purchased by the Trefethens, who proceeded to restore the 1886-built winery. Gradually, they planted the vineyard with CABERNET SAUVIGNON, CHARDONNAY, PINOT NOIR, and RIESLING. Grapes have been sold to other wineries since the first crop was harvested. The winery made its first wines in 1973 and annual production has grown to between 75,000 and 80,000 cases. Today, the winery produces Chardonnay, Cabernet Sauvignon (regular and RESERVE), Riesling, and two lower-priced blends—Eschol Red and Eschol White.

Trentino DOC [trehn-TEE-noh] This is a large DOC that covers the Trentino province—it's the southern portion of Italy's TRENTINO-ALTO ADIGE region. Most of the vineyards are scattered around the Adige River Valley that meanders from north to south. The northern third of this area is much like the neighboring ALTO ADIGE just to the north— both in the Austrian culture and in the wine. From the city of Trento south it becomes much more Italian. The Trentino DOC authorizes seventeen VARIETAL WINES—Cabernet (from Cabernet Sauvignon and Cabernet Franc), CABERNET SAUVIGNON, CABERNET FRANC, CHARDONNAY, LANGREIN, Marzemino, MERLOT, MUSCAT (both Moscato Giallo and Moscato Rosa), MÜLLER THURGAU, Noisiola, Pinot Bianco (PINOT BLANC), Pinot Grigio (PINOT GRIS), Pinot Nero (PINOT NOIR), Riesling Italico (WELSCHRIESLING), Riesling Renano (RIESLING), and Traminer Aromatico (GEWÜRZTRAMINER). There's also BIANCO (made from a blend of white grapes), ROSSO (made from a red-grape mixture), and VIN SANTO (made from Noisiola grapes). The Trentino province also has several individual DOCs including CASTELLER, Sorni, TEROLDEGO ROTALIANO, and VALDADIGE.

Trentino-Alto Adige [trehn-TEE-noh AHL-toh AH-dee-jeh] Wine-producing region located in northeastern Italy and bordered by LOMBARDY on the west, VENETO on the east, and Austria on the north. It consists of two provences—Alto Adige in the north and Trentino in the south—which, although linked together into one region, are quite different. **Alto Adige**, also known as *South Tyrol* or *Südtirol,* is officially bilingual. It has a German-speaking majority that still has strong ties to Austria, which ceded this area to Italy in 1918. Alto Adige wines reflect this bilingual approach on their labels—a wine made from the PINOT BLANC grape might be referred to as both *Weissburgunder* and *Pinot Bianco* (both synonyms for Pinot Blanc). In addition to the ALTO ADIGE DOC, which covers this whole provence, there are a number of smaller DOCs such as Colli di Bolzano, Lago di Caldaro, Meranese di Collina, SANTA MADDALENA, Terlano, and Valle Isarco. **Trentino**, the southern portion of this region, begins north of the city of Trento and continues south. This part of Trentino-Alto Adige is much more Italian. The TRENTINO DOC covers the whole southern portion and includes a number of VARIETAL WINES like CABERNET SAUVIGNON and MERLOT. In addition, there are several individual DOCs such as CASTELLER, Sorni, TEROLDEGO ROTALIANO, and VALDADIGE. Over half the total wine production of Trentino-Alto Adige is DOC wine (the highest percentage of Italy's twenty wine-producing regions), and a majority is red. The dominant red grapes are the local varieties LAGREIN, SCHIAVA (also called *Vernatsch*), and Lambrusco a Foglia Frastagliata (which is apparently unrelated to the other LAMBRUSCO varieties found throughout Italy). There are also wines made from Marzemino grapes. There are many well-known white-grape varieties grown in the region including CHARDONNAY, MÜLLER-THURGAU, Pinot Bianco (Pinot Blanc), Pinot Grigio (PINOT GRIS), RIESLING, SAUVIGNON BLANC, and GEWÜRZTRAMINER—the latter is thought to have originated in the Alto Adige village of Tramin (*Temeno*).

Treppchen *see* ERDEN; PIESPORT

Tricastin *see* CORTEAUX DU TRICASTIN

Trier [TREER] A city that has existed for over 2,000 years, with its wine-producing origins dating back to Roman times. It's located in Germany's MOSEL-SAAR-RUWER region along the Mosel River north of where the Saar River joins the Mosel. Trier, which is the largest and most important city in this region, is where many of the leading wine estates, like BISCHÖFLICHEN WEINGÜTER and FRIEDRICH-WILHELM-GYMNASIUM, keep their cellars. The city has nearly 1,000 acres of vineyards, which are included in the BEREICH of SAAR-RUWER and the GROSSLAGE of Römerlay.

trocken [TRAWK-uhn] German word meaning "dry." Officially, a wine labeled "trocken" must meet the following requirements: RESIDUAL SUGAR may not exceed 4 grams per liter (0.4 percent), but it may go up to 9 grams per liter (0.9 percent) as long as the TOTAL ACIDITY is within 2 grams per liter of the residual sugar. For example, if residual sugar is 9 grams, then total acidity must be at least 7; if total acidity is only 6 grams, then the residual sugar can't exceed 8 grams.

Trockenbeerenauslese [TRAWK-uhn-bay-ruhn-OWS-lay-zuh] The German term for "dry selected berries," used to describe wines made from specially selected, overripe grapes that are left on the vine until nearly dry. Because these grapes—picked one by one at fullest maturity—are very concentrated in flavor and sugar, they produce extremely rich, nectarous wines. Trockenbeerenauslese is the highest subcategory of QUALITÄTSWEIN MIT PRÄDIKAT and ranks above KABINETT, SPÄTLESE, AUSLESE, BEERENAUSLESE, and EISWEIN. To attain the Trockenbeerenauslese category, the natural sugar content of the grapes must reach a certain minimum (150 OECHSLE, approximately 35 percent sugar by weight), depending on the region and the variety. The grapes are usually infected with BOTRYTIS CINEREA (*Edelfäule* in German), which shrivels them and thereby concentrates the sugar. The superior wines made from these grapes are extremely sweet but have enough ACID for proper BALANCE. Because of the extraordinarily high sugar content, these wines frequently have trouble FERMENTING and often contain only 5.5 to 6 percent alcohol (from a potential of 21.5 percent or more if fermented DRY). Trockenbeerenauslese wines are exceptionally rare, extremely expensive (even more than Beerenauslese wines), and considered to be one of the world's premier DESSERT WINES. They will AGE for many years, during which time they'll develop even more complexity.

troisième cru [twah-zyem KROO] The French phrase for "third growth," referring to the third-highest subcategory of the MÉDOC area's CRUS CLASSÉS (classed growths), which were established in the CLASSIFICATION OF 1855. Fourteen CHÂTEAUS were ranked as *troisième cru* in 1855, and this hasn't changed.

Trollinger   *see* SCHIAVA

Troplong-Mondot, Château [sha-TOH troh-LAW*N* maw*n*-DOH] A GRAND CRU CLASSÉ estate located in the SAINT-ÉMILION AC in BORDEAUX. The vineyard covers about 72 acres planted with approximately 65 percent MERLOT, 15 percent CABERNET SAUVIGNON, 10 percent CABERNET FRANC, and 10 percent MALBEC. The estate annually produces about 10,000 to 11,000 cases of red wine. These wines (particularly the VINTAGES since 1985) are highly regarded and viewed as deserving an upgrade to PREMIER GRAND CRU CLASSÉ status. Recent vintages have been full-bodied (*see* BODY), full-flavored, and TANNIC enough to AGE 15 years or more. A SECOND LABEL **Mondot** was introduced in the mid-1980s for lower-quality batches of wine.

Trotanoy, Château [sha-TOH traw-tah-NWAH] A highly regarded CHÂTEAU located in the POMEROL AC in BORDEAUX. The quality of the wines is thought to be equivalent of a DEUXIÈME CRU (second growth) of the MÉDOC. Château Trotanoy has about 20 acres and produces from 3,000 to 5,000 cases of red wine annually. It uses 80 to 85 percent MERLOT, along with small amounts of CABERNET FRANC and CABERNET SAUVIGNON. The wines are generally dark and CONCENTRATED and capable of AGING for 15 to 20 years.

Trottevieille, Château [sha-TOH trawt-VYEH-yuh] One of the famous PREMIERS GRANDS CRUS CLASSÉS of the SAINT-ÉMILION AC in BORDEAUX. It consists of nearly 25 acres and produces about 4,000 to 5,000 cases of red wine each year. The blend of grapes used is approximately 50 percent MERLOT, 45 percent CABERNET FRANC, and 5 percent CABERNET SAUVIGNON. Although reviews have been mixed for VINTAGES prior to the mid-1980s, they've been quite positive since. Recent vintages appear capable of AGING for 15 to 20 years.

Trouchet Noir   *see* CABERNET FRANC

Trousseau Gris [troo-soh GREE] Gray mutation of the red Trousseau grape that is used to make white wines. It's grown principally in France's Jura region and in California, where it's called *Gray Riesling*. It's not as popular in California as it once was. Small amounts are also grown in New Zealand where it's called *Grey Riesling*. The wines produced from Trousseau Gris are generally mild, have muted aromas and flavors, and light ACIDITY. The styles can range from DRY to medium-sweet. In California, small amounts of CHENIN BLANC or SYLVANER are often blended with Trousseau Gris to enhance the resulting wines. Another name for Trousseau Gris is *Chauche Gris.*

Tschaggel *see* SCHIAVA

Tschaggelevernatsch *see* SCHIAVA

Tudal Winery [too-DAHL] Until urban sprawl compelled him to move in 1973, Arnold Tudal was a farmer in Alameda County, California. Tudal choose 10 acres in the NAPA VALLEY between the towns of St. Helena and Calistoga. After a try at growing walnuts, he planted CABERNET SAUVIGNON and produced his first wine in 1979. Initial wines were quite successful, although VINTAGES in the late 1980s have been less consistent than earlier releases. Only about 2,500 cases of wine are made each year.

Tunisia [too-NEE-zhuh] Like its neighbor ALGERIA, this north African country was greatly influenced by French winemaking traditions. Its modern vineyards were originally planted by the French, although they were nearly wiped out by the PHYLLOXERA epidemic that spread to this area in the 1930s. Tunisia produces mainly red and ROSÉ wines from French style grapes—ALICANTE BOUCHET, CARIGNAN, GRENACHE, MOURVÈDRE, CABERNET SAUVIGNON, and PINOT NOIR. Tunisia is also recognized for its MUSCAT wines, particularly the fortified DESSERT WINES. Its main vineyards are all located around the Gulf of Tunis.

Turkey It's conjectured that Turkey's winemaking history may go back as far as 6,000 years. The modern wine industry was reborn in the 1920s after being essentially shut down by Islamic traditionalists. Today the main growing areas are central and eastern Anatolia, Trakya, and the area around Izmir on the Aegean coast. Many of the vines are native, and a number of European varieties are grown in Trakya. Native red varieties include Adakarasi, Karasakiz, and Papazkarasi; native white grapes include Apincak (or Yapincak), Beylerce, Emir, and Narince. Imported vines include CABERNET SAUVIGNON, CARIGNAN, CHARDONNAY, CINSAUT, CLAIRETTE, GAMAY, MERLOT, MUSCAT, PINOT NOIR, RIESLING, SÉMILLON, and SYLVANER. Tekal, the state-run monopoly, dominates wine production and has over twenty wine-producing facilities scattered throughout the country. Turkey also has over 100 private wineries, the best known of which are Kutman's Villa Doluca and Kavaklidere.

Tuscany [TUHS-kuh-nee] Tuscany (*Toscana* in Italian), a wine-producing region in central Italy, has been producing its best-known wine CHIANTI for centuries. In addition to the Chianti DOCG, the Tuscany area has four other DOCGS—BRUNELLO DI MONTALCINO, CARMIGNANO, VINO NOBILE DI MONTEPULCIANO, and VERNACCIA DI SAN GIMIGNANO, all of which are red-wine areas. These Tuscan DOCGs represent five out of the total of fourteen in all of Italy. Tuscany, whose capital city is Florence, is also leading the shift to higher-quality wines, whether or not they're DOC/DOCG. These wines, known as **super-Tuscans**, are produced using unapproved methods (like AGING in small, nontraditional oak barrels), unapproved varieties (like CABERNET SAUVIGNON and MERLOT), or an unapproved composition (like using 100 percent SANGIOVESE, made in areas where it's not approved). Although placed in the VINO DA TAVOLA category, these super-Tuscans are in some cases superior to DOCG wines and are able to command higher prices. Examples of these super-Tuscans using red grapes are Ca' del Pazzo, COLTASSALA, FLACCIANELLO, Fontalloro, GRIFI, SASSICAIA (upgraded to DOC status in 1994) SAMMARCO, I SODIDI SAN NICCOLO, SOLAIA, TAVERNELLE, and TIGNANELLO. Super-Tuscan whites include GALESTRO and PRELUDIO. Tuscany also has numerous DOCs including ELBA, MONTECARLO, MORELLINO DI SCANSANO, MOSCADELLO DI MONTALCINO, POMINO, ROSSO DI MONTALCINO, and ROSSO DI MONTEPULCIANO. It is also well known for its VIN SANTO. The dominant red grape grown in Tuscany is SANGIOVESE, but CABERNET SAUVIGNON and CABERNET FRANC are also important. CANAIOLO, which historically played a meaningful role in Chianti production, is diminishing in importance. Tuscany's most important white grape is TREBBIANO. Other white grapes include MALVASIA, VERNACCIA DI SAN GIMIGNANO, CHARDONNAY, Pinot Gigio (PINOT GRIS), Pinot Bianco (PINOT BLANC), SAUVIGNON BLANC, and SÉMILLON.

gni Blanc *see* TREBBIANO

Ugni Noir *see* ARAMON

ullage [UHL-ihj] The empty space that develops in bottles, barrels, or casks as wine evaporates. It's important for the ullage in casks or barrels to be kept to a minimum by TOPPING so that the air exposure won't cause the wine to become OXIDIZED. Older bottles of wine may have a larger space between the CORK and the wine simply because of their age. However, a young bottle of wine with a large ullage could indicate a faulty cork.

Ull de Llebre *see* TEMPRANILLO

Umbria [UHM-bree-uh; OOM-bree-uh] Wine-producing region located in central Italy, bordered on the west by TUSCANY and on the east by the MARCHES. Some of Italy's most famous wines—like the whites from the ORVIETO DOC—come from Umbria. There are seven other DOCS in this hilly region including Colli Altotiberini, Colli del Trasimeno, Colli Perugini, MONTEFALCO, and TORGIANO (the red RISERVA wines have DOCG status). As in Tuscany, a fair amount of VIN SANTO is also made here. Umbria's most popular grapes are TREBBIANO, GRECHETTO, and Verdello for white wines and SANGIOVESE, Cilegiolo, CANAIOLO, and Sagrantino for red and ROSÉ wines.

Umpqua Valley AVA [UHMP-kwah] AVA that encompasses the towns of Umpqua and Roseburg, about 180 miles south of Portland, Oregon, and just south of the WILLAMETTE VALLEY AVA. It's located in the prime growing region between the coastal range to the west and the Cascade Mountains. Like the Willamette Valley, it's cool and therefore classified as a Region I growing area (*see* CLIMATE REGIONS OF CALIFORNIA). PINOT NOIR and CHARDONNAY are the most popular varieties. Small amounts of other grapes are planted including CABERNET SAUVIGNON, GEWÜRZTRAMINER, MÜLLER-THURGAU, RIESLING, and ZINFANDEL. Area wineries include Girardet, Henry Estate, and Hillcrest Vineyard (founded in 1963).

Umstadt, Bereich *see* HESSISCHE BERGSTRASSE

unfiltered A term for wine that has not been filtered (*see* FILTERING), a process which, according to some winemakers, removes some of a wine's flavor and body along with any SEDIMENT. An unfiltered wine has undergone other processes such as CENTRIFUGING, COLD STABILIZATION, FINING or RACKING to remove particles from the wine. Unfiltered wines, which are usually labeled as such, often leave a small deposit of sediment in the bottle.

unfined Some winemakers believe that FINING takes too much flavor and body out of wines, so they rely on other processes (CENTRIFUGING, COLD STABILIZATION, FILTERING, RACKING) to remove the particles from wine. Wines bottled without fining are sometimes labeled "Unfined" to point out that wine should be more flavorful. Unfined wines may throw off a small amount of SEDIMENT in the bottle.

Ungeheuer *see* FORST

United States Depending on annual production, the United States ranks as the world's fourth or fifth largest wine-producing nation. U.S. wine consumption has increased about 400 percent over the last 25 years. Even so, on a per capita basis Americans consume only one-seventh to one-eighth the wine that the French, Italians, or Portuguese do. About 95 percent of U.S. wines are produced in CALIFORNIA, which would rank California in about fifth or sixth place if it were a nation. California's CENTRAL VALLEY provides 75 to 80 percent of the state's wine, and although the quality of Central Valley wine is improving, most of it is considered rather ordinary. On the other hand, most higher-quality U.S. wine comes from California, although it's not the only state producing first-rate wine. WASHINGTON is now viewed as having the second largest fine wine production. And wine is produced in at least 42 other states. As for U.S. wine-production quantities, NEW YORK ranks second and OHIO third. Most of the wine from these states, however, is made from native American grapes and French-American HYBRIDS, neither of which produce top-notch wines. The resurgence in quality-wine production, which started in California in the mid-1960s (decades after PROHIBITION almost decimated the wine industry), has triggered a similar rally in other parts of country. Now there are over 1,400 wineries scattered throughout the nation. Over half of these are in California, but there are over eighty each in New York and Washington, seventy in OREGON, fifty in VIRGINIA, thirty in New Mexico, and twenty-five in TEXAS. In 1983 the United States implemented the AMERICAN VITICULTURAL AREA (AVA) system, which is designed to identify U.S. wines in a fashion similar to France's APPELLATION D'ORIGINE CONTRÔLÉE for French wines. Unlike the French regulations, however, AVA rules (under the jurisdiction of BATF—Bureau of Alcohol, Tobacco, and Firearms) are extremely lax and must be strengthed before they become truly meaningful. There are now over 120 AVA areas throughout the United States.

unripe; underripe A winetasting term used for wine made from grapes that have been picked before they're fully ripe. Such grapes generally have high ACIDITY, GREEN flavors, and a lack of CHARACTER.

Untermosel *see* ZELL

Ürzig [UHR-tsikh] A tiny village situated on the Mosel River in Germany's MOSEL-SAAR-RUWER region. Its highly regarded wines are known for their distinctive spicy character, which comes from the area's red clay soil. Urzig's best known vineyard is **Würzgarten**, which means "spice garden."

Utiel-Requena DO [oo-TYEHL *r*eh-KEH-nah] DO located west of the city of Valencia in the Levante region of eastern Spain. It encompasses the towns of Utiel and Requena and touches the Valencia DO on its eastern boundary. This area produces good ROSÉ wines and full-bodied (*see* BODY) reds, mainly from the Bobal grape, with minor use of TEMPRANILLO and Garnacha (GRENACHE). Utiel-Requena's rather ordinary white wines are made from MACABEO, Merseguera, and Planta Nova.

uva [OO-vah] The Italian word for "grapes."

Uva Abruzzi *see* MONTEPULCIANO

Uva Canina *see* CANAIOLO

Uva della Marina *see* UVA DI TROIA

Uva di Troia [OO-vah dee TROY-uh] A high-quality red wine grape grown primarily in the Italian region of APULIA. Uva di Troia is one of the basic grapes of several DOCs, most notably that of CASTEL DEL MONTE. This grape makes rich, concentrated wines with good aging potential. Uva di Troia, also known as *Sumarello* and *Uva della Marina,* is usually blended with other varieties such as BOMBINO NERO, MONTEPULCIANO, and SANGIOVESE.

Uva Merla *see* CANAIOLO

Uva Vermiglia *see* CROATINA

A *see* VOLATILE ACIDITY

Vacqueyras [va-keh-*R*AS] One of the better wine-making villages, which is located northeast of CHÂTEAU-NEUF-DU-PAPE in the southern portion of France's RHÔNE region. It's one of the seventeen villages entitled to use the CÔTES DU RHÔNE-VILLAGES AC, and the label also usually includes this village's name. Vacqueyras is best known for its red wines, which generally exhibit dark color, spicy fruit and enough TANNINS to age well. The main grapes used for red wines are GRENACHE, SYRAH, CINSAUT, and MOURVÈDRE.

Vaillons *see* CHABLIS

Valais [va-LEH; va-LAY] Canton that contains one of Switzerland's best growing climates—dry and sunny—and is therefore one of the two main growing regions (the other being VAUD). The vineyards are located in the upper valley of the Rhône in the southwestern part of Switzerland not far from the Italian border. Valais produces mostly white wines, and CHASSELAS (locally known as *Fendant*) is the dominant grape. GAMAY and PINOT NOIR are the most popular red grapes in this area. They're often blended together in a wine called **Dôle**, which is similar to a light-bodied, red BURGUNDY. Dôle, which must contain 51 percent Pinot Noir, is regarded as one of Switzerland's best red wines. Lower-quality versions (those with less than 51 percent Pinot Noir) of this same blend are called **Goron**. Valais also grows Amigne, Arvine, Johannisberger (RIESLING), Humagne, and Malvoisie de Valais (PINOT GRIS) grapes.

Valcalepio DOC [vahl-kah-leh-PEE-oh] DOC located in the center of Italy's LOMBARDY region northeast of Milan and just east of Bergamo. Valcalepio makes a BIANCO wine from Pinot Bianco (PINOT BLANC) and Pinot Grigio (PINOT GRIS) and a ROSSO from MERLOT and CABERNET SAUVIGNON. The best wines come from the vineyards next to the FRANCIACORTA DOC, along the Oglio River.

Valcarcelia *see* MONASTRELL

Valdadige DOC [vahl-DAH-dee-jay] This DOC, which covers vineyards scattered throughout northeastern Italy's TRENTINO-ALTO ADIGE region and into the VENETO region, is considered the lowest-quality DOC in the Adige Valley. Valdadige (*Etschtaler* in German) has two VARIETAL WINES—Pinot Grigio (PINOT GRIS) and SCHIAVA—and three basic wines—BIANCO, ROSSO, and ROSATO. The Bianco, Rosso, and Rosato wines, which can be DRY or AMABILE, have many approved varieties from which they can be made.

Valdeorras DO [bahl-deh-AW*R*-rahs] DO that is located in the mountainous area east of the town of Orense in the Galica region in northwestern Spain. Valdeorras produces mostly red wines made primarily from Alicante (GRENACHE) and much of it is sold off in BULK. The Mencía grape is now being planted in larger numbers, and wines made from it are more likely to show up in a Valdeorras DO bottle. White wines are made mainly from PALOMINO grapes, which produce rather ordinary TABLE WINES. The real rising star of Valdeorras, however, is the white wine made from the local grape Godello. This high quality grape grows well in this area and produces CRISP, FRESH, AROMATIC wines.

Valdepeñas DO [bahl-deh-PEH-nyahss] A large DO located south of Madrid in the southern part of Spain's CASTILLA-LA MANCHA region. The Valdepeñas DO, which is named after the town of the same name, is almost fully surrounded by the huge LA MANCHA DO. Valdepeñas is best known for its CLARETE, which has been made in this region for centuries. This clarete is a light red wine made from both red (Cencibel or TEMPRANILLO) grapes and white (AIRÉN) grapes. Even though Airén grapes are planted in about 85 percent of the vineyards, the red claretes make up the majority of Valdepeñas production. That's because the DO requirements state that the minimum amount of Cencibel to be used is 20 percent, which means that Airén could comprise up to 80 percent of the blend. This ratio produces wines that are light in both color and flavor. Nonetheless, red Valdepeñas wines are popular throughout Spain. The best wines have very high percentages of Cencibel. Authorities are now requiring that any new vineyard planting consist only of red Cencibel grapevines.

Valdepeñera Blanca *see* AIRÉN

Valencia DO [vuh-LEHN-shee-uh; bahl-LEHN-thyah] DO area that is located just west of the coastal city of Valencia in eastern Spain's region called the Levante. There are three subzones: the smallest, **Alto Turia**, which is situated northwest of the city of Valencia; **Clariano**, which is southwest of the city; and the largest area, **Valentino**, which includes vineyards from the former DO, Cheste, and is located directly west of the city of Valencia. The Valencia DO produces more white wines than reds or ROSÉS. Merseguera is the most widely planted white grape, but there are a variety of others including MALVASIA, Planta Fina, Moscatel (MUSCAT), and PEDRO XIMÉNEZ. Red and rosé wines are made mainly from Bobal, blended with Garnacha (GRENACHE), TEMPRANILLO, and MONASTRELL.

Valle d'Aosta; Valle d'Aosta DOC [VAHL-lay DAWSS-tuh]

Italy's smallest wine-producing region. It's located in the northwestern section of the country, with France on the west, Switzerland on the north, and PIEDMONT surrounding it on the south and east. Because of its location, the region is officially bilingual and part of the area (known as *Vallée d'Aoste* in French) is French speaking. Valle d'Aosta is surrounded by tall Alpine peaks, and the vineyards are planted mainly on hilly slopes and terraces near the valley floor. There is now only one DOC area, **Valle d'Aosta DOC**. The previous DOC areas of Donnaz and Enfer d'Arvier were incorporated into it and are now regarded as two of the seven subzones. The other five subzones are Arnad-Montjovet, Chambave, Morgex et La Salle, Nus, and Torrette. The Valle d'Aosta DOC covers ROSSO, BIANCO, and ROSATO wines. There are twenty-two approved grape varieties that can be grown throughout this DOC. The most popular white grapes are Blanc de Morgex, Moscato (MUSCAT), MÜLLER-THURGAU, and Pinot Grigio (PINOT GRIS). For red and rosé wines the most prominent grapes are GAMAY, NEBBIOLO, Petit Rouge, Pinot Nero (PINOT NOIR), and Vien de Nus.

Vallée de la Marne *see* CHAMPAGNE

Valley of the Moon *see* SONOMA VALLEY AVA

Valmur [vahl-MEW*R*] One of the seven GRAND CRU vineyards in CHABLIS. It consists of just over 29 acres and is located between GRENOUILLES and LES CLOS.

Val Nure *see* COLLI PIACENTINI

Valoux *see* BUSCAUT, CHÂTEAU

Valpantena [vahl-pahn-TEH-nah] A term referring to the Pantena Valley, which lies within the VALPOLICELLA DOC area near Verona in Italy's VENETO region. The name can be used on the label as Valpolicella-Valpantena.

Valpolicella DOC [vahl-paw-lee-CHEHL-lah] A very important red-wine DOC zone located in northeastern Italy's VENETO region. It's situated between BARDOLINO and SOAVE, just north of Verona. Valpolicella ranks just after the CHIANTI DOCG for Italy's total DOC red-wine production. The wine is made primarily from Corvina Veronese (CORVINA), Rondinella, and Molinara grapes, although four other varieties can comprise up to 15 percent of the blend. Valpolicella's standard DOC wines are rather LIGHT and very fragrant and fruity. Those labeled SUPERIORE have a 1 percent higher minimum ALCOHOL content and are AGED for a minimum of 1 year. The best wines are generally

those labeled CLASSICO, which indicates that they come from the inner classico zone with its steeply terraced vineyards. **Valpolicella-Valpantena** on the label indicates that the wines come from a separate area called the Pantena Valley. Valpolicella wines made by the RIPASSO PROCESS are richer in flavor and more full-bodied (*see* BODY) than standard renditions. To make a ripasso wine, the juice is FERMENTED in the usual way and then placed in casks containing the LEES from a prior batch of RECIOTO DELLA VALPOLICELLA or RECIOTO DELLA VALPOLICELLA AMARONE. This ripasso process, which lasts from 2 to 3 weeks, adds color, TANNINS, and complex flavors. Unfortunately, the term *ripasso* is not allowed on wine labels, so the consumer must know the producers who make this style of wine. Among the wines using this process are Boscaini's Le Canne, Masi's CAMPO FIORIN, and Santi's Castello.

Valréas *see* CÔTES DU RHÔNE

Valtellina DOC [vahl-teh-LEE-nah] DOC zone located in the LOMBARDY region in northern Italy, very close to the Swiss border. The special MICROCLIMATE of this Alpine area allows the grapes to ripen properly. Only red wines are covered by this DOC. Standard Valtellina wines are made from at least 70 percent Chiavennasca (the local name for NEBBIOLO), and the rest from a variety of red grapes. They require 1 year of AGING. Valtellina SUPERIORE wines must be made with at least 95 percent Chavennasca grapes and have 2 years of aging, one of which is in wood. Bottles labeled RISERVA have had 4 years of aging. Valtellina Superiore can be made only from vineyards surrounding four of Valtellina's villages—Grumello, Inferno, Valgella, and Sassella, the latter being considered best. The word *Sforzato* or *Sfursat* on the label indicates the wine was made by the PASSITO process and has a minimum ALCOHOL content of 14½ percent.

vanilla; vanillin A sensory term to describe the sweet, distinctively vanillalike smell of some wines that have been AGED in new OAK barrels.

varietal *see* VARIETAL WINE

varietal character The unique traits of a given grape variety once it's made into wine is called its varietal character. These traits include AROMA, flavor, COLOR, and BODY. Many elements, like soil, climate, winemaking techniques, and storage can influence a wine, but the grape variety is the dominant component. With practice, one can learn these characteristics and begin to identify VARIETAL WINES. For example, the characteristics of PINOT NOIR and CABERNET SAUVIGNON are distinct enough that, once the differences are understood, they usually can be distinguished even in a BLIND TASTING. Other grape varieties have characteristics so similar that they may be difficult to identify for all except a practiced palate. With some grapes, the varietal characteristics are simply not very distinctive, making identification extremely difficult. *See also* CHARACTER.

varietal wine; varietal [vuh-RI-ih-tuhl] A wine that uses the name of the dominant grape from which it's made, such as CABERNET SAUVIGNON, CHARDONNAY, and RIESLING. This practice occurs primarily in areas where many different grape varieties are grown in close proximity, principally in growing regions of North and South America, Australia, New Zealand, and recently in parts of Europe. There are rules in most areas about what can be called a varietal wine. For example, in the United States at least 75 percent of the wine must come from the grape variety named on the label, while in Australia it's 80 percent. Instead of using varietal names, Europeans have long labeled their better wines with the names of regions, districts, or villages, thereby giving the wine's origin utmost importance. In Europe most quality wines are governed by each country's APPELLATION system, which defines what grapes can be grown in specific areas and encourages the production of quality wines.

variety; varieties Winetasting term that refers to the single type of grape within a species that has its own distinct recognizable characteristics. Some of the better-known grape varieties include CABERNET SAUVIGNON, CHARDONNAY, CHENIN BLANC, MERLOT, PINOT NOIR, RIESLING, SAUVIGNON BLANC, SYRAH, and ZINFANDEL. Almost all grape varieties used in winemaking are part of the VITIS VINIFERA species. In the United States it's common practice to include the name of the grape variety on the label (*see* VARIETAL WINE), whereas in Europe the name of the producing region is the common identifier. Over 165 of the most popular grape varieties are defined in this book (*see* Grape Varieties, page 609, for a detailed list).

Varresana Bianca *see* VERMENTINO

Vaucoupin *see* CHABLIS

Les Vaucrains *see* NUITS-SAINT-GEORGES

Vaud [VOH] One of Switzerland's two main wine-producing cantons—the other is VALAIS. Vaud's vineyards are located along the Rhône, starting north of Valais, and along the north shore of Lake Geneva. The three main growing areas are CHABLAIS, just south of Lake

Geneva on the Rhône; LAVAUX, which is east of Lausanne on the lake's north shore; and LA CÔTE, which is on the lake's north shore west of Lausanne. Vaud is primarily a white-wine area, and CHASSELAS (locally known as *Dorin*) is the dominant grape. The most popular red grapes are GAMAY and PINOT NOIR. These two grapes are often blended together in a wine called **Salvagnin**, which is similar in style (like a light-bodied, red BURGUNDY) to the Valais canton's *Dole*. Other varieties grown in this region include PINOT GRIS, PINOT BLANC, and Riesling-Sylvaner (MÜLLER-THURGAU). Vaud has implemented a rudimentary AP-PELLATION system, which simply defines the region, the grape varieties, and the required sugar levels (*see* APPELLATION D'ORIGINE CONTROLEE for an explanation of the more extensive French system).

Vaudésir [voh-day-ZEE*R*] One of the seven GRAND CRU vineyards in CHABLIS. It consists of just under 32 acres, which are situated between LES PREUSES and GRENOUILLES.

Vau de Vey *see* CHABLIS

VDN *see* VIN DOUX NATUREL

VDQS *see* VIN DÉLIMITÉ DE QUALITÉ SUPÉRIEURE

vecchio [VEHK-ee-oh] Italian for "old," the word *vecchio* is used in the wine world to mean "aged." It can appear on DOC wines that have met certain aging conditions.

Vega Sicilia [BAY-gah see-SEE-lyah] Founded in 1864 and lo-cated in the RIBERA DEL DUERO DO, Vega Sicilia has established itself as Spain's most prestigious wine estate. The French varieties of CABERNET SAUVIGNON, MERLOT, and MALBEC are planted along with the native TEM-PRANILLO, Garnacha (GRENACHE), and Albillo. Tempranillo makes up about 60 percent of the blend, followed by Cabernet Sauvignon with about 25 percent. In addition to the unique blend of grapes used, Vega Sicilia wines go through extensive barrel AGING. This BODEGA'S premier wine—Vega Sicilia Unico—is made from grapes from the old-est vines and spends 10 years or more in wooden casks and barrels. Upon release, the highly sought-after Unico wines are generally RICH and full-bodied (*see* BODY). Two other wines, released under the name Valbuena, receive either 3 or 5 years of aging. They're rich and well-structured, although not quite as intense as the Unico.

vegetal [VEHJ-ih-tl] A winetasting term describing a wine in which the taste and smell have the characteristics of fresh or cooked vegeta-bles, particularly bell peppers and asparagus. Some grape varieties—such as CABERNET SAUVIGNON—have a degree of vegetal character to them. However, a strong vegetal quality is unpleasant and not a desirable trait. *See also* HERBACEOUS.

Velletri DOC [vay-LEH-tree] A DOC area located northeast of Lake Albano and northeast of Rome in Italy's LATIUM region. The area produces BIANCO and ROSSO wines. The Bianco, which is made from MALVASIA and TREBBIANO, may be DRY, AMABILE or DOLCE, and STILL or SPUMANTE. The Rosso is made primarily from SANGIOVESE, MONTEPULCIANO, and Cesanese and may be dry or amabile. Bottles labeled RISERVA are higher in ALCOHOL and have been AGED for 2 years.

velouté [veh-loo-TAY] French for the winetasting term VELVETY.

Veltliner *see* GRÜNER VELTLINER

Veltlini *see* GRÜNER VELTLINER

velvety A winetasting term for opulently HARMONIOUS wines that have a LUSH, smooth TEXTURE. Its English synonym is SILKY, its French is *velouté.*

vendange [vah*n*-dah*n*-ZH] French for VINTAGE, referring to the grape harvest. The Spanish equivalent is *vendimia;* the Italian is *vendemmia.*

Vendange Tardive [vah*n*-dah*n*-ZH tahr-DEEV] French for "LATE HARVEST," referring to wines made from late-picked grapes with higher sugar levels and more pronounced flavors. Such wines, which are a specialty of the ALSACE region, are generally VINIFIED totally DRY and are rich and very flavorful. They're made from several varieties—RIESLING, GEWÜRZTRAMINER, PINOT GRIS, and MUSCAT.

vendemmia [vayn-DAYM-myah] Italian for VINTAGE, referring to the time of the grape harvest. The Spanish equivalent is *vendimia;* the French is *vendange.*

vendimia [bayn-DEE-myah] The Spanish word for "VINTAGE", referring to the grape harvest. The French equivalent is *vendange;* the Italian is *vendemmia.*

Venegazzu [veh-neh-GAHD-dzoo] A well-known wine estate located in the Montello e Colli Asolani DOC zone in Italy's VENETO region. The estate, which was formerly owned by the Loredan Gasparini family, has a history of not following DOC rules. Even though Venegazzu makes highly regarded wine, it can be classed only as VINO DA TAVOLA. The best-known wine is the BORDEAUX-style *Venegazzu della Casa Riserva,* which uses CABERNET FRANC, CABERNET SAUVIGNON, MALBEC, and MERLOT.

Veneto [VEH-neh-toh] A large wine-producing region in northeastern Italy. Its capital, Venice, sits on the Adriatic Sea. Directly west of Venice is this area's other important city, Verona, which isn't far from Lake Garda on the region's western edge. The Veneto is one of Italy's top three or four regions in total wine production. It's by far the top producer of DOC-approved wines, with almost 21 percent of Italy's total DOC production. The best-known wines are from the three DOCs of BARDOLINO, SOAVE, and VALPOLICELLA, all of which are located around Verona. Between them, these three areas account for about 40 percent of the Veneto's DOC wine production. This region has ten other DOC areas including BIANCO DI CUSTOZA, BREGANZE, COLLI BERICI, GAMBELLARA, and LISON-PRAGAGGIORE. Popular red grapes in the Veneto include CABERNET FRANC, CABERNET SAUVIGNON, CORVINA, Molinara, MERLOT, and Rondinella. Among the favored white grapes are GARGANEGA, Pinot Bianco (PINOT BLANC), Pinot Grigio (PINOT GRIS), PROSECCO, and TREBBIANO.

Vennentino *see* VERMENTINO

Ventoux *see* CÔTES DU VENTOUX

Verbesco *see* BARBERA

Verdejo; Verdejo Palido [vehr-DAY-yoh pah-LEE-doh] A white-wine grape grown in and indigenous to Spain's RUEDA region. It's also cultivated in the neighboring regions of Toro and RIBERA DEL DUERO. Verdejo produces full-bodied (*see* BODY), yet CRISP wine with a rich, nutty flavor. Rueda's top category of wine, Rueda SUPERIOR, must contain at least 60 percent Verdejo; the very best wine is 100 percent Verdejo. The Rueda region also produces a SHERRY-style wine from Verdejo grapes.

Verdelho [vehr-DEH-lyoh] 1. MADEIRA'S most widely planted white-wine grape, Verdelho is classified as a noble or classic grape. On the Portuguese mainland, Verdelho is recommended in the DÃO region's white wines and in the production of white PORT. 2. A medium-dry style of Madeira wine, slightly richer than SERCIAL but less opulent than BOAL or MALMSEY. Originally made primarily with Verdelho grapes, this style of Madeira has recently utilized more TINTA NEGRA MOLE (which is considered only a *good* grape), especially in the cheaper versions. In 1986, however, Portugal entered the Common Market, whose regulations required that by 1993 any Madeira wine naming a variety on its label will have to contain at least 85 percent of that grape. Wines labeled "Verdelho-style" can contain less than the required 85 percent, and most likely contain more Tinta Negra Mole.

Verdicchio [vehr-DEEK-kyoh] A white-wine grape grown mainly in Italy's MARCHES region where it's been cultivated since the fourteenth century. Verdicchio's name is derived from *verde* (meaning green), referring to the yellow-green skin of the grape, which gives the wine a subtle greenish hue. The wines are generally CRISP and DRY, with a light but elegant aroma and flavor. The best known of the Verdicchio wines come from the DOC of VERDICCHIO DEI CASTELLI DE JESI, which can include small amounts of TREBBIANO and MALVASIA. Part of the notability of these wines comes from the unusual green, amphora (two-handled urn)-shaped bottle in which it comes. The wines from the DOC of VERDICCHIO DEI MATELICA are not as well known as those from Verdicchio dei Castelli di Jesi but are thought by many to be as good or better because they're more full-bodied (*see* BODY) and have better aging potential. The high ACIDITY of the Verdicchio grape makes it a good candidate for SPARKLING WINES, and the SPUMANTE made from this variety receives good reviews. Verdicchio is also known as *Marchigiano* and *Verdone*.

Verdicchio dei Castelli di Jesi DOC [veh*r*-DEEK-kyoh day kahs-TEHL-lee dee YEH-zee] Area that encompasses the hilly sites west of the town of Jesi in Italy's MARCHES region. This is the best known of the DOCs making wine from the VERDICCHIO grape. The wines, which can also contain up to 15 percent MALVASIA and TREBBIANO grapes, are generally CRISP and DRY, with a light but elegant aroma and flavor. Part of the notability of these wines comes from the unusual green, amphora (two-handled urn)-shaped bottle in which it comes. The CLASSICO zone covers all but a small section of the regular DOC area. SPUMANTE versions are made as well, some using the MÉTHODE CHAMPENOISE.

Verdicchio di Matelica DOC [veh*r*-DEEK-kyoh dee mah-TAY-lee-kah] Another DOC that produces wines based on the VERDICCHIO grape. It's located south of the better-known VERDICCHIO DEI CASTELLI DI JESI DOC in central Italy's MARCHES region. The wines of these two DOCs are similar, although some feel the Matelica wines are more full-bodied (*see* BODY). In addition to Verdicchio, the wines can also contain up to 15 percent of MALVASIA and TREBBIANO grapes.

Verdone see VERDICCHIO

Verdot Rouge see PETIT VERDOT

Verduzzo; Verduzzo Friulano [vehr-DOOT-soh froo-LAH-noh] A white-wine grape indigenous to Italy's FRIULI-VENEZIA GIULIA region. Verduzzo is best known for its AMABILE (semisweet) and DOLCE (sweet) wines, which exhibit floral and rich honey characteristics, balanced by good ACIDITY. The best of these sweet wines, Romandolo CLASSICO, comes from the northern part of the COLLI ORIENTALI DEL FIULI DOC. Verduzzo is also used in the production of DRY white wines. The *Verduzzo Trevigiano* grown in Italy's VENETO region is thought to be a different variety.

Aux Vergelesses *see* SAVIGNY-LÈS-BEAUNE

Les Vergelesses *see* PERNAND-VERGELESSES

Les Vergennes *see* CORTON

Les Vergers *see* CHASSAGNE-MONTRACHET AC

Vergine *see* MARSALA DOC

Vermentino [ver-mehn-TEE-noh] A white-wine grape thought to be related to MALVASIA and to a variety grown in Italy's PIEDMONT known as *Favorita*. Vermentino is most often associated with the French island of CORSICA. However, it's also grown on the neighboring Italian island SARDINIA and on Italy's mainland in the LIGURIA region. On Corsica, Vermentino is usually blended with Ugni Blanc (TREBBIANO). Corsica's best wines, however, are made with 100 percent Vermentino grapes and are deep-colored, fruity, and full-bodied (*see* BODY). In Liguria, where Vermentino is DOC classified as **Riviera Ligure di Ponente**, the wines are LIGHTER and CRISPER than the Corsican versions. Sardinian renditions, which are DOC classified as **Vermentino di Gallura** and **Vermentino di Alghero**, are similar to those from Liguria, but not as ACIDIC. Vermentino is also called *Varresana Bianca* and *Vennentino*.

vermouth [ver-MOOTH] White wine that has been FORTIFIED and flavored with various herbs and spices. The name *vermouth* comes from the German *wermut* ("wormwood"), which, before it was declared poisonous, was once the principal flavoring ingredient. There are several types of this wine, the most popular being **dry white vermouth**, commonly thought of as French, although it's made in other countries including the United States. It's served as an APÉRITIF and used in nonsweet cocktails like martinis. The reddish brown **sweet vermouth** (which is colored with caramel) is also served as an apéritif as well as used in slightly sweet cocktails such as the Manhattan. A third style called **Bianco** is white and slightly sweet, and not as popular as the other two.

Vernaccia di Oristano [ver-NAHT-chah dee aw-riss-TAH-noh] 1. A white-wine grape grown on the island of SARDINIA, primarily north of the city of Oristano. Vernaccia di Oristano grapes are processed much like those for sherry, producing good-quality, amber-colored wines reminiscent of DRY, aged Olorosos (*see* SHERRY). These wines are AGED in wood for a minimum of 2 years; 3 years for SUPERIORE, and 4 years for RISERVA. Although not as distinctive, there are also LIQUOROSO (FORTIFIED) versions that are vinified both sweet and dry. Vernaccia di Oristano is not related to VERNACCIA DI SAN GIMIGNANO. 2. A DOC encompassing the city of Oristano and areas to the north of the city, which is located on the western side of Sardinia.

Vernaccia di San Gimignano [ver-NAHT-chah dee sahn jee-mee-NYAH-noh] 1. A white-wine grape grown in Italy's TUSCANY region, primarily southwest of Florence around the medieval hilltop town of San Gimignano. Vernaccia di San Gimignano dates back as far as the thirteenth century and its origins are thought to be Greek. The wines produced from this variety vary tremendously. Traditionally made, they're golden in color, rich, and full-bodied (*see* BODY), with an OXIDIZED style and a slightly bitter edge to the flavor. More modern winemaking techniques produce paler-colored wines with crisper, lighter characteristics. 2. A DOCG area based around the town of San Gimignano that was the very first to receive DOC status when Italy began implementing its wine-classification system in 1966. In addition to the reputation for the wines produced from its namesake grape, the town of San Gimignano is renowned for its medieval atmosphere. It's replete with tall, narrow towers that were built during a time when higher was considered better and safer.

Vernatsch *see* SCHIAVA

Les Verroilles *see* GEVREY CHAMBERTIN

vertical tasting *see* WINETASTING

Vesuvio DOC *see* LACRYMA CHRISTI DEL VESUVIO DOC

Veuve Clicquot-Ponsardin [vu*rv* klee-KOH paw*n*-sahr-DA*N*] Large, important CHAMPAGNE house that is located in Reims in France's Champagne region. It's said that Madame Clicquot, a young window (*veuve* in French) who took over her dead husband's Champagne house in 1805, developed a way to remove the dead yeast cells from bottles. The process, called *remuage* (*see* RIDDLING), is now an important part of the MÉTHODE CHAMPENOISE used by all Champagne houses (although experiments are underway for techniques to eliminate the time-consuming manual labor involved). Veuve-Cliquot produces about 9 million bottles of champagne led by its premium brand, the well-known **La Grande Dame**, named after Madame Clicquot. Moet-Hennessy now owns Veuve-Cliquot, which was founded in 1772.

Vichon Winery [vee-SHAWN] Winery that is located southwest of the town of Oakville in the NAPA VALLEY AVA. Vichon was formed in 1980 as a partnership by a number of leading hotel and restaurant people. The name Vichon was formed by taking two letters from each of the three general partners' names—George Vierra, Peter Brucher, and Doug Watson. In 1985 Vichon Winery was sold to Robert Mondavi's three children, Tim (who runs the operation), Michael, and Marcia. The winery produces five wines: two CABERNET SAUVIGNONS—a Napa Valley bottling and a Stags Leap District (SLD) bottling; CHARDONNAY; MERLOT; and a SAUVIGNON BLANC-SÉMILLON blend called Chevrignon. The SLD bottling of Cabernet Sauvignon is the consensus star of the group. Vichon's annual production is nearing the 50,000-case mark. A SECOND LABEL **Vichon Coastal Selection** is being used for lower-priced, lower-quality wines.

Vidal 256 *see* VIDAL BLANC

Vidal Blanc [vee-dahl BLAHN (BLAHNGK)] A French-American HYBRID grape developed by crossing UGNI BLANC and Seibel 4986 (another hybrid). Vidal Blanc (officially known as *Vidal 256*) is grown in the eastern United States. The grapes have high sugar and good ACID levels, with nice but rather neutral flavors. The wines are vinified in a variety of styles from DRY to sweet. ICE WINES with good flavor and richness have been made from frozen Vidal Blanc grapes in a style similar to German EISWEIN.

VIDE *See* VINITIVINICOLTORI ITALIANI D'ECCELLENZA

Vidure *see* CABERNET SAUVIGNON

Viex-Château-Certan [vyew shah-TOH sehr-TAHN] Prior to World War II, this famous POMEROL AC estate was regarded as the best in this APPELLATION. Although Château PÉTRUS and several other Pomerol AC estates have surpassed it in quality during the last several decades, Viex-Château-Certan still makes high-quality wines that are comparable to those of a DEUXIÈME CRU (second growth) of the MÉDOC. The château's 33 acres produce about 5,000 to 7,000 cases of red wine each year. The grapes used are approximately 50 percent MERLOT, 25 percent CABERNET FRANC, 20 percent CABERNET SAUVIGNON, and 5 percent MALBEC. Better VINTAGES are capable of AGING for 15 to 20 years. The château's SECOND LABEL is called **Clos de la Gravette**.

vigna [VEE-nyah] Italian for "vineyard."

Vigne au Saint; La Vigne au Saint *see* CORTON

vigneron [vee-nyeh-ROHN] French term for "vine grower." *See also* VITICULTEUR.

vignoble [vee-NYOHBL] French for "vineyard."

Vignoles *see* RAVAT

vigorous A descriptive term for wines that are full-bodied (*see* BODY), LIVELY, and youthful.

Vila Nova de Gaia [vee-lah noh-vah deh GAH-yah] A quaint old town in northern Portugal that sits on the Douro River across from the city of OPORTO. PORT wines have been stored and matured in the LODGES (warehouses) in Vila Nova de Gaia for over 200 years.

Le Village *see* CORTON

Villa Mt. Eden [VIHL-luh mownt EE-dn] This NAPA VALLEY winery, which was founded in 1974 by Ann and James McWilliams, was purchased in 1986 by Washington State's Stimson Lane, a subsidiary of UST Inc. (owners of U.S. Tobacco). UST Inc. also owns Napa Valley's CONN CREEK WINERY, as well as CHÂTEAU STE. MICHELLE and Columbia Crest, both in Washington. The new owners have boosted Villa Mt. Eden's production from about 25,000 to nearly 150,000 cases per year, mainly through a lower-priced line labeled Cellar Select. The Grand Reserve line represents their high-quality wines. Villa Mt. Eden focuses on CABERNET SAUVIGNON, CHARDONNAY, MERLOT, PINOT NOIR, and ZINFANDEL.

Villard Blanc [vee-yahr BLAH*N*; BLAH*N*GK] A white French-American HYBRID widely grown in the south of France, particularly in the LANGUEDOC-ROUSSILLON region. It was developed by French hybridizer Seyve-Villard, who also created SEYVAL BLANC. Villard Blanc, also known as *Seyve Villard 12.375,* is grown in the eastern United States as well. It's highly productive and produces medium-quality wine with a flavor so pronounced that it's usually blended with other grape varieties to produce a more neutral wine. Villard Blanc acreage has declined over the last few decades because French authorities are encouraging its replacement with higher-quality white grape varieties.

Villard Noir [vee-yahr NWAH*R*] Although once quite popular in France, this red French-American HYBRID is gradually being replaced by higher-quality red varieties at the encouragement of French authorities. Villard Noir, which is still widely planted in southwestern France, produces wines of medium to low quality. Much of the crop is now distilled into SPIRITS. Villard Noir, also known as *Seyve Villard 18.315*, can be found in the eastern United States, as well.

Villeneuve de Cantemerle *see* CANTEMERLE, CHÂTEAU

Villeranque *see* CITRAN, CHÂTEAU

vin [VA*N*] The French word for "wine."

vina [BEE-nyah] Spanish for "vineyard."

vin blanc [va*n* BLAH*N*] French for "white wine."

vin bourru [va*n* boo-*R*EW] A French term for wine that is drawn from the vat or barrel just shortly after FERMENTATION is completed. Vin bourru wine has a fresh, slightly effervescent character and is a favorite in many European countries.

vin de carafe *see* CARAFE WINE

Vin de Consommation Courante [va*n* duh kaw*n*-saw-mah-SYAW*N* koo-RAH*M*] French for "Wine for Current Consumption," once the official name for France's VIN ORDINAIRE ("ordinary wine"). Vin de Consommation Courante has been replaced by the term VIN DE TABLE.

Vin de Corse AC *see* CORSICA

vin de cuvée [va*n* duh koo-VAY] A term used in France's CHAMPAGNE region to describe the juice produced from the first PRESSING of the grapes. The presses in champagne hold 4,000 kilograms (about 8,800 pounds) of grapes, which, up until 1990, were given four separate pressings. The first pressing (*serre*) could produce up to 2,050 liters (541 gallons) of *vin de cuvée*, which is the best juice and goes into the premium champagnes. The second pressing could yield up to 410 liters (108 gallons) of juice called *première taille*. The third pressing could produce up to 205 liters (54 gallons) of juice called *deuxième taille*. Both the second and third pressings were of lesser quality than the *vin de cuvée* and were used in lower-quality wines or sold off. The fourth pressing, called *rebêche*, was made from moistened grapes and produced insipid juice used by the workers for homemade wine. As of 1990, the deuxième taille (juice from the third pressing) category was officially eliminated and the maximum amount of juice for the première taille (juice from the second pressing) was increased from 410 liters to 500 liters (132 gallons).

vin de garde [van duh GAH*R*D] A French term that means "wine for guarding" or "keeping," referring to a wine with the proper attributes for long AGING. A vin de garde will improve and develop character as it matures.

vin de goutte *see* FREE-RUN JUICE; FREE-RUN WINE

vin de l'année [van duh lah-NAY] French term that means "this year's wine" and refers to wine from the latest VINTAGE. The expression is used in areas like BEAUJOLAIS, where many of the wines are drunk quite young.

Vin Délimité de Qualité Supérieure (VDQS) [van deh-lee-mee-TAY duh kah-lee-TAY soo-pehr-YUR] French for "Delimited Wine of Superior Quality." This is the second-highest classification level for French wines, the top category being APPELLATION D'ORIGINE CONTRÔLÉE (AC). There are two categories below VDQS—VIN DE PAYS and VIN DE TABLE. VDQS wines are controlled by regulations similar to AOC wines, although they are not quite as demanding. Many VDQS wines are of excellent quality, and the French have promoted over twenty VDQS areas to AOC status.

vin de liqueur [van duh lee-KEW*R*] Similar to a VIN DOUX NATUREL in that FERMENTATION is stopped by the addition of BRANDY (a vin doux naturel must be stopped by a neutral alcohol). The brandy is usually added to the grape juice before fermentation has begun, but it can be added during the process. The resulting FORTIFIED wine is sweet and high in ALCOHOL, generally ranging between 16 and 22 percent. FLOC DE GASCOGNE, PINEAU DES CHARENTES, and RATAFIA are all vins de liqueur.

vin de paille [van duh PAH-yuh] French for "straw wine," referring to wines made from grapes that are dried by spreading them out on mats or trays or by hanging them in bunches. The name comes from the original practice of using straw mats during the drying process. The dried grapes are full of sweet, concentrated juice. Once FERMENTATION begins, the sugar content is usually high enough to take the wine to a reasonable alcohol level (*see* ALCOHOL BY VOLUME) and still retain enough RESIDUAL SUGAR to make these wines fairly sweet.

vin de pays [van deu pay-YEE] French for "country wine." Officially, this is the third-highest wine quality level in France's quality control system. The two higher categories are APPELLATION D'ORIGINE CONTRÔLÉE (AOC) AND vin DÉLIMITÉ DE QUALITÉ SUPÉRIEURE (VDQS); VIN DE TABLE is lower. The rules for vin de pays are similar to the two higher categories, but they are slightly more relaxed in that higher YIELDS and lower minimum ALCOHOL levels are allowed. There are three types of geographically defined categories within vin de pays. The largest are *vin de pays régionaux,* which encompass entire regions. Within a region there may be several *vin de pays départementaux* (DÉPARTEMENTS) and within those, numerous *vin de pays de zone* (a localized area or community), the smallest defined areas. Some of the better known vin de pays regions are Vin de Pays du Jardin de la France and Vin de Pays D'Oc. Départements include Vin de Pays de l'Aude (AUDE) and Vin de Pays de l'Hérault (HÉRAULT). The term **Vin du pays**, which simply means "local wine," isn't the same as *vin de pays* and has no legal meaning.

vin de presse *see* FREE-RUN JUICE; FREE-RUN WINE

Vin de Qualité Produits dans des Régions Déterminées (VQPRD) [va*n* deu kah-lee-TAY proh-DWEE dah*n* day ray-ZHAW*N*S day-tehr-mee-NEES] A French expression that literally means "Quality Wine Produced in Determined Regions," and that is commonly shortened to simply "quality wine." Though "VQPRD" may be found on the label of some top-quality wines from countries in the European Economic Community, each member country has their own program to encourage the production of quality wines. For example, in France the APPELLATION D'ORIGINE CONTRÔLÉE and VIN DÉLIMITÉ DE QUALITE SUPÉRIEUR are such programs, as are Italy's DENOMINAZIONE DI ORIGINE CONTROLLATA and DENOMINAZIONE DI ORIGINE CONTROLLATA E GARANTITA, Spain's DENOMINACIÓN DE ORIGEN, and Germany's QUALITÄTSWEIN and QUALITÄTSWEIN MIT PRÄDIKAT.

Vin de Savoie AC *see* SAVOIE

vin de table [va*n* deu TAH-bl] French for TABLE WINE, also referred to as **vin ordinaire** ("ordinary wine"). This is France's lowest category of wine and includes all the wines that don't fit into the higher categories of APPELLATION D'ORIGINE CONTRÔLÉE (AOC), VIN DÉLIMITÉ DE QUALITE SUPÉRIEURE (VDQS), and VIN DE PAYS. The labels on vin de table wines don't mention regional or local origin and bear only the country's name. They're often sold with a proprietary brand name with the simple indication that they're either VIN ROUGE, VIN BLANC, or VIN ROSÉ. Vin de table replaces the term VIN DE CONSOMMATION COURANTE.

Vin Doux Naturel (VDN) [va*n* doo nah-tew-REHL] French for "naturally sweet wine." This refers to a category of sweet, FORTIFIED wines made from grapes that are high in natural sugar (capable of reaching 15 percent ALCOHOL) and whose FERMENTATION is stopped by the addition of a neutral alcohol (no more than 10 percent of the volume). The resulting wines are usually 15 to 18 percent alcohol but can range as high as 21½ percent. VDNs vary in sweetness, with white wines generally being sweeter and less alcoholic than reds. Most VDN white wines are made from MUSCAT, usually Muscat à Petits Grains or Muscat of Alexandria. APPELLATION D'ORIGINE CONTRÔLÉES (ACS) noted for their VDN whites include MUSCAT DE BEAUMES-DE-VENISE, MUSCAT DE FRONTIGNAN, Muscat de Lunel, Muscat de Mireval, MUSCAT DE RIVESALTES, and Muscat de St-Jean-de-Minervois. The best known VDN red and ROSÉ wines, produced primarily from GRENACHE, are from the ACs of BANYULS, MAURY, RASTEAU, and RIVESALTES.

vin du pays [van doo pay-YEE] The French term for "local wine." *See also* VIN DE PAYS.

vineal [vihn-EE-uhl] A general term describing anything characteristic of grapes, grapevines, wine, or winemaking.

vinegary A *vinegary* smell and flavor in wine is a sign of bacteriological breakdown—and the wine's demise.

vineyard An area planted with grapevines.

vineyard-designated A term indicating that a wine is made with grapes from the specific vineyard named on a wine's label. In the United States, a vineyard name on a label means that 95 percent of the grapes in the wine came from the named vineyard and that the named vineyard is located in the AVA indicated on the label.

vin fin [van FAN] French for "wine of quality." This is not an official term, however, and, because it's so freely used for marketing purposes, it doesn't have much meaning.

vin gris [van GREE] French for "gray wine," but referring to very pale ROSÉ wines. Vin gris wines are produced in various parts of France and are made from lightly pressed red grapes (CABERNET SAUVIGNON, PINOT NOIR, or GAMAY), which are separated from the juice before much color is transferred from the skins.

vinha [VEE-nyer] Portuguese for "vineyard."

vinho [VEE-nyoo] Portuguese for "wine."

vinho consumo [VEE-nyoo KAWN-soo-myoh] The Portuguese term for "wine to consume" or ordinary wine. Similar in meaning to the French VIN ORDINAIRE.

Vinho Verde DOC [VEE-nyoh VEHR-deh] Portugal's largest DOC, Vinho Verde is located in the Minho region in the northwestern part of the country. The term *vinho verde* means "green wine," referring not to this wine's color, but to its fresh, fruity, youthfulness. These slightly effervescent wines can be red or white, each representing about half the production. The red wines, which are often harsh with a SOUR, ACIDIC character, are primarily consumed by Portuguese and not exported in large quantities. The white wines are also acidic, but the acidity helps make them FRESH and CRISP. Although the best white wines are DRY, some are made in a sweet style. Both red and white wines are meant to be drunk young. The main grapes used for the red wines are Azal Tinto, Borraçal, and Espadeiro; the white wines use AL-VARINHO, Loureiro, and Trajadura grapes.

viniculture [VIHN-ih-kuhl-cher] The study or science of making wines. One who does so is called a viniculturist. *See also* ENOLOGY; VITI-CULTURE.

vinifera *see* VITIS VINIFERA

viniferous [vi-NIHF-uhr-us] Suitable for use in winemaking, as in a viniferous grape variety.

vinification [vihn-ih-fih-KAY-shuhn] The process of making wines.

vinify; vinified [VIHN-uh-fi] To produce wine from grapes or other fruit.

vin jaune [van ZHOHN] French for "yellow wine," referring to a type of wine made in eastern France's JURA region. AGED for 6 years, vin jaune undergoes a process similar to a fino-style SHERRY whereby a film of FLOR (a yeast) covers the wine's surface. This layer prevents oxidation (*see* OXIDIZED) while allowing evaporation, thereby creating the wine's subsequent concentration. The result is a sherrylike wine with a delicate, nutty richness that can age for decades. The best known vin jaune, made from SAVAGNIN grapes, is from the APPELLATION D'ORIGINE CONTRÔLÉE of CHÂTEAU-CHALON.

vin mousseux *see* MOUSSEUX

vin nature *see* NATURE

vin nouveau *see* NOUVEAU

vino [It. VEE-noh; Sp. BEE-noh] The Italian and Spanish term for "wine."

vino borracho *see* MALAGA DO

vino corriente [BEE-no koh-rree-AYN-tay] Spanish for "plain wine," referring to one that's young, inexpensive, and ordinary. Vino corriente is equivalent in meaning to France's VIN ORDINAIRE.

vino da pasto [VEE-noh dah PAH-stoh] Italian for TABLE WINE or "wine of the meal." This term has no official significance and is used to categorize wines served during the meal versus those taken as an APÉRITIF or DESSERT WINE. VINO DA TAVOLA, which also means "table wine," is an official category.

vino da taglio *see* TAGLIO

vino da tavola (VdT); pl. vini [VEE-noh dah TAH-voh-lah; pl. VEE-nee] Italian for "TABLE WINE," referring to Italy's lowest category of wine. The term is similar to France's VIN DE TABLE and Germany's TAFELWEIN. Generally, VdT wines are fairly ordinary; however, there are a number of surprises because many top producers don't conform to DOC regulations and make excellent wines that they register in this category. This occurs mainly when producers use unapproved grape varieties or when the proportions don't meet DOC regulations. Examples of such excellent wines are Tuscany's SOLAIA and TIGNANELLO (both are a blend of CABERNET SAUVIGNON and SANGIOVESE). Within the VdT category is a new premium category—**vino da tavola con indicazione geografica**. An area granted this higher designation may label their wines with the vintage, place of origin, and grape variety, whereas regular vini da tavola may list only the country on the label.

vino de color *see* MALAGA DO

vino de la tierra [BEE-noh theh lah TYEH*R*-*r*ah] This is the Spanish term for "country wines," a new category that's equivalent to the French VIN DE PAYS.

vino de mesa [BEE-noh theh MAY-sah] The Spanish term for "TABLE WINE," Spain's lowest official category of wine. This term has a similar status to France's VIN DE TABLE, Italy's VINO DA TAVOLA, and Germany's TAFELWEIN.

vino de pasto [BEE-noh theh PAHS-toh] An unofficial Spanish term for "wine of the meal" or "TABLE WINE." It's used to designate wines served during the meal versus those consumed as an APÉRITIF or DESSERT WINE. VINO DE MESA (which also means "table wine") is the official category.

vino espumoso natural método tradicional *see* CAVA DO

vino maestro *see* MÁLAGA DO

vinometer [vih-NAHM-ih-ter] A simple calibrated instrument used to measure the alcoholic content of finished DRY wines. A vinometer isn't accurate for sweet wines.

Vino Nobile di Montepulciano DOCG [VEE-noh NAW-bee-lay dee mawn-teh-pool-CHAH-noh] DOCG that is located in the hilly area around the town of Montepulciano, southeast of Siena in the eastern portion of Italy's TUSCANY region. The designated area is actually situated inside the large CHIANTI subzone of Colli Senesi. Vino Nobile di Montepulciano is named after the town and the historic notion that the wine was available only for the tables of nobility. This was the very first DOCG in Italy. Unfortunately, its first VINTAGE in 1983 was met with disappointing reviews. That and the fact that over 250,000 cases of this wine are now produced each year has somewhat diminished its noble aspect. Quality since that 1983 vintage has improved, however, and wines from the top producers are viewed as some of Italy's best. Vino Nobile di Montepulciano wines are made from 60 to 80 percent Prugnolo (SANGIOVESE), 10 to 20 percent CANAIOLO, and up to 20 percent of other varieties (although no more than 10 percent white). One of the other red varieties most often used is the Mammolo, which adds the scent of violets to the BOUQUET. White grapes like TREBBIANO and MALVASIA are no longer required, which allows winemakers to produce wines that are more intense and longer lived. The wines of this DOCG must be AGED for 2 years in oak or chestnut casks, 3 years for those labeled RISERVA. In 1989 a new DOC—ROSSO DI MONTEPULCIANO—was formed. It's located in exactly the same area and uses the exact same grape varieties as for the Vino Nobile di Montepulciano DOCG. This change has allowed producers to reclassify some of the wines originally intended from Vino Nobile di Montepulciano to the Rosso di Montepulciano DOC. As a result, lesser wines can be used in the new DOC, which should raise the overall quality of wines coming from the Vino Nobile di Montepulciano DOCG.

vino novello [VEE-noh noh-VEHL-oh] Italian for "new wine," used in the same sense as the French NOUVEAU to refer to light, fruity red wines. By law, vino novello (also called simply *novello*) must be bottled within the year of the harvest, but in practice they're bottled within a few weeks.

vin ordinaire [va*n* or-dee-NEH*R*] French for "ordinary wine." *See also* VIN DE TABLE.

vino rosso *see* ROSSO

Vinos de Madrid DO Established in 1990, this is a new DO for the vineyards surrounding Spain's capital city Madrid. The area, sometimes referred to as *Tierra de Madrid,* consists of three subzones— **Arganda, Navalcarnero,** and **San Martín de Valdeiglesias**. Arganda is by far the most important in terms of wine quantity and quality. The majority of wine it produces is white, made from Malvar and AIRÉN. But the area is best known for its red wines, which are made from TEM-PRANILLO. The better reds can be full-flavored and full-bodied.

vinosity [vi-NAHS-ih-tee] The collective characteristics of a wine, such as aroma and taste.

vino tipico [VEE-noh TEE-pee-koh] Initiated in 1989, this quality category for Italian wines ranks between the VINO DA TAVOLA and DE-NOMINAZIONE DI ORIGINE CONTROLLATA (DOC) categories. It's similar to France's VIN DE PAYS and Germany's LANDWEIN. Vino tipico wines are officially approved as being representative of their area.

vinous [VI-nuhs] 1. When used as a winetasting term, vinous describes a generically pleasant, winey flavor and/or aroma. 2. A general term describing anything characteristic of wine. For example, a vinous color or vinous fragrance.

vin rosé [va*n* roh-ZAY] French for "rosé wine."

vin rouge [va*n* ROOZH] French for "red wine."

Vin Santo [VEEN SAHN-toh] Vin Santo, also called *Vino Santo,* is a wine made primarily in TUSCANY but also in the UMBRIA, TRENTINO-ALTO ADIGE, and VENETO regions of Italy. The wine is made by drying grapes either by hanging them up or by laying them on trays in airy rooms or barns. After 3 or 4 months the semidried grapes are full of concentrated sugars and flavors. They're PRESSED and then FERMENTED in small oak or chestnut barrels (called **caratelli**), which contain a small amount of **madre**—thick wine left from the prior year. The wine is kept in these barrels for 2 to 3—sometimes as long as 6—years. The barrels, which are not completely full, are exposed to varying temperatures—hot in the summer, cool in the winter. This oxidation (*see* OX-IDIZED) treatment is part of the AGING process and produces wine with a characteristic nutty-caramel flavor, a deep golden color, and an AL-

COHOL content that ranges from 14 to 17 percent. Most Vin Santo is sweet and served as DESSERT WINE, although some versions are DRY and better suited for an APERITIF. The grapes used to make Vin Santo vary. In Tuscany, for example, the grapes are primarily TREBBIANO, MALVASIA, and CANAIOLO. The POMINO DOC, however, makes a red Vin Santo from SANGIOVESE, CABERNET SAUVIGNON, CABERNET FRANC, and MERLOT, and a white version from PINOT BLANC and CHARDONNAY. In TRENTINO, the Noisola grape is used, while in the VENETO region's GAMBELLARA DOC, GARGANEGA is the main grape.

Vin Santo di Gambellara *see* GAMBELLARA DOC

Vin Sec de Château Broustet *see* BROUSTET, CHÂTEAU

Vin Sec de Château Caillou *see* LE CAILLOU, CHÂTEAU

Vin Sec de Château Coutet *see* COUTET, CHÂTEAU

Vin Sec de Doisy-Daëne *see* DOISY-DAËNE, CHÂTEAU

vins mousseux *see* MOUSSEUX

Vinsobres *see* CÔTES DU RHÔNE

vintage [VIHN-tihj] Term that describes both the year of the actual grape harvest and the wine made from those grapes. In the United States, the label may list the **vintage year** if 95 percent of the wine comes from grapes harvested that year. If a blend of grapes from 2 years or more is used, the wine is called *non-vintage* or *NV*. Some CHAMPAGNE and SPARKLING WINE producers are using the term *multi-vintage* to describe wines made from a blend of two or more years. The multivintage designation is to reflect the fact that the vintners are purposefully blending cuvees from different years to achieve a superior house style. Although it's often assumed that a **vintage wine** is one of superior quality, that's not necessarily true. Some vintages are simply considered better overall than others. That's because the quality of the harvest varies from one year to another. In addition, an individual wine may be better or worse than others of a particular vintage because of the originating vineyard's MICROCLIMATE or because of the winemaking process it underwent. An excellent year for a growing region translates to a generally superior quality, which means there are more choices for fine wines of that vintage. So consumers should view a vintage year only as a general guideline. In the end, each wine must be judged on its own merit.

vintage port *see* PORT

Vintage Tunina [too-NEE-nah] The proprietary name for a VINO DA TAVOLA produced by Jermann, a wine estate in the COLLIO DOC in northeast Italy's FRIULI-VENEZIA GIULIA region. Vintage Tunina combines primarily fully ripened CHARDONNAY and SAUVIGNON BLANC with RIBOLLA, MALVASIA, and PICOLIT. The result is a CRISP, DRY, medium-bodied white wine with marvelously complex flavors.

vinted by [VIHN-ted] Occasionally seen on labels, this phrase has no legal or established significance. In general, it means "made by." *See also* BOTTLED BY; ESTATE BOTTLED; GROWN, PRODUCED AND BOTTLED BY; MADE AND BOTTLED BY; PRODUCED AND BOTTLED BY.

Vintivinicoltori Italiani d'Eccellenza; VIDE [veen-tee-vee-nee-koh-loh-TOH-ree ih-tah-lee-AH-nee dayt-chayl-LEHN-tzuh] Italian for "Italian growers and makers of excellence," a voluntary group of wine producers that has established more stringent standards than those imposed by DOC or DOCG regulations. Vintivinicoltori Italiani d'Eccellenza (VIDE) member organizations market only ESTATE BOTTLED wines, which can be submitted for demanding chemical analysis and tasting panel review. Approval by the Vintivinicoltori Italiani d'Eccellenza entitles the wine bottle to bear the VIDE neck label, indicating its high quality. Wines from each new VINTAGE must be submitted for testing in order to earn the VIDE neck label so members can't rest on the reputation of the prior year's wine.

vintner [VIHNT-ner] One who makes or sells wine.

Vintner's Reserve *see* RESERVE

Vinzelles *see* POUILLY-VINZELLES AC

Viognier; Vionnier [vee-oh-NYAY] An esteemed white-wine grape considered very rare because of the limited acreage planted throughout the world. In addition, its low yield and susceptibility to vineyard diseases make Viognier wines extremely difficult to find. This grape gained its distinguished reputation from the northern RHÔNE wines of CHÂTEAU-GRILLET and CONDRIEU. Connoisseurs crave these intense, DRY white wines with vibrant floral qualities and an intriguing BOUQUET reminiscent of apricots, peaches, and pears. Within the CÔTE RÔTIE vineyards, a small amount of Viognier is interplanted with SYRAH, a red grape. The Viognier grapes are harvested and vinified with the Syrah to produce the highly valued Côte Rôtie red wines. It's extremely rare for France to officially sanction the use of a white grape in such high-quality red wines. California has a small but increasing amount of Viognier planted, with JOSEPH PHELPS VINEYARDS being one of the early innovators with this variety.

Vionnier see VIOGNIER

Vire see MÂCON AC

Virginia In the early 1600s Virginia was one of the first states to plant grapes and make wines. Starting in 1773, Thomas Jefferson made repeated attempts (with little success) to grow VITIS VINIFERA vines on his estate, Monticello. By the end of the nineteenth century, Virginia was one of the more important wine-producing areas in the United States. Unfortunately, the temperance movement and PROHIBITION scuttled most of the existing industry. A resurgence began in the early 1970s when VINTNER Dr. Archie Smith III first planted HYBRIDS like SEYVAL BLANC and then later VITIS VINIFERA vines at his Meredyth Vineyards. Today, Virginia has almost fifty wineries and over 1,400 vineyard acres, over 70 percent of which are planted with vitis vinifera grapes like BARBERA, CABERNET FRANC, CABERNET SAUVIGNON, CHARDONNAY, RIESLING, SAUVIGNON BLANC, and VIOGNIER. Chardonnay is the most popular variety and seems to do best in this climate. Virginian vineyards are scattered throughout the state, but the majority are between Charlottesville and the Maryland border, on the eastern slopes of the Blue Ridge Mountains. Virginia wineries include Barboursville, Ingleside Plantation, Meredyth, Montdomaine Cellars, Oakencroft, Piedmont, Prince Michel, and Rapidan River

Visan see CÔTES DU RHÔNE

viscous; viscosity [VIHS-kuhs; vih-skahs-ih-tee] A wine described as viscous is generally RICH, CONCENTRATED, and high in GLYCEROL and EXTRACT. Viscosity leaves a strong impression of TEXTURE on the palate and is discernible visually by distinct LEGS or SHEETS on the sides of the glass.

Vita Nova [VEE-tuh NOH-vuh] SANTA MARIA VALLEY AVA winery that was formed in 1986 by Jim Clendenen of AU BON CLIMAT, Bob Lindquist of Qupe, Steve Arcriono, and Doug Margerum. Vita Nova set out to make high-quality red BORDEAUX-BLEND wines but ended up producing high-quality white wines as well. It began with **Reservatum**, a red Bordeaux-blend, but has gained as much or more exposure from its excellent CHARDONNAY wines. A successful SAUVIGNON BLANC-SÉMILLON blend (also labeled Reservatum) has also been produced. Vita Nova's annual production, all from purchased grapes, is only about 3,000 cases.

viticulteur [vee-tee-kuhl-TEW*R*] The French term for "vine grower," which generally refers to someone who has his own vineyards, as opposed to a VIGNERON, one who generally doesn't own the property but either rents the land or works as an employee.

viticultural area [VIHT-ih-kuhl-cher-uhl] A region where grapes are grown. *See also* AMERICAN VITICULTURAL AREA.

viticulture [VIHT-ih-kuhl-cher] The cultivation of grapevines, or the study or science of grapes and their culture.

vitis aestivalis [VEE-tihs ehs-tuh-VEHL-uhs] A species of vine native to America and grown primarily in the area in and around Missouri, Arkansas, and Tennessee. The best-known variety is the red grape *Cynthiana,* sometimes called *Norton.*

vitis labrusca [VEE-tihs luh-BRUHS-kuh] One of the main North American vine species, vitis labrusca is found primarily in Canada and the northeastern United States, although some grapes of this species are grown in South America. The CONCORD variety is the best known, followed by the CATAWBA and the Delaware. Grapes from this species have a pronounced musky, grapey, FOXY quality that's often criticized by VITIS VINIFERA aficionados.

vitis riparia [VEE-tihs rih-PEHR-ee-uh] A native America vine species noted for its resistance to PHYLLOXERA and best known for breeding ROOTSTOCKS that can withstand this disease. There are some grape VARIETIES of this species used in winemaking, although the best known are HYBRIDS (such as BACO NOIR) that have been developed from breeding vitis riparia with VITIS VINIFERA varieties.

vitis rotundifolia [VEE-tihs roh-tuhn-dih-FOHL-ee-uh] Vine species that is native to the region around the Gulf of Mexico and is part of the MUSCADINE family. This species, whose name is attributed to the vines' round leaves, produces grapes with a strong, musky flavor. The best known VARIETY—the bronze-colored SCUPPERNONG—is used to make sweet wines that are still popular in some areas of the South.

vitis vinifera [VEE-tihs vihn-IHF-uh-ruh] The vine species that produces over 99 percent of the world's wines today. It is native to Europe as well as East and Central Asia, but it has been planted all over the world. There are estimated to be thousands of VARIETIES of this species, some of the best known being CABERNET SAUVIGNON, CHARDONNAY, CHENIN BLANC, MERLOT, PINOT NOIR, RIESLING, SAUVIGNON BLANC, SYRAH, and ZINFANDEL.

Viura *see* MACABEO

Vlassky Riesling *see* WELSCHRIESLING

VLM *see* RIDDLING

Vogelsang *see* JOHANNISBERG

volatile acid *see* ACIDS

volatile acidity Also called simply VA, volatile acidity is as much a part of wine as body temperature is in a human. A balanced amount of VA is necessary for aroma and flavor but, just as a fever indicates a problem in man, excess volatile acidity in wine signals trouble. VA can be caused by several acids, even though its primary source is acetic acid (*see* ACIDS), and is the result of bacteriological infection through oxidation (*see* OXIDIZED) during winemaking. In quantities of less than 0.05 percent, volatile acidity doesn't affect a wine's quality. At higher levels, however, VA can give wine a sharp, vinegary tactile sensation, which is caused by acetic acid. In wines with excessive volatile acidity, the acetic acid is accompanied by ETHYL ACETATE, which contributes a sweet, vinegary smell. Extreme volatile acidity signifies a seriously flawed wine. Such a wine can be referred to as *volatile*.

Vollrads *see* SCHLOSS VOLLRADS

Volnay AC; Volnay-Santenots AC [vawl-NAY sahn-tuh-NOH] The village of Volnay sits high up on the hill between MEURSAULT and POMMARD in the CÔTE DE BEAUNE area of France's BURGUNDY region. As one heads south, the **Volnay AC** is the last APPELLATION in the Côte de Beaune (until the SANTENAY AC) that focuses on red wines. These PINOT NOIR-based wines are generally of high quality, and the Volnay AC has an above-average reputation. Their reputation extends back to the 1300s, when they were a favorite of Phillipe de Valois, the Duke of Burgundy. In the 1400s, these wines were a favorite of Louis XI. Although Volnay has no GRAND CRU vineyards, it has twenty-six PREMIER CRU vineyards, with more acreage assigned to them than to those for the regular Volnay AC. The better premier cru vineyards include **Bousse d'Or**, **Les Caillerets**, **Les Champans**, **Clos des Chênes**, and **Clos des Ducs**. The wines range from a LIGHTER, elegant, silky style to those that are more full-bodied (*see* BODY) and TANNIC. The **Volnay-Santenots AC** is for six red-wine producing vineyards which, although actually located in Meursault, are allowed to use Volnay-Santenots AC on their label.

voros Hungarian for "red."

Vosgros *see* CHABLIS

Vosne-Romanée AC [vohn raw-ma-NAY] The village of Vosne-Romanée is located in the CÔTE DE NUIT area of BURGUNDY. The top red wines from this village are considered to be the finest in BURGUNDY—possibly in all of France—with wines from the PAUILLAC AC in BORDEAUX the most often mentioned contenders. Vosne-Romanée contains five prestigious GRAND CRU vineyards—RICHEBOURG, LA ROMANÉE, ROMANÉE-CONTI, ROMANÉE-SAINT-VIVANT, and LA TÂCHE—which produce some of the world's highest-priced wines. The grands crus ECHÉZEAUX and GRANDS-ECHÉZEAUX, which are located in the neighboring village of Flagey-Echezeaux, are also often associated with Vosne-Romanée. This is because the Flagey-Echézeaux village wines can be sold with the Vosne-Romanée appellation. In addition to the grands crus, there are fifteen PREMIER CRU vineyards that have a reputation for producing generally high-quality wine. Of these, **Clos des Réas, Les Gaudichots, La Grande Rue, Les Malconsort,** and **Les Suchots** are considered some of the best. High-quality wines from Vosne-Romanée demonstrate a richness and elegance, along with a spiciness that's difficult to find in other red Burgundies. Many critics believe that the quality of standard Vosne-Romanée AC wines is variable and inconsistent, which is disappointing because they're expensive. More often than not, these wines coast on the reputation of the grands crus and premiers crus of this village.

Vougeot AC [voo-ZHOH] The village of Vougeot, which is located in the CÔTE DE NUITS area of BURGUNDY, is most often associated with the 124-acre GRAND CRU vineyard, CLOS DE VOUGEOT. There are about 40 other acres in this APPELLATION, split between the village vineyards and several PREMIER CRU vineyards. The premier cru of **Les Petits Vougeots** and its subvineyard of **Clos de la Perrière** are thought to be the best. Most of the wine is red, made from PINOT NOIR, although there's a small amount of white made from CHARDONNAY. These white wines are produced from the premier cru vineyard Le Clos Blanc and labeled **Clos Blanc de Vougeot.**

Vouvray AC [voo-VREH; voo-VRAY] APPELLATION that is just east of Tours in the center of France's LOIRE Valley. CHENIN BLANC, which is noted for its high ACIDITY, is the only variety grown in the vineyards that surround the village of Vouvray. The white wines vary greatly in style—they can be very sweet to very DRY, and STILL or SPARKLING. The best are generally well-made, medium-dry wines, with a touch of sweetness to help balance the sharp acidity. Very sweet wines, especially those created from BOTRYTIS CINEREA-infected grapes, can also be wonderful because Chenin Blanc's acidity cuts what could be an over-bearing sweetness and heightens the COMPLEX, HONEYED flavors. It also enables many of these wines to age quite well, with some lasting 40 to 50 years. The same high acidity that benefits sweet wines can make DRY wines harsh and sharp when young. The best of these will SOFTEN and their flavors evolve as they mature. CRISP, dry wines are usually the best choice for further processing into fully sparkling (MOUSSEUX) or slightly sparkling (PETILLANT) wines. Vouvray Moussex AC and Vouvray Petillant AC are both made via MÉTHODE CHAMPENOISE.

VQPRD *see* VIN DE QUALITÉ PRODUITS DANS DES RÉGIONS DÉTERMINÉES

achenheim [VAHKH-uhn-hime] One of the top wine-producing villages of Germany's RHEINPFALZ region. Wachenheim is located south of BAD DÜRKHEIM in the BEREICH Mittelhaardt/Deutsche Weinstrasse. The wines from Wachenheim, although slightly lighter than those from the neighboring villages of DEIDESHEIM and FORST, is still full-bodied (*see* BODY) and RIPE. They're often described as ELEGANT. The best individual vineyard sites (EINZELLAGEN) are **Goldbächel** and **Gerümpel**, followed by **Böhlig** and **Rechbächel**.

Walla Walla Valley AVA Small VITICULTURAL AREA located in the southern part of the large COLUMBIA VALLEY AVA. Most of the Walla Walla Valley area is in Washington but a tiny portion dips into northeast Oregon. The area, which is just developing, has less than 100 acres of vines planted. It appears to have one of the most diverse climates and is regarded as having good potential. Dominant varieties are CABERNET SAUVIGNON, CHARDONNAY, and MERLOT, plus a small amount of GEWURZTRAMINER. Area wineries include LEONETTI CELLARS, Seven Hills, and WOODWARD CANYON WINERY.

Walporzheim/Ahrtal, Bereich *see* AHR

Walschriesling *see* WELSCHRIESLING

 Warre [WEHR] Founded in 1670, this is the oldest English-owned PORT company. The first Warre family members were not involved with the business until 1729. The company is now owned by the Symington family, which also owns Dow (*see* SILVA & COSENS), GRAHAM, and SMITH WOODHOUSE—all premium port producers. Warre vintage ports are generally ranked within the top eight or nine of its kind. This company also produces a highly regarded single-quinta port from Quinta da Cavadinha, during undeclared years (*see* PORT). Warre also makes a good Late Bottled Vintage port.

Washington Washington winemaking is thought to have begun in the 1870s, although the first VITIS VINIFERA vines weren't planted until the early 1900s. PROHIBITION and Washington state laws managed to put a damper on most activity from 1920 to the 1960s. However, Washington has blossomed since the mid-1960s and now has over eighty wineries and 11,000 acres of vitis vinifera vineyards. It's the second largest producer (after California) of high-quality wine in the United States. Most of Washington's better vineyards are located in the eastern portion of the state, where the Cascade Mountains block the cool, damp weather prevalent in the western part. Washington's three primary growing regions are here—COLUMBIA VALLEY AVA, YAKIMA VALLEY

AVA, and WALLA WALLA AVA (the latter two are encompassed by the huge Columbia Valley AVA). These APPELLATIONS are the warmest growing areas in the Pacific Northwest, ranging from Region I to Region III (*see* CLIMATE REGIONS OF CALIFORNIA). The eastern region has the dry climate that is ideal for grapes and requires some irrigation during the growing season. Because of the varying temperatures throughout the eastern part of Washington, different grape varieties do well in its various locations. This means that MERLOT, a warm-weather grape, and RIESLING, a cool-weather grape, can both flourish. CABERNET SAUVIGNON, CHENIN BLANC, SAUVIGNON BLANC, and SÉMILLON are also grown, as well as CONCORD and other VITIS LABRUSCA varieties. There is another small growing area around Puget Sound in western Washington, but the cool, damp climate stipulates grape varieties like MÜLLER-THURGAU. Another area worth noting is in southwest Washington (Clark County) just north of Portland, Oregon. Its climate is similar to Oregon's Willamette Valley, which has great success with PINOT NOIR, Riesling, and CHARDONNAY.

watery A winetasting term for wines that are lacking in BODY, ALCOHOL, ACIDITY, and flavor.

weeper Term that describes a bottle of wine that is *weeping* or leaking slightly around its cork. This can be caused by a faulty cork or by poor storage where a cork that wasn't kept moist shrank. Weepers aren't necessarily bad bottles of wine, although it's possible that spoilage could have occurred.

Wehlen [VAY-luhn] A small wine-producing town located between BERNKASTEL and ZELTINGEN in Germany's MOSEL-SAAR-RUWER region. It's considered one of the region's top producers, primarily because of the wines from the famous vineyard site (EINZELLAGE) **Sonnenuhr** (the name of which means "sundial," which comes from the massive sundial on the property). Wehlen owes much of its reputation to the high-quality wines from the PRÜM family, who've made wine in Wehlen since the eighteenth century.

weighty A word that's sometimes used to describe a powerful, full-bodied (*see* BODY) wine.

wein [VINE] The German word for "wine."

Weinbaugebiet [vine-BOW-geh-beet] The term for a basic wine region designated for DEUTSCHER TAFFELWEIN (German TABLE WINE) production. There are four *Weinbaugebiete*—BAYERN, NECKAR, OBERHEIN, and RHEIN MOSEL. They are further divided into eight Untergebiet (subdistricts) and nineteen Gebiet (districts identified for LANDWEIN production).

weinberg [VINE-behrk] German term for "vineyard." *See also* WEIN-GARTEN.

weingarten [VINE-gahr-tuhn] Term for "vineyard" used in Germany's WÜRTTEMBERG region. *See also* WEINBERG.

weingärtnergenossenschaft [VINE-gahrt-nuhr-geh-NAW-sehn-shahft] Term for "cooperative cellar" in Germany's WÜRTTEMBERG region. *See also* WINZERGENOSSENSCHAFT.

weingut [VINE-goot] German for "wine estate." The term *weingut* usually refers to a winemaking facility, its cellar, and the vineyards. It can be used on a label only if the wine and any SUSSRESERVE have been made exclusively from estate-grown grapes.

weinkellerei [vine-KEHL-ler-ri] German for "wine cellar." Use of this term on a label usually means that the producer buys their grapes, MUST, or wine and may not have their own vineyards. Use of *Weingut-Weinkellerei* on a label indicates the producer owns his vineyards but also buys grapes from others.

Weissburgunder *see* PINOT BLANC

Weisserburgunder *see* MELON DE BOURGOGNE; PINOT BLANC

Weisser Gutedel *see* CHASSELAS

Weisser Klevner *see* PINOT BLANC

Weisser Riesling *see* RIESLING

weissherbst [VICE-hehrbst] A German word that translates to "white autumn" or "white harvest." It originally referred to red grapes that had lost their color because of Edelfaüle (BOTRYTIS CINEREA). Today *weissherbst* refers to ROSÉ wines produced from a single grape variety and of at least QUALITÄTSWEIN quality. The best-known wines of this type are made from Spätburgunder (PINOT NOIR) in Germany's BADEN and WÜRTTEMBERG regions.

well rounded *see* ROUND

Welschriesling [VELSH-reez-ling; VELSH-rees-ling; velsh-REEZ-ling] A white-wine grape that—in spite of its spelling—is not related to the true RIESLING of Germany, but which is a distinctly separate variety. Welschriesling's origin is a mystery, but it is well suited for the climate of central Europe, where it's extensively cultivated. It's known as Welshriesling (or *Walschriesling*) in Austria, *Vlassky Riesling* in Czechoslovakia, *Olaszriesling* in Hungary, *Riesling Italico* in Italy, and

Grasevina or *Laskiriesling* in the former Yugoslavia. Welschriesling is a high-yielding vine that, in most cases, produces fairly bland wines. At its best, this grape delivers LIGHT wines with pronounced flowery aromas, but it's quite different from the true Riesling. Some areas, like northeast Italy, blend Welschriesling with true Riesling and label the result "Riesling," which causes some confusion. In parts of Rumania, Welschriesling is used in SPARKLING WINES, whereas Austria occasionally turns it into a delightful TROCKENBEERENAUSLESE.

Wente Bros. [WIHN-tee] Wine-producing enterprise that was established in 1883 by Carl H. Wente on 50 acres he purchased in the LIVERMORE VALLEY. Over the years, Wente Bros. has been responsible for a number of firsts: in 1933 it produced California's first SAUVIGNON BLANC-labeled VARIETAL WINE; in 1936 it produced California's first CHARDONNAY-labeled varietal; and in 1969 it produced the first LATE-HARVEST RIESLING made from BOTRYTIS CINEREA-infected grapes. As it grew, Wente Bros. accumulated nearly 1,200 acres of vineyards in the Livermore Valley (plus a 2,000-acre cattle ranch) and another 650 acres of vineyards in the ARROYO SECO AVA (MONTEREY COUNTY). Today, Wente Bros. produces Chardonnay, GEWÜRZTRAMINER, Late-Harvest Riesling, and Sauvignon Blanc from their various vineyards. The wines are sold in two categories—estate-grown VARIETAL WINES and estate RESERVE, the latter in limited quantities. The neighboring Cresta Blanca Winery, which was purchased in 1981, has been refurbished and turned into Wente Bros. Sparkling Wine Cellars, which now produces MÉTHODE CHAMPENOISE-style SPARKLING WINES. Production for Wente Bros. is nearing 600,000 cases per year. The Wente family is also involved in the **Murrieta's Wells** winery, producer of two upscale BORDEAUX BLEND wines—the white is a blend of Sauvignon Blanc and SÉMILLON, and the red is a combination of CABERNET FRANC, CABERNET SAUVIGNON, and MERLOT. In 1992 Wente Bros. was involved in a syndicate that purchased **Concannon Vineyard**, another historic Livermore Valley winery.

Whitehall Lane This NAPA VALLEY winery was founded in 1980 by brothers Art Finkelstein and Alan Steen. In 1988 it was acquired by Japanese businessman Hideaki Ando, and in 1993 it was sold to San Francisco Bay area wine retailer Tom Leonardini. PHYLLOXERA infestation in the early 1990s necessitated replanting of Whitehall Lane's 26-acre vineyard (with CABERNET SAUVIGNON, CABERNET FRANC, and MERLOT). The winery is now focusing on high-quality Cabernet Sauvignon (regular and RESERVE), Cabernet Franc, CHARDONNAY, and Merlot. Their annual production is nearing 20,000 cases.

white port *see* PORT

White Riesling *see* RIESLING

white wine Any wine that's made from light-skinned grapes or from dark-skinned grapes whose juice doesn't contain any extracted color (which happens when the juice is immediately separated from the grape skins, seeds, and pulp). A white wine's hue may range from almost no color to very pale yellow to golden yellow to amber. As white wines age, they tend to darken.

White Zinfandel White Zinfandel is not a white wine but rather what's called a BLUSH WINE in the United States and a ROSÉ or BLANC DE NOIR in France. It's made from ZINFANDEL (a red-wine grape) and kept pale in color by quickly removing the skins from the juice after the grapes are pressed, which stops the transfer of color from the grape skin's dark pigments. The wine is then processed as for white wine. The resulting color generally varies from pale pink to apricot to salmon. Most White Zinfandels are slightly sweet, although some are quite DRY with just a whisper of RESIDUAL SUGAR. Introduced in the United States in the late 1970s, White Zinfandel wines found a niche in the early 1980s as the white-wine boom took off and producers searched for a channel for the red-grape surplus.

whole berry fermentation Fermentation method that could be considered a variation of the CARBONIC MACERATION technique but differs in that it's normally used with full-bodied (*see* BODY), TANNIC red wines. Whole berry fermentation consists of leaving some of the grape berries intact during the CRUSHING process. Some winemakers like to hold some of these whole berries back and add them at various points, thereby extending the FERMENTATION process. The chemical process involved with whole berry fermentation lends these sturdy red wines a lively, berryish character with fewer TANNINS and less ALCOHOL.

Willamette Valley AVA This Oregon VITICULTURAL AREA is in the state's northern portion, starting north of Portland and stretching to just south of Eugene. The Willamette Valley AVA nestles between the coastal range to the west and the Cascade Mountains to the east in Oregon's best grape-growing areas. It stretches for about 175 miles and is this state's main wine-producing area. The Dundee Hills area with its red soil and steep hills is regarded as one of the best sections, as is the Eola Hills area. PINOT NOIR, RIESLING, and CHARDONNAY are the most popular grape varieties, followed by PINOT GRIS. Other grapes, planted in small amounts, include CABERNET SAUVIGNON, GEWÜRZTRAMINER, MÜLLER-

THURGAU, SÉMILLON, and ZINFANDEL. Area wineries include Adelsheim, Amity, Bethel Heights, DOMAINE DROUHIN (the Drouhins of Burgundy), Elk Cove, Eyrie Vineyard, Knudsen-Erath Winery, Montinore Vineyard, Panther Creek, Ponzoi, Rex Hill, Sokal Blosser Winery, Tualatin Vineyards, and Yamhill Valley Vineyards.

Wiltingen [VIHL-ting-uhn] A famous wine-producing village located on the SAAR River in Germany's MOSEL-SAAR-RUWER region. Wiltingen is surrounded by numerous vineyards, including the 67-acre SCHARZHOF-BERG vineyard, which produces the village's best wines. Scharzhofberg is classified as an ORTSTEIL, and its wines, therefore, don't use Wiltingen in the name but are simply labeled Scharzhofberg. Wiltingen gives its name to the GROSSLAGE covering the area, Wiltingener Scharzberg, which can cause some confusion with the Scharzhofberg name. Other good vineyards include **Braune Kupp**, **Braunfels**, **Hölle**, **Kupp**, and **Rosenberg**. Area vineyards are planted with a high proportion of RIESLING.

Wiltinger Scharzberg *see* SAAR

wine The naturally fermented juice of grapes, unless otherwise specified. More broadly, the term can include alcoholic beverages created from other fruits and even vegetables and grains. Such potables are usually specified with the name of the fruit, as in "apricot wine." Wine has a rich history that has evolved along with that of man. Its historical roots reach back almost 12,000 years. As various cultures spread out into new parts of the world, so did the grapevine and the art of winemaking. Today there are vineyards throughout the world with good wine being produced in far-ranging locations from the United States to South Africa to Australia to South America to Europe. Wine is broadly classified in the following categories: 1. STILL (nonsparkling) WINES—including red, white, and ROSÉ—which can be DRY (nonsweet), semisweet, and sweet; 2. SPARKLING WINES, including French CHAMPAGNES as well as effervescent wines from other parts of the world; 3. FORTIFIED wines (such as SHERRY, PORT, and some DESSERT WINES), which have been augmented with BRANDY or other spirit; and 4. Aromatic Wines, like VERMOUTH, which have been flavored with ingredients like herbs or spices.

wine bottles Wine bottles come in many sizes, shapes, and colors. Bottle shapes and colors have some standard usage, but none are official so they cannot be completely relied on for accuracy (*see* Common Wine Bottle Shapes, page 586). The high-shouldered, straight-sided bottles made of dark green glass are the standard for BORDEAUX red wines. They're also generally used in other countries around the world for wines made from grapes associated with Bordeaux (like CABERNET SAUVIGNON and MERLOT), as well as others like California's ZINFANDEL and Italy's CHIANTI (the higher-quality ones). A similiarly shaped bottle in clear glass is used for Bordeaux white wines and is in general use around the world for wines made from SAUVIGNON BLANC and SÉMILLON. Some of these bottles are now showing up in taller versions that are slightly wider at the shoulders than at the bottom and have deeper PUNTS. The sloped-shouldered bottles used throughout BURGUNDY and the RHÔNE are also generally used throughout most of the world for wines made from grape varieties associated with those regions, such as CHARDONNAY, PINOT NOIR, and SYRAH (although Australian Syrah generally comes in Bordeaux-style bottles). Many Italian and Spanish wines also come in the sloped-shouldered bottles. Tall slender bottles called FLUTES or Rhine bottles are used in the RHINE region (where they're colored brown) and in ALSACE and the MOSEL (where they're usually green). This shape is used elsewhere for wines made with grape varieties associated ꓫvith Germany, like RIESLING and GEWÜRZTRAMINER. ROSÉ wines from Europe generally use this same bottle, only made of clear glass. U.S. BLUSH wines generally use a clear Bordeauxstyle bottle. The squat, straw-covered FIASCO used in Chianti has generally been replaced by the Bordeaux bottle. Since 1979 metric standards have been in use in the United States and the *standard wine bottle* size was set at 750 milliliters (ml) or approximately 25.4 ounces, which is almost exactly equivalent to an American fifth (⅕ of a quart or 25.6 ounces). In answer to the stricter driving/alcohol limits in many U.S. states, the wine industry recently introduced a new 500-ml bottle size, which is two-thirds of a standard bottle. In France's BEAUJOLAIS area a 500-ml bottle (which they call a POT) has long been used. In the United States, other legal bottle sizes include 50 ml, 100 ml, 187 ml, 375 ml, 1 liter, 1.5 liter, and 3 liter. Wine may also be bottled in sizes large than 3 liters if the capacity is in even-liter sizes—4 liters, 5 liters, 6 liters, etc. Other bottle terminology, although not legally defined in the United States, is still sometimes used in wine circles. These terms, which include French bottle descriptions and approximate bottle sizes, are: **split**—equivalent to 187 ml or one-quarter of a standard wine bottle; **half bottle**—375 ml; **magnum**—1.5 liters/2 standard bottles; **double magnum**—3 liters/4 standard bottles (in BORDEAUX); **Jeroboam**—3 liters/4 standard bottles (in CHAMPAGNE) or 4.5 liters/6 standard bottles (in BORDEAUX); **Rehoboam**—4.5 liters/6 standard bottles (in CHAMPAGNE); **Methuselah**—6 liters/8 standard bottles (in CHAMPAGNE); **Imperial**—6 liters/8 standard bottles (in

Bordeaux); **Salmanazar**—9 liters/12 standard bottles; **Balthazar**—12 liters/16 standard bottles; and **Nebuchadnezzar**—15 liters/20 standard bottles.

wine bucket *see* TEMPERATURE

wine cellar A storage area for wines, as well as the wines stored there. Traditionally, a wine cellar was underground because such a location keeps the wines at the proper temperature. Subterranean cellars certainly aren't a requirement today with the advent of temperature-controlled units that can be placed anywhere. Ideally, a wine cellar should be dry (but not overly, since a modicum of moisture helps keep the corks from drying out), well ventilated, vibration free, and cool. The ideal temperature is 50° to 55°F, but a reasonably consistent temperature between 45° and 70°F is acceptable. What's important is that the temperature remain constant—if it changes, the change shouldn't be drastic. Although wines age faster in warmer temperatures, they shouldn't be damaged unless the temperature is excessively hot. Bottles should be stored on their sides so that the wine is in contact with the cork to keep it moist and airtight. A cork that shrinks can expose the wine to oxygen (*see* OXIDIZED), which can ruin a wine.

wine cooler 1. An alcoholic beverage based on wine, fruit juice, sugar, and carbonated water. Wine coolers were first introduced in the United States during the early 1980s and became very popular over the next 5 to 6 years. 2. Another name for an ice bucket or wine bucket (*see* TEMPERATURE).

wineglasses *see* GLASSES, WINE

wine lake A reference to the low-quality wine produced in huge volumes from the warmer growing areas in the European Economic Community. Unlike quality wines, these potables don't fit into any of the supervised quality categories and therefore the vineyards are not governed by YIELD limitations. In addition, the grape VARIETIES are usually high producers of neutral character. Authorities in the various European countries are encouraging improvements through advanced VINIFICATION techniques and replanting with higher-quality grape varieties.

winemaker 1. An expert at making wine, who's usually in charge of all the steps of wine production at a winery. 2. Any person who makes wine, as in home winemaker.

wine press *see* PRESS

winery The American name for the place, including the building and required winemaking equipment, where wine is made.

wine-serving temperatures *see* TEMPERATURE

wine-storing temperatures *see* TEMPERATURE

winetaster 1. A person who evaluates wine by tasting. Generally, the term is applied to professionals or serious amateurs who have knowledge of and experience in the proper evaluations techniques. It can apply to writers, critics, buyers, and judges of winetasting events.

winetasting There's drinking wine and *tasting* wine, the latter being a more serious (but enjoyable) endeavor. The primary objective of a winetasting is to analyze the wine to determine its quality. The most simple, straightforward approach is to assess whether a wine tastes *good*. Dedicated winetasters (who vary broadly in their degree of seriousness) have more exacting criteria, however. There are many guidelines on how to taste wine formally, such as using the proper equipment, like white tablecloths, DECANTERS and appropriate GLASSES; having the wines at the right TEMPERATURE; decanting the wine, if necessary, and so on. The tasting process itself involves three basic steps, all of which have their own nuances: examining the wine's appearance, smelling the wine, and tasting it. **Examining the wine's appearance** generally consists of tilting the glass slightly away from you over a white background so the wine's color, clarity, and brilliance are obvious. Next, with the glass in an upright position, swirl the wine (wetting the sides of glass) and then check its VISCOSITY by observing the LEGS or SHEETS that cling to the sides of the glass. The wine's appearance tells an experienced winetaster several things including how it's AGING (whether it may be past its prime) and possible quality. **Smelling the wine** generally consists of swirling the wine to release its AROMA and/or BOUQUET and then putting your nose just inside the glass and inhaling gently. If you don't get much aroma from the wine, cover the top of the glass with one palm and swirl again; quickly remove your palm just before you smell the wine. Because smell and taste have a symbiotic relationship, just smelling the wine can reveal much of its character. If there's something wrong with wine, the nose will usually detect it. Conversely, the first hint of a delightful wine will be perceived through the sense of smell. By the final step of **tasting the wine**, a number of clues about it will already have been revealed. Some serious tasters suck in a little air as they take the wine into their mouth. This technique aerates the wine (which brings out the flavor) but also creates a slurping noise. Other tasters "chew" or slosh the wine around in their mouth. Both procedures are intended to expose the wine's full flavors while bringing the olfactory senses into play. In **blind tastings**, the identity of the wines is not known to the tasters. This is often done so that knowledge of the wine's origin doesn't influence the tasters' opinion. In some blind tastings, participants will know what type of wines are being tasted, but not which winery or CHÂTEAU they're from. For example, a group in a blind tasting might know that the wines are all California CABERNET SAUVIGNONS from the 1985 VINTAGE or that the same vintage of California and Bordeaux wines are being compared. In other blind tastings, the participants are told the various wines' identities (such as six CHARDONNAYS from six named wineries), but they don't know which glass which wine is in. Part of the fun and educational value of a blind tasting is learning how to determine the regional traits of wines and, eventually, those of the individual wineries and châteaus. Occasionally, there are **double blind tastings** where different VARIETAL WINES are tasted together. This adds the challenge of trying to ascertain the VARIETAL CHARACTER of each wine, in addition to where it's from. A **horizontal tasting** is one where all the wines are from the same vintage but from different wineries, wine estates, or châteaus. In a **vertical tasting** wines are from different (often contiguous) years but from the same winery, wine estate, or château. For example, a vertical tasting could include the 1981, 1982, 1983, 1984, 1985, and 1986 vintages of SILVER OAK Napa Valley CABERNET SAUVIGNON. The idea of a vertical tasting is to try to identify traits that exist in the same wine year after year. There are numerous descriptors used for winetasting. Knowing these terms is certainly not a requirement for enjoying wine. But knowledge of wine terminology will help you better understand wine newsletters, magazine and newspaper articles on wine, wine reviews, and restaurant winelists. This book includes many of these winetasting terms, a full list of which can be found on page 605. *See also* Winetasting, page 598.

winetasting terms *see* individual listings; Winetasting Terms, page 598.

wine thief A long glass or metal tube used for withdrawing samples of wine from barrels or CARBOYS.

Winkel [VINGK-uhl] A prominent wine-producing village located near the Rhine River in Germany's RHEINGAU region. It's situated in an area of premium vineyards, along with other villages like GEISENHEIM, Mittelheim, OESTRICH, and HATTENHEIM. Winkel's most famous vineyard is the 125-acre SCHLOSS VOLLRADS, which is situated in the hills above the village. Schloss Vollrads is classified as an ORTSTEIL and, therefore, simply uses its name on wine labels. Other quality vineyard sites (EINZELLAGEN) are **Hasensprung** and **Jessuitengarten**.

Winkler Scale *see* CLIMATE REGIONS OF CALIFORNIA

winzergenossenschaft [vine-zer-geh-NAW-sehn-shahft] The literal translation of this German term is "wine grower association," although it's more generally known as a "cooperative cellar." Wines sold by cooperative cellars can use the term ERZEUGERABFÜLLUNG—which has the same connotation as ESTATE BOTTLED—on labels. Although most of the better wines come from private estates, some of the *winzergenossenschaft* wines, particularly in Germany's RHEINPFALZ and BADEN regions, can be quite good. *Winzerverein* ("wine grower society") sometimes appears on labels and has the same meaning as *winzergenossenschaft*. *See also* ZENTRALKELLEREI.

winzerverein *see* WINZERGENOSSENSCHAFT

Wisselbrunnen *see* HATTENHEIM

withered A winetasting term used to describe an over-the-hill wine that's lost its FRUITY characteristics, both in flavor and BOUQUET.

Wonnegau, Bereich *see* RHEINHESSEN

wood-aged port *see* PORT

wood aging *see* AGING

Woodward Canyon Winery Small Washington State winery located in the WALLA WALLA AVA just west of the town of Walla Walla. Rick Small established his Woodward Canyon Winery in 1981 after planting a small 10-acre vineyard in the 1970s. The winery produces four wines—CHARDONNAY, CABERNET SAUVIGNON, a Cabernet Sauvignon-MERLOT blend called Charbonneau Red, and a SAUVIGNON BLANC-SÉMILLON blend called Charbonneau White. The Cabernet Sauvignon, Charbonneau Red, and Chardonnay have elicited high ratings from reviewers in the late 1980s and into the 1990s. Production is limited at 5,000 cases per year.

woody A wine that's been kept too long in barrels will take on an exaggerated OAKY flavor and BOUQUET. This *woody* trait can overwhelm a wine's other components and is considered undesirable.

Wülfen *see* RAUENTHAL

Württemberg [VURT-uhm-behrk] One of Germany's thirteen AN-BAUGEBIETE (quality wine regions), located along the Neckar River and its tributaries where they flow east of the Rhine River before turning west to join the Rhine. The majority of the region's vineyards are situated just north of the city of Stuttgart. The region is divided into three main BERE-ICHE—**Kocher-Jagst-Tauber**, **Remstal-Stuttgart**, and **Württemberg-isch Unterland**. There are many small vineyards in the region and almost 90 percent of the crop is processed by grower's cooperatives. Unlike most Anbaugebiete, red varieties make up over 50 percent of the planted acreage in Württemberg. RIESLING is the most widely planted grape, but there are several widely planted red varieties—Trollinger (SCHIAVA), Müllerrebe (MEUNIER), Limberger, PORTUGIESER, and Spätburg-under (PINOT NOIR). Red wines are generally slightly sweet and light in both color and TANNINS. Because many of the red grapes lack adequate color, they're made into WEISSHERBST (a ROSÉ) rather than red wine. This region's other specialty is SCHILLERWEIN, a pink wine made by combining red and white grapes prior to FERMENTATION.

Württembergisch Unterland, Bereich *see* WÜRTTEMBERG

Würzburg [VUH*R*TS-beh*r*k] University city that is the capital of Germany's FRANKEN region and the site of many of the old cellars of the region's finest wine-producing estates. Among the best cellars are: the Staatlicher Hofkeller, which is the Bavarian State Domain; the Juliusspital, the local church charity; and Bürgerspital, a city-run charitable institution. The vineyards on the city's outskirts along the Main River are planted primarily with MÜLLER-THURGAU, RIESLING, and SYLVANER. **Stein** is the most famous vineyard (EINZELLAGE) in Würzburg (and Franken). Its 210 acres cover the best sections, which have an ideal southern exposure and look down on Würzburg. Wines from the Franken region are sometimes called Steinwein, in reference to this famous vineyard.

Würzburger Stein *see* FRANKEN; WÜRZBURG

Würzgarten *see* HALLGARTEN; ÜRZIG

Wyndruif *see* SÉMILLON

arel-lo [sah-REHL-loh] Grown extensively in Spain's CATALONIA region, this white-wine grape is one of the three main varieties used to make most Spanish SPARKLING WINES. It is considered a medium- to low-quality grape, used mainly to add BODY, and is customarily blended with the higher-quality MACABEO and PARELLADA grapes. Xarel-lo is also used to make a STILL WINE, which is usually a blend of these same grapes. It's the primary grape in the Alella DO, where it's known as *Pansa Blanca*.

Xérès [seh-REHS] The former name for JEREZ DE LA FRONTERA.

"Y" *see* D'YQUEM, CHÂTEAU

Yakima Valley AVA [YAK-uh-maw] Although Yakima Valley, which is in the south central part of Washington State, was the first designated AVA in the northwest, it's now encompassed by the much larger CO-LUMBIA VALLEY AVA. It has some of the coolest weather in the Columbia Valley and grows a great number of CONCORD grapes, most of which are used for juice. The grapes that go into wines include CABERNET SAUVIGNON, CHENIN BLANC, CHARDONNAY, MERLOT, RIESLING, SAUVIGNON BLANC, and SÉMILLON. Among the wineries in this area are Blackwood Canyon Vintners, Cascade Estates, Coventry Vale, Covery Run, Hinzerling, and Hogue.

Yarra Valley A small Australian growing area situated just northeast of the city of Melbourne in the state of Victoria. The principal grape varieties here are CHARDONNAY, PINOT NOIR, and CABERNET SAUVIGNON, followed by Shiraz (SYRAH), SAUVIGNON BLANC, MERLOT, RIESLING, CABERNET FRANC, and SÉMILLON. Yarra Valley is best known for Pinot Noir and Cabernet Sauvignon wines. Area producers include Coldstream Hills, De Bortoli, Domaine Chandon, Lillydale Vineyards, Long Gully, Lovegrove of Cottles Bridge, Seville Estates, Yarra Ridge, Yarra Yering, and Yeringberg.

yeast [YEEST] A living, microscopic, single-cell organism. Wild yeast spores are always floating in the air. Just when these wild spores first interacted with foods and liquids is uncertain, but we do know that Egyptians used yeast as a leavening agent over 5,000 years ago and that wine and other fermented beverages were made for millennia before that. It was in 1857 that France's famous microbiologist Louis Pasteur discovered that FERMENTATION was caused by yeasts. During fermentation, yeast converts food (in the form of sugar or starch) into ALCOHOL and CARBON DIOXIDE. In the production of wine, the conversion of yeast to alcohol is necessary for the final product, and carbon dioxide is what makes SPARKLING WINES effervescent. To multiply and grow, all yeast needs is the right environment—moisture, food, and a warm, nurturing temperature. Today, scientists have been able to isolate and identify the specific yeasts that are best for winemaking. Modern winemakers carefully choose the yeasts they use in combination with different varieties of grapes. Various yeasts have specific properties and are better suited for particular winemaking styles. For example, some yeasts produce less foam and are therefore well suited for BARREL FERMENTATION. Those styles of yeast that are resistant to cold temperatures are best for making white wines. Other yeasts ferment more rapidly, tolerate alcohol better, or impart flavors to the wine (some desirable, others not). Popular commercially available yeasts used today include Champagne, Epernay, Montrachet, Pasteur Champagne, and Steinberg. Rather than resorting to using cultivated yeasts, some winemakers prefer **native yeast fermentation**, which relies simply on natural wild yeast spores. *See also* BRETTANOMYCES.

yeasty A winetasting term used to describe the yeasty, fresh-bread BOUQUET found in certain wines that have been aged *sur lie*—"on the LEES" (the fermentation-created sediment that consists mainly of dead yeast cells and small grape particles). Some wines—such as CHARDONNAY or SAUVIGNON BLANC—are aged this way to add complexity. SPARKLING WINES made via MÉTHODE CHAMPENOISE can also assume a yeasty characteristic because they undergo a second (*sur lie*) fermentation in the bottle. In most wines, however, a yeasty smell is considered a flaw.

Yecla DO [YAY-klah] A DO located in the Levante region in eastern Spain, northwest of the city of Alicante. Yecla produces mainly high-ALCOHOL (14 to 16 percent) red wines, primarily from MONASTRELL grapes, along with some Garnacha (GRENACHE). Recent efforts suggest that a shift toward lower-alcohol (12 to 13 percent) wines may be underway.

yeso *see* PLASTERING

yield [YEELD] A term used in grape-growing and winemaking circles to express the productivity of a set amount of vineyard land. Yield is a way of comparing the relative productivity of different grape varieties in different locations. In the United States and Australia, grape yield is generally expressed in terms of tons per acre; in Europe and South America, it's expressed in HECTOLITERS per HECTARE. In comparing European yields to U.S. yields, 1 hectoliter of grapes per hectare would be equivalent to .0741 tons of grapes per acre; 1 ton per acre is equivalent to 13.5 hectoliters per hectare. A hecoliter produces approximately 133 bottles or 11.1 cases of wine (a standard bottle is 750 milliliters). A ton of grapes produces about 727 bottles or just over 60 cases of wine. Therefore, a vineyard in France that produces 50 hectoliters of grapes per hectare would be equivalent to one in the United States that produces 3.7 tons of grapes per acre. A U.S. vineyard producing 5 tons per acre is equivalent to a European vineyard producing 67.5 hectoliters per hectare. A 50-hectare vineyard producing 45 hectoliters of grapes per hectare would produce just under 25,000 cases of wine. Yield is important because the higher the yield, the more productive the vines and the more grapes the grower has to sell. However, it's generally agreed that lower yields produce higher-quality wines and that the higher the yield, the more diluted the resulting wine will be. With that in mind, one of the criteria for meeting French APPELLATION D'ORIGINE CONTRÔLÉE (AC) regulations is permissible yield. Each AC area has a maximum allowable yield, depending on the grape variety and quantity of land. Yields are kept down by pruning the vines so that there's an optimum ratio between fruit production and vegetative growth (important for the next year's production). As more is learned about viticultural techniques, higher yields are being achieved without loss of quality. However, it still holds true that higher yields from the same set of vines grown the same way will dilute the concentration in the grapes. Some vineyards in Germany's RHINE and MOSELLE district can yield 100 hectoliters per hectare without loss of quality. On the other hand, in Spain much of the vineyard land is very arid and can't be densely planted because the vines won't get enough moisture. This climate, plus rather antiquated viticultural practices, limits yields in most parts of Spain where the average is around 23 hectoliters of grapes per hectare. In California's coastal areas, where higher quality wines are made, growers expect 3 to 6 tons per acre (equivalent to 40 to 80 hectoliters per hectare), depending on the location and grape variety.

York Mountain AVA A small California APPELLATION located just west of the PASO ROBLES AVA in SAN LUIS OBISPO COUNTY. It sits east of the San Lucian Mountains and receives the ocean breezes that are generally blocked from the Paso Robles area. York Mountain therefore is considered a cool Region I area (*see* CLIMATE REGIONS OF CALIFORNIA) and does well with PINOT NOIR grapes. It currently has only one winery, York Mountain Vineyard, although there are other vineyards in the area.

young; youthful In winetasting parlance, *young* describes a fresh, light, generally fruity wine.

d'Yquem, Château [sha-TOH dee-KEHM] When the wines of SAUTERNES were ranked in the CLASSIFICATION OF 1855, one wine, Château d'Yquem, stood out from all the rest. It was elevated to a class all by itself—known variously as *Premier Grand Cru, Grand Premier Cru,* and *Premier Cru Supérieur*. Although Château d'Yquem is allowed to label its wines "Premier Grand Cru Classé," it doesn't. Today, this CHÂTEAU undisputedly still makes the best wines in the area, and some feel in all of Bordeaux (including the red wines). In addition to Château d'Yquem's microclimate, it's the meticulous selection process that occurs every step of the way that makes these wines so great. If the grapes aren't perfectly ripe, they simply aren't picked. This necessitates multiple passes through the vineyards—up to ten to twelve times during some VINTAGES. In difficult years the picking process itself can take 8 to 9 weeks. If the picked grapes aren't of high enough quality, they're rejected. Even after the wines have been made and AGED in OAK, some barrels may be rejected before finishing the wines. In a few years—like 1978 and 1979—over 60 percent of the wine was rejected as unsuitable. Some vintages (1964, 1972, and 1974, for example) were rejected totally, and no Château d'Yquem wine was produced at all. Rejected wines are sold to other VINTNERS. Château d'Yquem declares that, because of this selective process, only one glass of wine per vine is produced. One consequence of this careful selection is that the wines are very expensive—the last few vintages have been released at from $125 to $200 per bottle. Another is that the wines are extremely RICH, full-bodied (*see* BODY), and powerfully flavored, with the best vintages capable of aging for 40 to 60 years or longer. Although Château d'Yquem has about 250 acres of vineyards, annual production is only 5,000 to 6,000 cases of sweet Sauternes AC wines and about 2,000 cases of DRY white wine. The grapes used are approximately 80 percent SÉMILLON and 20 percent SAUVIGNON BLANC for the sweet Sauternes wines. The dry white wine, which is called **"Y,"** uses almost equal parts Sémillon and Sauvignon Blanc.

Yvorne [ee-VAW*RN*] A wine named for a village in the CHABLAIS district in Switzerland's VAUD canton. Yvorne wines are produced from CHASSELAS grapes, locally called *Dorin*. They're known for their ripe fruit and FLINTY character and are considered some of the best of the district.

apponara Bianca *see* BOMBINO BIANCO

ZD Wines This winery was originally established in the SONOMA VALLEY in 1969 and moved to its present location in the NAPA VALLEY just off the Silverado Trail in 1979. The founders, Gino Zepponi and Norman De Leuze, started with CHARDONNAY and PINOT NOIR, but the line was eventually expanded. Today the winery produces nearly 21,000 cases each year. Over 70 percent of the production is made up of the highly regarded Chardonnay wines, blended from grapes from MONTEREY COUNTY, Napa Valley, SANTA BARBARA COUNTY, and Sonoma County. ZD Pinot Noir also receives high scores from some reviewers. The ZD line is completed with CABERNET SAUVIGNON and an occasional LATE HARVEST wine made from RIESLING or GEWÜRZTRAMINER.

Zell [TSEHL] Although there are a number of German towns and villages named Zell, the best known in wine circles is the village on the Mosel River in Germany's MOSEL-SAAR-RUWER region. It's this village that's the genesis of **Zeller Schwarze Katz**, the wine with the familiar black cat (Schwarze Katz) on the label. In 1971 Zeller Schwarze Katz became the name of the GROSSLAGE covering vineyards around Zell, and only wines from this Grosslage can use the name. Most wines using the Zeller Schwarze Katz name are simple, light wines, although quality can vary immensely. Zell also lends its name to the BEREICH that covers this region, **Bereich Zell/Mosel**, which encompasses the land from Zell northeast to Koblenz. This area is also referred to as *Untermosel* or *Lower Mosel*.

Zeller Schwarze Katz *see* ZELL

Zellerbach Vineyards *see* KENDALL-JACKSON VINEYARDS

Zell/Mosel, Bereich *see* ZELL

Zeltingen [TSEHL-tihn-guhn] A top wine-producing village in Germany's MOSEL-SARR-RUWER region. It's located in the same area as other esteemed villages of the Mosel—BERNKASTEL, GRAACH, and WEHLEN. The vineyards of Zeltingen-Rachtig (its full name) exist on both sides of the Mosel River. Top EINZELLAGEN include **Deutschherrenberg**, **Himmelreich**, **Schlossberg**, and **Sonnenuhr** (which lies adjacent to the Sonnenuhr vineyard of Wehlen). Zeltingener RIESLING wines are known to be full-bodied (*see* BODY) yet ELÉGANT.

zentralkellerei [TSEHN-trahl-KEHL-lehr-ri] A German term meaning "central cellar," referring to a very large cooperative cellar that gets its wine or MUST from smaller cooperative cellars (*see* WINZ-

ERGENOSSENSCHAFT). A large *zentralkellerei* may have as many as 4,000 to 5,000 members and produce their own brand names of wine.

Zibibbo *see* MUSCAT

Zinfandel [ZIHN-fuhn-dehl] Grape that is considered California's red-wine grape because it's not widely grown in other parts of the world. Zinfandel vines were brought to California by Agoston HA-RASZTHY (known as "the father of California wine") in the 1850s. By the 1880s this variety was rapidly gaining acceptance by California growers, and it is now that state's most extensively planted red grape. For years Zinfandel's origins were very mysterious. Now, however, a relationship between Zinfandel and *Primitivo* (a variety grown in Italy's PUGLIA region) has been established. Outside of the Zinfandel grown in California (and Italy's Primitivo), there are only isolated plantings of this grape—mainly in South Africa and Australia. Zinfandel is vinified in many styles, which vary greatly in quality. One popular style is *White Zinfandel,* a fruity-flavored white wine that's usually slightly sweet and ranges in color from light to dark pink. The Zinfandel grape is also used as a base for SPARKLING WINES. When made into red wine, Zinfandel can produce wines ranging from light, NOUVEAU styles to hearty, robust reds with berrylike, spicy (sometimes PEPPERY) flavors, plenty of TANNINS and ALCOHOL, and enough DEPTH, COMPLEXITY, and LONGEVITY to be compared to CABERNET SAUVIGNONS. Another style is LATE-HARVEST Zinfandel, which exhibits higher alcohol levels and some RESIDUAL SUGAR. Occasionally, Zinfandel is fortified and marketed as a California PORT-style wine. Large Zinfandel plantings exist in California's CENTRAL VALLEY where the hot weather tends to produce lower-quality grapes, which often make their way into JUG WINE. The Italian DOC, PRIMITIVO DI MANDURIA, produces dry red Primitivo grape-based wines that are similar to some California Zins. As Zinfandel's popularity increases, more and more enterprising Italian Primitivo growers are labeling their wines "Zinfandel" and exporting them to the United States.

zucchero [TSOOK-kay-roh] Italian for "sugar." *Zuccheraggio* is the Italian term for CHAPTALIZATION and *residuo* refers to RESIDUAL SUGAR.

APPENDIX

TIPS FOR BEGINNERS ON BUYING WINE

Buying wine can be an interesting and endlessly adventurous journey of discovery. However, unlike other consumables, which generally have a predictable level of consistency year after year, wine VINTAGES can be noticeably different in varying degrees from subtle to conspicuous. Such annual differences could have any of myriad reasons including different weather conditions, change in winemaker or winemaking style, or grapes from a different supplier. Newcomers needn't be intimidated when buying wine, however, and the following tips should help facilitate forays to the wine store.

1. Plan ahead by reading about wine—unplanned or spur-of-the-moment purchases are often disappointing. Put your name on the mailing list of several wine stores that send newsletters with information such as current releases, award winners, and what's new in the wine world. Compare several different wine store flyers to help in shopping for the best prices.

2. Choose a wine retailer *carefully*. The store you select should be air-conditioned—heat and erratic temperature fluctuations can drastically alter a wine's flavor. Avoid wine stored near heat outlets or in the glare of bright, intense light, such as a sun-drenched window. Ideally, a store should have rapid turnover, and the wine should be stored on its side, neither of which is always the case in supermarkets or drug stores. If the store has speedy turnover, however, wine standing in an upright position shouldn't suffer the consequences of a cork drying out. The store's staff should be well informed, just as able to suggest a wine to go with a particular dish as they are to advise you on a specific vintage of a particular wine. The bottom line is that you'll generally get more personalized and informed service at a wine store than you will at a supermarket or other store where wine isn't the focus.

3. Try to do most of your shopping in one or two wine establishments so that you can get to know the salespeople.

4. Familiarize yourself with a store's system of arranging wines. Most establishments organize their wines by grape variety (CABERNET SAUVIGNON, CHARDONNAY, ZINFANDEL, etc.) for American wines, as well as place of origin (France, Italy, Spain, etc.) for foreign wines. There are also often sections for discounted wines, odd lots, special promotions, etc. Taking time to check out the aisles of your favorite wine store will give you a head start the next time you dash in for a last-minute purchase.

5. When you go into a wine store to ask advice, have a good idea of what you want. What is the wine for? If it's to go with a meal, what will be served? What are your personal preferences? How much do you want to spend? The more informed you are as a shopper, the happier you'll be as a consumer.

6. Your personal taste should *always* be the deciding factor in your wine choice. If possible, taste a wine before you buy it. Many wine stores have tasting bars that let you sample selected wines.

7. Inspect the wine you buy to make sure that the bottle's fill level is not lower than other bottles. Neither should the bottle show any sign of leakage. Both are a warning that air (one of wine's worst enemies) is getting into the bottle.

8. Buying wine in case lots generally saves you money because many wine stores offer discounts of 10 percent or more on case purchases. But there's one caveat: *always* try a bottle first. You're setting yourself up for potential disappointment (not to mention wasted money) if you buy a case of wine simply because a co-worker, friend, or wine writer likes it. You might think it's *dreadful.* Your personal taste should always be the final word.

See also Opening and Serving Still Wine, page 590; TEMPERATURE; WINE BOTTLES; WINE CELLAR.

TIPS ON ORDERING WINE IN A RESTAURANT

Ordering wine in a restaurant isn't really much different than buying it in a wine store; the main distinction is that you have an audience—your dining companion(s). There is a certain procedure, however, that the following tips should help you quickly master.

1. It pays to be prepared when you know you'll be ordering wine in a restaurant. If possible, do a little reading about wines so you'll have an idea of what you might want to order. Today, all but the most modest of restaurants have a wine list. Restaurants without wine lists might simply offer a red and white HOUSE WINE; some have a daily "blackboard" with the selection of wines. If you order the house wine (which should be available by glass or carafe), be sure to ask what it is. The server should be able to tell you the variety (Chardonnay, Merlot, etc.), brand name, and VINTAGE (if any) of a house wine. Most wine lists are presented as a printed menu, with the wines arranged by color (red or white) and region or country (American, French, Italian, etc.). A good wine list will indicate the wine's name, vintage, and region or winemaker, such as: "1989 Heitz Cabernet Sauvignon, Napa Valley, Martha's Vineyard." Some even add a descriptive comment about the wine, such as: "Dark, rich, and intensely flavored, with hints of mint and cherries and a long-lasting finish." Additionally, many wine lists number their wines, which facilitates the server in locating them in the cellar. Numbers are also a help if you don't know how to pronounce a wine—you can simply say, "I'd like a bottle of number 13." Lastly, expect the standard markup for wines in restaurants to be 2 to 2½ times retail.

2. You've perused the wine list and made a selection. Or, maybe you've reviewed the list, know you want a Pinot Noir, but are unfamiliar with those on the wine list. This is where the SOMMELIER or wine steward can help. A *good* sommelier will assist you in choosing a wine in your price range, while at the same time making you feel comfortable, never uninformed. In some restaurants, the server will perform the sommelier's duties.

3. Once the wine is ordered, it's brought to the table and presented to the individual who ordered it. This is the point where you examine the label to make sure it's the wine you ordered. Be sure and check the vintage—sometimes a restaurant will deplete its supply of one vintage and simply bring out the succeeding year. This may not make a difference, but if you love the 1985 vintage of a wine and are presented a 1986 instead, know there will most certainly be some difference. In such an instance, you may decide to order a different wine.

4. Once the wine is opened, the sommelier or server will present the cork to whomever ordered it. According to tradition, the cork may then be sniffed to detect any off odors, although this step certainly isn't necessary. You may want to examine the cork to be sure the end that was in contact with the wine is wet—a sign that the wine was stored properly. If the cork is moldy or crumbles between your fingers, it's certainly a sign of deterioration—order another bottle.

5. Smell and taste are the best criteria of whether or not a wine is sound, and the next step is for the sommelier to pour a small amount of wine for the person who ordered it. Gently swirl the wine in the glass to release the aroma, smell the wine, and then take a tiny sip. If the wine doesn't emit any rank or off-putting odors (such as vinegar) or flavors, it is most probably acceptable. Remember that the flavor and aroma of wine will expand and develop as it aerates. It's not appropriate to return a wine simply because you don't like it as much as you thought you would. Lastly, the tasting process should not be a long, involved procedure—the server has other tables to attend.

6. Once you've tasted and approved of a wine, simply say "thank you" to the server, a signal that he or she may pour it for the others in your party.

7. Many restaurants will open and serve a bottle of wine brought by the diner. A quick call will confirm if this is possible and, if so, the amount of the corkage fee—a charge for opening and serving the wine. Some restaurants charge a lower fee if the wine brought is not on their wine list, such as might be the case with an older or particularly distinctive wine.

DEMYSTIFYING THE WINE LABEL

The information on a wine label can provide the consumer with pertinent details about the wine in the bottle. Unfortunately, some foreign wine labels can be extremely confusing. In the United States, however, certain mandatory label information is required, even for imported wines (on which the data must be in English). The following information should bolster your wine label knowledge and help decipher even the most complicated label.

MANDATORY LABEL INFORMATION FOR WINES SOLD IN THE UNITED STATES:

1. Name of the wine
2. Name of the producer
3. Name and address of the bottler (if different from the producer)
4. Name of the importer of a non-U.S. wine
5. Name of the shipper if different from the importer
6. Alcohol content, expressed as a percentage of the volume
7. Volume of the bottle's contents
8. Country of origin
9. Sulfite advisory
10. Government warning

OPTIONAL LABEL INFORMATION:

11. Quality of the wine
12. Vintage of the wine
13. Type of wine
14. Appellation or growing region
15. Descriptive information about the wine

Details on Mandatory and Optional Wine Label Information

1. Name of the Wine

The standards for naming a wine vary depending on its origin. Some of the foundations for wine names follow.

- In many European countries a wine is named for the growing area or APPELLATION where it originated. For example, Bordeaux Supérieur, Brouilly, and Chablis are all French ACs (APPELLATION

D'ORIGINE CONTRÔLÉE); Chianti is an Italian DOCG (DENOMINAZIONE DI ORIGINE CONTROLLATA GARANTITA), and Rioja is a Spanish DOCa (DENOMINACIÓN DE ORIGEN CALIFICADA).

- In some areas like the United States, Australia, New Zealand, South Africa, and South America, and in France's Alsace region, the grape variety (such as cabernet sauvignon or chardonnay) is often the name of the wine.

- Proprietary names are sometimes used when a wine doesn't fit into either of the previous guidelines. For example, JOSEPH PHELPS VINEYARDS' Insignia which, because it's a Cabernet Sauvignon–Cabernet Franc–Merlot blend and doesn't contain 75 percent of one grape variety, cannot (in the United States) be named after a specific grape variety.

2. Name of the Producer

The name of the producer is often the most important information on the label. That's because some producers have a reputation for producing high-quality wines year after year, whereas others have sporadic or less than stellar records. For example, a single GRAND CRU vineyard in BURGUNDY can have numerous producers, with some making consistently higher-quality wine than others. The name of the producer can be the name of a winery in countries like the United States and Australia, of a CHÂTEAU in some parts of France like BORDEAUX, of a DOMAINE in other French areas like Burgundy, and of wine estates in Italy, Spain, and Germany. The exact name of the producer is important because in many areas, such as France and Germany, there are a number of producers with the same surname. Therefore, knowledge of both Christian name and surname is necessary to differentiate producers. For instance, the name of the PRÜM family is attached to numerous wine estates in Germany's MOSEL-SAAR-RUWER region, the best known of which is Joh. Jos. Prüm.

3. Name and Address of the Bottler

The name of the bottler is often the same name as the producer, but occasionally a company other than the producer actually bottles the wine, in which case the label would read something like: "Bottled For ABC Winery by XYZ Company." A label that says "Estate Bottled" (*see listing*) means the wine was bottled by the producer.

4. Name of the Importer

When wines are brought into the United States, an importer handles the arrangements for shipping and storing the wines until they reach the establishment where they'll be sold.

5. Name of the Shipper

If a company other than the importer handles the shipping, that organization's name is also listed on the label.

6. Alcohol Content

The United States requires that alcohol by volume (*see* ALCOHOL) information be included on wine labels. For TABLE WINE, the U.S. requirement is a minimum alcohol level of 7 percent, a maximum of 14 percent. The label variance can be up to 1.5 percent. For example, a wine label stating "Alcohol 12.5% By Volume" can legally range anywhere from 11 to 14 percent. However, wines cannot exceed the upper or lower limit. The alcohol-by-volume range for SHERRIES is 17 to 20 percent, for PORTS it's 18 to 20 percent; both have a label variance of 1 percent.

7. Volume of the Bottle's Contents

The volume figure, such as 750 ml (milliliters) or 1.5l (liters), is sometimes molded into the bottle glass rather than printed on the label. Therefore, if the label doesn't designate the bottle size, look along the base of the bottle for the indication. For details on the various bottle sizes allowed in the United States, see listing for WINE BOTTLES.

8. The Country of Origin

The country of origin is the country where the wine is produced. However, depending on that country's laws, it may not necessarily be where all the grapes were grown.

9. Sulfite Advisory

The words "Contains Sulfites" indicate that sulfur dioxide (SO_2)—a colorless, water-soluble, nonflammable gas—was used somewhere in the grape-growing or winemaking process and that the resulting wine contains 10 ppm or more of sulfites, which can cause severe allergic reactions in certain individuals.

10. Government Warning

A U.S. Surgeon General warning states that drinking alcoholic beverages can: 1. cause birth defects, 2. impair ability to drive a car or operate machinery, and 3. cause health problems.

11. Quality of the Wine

The quality of the wine is often implied by the rating the wine receives in the producing country's appellation system. For example at the lowest level of Italy's quality ranking are the VINO DA TAVOLA wines, surpassed by VINO TIPICO wines, DENOMINAZIONE DI ORIGINE CONTROLLATA (DOC) wines, and the highest level, DENOMINAZIONE DI ORIGINE CONTROLLATA E GARANTITA (DOCG) wines. Although choosing an Italian wine of DOCG status doesn't always mean it will be better than those of lesser rankings, it usually indicates a wine of high quality. (See individual country entries for their hierarchy of quality rankings.)

12. Vintage of the Wine

The year indicated on a wine label is the *vintage,* or the year the grapes were harvested. In the United States, a wine label may only list the vintage if 95 percent of the wine comes from grapes harvested that year. If a blend of grapes from 2 years or more is used, the wine is either labeled *non-vintage (NV)* or there's no mention of date. *See also* VINTAGE.

13. Type of Wine

The label information regarding the type of wine is very general, usually in the form of basic terms like "red table wine," "dry red wine," "white wine," "still white wine," or "sparkling wine." Such terms simply place the wine in a generic category. Don't assume, however, that because a wine is described as, say, a "red table wine" that it's a simple or mediocre wine. In the United States, for example, unless a wine contains at least 75 percent of a particular grape variety, it cannot use the grape's name on the label. For instance, CAIN CELLARS simply uses the descriptor "red table wine" for its Cain Five—a wine this winery considers its premium red, which happens to be a blend of the five Bordeaux grape varieties— CABERNET SAUVIGNON, CABERNET FRANC, MERLOT, MALBEC, and PETIT VERDOT.

14. Appellation or Growing Region

As mentioned previously under *Name of the Wine,* the actual growing area or APPELLATION becomes the name of many European wines. In other areas like the United States and Australia, where the wine is more often named for the grape variety, some producers also list the growing region on the label, particularly if the area is prestigious. The NAPA VALLEY in the United States and the HUNTER VALLEY in Australia are examples of such well-known growing regions. In the United States, where such growing regions are called AMERICAN VITICULTURAL AREAS (AVA), at least 85 percent of the grapes must come from a single AVA for the region's name to be used on the label.

15. Descriptive Information

Occasionally, wine labels include descriptive words or phrases designed to give the consumer added information. For example, a label might indicate the wine was BARREL-FERMENTED, a process thought to imbue a wine with rich, creamy flavors, delicate oak characteristics, and better aging capabilities. Many terms, however, are simply marketing jargon with no legal or standard usage.

See the labels on the following pages for examples of mandatory and optional wine label information.

SAMPLE WINE LABELS AND THE INFORMATION THEY INCLUDE

WINE LABEL KEY

1. Name of the wine
2. Name of the producer
3. Name and address of the bottler (if different from producer)
4. Name of the importer of a non-U.S. wine
5. Name of the shipper if different from the importer
6. Alcohol content, expressed as a percentage of the volume
7. Volume of the bottle's contents
8. The country of origin
9. Sulfite advisory
10. Government health warning
11. Quality of the wine
12. Vintage of the wine
13. Type of wine
14. Appellation or growing region
15. Descriptive information about the wine

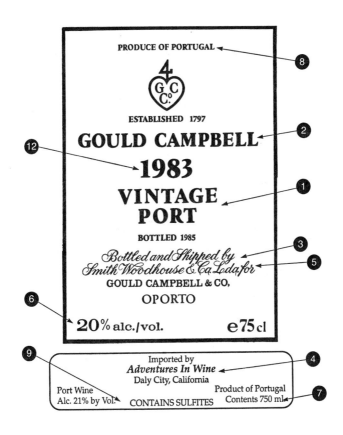

PRODUCE OF PORTUGAL ◄ **8**

ESTABLISHED 1797

GOULD CAMPBELL ◄ **2**

12 ►**1983**

VINTAGE **1**
PORT

BOTTLED 1985

Bottled and Shipped by ◄ **3**
Smith Woodhouse & Ca Lda for ◄ **5**
GOULD CAMPBELL & CO.
OPORTO

6 ►**20**% alc./vol.   e**75**cl

9   Imported by   **4**
          Adventures In Wine ◄
          Daly City, California

Port Wine   Product of Portugal
Alc. 21% by Vol.   CONTAINS SULFITES   Contents 750 ml ◄ **7**

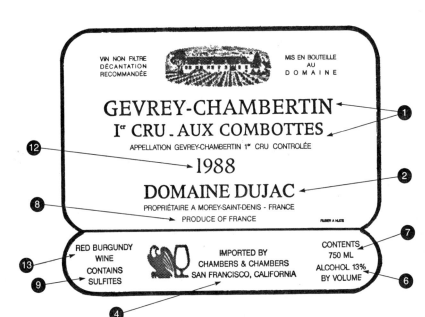

VIN NON FILTRE
DÉCANTATION
RECOMMANDÉE

MIS EN BOUTEILLE
AU
DOMAINE

GEVREY-CHAMBERTIN
Ier CRU - AUX COMBOTTES

APPELLATION GEVREY-CHAMBERTIN 1er CRU CONTROLÉE

1988

DOMAINE DUJAC

PROPRIÉTAIRE A MOREY-SAINT-DENIS - FRANCE

PRODUCE OF FRANCE

RED BURGUNDY
WINE

CONTAINS
SULFITES

IMPORTED BY
CHAMBERS & CHAMBERS
SAN FRANCISCO, CALIFORNIA

CONTENTS
750 ML

ALCOHOL 13%
BY VOLUME

CHÂTEAU
LA TOUR DE BY

1982

CRU BOURGEOIS DU MÉDOC

MÉDOC

APPELLATION MÉDOC CONTROLÉE

Sté VITICOLE DU MEDOC "CHATEAU LA TOUR DE BY" 33340 BÉGADAN

CONTENTS 750 ml (25.4 Fl. Oz)

PRODUCE OF FRANCE ALCOHOL 12% BY VOL. RED BORDEAUX WINE

Shipped by : Crus et Châteaux de Bordeaux

Imported by : LEFCOURT CELLARS Inc, SAN FRANCISCO, CA.

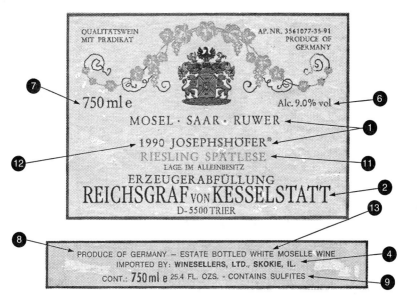

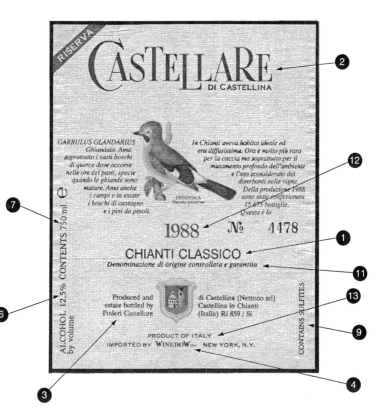

COMMON WINE BOTTLE SHAPES

1. Slope-shouldered, pale green bottle, used in BURGUNDY and the RHÔNE as well as throughout most of the world for wines such as CHARDONNAY, PINOT NOIR, and SYRAH.
2. High-shouldered, dark green glass bottle, the standard for BORDEAUX red wines; also generally used around the world for wines such as CABERNET SAUVIGNON, MERLOT, ZINFANDEL, and higher-quality CHIANTI. In clear glass, this shape bottle is used for Bordeaux white wines and in other countries for SAUVIGNON BLANC and SÉMILLON wines.
3. Tall slender bottle called a FLUTE or Rhine, colored brown in Germany's RHINE region and green in ALSACE and the MOSEL. This shape is used elsewhere for grape varieties associated with Germany, such as RIESLING and GEWÜRZTRAMINER.
4. Straw-covered FIASCO, used for less-expensive Chiantis.
5. CHAMPAGNE (or other sparkling wine) bottle.
6. Broad-shouldered, long-necked bottle used for SHERRY and PORT.

See also WINE BOTTLES.

WINE STYLES

In most instances, when pairing wine with food, you should drink a better wine and forgo its compatibility with the food rather than settle for a mediocre wine just to achieve a food-wine match. But it's also worth the extra effort to try to balance the style of the wine with that of the food. A hearty dish like osso buco, for example, is better paired with a rich, intense wine like a MERLOT, ZINFANDEL, or red RHONE. On the other hand, a lighter dish like a simple pasta primavera (fresh vegetables and olive oil) is better complemented with a white wine or even a lighter red wine such as BEAUJOLAIS, LAMBRUSCO, or VALPOLICELLA. The goal in pairing wine with food is compatibility—neither should overpower the other.

The following information provides a general guide to the style of various wines in terms of the BODY they usually exhibit. Keep in mind that individual winemaking styles and a given VINTAGE may influence the weight of these wines. For example, the 1981 vintage in BORDEAUX generally produced medium-bodied wines, whereas those from Bordeaux's 1982 vintage are much more CONCENTRATED and full-bodied. In California, the CABERNET SAUVIGNON wines from LOUIS M. MARTINI WINERY are a much lighter style than the BIG, TANNIC wine styles from MAYACAMAS VINEYARDS.

In the following lists, white and red wines are noted separately and grouped into one of three sections—light-, medium-, and full-bodied. Note: In each section the wines are ordered (top to bottom) from the lightest to the heaviest.

WHITE WINES

Light-bodied (from lightest to heaviest)

- Italian—like those from FRASCATI, GALESTRO, ORVIETO, SOAVE, TREBBIANO D'ABRUZZO, VERDICCHIO DEI CATELLIDI DI JESI

- German, nonsweet (TROCKEN or HALBTROCKEN) from grape varieties such as MÜLLER-THURGAU, SYLVANER, or SCHEUREBE

- PINOT GRIS (also called *Pinot Grigio*)

- German, nonsweet (trocken or halbtrocken) from RIESLING grapes

- MELON DE BOURGOGNE—like French MUSCADET, U.S. Melon de Bourgogne, and some U.S. PINOT BLANC (some of which are actually made from Melon de Bourgogne grapes)

- CHAMPAGNE and other better sparkling WINES—Blanc de Blanc (lighter, less-yeasty styles)
- Riesling from the United States and ALSACE
- Pinot Blanc from Alsace and the United States (unoaked)

Medium-bodied (from lightest to heaviest)

- CHENIN BLANC—French from SAVENNIERS and VOUVRAY, from the United States
- Champagne and other better sparkling wines—all but the less yeasty-style Blanc de Blanc
- Pinot Blanc—United States (oaky styles)
- Southern Rhône wines—like CÔTE DU RHÔNE
- U.S. SAUVIGNON BLANC wines (unoaked)
- Bordeaux
- U.S. and Alsatian GEWÜRZTRAMINER
- POUILLY-FUMÉ, SANCERRE, and U.S. Sauvignon Blanc (oaky styles)
- Italian—like those from GAVI
- CHARDONNAY—unoaked U.S. or French (like those from CHABLIS)
- BURGUNDY—those from POUILLY-FUISSÉ, SAINT VÉRAN, and other MÂ-CONNAIS wines (MÂCON, MÂCON-VILLAGES)

Full-bodied (from lightest to heaviest)

- Chardonnay—United States, BARREL-FERMENTED and AGED in oak
- Burgundy—those from premier Burgundian villages like CHAS-SAGNE-MONTRACHET, PULIGNY-MONTRACHET, MEURSAULT
- Northern Rhône wines, especially those from HERMITAGE but also SAINT JOSEPH and CROZES-HERMITAGE

RED WINES

Light-bodied (from lightest to heaviest)

- BARDOLINO
- Lambrusco
- NOUVEAU-style—French, United States, and others

- Beaujolais (except for CHÉNAS, JULIÉNAS, MORGON, MOUIN-À-VENT, and RÉGNIÉ)
- Most German red wines—like SPÄTBURGUNDER or PORTUGIESER
- Valpolicella (except AMARONE-style)
- DOLCETTO—United States and Italian
- Beaujolais from CHÉNAS, JULIÉNAS, MORGON, MOUIN-À-VENT, and RÉGNIÉ
- Burgundy—most CÔTE DE BEAUNE

Medium-bodied (from lightest to heaviest)

- Valpolicella (Amarone-style only)
- RIOJA
- BARBERA—U.S. and Italian
- CHIANTI CLASSICO
- U.S. PINOT NOIR
- Burgundy—most CÔTE DE NUITS
- Bordeaux—most vintages

Full-bodied (from lightest to heaviest)

- Burgundy—from the better vintages of top GRAND CRU and PREMIER CRU vineyards
- U.S. Merlot
- U.S. SYRAH and Australian Shiraz
- U.S. Zinfandel
- Bordeaux (the best vintages)
- U.S. Cabernet Sauvignon
- AGLIANICO wines from southern Italy, particularly TAURASI and AGLIANICO DEL VULTURE
- Rhône (especially Hermitage, CÔTE ROTIE, and CORNAS)
- BRUNELLO DI MONTALCINO
- BARBARESCO
- BAROLO

OPENING AND SERVING WINE

STILL WINE

Serving wine at home is neither difficult nor does it need to be overly formal. The first thing to consider is a wine's serving temperature, which depends on the style of the wine as well as your personal preference. Serving wine overly cold can mute its aroma and flavor, while serving it inordinately warm can make the wine seem dull and harshly ALCOHOLIC. For more details on a wine's serving temperature, see TEMPERATURE, as well as "Optimum Wine-Serving Temperatures," page 594.

Better wines are sealed with a CORK (although some vintners are exploring alternatives), so make sure you have a corkpuller or CORKSCREW (see listing for detailed information). But the first step in opening wine is to remove the CAPSULE, a casing (most often made of metal or plastic) that covers the bottle's lip and cork. Using a sharp knife or special foil-cutting tool (available at wine or gourmet shops), cut through the capsule about ¼ inch below the bottle's lip. Remove the capsule at the point it's cut. Wipe the rim of the bottle and the top of the cork with a damp towel to remove any residue.

The technique of removing the cork itself varies depending on the type of corkscrew or corkpuller. Most corkscrews are designed to maximize leverage so that Herculean strength isn't necessary. Some seimiautomated corkscrews actually insert the screw into the cork and extract it in one motion, while others continuously turn in one direction until the cork's expelled. Corkpullers consist of two thin parallel metal prongs connected by a handle. The prongs are pushed down between the inside of the bottle neck and the sides of the cork, and then the instrument is simultaneously pulled and turned until the cork comes out.

To open the wine, position a corkscrew in the cork's center, twist the screw clockwise into the cork as far as it will go without piercing the bottom of the cork. Doing so will reduce the prospect of pieces of cork falling into the wine, as well as improve the chances of keeping the cork intact for reuse, if necessary. Once the screw is firmly seated, gently ease the cork out of the bottle. If a cork breaks off during the process, gently try to reinsert the corkscrew. Or, use the thin prongs of a corkpuller to capture the cork left in the bottle. If you mistakenly push the cork remnant into the bottle, try extracting it with a special cork retrieval tool, available at wine and gourmet shops. If you can't get the cork out of the wine, either decant it, or simply pour the wine with the cork in the bottle, but very carefully.

Once the cork has been extracted, wipe the lip of the bottle again to remove any errant bits of cork. If tiny cork fragments break off into the wine, strain the wine through a fine sieve into a decanter.

Red wines over 8 years old often have a natural SEDIMENT, which, although harmless, leaves an unpleasantly gritty residue in the mouth. Holding the wine bottle up to or over a strong light will sometimes reveal this sediment. Removing sediment is a simple process through DECANTING (see listing for complete details). Decanting may also be done to allow wine to BREATHE (aerate) before it's served, a process some wine enthusiasts believe enhances a wine's flavor.

The wineglass you use should have a rim that curves in slightly (some champagne FLUTES are an exception), which captures the aroma and BOUQUET and makes it possible to swirl the wine properly in order to release its fragrance. A wineglass should always be made of clear glass so that the wine's true color and clarity are plainly visible.

When pouring wine, fill the glass only half full, again to leave room for swirling. Just as you finish pouring each glass and are returning the bottle to the upright position, give the bottle a slight twist. This simple technique eliminates dripping.

All that's left to serving wine is to savor and enjoy it!

See also "Optimum Wine-Serving Temperatures," page 594; "Winetasting," page 598; "Opening and Serving Champagne," below; GLASSES, WINE

CHAMPAGNE AND SPARKLING WINES

CHAMPAGNE and other SPARKLING WINES should be served quite cold, between 39° and 50°F, depending on the quality. The less expensive the champagne, the colder it should be served, because cold mutes flavor. Conversely, VINTAGE champagnes—with their complexity and delicate balance of flavors—are much better served at between 45° and 50°F.

It's best not to chill sparkling wines for much more than 2 hours before serving. Longer refrigeration can dull both the flavor and bouquet of such wines. Champagne can be speed-chilled by submerging the bottle in a bucket or large pan filled with equal amounts of ice and cold water. This procedure chills the wine much faster than ice alone.

The first step in opening champagne is to remove the foil, which sometimes has a "zipper" or perforation to expedite the process. Untwist and remove the wire cage that encloses the cork, being careful to shield the cork with your hand, just in case it ejects prematurely (a rare occurrence). Holding the bottle at a 45° angle (making sure it's not pointed at anyone), and with the fingers of one hand over the cork, gently rotate the bottle (not the cork) with your other hand. As you feel the cork begin to loosen and lift, use your thumb to gently ease it from the bottle. If properly handled, the cork should release from the bottle with a muted "poof," not a loud "POP." Although properly opened champagne should never gush from the bottle, it's a good idea to have a glass standing by, just in case.

Champagne and other sparkling wines should always be served in the tall, slender glasses known as flutes, which have a very small surface from which bubbles can escape and showcase more of the wine's bouquet. The old-fashioned shallow, "saucer" champagne glass allows both effervescence and bouquet to escape twice as fast as the flute.

See also "Optimum Wine-Serving Temperatures," page 594; CHAMPAGNE.

COMMON WINEGLASS SHAPES

1. CHAMPAGNE flute.
2. Classic Tulip, suitable for both white and red wines.
3. ISO (International Standards Organization) glass, specifically designed for winetasting.
4. Classic red wineglass.
5. Paris goblet, common all-purpose restaurant glass.
6. Sherry *copita,* traditional for tasting SHERRY; also good for PORT.

See also GLASSES, WINE; WINETASTING; Winetasting, page 598.

OPTIMUM WINE-SERVING TEMPERATURES

The serving temperature for wine varies depending on the style of wine and one's personal preference. Serving wine too cold reduces its aroma and flavor and highlights any bitterness. Serving it too warm can make the flavors unpleasantly FLAT and DULL and the wine seem harshly ALCOHOLIC. White wines are served chilled, but how cold is a matter of individual taste. Generally, SPARKLING WINES, CHAMPAGNE, and young, sweet white wines are served colder, about 40° to 50°F. On the other hand, RICH, full-bodied (*see* BODY) whites like California and Australian CHARDONNAYS and French white BURGUNDIES are better served at around 50° to 55°F. Other white wines should be served somewhere in the 43° to 53°F range, depending on their complexity of flavor. More intricately flavored wines should be served in the warmer side of this range in order to reveal their full scope of aromas and flavors. Because cold masks flavor, flawed or less expensive wines (except those with a bitter characteristic) should be served slightly cooler so detriments aren't so glaringly obvious. Lighter red wines like BEAUJOLAIS or VALPOLICELLA are best served at 50° to 60°F, whereas bolder reds like BORDEAUX, RHÔNE, BAROLO, CHIANTI, and California CABERNET SAUVIGNON and ZINFANDEL are best at about 62° to 67°F. Other red wines, such as California PINOT NOIR and red Burgundies, are best served in the 55° and 65°F range, depending how rich and full-bodied they are.

CHAMPAGNE AND OTHER SPARKLING WINES

Type of Wine	Serving Temperature (approximate °F)
Inexpensive versions	40 to 44
Better non-vintage	42 to 47
The best vintages	45 to 50

SWEET AND SEMISWEET WHITE WINES

Type of Wine	Serving Temperature (approximate °F)
Dessert wines (younger)	45 to 50
German semisweet wines—QbA (Qualitätswein Bestimmter Anbaugebiet), Spätlese, and Auslese	45 to 50
German sweet wines (older)—Auslese, Beerenauslese, Eisewein, and Trockenbeerenauslese	50 to 55
Sauternes (older)	50 to 55
Vouvray	43 to 48

WHITE WINES (DRY AND OFF-DRY)

Type of Wine	Serving Temperature (approximate °F)
Bordeaux—like those from Graves	45 to 50
Burgundy—medium quality	45 to 50
Burgundy—premium quality	50 to 55
Chardonnay—medium quality	45 to 50
Chardonnay—premium quality	50 to 55
Chenin Blanc U.S.	43 to 48
German, high-quality, nonsweet (Trocken or Halbtrocken)	48 to 53
Gewürztraminer—U.S. and Alsatian	45 to 50
Italian—like those from Frascati, Galestro, Orvieto, Soave, Trebbiano d'abruzzo, Verdicchio dei Catellidi di Jesi	42 to 47
Italian—like those from Gavi	45 to 50
Melon de Bourgogne	43 to 48
Muscadet	43 to 48
Pinot Blanc from Alsace and the United States	45 to 50
Pinot Gris (also called *Pinot Grigio*)	45 to 50
Pouilly-Fumé	43 to 48
Rhône (northern)	48 to 53
Rhône (southern)	45 to 50
Sancerre	43 to 48
Sauvignon Blanc	43 to 48
Savenniers	43 to 48

ROSÉ AND BLUSH WINES

Type of Wine	Serving Temperature (approximate °F)
Almost all Rosé and Blush Wines	40 to 45
High-quality dry rosé	43 to 48

RED WINES

Type of Wine	Serving Temperature (approximate °F)
Aglianico wines from southern Italy, particularly Taurasi and Aglianico Del Vulture	62 to 67
Barbaresco	60 to 65
Barbera (U.S. and Italian)	57 to 62
Bardolino	48 to 53
Barolo	62 to 67
Beaujolais (except for Chénas, Juliénas, Morgon, Moulin-à-Vent, and Régnié)	50 to 55
Beaujolais from Chénas, Juliénas, Morgon, Moulin-ā-vent, and Régnié	53 to 58
Bordeaux (most vintages)	58 to 63
Bordeaux (the best vintages)	62 to 67
Brunello di Montalcino	62 to 67
Burgundy—from the better vintages of top Grand Cru and Premier Cru vineyards	58 to 63
Burgundy—most Côte de Beaune	55 to 60
Burgundy—most Côte de Nuits	58 to 63
Cabernet Sauvignon, U.S.	62 to 67
Chianti Classico	57 to 62
Chianti Classico Reserva	60 to 65
Côtes du Rhône (and other southern Rhônes)	53 to 58
Dolcetto, U.S. and Italian	53 to 58
German red wines—like Spätburgunder or Portugieser	52 to 57
Lambrusco	48 to 53
Merlot, U.S.	59 to 64

RED WINES

Type of Wine	Serving Temperature (approximate °F)
Nouveau-style—French, U.S., and others	48 to 53
Pinot Noir, U.S.	58 to 63
Rhône (northern)	62 to 67
Rioja	57 to 62
Rioja Reserva	60 to 65
Shiraz, Australian	59 to 64
Syrah, U.S.	59 to 64
Valpolicella (Amarone-style only)	55 to 60
Valpolicella (except Amarone-style)	52 to 57
Zinfandel (light)	57 to 62
Zinfandel (heavy)	62 to 67

FORTIFIED WINES

Type of Wine	Serving Temperature (approximate °F)
Madeira	55 to 60
Muscat de Beaumes de Venise	42 to 47
Port, Ruby	57 to 62
Port, Tawny (older)	55 to 60
Port, Tawny (younger)	50 to 55
Port, Vintage	62 to 67
Port, white	45 to 50
Sherry, amontillados	60 to 65
Sherry, most finos, except amontillados	45 to 50
Sherry, olorosos	60 to 65

WINETASTING

EVALUATING THE APPEARANCE, SMELL, AND TASTE OF WINE

To begin with, it should be noted that evaluating wine is a very personal process. Besides individual likes and dislikes, everyone has varying levels of tolerance for qualities like sweetness, bitterness, TANNINS, and ACID. Such personal variables can result in passionate disagreements at a winetasting where some participants might view a wine as outstanding while others consider the same potable inferior or, at best, mediocre. What's the bottom line? There are really no wrong answers when it comes to your particular preferences.

In truth, evaluating a wine can be quite easy—you simply taste it and decide whether or not you like it. Some wine enthusiasts, however, carefully consider three basic components—the wine's appearance, smell, and, of course, taste—each of which possess distinct and important nuances.

To begin tasting for evaluation, pour about 1½ ounces of wine into a 7- or 8-ounce wineglass to allow plenty of room for swirling. Start by tilting the glass slightly away from you at about a 45° angle, preferably over a white background so that the wine's color and clarity are more obvious. When comparing several similar wines, the color intensity (or depth) can also be examined by placing glasses (with the same fill level) on a white background and viewing them from the top.

Next, begin gently swirling the wine, a technique that can initially be learned by leaving the wineglass on the table, holding it by the stem and rotating it in small circles. The object is to get the wine to move up the sides of the glass at least halfway. Once you can swirl on the table without sloshing, lift the glass off the table and use the same technique (the noise of moving the glass around on the table can be distracting to other tasters). Swirling is done to help release a wine's aroma. It also wets the inside of the glass, leaving a coating that separates into viscous-looking rivulets called LEGS (or *tears*)—extremely wide legs are called *sheets*. Legs that take a long time to slide down the glass are a clue to the taster that the wine is probably RICH and full-bodied (*see* BODY).

Now, let's get down to the details of the appearance, smell, and taste of wine.

A WINE'S APPEARANCE

A wine's appearance is the first indicator of its condition and a clue of what's to come in the smell and taste. Three elements are usually considered when examining the appearance of wine—color depth, color hue, and clarity.

Color Depth

Color depth (or intensity) is an indicator of quality that, in most instances, accurately predicts (particularly with red wine) how full-bodied a wine will be. Grape varieties and their intrinsic degree of color most certainly influence the depth of color, which can confuse the issue when comparing wines made from different varieties. When comparing like wines, however, the rule of thumb is that the deeper-colored wines are generally made from higher-quality grapes and will therefore have fuller flavor and body. A pale color intensity, especially in a red wine, can have several meanings—from overplanted vineyards to underripe grapes—any of which diminish a wine's character and flavor.

Color Hue

Color hue in a wine is an extremely important gauge of how well the wine has aged. As wine ages, the small amount of oxygen in the bottle affects its color, which therefore becomes an indicator of whether or not the wine is maturing at an appropriate rate. If the wine's color seems older than it should, it could indicate a problem such as mishandling during production or bottling or possibly a bad cork. Likewise, an older wine that still exhibits the bright color of one much younger most certainly has aged well and will probably also have a youthful aroma and taste. Following is a brief description of the color changes wines undergo during aging.

White wine color transitions during aging

- *Pale greenish-yellow* is common in very young wines that are still exhibiting small amounts of chlorophyll (found in grapes); this generalization is especially true of wines from cooler growing climates.

- *Straw color* is representative of many recently released DRY white wines.

- *Yellow-gold* is found in younger sweet DESSERT WINES and in dry wine with 3 to 4 years of aging.

- *Gold* is indicative of dry wines with substantial (6 years or more) bottle-aging and of full-bodied dessert wines with additional age. Dessert wines of considerable age and good condition will exhibit an even deeper golden color.

- *Brown* tinging indicates excessive aging and the flavor and smell of such a wine will most probably be somewhat OXIDIZED. The only exceptions are some SHERRIES that are still quite good.

Red wine color transitions during aging

- *Purple* is indicative of a very young wine.

- *Crimson or ruby* is common in dry TABLES WINES with brief aging as well as very young vintage PORTS.

- *Red* is indicative of table wines with several years of bottle age, such as a 2- to 5-year-old CABERNET SAUVIGNON or red BORDEAUX or a 1- to 3-year-old PINOT NOIR or red BURGUNDY. This is the optimum stage for most red wines unless they're made for long aging.

- *Brick-red* (the red color begins to fade and assume a hint of brown) is an indicator of maturity in a wine. Examples are Bordeaux wines that are generally 6 years or older and Burgundies over 3 years old.

- *Reddish-brown* (even lighter than brick-red, with more brownish hues) suggests a very mature bottle of wine, such as a Bordeaux over 10 years old or a Burgundy over 7 years. This stage is about as far as a dry table wine can go and still be good; those capable of long aging can remain in this stage for years.

- *Tawny* is only desirable with old tawny ports; tawny-colored dry table wines are generally not worth drinking.

- *Amber-brown* is an indication in most cases of deterioration and oxidization, which produces a stale, sherrylike character.

Clarity

Wines should be brilliant without any cloudiness or haziness, factors that generally signal a flaw in the wine. A clear wine will occasionally have some SEDIMENT in the shoulder or the bottom of the bottle, which is acceptable, especially in older wines. DECANTING a wine prior to serving will remove the sediment.

A WINE'S SMELL

Because smell and taste have a symbiotic relationship, just smelling a wine can reveal much of its character. If there's something inherently wrong or wonderful with a wine, the nose will usually detect it. Swirling a wine releases its AROMA and BOUQUET, which can be perceived by putting your nose just inside the glass and inhaling gently. If you don't get much odor from a wine, cover the top of the glass with one palm and swirl again, quickly removing your palm just before you smell again. The caliber of an aroma or bouquet can be gauged by its intensity, quality, and character.

Intensity

The intensity of a wine's aroma or bouquet can vary greatly and is generally reflective of the taste that will follow. A light aroma usually heralds a light taste; wines with a more intense or aromatic NOSE, assuming other factors are favorable, are considered desirable.

Quality

The quality of an aroma or bouquet can be stated in generalities such as pleasant versus unpleasant, complex versus simple, and harmonious versus unbalanced. The best wines are pleasant, complex, and harmonious, with no off odors.

Character

The aroma's *character* pertains more specifically to the various odors that are detectable in a wine. The nose of a complex wine might exhibit a plethora of odors including black cherries, chocolate, violets, leather, and cinnamon. On the other hand, a simple wine might reveal only a couple of scents such as raspberry and vanilla. Experienced tasters usually have better-developed sensory memories than beginners and are therefore more adept at identifying the intricacies of a wine's aroma. Training your "aroma memory" can be helpful when trying to determine a wine's characteristics, and you can do so by spending time in a garden smelling (and tasting) various fruits, vegetables, and flowers. Or, gather a variety of items representative of other smells that can be found in wine, such as leather, rubber, or tobacco. Some wine specialty shops have kits that will help you identify various smells found in wine. Review the Wine Aroma Wheel, page 607, for detailed descriptors for a wine's smell. *See also* Winetasting Terms, page 605.

A WINE'S TASTE

Now it's time for the final evaluation step—tasting the wine. Begin by taking a small sip of wine—some serious tasters suck in a little air just as they do so, a technique that aerates the wine (accentuating the flavor) but that, unless done discreetly, creates a slurping noise. Other tasters "chew" or slosh the wine around in their mouth. Both techniques are intended to expose the wine's full flavors while bringing the olfactory senses into play. As you swallow the wine, notice the impression that lingers in your mouth and throat.

The wine's flavors are often forecasted by the aroma and bouquet, although different or additional flavor characteristics may be detected while tasting. Certain important properties affect the final evaluation of the wine that only tasting can determine. These include discernible levels of *sweetness* or *dryness, acidity, bitterness,* tactile sensations generated by the wine's *body, tannins* (in red wine), *alcohol* level, *finish,* and, finally, the overall *balance* of these combined properties. Now, let's talk about these tasting properties in detail.

Sweetness or Dryness

Levels of sweetness or dryness are generally more important in white wines because most reds are vinified DRY (no RESIDUAL SUGAR). The style of wine usually dictates the level of sweetness. For example, most CHARDONNAY and SAUVIGNON BLANC wines are dry, whereas CHENIN BLANC, GEWÜRZTRAMINER, and RIESLING wines often have a touch of sweetness, and dessert wines like SAUTERNES or LATE HARVEST wines are usually very sweet. Sometimes sweetness, which is most recognizable at the tip of the tongue, is required to balance the high acidity of a particular grape, such as the highly acidic Chenin Blanc used in France's VOUVRAY wines. Occasionally, a completely dry but very fruity wine has a seemingly sweet quality to it, which is due to the ETHYL ALCOHOL produced during fermentation.

Acidity

A wine's acidity, which is detected by its tartness, accomplishes several things: it contributes to a wine's aging capabilities by working as a preservative, protecting both color and flavor; it enlivens the flavor—wines with low acid are usually flat; and it gives a wine that would ordinarily be cloyingly sweet enough balance to be desirable. Excess acid, however, can give a wine a sharp, harsh edge and throw it out of balance.

Bitterness

Most evident on the back of the tongue, bitterness is not a desirable character in most wines. In young reds, however, a small amount is not generally considered a detriment.

Body

A wine's body, perceived in the mouth as TEXTURE or WEIGHT, is produced by a combination of elements including ALCOHOL, GLYCEROL, ACID, and EXTRACT. A rich, complex wine that feels luxuriously heavy in the mouth is considered *full-bodied*, whereas one that seems watery or flimsy is referred to as *light-bodied* or *thin*. A *medium-bodied* wine falls somewhere between the two. Not all wines seek to be full-bodied, however, particularly those like CHAMPAGNE, which strive for finesse. Rich dessert wines like Sauternes are generally full-bodied partly because their residual sugar adds weight and texture.

Tannins

Detectable by a dry, sometimes puckery, sensation in the mouth and back of the throat, tannins are noticeable in many red wines but not whites. That's because, during red winemaking, the juice is left in contact with the grape skins, seeds, and stems, all of which contribute astringent substances known as tannins. The length of contact partially determines the amount of tannins in a wine, but additional tannins are extracted from oak barrels (especially new ones) during extended aging. Although tannins are noticeable in young red wines, they are generally most prominent in high-quality, red wines meant for aging and give such wines structure as well as an antioxidant (preservative) capability. The harsh, rough qualities of tannins diminish over time, producing a wine that has backbone without being overtly tannic. Ideally, this process occurs while the wine still has other positive attributes like good flavor, fruit, and acidity. Occasionally, wines have excess tannins that never come into balance before the rest of the components fade.

Alcohol

Even though alcohol plays a role in giving a wine more body, it shouldn't be singularly noticeable in a balanced wine. Excess alcohol that isn't balanced by other components can produce a warm, sometimes even hot, burning sensation in the mouth and throat. Such a wine is referred to as HOT or ALCOHOLIC.

Finish

A wine's finish is the lingering impression of flavor and tactile sensation that remains in the mouth after the wine is swallowed. The palate impression should be favorable, and the longer the finish, the higher the quality of the wine. This length of time, sometimes referred to as *persistence,* is often described in terms such as "it had a long finish," "the finish was lacking," or "the finish was short."

Balance

All the individual factors of a wine's flavor must be viewed from their relationship to each other—their *balance.* A wine where none of the components overpowers the others is considered well balanced. For example, a wine with a very light fruit flavor could easily be overpowered by alcohol or tannins, whereas a fruity, full-flavored wine with the same levels of alcohol and tannins would be well balanced. A sweet wine with moderate acid might not be balanced, but a dry wine with that same acid level might be excellent.

See also GLASSES, WINE; WINETASTING.

WINETASTING TERMS

There's a special winetasting vocabulary, and knowing the language will help you better understand wine newsletters, magazine and newspaper articles on wine, wine reviews, and even menus and wine lists. The meanings of some winetasting terms are analogous to the word. Such terms include banana, butterscotch, candylike, coconutty, coffee, cranberry, grapefruity, licorice, melon, mushrooms, pineapple, plums, raspberry, strawberry, and truffles. Definitions for these self-explanatory terms will not be found in this volume. There are listings, however, for the following winetasting terms:

abboccato
acescence
acetic
acetone
acidic
aftertaste
aggressive
aigre
aimable
alcoholic
amabile
angular
appley
aroma
aromatic
astringent
attack
attenuated
austere

backward
baked
balance
barnyard
berrylike
big
bitter
black
  currant
body

botrytised
bouquet
brambly
brawny
breed
brettano-
  myces; brett
briary
brick red
bright
brilliant
browning
brut
burning
burnt matches
buttery
butyric

caramel
cassis
cedar
character
cherry
chewy
chocolaty
cigar box
citrusy
clarity
classic
clean

closed
cloudy
cloying
coarse
color
common
complex
cooked
corked
creaming
creamy
cremant
crisp
crystals

deep
delicate
demi-sec
depth
developed
dirty
distinguished
doux
dried out
dry
dull
dumb
dusty

earthy
eggs

elegant
empty
esters
eucalyptus
extract
exuberant

faded
farmyard
fat
feeble
finesse
finish
firm
flabby
flat
fleshy
flinty
floral
forward
foxy
fresh
frizzante
fruity
full-bodied

gamey
gassy
geranium
glycerol
goût

goût de terroir
grapey
grassy
gravelly
green
grip

hard
harmonious
harsh
hazy
heady
hearty
heavy
herbaceous
hollow
honeyed
hot

inky
insipid

jammy

leafy
lean
leathery
legs
length
light
limpid
lingering
liquoreux
lively
long
luscious
lush

maderisé
maderized
masculine
massive
mature
meaty
mellow

meniscus
mercaptans
metallic
minty
moelleux
moldy
mousy
mouth-
  filling
muscular
musky
musty

nerveux
neutral
noble
nose
nutty

oaky
oeil de perdrix
off
off-dry
oily
open
opening
overripe
oxidized

pelure d'oignon
penetrating
peppery
perfume
perlant
persistence
petillant
petit
petrol
pierre-à-fusil
piqué
plump
powerful
pricked
pruney

puckery

race
raisiny
raw
refined
resinous
rich
ripe
robust
rotten eggs
rough
round
rubbery

savory
sec
shallow
sharp
sheets
sherrified
short
silky
simple
skunky
smoky
smooth
soapy
soft
soften
solid
sound
sour
sparkling
spicy
spritzig
spritzy
stale
stalky
steely
stemmy
strong
structure

sturdy
sulfur
supple
sweet
syrupy

tannic
tar
tart
tartrates
tears
texture
thick
thin
tight
tired
toasty
tobacco
tough

unripe

vanilla
varietal
  character
vegetal
velouté
velvety
vigorous
vinegary
vinosity
vinous
viscous
volatile acidity

watery
weighty
withered
woody

yeasty
young

WINE AROMA WHEEL

In the 1980s, Ann Noble, a professor at the University of California at DAVIS, was the guiding light in developing what is now known as the wine aroma wheel—a reference for aroma traits commonly found in wines. The terms closer to the center of the wheel are more general; those toward the outside are more specific. Review and use of this aroma wheel helps evolving winetasters increase their descriptive abilities. Many of these sensory terms are defined in this book. *See also* Winetasting Terms, page 605.

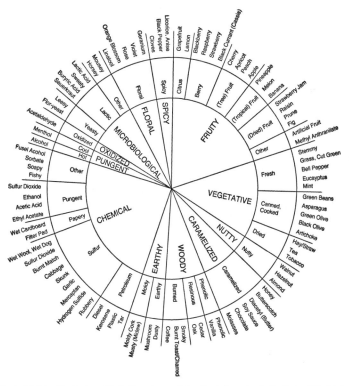

A. C. Noble, R. A. Arnold, J. Buechsenstein, E. J. Leach, J. O. Schmidt, and P. M. Stern. "Modification of a standardized system of wine aroma terminology." *American Journal of Enology and Viticulture,* 1987. Reproduced by permission.

HOW TO STORE LEFTOVER WINE

Careful handling of an unfinished bottle of wine is necessary because prolonged contact with air will ruin a wine's flavor.

One way to save leftover wine is to transfer it to a smaller bottle, thereby minimizing airspace in the bottle. Save splits or half bottles (see WINE BOTTLES) just for this purpose, or use other clean small bottles. Always seal the bottle tightly to keep more air from getting in.

Another option is to "gas" leftover wine. There are several harmless canned gases on the market today that are a combination of nitrogen (N_2) and carbon dioxide (CO_2). They're designed to be squirted directly into a partially full bottle of wine, thereby blanketing the wine's surface and protecting it from flavor-destroying oxygen. These special gases are available in cans (which feel empty because gas is weightless) in most wine stores and many gourmet specialty shops.

There's another gadget on the market called a vacuum wine saver, which is designed to remove excess air from a partially full wine bottle. To use it, you simply insert a specially designed reusable rubber stopper in the bottle neck. Then you position a pump over the stopper and pump up and down until you can feel some resistance, an indication that the air has been sucked from the bottle, meaning that the bottle is vacuum sealed.

For champagne and other sparkling wines, a special champagne stopper can be purchased at gourmet shops and some wine stores for only about five dollars. It fits on top of the bottle opening and has two clamps that lock the seal tightly.

Store leftover wine—red, white, and sparkling—in the refrigerator and, if possible, drink it within a day or two. If the room temperature is cool (65°F), red wine does not need to be refrigerated.

GRAPE VARIETIES

Following are the names of the grape varieties that can be found throughout *Wine Lover's Companion*. The main listings (with full definitions) are in **boldface** type. The other entries are generally the regional or country names for the grape variety to which they are cross–referenced.

Ablan *see* PALOMINO
Aglianico
Agliano *see* ALEATICO
Airén
Albana
Albariño *see* ALVARINHO
Alcanol *see* MACABEO
Alcayata *see* MONASTRELL
Aleatico
Alicante *see* ALICANTE BOUSCHET; GRENACHE
Alicante Bouschet
Alicante Ganzin *see* RUBIRED
Aligoté
Allianico *see* ALEATICO
Altesse
Alvarinho
Americano *see* ISABELLA
Aramon
Arinto
Arneis
Aurora; Aurore
Auxerrois *see* MALBEC
Auxerrois Blanc
Auxerrois Gris *see* PINOT GRIS

Bacchus
Baco Blanc
Baco Noir
Baga
Balbi *see* PROSECCO
Balzac *see* MOURVÈDRE
Barbera
Beaunois *see* CHARDONNAY

Beli Pinot *see* PINOT BLANC
Bellina *see* ISABELLA
Biancame *see* ALBANA
Bigney *see* MERLOT
Black Muscat *see* MUSCAT
Blanca-Roja *see* MALVASIA
Blanc de Troyes *see* ALIGOTE
Blanc Fumé
Blanquette *see* CLAIRETTE
Blauburgunder *see* PINOT NOIR
Blauer Klevner *see* PINOT NOIR
Blauer Limberger *see* BLAUFRÄNKISCH
Blauer Portugieser *see* PORTUGIESER
Blauer Spätburgunder *see* PINOT NOIR
Blaufränkisch
Boal
Bombino Bianco
Bonarda
Bonarda di Chieri *see* BONARDA
Bonarda di Gattinara *see* BONARDA
Bonarda Piemontese *see* BONARDA
Bordo *see* CABERNET FRANC
Bouche *see* CABERNET FRANC; CABERNET SAUVIGNON
Bouchet *see* CABERNET FRANC; CABERNET SAUVIGNON
Bourguignon Noir *see* GAMAY
Brenton *see* CABERNET FRANC
Brown Muscat *see* MUSCAT

Brunello *see* SANGIOVESE
Bual *see* BOAL
Buisserate *see* JACQUÈRE
Burger *see* ELBLING
Burgundac Crni *see* PINOT NOIR

Cabernet Franc
Cabernet Sauvignon
Caccione Nero *see* CANAIOLO
Cadarca *see* KADARKA
Calabrese *see* SANGIOVESE
Camobraque *see* FOLLE BLANCHE
Canaiolo
Cannonau *see* GRENACHE
Cape Riesling *see* CROUCHEN
Carignan; Carignane
Carignan Rosos *see* GRENACHE
Cariñena *see* CARIGNAN
Carmelin *see* PETIT VERDOT
Carmenet *see* CABERNET FRANC
Carnelian
Castelhão Frances *see* PERIQUITA
Catawba
Cayuga White
Cencibel *see* TEMPRANILLO
Centurion
Chambourcin
Chancellor
Charbono
Chardonnay
Chasselas
Chaudenet Gris *see* ALIGOTÉ
De Chaunac
Chelois
Chenin Blanc
Chevrier *see* SÉMILLON
Chiavennasca *see* NEBBIOLO
Cinsaut, Cinsault
Clairette
Clairette Ronde *see* TREBBIANO
Clairette Rosé *see* TREBBIANO
Clare Riesling *see* CROUCHEN

Clevner *see* PINOT BLANC
Colombar *see* COLOMBARD
Colombard
Concord
Cordisco *see* MONTEPULCIANO
Cortese
Corvina
Cot *see* MALBEC
Crabutet *see* MERLOT
Criolla *see* MISSION
Croatina; Croattina
Crouchen
Cruian *see* CORVINA
Cugnette *see* JACQUÈRE

Dolcetto
Dolsin; Dolsin Nero *see* DOL-
 CETTO
Dorin *see* CHASSELAS
Durif
Dutchess

Edeltraube *see* GEWÜRZTRAMINER
Ehrenfelser
Elbling
Elysium *see* MUSCAT
Emerald Riesling
Erbaluce
Espagne *see* CINSAUT
Esparte *see* MOURVÈDRE
Essencia *see* MUSCAT

Faber
Favorita *see* VERMENTINO
Fendant *see* CHASSELAS
Fetească *see* LEÁNYKA
Flora
Folle Blanche
Freisa
French Colombard *see* COLOM-
 BARD
Fresa *see* FREISA

Fresia *see* FREISA
Friulara *see* RABOSO
Friularo *see* RABOSO
Frontignan *see* MUSCAT
Früher Roter Malvasier *see* MALVASIA
Fumé Blanc *see* SAUVIGNON BLANC
Furmint

Gamay
Gamay Beaujolais
Gamay Blanc *see* CHARDONNAY
Gamza *see* KADARKA
Gargana *see* GARGANEGA
Garganega
Garnaccia *see* GRENACHE
Garnacha *see* GRENACHE
Garnacha Blanca *see* GRENACHE
Garnacha Tinta *see* GRENACHE
Garnacho Tinto *see* GRENACHE
Gewürztraminer
Glera *see* PROSECCO
Golden Chasselas *see* PALOMINO
Goldmuskateller *see* MUSCAT
Gordo Blanco *see* MUSCAT
Graciano
Graševina *see* WELSCHRIESLING
Grauvernatsch *see* SCHIAVA
Grechetto
Greco
Greco Bianco di Perugia *see* GRECHETTO
Greco del Vesuvio *see* GRECO
Greco delle Torre *see* GRECO
Greco di Ancona *see* ALBANA
Greco Spoletino *see* GRECHETTO
Green Grape *see* SÉMILLON
Green Hungarian
Grenache
Grignolino
Gris Meunier *see* MEUNIER

Grolleau *see* GROSLOT
Groppello
Groslot
Gros Plant *see* FOLLE BLANCHE
Grosse Roussette *see* MARSANNE
Grosse Syrah *see* MONDEUSE
Grossriesling *see* ELBLING
Grossvernatsch *see* SCHIAVA
Grüner *see* GRÜNER VELTLINER
Grüner Veltliner
Grünmuskateller *see* GRÜNER VELTLINER
Gutedel *see* CHASSELAS

Hanepoot *see* MUSCAT
Hárslevelü
Hermitage *see* CINSAUT
Hermitage Blanc *see* MARSANNE
Huxelrebe

Isabella

Jacquère
Joannes Seyve 26205 *see* CHAMBOURCIN
João de Santarem *see* PERIQUITA
Johannisberger *see* RIESLING
Johannisberg Riesling *see* RIESLING

Kadarka
Kéknyelü
Kerner
Kleinberger *see* ELBLING
Kleinvernatsch *see* SCHIAVA
Klingelberger *see* RIESLING
Kuhlmann 1882 *see* MARÉCHAL FOCH
Kuhlmann 1942 *see* LEON MILLOT

Lagarino see LAGREIN
Lagrain see LAGREIN

Lagrein
Lairén see AIRÉN
Lambrusco
Lardot see MACABEO
Laskiriesling see WELSCHRIESLING
Leányka
Leon Millot
Lexia *see* MUSCAT
Listan *see* PALOMINO
Lizzana *see* GARGANEGA
Lyonnaise Blanche see MELON
    DE BOURGOGNE

Macabeo
Maccabeu *see* MACABEO
Mâconnais *see* ALTESSE
Mädchentraube *see* LEÁNYKA
Málaga *see* CINSAUT
Malbec
Malmsey *see* MALVASIA
Malvasia
Malvoisie *see* MALVASIA
Manchega *see* AIRÉN
Marchigiano *see* VERDICCHIO
Maréchal Foch
Marsanne
Marzemina Bianca *see* CHASSELAS
Mataro *see* MOURVÈDRE
Mavrodaphne
Mazuelo *see* CARIGNAN
Médoc Noir *see* MERLOT
Melon d'Arbois *see* CHARDONNAY
Melon de Bourgogne
Merlau *see* MERLOT
Merlau Blanc *see* MERLOT BLANC
Merlot
Merlot Blanc
Meunier
Mission
Mittervernatsch *see* SCHIAVA
Molette Noire *see* MONDEUSE
Monastrell

Mondeuse
Monestel *see* CARIGNAN
Montepulciano
Montonec *see* PARELLADA
Morastel *see* MONASTRELL
Morellone *see* MONTEPULCIANO
Morillon *see* NEGRETTE
Morio-Muskat
Morrastal *see* MONASTRELL
Morrastel *see* GRACIANO
Mortágua *see* TOURIGA NACIONAL
Moscatel *see* MUSCAT
Moscatel de Málaga *see* MUSCAT
Moscatel Gordo *see* MUSCAT
Moscatello *see* ALEATICO
Moscatel Rose *see* MUSCAT
Moscato Bianco *see* MUSCAT
Moscato di Amburgo *see* MUS-
    CAT
Moscato Giallo *see* MUSCAT
Moscato Rosa *see* MUSCAT
Mourvèdre
Müllerrebe *see* MEUNIER
Müller-Thurgau
Muscadelle
Muscadet *see* MELON DE BOUR-
    GOGNE
Muscadet Doux *see* MUSCADELLE
Muscadine
Muscat
Muscat Blanc *see* MUSCAT
Muscat Blanc à Petits Grains
    see MUSCAT
Muscat Canelli *see* MUSCAT
Muscat d'Alsace *see* MUSCAT
Muscatel de Grano Menudo *see*
    MUSCAT
Muscateller *see* ALEATICO
Muscat Frontignan *see* MUSCAT
Muscat Hamburg *see* MUSCAT
Muscat of Alexandria *see* MUS-
    CAT

Muscat Ottenel *see* MUSCAT
Muskateller *see* MUSCAT
Muskotaly *see* MUSCAT
Musquette *see* MUSCADELLE

Nagyburgundi *see* PINOT NOIR
Napa Gamay *see* GAMAY
Nebbiolo
Negra Mole
Negramoll *see* NEGRA MOLE
Negrette
Negron *see* RABOSO
Neretto *see* CROATINA
Niagara

Oeillade *see* CINSAUT
Ojo de Liebre *see* TEMPRANILLO
Olaszriesling *see* WELSCHRIESLING
Oporto *see* PORTUGIESER
Optima
Orange Muscat *see* MUSCAT
Oremasco *see* DOLCETTO
Ortega
Ottaianello *see* CINSAUT

Paarl Riesling *see* CROUCHEN
Pais *see* MISSION
Palomino
Parellada
Pedernão *see* ARINTO
Pedro Jiménez *see* PEDRO
    XIMÉNEZ
Pedro Ximen *see* PEDRO
    XIMÉNEZ
Pedro Ximénez
Periquita
Perlan *see* CHASSELAS
Petite-Cabernet *see* CABERNET
    SAUVIGNON
Petite Sirah; Petite Syrah
Petit Gamai *see* GAMAY
Petit Gris *see* PINOT GRIS

Petit Noir *see* NEGRETTE
Petit Verdau *see* PETIT VERDOT
Petit Verdot
Picardan Noir *see* CINSAUT
Picolit
Picotener *see* NEBBIOLO
Picpoule *see* FOLLE BLANCHE
Pigato
Pineau *see* PINOT NOIR
Pineau d'Anjou *see* CHENIN
    BLANC
Pineau de la Loire *see* CHENIN
    BLANC
Pinotage
Pinot Beurot *see* PINOT GRIS
Pinot Bianco *see* PINOT BLANC
Pinot Blanc
Pinot Buot *see* PINOT GRIS
Pinot Chardonnay *see* CHARDON-
    NAY
Pinot de l'Ermitage *see* DURIF
Pinot de Romans *see* DURIF
Pinot Grigio *see* PINOT GRIS
Pinot Gris
Pinot Meunier *see* MEUNIER
Pinot Nero *see* PINOT NOIR
Pinot Noir
Piqupoul de Pays *see* BACO
    BLANC
Pisse-vin *see* ARAMON
Plante Riche *see* ARAMON
Plant Gris *see* ALIGOTE
Plant Meunier *see* MEUNIER
Portugais Bleu *see* PORTUGIESER
Portugieser
Pressac *see* MALBEC
Primaticcio *see* MONTEPULCIANO
Primitivo *see* ZINFANDEL
Prosecco
Prugnolo *see* SANGIOVESE
Prunella *see* CINSAUT
Pugent *see* NEBBIOLO

Raboso
Raisinotte *see* MUSCADELLE
Ravat
Rebula *see* RIBOLLA
Refosco *see* MONDEUSE
Refosco del Peduncolo Rosso
    see MONDEUSE
Refosco Nostrano *see*
    MONDEUSE
Rheinelbe *see* ELBLING
Rhine Riesling *see* RIESLING
Ribolla
Riesling
Riesling Italico *see* WELSCHRIES-
    LING
Riesling Renano *see* RIESLING
Riesling-Sylvaner *see* MÜLLER-
    THURGAU
Rivaner *see* MÜLLER-THURGAU
Riviera Ligure di Ponente *see*
    VERMENTINO
Rizlingszilvani *see* MÜLLER-
    THURGAU
Rkatsiteli
Robola *see* RIBOLLA
Romondolo Classico *see* VER-
    DUZZO
Rosenmuskateller *see* MUSCAT
Rotor Traminer *see* GEWÜRZ-
    TRAMINER
Roussanne
Rousselet *see* GEWÜRZTRAMINER
Roussette
Roussillon *see* GRENACHE
Roussillonen *see* CARIGNAN
Royalty
Rubired
Ruby Cabernet
Rülander *see* PINOT GRIS

Saint-Émilion *see* TREBBIANO
Sangiovese

San Gioveto *see* SANGIOVESE
Sangioveto *see* SANGIOVESE
Sanvicetro *see* SANGIOVESE
Sauvignon *see* TOCAI FRIULANO
Sauvignonasse *see* TOCAI FRIU-
    LANO
Sauvignon Blanc
Sauvignon Jaune *see* SAUVIGNON
    BLANC
Sauvignon Musqué *see* SAUVI-
    GNON BLANC
Sauvignon Rouge *see* CABERNET
    SAUVIGNON
Sauvignon Vert *see* MUSCADELLE
Savagnin
Savagnin Noir *see* PINOT NOIR
Savagnin Rosé *see* GEWÜRZ-
    TRAMINER
Savoyance *see* MONDEUSE
Scheurebe
Schiava
Schioppettino
Schwarzriesling *see* MEUNIER
Scuppernong
Seibel 5279 *see* AURORA
Seibel 7053 *see* CHANCELLOR
Seibel 9549 *see* DE CHAUNAC
Seibel 10878 *see* CHELOIS
Sémillon
Sercial
Serprina *see* PROSECCO
Seyre-Villard 5276 *see* SEYVAL
    BLANC
Seyval Blanc
Silvaner *see* SYLVANER
Skadarska *see* KADARKA
South African Riesling *see*
    CROUCHEN
Souzão, Sousão
Spanna *see* NEBBIOLO
Spätburgunder *see* PINOT NOIR
Steen *see* CHENIN BLANC

Stein *see* CHENIN BLANC
Sultana
Sumarello *see* UVA DI TROIA
Sylvaner
Symphony
Syrah
Szükerbarat *see* PINOT GRIS

Tempranilla *see* TEMPRANILLO
Tempranillo
Terrano *see* MONDEUSE
Thalia *see* TREBBIANO
Thompson Seedless *see* SULTANA
Tindilloro *see* CANAIOLO
Tinta *see* GRENACHE
Tinta Cão *see* RUBIRED
Tinta Madeira
Tinta Negra Mole *see* NEGRA
MOLE
Tinta Roriz *see* TEMPRANILLO
Tinto *see* GRENACHE
Tinto del Pais *see* TEMPRANILLO
Tinto de Toro *see* TEMPRANILLO
Tinto Fino *see* TEMPRANILLO
Tocai Friulano; Tocai
Tocai Italico *see* TOCAI FRIULANO
Tokai *see* TOCAI FRIULANO
Tokay *see* MUSCADELLE
Tokay d'Alsace *see* PINOT GRIS
Tondo *see* PROSECCO
Touriga Francesa
Touriga Nacional
Traminac *see* GEWÜRZTRAMINER
Traminer *see* GEWÜRZTRAMINER
Traminer Aromatico *see*
GEWÜRZTRAMINER
Traminer Aromatique *see*
GEWÜRZTRAMINER
Traminer Musqué *see* GEWÜRZ-
TRAMINER
Traminer Parfumé *see* GEWÜRZ-
TRAMINER

Tramini *see* GEWÜRZTRAMINER
Trebbiano
Trebbiano Abruzzo *see* BOMBINO
BIANCO
Trebbiano d'Abruzzo *see*
BOMBINO BIANCO
Trebbiano Romagnolo *see* TREB-
BIANO
Trebbiano Toscano *see* TREB-
BIANO
Trollinger *see* SCHIAVA
Trouchet Noir *see* CABERNET
FRANC
Tschaggel *see* SCHIAVA
Tschaggelevernatsch *see* SCHIAVA

Ugni Blanc *see* TREBBIANO
Ugni Noir *see* ARAMON
Ull de Llebre *see* TEMPRANILLO
Uva Abruzzi *see* MONTEPULCIANO
Uva Canina *see* CANAIOLO
Uva della Marina *see* UVA DI
TROIA
Uva di Troia
Uva Merla *see* CANAIOLO
Uva Vermiglia *see* CROATINA

Valcarcelia *see* MONASTRELL
Valdepeñera Blanca *see* AIRÉN
Varresana Bianca *see* VER-
MENTINO
Veltliner *see* GRÜNER VELTLINER
Veltlini *see* GRÜNER VELTLINER
Vennentino *see* VERMENTINO
Verdejo; Verdejo Palido
Verdelho
Verdicchio
Verdone *see* VERDICCHIO
Verdot Rouge *see* PETIT VERDOT
Verduzzo; Verduzzo Friulano
Vermentino
Vernaccia di Oristano

Vernaccia di San Gimignano
Vernatsch *see* SCHIAVA
Vidal 256 *see* VIDAL BLANC
Vidal Blanc
Vidure *see* CABERNET SAUVIGNON
Vignoles *see* RAVAT
Villard Blanc
Villard Noir
Viognier
Vionnier *see* VIOGNIER
Viura *see* MACABEO
Vlassky Riesling *see* WELSCHRIES-
    LING

Walschriesling *see* WELSCHRIES-
    LING

Weissburgunder *see* PINOT BLANC
Weisserburgunder *see* MELON DE
    BOURGOGNE; PINOT BLANC
Weisser Gutedel *see* CHASSELAS
Weisser Klevner *see* PINOT BLANC
Weisser Riesling *see* RIESLING
Welschriesling
White Riesling *see* RIESLING
Wyndruif *see* SÉMILLON

Xarel-lo

Zapponara Bianca *see* BOMBINO
    BIANCO
Zibibbo *see* MUSCAT
Zinfandel

OFFICIAL WINE CLASSIFICATIONS OF BORDEAUX

CLASSIFICATION OF 1855—BORDEAUX (MÉDOC)

PREMIERS CRUS (FIRST GROWTHS)

Châteaus	Appellations
Lafite-Rothschild	Pauillac
Latour	Pauillac
Margaux	Margaux
Haut-Brion[1]	Graves (Pessac-Léognan)

DEUXIÈMES CRUS (SECOND GROWTHS)

Châteaus	Appellations
Mouton-Rothschild[2]	Pauillac
Rausan-Ségla	Margaux
Rauzan-Gassies	Margaux
Léoville-Las Cases	Saint-Julien
Léoville-Poyferré	Saint-Julien
Léoville-Barton	Saint-Julien
Durfort-Vivens	Margaux
Lascombes	Lascombes
Gruaud-Larose	Saint-Julien
Brane-Cantenac	Margaux
Pichon-Longueville Baron	Pauillac
Pichon Lalande	Pauillac
Ducru-Beaucaillou	Saint-Julien
Cos d'Estournel	Saint-Estèphe
Montrose	Saint-Estèphe

[1] Château Haut-Brion is actually located in Graves, although this classification presumably only included châteaus in the Medoc.
[2] Château Mouton-Rothschild was upgraded to a premier cru (first growth) in 1973.

TROISIÈMES CRUS (THIRD GROWTHS)

Châteaus	Appellations
Giscours	Margaux
Kirwan	Margaux
d'Issan	Margaux
Lagrange	Saint-Julien
Langoa-Barton	Saint-Julien
Malescot St-Exupéry	Margaux
Cantenac-Brown	Margaux
Palmer	Margaux
La Lagune	Haut-Médoc
Desmirail	Margaux
Calon-Ségur	Saint-Estèphe
Ferrière	Margaux
Marquis d'Alesme-Becker	Margaux
Boyd-Cantenac	Margaux

QUATRIÈMES CRUS (FOURTH GROWTHS)

Châteaus	Appellations
St.-Pierre	Saint-Julien
Branaire-Ducru	Saint-Julien
Talbot	Saint-Julien
Duhart-Milon-Rothschild	Pauillac
Pouget	Margaux
La Tour-Carnet	Haut-Médoc
Lafon-Rochet	Saint-Estèphe
Beychevelle	Saint-Julien
Prieuré-Lichene	Margaux
Marquis-de-Terme	Margaux

CINQUIÈMES CRUS (FIFTH GROWTHS)

Châteaus	Appellations
Pontet-Canet	Pauillac
Batailley	Pauillac
Grand-Puy-Lacoste	Pauillac
Grand-Puy-Ducasse	Pauillac
Haut-Batailley	Pauillac
Lynch-Bages	Pauillac
Lynch-Moussas	Pauillac
Dauzac	Margaux
Mouton-Baron-Philippe	Pauillac (now D'Armhailac)
du Tertre	Margaux
Haut-Bages-Liberal	Pauillac
Pédesclaux	Pauillac
Belgrave	Haut-Médoc
de Camensac	Haut-Médoc
Cos Labory	Saint-Estèphe
Clerc-Milon-Rothschild	Pauillac
Croizet-Bages	Pauillac
Cantermerle	Haut-Médoc

CLASSIFICATION OF 1855—BORDEAUX (SAUTERNES/BARSAC)

PREMIER GRAND CRU (FIRST GREAT GROWTH)

Châteaux

d'Yquem

PREMIERS CRUS (FIRST GROWTHS)

Châteaux

Guiraud	Sigalas-Rabaud	Climens
La Tour Blanche	Rabaud-Promis	Suduiraut
Lafaurie-Peyraguey	Haut-Peyraguey	Rieussec
de Rayne-Vigneau	Coutet	
d'Arche	Doisy-Védrines	Caillou
Filhot	Doisy-Daëne	Nairac
Lamothe	Suau	de Malle
de Myrat	Broustet	Romer

CLASSIFICATION OF 1959—GRAVES

CRUS CLASSES—RED WINES

Châteaux

Haut-Brion	Haut-Bailly	Malartic-Lagravière
Bouscaut	La Mission-Haut-Brion	Oliver
Carbonnieux	La Tour-Haut-Brion	Pape-Clément
Domaine de Chevalier	La Tour-Martillac	Smith-Haut-Lafitte
de Fieuzal		

CRUS CLASSES—WHITE WINES
Châteaus

Bouscaut	Couhins	Malartic-Lagravière
Carbonnieux	La Tour-Martillac	Olivier
de Chevalier	Laville-Haut-Brion	

CLASSIFICATION OF 1985—SAINT-ÉMILION
PREMIERS GRANDS CRUS CLASSÉS (FIRST GREAT CLASSED GROWTHS)

Châteaus

Ausone	Canon	Magdelaine
Cheval Blanc	Clos Fourtet	Pavie
Beauséjour (Duffau	Figeac	Trottevieille
Lagarrosse)	La Gaffelière	
Belair		
L'Angélus	Curé-Bon	Mauvezin
L'Arrosée	Dassault	Moulin-du-Cadet
Balestard-La-	La Dominique	L'Oratoire
Tonnelle	Faurie-de-Souchard	Pavie-Decesse
Beau Sejour-Becot	Fonplégade	Pavie-Macquin
Bellevue	Fonroque	Pavillon Cadet
Bergat	Franc-Mayne	Petit-Faurie-de-
Berliquet	Grand Barrail	Soutard
Cadet-Piola	Lamarzelle Figeac	Le Prieuré
Canon-La-Gaffelière	Grand-Corbin-	Ripeau
Cap de Mourlin	Despagne	Sansonnet
Le Chatelet	Grand Corbin	Saint-Georges-Cote-
Chauvin	Grand Mayne	Pavie
Clos des Jacobins	Grand Pontet	La Serre
Clos La Madeleine	Guadet-Saint-Julien	Soutard
Clos Saint-Martin	Haut-Corbin	Tertre-Daugay
La Clotte	Haut-Sarpe	La Tour-du-Pin
La Clusière	Laniote	Figeac
Corbin	Larcis-Ducasse	La Tour-Figeac
Corbin-Michotte	Lamarzelle	Trimoulet
Couvent-des-	Larmande	Troplong-Mondot
Jacobins	Laroze	Villemaurine
Croque-Michotte	Matras	Yon-Figeac

WINE MAPS

The maps on the following pages identify the most popular growing areas for today's primary wine-producing countries. In many cases the areas identified conform to that country's APPELLATION system. For the United States, state maps are included for CALIFORNIA, NEW YORK, and OREGON/WASHINGTON. Following is a brief description of the wine maps.

MAP KEY

- - - - - - - - - - - - - - - Wine growing regions

————————————→ Wine-growing region

● Cities

★ Capitals

FRANCE

The map of FRANCE displays the six primary premium wine-producing regions—ALSACE, BORDEAUX, BURGUNDY, CHAMPAGNE, the LOIRE, and the RHÔNE, plus three other highly productive regions—Southwest France, LANGUEDOC-ROUSSILLON and PROVENCE. More detailed maps are included for France's Bordeaux and Burgundy regions, two of the best-known growing regions in the world.

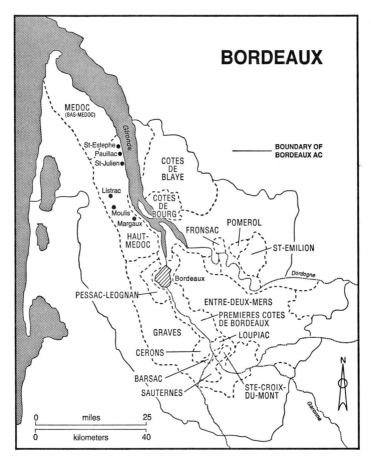

BORDEAUX

MEDOC
(BAS-MEDOC)

Gironde

St-Estephe
Pauillac
St-Julien

BOUNDARY OF
BORDEAUX AC

COTES
DE
BLAYE

Listrac

COTES
DE
BOURG

Moulis
Margaux

POMEROL

HAUT-
MEDOC

FRONSAC

ST-EMILION

Bordeaux

Dordogne

PESSAC-LEOGNAN

ENTRE-DEUX-MERS

PREMIERES COTES
DE BORDEAUX

GRAVES

LOUPIAC

CERONS

BARSAC

SAUTERNES

STE-CROIX-
DU-MONT

Garonne

N

0   miles   25

0   kilometers   40

The map of BORDEAUX denotes the primary APPELLATION D'ORIGINE CONTRÔLÉE
(AC) areas (such as the MÉDOC, the HAUT-MÉDOC, GRAVES, and SAINT-ÉMILION),
along with some of the more famous ACs within the Haut-Médoc AC (like
PAUILLAC and MARGAUX).

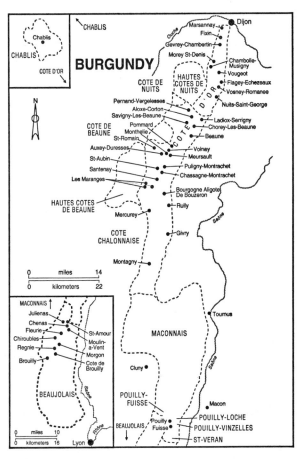

The center segment of the BURGUNDY map indicates the CÔTE D'OR, CÔTE CHALONNAISE and the MÂCONNAIS growing areas. The CÔTE D'OR, which is the most famous section of Burgundy and produces premium PINOT NOIR and CHARDONNAY wines, is split into the CÔTE DE NUITS and the CÔTE DE BEAUNE. Within these two areas many of the world-famous communal ACs—such as VOSNE ROMANÉE, MEURSAULT, and PULIGNY-MONTRACHET—are identified. The inset for CHABLIS, indicates it is to the far north of the rest of Burgundy; that of BEAUJOLAIS shows it to the far south.

The map of ITALY, which is the world's largest producer of wine, shows the twenty major growing regions including the islands of SICILY and SARDINIA.

GERMANY's map identifies the thirteen ANBAUGEBIETE including the two recently added from the former East Germany—SAALE-UNSTRUT and SACHSEN.

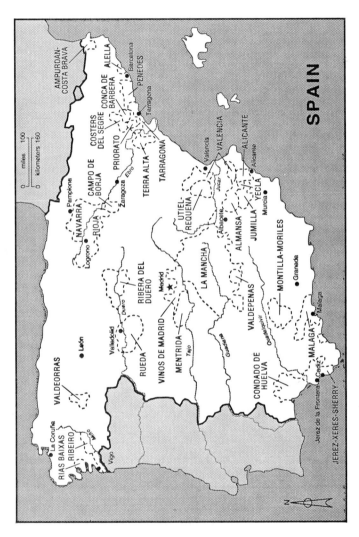

The map of SPAIN denotes the primary DENOMINACIÓN DE ORIGEN (DO) areas, as well as that of RIOJA—the only DENOMINACIÓN DE ORIGEN CALIFICADA (DOCA) area.

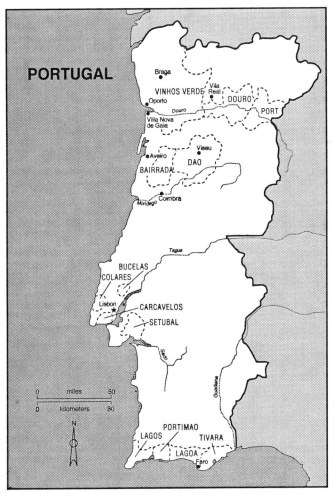

PORTUGAL's map indicates the primary DENOMINAÇÃO DE ORIGEM CONTROLADA (DOC) areas including that of the PORT DOC, which produces one of the world's famous FORTIFIED wines.

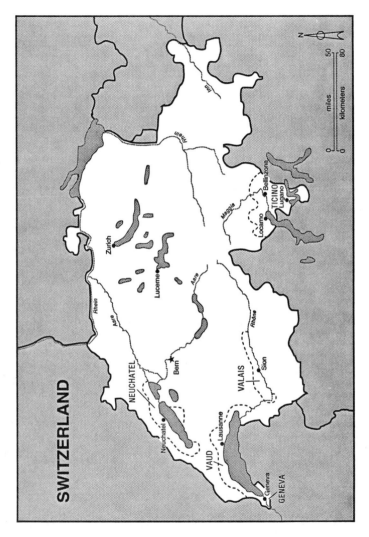

The map of SWITZERLAND shows the location of the five primary growing areas—GENEVA, NEUCHATEL, TICINO, VALAIS and VAUD.

There are two maps for CALIFORNIA (which produces about 95 percent of the total U.S. wine production)—one for the northern portion, and one for the Central and Southern sections. Among the areas identified are primary AMERICAN VITICULTURAL AREAS (AVAS), such as SANTA MARIA VALLEY and PASO ROBLES in the central part of the state, and famous areas like NAPA VALLEY, CARNEROS, SONOMA VALLEY and RUSSIAN RIVER VALLEY in the northern section.

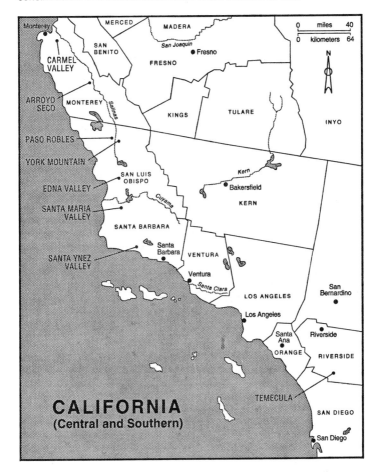

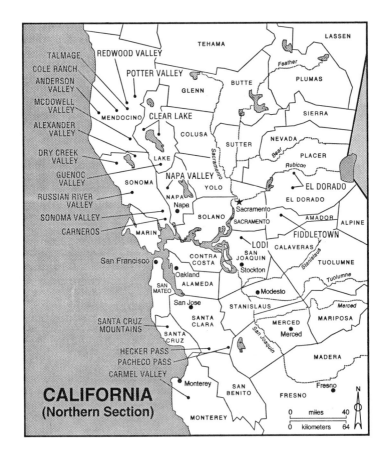

TALMAGE
COLE RANCH
ANDERSON VALLEY
MCDOWELL VALLEY
ALEXANDER VALLEY
DRY CREEK VALLEY
GUENOC VALLEY
RUSSIAN RIVER VALLEY
SONOMA VALLEY
CARNEROS

REDWOOD VALLEY
POTTER VALLEY
MENDOCINO
CLEAR LAKE
NAPA VALLEY
SANTA CRUZ MOUNTAINS
HECKER PASS
PACHECO PASS
CARMEL VALLEY

TEHAMA
LASSEN
Feather
BUTTE
PLUMAS
GLENN
SIERRA
COLUSA
NEVADA
SUTTER
Bear
PLACER
Rubicon
LAKE
Sacramento
EL DORADO
SONOMA
YOLO
NAPA
Napa
EL DORADO
SOLANO
Sacramento
AMADOR
ALPINE
SACRAMENTO
MARIN
FIDDLETOWN
LODI
CALAVERAS
San Francisco
CONTRA COSTA
SAN JOAQUIN
Stanislaus
TUOLUMNE
Oakland
Stockton
Tuolumne
SAN MATEO
ALAMEDA
Modesto
San Jose
STANISLAUS
Merced
SANTA CLARA
MARIPOSA
SANTA CRUZ
MERCED
San Joaquin
Merced
MADERA
Monterey
SAN BENITO
Fresno

CALIFORNIA
(Northern Section)

MONTEREY
FRESNO

N

0 miles 40
0 kilometers 64

OREGON and WASHINGTON (which are fast becoming first-rate producers of fine wines) are combined on one map, which indicates principal AVAS such as the WILLAMETTE VALLEY in Oregon and the COLUMBIA VALLEY, which extends into both states.

The map of NEW YORK (which is the second largest wine producer in the U.S.) identifies primary AVAS such as the HUDSON RIVER REGION, the FINGER LAKES, and THE HAMPTONS on Long Island.

The map of ARGENTINA identifies the location of the Mendoza growing region, which produces about 70 percent of Argentina's wines along with some of the lesser areas like Rio Negro, San Juan and Salta.

Antofagasta

NORTH CENTRE
REGION

ACONCAGUA
VALLEY

MAIPO VALLEY

Valparaíso
Santiago ★ RANCAGUA DISTRICT

COLCHAGUA
Curicó ● DISTRICT

CURICO DISTRICT

Concepción MAULE VALLEY

BIO-BIO BIO-BIO

CHILE

| 0 | miles | 400 |
| 0 | kilometers | 640 |

CHILE's map shows the famous Maipo Valley located just outside of Santiago,
along with Chile's other primary growing areas.

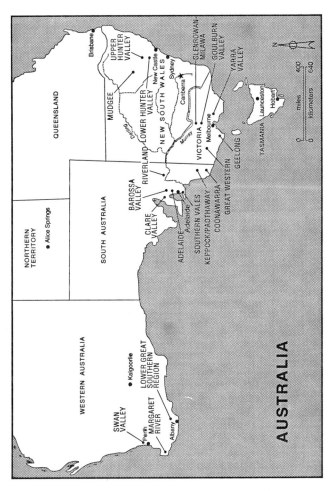

Most of AUSTRALIA's growing regions are centered in the southeastern section of the country where areas like HUNTER VALLEY, YARRA VALLEY, COONAWARRA and BAROSSA VALLEY are located. There are a few areas in the southwest, such as that of MARGARET RIVER around the city of Perth.

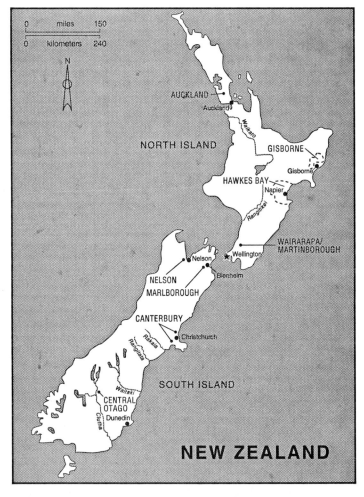

NEW ZEALAND's North Island—with growing areas in Auckland, Gisborne/Poverty Bay, Hawkes Bay and the Wairarapa/Martinborough area—was the first of the islands to start producing wines. The South Island subsequently followed and now has growing areas in Marlborough, Canterbury and Central Otago.

BIBLIOGRAPHY

Adams, Leon D. *Leon D. Adams' Commonsense Book of Wine (3rd ed.).* Boston: San Francisco Book Company/Houghton Mifflin, 1975.

Amerine, M. A., and V. L. Singleton. *Wine (2nd ed.).* Berkeley: University of California Press, 1977.

Anderson, Burton. *The Wine Atlas of Italy.* New York: Simon & Schuster, Inc., 1990.

Anderson, Stanley F., and Raymond Hull. *The Art of Making Wine.* New York: Hawthorn Books, Inc., 1970.

Ashley, Maureen. *The Encyclopedia of Italian Wines.* New York: Fireside/Simon & Schuster, Inc., 1991.

Barr, Andrew. *Pinot Noir.* London: Viking/Penguin, 1992.

Benson, Jeffrey, and Alastair Mackenzie. *Sauternes (2nd ed.).* London: Philip Wilson Publishers Ltd., 1990.

Bespaloff, Alexis. *Alexis Bespaloff's Complete Guide to Wine.* New York: Signet/Penguin, 1994.

————. *The New Frank Schoonmaker Encyclopedia of Wine.* New York: William Morrow and Company, Inc., 1988.

Broadbent, Michael. *The New Great Vintage Wine Book.* New York: Alfred A. Knopf, 1991.

————. *The Simon & Schuster Pocket Guide to Wine Tasting.* New York: Fireside/Simon & Schuster, Inc., 1988.

Clarke, Oz. *New Classic Wines.* New York: Simon & Schuster, Inc., 1991.

————. *Oz Clarke's New Encyclopedia of French Wines.* New York: Simon & Schuster, Inc., 1990.

————. *Oz Clarke's Wine Handbook 1993.* New York: Fireside/Simon & Schuster, Inc., 1992.

————. *The Wine Book.* New York: Portland House, 1990.

Conaway, James. *Napa.* Boston: Houghton Mifflin Company, 1990.

Cooke, George M., and James T. Lapsley. *Making Table Wine at Home.* Oakland, CA: University of California, 1988.

Cooper, Rosalind. *The Wine Book.* Tucson: HPBooks, 1981.

Cox, Jeff. *From Vines to Wines.* Pownal, VT: Garden Way Publishing/Storey Communications, Inc., 1985.

Dallas, Phillip. *Italian Wines (3rd ed.).* London: Faber and Faber, 1989.

Duijker, Hubrecht. *The Wine Atlas of Spain.* New York: Simon & Schuster, Inc., 1992.

Eyres, Harry. *Cabernet Sauvignon.* London: Viking/Penguin, 1991.

Faith, Nicholas. *The Story of Champagne.* New York: Facts On File, 1989.

George, Rosemary. *The Wine Dictionary.* Essex England: Longman, 1989.
————. *The Simon & Schuster Pocket Wine Label Decoder.* New York: Fireside/Simon & Schuster, Inc., 1989.
Gleave, David. *The Wines of Italy.* London: Salamander, 1989.
Grossman, Harold J. *Grossman's Guide to Wines, Beers, and Spirits (6th ed.).* New York: Charles Scribner's Sons, 1977.

Halliday, James. *Wine Atlas of Australia and New Zealand.* North Ryde, NSW Australia: Angus & Robertson/HarperCollins Publishers, 1991.
————. *Wine Atlas of California.* New York: Viking/Penguin, 1993.
Hazan, Victor. *Italian Wine.* New York: Alfred A. Knopf, 1982.
Herbst, Sharon Tyler. *Food Lover's Companion.* Hauppauge, NY: Barron's Educational Series, Inc., 1990.
Howkins, Ben. *Rich, Rare & Red: A Guide to Port.* London: Christopher Helm, 1987.

Jackisch, Philip. *Modern Winemaking.* Ithaca, NY: Cornell University Press, 1985.
Jamieson, Ian. *German Wines.* London: Faber and Faber, 1991.
————. *The Simon & Schuster Guide to the Wines of Germany.* New York: Fireside/Simon & Schuster, Inc., 1992.
Jeffs, Julian. *Sherry.* London: Faber and Faber, 1982.
Johnson, Hugh. *Hugh Johnson's Modern Encyclopedia of Wine (3rd ed.).* New York: Simon & Schuster, Inc., 1991.
————. *The Atlas of German Wines.* New York: Simon & Schuster, Inc., 1986.
————. *The World Atlas of Wine (3rd ed.).* New York: Simon and Schuster, 1985.
Joseph, Robert. *The White Wines of France.* Los Angeles: HPBooks, 1987.
————. *The Wines of the Americas.* Los Angeles: HPBooks, 1990.

Kaufman, William I. *The Pocket Encyclopedia of Pacific Northwest Wines and Wineries*. San Francisco: The Wine Appreciation Guild, 1992.

Kramer, Matt. *Making Sense of Burgundy*. New York: Quill/William Morrow, 1990.

————. *Making Sense of California Wine*. New York: William Morrow and Company, Inc., 1992.

————. *Making Sense of Wine*. New York: William Morrow and Company, Inc., 1989.

Laube, James. *California's Great Cabernets*. San Francisco: Wine Spectator Press, 1989.

————. *California's Great Chardonnays*. San Francisco: Wine Spectator Press, 1990.

Librarie Larousse. *Larousse Wines and Vineyards of France*. New York: Arcade Publishing/Little, Brown and Company, 1991.

Lichine, Alexis. *Alexis Lichine's New Encyclopedia of Wines & Spirits (5th ed.)*. New York: Alfred A. Knopf, 1987.

Livingstone-Learmouth, John, and Melvyn Master. *The Wines of the Rhône*. London: Faber and Faber, 1983.

Loftus, Simon. *Puligny-Montrachet: Journal of a Village in Burgundy*. New York: Alfred A. Knopf, 1993.

MacQuitty, Jane. *The Simon & Schuster Pocket Guide to Australian & New Zealand Wines*. New York: Fireside/Simon & Schuster, Inc., 1990.

May, Oliver. *The Wines of Australia (new ed.)*. London: Faber and Faber, 1991.

Mayson, Richard. *Portugal's Wines and Wine Makers*. San Francisco: The Wine Appreciation Guild/Ebury Press, 1992.

McWhirter, Kathryn, and Charles Metcalfe. *Encyclopedia of Spanish and Portuguese Wines*. New York: Fireside/Simon & Schuster, Inc., 1991.

Metcalfe, Charles, and Kathrun McWhirter. *The Wines of Spain & Portugal*. Los Angeles: HPBooks, 1988.

Norman, Remington. *The Great Domaines of Burgundy*. New York: Henry Holt and Company, 1992.

Parker, Robert M. *Bordeaux: A Comprehensive Guide to the Wines Produced from 1961–1990*. New York: Simon & Schuster, Inc., 1991.

————. *Burgundy: A Comprehensive Guide to the Producers, Appellations, and Wines.* New York: Simon & Schuster, Inc., 1990.

Peppercorn, David. *Bordeaux (2nd ed.).* London: Faber and Faber, 1991.

Peynaud, Émile. *The Taste of Wine.* San Francisco: The Wine Appreciation Guild, 1987.

Philpott, Don. *The Vineyards of France.* Chester, CT: The Globe Pequot Press, 1987.

Pigott, Stuart. *Riesling.* London: Viking/Penguin, 1991.

Prial, Frank J. II, with Rosemary George and Michael Edwards (eds.). *The Companion to Wine.* New York: Prentice Hall General Reference, 1992.

Ray, Cyril. *The New Book of Italian Wines.* London: Sidgwick & Jackson, 1982.

Read, Jan. *The Simon & Schuster Pocket Guide to Spanish Wines (2nd ed.).* New York: Fireside/Simon & Schuster, Inc., 1988.
————. *The Wines of Portugal.* London: Faber and Faber, 1987.
————. *The Wines of Spain.* London: Faber and Faber, 1982.

Ribéreau-Gayon, Pascal (ed.). *The Wines and Vineyards of France* New York: Viking/Penguin, 1990.

Robards, Terry. *California Wine Label Album.* New York: Workman Publishing, 1981.

Robinson, Jancis. *Vines, Grapes and Wines.* New York: Alfred A. Knopf, 1986.

Roby, Norman S. and Charles E. Olken. *The New Connoisseurs' Handbook of California Wines (2nd ed.).* New York: Alfred A. Knopf, 1993.

Schuster, Michael. *The Simon & Schuster Beginner's Guide to Understanding Wine.* New York: Simon & Schuster, Inc., 1989.

Spurrier, Steven. *French Country Wines.* London: Collins Willow, 1984.

Stevenson, Tom. *Champagne.* London: Sotheby's, 1986.
————. *Sotheby's World Wine Encyclopedia.* London: Sotheby's/Dorling Kindersley, 1988.

Suckling, James. *Vintage Port.* San Francisco: Wine Spectator Press, 1990.

Sullivan, Charles L. *Like Modern Edens: Winegrowing in Santa Clara Valley and Santa Cruz Mountains 1798–1981.* Cupertino, CA: California History Center, 1982.

Sutcliffe, Serena. *The Wine Handbook*. New York: Fireside/Simon & Schuster, Inc., 1987.
————. *The Wines of Burgundy*. New York: Fireside/Simon & Schuster, Inc., 1992.

Thompson, Bob. *The Simon & Schuster Pocket Guide to California Wines*. New York: Fireside/Simon & Schuster, Inc., 1990.
————. *The Wine Atlas of California and the Pacific Northwest*. New York: Simon & Schuster, Inc., 1993.

Voss, Roger. *The Simon & Schuster Pocket Guide to Fortified and Dessert Wines*. New York: Fireside/Simon & Schuster, Inc., 1989.

Wagner, Philip M. *Grapes Into Wine*. New York: Alfred A Knopf, Inc., 1976.
Wasserman, Sheldon and Pauline. *Italy's Noble Red Wines*. New York: MacMillan Publishing Company, 1991.

Zraly, Kevin. *Windows On The World Complete Wine Course (1994 ed.)*. New York: Sterling Publishing Company, 1992.

ABOUT THE AUTHORS

Ron Herbst is a food and wine writer, consultant, and connoisseur who has extensive experience in the restaurant business, and a B.S.B.A. degree in Hotel and Restaurant Management.

Sharon Tyler Herbst is an award-winning food-reference and cookbook author of seven books, the Past President of the International Association of Culinary Professionals, and regularly appears on national TV.